Thirteenth Edition

Those Who Can, Teach

Thirteenth Edition

Those Who Can, Teach

Kevin Ryan

Boston University

James M. Cooper

University of Virginia

WADSWORTH
CENGAGE Learning™

Australia • Brazil • Japan • Korea • Mexico • Singapore • Spain • United Kingdom • United States

WADSWORTH
CENGAGE Learning™

Those Who Can, Teach, **Thirteenth Edition,**
Kevin Ryan and James M. Cooper

Executive Editor: Mark D. Kerr

Developmental Editor: Kate Scheinman

Assistant Editor: Genevieve Allen

Editorial Assistant: Greta Lindquist

Media Editor: Ashley Cronin

Marketing Manager: Kara Kindstrom

Marketing Coordinator: Klaira Markenzon

Marketing Communications Manager:
Heather Baxley

Content Project Manager: Samen Iqbal

Design Director: Rob Hugel

Art Director: Jennifer Wahi

Print Buyer: Rebecca Cross

Rights Acquisitions Specialist: Tom McDonough

Production Service: Jill Traut, MPS

Cover Designer and Text Designer:
Liz Harasymczuk

Photo Researcher: Jeremy Glover

Text Researcher: Sue Howard

Copy Editor: Jill Pellarin

Cover Image: Getty/Stockbyte/57444186

Interior Design Images: Images from Shutterstock
.com: 3D graph, Martan; pencil/apple on books,
Karen Roach; coffee, Mark Aplet; pencil/pastel,
Denis Ponkratow; half apple, Roman Kholodov;
light bulb, Zoran Vukmanov Simokov; magnifying
glass, Brian A Jackson; notebook and pencil, Ilona
Baha; jigsaw puzzle piece, STILLFX; red and green
apples, Gunnar Pippel; clock, Smit; school bag,
Qeen; mobile phone, cobalt88; highlighter pens,
Elaine Barker

Compositor: MPS Limited, a Macmillan
Company

For product information and technology assistance, contact us at
Cengage Learning Customer & Sales Support, 1-800-354-9706.

For permission to use material from this text or product,
submit all requests online at **www.cengage.com/permissions.**
Further permissions questions can be e-mailed to
permissionrequest@cengage.com.

Library of Congress Control Number: 2011928898

Student Edition:

ISBN-13: 978-1-111-83028-1

ISBN-10: 1-111-83028-2

Advantage Edition:

ISBN-13: 978-0-8400-2877-8

ISBN-10: 0-8400-2877-6

Wadsworth
20 Davis Drive
Belmont, CA 94002-3098
USA

Cengage Learning is a leading provider of customized learning solutions
with office locations around the globe, including Singapore, the United
Kingdom, Australia, Mexico, Brazil, and Japan. Locate your local office at
www.cengage.com/global.

Cengage Learning products are represented in Canada by Nelson Education, Ltd.

To learn more about Wadsworth, **visit www.cengage.com/wadsworth**

Purchase any of our products at your local college store or at our preferred
online store **www.CengageBrain.com.**

Printed in the United States of America
1 2 3 4 5 6 7 15 14 13 12 11

Brief Contents

Contents

PART II: Teachers 162

6 What Makes a Teacher Effective? 162

7 What Should Teachers Know about Technology and Its Impact on Schools? 193

PART IV: The Teaching Profession

411

Writing the thirteenth edition of *Those Who Can, Teach*, we were guided by the goals and challenges of teaching an "Introduction to Education" or a "Foundations of Education" course to *today's students*. Both authors have long taught aspiring teachers in their very first education course. Therefore, instructors teaching the introductory course in education were very much on our minds. As we saw it, instructors want to:

- **Help students examine their motives for teaching** so they can determine whether teaching is right for them.

- **Inspire these future teachers to form and sustain a commitment to teaching**—a commitment that is grounded in a realistic understanding of the teaching profession.

- **Offer instructional activities** that incorporate the way today's students learn, particularly with regard to their use of technology.

- **Prepare aspiring teachers to teach students whose cultural complexities**—such as race, socioeconomic status, and orientation to learning—may differ from their own.

- **Provide course experiences** that help prospective teachers bridge the "theory-to-practice" divide.

- **Make the history and philosophies of education relevant** to the lives and careers of future teachers.

- **Help prospective teachers develop the habits and skills of a** reflective practitioner.

- **Prepare all students to do well on mandatory, high-stakes standardized tests** based on national, state, and local standards.

Another reality that we have kept in mind as we have revised this text is that today's college students are part of a fresh, new generation, which has grown up in this era of technological and social change. For these students, **technology is a way of life.** They are both connected and insulated through technology, and are accustomed to processing information differently than the generations before them.

- They are **team oriented** due to the significant time spent on social networking sites and on instant messaging platforms.

- Many of today's students are **unaccustomed to academic difficulty.** Rather, they are used to rewards and accolades, and have high expectations for achievement and little tolerance for failure.

- The lives of today's students **are often quite programmed.** They suffer more stress and often feel more overwhelmed compared to those in past generations.

How Does *Those Who Can, Teach* Meet the Needs of Today's Learners?

How have we addressed the challenges of teaching today's students while meeting the goals of an introduction to education course in this edition of *Those Who Can, Teach?*

We know that students who will use this text are facing many challenges. Many are at the beginning of their college experience and are still getting accustomed to their independence. There are almost certainly many activities—other courses, social events, and jobs, to name a few—competing for their time and attention. They, like all of us, struggle to balance all that is on their plate. Still, we believe that exploring what might be their life's work requires that they fully engage in the course and with the questions posed in this text. To help them do this, we have used a number of instructional tools, described below, to gain and keep the readers' attention and to inspire them to carefully consider all aspects of becoming one of Those Who *Can*.

- **Examining motives for teaching.** We begin and end the book with chapters that focus on examining "Why Teach?" Two or three times in each chapter, students are asked to **Pause and Reflect** on questions of self-examination and understanding. At the end of each chapter, we provide the reader opportunities to consider and reflect in the sections entitled, **Why Teach? Your Final Word.** In addition, two "bookend" sections, **Let's Get Started** and **Before You Close This Book**, offer important reflection questions before and after students read the text. These appear as interactive activities on the Education CourseMate website as well. **Let's Get Started,** in particular, was written to make clear to student-readers what we hope they get out of *Those Who Can, Teach* and what we believe is the most productive way to engage the book.

- **Developing a realistic understanding of teaching.** A frequent complaint of beginning teachers is "that no one ever told us what it would *really* be like in the classroom." Although these complaints are sometimes unfair (people tried to tell them but they may not have been listening), we have tried to reflect the real world of schooling. Throughout the book, we have presented many case studies of teachers in our **From Pre-service to Practice** feature that portrays the realities (both the good and bad) of teaching. The **Voices from the Classroom** feature is a reflection or comment on one of each chapter's key topics from actual classroom teachers. The classroom voices bring a realistic perspective on these topics and issues. We have also interspersed through the book numerous **TeachSource Video Cases,** which provide students with real-life teaching examples of problems, methodology, and teaching styles in online video clips that add another layer of richness to the realistic case studies offered by this book.

- **Learning through technology.** Because today's students learn so much through technology, we have integrated technology throughout the book. One whole chapter, "What Should Teachers Know about Technology and Its Impact on Schools?" addresses the many uses of technology to increase and enhance learning for all students, including those with disabilities. The **TeachSource Video Cases,** mentioned above, provide multi-media ways of observing and studying teaching. Education CourseMate, accessible through www.cengagebrain.com, provides many supplementary materials for students to deepen their understandings.

- At the end of each chapter, there are three or four **websites** for students to explore in greater depth the topics and issues discussed in the chapter.

- **Understanding cultural complexities.** Women and whites predominate in both teacher education programs and in the teaching force, whereas over 40 percent of students in public schools are students of color. Many education students have had few interactions with students who differ from them in terms of race, ethnicity, and socioeconomic status. The chapter "Who Are Today's Students in a Diverse Society?" describes various diversities and implications for teachers.

Throughout the book, we provide multiple examples of the diversities that teachers will encounter, and discuss implications for teachers and schools.

- **Bridging the "theory-to-practice" divide.** The book assists students to bridge this gap by providing realistic **case studies, TeachSource Video Cases, Reflection Questions, Voices from the Classroom,** and many **Pause and Reflect** questions throughout the book.

- **Bringing history and philosophy "alive" to students.** We try to enliven the history of American education through a lively writing style and by focusing on the people who have made educational history. Our **Leaders in Education** feature, found both in the book and on the website, presents biographical sketches of both historical (e.g., Horace Mann, John Dewey, and Anne Sullivan), as well as contemporary educational leaders (e.g., Michelle Rhee, Erin Gruwell, Kay Tolliver, and Ron Berger). In discussing educational philosophies, we have developed statements by teachers who embrace each philosophy, so readers can see how those individual philosophies guide teachers' actions and behavior in classrooms. Chapter 9 includes **Your Philosophy of Education Self-Inventory** to help students bring their educational views to great consciousness. An interactive version of this instrument is available on the Education CourseMate website.

- **Reflective practice.** Throughout the book, we ask readers to stop and think: to reflect. We are convinced that our readers, like ourselves, live in a noisy world of words and pictures that is continually competing for our attention. We have tried to make a case for reflection but have also built into the text requests that the reader stop and reflect what particular content means personally. Using a variety of devices throughout the book, such as, cartoons, and boxed inserts on research findings, we are unabashedly committed to helping students start on the road to become reflective practitioners. New in this edition is a special feature, **Truth or Fiction?** which appears at the beginning each chapter. To quickly engage the readers in the chapter's subject, we present them with three or more statements having to do with the subject of the chapter and ask them to make a judgment as to whether each statement is true or false. Later in the chapter, they will encounter the subject of each statement (marked with a special "Truth or Fiction" icon) and discover whether the statement was "truth" or "fiction."

- **Team-orientation of students, students' high success rates and busy lives.** The Instructor's Manual, Test Bank, Student Website (Education CourseMate), and Course Management System provide many materials (described below) to save students and instructors time and to assist them in achieving the objectives of each chapter. Many group activities are also suggested, and **Video Cases** can be shown in class to provide a common viewing experience that can then be deconstructed through group activity.

- **Informal writing style.** Although there are many changes in the thirteenth edition, key qualities have been retained. Chief among them is the book's informal writing style. We have tried to communicate the seriousness surrounding professional topics and at the same time reflect the humor and humanity that is part of the professional life of a teacher. We are helped in this "experiential" aspect of our book by the presence in the text of the actual words of practicing classroom teachers. We believe (and hope) that this writing style and heavy use of narrative give the text a greater sense of reality.

- **Standards testing for teachers.** Recognizing that virtually all prospective teachers must meet state and national standards to be licensed, *Those Who Can, Teach* tries to make the connection between standards and content crystal clear by including a correlation chart in the back of the book. The 10 core principles of INTASC are correlated to the chapters and pages in the book (see inside cover), and at the beginning of each chapter we identify the principles addressed in that chapter.

- **Finally, currency.** The field of education is in a particularly dynamic state. The federal government has initiated new programs such as "The Race to the Top," and changes are being made in the landmark No Child Left Behind legislation. State and local educational authorities are deeply involved in educational reform efforts. The policies of key players such as teachers unions, as well as foundations such as the Gates Foundation, are changing. New groups and organizations are influencing the lives of teachers. All this and the ever-increasing research base in education need to be brought to the attention of those considering becoming teachers.

Accompanying Teaching and Learning Resources

The thirteenth edition of *Those Who Can, Teach* is accompanied by an extensive package of instructor and student resources.

- *Kaleidoscope: Contemporary and Classic Readings in Education,* **thirteenth edition** is a companion book of readings that can be used either in conjunction with the text or as a separate volume. This collection of 55 selections, approximately 40 percent of which are new in the current edition, contains works by some of the most distinguished scholars in education, along with the writings of practicing teachers. Several of the authors and reports of research cited in *Those Who Can, Teach* are included in this book of readings. We have specially marked several key readings, like those of John Dewey and John Goodlad, as educational classics for their impact on the field. We believe that a certain level of literacy about the field of education—that is, knowing the key figures who have shaped educational practice—is a requirement of being a professional teacher. Other readings typically reflect more recent developments in the field.

- An **Online Instructor's Manual with Test Bank,** prepared by Amy Thompson, Professional Development Coordinator in the Hanover County Public Schools in Virginia, is offered at the Instructor's website. It includes a transition guide, sample syllabi, learning objectives, chapter overviews, supplementary lecture and discussion topics, class activities, student study guides, practice quizzes, selected references and media resources, school observation activities, and a section of five or six case studies with discussion questions. The Instructor's Manual also includes a correlation guide to *Kaleidoscope,* the companion reader. For assessment support, the updated Test Bank includes multiple-choice, short-answer, and essay questions for each chapter.

- **ExamView® Test Bank,** available for download from the Instructor's website, includes all the test items from the Test Bank in electronic format, enabling you to create customized tests in print or online.

- **Presentation Slides,** also prepared by Amy Thompson, are available from the Instructor's website and include preassembled Microsoft PowerPoint lecture slides that cover content for each chapter of the book.

- **Education CourseMate,** accessible by students at CengageBrain.com, brings course concepts to life with interactive learning, study, and exam preparation tools that support the printed textbook. CourseMate includes an integrated eBook, quizzes, flashcards, TeachSource Video Cases, and other book-specific resources such as reflection activities and the Your Philosophy of Education Self-Inventory. For instructors, Education CourseMate includes access to EngagementTracker, a first-of-its-kind tool that monitors student engagement in the course. The accompanying instructor website, accessible by instructors at login.cengage.com, includes protected resources such as an electronic version of the instructor's manual, test bank, and PowerPoint slides.

- **The award-winning Video Cases** add the sharp bite of life in schools to our text. Available online and organized by topic, each case is a 4- to 6-minute module consisting of videos presenting actual classroom scenarios that depict the complex problems and opportunities teachers face every day. The video clips are accompanied by "artifacts" that provide background information and allow preservice teachers to experience true classroom dilemmas in their multiple dimensions. Also, a number of ABC video news stories pertaining to topics treated in the text are accessible to the reader.

- **WebTutor.** Jump start your course with customizable, rich, text-specific content within your Course Management System. Whether you want to Web-enable your class or put an entire course online, WebTutor™ delivers. WebTutor™ offers a wide array of resources, including access to the eBook, quizzes, videos, web links, exercises, and more.

- **The Educator's Guide Series.** These are brief paperbacks that examine important topics in more depth, such as Diversity in the Classroom, Classroom Assessment, Inclusion, Technology Tools, Teacher Reflection, Motivation, and Differentiated Instruction.

Acknowledgments

Whenever any of us puts pen to paper or fingers to the keyboard, we stand on the shoulders of others. This is certainly true of this book. We are indebted to many people. In the writing of this book, we are especially appreciative of the help given by the following individuals. Most notably, Helen Crompton for her contribution to the chapter entitled "What Should Teachers Know about Technology and Its Impact on Schools?" Additionally, we thank a number of scholars for the invaluable contribution of their research and writing to various chapters, specifically: Cathleen Kinsella Stutz for Chapters 2 and 8; Susan Tauer for Chapters 9 and 12; and Larry Kaufman for Chapter 10. We also wish to thank Steven Tigner for his helpful suggestions on the chapter entitled "What Are the Philosophical Foundations of American Education?" Special thanks go to our colleagues and students for their many good ideas and continuing support, in particular, the teacher contributors to the Voices from the Classroom feature. An advisory board of reviewers also made key contributions to the organization and content of this edition, most notably:

Patricia Blaine, West Kentucky Community & Technical College

Diane Corrigan, Cleveland State University

Rosanne Dlugosz, Maricopa Community College, Scottsdale

Melanie Felton, College of Saint Mary

Carmen Garcia-Caceres, The University of Texas at Brownsville

Sam Guerriero, Butler University

Leanna Manna, Villa Maria College

Barbara Stern, Madison University

A special acknowledgment is due to Marilyn Ryan for the substantial intellectual and psychological contributions she made to the several editions of this book. Writing and revising a textbook is a multifaceted process, particularly today with the addition of ancillary supports such as video cases and our website. Many people provide advice—some solicited and some not. We believe, however, that our best source of advice on this book and its companion, *Kaleidoscope,* has been the team we've worked with at Cengage Learning. Mark Kerr, executive editor, education, had the responsibility of overseeing the "big picture" surrounding this project. We are enormously appreciative of his energetic and insightful leadership. Samen Iqbal, content project manager, has deftly handled the copyediting process and all of the final stages of production. The developmental editor plays a key role in the production of a textbook and we count ourselves enormously fortunate to have been assisted by Kate Scheinman. Kate has been a font of organizational wizardry and a rock of sanity throughout the long and complicated revision process. Finally, we acknowledge the thousands of students for whom this book is written. Your new learning as you become teachers is central to our work as authors. We value your feedback on how we are doing and invite you to respond by sending us your comments through the Cengage Learning website.

Kevin Ryan
James M. Cooper

So Let's Get Started . . .

And get to what this book is all about: students and teachers, schools and subject matter, ideas about learning, and the fascinating challenges of education today. If you take a look at the chapter titles, you can see that we have built the book around questions—questions you should try to answer if you are thinking about becoming a teacher such as, "What makes a teacher effective?" and "How should our schools be reformed?" The *most important question*, however, is the first chapter's question, "Why teach?" This question—and its potential answers—is the focus not only of the initial chapter; it captures the purpose of the entire book.

One of life's most important questions is this: "What am I going to do with my life?" How you spend most of your time and energy—what *work* you decide to do—will determine, more than anything else, how content you are in life. Ideally, a career decision should be based on the best information available about the chosen field and on a deep understanding of who you are.

Knowing Your Own Motives

Centuries ago, Francis Bacon told us, "Knowledge is power." Much earlier, Socrates (one of civilization's great teachers, whom we discuss in the chapter entitled "What Are the Philosophical Foundations of American Education?") recognized the enormous power of self-knowledge when he urged his students to "know thyself." Understanding yourself and your motives, especially in something as important as a career choice, is crucial to good decision making. Becoming a teacher without taking the time to carefully consider whether you're truly meant to teach, or without examining *the reasons you want to teach*, can lead to disappointment. For instance, let's say your fifth-grade teacher had an enormous influence on you. She took the time to get to know you, taught you new and interesting subjects, had loads of patience, and was just plain fun. In fact, you have considered becoming a teacher since fifth grade. You get to college and declare yourself an education major, without ever analyzing precisely why you want to teach or whether you have the ability, skills, attitudes, or drive to become a teacher.

Equally as important as knowing *who you are* is clarifying your motives for teaching. Why is knowing *why* you want to teach so important? Because understanding the reasons you want to teach will help you determine whether teaching is right for you. It will also help you uncover and plan for the unique challenges you may face as a teacher. Let's say your desire to teach stems from a passion for a particular subject. Someone whose desire to teach grows out of a passion for history, for example, will have to prepare for the reality that not all of his students will share that passion. How will such a teacher motivate students who would rather be learning math? Or playing soccer?

We have written this book to help you to uncover whether you have what it takes to become a successful, fulfilled teacher and to help you understand the reasons you are considering teaching as a profession. We hope that you will use this book to gain a greater understanding of how you and a career in education might fit together.

The Habit of Reflection

As you will see throughout this book, we believe that effective teachers, indeed effective people in many areas of life, succeed in part because they are mindful of what they are doing. Always looking for ways to improve, they reflect on their performance and on what they are engaged in. Having acquired the habit of reflection, these people are called *reflective practitioners*.

Everyone has experiences. We meet new people. Someone sends us a fascinating Web link. We encounter a destitute, homeless person on the street. We have an unexpected and deeply personal conversation with a roommate. We all have special experiences. Truly effective people, however, use their experiences to understand their past and to chart their future. This very crucial practice of *reflection* is a habit you can start developing even now, as part of your career choice process. The way you use this book can help you on the path to be a reflective person. We think that recording what you think today, revisiting your thoughts throughout the term, and then noting what you think at the end of your course work will help solidify any choice you make about teaching.

Everyone can develop the habit of reflection. Begin right now by answering four questions. Take time to write your answers to these questions. By doing so, you will take your first steps to becoming a reflective practitioner, which will help you in your life and in your career, whatever that may be.

Your Motives Exam

The questions below will help you get in touch with your true motives for considering teaching as a career path and your personal thoughts about teaching. You can respond on the blank lines that follow, on a separate sheet of paper, or on the Education CourseMate website, where an interactive version of this exercise is available. In the exercise, we ask you to think about four main questions: Why do you want to become a teacher? Which teachers have you admired most and what made them so admirable? What strengths or qualities do you have that will make you a successful teacher? And, finally, what concerns do you have about either becoming a teacher or the teaching field itself?

First, list all of the reasons to become a teacher, and all of the reasons to choose another profession (or why *not* to become a teacher). Be sure to list not only the altruistic reasons you may want to teach—to help others or to inspire children, for example—but also the more selfish motives you may have, such as having the summers off to travel or finishing work at 3:00 in the afternoon. Do the same for choosing another profession in the second column. For this exercise to be valuable, you need to paint a full, complete picture of how you feel and what you think about teaching as well as possible other professions you may consider. As teacher Elida Laski asks in the "Voices from the Classroom" feature in Chapter 1, "Do you have to be born with that certain something in order to be a good teacher? If you are born with *it,* do you always know that teaching is the profession for you?"

Visit the Education CourseMate website and answer these questions online.

1) Why do you want to become a teacher?

Motives for becoming a teacher

Motives for choosing another profession

_____   _____

_____   _____

_____   _____

_____   _____

_____   _____

_____   _____

_____   _____

_____   _____

Now, think about some of the people—your teachers—who may have inspired you to consider teaching as a profession.

2) Who are three teachers you had in your elementary and secondary education whom you admire most? What made them so admirable?

1. _____

_____

_____

_____

2. _____

_____

_____

_____

_____

3. _____

_____

_____

_____

Next, take an initial look at yourself.

3) What are your strengths? List at least five qualities you have that will make you a successful teacher.

1. _____

2. _____

3. _____

4. _____

5. _____

Lastly, think about what concerns you have.

4) What concerns do you have about either becoming a teacher or the teaching field itself? List three questions about teaching and education that you want to know more about by reading this book.

1. _____

_____

2. _____

_____

3. _____

_____

If you did not stop reading to think about your motives for becoming a teacher or if you failed to commit yourself in writing, please stop now and think about what kept you from seriously engaging one or more of the questions. Your answer may tell you a good deal about yourself as a learner, about the educational system of which you are a product, and possibly about how you will behave as a teacher. Have you been trained to devour pages and pages of textbook reading without really confronting the issues conveyed by the words? Have you learned to disregard your own views, even about issues quite central to you? If your answers to these questions are *yes,* you are like many, many other students. But take heart.   With practice, everyone can develop the habit of reflection.

We sincerely hope that this will be a different kind of book and a different kind of reading-questioning-thinking experience for you. Precisely because we are teachers, we want this book to have a very special impact on you. We want to help you make good decisions about whether you want to be a teacher and about what kind of teacher you want to become. For these reasons, you need to read this book in a different way. Take the book on fully. Encounter it. Fight with it! Improve it by adding yourself to it. The truism you probably heard from your parents, "You get out of it what you put into it," truly applies here.

Our hope is that by the end of the semester, when you have finished reading this text, you will have acquired the habit of reflection and developed a greater understanding of what it means to teach, of what teachers do, of how schools operate within their communities and society, and of several other issues you will need to consider as you think through the question, "Why teach?"

1 why teach?

InTASC Standard 9

FOCUS POINTS

- A great variety of motivations lead people to select teaching as their occupation, and often the same person has more than one reason for doing so.

- Teaching, like other occupations, often attracts people because of the rewards it offers them. These can be divided into extrinsic and intrinsic rewards.

- In deciding whether to become a teacher, you can draw on many useful experiences, including actual encounters with teachers and children, vicarious classroom experiences, guidance from friends and acquaintances in the profession, and—most important—your own reflections.

- The views of teaching held by the public, those hiring and working with new teachers, and the new teachers themselves are supportive and positive.

(© Jim Craigmyle/Corbis)

People take education courses for many reasons, but three are particularly common: First, as citizens, people need to know how a major institution like the school system works so that they can make informed choices within their communities and at the voting booth. Second, as parents or potential parents, they need to know a great deal to be intelligent partners with the schools in their children's education. Third, those who consider a career in teaching need to understand the profession they may be entering.

This text is written with this third group in mind. And this chapter, more than any other, focuses on those people who are exploring the teaching profession. Its purpose is to help you answer a fundamental question: Why should you become a teacher? As you read about the following teachers, we hope you come to understand more fully your own motivations for teaching.

Truth or Fiction?

T   F   The percentage of teachers reporting to be "very satisfied" with their choice of teaching as a career has almost doubled in the last 25 years.

T   F   Most school superintendents and principals claim that the quality of new teachers has declined.

T   F   American teens claim teachers contribute most to our society's well-being.

examining your motives for teaching

If you teach, it is quite likely that by the end of your second year of teaching you will have had the following experiences:

1. Someone at a party or other social gathering will ask you what you do and how you like teaching. Soon the person will tell you that he or she has always wanted to be a teacher and regrets having become a stockbroker/bookkeeper/sales representative/flight attendant/disk jockey, and that he or she may still give it all up and become a teacher.

2. You will get to know an experienced teacher who confides that he or she deeply regrets having become a teacher. While in college, the person felt cut out for teaching and actually enjoyed it initially. But gradually, he or she became fed up with the whole thing—bratty kids, pushy administrators, the same old faces in the teachers' lounge, the instant-expert parents, and the overemphasis on standards and high-stakes testing. Now the person feels trapped in teaching and sees no way out.

The purpose of this chapter is to keep you from becoming "the other person" in either of these situations. It is intended to help you make a well-thought-out decision about what to do with your life, particularly if you are still undecided about becoming a teacher.

COMPARING YOUR MOTIVES TO OTHERS'

At this point, you have likely answered the question "What are my motives for wanting to become a teacher?" (and we surely hope you have). Here are a few motives you might check against your own list:

- I really like the idea of having a positive influence on 25 (or 150) kids every day.
- I can't think of anything else to do with my major.
- Teaching seems to be a fairly secure, low-risk occupation with many attractive benefits, including lots of vacation time and time to raise a family.
- I always loved history (or mathematics or science or literature), and teaching seems to be a career that will allow me to work with a subject matter that I love.
- I can't imagine anything more important to do with my life than helping children with disabilities learn to cope with, and even overcome, their barriers.
- The instruction I had in school was incredibly bad, and I want to correct that situation.
- My parents would really be pleased and proud if I were a teacher.
- Quite simply, I love children.

TABLE 1.1 Principal Reasons Selected by all Teachers for Originally Deciding to Become a Teacher, 1971–2006 (%)					
Reason	1971	1981	1991	2001	2006
Desire to work with young people	72	70	66	73	71
Value or significance of education to society	37	40	37	44	42
Interest in subject-matter field	35	44	34	36	39
Influence of teacher in elementary or secondary school	18	25	27	32	31
Influence of family	21	22	21	19	19

Sources: Adapted from Table 49, Status of the American Public School Teacher (Washington, DC: National Education Association, 2003), p. 68; and prepublication data derived from the 2005–2006 administration of the Status survey (courtesy of the National Education Association).

- I enjoy being in charge and being a positive influence on students.
- I really don't know what else I could do. I know about teaching, and I think I could do it.
- I'm concerned that society is falling apart, and I want to look out for the kids.
- Education seems as if it's going to be the action field of the future, and I want to be part of it.
- One of my students might become a famous painter, or the president of a major foundation, or who knows what. It would be great to have a strong impact on just one significant life.
- I really want to become a principal/coach/guidance counselor/college professor/ educational researcher, and teaching seems to be the way to start.
- I have strong religious beliefs and see teaching as a good and useful way to live my life.
- Businesses are increasingly interested in training and educating their employees, and I want a career as a private-sector educator working in corporate America.
- I want to have fun in life, and as a teacher, I'll have fun and get paid for it!
- I have always felt I have a calling— a vocation—to be a teacher.[1]

You may be interested in seeing whether answers to the question "Why teach?" have changed over time. Why did the teachers you had select teaching as a career? Why did your parents' teachers decide to teach? The data in Table 1.1 come from a study conducted every five years by the National Education Association. Notice the striking stability from one generation to the next of the prime motivation for teaching—"desire to work with young people." From 1971 to 2006, the change is only 1 percent. Although not as dramatic, the generational stability of the other motivations is remarkable. Amid all of the social change in recent decades, men and women continue to be drawn to the work of teaching by the same desires. As we'll see, the rewards often match the desires of those who teach.

the rewards of teaching

As we have seen, responses to the question "Why teach?" run the gamut from "Teaching will satisfy me" to "I want to help others." Our individual motivations can change and may be quite different at different times and when we are in different moods.

> *At twenty-two, I graduated Phi Beta Kappa. I had choices at my fingertips: law school, grad school . . . corporate America, here I come! Adults swelled their chests in pride. My peers practiced the "on my way to a Lexus" shuffle. Then the question: "And what are your plans after graduation?" Answer: "I'm moving to New York to teach elementary school in the South Bronx." As a twenty-three-year-old teacher with sore feet and twenty-eight incredible kids, my explanation reminds me of a song. I had a choice to sit it out or dance. I chose to dance.*
>
> —THALIA THEODORE,
> Washington Post (December 2, 2001), p. F1

As social psychologist Peter Drucker quipped, "We know nothing about motivation. All we can do is write books about it."

At the same time, the motivational *factors*—those qualities that reside within teaching—are clearer and relatively constant. Researchers have identified a set of occupational rewards that can help us sort out both the attractive and unattractive qualities of a teaching career.[2] These rewards are classified into two broad categories: extrinsic and intrinsic. **Extrinsic rewards** are the public, external attractions of an occupation, such as money, prestige, and power. The **intrinsic rewards** of an occupation are the internal psychic or spiritual satisfaction one receives from one's work, such as a personal sense of accomplishment or an enjoyment of the work itself. It will come as no surprise that, comparatively speaking, teaching is somewhat out of balance, receiving generally high marks on one set of rewards and low marks on the other.

EXTRINSIC REWARDS

Teaching has rarely been cited for its abundance of extrinsic rewards. Although it offers more extrinsic rewards than many other occupations, such as law enforcement and coal mining, when compared with other professions, teaching ranks low in extrinsic compensations.

Salaries

Teachers' salaries and benefits (such as retirement plans and health care) have improved substantially in recent years, as you will see in Chapter 13, "What Are Your Job Options in Education?"; there are also encouraging signs that steady gains can be expected. Nevertheless, relative to salaries in occupational fields with similar educational requirements (e.g., a college degree and specialized training), teachers' salaries do not compare favorably. Whereas salaries in some professions usually begin low and then increase significantly, salaries for teachers may rise only modestly over the course of an entire teaching career. However, the importance of salary, like the whole issue of monetary needs, varies enormously from one person to the next. And teachers' salaries vary significantly from one geographical location to the next, as you will also see in Chapter 13.

Status

Status refers to one's position in a group—that is, where one stands in relation to others. The status of a doctor or a beggar is rather clear, but the status of a teacher is more difficult to gauge. To young parents entrusting their child to school for the first time, the status of the teacher is quite high. To the same parents 12 or 15 years later, on hearing that their child wants to become a teacher, the status may be somewhat diminished. The United States' current commitment to massively reform its educational system is, however, having a positive effect on the status of teaching.

Figure 1.1 shows the results of a turn-of-the-century public opinion survey that asked which of eight professions (including physician, lawyer, nurse, and journalist) "provides the most important benefit to society." Respondents put teaching first by close to a four-to-one margin over physicians (62% versus 17%). This was a big improvement over a poll taken a decade earlier, in which only 35 percent of respondents put teaching first.[3]

FIGURE 1.1

Profession That Provides the Most Benefit to Society

Source: David Haselkorn and Louis Harris, "The Essential Profession: A National Survey of Public Attitudes Toward Teaching, Educational Opportunity, and School Reform." Reprinted with permission of Recruiting New Teachers, Inc., 1998.

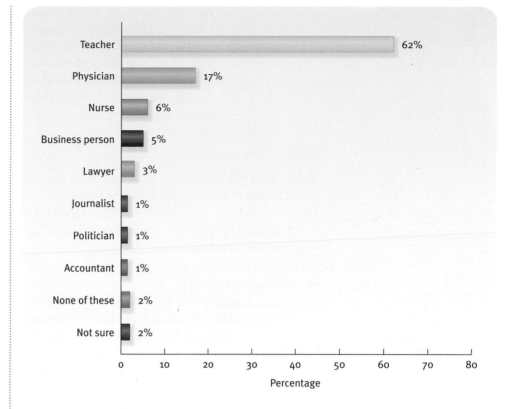

Power

Power is not usually seen as a reward of teaching, but it nevertheless is a quality that "resides in the office." Anyone who claims that teachers do not have power has forgotten what it was like to go to school without having done the homework and to sit in fear of being called on by Mrs. Gotcha. The power of the teacher is not a dollars-and-cents power, like that of a corporate chief executive officer, but any person who can make another's day or ruin another's year has power. Although, as sociologist Dan Lortie observed, "Teachers are not supposed to *enjoy* exercising power per se,"[4] the public opinion survey discussed earlier clearly indicates that the public sees the quality of teachers as the greatest influence on student learning.[5]

A recent study by Harvard economists, coined by the press as "The $320,000 Kindergarten Teacher," will surely boost the power and prestige of teachers. The study focused on the impact of early education on the lifetime earnings of people who attended and did not attend kindergarten. The cumulative financial impact on a single class of early school attendees was a staggering $320 million!

Work Schedule

There is an old joke about a student in an education course being stumped on an exam by the question "What are the three best things about a career in teaching?" Finally, in desperation, he writes, "June, July, and August."

That student probably flunked, but he did have a point. Compared with other workers, teachers spend much less time at their work sites. If we ignore what teachers do at home by way of preparing lessons, correcting papers, and checking homework, we can say they work six or seven hours per day for fewer than half the days of the year. Compared with those in power-and-status occupations, such as corporate finance or law, teachers have less demanding work schedules. Also, teachers have much more flexibility and personal control over how they use their time. For many men and women, family life is a top priority, and the time spent close to home and on summer vacations is a major plus associated with a teaching career. These teachers see sharing a schedule with their children as a significant benefit. Teachers' work schedules, therefore, are one extrinsic reward that carries a great deal of weight.

INTRINSIC REWARDS

Extrinsic rewards, like company stock options or year-end bonuses, are tangible. Intrinsic rewards are, by their very nature, "in the eye of the beholder." What might be one person's intrinsic reward, such as taking a busload of students on an overnight fieldtrip to the state capital, is another's living nightmare. However, the most satisfied teachers are usually those attracted to such intrinsic rewards.

Students

The attraction of working with students has long been one of the strongest rewards perceived by teachers. The daily contacts, the conversations and exchanges, and even the struggles to motivate students are a deep source of satisfaction for many teachers. Seeing children learn, grow, and develop—seeing them able to do things in May that they were unable to do at the beginning of the school year—is a genuinely fulfilling experience. Being important to others satisfies profound human needs, and teachers know about and appreciate this potential to affect the lives of others. Nearly three out of five (58%) teenagers surveyed mentioned teachers when asked by researchers who or what had influenced them to become the kinds of people they are.[6]

This reward is particularly meaningful to elementary school teachers, who spend so much time with the same group of 15 to 30 children. Secondary school teachers, who focus on a particular subject matter and may see as many as 150 students in a day, identify working with students as an important attraction, but not always to the same degree as their elementary school counterparts.

Performance of a Significant Social Service

In the award-winning film about early Renaissance England, *A Man for All Seasons,* Sir Thomas More says to Richard Rich, the man who eventually betrayed him, but who at the time was seeking a cushy job at court, "Why not be a teacher, Rich? You'd be a fine teacher. Perhaps a great one." Disappointed, Rich replies, "And if I were, who would know it?" Thomas More then says, "You . . . your pupils . . . your friends . . . God—not a bad public, that."[7]

To many teachers, their greatest satisfaction is the sense that they are doing important work for the common good. This realization buoys them up and helps them tolerate the less attractive aspects of teaching. As we saw in Figure 1.1, the general public seems to agree that teaching provides valuable benefits for society. Whereas workers in government and business are aware in an abstract sense that they are contributing to the social good, teachers have daily flesh-and-blood testaments to the importance of their service right before them. Many college professors report that they see more college students not only seriously considering teaching as a career but also selecting teaching specifically because they see it as service to the nation and a way to pay back the country. For some students, the deeper motive behind this service for others is a religious one; that is, they see teaching as a way to serve God by serving the young.

> *A man of humanity is one who, in seeking to establish himself, finds a foothold for others and who, desiring attainment for himself, helps others to attain.*
>
> —CONFUCIUS (551–479 B.C.),
> Chinese Philosopher

▶❚❚ TeachSource VIDEO CASE

Teaching as a Profession: Collaboration with Colleagues

Go to the Education CourseMate website to watch the video clips, study the artifacts in the case, and reflect on the following questions:

1. Were you aware that the collaborative process shown in this case goes on among teachers? In your own education, have you seen evidence of this collaborative planning process?

2. Does the planning process these teachers engaged in look like something you would enjoy as part of your career?

Stimulation and Support from Fellow Teachers

When describing the work of teaching, researchers often report on the sense of isolation many teachers experience.[8] Nevertheless, for many teachers their contacts and interactions with colleagues are an important intrinsic reward. Teachers enjoy the shoptalk and camaraderie that are a natural part of school life. Because teachers are not always rewarded for their individual job performance or for their expertise, feelings of competition are less prevalent than among such occupational groups as salespeople or lawyers who must establish and grow their clientele. Teachers know they are part of a highly and increasingly cooperative venture. (The Video Case, *Teaching as a Profession: Collaboration with Colleagues* provides a more in-depth look at how teachers can work together.)

The Work of Teaching

For many teachers, the process of teaching is a significant reward in itself. Whether it is explaining an idea, working with small groups, or designing instructional units, the actual work itself is highly gratifying. Like a pianist moving through a favorite sonata or a lawyer cross-examining a witness, teachers often draw their deepest satisfactions from the act of applying their craft. One teacher describes this feeling in this chapter's Voices from the Classroom feature. Of course, teachers vary in which activities they find rewarding. Some draw their rewards from establishing a nurturing, cooperative environment; some from unraveling complicated problems for students; and some from seeing students work and learn independently. For many teachers, all else pales before their deep sense of fulfillment in simply doing the work of teaching.

This teacher obviously enjoys her students and the work of teaching.

As you continue reading and doing the work of this course, we urge you to keep in mind the issues of intrinsic and extrinsic rewards, personal satisfactions, and the "fit" between you and the work of the teacher. Begin now with some quiet reflection.

VOICES from the classroom

Are You Born with It?

Elida Laski taught kindergarten for three years in Chula Vista, California, was a literacy coach in the Boston public school system, and is now an assistant professor at Boston College.

In my second year of teaching, a colleague told me, "Good teachers are born, not made, and you were born with it." After four years of teaching, I still wonder about this comment. What is *it*—that certain something that distinguishes excellent teachers? Do you have to be born with that certain something to be a good teacher? If you are born with *it*, do you always know that teaching is the profession for you? Is it true that some people are just not made for teaching, or can anyone learn what it takes? How do you know whether you are meant to be a teacher?

I never intended to be a teacher. In fact, it was not until my senior year of college that, as a frustrated pre-med student, I entertained the idea of teaching and took two education courses. Immediately, I knew that teaching was for me! I had done very well in the pre-med track, but I never felt invested in what I was studying. Education courses required just as much, if not more, time and thought, and they were exciting in a way pre-med had never been. Education offered the academic rigor of the sciences but also appealed to my heart.

Teaching demands systematic thought and reflection to deliver instruction and analyze situations. It requires a solid understanding of content and pedagogy to be critical of new trends and develop curriculum. However, I believe it is instincts that humanize teaching—the gut feeling of what will work or not, the sense of how to connect with each child, and the ability to juggle 10 things at once and be fired up rather than stressed out, and so much more. Being in the classroom is still an adrenaline rush. I put in 12-hour days without thinking twice. I cannot go to a store, museum, or park without thinking how I might apply what I see to my classroom. The joy of teaching, itself, drives me. That, I think, is the *it*. Whether you can learn *it* or must be born with *it*, I still cannot say.

> ### PAUSE AND REFLECT
>
> 1. Which of the extrinsic rewards discussed in this section apply to you most? Which of the intrinsic rewards? Are there other rewards not mentioned here?
>
> 2. As you probe your own motives for considering teaching, what have you learned about yourself?

sources of useful experience

One of the major educational insights applied to schooling in recent years concerns individual differences. There is a new appreciation for the unique learning styles and learning problems of children and youth. As a result, the "one true way" approach to education is gradually slipping by the boards. The same insight about individual differences applies to making an intelligent career choice. Because people learn in such diverse ways and differ so much in what they already know and need to learn, we can offer only sketchy guidelines here. We consider four categories of experience, however, that may help you answer the question "Should I teach?" You should use the four sources in whatever combination best fits your present stage of life and career decision making.

REAL ENCOUNTERS

Students who aspire to be teachers should test their commitment by putting themselves in actual school situations. As much as possible, students of teaching should observe in schools and participate in various activities that give them **real encounters** with students. Some teaching candidates avoid contact with the young until they begin student teaching, only to find that young people are much different from the romantic images they have manufactured. "Those nasty little fifth-graders are so disgustingly . . . juvenile!" one shocked student teacher told us. All too frequently, teaching candidates limit their encounters to typical elementary and secondary school students. They do not consider teaching children with mental or physical disabilities or even becoming a specialist such as a reading teacher. As a result of their past experiences, they may have been exposed to only a narrow segment of the opportunities and challenges of teaching.

Increasingly, school districts are using college students as teacher aides and assistant teachers, both during the school year and in summer school. Also, a large number of teacher education programs have cooperative arrangements with schools that give college students opportunities to play various roles within the school, usually as part of their coursework in teacher education. In addition, we urge prospective teachers to explore opportunities to be substitute teachers in nearby schools. Although the work is demanding, much can be learned from it. Besides the valuable experience and the money earned, these substitute teaching stints often lead to regular teaching positions. School districts typically are more interested in hiring someone they have seen "in action" and who is a "known quantity" rather than strangers they only know from résumés and references. If your schedule doesn't permit substitute teaching, many schools will gratefully accept part-time volunteer help from education students.

> *You cannot acquire experience by making experiments. You cannot create experience. You must undergo it.*
>
> —ALBERT CAMUS (1913–1960),
> French Author

Real-world experience with children can help you make an informed decision about teaching as a career.

(© Bob Daemmrich/PhotoEdit)

Schools, however, do not exhaust the opportunities. There is much to be said for nonschool contact with children, such as camp counseling, playground work, after-school recreation projects, work in orphanages and settlement houses, and youth-related church work. Other possibilities include coaching a team or sponsoring a youth club. The most important thing is to get your feet wet—to get the feel of working with young people in a helping relationship.

VICARIOUS EXPERIENCES

Not all learning has to take place in the school of hard knocks. In fact, civilization itself requires that we be able to capitalize on the experiences of others. Artists and other talented people can make others' experiences accessible to us for enjoyment, edification, or both. Great fictional classics such as *Good-bye, Mr. Chips* by James Hilton and *The Corn Is Green* by Emlyn Williams, portray teachers and schools, as do somewhat more contemporary novels like Bel Kaufman's *Up the Down Staircase* and Evan Hunter's *Blackboard Jungle.* (All four of these books have been made into films.) There have also been some fine nonfiction accounts of teaching; among the best are Rafe Esquith's *Teach Like Your Hair Is on Fire*, Tracy Kidder's *Among Schoolchildren*, Samuel G. Freedman's *Small Victories*, and Esmé Raji Codell's *Educating Esmé.*

Films such as *Freedom Writers, The History Boys, The Emperor's Club, Mr. Holland's Opus, Music of the Heart, Lean on Me, Dangerous Minds, Pay It Forward, Dead Poet's Society*, and *Stand and Deliver* are other sources of **vicarious experiences** that help us both relive our own school experiences and see them in a different light. However, that light is often distorting. Leslie Swetnam has reported on how the media—particularly film and television—twist the public's image of the teacher. Swetnam states, "Problems arise from the misrepresentation of who teaches, where they teach, how they teach, and what demands are placed on teachers, thereby creating an alarming distortion with consequences serious enough to warrant the concern of all educational professionals."[9] Her analysis of the most popular media presentations of teachers and schools shows that they overrepresent male teachers, secondary schools, minority teachers, and urban schools. Other distortions are that classes are small; teaching typically means the adult is talking (often with the skill of a Stephen Colbert or Steve Carrell!), and when the class finally gets around to it, learning is fun, fun, fun.[10]

One genre of films that is especially distorting includes those that present teachers as perverts and sadists—films such as *The Breakfast Club, Election,* and *Sugar and Spice,* as well as hoards of others. These dark portrayals of teachers may be entertaining but are hardly useful. Then there has also been a parade of comedies about school life, such as *The School of Rock, Ferris Bueller's Day Off, Summer School* and *Bad Teacher,* which don't exactly flatter traditional teachers either.

Despite their occasional inaccuracies, a careful analysis of these images can prepare us for certain aspects of teaching and school life. We must remember, however, that books, films, and television often portray school life at its extremes, featuring heightened situations well beyond the typical experiences of most teachers. The true drama of teaching is quiet, long term, and terribly real.

GUIDANCE

Another aid in determining whether teaching is right for you is the advice and counsel gained from those who know you. Besides parents and friends (who may be too close to you to be objective), you can consult former teachers, career placement counselors, and your college professors. The latter can be particularly helpful because, besides knowing you, they are familiar with the realities of teaching.

You should use caution when seeking guidance from others, however. First, choose people who know you well rather than those who have seen you just at your better moments. Second, do not expect a comprehensive computer printout of hard data with a firm decision at the bottom line. If you get a few glimpses of insight from the advice given, be satisfied. Third, be wary because many people are compulsive advice givers. People often generalize on the basis of too little knowledge, and they are sometimes just plain wrong. Receive advice openly, but follow it cautiously.

> "
> *Write down the advice of him who loves you, though you like it not at present.*
> —ENGLISH PROVERB

REFLECTION

The most important aspect of the real school encounters, guidance, and vicarious experiences you collect is that they provide you with data for **reflection**. Indeed, the value of these experiences will be lost if you do not think seriously about them. People are often so busy experiencing things—or getting ready to experience them— that they fail to reflect on what they have done to ensure that they get the most from the experience.

Admittedly we are nags, but we cannot stress this point strongly enough. Reflection goes to the very heart of why we have written this book. Both of us are convinced that many people make sloppy decisions about becoming teachers. Often, they have not asked fundamental questions about themselves and about schools. This is precisely why we have organized this book around questions such as "Why teach?" and "What is a school and what is it for?"

Getting Started as a Reflective Practitioner

All of us "reflect" in some way on what we experience. Typically, our reflections are brief and unsystematic. The *reflective practitioner* thinks more thoroughly and more systematically about experiences. The next time you visit a school or view a Video Case of classroom life, use these questions to stimulate your thinking:

1. What surprised you about what you observed? What was unexpected?
2. What were the teacher's goals? From what you could tell, were they achieved?
3. If you had the same goals, what would you have done?
4. How did the students appear to be responding during the class? Were they all involved? Most of them? Just a few? What could have been done to improve their involvement?
5. What, if anything, was different about these students from the way you and your classmates were at their age? Were there striking similarities?

PAUSE AND REFLECT

1. Are you really and truly using all the resources available to you to help you make a conscious, clearly thought-out decision about your future career? What can you do to enhance your chances of making a good decision?
2. Have you *really* acquired the mental habit of reflecting on your experiences?

case studies in the motivation to teach

This section offers two case studies illustrating common motives for going into teaching. Each case study is followed by a set of questions and a comment that raises important issues about the nature of teaching. The cases provide examples of how particular abstract motives take shape in teachers' lives. You may want to discuss the cases and the accompanying questions with other people. The shared experience of reading the cases and responding to the questions should help you probe and understand your own motivations.

COMMENT

All of us have had teachers whose excitement and enthusiasm for their subject were contagious. Love for a particular subject matter or content is an important and commendable motive for teaching. A major purpose of school is to pass on the best of society's knowledge. Another important purpose is to help young people develop basic skills and attitudes, especially a love for learning. A teacher who has a passion to convey the subject matter is effective at both of these goals. Such teachers may push students hard, but they are frequently the ones who have the greatest impact on students.

But carrying love for a particular subject to an extreme can cause trouble. Real learning is usually built on students' interest. Their interest in or love of learning can be blunted when the lover (the teacher) is too overpowering or insistent. The great teacher, like the great lover, knows how to draw out others' interests and help students "fall in love."

Another danger awaits the teacher who is "blinded" by love of a subject. This teacher may be so busy teaching what she or he enjoys that the rest of the curriculum gets shortchanged. For example, the English teacher who loves interpreting literature often finds it easy to avoid slugging it out with grammar, punctuation,

from PRESERVICE to PRACTICE

The Desire to Teach a Particular Subject

Julia Tucker had been a star science student since junior high school. She received a partial scholarship to study chemistry in college and earned high marks in everything connected with science. She also derived a good deal of personal satisfaction from quietly showing her mostly male teachers and fellow students that a female could excel at science.

When she graduated from college, Julia was heavily recruited by a chemical engineering firm and immediately fell in love with her job. It took a little longer—two years—but she fell even more in love with Nicholas, a chemist, who was working on the same project. They got married, and a year and a day later, Justin was born. Julia was back at work in six weeks. Both Nicholas and she hoped to have four children, but it didn't work out that way. There was no second pregnancy.

Julia was disappointed, but she took it philosophically. After all, she had a wonderful job, a loving husband, and a son who was the joy of her life. Everything was fine until Justin went off to middle school and began taking science courses. Julia couldn't wait to help him with his science homework. She stayed up late reading his science textbooks.

She found all sorts of excuses to talk to Justin's teachers about science education. She found herself daydreaming at work about how to teach scientific concepts to children. Somewhere along the way, Julia also began losing interest in the highly specialized type of chemistry she was doing. So, after a great deal of soul searching and several late-night conversations with Nicholas, she quit her job and went back to school to get a teaching license in chemistry.

That was more than a year ago. Now Julia has a job—but it is hardly the job she fantasized about in her old lab or the teaching position for which she prepared. To her surprise, when she obtained her teaching license, the only available position (other than ones that would force her to move the family) was at the elementary level, as a fifth-grade teacher. The school superintendent realized that Julia would be a real asset to his school district but did not have an opening in the high school for two more years, when the chemistry teacher was scheduled to retire. So he presented Julia with a proposition: she could take some methods courses over the summer (at district expense), then teach fifth-grade for two years

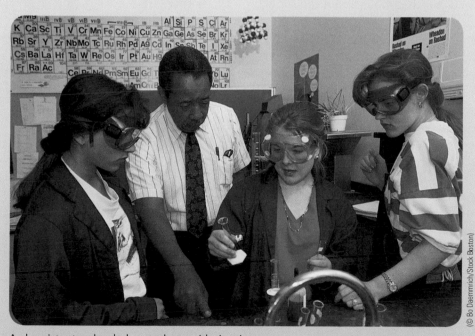

A chemistry teacher helps students with titrations.

(© Bo Daemmrich/Stock Boston)

(continued)

helping establish a new elementary science curriculum, and be the coordinator of the annual science fair.

At first, Julia was wary. She thought it would mean throwing away a good deal of her specialized knowledge and risking failure as an elementary school teacher, although the fifth-grade job would last only two years. But after talking it over with Nicholas and getting great support from her son, she reluctantly agreed.

A funny thing happened during the summer as Julia took the methods courses and prepared herself for her fifth-graders. She became more enthused about teaching children who she believed were "just becoming interested in the outer world." When Julia actually started working with her fifth-graders, she was hooked. They were so alive, responsive, and hungry to know about the world. What a challenge! Thoughts of ever becoming a chemistry teacher took a back seat to the elementary classroom.

By November, however, Julia had begun to have misgivings. A certain flatness in her class worries her. Much of the September curiosity has turned into an early case of midwinter blahs. Her supervisor has conducted the first formal observation of her teaching, and Julia is curious about the supervisor's opinion.

"So, Suzanne," Julia says at their post-observation conference. "How did I do? You were writing up such a storm, I thought you would need another notebook!"

"Oh, I hope you didn't find that distracting. I probably should have warned you that I would be scribbling away."

"No, that's fine. I'm just curious to know how I did."

"I'd much rather hear what *you* think, Julia. How do you think the class went?"

"Well, I think pretty much as usual. They were a little quieter, perhaps because you were in there, but in general it was an average class."

"I did notice it being quiet, Julia. How do you feel about that?"

"As a matter of fact, I'm confused by it. Since September, the decibel level has been steadily falling in all my classes, but particularly when we are doing science. I couldn't get them to shut up in September.

> *I love to learn in order that I might teach; and I get no joy from learning anything if I alone am to know about it.*
>
> —SENECA (1 BCE–AD 65), Roman philosopher

They ate up everything I presented, especially science. They just seem to have lost interest."

"From what I just saw, and from what I have observed passing by your door these weeks, I'd agree. Interest looks low."

"Suzanne, I've really worked to find topics that will interest them. I built a whole unit on pollution last month, with writing assignments and mathematics worked in. They said they were interested in heredity, so next month we're going to do family histories with interviews and collections of family facts and artifacts. They were all excited about this project in September, but now I'm stumped. What's the matter?"

"Quite honestly, Julia, I had a feeling this would happen."

"What do you mean?"

"When you came to interview last June, we were thrilled at the possibility of getting someone so knowledgeable and experienced, and particularly someone who loves science so much. But those same qualities made us hesitate too."

"I'm not getting you, Suzanne. I know we were all concerned that I didn't have traditional preparation for elementary teaching. You're not saying I know too much and I like science too much, are you?"

"Yes and no. No, you don't know too much. And yes, your love of science is a terrific asset. But at the same time, these qualities are keeping you from being the potentially fine teacher you can become. Julia, let me be honest. You are drowning these kids with information—and not just in science. You seem to be doing all the work. What worked so well for you during your student teaching with high school juniors and seniors just doesn't work with these elementary school wigglers."

"Honestly, Suzanne, I'm not giving them high school material. This work is within their range. I don't mean to sound defensive, but really. . . ."

"Julia, think 'romance.'"

"Romance? I thought you told me to do health and human sexuality in the spring!"

"No, no. Romance. Like in 'the romance of science' and 'the romance of writing.' Do you remember telling us during your interview how you fell in love—your words, Julia—fell in love with science in the fifth grade when you had to do a project for the science fair? Well, I think you ought to do a little time traveling and think about what caused *your* romance with science. Was it a fascinating question? An unsolved problem? The excitement of maybe solving a problem the adults couldn't? Or was it a teacher pumping facts and theories into you?"

"Uh-oh. I think the dawn is breaking. I've been too busy talking at them and trying to teach them some basic information."

"Right. You've been so busy telling them about what you love that you forgot that romance is a two-way street. It's a classic mistake of rookie teachers, even ancient ones like you. Sometimes you can get away with it in high schools, but not in elementary schools."

"So what do I do now?"

"Well, let me put aside these notes, and let's see whether you and I can put a little romance into the rest of the week's lessons."

"A little pedagogical seduction! Suzanne, I think you found the key!"

CASE QUESTIONS

1. How would you characterize Julia's motivation to teach?

2. What do you think her students were thinking and feeling about her classes?

3. Julia is clearly an outstanding resource to the school. What are her liabilities?

4. Which clues should Julia have been picking up on?

5. What are some things Julia might do to stimulate romance for science in her students?

and other essential writing skills. The elementary school teacher who loves science, like Julia, may fail to give the other subjects their due. Although this tendency to focus on what we know and love—and to avoid what we do not know or like—is understandable, it is also irresponsible. It is unfair to both the students and their later teachers, who will expect students to have a command over the avoided or neglected content.

Neither Julia's motive nor her problem is uncommon. Teachers who are strongly motivated by the desire to teach a particular subject matter have to be somewhat cross-eyed. While keeping one eye on what they want to teach, they need to keep the other eye on the students and their day-to-day progress and needs.

COMMENT

In addition to the serious injustice of underchallenging many students, Fred was reacting against the perversion of an important idea: teaching good citizenship. In Fred's school, as in many others, the idea of teaching good citizenship has been badly distorted.

During the 1930s, in a reform started by U.S. educator and philosopher John Dewey, many schools adopted the policy of awarding a grade for citizenship. Dewey and many of his followers envisioned training for citizenship as a process of working out in class actual problems that arise in a democracy. They saw the schools as an appropriate place to teach students about democratic decisions and to give them low-risk but real practice in such decision making in a context where mistakes were not "for keeps."

As sometimes happens with reforms, educational and otherwise, the processes introduced to the classroom by these reformers gradually degenerated into empty forms. Good citizenship came to mean docility, doing what one is told. Students could earn "good citizenship" grades by "playing the game"

> *The role of the teacher remains the highest calling of a free people. To the teacher, America entrusts her most precious resource, her children; and asks that they be prepared, in all their glorious diversity, to face the rigors of individual participation in a democratic society.*
>
> —SHIRLEY HUFSTEDLER,
> former U.S. Secretary of Education

LEADERS in education

Erin Gruwell (1969–)

(Courtesy of Erin Gruwell)

Nothing could have prepared Erin Gruwell for her first day of teaching at Wilson High School in Long Beach, California. A recent college graduate, Erin landed her first job in Room 203, only to discover that many of her students had been written off by the education system and deemed "unteachable." As teenagers living in a racially divided urban community, they were already hardened by first-hand exposure to gang violence, juvenile detention, and drugs.

Enter Erin Gruwell. By fostering an educational philosophy that valued and promoted diversity, she transformed her students' lives. She encouraged her students to rethink their rigidly held beliefs about themselves and others, reconsider their daily decisions, and rechart their futures. With Erin's steadfast support, her students shattered stereotypes to become critical thinkers, aspiring college students, and citizens for change. They even dubbed themselves the "Freedom Writers"—in homage to the civil rights activists known as "Freedom Riders"—and published a book.

Inspired by Anne Frank and Zlata Filipovic (who lived through the chaos of war-torn Sarajevo), Erin and her students captured their collective journey in *The Freedom Writers Diary: How a Teacher and 150 Teens Used Writing to Change Themselves and the World Around Them*. Through poignant student entries and Erin's narrative text, the book chronicles their "eye-opening, spirit-raising odyssey against intolerance and misunderstanding."

Although Erin has been credited with giving her students a "second chance," it was perhaps she who changed the most during her tenure at Wilson High. Today, her impact as a "teacher" extends well beyond Room 203. Currently, Erin serves as president of the Freedom Writers Foundation (www.freedom-writersfoundation.org) and raises awareness by traveling across the United States to speak inside large corporations, government institutions, and community associations. But Erin's capacity to convert apathy into action matters most at schools and juvenile halls, where any observer can watch the expressions of troubled teens shift from guarded cynicism to unabashed hopefulness.

Erin and her students have appeared on numerous television shows, including *Oprah*, *The Rosie O'Donnell Show*, *Prime Time Live with Connie Chung*, *The View*, *Good Morning America*, and CSPAN's *Book TV*. Her class has been featured on National Public Radio and in national newspapers and *People* magazine. In January 2007, Paramount Pictures released *Freedom Writers*, a film based on this remarkable story, featuring Hilary Swank as Erin. That same year, her personal account of becoming a teacher, *Teach with Your Heart: What I Learned from the Freedom Writers*, was published.

Erin is a graduate of the University of California, Irvine, where she received the Lauds and Laurels Distinguished Alumni Award. She earned her master's degree and teaching credentials from California State University, Long Beach, where she was honored as Distinguished Alumna by the School of Education.

and not bothering anyone. Citizenship became a code word among teachers. A teacher who was given a class of "low achievers" or "discipline problems" was sometimes told, "Don't worry about academic concerns with these children. Just make them good citizens." Parents were told that their child wasn't a very good student but was "an excellent citizen." This euphemism meant that even though he or she didn't learn anything, the child did without question everything that students were supposed to do.

from PRESERVICE to PRACTICE

The Desire to Aid in the Renewal of Society

Fred Harvey was in his late thirties. His disposition was so pleasant, and a smile came so readily to his face, that one of the other teachers in the large metropolitan high school referred to him as "everybody's Dad." Fred had a remarkable ability to remain relaxed when everyone else was tense, and he often broke up emotionally charged faculty-room situations and staff meetings with an appropriate quip or humorous question.

Each year, Fred asked to teach the Curriculum II freshman history class. Of course, his request was always granted because the Curriculum II classes were considered the dumping ground for slow students and students who had given up. Some of the other teachers regarded the Curriculum II classes as "punishment." Yet, year after year Fred worked happily with students nobody else really wanted.

Fred's freshman history class was one of the most active in the school. He often took his students beyond the walls of the school on expeditions to day court, the police station, jail, and industrial plants in the area—and he also managed to sneak a baseball game into the field-trip lineup. Yet his classes were not characterized by fun and games. Students worked hard on long and involved homework assignments, intricate discussions of problems, and demanding tests.

One year, Fred invited another teacher to speak to the class about shipbuilding in the eighteenth century. The talk went well, and after the session the other teacher, Todd Vincent, commented to Fred that the discussion following his talk had been very different from what he had anticipated: the questions were thoughtful and displayed observation of detail that the guest speaker had not expected from a "bunch of Curriculum IIs."

Fred laughed. "You know, Todd," he said, "they amaze me too sometimes. Most of these kids really have behavior problems, not intellectual ones. If

> *Those who educate children well are more to be honored than they who produce them; for these only give them life, those the art of living well.*
>
> —ARISTOTLE (384–322 BCE), Greek Philosopher

you looked at their case histories, you'd find that the majority of them were 'dropped through the ranks.'"

"What do you mean?" asked Todd.

"They were in regular classes a good bit of their scholastic lives, but when they became problems in class, their teachers decided that the cause of their poor behavior was that the work was too hard for them. Most of the children in this class really represent the rebels, the nonconformists, the 'antisocials'—the kids who some teachers claim 'won't go along with the system.' They're the kids about whom many teachers say, 'I don't care whether they learn history as long as they become good citizens.'"

"Yes, but you must admit that very few of them will go to college. Most Curriculum IIs just drop out," said Todd.

"Maybe you're missing my point," replied Fred. "I guess I'm saying that people can't be 'good citizens' unless they are contributing members of society, and that they should contribute something they think is worth contributing. If they can't get the basic tools that make a person productive, how can they be good citizens? It's a lot more than getting a job or making a decent living. In fact, I believe these kids are much more capable than the kids we send to the university."

"In what sense?"

"In the sense that they are the least accepting of society as it exists now," replied Fred. "If you talked to some of them for an hour or so, you'd find that they really feel the school is hypocritical in many ways, and they aren't afraid to point out the hypocrisies. They'll tell you, for instance, that there are two sets of rules in the school, two sets of discipline procedures, two sets of privileges, and all the rest."

"But I hear the same thing from my 'honors' classes," Todd protested. "Those kids know about the double standard too. They often tell me that

(continued)

an honors student here can get away with anything from cutting class to smoking in the john."

"You've got me wrong again, Todd. What these kids are saying is not that we expect too much of them, but rather that we expect too little. For instance, if a kid dropped from an A to a C in your honors history course, what would happen?"

"The kid would probably get a 'request' to go in and see the counselor," Todd replied.

"That's right," Fred continued. "When a kid everyone believes is bound for college does poorly, bells go off and people get concerned. They try to help the kid take a look at what's wrong. If one of these students goes from a C to an F, though, everyone says, 'Well, what more do you expect? The kid's only a Curriculum II and doesn't have the ability to sustain a C.' And they get all the inexperienced teachers and martinets in the school. Oh, they know that if they become real problems, they'll get counseling and possibly even better teaching. But that isn't their complaint. They know that the system isn't out to punish them; they know the system would rather they just float along and not bother anyone. That's the double standard in this school: those who are cared about and those who aren't."

"You know," said Todd, "you're not just talking about the Curriculum II classes. I think the same thing is generally true of Curriculum I classes. It seems that a kid who's really bright gets a lot of attention, and so does the kid who is really slow, but it's that kid in the middle. . . ."

"Right," said Fred. "The kids in this class are the bottom of that middle group in terms of the concern they arouse from the system—and they know it. Yet, as you saw today, they are capable. We owe them a decent set of expectations. I've maintained high expectations for the kids. I would prefer to slightly overmatch them intellectually than undermatch them, because no development is possible when you're being undermatched constantly."

"Don't they complain about being pushed too hard?" asked Todd.

"Oh, sure! There's always a good deal of moaning, particularly in the early weeks, until they realize I don't dance to that tune. Pretty soon they settle in and decide to go along with the program. But then they realize that they are actually learning. At that point, they're hooked. They're mine, and I wouldn't trade teaching them for anything!"

"Well, Fred, this has been most instructive. I came to teach and I ended up learning."

"Me too. That's what keeps me going. And Todd, please come back next semester."

CASE QUESTIONS

1. How is Fred's commitment to social renewal specifically shown in his classroom teaching?

2. According to Fred, what is the criterion for assignment to Curriculum II classes in his school? Was this true of your high school?

3. What is the double standard Todd spoke of, and how do you explain it? What is the double standard Fred spoke of, and how do you explain it? Did either of these double standards exist in your school?

4. How do Fred's expectations for his students differ from those of most teachers you have known? In what other ways is he different from most of the teachers you have known?

5. What do you think were Todd's major misconceptions as a teacher?

6. What does Fred see as the role of academic disciplines in education? If you had to, how would you argue against his position?

The use of a citizenship grade as a conduct mark is an absolute travesty of the system Dewey and the reformers designed. As Fred noted, in reality good citizens are not docile sheep who can be "conned" with impunity. The long-term effect of the misinterpretation of citizenship as conformity and docility has been to discredit it as an appropriate goal for schooling. Yet, in Fred we see a person consciously attempting to develop educated citizens. His class visits to courthouses, legislative sessions, and factories, as well as the classroom study of major social problems, are very much in keeping with what Dewey—and, indeed, Thomas Jefferson and James Madison—had in mind when they spoke of educating for freedom.

opinions about teachers and teaching

The "Why teach?" question and the decision about whether teaching is the right career for you is intensely personal. Although what you think about teaching and whether it is a "good fit" for you is of primary importance, it may be useful to know what others think about teachers too. Here we'll consider the views of the general public, students, and administrators, and what teachers who are new to the field have to say about their work.

WHAT DOES THE PUBLIC SAY ABOUT TEACHERS AND TEACHING?

The education of America's children regularly tops the list of the public's social concerns. Particularly now, in the second decade of the twenty-first century, our educational system is receiving major attention from social critics and politicians. Americans are relying on their teachers to instruct, guide, inspire, motivate, and occasionally prod their children to learn more than ever before.

The public—that is, the people whose taxes pay the salaries of public school teachers—overwhelmingly acknowledges and supports the nation's teachers. When asked to select which group provided "the most benefit to society," 62 percent selected teachers, whereas only 17 percent selected physicians (the second choice). Only 5 percent chose people in business, 3 percent chose lawyers, and only 1 percent chose journalists and politicians.[11] When asked to rate which factors have the greatest impact on student learning, 44 percent selected the qualifications of the teacher over other factors such as class size, socioeconomic status of the family, or the family's involvement and support.[12]

Finally, the public has a great deal of trust in teachers. According to the *National Credibility Index,* when asked which people were "the most believable when speaking out on public issues," teachers were rated the highest, above members of the armed forces, national experts, and community activists.[13]

WHAT DO STUDENTS THINK ABOUT TEACHERS?

The old ditty sung by generations of students, "No more pencils. No more books. No more teachers' dirty looks!" may be giving way to a new appreciation. As shown in Figure 1.2, in a 2010 survey of students ages 12 to 17, high school students, often thought to be somewhat cool toward their teachers, view them as the top contributors (32%) to society's well-being, ahead of the next two contributors, doctors (23%) and scientists (19%). Although many students may fail to show it in their daily dealings with their teachers, this survey shows the deep wellsprings of their appreciation for the work of teachers.

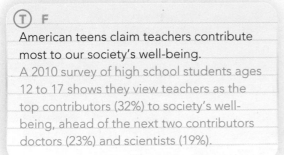

(T) F

American teens claim teachers contribute most to our society's well-being.

A 2010 survey of high school students ages 12 to 17 shows they view teachers as the top contributors (32%) to society's well-being, ahead of the next two contributors doctors (23%) and scientists (19%).

PAUSE AND REFLECT

1. Does this information about students' high regard for teachers surprise you?

2. What are your personal reactions to this endorsement of teachers?

FIGURE 1.2

The Lemelson-MIT Invention Index of American Youth Ages 12 through 17

Source: Available at http://web.mit.edu/invent/n-pressreleases/n-press-10index.html

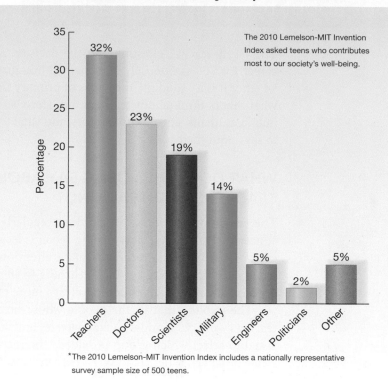

Teens' View of Society's Top Contributors

The 2010 Lemelson-MIT Invention Index asked teens who contributes most to our society's well-being.

Teachers 32%, Doctors 23%, Scientists 19%, Military 14%, Engineers 5%, Politicians 2%, Other 5%

*The 2010 Lemelson-MIT Invention Index includes a nationally representative survey sample size of 500 teens.

WHAT DO ADMINISTRATORS SAY ABOUT *NEW* TEACHERS?

The high regard the public and students have for teachers is encouraging. But what about new teachers, those who have recently entered the field? What do the administrators who work with new teachers and supervise them on a daily basis say about them?

The opinions of principals and superintendents support those of the general public. A stunning 98 percent of superintendents and principals surveyed agreed

Surveys reveal that most people consider an effective teacher to be a vitally important factor in a good education.

(© Elizabeth Crews)

with the descriptions of their new teachers as "motivated" and "energetic."[14] Rumors that the quality of new teachers has deteriorated are hardly borne out by those who do the hiring. A majority (52%) of these frontline administrators believe that the quality of those entering the profession has improved; only 9 percent of these educators believe it is declining.[15] We suspect that there are few professions or occupations where supervisors have such high regard for newcomers.

T (F)

The majority of school superintendents and principals claim that the quality of new teachers entering the field has declined. In a recent survey of frontline school administrators, the majority (52%) believed that the quality of those entering the profession has improved.

WHAT DO NEW TEACHERS THINK ABOUT TEACHING?

An in-depth study, conducted at the beginning of the twenty-first century with 664 public school teachers and 250 private teachers who had all taught for five or fewer years, paints a picture of how today's newest teachers feel about their work. The researchers aptly titled their report *A Sense of Calling: Who Teaches and Why*, and they concluded that "most new teachers are highly motivated professionals who bring a strong sense of commitment and high morale to their work."[16] New teachers see themselves as talented and dedicated professionals.

> *The best prize life offers is the chance to work hard at work worth doing.*
>
> —THEODORE ROOSEVELT (1858–1919), 26th U.S. President

Reflecting the title of the report, 86 percent of new teachers affirmed the notion that only those "with a true sense of calling" should teach.[17] Nine out of 10 claimed that the teaching profession demands a high level of energy and effort, requiring more talent and hard work than many other professions. The teachers in this study continually commented on the need for enthusiasm to do the job well. An overwhelming 98 percent described other new teachers with whom they work as sharing in their sense of commitment and enthusiasm. This is hardly the portrait of a disappointed and disgruntled group of newcomers.

PAUSE AND REFLECT

1. Do the opinions of one of these groups—the public, students, administrators, other new teachers—matter more to you than the opinions of the others? Why?

2. How important is it to you to know what other people will think about you as a teacher?

why teachers teach

Let's get back to the question "Why teach?" by considering those already in the field. First, are teachers personally satisfied with their career choice, and second, why do they teach? The answer to the satisfaction question reveals a dramatic and encouraging increase in teacher satisfaction in the last half century, going from a low in 1986 of 33% reporting being "very satisfied" to the most recent figure of 59% in 2009[18] (see Table 1.2).

Next, "Why teachers teach": *Attitudes about Teaching*, a 2003 study, reveals some answers that are surprisingly consistent with the results reported in *A Sense of Calling*. As shown in Table 1.3, nearly all of these new teachers (96%) reported that teaching is the work they love to do. Four out of five claimed that they would choose teaching

TABLE 1.2	Satisfaction with Teaching as a Career through the Years

(Percentage of teachers responding "very satisfied)

1984—40%	1987—40%	1995—54%	2006—56%
1985—44%	1988—50%	2001—52%	2008—62%
1986—33%	1989—44%	2003—57%	2009—59%

Source: From The MetLife Survey of the American Teacher: Collaborating for Student Success, April, 2010. Available at http://www.metlife.com/assets/cao/contributions/foundation/american-teacher/MetLife_Teacher_Survey_2009.pdf.

Ⓣ F

The percentage of teachers reporting to be "very satisfied" with their choice of teaching as a career has almost doubled in the last 25 years.

The answer to this teacher satisfaction question reveals a quite dramatic and encouraging increase in teacher satisfaction in the last half century, going from a low in 1986 of 33 percent reporting being "very satisfied," to the most recent figure of 59 percent in 2009.

> *Pleasure in the job puts perfection in the work.*
>
> —ARISTOTLE (384–322 BC),
> Greek Philosopher

again if starting over. Three out of four insisted that "teaching is a lifelong choice," and two out of three reported that they get a great deal of satisfaction out of teaching. Contrary to the rumor that many people simply drift into teaching, a mere 12 percent said that they "fell into teaching by chance." All but a handful had very altruistic attitudes about their work, telling the researchers that teaching offers them an opportunity for "contributing to society."

For some teachers, teaching is clearly a short-term career. One in five respondents in the *A Sense of Calling* survey indicated that they would probably change careers at some point. Although this figure contrasts sharply with the 50 percent of young college graduates in other fields who say that they expect to change careers at least once,[19] the reference to teaching as a short-term career brings up an important point. The desire to teach for a few years and then to move on to another career or to raise a family is both common and to be respected. Also, our schools are filled with people who "dropped in" on teaching and stayed to make it their professional home.

Judging from this study, new teachers show a remarkable certainty that they made the right choice in pursuing a teaching career. It also appears that most of today's new teachers have taken the time to reflect on whether teaching is the right career choice for them.

In *A Sense of Calling*, the researchers asked new teachers, "Is teaching satisfying?" They also asked the study participants specifically how important it was that their work has certain characteristics. Table 1.4 summarizes the new teachers' responses. An impressive 96 percent reported

TABLE 1.3	Why Teachers Teach

What Teachers Say	Percentage Who Say It
Teaching is work they love to do.	96
They would choose teaching again if starting over.	80
Teaching is a lifelong choice.	75
They get a lot of satisfaction out of teaching.	68
They fell into teaching by chance.	12

Source: Public Agenda, *Attitudes About Teaching* (New York: Public Agenda, 2003), p. 12.

TABLE 1.4 **Is Teaching Satisfying?**

How important is it to you that a job has each of the following characteristics?

	New Teachers' Responses (%)	
	"Absolutely Essential"	"My Current Teaching Position Has It"
Involves work you love to do	83	96
Allows enough time to be with family	81	79
Contributes to society and helps others	72	97
Provides the supervision and support you need	64	78
Has job security	60	84
Gives the sense that you are respected and appreciated	59	66
Has good opportunities for advancement	33	59
Pays well	30	31

Source: Public Agenda, *A Sense of Calling* (New York: Public Agenda, 2000), p. 10.

that they are involved in work they love, and 97 percent were convinced they were doing important work for the good of society. Eighty-four percent had the peace of mind that comes with knowing one's job is secure.[20] Although not surprising, only 31 percent claimed that teaching pays well. Clearly, today's new teachers, although not painting a perfect picture, are personally "happy in their work."

Teachers' widespread satisfaction and love for their work is largely unknown, even among teachers. This "good news" has been lost in the headlines focusing on students' cyberbullying, low test scores, and other educational problems. The reality is that most teachers love the job of teaching. Consider the following:

- Seventy-nine percent of teachers agree "strongly" with the following statement: "I am passionate about teaching."
- Seventy-four percent of teachers say that teaching is a lifelong career choice.
- Ninety-one percent of new teachers believe that teaching matches their skills and interests very well.[21]

A SPECIAL INTRINSIC REWARD

It is certainly encouraging news that others apparently are happy and satisfied as teachers. Nevertheless, it is your life—and your choice to enter the teaching field. Clearly, selecting a career is a personal decision and involves answering many questions: "Will I be happy?" "Will this career provide me with a satisfying lifestyle?" "Will I be up to the challenge, and will I find the work satisfying?" "Will I grow in the experience?" People who are considering teaching as a life's work should grapple with these questions, which relate to the motives for their choice, but they must also scrutinize other, deeper motives.

"

vo.ca.tion *n. 2. An inclination, as if in response to a summons, to undertake a certain kind of work.*

—AMERICAN HERITAGE DICTIONARY

Teaching, like nursing, the ministry, and social work, is a service occupation. More correctly, teaching is a **vocation**. Built into teaching is the idea of contributing to the lives of others. For many people, the root of their decision to teach is deeper than a love of subject matter or an attraction to the life of a teacher. Many men and women select teaching for reasons that are, at heart, religious or humanitarian. They see themselves as *called* to the work.

OUR FINAL WORD

We have said much in this chapter about the extrinsic and intrinsic rewards that come with teaching. One of the intrinsic rewards mentioned was the knowledge that as a teacher you are involved in crucially important work. This particular **psychic reward** is captured by the story of a U.S. television reporter who was filming a documentary on the work of the late Mother Teresa and her community of nuns in the slums of Calcutta, India. The reporter came upon a young American nun cleaning the running sores, filth, and infections covering the body of a dying beggar. After filming the young woman as she carefully cleansed the ruined body of this near-death man, the reporter looked down at the nun and declared, "Sister, I wouldn't do that for a million dollars!" Without taking her eyes off her dying patient, the young nun quietly replied, "Neither would I."

One of the great intrinsic benefits of a career in teaching—and one not shared by the vast number of other occupations—is the inner certainty that you are doing important work and that you are spending your life well. *Those who can, teach.*

WHY TEACH? YOUR FINAL WORD

In your journal or online at this textbook's website, respond to the following questions:

1. As a result of reading this initial chapter and participating in the activities, you may be closer to clarifying your answer to the question "Why teach?" Describe what you discovered as you read this chapter and what you intend to do as a result.

2. Which of the intrinsic and extrinsic motivations cited in this chapter do you think most closely match your current motivations to teach?

3. This chapter includes several sources for experiences to gain greater understanding of teaching and its "fit" with your own motivations and values. Specifically which of these do you think you will pursue?

KEY TERMS

extrinsic reward (4)
intrinsic reward (4)
psychic reward (24)
real encounter (9)

reflection (11)
vicarious experience (10)
vocation (24)

FOR FURTHER INFORMATION

TEACHSOURCE VIDEOS

Becoming a Teacher: Voices and Advice from the Field

This video shows several teachers, new and experienced, discussing how to become a teacher and providing practical advice.

Freedom Writers: Teachers Can Inspire Students to Learn and Achieve

This video is an interview with Erin Gruwell, the subject of a profile in this chapter.

WEB RESOURCES

About.com. Available at **http://careerplanning. about.com/**

This all-purpose information website has sites ranging from the nature of teaching to something called "workplace survival."

The Apple Monster: Where Teachers Meet and Learn. Available at **http://theapple.monster.com/.**

This site has multiple sources of information and support for teachers, from job openings to interviewing techniques, lessons plans, and disciplinary tips.

Association for Supervision and Curriculum Development. Available at **www.ascd.org**.

This site of a major educational organization has many different features and supports for those exploring careers in education and for new teachers.

PRINT RESOURCES

Marva Collins and Civia Tamarkin, *Marva Collins' Way* (Los Angeles, CA: Tarcher, 1982).

This book takes the reader inside the world of one of America's most inspiring and controversial teachers, Marva Collins, who describes her method of educating the children others forgot.

Rafe Esquith, *Teach Like Your Hair Is on Fire* (New York: Viking Adult/Penguin Group USA, 2007).

The title captures the intensity and excitement of this inspired teacher's approach to teaching. Rafe Esquith's Los Angeles fifth-grade classroom is the scene of poor, immigrant children being exposed to Shakespeare, classical music, and the world of ideas—and loving it.

Erin Gruwell, *Teach with Your Heart: Lessons I Learned from the Freedom Writers* (New York: Broadway Books, 2008).

Erin Gruwell, featured in this chapter's Leaders in Education, has written a personal, poignant account of her struggles as a beginning teacher and of finally reaching her goal of inspiring young students to become powerful writers.

Tracy Kidder, *Among Schoolchildren* (Boston: Houghton Mifflin, 1989).

The author spent an entire school year observing a fifth-grade teacher and produced a rich, fascinating account of a teacher's year that shows how one teacher shaped and moved the lives of her students.

National Education Association, *Status of the American Public School Teacher* (Washington, DC: National Education Association, 2003). Available at **http://www.nea.org/edstats/images/status.pdf**

This report is a goldmine of information on topics ranging from teachers' attitudes toward their work to salary information. Compiled every five years, the report gives us a snapshot of the profession today in a historical perspective.

The Education CourseMate website for this text offers many helpful resources. Go to www.cengagebrain.com to access the TeachSource Video Cases and other TeachSource videos, flashcards, interactive quizzes, the eBook, reflection and enrichment activities, a state standards resource center, and other study aids.

2 what is a school and what is it for?

(© Bob Daemmrich)

I n this chapter, we explore with you two related and fundamental questions: What is a school? and What is it for? We pose and discuss these questions to aid you in forming your ideas about the underlying issues. It is unlikely that you can make a good career choice if you lack a fundamental understanding of the institution in which your career is centered. Also, if you hope to thrive and be happy within an institution, you have to know how it is put together and how it works. For example, you must know what the institution says it is doing and what, in fact, it actually does. If you are considering a job in a particular school, you need to know what the leadership of the school *really* expects of their teachers to know whether you want to work there. Finally, if you hope to improve the schools—that is, make them better because of your involvement with them—you must have a realistic view of what is going on in the schools now and develop your vision of what the schools can and should become in the future.

FOCUS POINTS

- Education is a large, all-encompassing endeavor, whereas schooling is a specialized activity and simply one aspect of an individual's education.

- Schools have cultures and play a critical part in passing on a society's values to the young.

- The purpose of school determines much of what happens in school. There are universal purposes, and those of a particular school can be determined by methods discussed in this chapter.

- Research is giving us more accurate answers to the age-old question, "What is a good school?"

Truth or Fiction?

T F By the time you graduated from high school, you had experienced the equivalent of 10,000 movies of life in school.

T F The middle school years are characterized by a growth in independence and social interests.

T F Research shows that academically effective schools are good at remaining independent of parental involvement.

what is a school?

What is a school? This may not sound like a profound question; in fact, it probably seems rather tame. But, as the late U.S. Senator and linguist S. I. Hayakawa once wrote, "If fish were scientists, the last thing they would study would be water." Our point is that schools have been so much of your life that what they *actually* are may have become almost invisible to you. Again, we ask you to stop reading and seriously to reflect: What is a school?

The average child will spend more than 7,000 hours in elementary school (including kindergarten) by the end of sixth grade. By the time a student graduates from high school, this time totals 14,000 hours—the equivalent of watching 10,000 full-length movies!

Your reaction to this question reflects who you are and what your experience with school has been. Perhaps you responded in one of the following ways:

(T) F

By the time you graduated from high school, you had experienced the equivalent of 10,000 movies of life in school.

By the time a student graduates from high school, this time totals 14,000 hours—the equivalent of watching 10,000 full-length movies!

- A school is an agency that weans children from the protective warmth of the family and trains them for what society has decided is useful work.
- A school is a place where they fix your mind so you think like everyone else.
- A school is where children fall in love with learning.
- A school is a tax-supported baby-sitting agency.
- A school is a place where young savages have a chance to become civilized by engaging the world's most precious wisdom.
- A school is a place where we explore who we really are and how we can become full, creative human beings.
- A school is an institution where the dead wisdom and worn-out skills of the past are force-fed to the young.
- A school is where *real* education takes place.

Each of these descriptions says a great deal about the school experience of the person who formulated it. Our conviction is that your definition of *school* is a crucial cognitive map that greatly affects how you put together information and impressions of schools.

> **PAUSE AND REFLECT**
>
> 1. Before you read on, how would you answer the question "What is a school?"
>
> 2. Which of the descriptions best describe your understanding of schools? Which least describes your understanding? If none of them fit, write your own one-sentence description.

education and schooling

Before we burrow in on schools, we need to clarify an important distinction—namely, the difference between *education* and *schooling*. In simpler, premodern societies, when a boy could learn to be a man by following his father around and imitating him and the men of the village, and a girl could learn to be a woman by doing the same with her mother and the other women, schools were not necessary. Formal schooling became a social necessity when the home and the community were no longer effective or competent at training the young through informal contacts.

Most modern societies have realized for some time that education is too important to be left to chance. Whereas important things are sometimes learned on street corners, and grandparents often are excellent teachers, the informal educative process is simply too unreliable. Still, there are nagging and growing doubts that herding youngsters into school buildings for six or seven hours a day, five days a week, is the most effective way to prepare our children for life in our modern world—more on that topic later.

It has been jokingly suggested that in today's society, children interrupt their education to go to school. The distinction between schooling and education implied by this remark is important. Both schooling and education have myriad definitions. We have sprinkled a few such definitions here and there throughout the book for you to sample. Before we go further, though, we should look at these two related but distinct concepts in greater detail.

EDUCATION

For the moment, let us say that **education** is a process of human growth by which one gains greater understanding and control over oneself and one's world. It involves our minds, our bodies, and our relations with the people and the world around us. Education is also characterized by continuous development and change.

Education is much more open-ended and all-inclusive than schooling and knows few boundaries. It includes both the formal learning that takes place in schools and the entire universe of informal learning, from how to hook a worm on a line to how to burp a baby.

The agents of education can range from a revered grandparent to the guests on a late-night television talk show; from a child with a disability to a distinguished scientist. Whereas schooling follows a routine and has a certain predictability, education quite often takes us by surprise. We go to the movies to relax—and come home with a vivid sense of the horrors of warfare. We get into a casual conversation with a stranger and discover how little we know about other religions. Education is a lifelong process: it starts long before we begin school and should be ongoing our entire lives.

> *All of us have two educations: one which we receive from others; another, and the most valuable, which we give ourselves.*
>
> —JOHN RANDOLPH (1773–1833),
> U.S. Congressman

Teachers come in many shapes and sizes—even as parents!

(© Somos/Veer/Getty Images)

SCHOOLING

In contrast to education, **schooling** is a specific, formalized process, usually focused on the young (but this is changing), and whose general pattern traditionally has varied little from one setting to the next. Despite minor variations in teaching practices among schools, for example, schooling remains a rather uniform practice throughout the United States. Children arrive at school at approximately the same time, take assigned seats, are taught by adults, use the same or similar textbooks, do homework, take exams, are given grades, and so on. The topics they learn—from fractions to the three branches of the U.S. government—have usually been mandated in advance.

Schools are created for the express purpose of delivering a certain type of educational experience called the *curriculum*. Teachers receive preparation to fulfill the purposes of schooling as defined by the curriculum. The curriculum (discussed more fully in Chapter 5, "What Is Taught?") represents what a community believes young people need to know to develop into good and productive adults, or at least includes what the school policymakers in a particular community believe young people need to know. In effect, what you were taught in elementary and high school represents your community's wager—that is, its *social bet*, what the older generation thinks you and your schoolmates will need to know to live well in the future. If the curriculum a community chooses turns out to be a losing bet, the individual and social consequences are indeed severe.

Keeping the differences between education and schooling clearly in mind is often particularly difficult for the people who should be most sensitive to them— that is, teachers who *do* education *in* schools. Most people enter teaching because they wish to educate others. Consciously or unconsciously, they are committed to a particular educational philosophy. Over time, the everyday experiences of working

> *I have never let my schooling interfere with my education.*
>
> —**MARK TWAIN (1835–1910),**
> American Author and Humorist

in a school inevitably cause their allegiances to shift from abstract educational ideals to the network of personalities and ideas surrounding the particular schools in which they teach. They become invested in schooling, in the way things are—that is, the routines of questioning, assigning homework, quizzes, and faculty meetings—and to varying degrees they tend to lose focus on the larger issues of education. For this reason alone, it is important for the teacher to keep alive the questions "What is a school for?" and "What is my contribution to this child's and this class's education?" We will have more to say on this topic when we examine ideas about education in Chapter 9, "What Are the Philosophical Foundations of American Education?"

PAUSE AND REFLECT

1. Which have been the most important learnings in your life—those from your nonschool education or from your schooling?

2. What is the most important thing you learned in school? What is the most important thing you learned outside school?

schools as cultures

A **society** is a grouping of individuals bound together by a variety of connections. Some of these connections might be shared geographic space or similar racial features. What really connects people, however, is their shared **culture**, composed of beliefs about what is right and wrong, and what is good and bad. Culture also includes the dominant ideas, stories and myths, artistic works, social habits, and organizations of a group. Another of its key aspects is language and the ways people use it in relationship to one another. Every group of people who live together in relative harmony can be said to share a culture, once defined as simply "just the way we are round here." Without a common culture, every time we walked into a room or passed someone on the street, we would grope for a way to respond. Our culture *tells* us what is the appropriate thing to do.

All sorts of cultures exist. A family possesses a culture, as does the U.S. Marine Corps; after a few weeks, a college dormitory assumes a distinctive culture. So too with a school. Think about it: each school you have attended has had its own culture—a set of beliefs, values, traditions, and ways of thinking and behaving toward one another—that distinguishes it from other social institutions and other schools.

Cultures, including **school cultures**, can be good or bad, leading to good human ends or poor ones. A strong, positive school culture engages the hearts and minds of children, stretching them intellectually, physically, morally, and socially. A school with a weak, negative culture may have the same type of facilities, student–teacher ratio, and curriculum as a neighboring good school, yet have a weak, negative effect on students, where everyone—students and teachers—goes through the motions, but with few of the positive effects that the strong-culture school provides.

SOCIALIZATION

Along with food, shelter, and loving care, adults pass their culture on to their young. A major part of any culture is the skills and attitudes necessary to function in that particular society. In our contemporary American society, we expect that most people will try to get along with one another, work cooperatively, and look after their families. The task of passing on a society's culture to the young is called **socialization**, defined as the general process of social learning whereby the child learns the many things necessary to become a well-functioning and acceptable member of a particular social environment.

Besides the family, the major socializing agencies in the life of a young person are schools, peer groups, religious institutions, youth organizations, the mass media, and in some cases work environments. Each of these agencies has its own values, norms, and mores that it attempts to teach so that the child will know how to act and behave in a manner acceptable to other agency members. Some agencies, such as the school, are formally created and organized. Others, such as peer groups, are informally created and casually organized.

Schools, as one of the most common institutions in the United States, have a significant role in teaching young people how to be social in the American context. Every school attempts to socialize children by getting them to value those things the school teaches both explicitly and implicitly. The students who tend to succeed in school typically accept these values, whereas many of the less successful students reject the ways of thinking and behaving that the school tries to teach.

> Our fundamental task as human beings is to seek out connections—to exercise our imaginations. It follows, then, that the basic task of education is the care and feeding of the imagination.
>
> —KATHERINE PATERSON,
> American Author

What are these values and how are they communicated to students? One researcher suggests that schools value several specific ways of thinking and behaving.[1] For example, schools encourage compliant behavior as opposed to personal initiative. Students soon learn to give the teacher what is wanted or expected. Reward systems used by schools teach students to "read" both the teacher and the system to determine just what is expected to get the grade, the teacher's attention, or the sticker with the smiling face. Similarly, competitiveness is learned through athletics, grading systems that compare students to one another, and ability grouping to separate students into classes according to their achievement levels. The many ways in which students learn what a school values include the amount of time allocated to each subject of study, the established school rules, and even the architecture of the school.

As a future teacher, you should work to be able to *read school cultures*. Which rules of behavior, rituals and ceremonies, and accepted patterns of teacher–student interaction are communicated to students at a particular school? Does the "climate" of the classrooms and the school suggest warmth, support, and nurturing of individuals, or do you observe a mood of disinterest, regimentation, and antipathy among staff and students? Most importantly, what is the school's deeper message about how its students should participate in society in the future and what stance they should take toward its culture?

schools as transmitters or re-creators of culture

There are two views, or models, of how U.S. schools should socialize students: (1) the school as the social institution where the young receive from the older generation the very best of their culture and (2) the school as the social institution where the young learn skills and become agents of social change.

We hope their intense curiosity is related to school work!

(Rubberball/Mike Kemp/jupiterimages)

TRANSMITTING CULTURE

In the model of the school as acculturator, schools exist to advance society by ensuring that the young know and appreciate the dominant ideas and values of their society's culture. The goal of cultural transmission in U.S. public schools is to teach the American way of looking at the world and the American way of doing things. This desire to ensure that the young share the common culture may explain why, in many U.S. school systems, we teach American history in the third, seventh, and eleventh grades. It can also explain why, for instance, we give little attention to the histories of China and India, even though they are among the most populous nations on earth and both have old, rich cultural heritages.

> *Education is simply the soul of a society as it passes from one generation to another.*
>
> —GILBERT K. CHESTERTON (1874–1936),
> British Author

Without even being conscious of it, our teachers instruct our young in our version of reality and our way of handling the real world. The schools of other countries do the same for their own young, of course. Schools in Iran, for instance, differ markedly from schools in Ghana, and both differ dramatically from their counterparts in the United States. Even so, the schools of each country are attempting to perform a similar function: to transmit the unique culture of the country to its newest members, the young.

People who view schools as transmitting culture usually talk about society as an organism—that is, as a living thing that can thrive or deteriorate based on how well different elements of society function together. When a society is healthy, each of its various components (the government, schools, communities, families, and individuals) does what it ought to be doing and works in concert with all the other components. Conflict is viewed negatively, and society works toward finding consensus among different groups and eliminating any conflict. From this perspective, it is vitally important that the older generation, including parents and teachers, help the young find value and meaning in their own culture so that they will internalize its values and contribute to its smooth functioning.

Acculturation and Diversity

Several dangers lurk beneath the surface when schools adopt the position that they should concentrate on transmitting the dominant culture. If schools offer the young an understanding of only the prevailing culture, the result may be an attitude of smug cultural superiority, which often leads nations and individuals to commit foolish actions. In cultural terms, what we do not know we often do not respect, and without mutual respect people easily become enemies. In recent decades, instantaneous electronic communications, missile-delivered nuclear weapons, and interdependent national economies have increasingly made the world a global village, and our students must learn how to function in this new world.

In recent decades, the United States has also experienced a surge of immigration from Central America, the Middle East, Southeast Asia, and elsewhere. These new Americans tend to be young, and both the newly arrived parents and their children are hungry for schooling. Although most are eager to learn American ways and American culture, teachers and students alike need to consider these students' native cultures. The majority of these immigrant children speak a language other than English at home. Sometimes schools, as part of acculturating children, unintentionally pull them away from their individual ethnic backgrounds. For example, one in five U.S. students goes home at night to a family in which English is a second language. As they become acculturated, using English becomes more important for these children, and their first languages become something private, rarely used in public.

Other school models try to acculturate the child while supporting his or her ethnic heritage. For example, elementary schools in Calexico, California, serve large populations of newly arrived Mexican children. Teachers design the classrooms so that American and Hispanic cultures are honored, and children learn to operate effectively in both languages.[2]

The presence of new Americans in a school can be a valuable resource in the effort to increase multicultural understanding and appreciation. Although U.S. schools need to transmit American culture, we must realize that what we call "American culture" has always embraced many cultures. Nevertheless, a primary responsibility of the schools is to assist foreign-born students in the acquisition of a high level of English proficiency, a delicate and politically charged balancing act. We will return to this thorny issue when we discuss multiculturalism and bilingual education in Chapter 3, "Who Are Today's Students in a Diverse Society?"

RECONSTRUCTING SOCIETY

The realization that the modern world is a dangerous place, faced with many complex issues, from international terrorists and nuclear weapons to wide-spread hunger and social injustice, has led some educators to posit that schools must become the tool of social reconstruction. Instead of seeing schools as places where past collective wisdom flows down to those who have the capacity and interest to make use of it, these educators assume a much more active, even assertive role for the school. According to this perspective, schools and teachers should work toward activating student interest and commitment to improving society. Unlike those who wish to transmit culture, educators who wish to reconstruct society accept the existence of conflicts among different groups and look at them as important tools to understand these groups' view of social problems.

Called **social reconstructionists**, these people see the role of schools as forming the young into agents of change and participating in the decision about how society needs to change. Compared to those committed to cultural transmission, they have less reverence for the accumulated wisdom of the past and more concern for the world's problems and the necessity to create a new order. They reject the idea

> *The great aim of education is not knowledge but action.*
>
> —HERBERT SPENCER (1820–1903),
> British Philosopher

of schools being "sorting machines," separating students for different life roles and see the successful student not so much as a cultivated person, but as an autonomous citizen ready to join with others to tackle the world's ills and help in the reconstruction of society. Currently, the most influential advocate of this position is William Ayers.

Even among social reconstructionists, however, a wide range of emphases and views are evident. Social reconstructionists fall into two broad categories: *democratic reconstructionists* and *economic reconstructionists.*

Democratic Reconstructionists

Democratic reconstructionists see the solution to certain trends and current issues, such as racism, poverty, and the destruction of the ecosystem, as lying in an aroused and skilled citizenry.[3] The school's mission, then, is to prepare students for vigorous participation in their government. The focus of schooling is on developing knowledge of democratic processes, critical thinking skills, and group process skills so the student can fruitfully work with others for social improvement. In more active programs, students select, study, and work on a community environmental problem, such as the polluting of landfills with unrecycled garbage. (We will return to this concept of democratic reconstructionism later in this chapter, in the discussion of Thomas Jefferson.)

Economic Reconstructionists

Economic reconstructionists tend to take a harsher view of the dominant culture and see schools as the pliant servants of those in power. The influence of corporate values is seen in many phases of school life, from the way textbooks are used to the widespread use of testing.[4] Moreover, economic reconstructionists often argue that schools *claim* to serve the needs of all but, in fact, serve the needs of the elites (i.e., the people with the most power). Economic reconstructionists suggest that schools disguise this fact, either by their own naiveté or by their willing support of the existing system. Because of their deep suspicions of, and sometimes outright disgust with, capitalism, economic reconstructionists are often labeled neo-*Marxists.*

One noted economic reconstructionist was the Brazilian educator Paulo Freire. Freire's first book, *The Pedagogy of the Oppressed*, describes his work with poverty-stricken, illiterate peasants in his native Brazil.[5] As Freire tried to teach these adults to read, he saw they were trapped in an economic and social web over which they had little control. Likewise, the normal mechanisms of education, such as grading and control by the teacher, imposed on the peasants a passivity and subservience to authority. For Freire, the typical methods and routines of schooling are a form of oppression in that they keep people from becoming fully free and independent. To counter this tendency, Freire taught literacy by helping the peasants to (1) name their problem (a polluted water supply); (2) analyze the problem (sewage contamination of the springs); and (3) collectively take action (design and build a new sewage system) to solve the problem.

When used in this manner, education becomes a tool both to develop the human potential of people, such as the ability to read, and to free them from oppressive conditions such as poverty and disease. Currently, two U.S. educators, Henry Giroux and Michael Apple, are major advocates for this economic reconstructionist view.

Although both democratic and economic reconstructionists focus on social problems and try to foster in students the attitudes and skills necessary to solve them, economic reconstructionists question more deeply the fundamental economic and social arrangements in a society. They see education as a necessary means for restructuring the power structures in a society. For them, money, power, and control of education are tightly bound together. Critics of the social reconstructionists' approach to education see it as naive and wrong-headed. They emphasize two points: (1) Our young need to acquire the basic skills and background before they become social activists, and (2) our current economic and social relations are too fragile and too serious to be toyed with by innocent and immature children.

> ### PAUSE AND REFLECT
>
> Which of these two broad educational approaches—transmitting the culture or reconstructing the culture—has the most appeal to you? Why?

the four basic purposes of school

Having most likely spent 12 or 13 years in school—the better part of your life—you are probably convinced you know the territory. Isn't it obvious what schools are and what they do? Perhaps. Yet most of us tend to think of schools in limited ways. Our own experiences within a relatively few schools influence what we think about all schools and what we understand of schools in general. Thus to gain a greater perspective, it is important to look at schools from different vantage points. The two missions we just examined, schools for "transmission of the culture" or for "reconstructing society," represent rather broad, general purposes for schools. Now we examine four purposes for schools that are closer to the everyday reality of teachers and students.

What should our schools be trying to do? This fairly straightforward, almost innocent question is, however, also perennial and has stirred fierce arguments among different groups. If residents have strongly conflicting views about what their community's schools should do, the question can rip apart the fabric of a community. It taps into serious disagreements about what different people think of contemporary American culture and society and what they want the schools to do for their children.

To illustrate that point, we have included several quotes about schools in this section. Some were written centuries ago, others more recently. As you read each, think about how the speaker characterizes the functions of schools and education. Also think about your own schooling.

The teacher has clearly captured their attention.

(iStockphoto.com/ranplett)

The function of schools that comes first to most people's minds is the intellectual function.

(© Bob Daemmrich/The Image Works)

INTELLECTUAL PURPOSES

Jacques Barzun is a cultural historian who writes frankly about the current state of schools in America.

> What do we really want from our schools? . . . Given the public's muddled feelings about brainwork (which is what "excellence" refers to) and the parental indifference up to now about what their children are being taught, the school has a double fight on its hands: against ignorance inside the walls and against cultural prejudice outside, the prejudice lying so deep that those who harbor it do not even know they do. . . . The difficulties of schooling . . . do not change. . . . Difficulties remain. It will always be difficult to teach well; to learn accurately; to read, write and count readily and competently; to acquire a sense of history and develop a taste for literature and the arts. . . . For this purpose no school . . . is ever just right; it is only by the constant effort of its teachers that it can even be called satisfactory.[6]
>
> —Jacques Barzun

If you said that Barzun is emphasizing the academic or *intellectual* purposes of schools, you would be right. One longstanding purpose of schools has been to foster the intellectual development of the young. Barzun is one of many observers who contend that promoting academic learning is the single most important purpose of schools.

Most people who highlight the intellectual purpose of schools believe that the development of reason, through intellectual pursuits, leads to individual enlightenment. Rationality—that is, the ability to know, to think, and to reason—is seen as an attribute distinct to humans and, more importantly, as the capacity that *makes us human.* Many of those who rank intellectual purposes as the highest priority see school as the one institution most common to all people. They believe, therefore, that promoting intellectual development in schools is essential so that all children have the opportunity to become rational human beings.

The intellectual purpose of school is included in every school's mission. The way it is manifested, however, can look different from school to school. Some schools exist for the primary purpose of helping students develop their intellects.

You may have heard about or even attended a secondary school that requires students to study "the Great Books" or one that has adopted the International Baccalaureate (IB) curriculum, currently taught in over 11,000 U.S. schools and growing in popularity.[7]

POLITICAL AND CIVIC PURPOSES

Now, let's consider a quote from Thomas Jefferson that highlights a different purpose of school. Although the writing style is dated, the idea is one that has been constant in American public schools since their beginning.

> [E]ven under the best forms [of government], those entrusted with power have, in time . . . perverted it into tyranny; and it is believed that the most effectual means of preventing this would be to illuminate . . . the minds of the people at large, and more especially to give them knowledge of those facts, which history exhibiteth . . . [that] they may be enabled to know ambition under all its shapes.[8]
>
> —THOMAS JEFFERSON

You will read more about Jefferson's contributions to the American public schools in Chapter 10, "What Is the History of America's Struggle for Educational Opportunity?" For now, note that Jefferson hoped that American schooling would help establish and sustain the United States of America, an infant nation. One of the overriding concerns of the early political leaders was, in fact, how people would learn to be American citizens and *not* English subjects.

The Jefferson quote underscores the *political and civic* purposes of schooling. Jefferson thought schools could help people learn how to govern themselves wisely and justly. The only sure way for any country to have a well-informed citizenry is through the systematic education that schooling can bring. That need may be more or less prominent at times, but the political purposes of schools have always been a primary reason why public schools exist.

In your own schools, you may have seen political and civic purposes emphasized through student government elections, voter registration drives, citizenship education programs, and even community service and outreach programs. Schools also promote these purposes by *how* they teach students to read, write, and discuss ideas rationally.

> *Never doubt that a small group of thoughtful committed citizens can change the world. Indeed, it is the only thing that ever has.*
>
> —MARGARET MEAD (1901–1978),
> Anthropologist

ECONOMIC PURPOSES

Let's consider one more perspective in light of your own school experiences. Jean Anyon, an educational researcher, has investigated the connection between economics and schooling for a number of years.

> When inner city students and their access to the range of services provide a realistic expectation that education will lead to better jobs, life, and future, as is expected in most middle-class and affluent homes, then the students will have a reason to make an educational effort. Realistic expectations that education will make a substantial, positive difference in the lives of their students may also motivate teachers and other school staff to a higher level of performance. At that point teachers, principals, and a quality curriculum can more easily make a difference in the lives of the inner city poor.[9]
>
> —JEAN ANYON

What is the implicit criticism that Anyon raises about the connection between a student's schooling and his or her occupation? As this quote suggests, many Americans think that schools primarily serve an *economic* purpose—that is, they believe that schools help students climb the economic ladder, obtaining the skills and knowledge required to attend college or to get a job.

Think about how you approach your own college education. If you and the rest of the student body of your campus were interviewed right now about why you are attending college, many of you would say that you attend college because you expect to earn a more comfortable living with a college degree than without one. Americans generally expect that more schooling will lead to greater personal wealth, and so far they are right. On the whole, high school graduates do obtain higher paying jobs than those who didn't complete high school, and college graduates earn more than high school graduates.

Americans also expect that schools will prepare students for their future, regardless of whether that future includes a college education. High schools support that expectation by including courses of study that are *college preparatory* or *vocational* (more currently called CTE for Career and Technical Education). Many Americans accept without question that schools guide students into curricular tracks that seem matched to their abilities and inclinations: mathematically inclined students enroll in such courses as calculus and advanced placement (AP) physics, whereas labor-oriented students enroll in cosmetology or computer repair courses. The assumption underlying the economic purposes of schools is that well-schooled people and people *appropriately schooled* are vital to a strong national economy, regardless of whether they become business leaders or laborers. We will see later in the chapter that Anyon, among others, has questioned the practices that rest on this assumption, pointing out that curricular tracking and instructional practices are not always related so much to students' individual abilities as to their expected role in the work world.

The economic purposes of schooling have profound effects both on the student and on society as a whole. You may have heard news accounts of the need for a "well-educated workforce" or the "new demands of working in 'green' industries." Pundits pronounce to one another what the new global economy will demand, and those predictions trickle down to schools. For instance, many school systems have placed emphasis on teaching computer skills and technology, with the goal of equipping graduates for the new realities of the workplace.

SOCIAL PURPOSES

We have identified intellectual, political, and economic purposes of schools. A fourth purpose is called the *umbrella purpose* because it is so all encompassing. Consider this last quote and think about what it means.

> If . . . education has a collective function above all, if its object is to adapt the child to the social milieu in which he is destined to live, it is impossible that society should be uninterested in such a procedure. . . . It is, then, up to the State to remind the teacher constantly of the ideas, the sentiments that must be impressed upon the child to adjust him to the milieu in which he must live.[10]
>
> —ÉMILE DURKHEIM

This quote draws attention to the *social purpose* of schools. How would you paraphrase this quotation? At some point in your life, you may have heard that schools also teach "social skills." What exactly does that mean to you? You may have heard the old adage "It's good to be smart, but if you can't get along with people or don't know how to work with others, then it doesn't make much difference how much you know."

Émile Durkheim was a French sociologist in the early twentieth century. One of his primary interests was the school's responsibility in promoting a healthy social order. For Durkheim, schools existed to help mold or guide students into what their society needed and expected of them. A teacher's job was to help students understand their role in the broader social order.

Durkheim's idea that schools must work to help students adapt to social expectations still holds currency today. Think of how many times elementary school teachers impress on pupils how important it is to *share*. Who decided that we needed to learn to share? Think of how frequently middle and high school teachers remind students to give their best effort on their homework or a project. What does "best effort" mean? Why not encourage students to "kick back and go with the flow"? Think also how schools and teachers emphasize punctuality and the importance of meeting commitments on time. These attributes are emphasized, in part, because they are characteristics prized by most employers. Further, the capacity to share, being sensitive to issues of time, and keeping commitments are habits that have wide value in marriage, family life, and community life. Sharing, concern for others, and promise keeping are three human qualities that illustrate how schooling helps children learn and adapt to social conventions. Because the social nature of schooling is so important, we will return to it later in the chapter.

> ### PAUSE AND REFLECT
>
> 1. Thinking back on your high school experiences, how were these four purposes (intellectual, political and civic, economic, and social) evident in your schooling? Was one more dominant than the others? Which one? Why was this one purpose more dominant in your community?
>
> 2. Which of these four purposes of education do you believe ought to be given the greatest weight in the organization of schools?

what do studies reveal about the nature of schools?

What happens in schools and how does the activity in a school contribute to or detract from its purpose? Researchers often look at the everyday events of human life and see patterns the rest of us may be only vaguely aware of. In the next several pages, we present a few of these studies and examine the patterns the researchers noticed, focusing first on elementary schools, then on middle schools and junior high schools, and finally on high schools.

LIFE IN ELEMENTARY SCHOOLS

One of the best perspectives on how time is usually spent in the elementary classroom is Philip W. Jackson's classic study *Life in Classrooms*.[11] Anthropologists have taught us that the humdrum aspects of human existence have cultural significance and that we must look at the most routine events in an elementary classroom if we are to understand what happens there. Are certain trivial acts repeated many times? How often do they occur? What is their cumulative effect on the child? What do they teach the child? Jackson's careful observations of elementary school classrooms show how revealing the answers to these questions can be.

Have you ever figured out how many hours a child spends in school? In most states, the school year is 180 days. The day typically begins at 8:30 A.M. and ends at 3 P.M., so it lasts a total of six and one-half hours. If a child doesn't miss a day of school, he or she spends more than 1,000 hours in school each year. Including kindergarten, the average child, by the end of sixth grade, will spend more than 7,000 hours in elementary school. How are those hours typically spent?

In pondering this question, you may think first of the curriculum, which specifies so many hours of reading, language arts, mathematics, science, play, social studies, music, art, and so on. But what do students really *do* when they are studying these subjects? They talk to each other or the teacher. They read silently and aloud. They yawn. They look out the window. They raise their hands. They line up. They stand up. They sit down. In short, they do a number of different things, many of them commonplace and trivial. To understand why some of these things happen, we must first look at what the teacher does.

The Teacher's Role

Jackson has observed that the elementary school teacher engages in as many as a thousand interpersonal interchanges each day.

The teaching–learning process consists, for the most part, of talking, and the teacher controls and directs discussion. The teacher acts as a *gatekeeper*, deciding who shall speak. (One may debate whether this *should* be the teacher's role, but clearly most teachers function this way.)

The teacher also acts as a *dispenser of supplies*. Because both space and resources are limited, and because the number of students wishing to use them at any one time is likely to be greater than the supply, the teacher must dole them out. A related function is as *granter of special privileges* to deserving students: passing out the milk, sharpening pencils, taking the roll, or spending free time at the computer. Although little teacher time is involved in awarding these special jobs, they are important because they help to structure the classroom socially as a system of rewards and punishments.

Timekeeper is another teacher responsibility. It is the teacher who decides when a certain activity ends and another begins, when it is time to stop science and begin spelling, and when students go outside for recess. In some schools, the teacher is assisted in timekeeping by bells and buzzers that signal when a period is over. As Jackson observes, things happen because it is time for them to occur, not because students want them to happen.

All these teacher functions can be seen as responses to the crowded conditions in the classroom. If the teacher were dealing with one student at a time in a tutorial situation, then gate keeping, dispensing supplies, granting special privileges, and timekeeping would not be necessary. Given that a tutorial setting is not possible, much time and energy are spent *keeping order*. The resulting atmosphere has unavoidable effects on the students. What are some of the consequences for students in crowded classroom conditions?

What Students Experience

One inevitable outcome for students that results from the teacher's "traffic management" functions is *delay*. Because students' actions are limited by space, material resources, and the amount of teacher attention they can command, there are definite limits on their freedom in class. In addition, because the class ordinarily moves toward a goal as a group rather than as individuals, its slowest members often determine the pace of progress. *Waiting* is a familiar activity for elementary school children—that is, waiting in line to get a drink of water, waiting with arm propped at the elbow to be called on to answer a question, waiting to use the scissors, waiting until others have finished their work to go on to the next activity, waiting until four other students have finished reading aloud for a chance to do so, and on and on.

Denial of desire is another common experience for the elementary student. A question goes unanswered, a raised hand is ignored, talking out of turn is not permitted, relief of bodily functions is allowed only at specified times. Some denial is necessary and probably beneficial, but one thing is certain: delayed gratification and denied desire are learned in school, and a certain amount of student frustration is bound to develop.

Students also experience frequent *interruptions* of many sorts, such as interruptions of seatwork by the teacher to give additional instructions or to clarify one student's question, interruptions when messages from the principal's office are read aloud to the class, interruptions for fire drills, interruptions when the teacher is working with one student and another student misbehaves, and so on. Students are expected either to ignore these intrusions or to quickly resume their activities. The emphasis on an inflexible schedule contributes to the sense of interruption by often making students begin activities before their interest has been aroused and

Waiting and delayed gratification are common occurrences in elementary school classrooms.

(© Elizabeth Crews)

stop at the height of their interest when the schedule dictates that they must begin another task.

A related phenomenon is *social distraction*. Students are often asked to behave as if they were alone, when they are actually surrounded by 20 to 30 other people. During assigned seatwork, for example, communication among students is often discouraged, if not forbidden. To be surrounded by friends, sometimes seated across from each other at a table, and not be allowed to talk is a difficult and tempting situation. As Jackson remarks, "These young people, if they are to become successful students, must learn how to be alone in a crowd."[12]

Delay, denial, interruption, and social *distraction*, then, are characteristic of life in elementary classrooms. Given these classroom conditions, it seems likely that the student who either possesses or quickly develops patience would find school more tolerable than the student who lacks it. The ability to control desires, delay rewards, and stifle impulses seems to be characteristic of successful students, whereas less successful students exhibit less patience and more impulsiveness.

(T) F

The middle school years are characterized by a growth in independence and the social interests.

Typically, in the "middle years," ages 11 to 13, students become more independent, more social, and more involved in the world around them.

LIFE IN MIDDLE AND JUNIOR HIGH SCHOOLS

In the "middle years," ages 11 to 13, students change in fundamental ways, becoming more independent, more social, and more involved in the world around them. It can be a stressful period for parents and teachers and, most especially, for the students themselves. Increasingly, these "middle years" are seen as a crucial time in an individual's formation. Early adolescence is characterized by a variety of developmental changes and needs that dramatically impact the school experience.

Among the major changes are:

Biological Changes. Early adolescence witnesses dramatic biological changes (Susman & Rogel, 2004). First, girls enter puberty an average of 18 months before boys during this stage. Second, even within gender the onset of puberty varies considerably, which complicates both genders' relationships with their classmates. Further, early-maturing girls, that is, the first to experience pubertal changes, often feel out of sync with their peers, resulting in emotional and adjustment issues (see, e.g., Ge, Conger, & Elder, 2001; Ge et al., 2003).

Cognitive Changes. Thinking also changes in significant ways during this period of development (Keating, 2004; Wigfield et al., in press). Students increasingly engage in abstract thinking and more sophisticated and elaborate information-processing strategies. They begin to use what Benjamin Bloom calls higher-order thinking.[13] Recent advances in cognitive research are revealing that the brain changes in significant ways during this period (Byrnes, 2001; Keating, 2004). Continuing advances in this emerging field of brain structure and function will undoubtedly increase educators' understanding of adolescents' cognition and behavior.

Changes in Self-Concept, Self-Esteem, and Identity Development. These three interrelated terms—self-concept, self-esteem, and identity development—all deal with slightly different aspects of an individual's *sense of self*. Early adolescence is a prime time for strong emergence of self-awareness. Children become vividly aware of their gender, race, and ethnicity during this period. Psychologists insist that integrating these experiences and characteristics into a coherent sense of self is fundamental to healthy development (Marcia, 1980; Waterman, 1982).

Changes in Achievement Motivation. Behavioral scientists have observed the somewhat obvious fact that some people have an intense desire to achieve something, whereas others may not seem that concerned about their achievements. They have labeled this phenomenon *achievement motivation*, the tendency to strive for success and to be goal oriented. Current criticism of middle schools frequently blames declines in achievement motivation as the direct cause of student disengagement.[14]

Although both younger and older students have these developmental needs, it is particularly important that schools serving children in the middle years meet these needs. Not meeting them often results in a young person's alienation from peers, loss of a sense of self-worth, and the onset of all sorts of destructive behavior, from fighting to escapism into drug use, to promiscuity. As one specialist observed, "Every child wants to believe in himself or herself as a successful person; every youngster wants to be liked and respected; every youngster wants physical exercises and freedom to move; and youngsters want life to be just."[15]

Types of Schools

Although many things in American schools remain constant, the way we educate young adolescents seems to be in constant flux. As discussed more fully in Chapter 10 "What Is the History of America's Struggle for Educational Opportunity?", our knowledge about this topic is circumscribed somewhat by the plethora of grade-clustering patterns evident in U.S. schools. Up until the beginning of the nineteenth century, students went through eight grades of one-teacher-to-a-classroom elementary schools and then some went on to multiple-teacher high schools. Reformers at the time thought the transition was too late and moved seventh, eighth, and ninth grade into what they called "junior" high school. This pattern was predominant until the 1960s, when theorists and reformers came to the conclusion that junior highs were becoming overly content focused and ignoring intellectual and development needs of young adolescents. Their answer was the "middle school," which stressed developmental goals in addition to more integration and exploration of subject matter. Since then, middle schools have become the dominate pattern, but with continuing debate about which particular pattern (grades 6–7, 5–7, 6–8, or 5–8) is most effective.[16] It is worth noting that most private and religious schools have traditionally resisted these changes and kept to the eight-grade elementary model.

Although the middle school model is dominant in public education today, it is not without its critics. These middle school opponents site the "drop-off" that is occurring between elementary and middle school. Recent test results in math and reading in all 50 states show that "between 1999 and 2004, elementary school students made solid gains in reading and math, while middle school students made smaller gains in math and stagnated in reading."[17] Describing "the lost years of middle schooling" in the United States (grades 6, 7, and 8) as "an intellectual wasteland" and "the 'Bermuda Triangle' of American education," such critics call for a return to the K–8 pattern and a more rigorous, discipline-focused curriculum.[18] Although supporters insist that the nature of the "middle years" requires a specially designed environment, opponents characterize the curriculum as soft and disorganized, with the middle school's academic mission taking a backseat to addressing students' social and emotional needs. Urban school leaders in particular are moving back to the K–8 and 9–12 model.[19] Sometimes this is part of a reform agenda to "shake up" a failing status quo situation; sometimes to restore a more direct and rigorous academic focus; and sometimes for social and

"
Schooling, instead of encouraging the asking of questions, too often discourages it.

—MADELEINE L'ENGLE (1918–2007), Author

behavioral purposes. This last motive is supported by recent research that found that sixth-graders in middle schools got into significantly more discipline problems than those in K–8 schools, and further that this pattern of misbehavior and concomitant academic problems persisted.[20]

Developmental or Academic Purposes Foremost?

Is there one right way of educating students in the middle grades best? Probably not. No one pattern is superior for all students. Increasingly, the debate over middle schools versus junior high versus K–8 elementary school is being influenced by a greater focus on academic achievement, concerns over the earlier and earlier arrival of puberty in children, and even district financial and building issues affecting the configuration of grades. Like many issues in school, this one involves a series of trade-offs. However, what is consistently identified as important for educating students in the middle grades is that the developmental needs of early adolescents, such as self-esteem and interpersonal skills, must be acknowledged and considered in developing and organizing programs.

PAUSE AND REFLECT

1. What was the grade-clustering pattern in your junior high or middle school? Do you believe it was the best pattern for you?

2. Do you think that meeting the developmental goals cited above is more crucial during middle school years than at other periods in students' lives? Why or why not?

3. Has your experience led you to agree or disagree with those who believe that academic achievement takes second place to personal growth in many of today's middle schools?

LIFE IN HIGH SCHOOLS

"The main hope of a nation lies in the proper education of its young." So declared the Renaissance philosopher Erasmus. Recently a New York Times columnist wrote an op-ed piece, "Putting Our Brains on Hold," in which he stated that "the world leadership qualities of the United States, once so prevalent, are fading faster than the polar ice caps."[21] Herbert was reporting on a recent study of the College Board that found that the U.S. has fallen in a very short time from the leader in percentage of college graduates to 12th out of the 36 developed nations surveyed.

Much criticism of our nation's secondary schools, such as Herbert's, comes from a growing recognition of the truth of Erasmus's quote and from a fresh awareness of the poor performance of many high schools. In the past, however, much of the censure and complaint has come from college professors and college students, both claiming incoming students had not received the necessary preparation to do college work. In a 2005 survey of nearly 1,500 recent graduates, "just 24 percent of graduates said they were significantly challenged during high school. Twenty percent of these high school graduates said that 'expectations were low and . . . it was easy to slide by.'"[22] The college instructors in this study claimed that 42 percent of college students are not adequately prepared by their high schools to meet college expectations.

The more recent criticism is of a different nature: concern over what some see as our high schools' failure to prepare graduates for the world of work. A recent report on American high schools states:

Our nation's public high schools are where most young people go to receive that crucial preparation. Yet, in many communities, particularly in our cities, upwards of half of all high school students drop out, and too many of those who finish high school are not ready for higher education, training, or the workplace.[23]

A government website recently reported that "Nationwide, 7,000 students drop out every day and only about 70 percent of students graduate from high school with a regular high school diploma. Two thousand high schools in the U.S. produce more than half of all dropouts and a recent study suggests that in the 50 largest cities, only 53 percent of students graduate on time. Research shows that poor and minority children attend these so-called "dropout factories"—the 2,000 schools that produce more than 50 percent of our nation's dropouts—at significantly higher rates.[24]

Not long ago, Microsoft founder, Bill Gates, who has focused on the reform of U.S. secondary education as a primary target of his philanthropy, offered the following analysis of our high schools:

> America's high schools are obsolete. By "obsolete," I don't just mean that our high schools are broken, flawed, and underfunded—though a case could be made for every one of those points. By "obsolete," I mean that our high schools—even when they're working exactly as designed—cannot teach our kids what they need to know today. Training the workforce of tomorrow with the high schools of today is like trying to teach kids about today's computers on a fifty-year-old mainframe. It's the wrong tool for the times. Our high schools were designed fifty years ago to meet the needs of another age. Until we design them to meet the needs of the 21st century, we will keep limiting—even ruining—the lives of millions of Americans every year.[25]

Multiple Purposes

As the U.S. economy struggles out of recession and faces increasing competition from our trading partners around the globe, the intensity of criticism of our high schools has increased.

The Comprehensive High School. The high school years bring people to the front door of adulthood. They begin to think about and sense what their futures might become. In many developed countries, this is the moment when young people are separated into different schools, such as the European gymnasiums for those planning to go to college and onto the professions, and trade and technical schools for those who will take a more direct route into the work world. Americans, by and large, have chosen to educate young people in **comprehensive high schools**, multipurpose schools with different tracks. *Academic* tracks stress the traditional subjects of English, history, mathematics, science, and foreign languages as preparation for college. A *general* track usually allows a greater number of elective courses and less rigorous versions of the traditional subjects. *Vocational* tracks may include a combination of academic and job-related courses; students in these tracks are preparing for a job after graduation.

The comprehensive high school is part of our nation's democratic tradition, and like our focus on diversity, is meant to strengthen our democratic traditions. Nevertheless, because of the variations in courses required for these different tracks and the differing standards for student achievement among them, the reality of the

> *Civilization is a race between education and catastrophe.*
>
> —H. G. WELLS (1866–1946),
> Anthropologist

term *high school education* takes on myriad meanings. Americans seem to want high schools to accomplish everything. The resulting confusion of goals is evident in the variety of goal statements adopted by states for their schools, in the written goals found in teachers' manuals or school district curriculum guides, and in teacher and student responses when asked about school goals. This is a major reason why our schools presently are making a fundamental shift: graduation from high school will now mean the achievement of certain academic standards rather than 12 or 13 years of school attendance.

The Shopping-Mall High School

The important move toward standards-based education, which will be discussed more fully in Chapter 5, "What Is Taught?" and Chapter 12, "How Should Education Be Reformed," has been fueled from many sources. One of the most severe and therefore influential criticisms was that not only did our high schools have a confusion of goals, but also they had become quite lax. This goal confusion and laxity was brought to the attention of educators and the general public a few decades ago by a research study that compared our comprehensive high schools to shopping malls. The metaphor states that, like a shopping mall, our schools cater to a variety of student consumers, emphasizing variety and choice, trying to have something for everyone.[26] Schools have offered a diverse curriculum in an attempt to appeal to all comers. The student-customers, on the other hand, are expected to make their own course selections. The schools essentially maintain neutrality in regard to students' or parents' choices among the many alternatives offered. The customer has the final word.

> *Kids may do poorly in school not simply because they aren't motivated to study or because they lack ability, but because they are intent on maintaining their standing in a crowd that regards academic achievement as uncool.*
>
> —B. BRADFORD BROWN,
> Professor and Author

Staying with the shopping mall metaphor, this study found that some customers (students) are serious about buying, others are just browsing and looking for ideas on what to buy, and still others are at the mall to meet their friends and "cruise." Faced with customers with such different levels of commitment, teachers reach accommodations, or treaties, that promote mutual goals or keep the peace. For example, some teachers make their deals crystal clear when they advise students, "Don't take my class if you don't want to work." If students don't want to play by these rules, they don't have to take the course. Another teacher in the study said, "Don't hassle me and I won't hassle you. I'll let you slide through if you don't interfere with the students who want to work."[27]

Within the "shopping-mall" high school can be found "specialty shops," the niches for students and families wanting more learning and school engagement. These venues include top-track programs, special education programs, vocational and technical education programs, and extracurricular programs, such as marching band or football. Because the students in these programs have been designated as special, they tend to receive special attention.

In contrast, the average or unspecial students (often called average, *general, normal,* or *regular*) are generally ignored by the specialty shops; they do not receive the additional commitment of time, personal relationships, and intensity of learning generally given to "specialty-shop" students. They have no important allies or advocates, and their treaties are characterized by avoidance of learning, not engagement. Schools may try to nurture these students' self-esteem, but they do not make academic demands of them.

This picture is undoubtedly unfair to many high schools with high expectations for students and demanding and creative programs. Two recently popular high school innovations are examples of this countertrend: the International Baccalaureate (IB) and career academies. The IB is a rigorous, off-the-shelf program of academic study, started in Switzerland by a nonprofit foundation over 40 years ago, and has become increasingly common throughout the world.[28] Although the IB has curricular programs for all the grades, it is most popular at the secondary level. Currently, over a thousand U.S. schools have adopted the IB curriculum.[29]

A recent reaction to large comprehensive high schools has been to restructure a school into small units or schools within schools (which will be discussed more fully in Chapter 12, "How Should Education Be Reformed?"). The career academy is one popular example of this trend. Typically, a career academy is a small learning community of students (30–60 per grade) and teachers dedicated to bridging the gap between the academic goals of secondary school and realistic preparation for work in a particular career, such as health care or computer technology. Besides their academic course work, students study vocational subjects that typically involve internships and other opportunities to gain work experience and earn money. Often, these career academies involve cooperative programs with nearby community colleges.

Nevertheless, it has been criticisms of the *process* of our high schools (i.e., ambiguous goals and laxity) and the *product* (graduates ill-prepared for the workplace) that have propelled many of the standards-based reform efforts.

> *Expecting all children the same age to learn from the same materials is like expecting all children the same age to wear the same size clothing.*
>
> —MADELINE HUNTER,
> Psychologist, Principal, and
> Assistant Superintendent

PAUSE AND REFLECT

1. Are these findings and descriptions of high school similar to what you saw in your own high school experience?

2. The high school years are often said to be "the best years of your life." Do you agree with this assertion? If so, why? If not, what could and should be done to change the high school experience?

what is a good school?

First, the obvious: not all schools are good schools. Second, good schools do not just happen—they are *made*. A school is the *product* of people's intellectual and physical energies. At any particular moment, the way a school is reflects the multiplicity of efforts that have gone into creating and maintaining it. Further, like towns and civilizations, schools rise and fall. They are human creations—dynamic and continually on the move.

No school, at least in the authors' experience, is "right" or "good" for all students. Nevertheless, some schools are strikingly better than others—that is, some schools provide a significantly better education for a much larger percentage of their students than do others. These schools, referred to in the educational literature as **effective schools**, are the focus of this section.

Defining an effective school has been a major concern of educators for several decades. A popular definition of an effective school is one in which learning for all students is maximized. Although this definition is certainly compelling, it is hardly precise. Besides the question of what constitutes learning, the meaning of *effective* is uncertain. Effective or good in what dimension? In academically engaged and happy students? In a teaching staff with high morale? In the percentage of students who get promoted or graduate? Those who go on to college? What kinds of colleges? How many students become skilled technicians and accomplished artisans? How many succeed in business or professional life? In athletics? Socially? Ethically?

Effective, as currently defined in most of the educational research literature, refers to students' achievement test scores in basic skills such as reading and mathematics. Although such tests measure skills that are not the only objectives of education, achievement in these academic areas is an important and widely acclaimed outcome of schooling. Also, achievement in reading and mathematics is easier to measure than good citizenship, artistic development, or passion for ideas.

CHARACTERISTICS OF AN EFFECTIVE SCHOOL

Beginning almost 30 years ago, a number of educational researchers began looking for the characteristics or qualities of effective schools.[30] Among the most significant characteristics they found to be correlated with high achievement in the basic skills were high expectations for student performance, communication among teachers, a task orientation among the staff, the ability to keep students on task, the expenditure of little time on behavior management, the principal's instructional leadership, the participation of parents, and the school environment.

The Teacher's Expectations

Through their attitude and regular encouragement, teachers in effective schools communicate to students their belief that the students will achieve the goals of instruction. In effect, the teachers get across to students a "can-do" attitude about learning. We discuss teacher expectations more in Chapter 6, "What Makes a Teacher Effective?"

Communication among Teachers

Teachers in effective schools do not operate in a vacuum, each in his or her isolated classroom. Instead, they talk among themselves about their work and converse about one another's students. They know the curricular materials and activities that go on in one another's classrooms, and they are helpful to one another. In short, effective schools have teachers who are good colleagues.

Task Orientation

The faculties of effective schools are highly task oriented. They begin instruction early in the class period and end instruction late in the period. The staff approaches its teaching responsibilities with a serious air and wastes little time in class. Whether the classes are formal or informal, underneath the surface of events lies a seriousness of purpose that is communicated to students.

Academic Engaged Time

Academic engaged time (or *academic learning time*) refers to the amount of time students are actually engaged in relevant content-related activities while experiencing a

VOICES from the classroom

What Is a Good School?

Denis Gray is a law and justice teacher at Brighton High School in Boston, Massachusetts

I teach in an urban high school, and it's a good school. For me, there are three criteria for what makes a good school:

1. The vast majority of its teachers want to have maximum impact on students through instruction.

2. Students have internalized the value of education and want to learn.

3. Most importantly, the educational and ancillary needs of all students are met.

To say the least, making this a reality in the lives of students does not go unchallenged. Students continually test us to determine whether we are "for real." Someone has said, "Students do not care what you know until they know that you care." Difficult students, in particular, test us. They test our patience, our self-control, our professionalism, our integrity, our faith, and our hope. Then, there are the self-doubt questions: "Am I a good teacher?" "Could my actions be interpreted as racist?" "What could/should I be doing that I'm not?"

There are many models and methodologies for instructing and learning. Most of them assume that students *want* to learn. Yet the reality is that for many students, there is a profound disconnect between education and success. They see that high school students sign multimillion-dollar athletic contracts. Colleges that should know better are not interested in ensuring that their athletes graduate. Many parents shower their children with the latest designer clothes and sneakers. Many students have part-time jobs to ensure that they always have pocket money. In their minds is the question, "If I get what I want now, why do I need an education?" Then there are issues of alienation and mistrust. Many students view the education we are trying to give them as an attempt by the "establishment" to "mess with their heads."

Of the three criteria, I believe the last to be the most important. Today's urban school, as a matter of social conscience, must address the psychosocial needs of its students as never before. Today's teacher, as a matter of personal conscience, is required to assume many roles in students' lives, including parent, protector, counselor, and confidant. It is a tough and complex job, but it's a job I love.

high rate of success. As we describe in Chapter 6, this characteristic involves the ability of a teacher to get students engaged in academic tasks, such as reading or solving math problems, and to keep their attention on these instructional activities. Research has demonstrated a tight link between the amount of time devoted to academic learning tasks and students' achievement.[31]

Behavior Management

We have all been in classrooms with teachers who spent huge chunks of time trying to quiet students to get them "on task" or who, in the course of correcting one student, disturbed all the rest, causing a ripple of distraction throughout the room. Teachers in effective schools have learned techniques to minimize the time devoted to managing students. They are efficient both in handling discipline problems and in implementing the learning activities. In addition, these teachers do not routinely resort to corporal punishment, because they use other techniques to deal with student

Good communication among teacher, student, and parents is key to good teaching.

(© Bob Daemmrich/The Image Works)

▶❙❙ TeachSource VIDEO CASE

Parental Involvement in School Culture

Go to the Education CourseMate website to watch the video clips, study the artifacts in the case, and reflect on the following questions:

1. Which of the other aspects of an effective school and effective teaching can you see in the portrayals in this video case?

2. Were parents involved in the schools you have attended? How? How could their involvement have been improved?

3. Do you as a teacher feel comfortable about involving parents in your classroom? If not, what can you do now to address your concerns?

behavior. (See Chapter 6, "What Makes a Teacher Effective?" for more on classroom management.)

The Principal

Principals play an important role in effective schools. Instead of being faceless bureaucrats aimlessly shuffling papers, the principals of effective schools are instructional leaders. They have strong views on the purposes of education and are vitally concerned about the quality of teaching and learning in their schools. Still, the principal is perceived as democratic in approach and cooperative in relationships with faculty. The effective principal gains teachers' confidence and clearly communicates to them a vision of what the school should accomplish and how each teacher can contribute toward this end.

Parents

An effective school reaches out and draws in parents instead of ignoring them or keeping them at arm's length. Parents are treated as key members of the learning team, as partners with the professional staff in helping their children achieve academic success. In addition to aiding in students' intellectual achievement, the involvement of parents can help improve their children's self-concepts, work habits, and attitudes toward school. The video case *Parental Involvement in School Culture* lets you view one example of how parents can contribute to an effective school.

The School Environment

Schools that promote learning have climates or environments that support a teacher's efforts to teach and students' efforts to learn. A school that has an environment that is calm, safe, pleasant, and orderly is conducive to learning. Conversely, a school with an environment that is unsafe, hostile, and generally unruly is rarely a place of learning—at least not academic learning.

Attempts to answer the question "What is a good school?" are still incomplete. Although the characteristics cited are those identified by several extensive research projects, studies continue. For instance, researchers at the recently formed national Center on Scaling up Effective Schools reports that "a consensus has grown among practitioners and researchers around the essential components of a successful *urban* school, such as:

- Quality instruction
- A rigorous curriculum
- A culture of learning
- Professional behavior
- Connections to external communities
- Systemic use of data
- System performance accountability
- Learner-centered leadership.[32]

> *Good schools . . . arise from the crucible of their culture.*
>
> —HOWARD GARDNER, Psychologist

Although there is much overlap with the long-standing list of characteristics, the new emphasis on assessment and evaluation is reflected in the inclusion of "systemic use of data" and "system performance accountability."

We strongly suspect that a number of qualities besides those mentioned here make major contributions to the establishment of a good school. Among these are a pervasive sense of curiosity, a passion for excellence, a strong belief in students' capacity to grow, and an environment of kindness and support.

the unfinished work of the schools

The question that we asked at the beginning of this chapter—What is a school?—has no single, satisfactory answer. Schools are human inventions. People bring schools into being for a variety of intellectual and social purposes. Ideally, the primary purposes of schools are to advance the common good and to help people live happy and successful lives. However, if schools are to serve a society, they must at least keep pace with that society. Many people who are concerned about our schools believe that the schools are moving very slowly, while the rest of society experiences dynamic change. They believe, in effect, the schools are out of step with society, usually being either too far ahead (a rarity) or lagging behind (the more common situation) the needs of the people they exist to serve. Schools, like every social institution, need to continually assess what they are *really doing*. They must first decide whether their purposes and goals are the right purposes and goals, and second to determine whether they are actually achieving those purposes. If you become an educator, you must have this commitment to continual examination and renewal of the schools.

The purposes for which schools are brought into being remain vital to our society. People—particularly parents—have a great desire for good schools for their children, and, as you will see later in this book, many excellent ideas are being generated and movements are underway for the renewal of our schools.

OUR FINAL WORD

Some readers may be uncomfortable with the idea that it is their job to renew the schools. Many may believe that becoming a good classroom teacher is sufficient. On the other hand, teachers are more than technicians in charge of their classrooms. As professional people, they and their teacher colleagues must have a forceful, clear voice in deciding how they render their services. It follows that the teacher is not simply responsible for his or her own performance, but bears some responsibility for the total educational enterprise. To live up to this responsibility requires a deep understanding of the schools and much hard work. Indeed, it is the very critical nature of the problems confronting the schools that makes teaching such an exciting occupation today. In the immediate future, education is where the action will be. You have a chance to bring fresh new ideas and energy and to complete this *unfinished work of the schools.*

WHY TEACH? YOUR FINAL WORD

In your journal or online at this textbook's website, respond to the following questions:

1. Had you thought about your school being a "culture"? In what ways do you think the cultures in the schools you attended affected and changed you?

2. Review the four purposes of schooling described in the text. Which one appeals most to you as a potential educator? Why?

3. What do you see as "the unfinished work of the schools?" Specifically, what changes do you believe must take place for schools to serve the current generation of children?

KEY TERMS

comprehensive high school (45)
culture (30)
democratic reconstructionists (34)
economic reconstructionists (34)
education (28)
effective schools (47)
school cultures (30)
schooling (29)
social reconstructionists (33)
socialization (31)
society (30)

FOR FURTHER INFORMATION

TEACHSOURCE VIDEO

Effective Schools Correlates Visible in Gates Foundation Schools

This video deals with many of the educational variables needed to provide to quality education.

WEB RESOURCES

Teachnet.com. Available at: **www.teachnet.com**

This website contains many resources for teachers, including links to information on such topics as classroom management and advice to student teachers; it also offers lesson plans and numerous resources.

StuckSchools.pdf [2]. The Education Trust. March 1, 2010. Available at **www.edtrust.org/print/1501**

Stuck Schools reports on how schools are often lumped together as "low performing," but, in fact, are not all alike. Some low-performing schools remain "stuck" year after year, whereas others that started as low performers are among the fastest improvers in their states.

Jacquelynne S. Eccles. Can Middle School Reform Increase High School Graduation Rates? California Dropout Research Project Report #12. June 2008. Available at **http://cdrp.ucsb.edu/dropouts/ projectsummary.pdf**

Although based on only one state, this report focuses on why students tend to drop out during middle school. In addition, the final section suggests what can be done about it.

PRINT RESOURCES

Laura Greenstein. *What Teachers Really Need to Know about Formative Assessment.* ASCD Books, 2010.

A comprehensive resource on formative assessment, covering the history and research base, data-gathering and decision-making procedures, and implications for formative assessment's role in education reform.

John Merrow, *Below C Level: How American Education Encourages Mediocrity and What We Can Do about It*, John Merrow, 2010.

One of America's most prominent media analysts and a regular contributor to the PBS *Nightly News* has offered his analysis of what is troubling America's schools and what can be done to correct them.

Diane Ravitch, *The Death and Life of the Great American School System: How Testing and Choice Are Undermining Education* (New York: Basic Books, 2010).

Historian and school reform advocate, Diane Ravitch, in the past a strong support of testing and charter schools, retracts her former support for No Child Left Behind, the testing movement, and calls for a different kind of school reform.

The Education CourseMate website for this text offers many helpful resources. Go to www.cengagebrain.com to access the TeachSource Video Cases and other TeachSource videos, flashcards, interactive quizzes, the eBook, reflection and enrichment activities, a state standards resource center, and other study aids.

3 who are today's students in a diverse society?

(© Susie Fitzhugh)

InTASC Standards 1, 2, 3, 5, 7, and 10

FOCUS POINTS

- Studies of the demographic makeup of the United States indicate dramatic shifts in ethnic composition, particularly in the increase of the Hispanic population.

- All children have basic needs. Being aware of and understanding these commonalities help us accommodate these diverse needs.

- Students have many strengths and abilities that extend beyond the traditional emphasis in our schools on linguistic and analytic abilities. Approaches that recognize multiple views of intelligence and differing learning styles emphasize the great diversity in student learning and ability.

- Gender issues affect the curriculum, classroom interactions, and achievement levels.

- Schools address the individual needs of students through multicultural, bilingual, special education, and gifted and talented programs.

In some ways, children never change. The pictures of children in classic literature are as true today as when they were first written. Look at the conniving, mischievous Tom Sawyer, the overly curious Alice in Wonderland, the tenacious Mafatu in *Call It Courage*, or the foolish Juan Bobo. These characters are endearing to us in part because we have all known children like them. Real children of today are also very much like the children of yesterday or the children of tomorrow. Certain stages of cognitive, social, emotional, and physical development have been identified, and a similar progression through these stages occurs for everyone. We all have basic psychological and physical needs that cut across racial, cultural, age, ability, and gender boundaries. You learn a great deal about these subjects in your courses in child or adolescent development and educational psychology. As a teacher, understanding these stages of development and areas of common needs gives you insight into student behavior and helps you develop appropriate classroom experiences.

- To succeed in today's classroom, teachers must be aware of many dimensions of student diversity.

Truth OR Fiction?

T F Over 40 percent of students in public elementary and secondary schools are from minority groups.

T F The majority of English language learners were born in the United States and are U.S. citizens.

T F Most children receiving special education services do so in separate classrooms with special education teachers.

T F After lagging men for many years, women now hold a similar number of jobs in science and mathematics fields.

Even so, it is also important to be sensitive to the great differences among students and to factors in our society that are directly affecting their lives. In this chapter, we hope to make you more fully aware of the diversity in our society and classrooms, the range of abilities among the students you will encounter, and schools' attempts to address all these areas of diversity. We also hope to make you more aware of and sensitive to the sorts of issues, potential problems, and benefits related to this diversity.

sources of student diversity

You will see diversity in your students along a number of dimensions, including who they are, what they need, and what kinds of abilities they have.

- Students in your classroom are likely to come from a variety of *racial and ethnic backgrounds*, representing many different cultures and ways of looking at the world. Cultural differences among teachers and students can give rise to misunderstandings unless you learn more about your students' backgrounds and expectations. Multicultural educational approaches help students learn to appreciate the contributions of all people.

- Some of your students may speak a primary *language other than English*. We will see that parents, educators, and policymakers have become divided, often bitterly so, over the best way to teach these English language learners in U.S. public schools.

- Another dimension of diversity will be seen in the *academic abilities, achievements, and learning styles* of your students. Some students will enter the school environment and immediately do well. Others will appear not to respond to your teaching. One of your biggest challenges as a teacher will be to provide a variety of learning experiences.

- Students in your classroom will develop at different rates and display *diverse needs*. Recognizing these needs will help you better understand some student behaviors and increase your insight into how to respond.

Diversity in the classroom means that your students will come from a wide range of cultural backgrounds, may speak a first language other than English, and will have a variety of learning abilities and learning styles.

(© Laura Dwight)

- *Boys and girls*, even when they come from the same socioeconomic, racial, or ethnic group, are different. They are raised differently even within the same families, and often society has different expectations of them. Treating boys and girls equitably as individuals and not as gender stereotypes is a constant challenge for both male and female teachers.

- Regardless of your own beliefs on the subject of homosexuality, if you are going to teach in the public schools, you may very well teach lesbian, gay, bisexual, or transgendered (LGBT) students, work with LGBT fellow educators, or interact with LGBT families. As a teacher, you will be challenged to establish and maintain a safe and supportive classroom environment for these and all of your students.

- Your students will come from families with varied *socioeconomic backgrounds*. The benefits of being a child from a family in a higher socioeconomic class often show up in school performance; children from such families typically do much better academically than students from families in lower socioeconomic classes. Teachers and schools are challenged to help students from these families. This topic is discussed in more detail in Chapter 4, "What Social Problems Affect Today's Students?"

racial, ethnic, and cultural diversity

Although American society has always been composed of various races, ethnicities, and cultures, today we are experiencing even greater cultural diversity. The term *race* refers to people with common ancestry and physical characteristics, whereas the term *ethnicity* applies to people who may be racially similar or different but who share a common culture, usually including language, customs, and religion.

Public school classrooms include an even higher percentage of minorities than the population as a whole. Although about 34 percent of the total population are members of racial or ethnic minority groups, 44 percent of school-age children are minorities—a figure that will continue to increase in the coming years.[1] As shown in Table 3.1, birth rates among minority groups are higher than those of

TABLE 3.1	Projections of the U.S. Population Ages 0–19, 2010–2020 (millions)			
	2010	**2015**	**2020**	**2010–2020**
Youth				**Change**
Total youth*	84.2	86.7	90.7	+7.8%
White, non-Hispanic	46.7	46.0	46.2	–1.0%
Hispanic (of any race)	18.9	21.5	24.3	+28.6%
Black, non-Hispanic	12.5	12.5	12.8	+2.4%
Other races, including mixed races†	5.1	5.2	5.7	+11.8%

Increase in total minority youth = +6.3 million, or +17.2%

Decrease in total white youth = –0.5 million, or –1.0%

*May not add exactly because of rounding.
†Includes American Indians, Alaskan Natives, Asian and Pacific Islanders.

Source: U.S. Bureau of the Census, *U.S. Population Projections*, released 2008.
Available at www.census.gov/population/www/projections/summarytables.html.

Ⓣ F

Over 40 percent of students in public elementary and secondary schools are from minority groups.
Minority groups, particularly Hispanics, have high birth rates; so, although minorities only constitute 34 percent of the total population, they make up 44 percent of the public school students.

white Americans, and immigration patterns are contributing to the increasing size of the minority population.

These national averages disguise the fact that minority groups are unequally distributed across the country. For example, minority groups are in the majority in California, Texas, New Mexico, Hawaii, and the District of Columbia, whereas minorities constitute less than 10 percent of the population in Maine, New Hampshire, Vermont, Iowa, and West Virginia.[2] In the 47 urban school districts that constitute the "great city schools," including those in New York City, Los Angeles, and Chicago, an overwhelming majority of students are from minority groups.

As might be expected with increasing cultural diversity, teachers will encounter more students whose native language is not English and whose ethnic and cultural backgrounds reflect a Hispanic or Asian heritage. We discuss these English language learners later in this chapter.

Students from biracial or multiracial backgrounds represent a small, but growing, segment of the U.S. population. These students often face unique issues, such as being asked to declare a single racial identity, thereby denying the rest of their heritage. Tiger Woods, an example of such an individual, declared himself to be a "Cablinasian"—a mixture of Caucasian, black, American Indian, and Asian. Students without the international renown of Tiger Woods may face rejection from both members of the mainstream culture and members of racial or ethnic minority groups whose heritage they share. Teachers need to be aware of the difficulties such children may face, and be willing to accept whatever identities the students choose for themselves.

With the development of a richer, more varied society, differences in values and family expectations are also more evident. For example, some families may place a premium on school and higher education, whereas other families may emphasize early entry into the workplace. Even though you will encounter a range of familial expectations for school achievement, be aware that all children deserve the best educational experience they can get while in school. Recognition of racial and ethnic differences can provide the understanding and insight needed for more effective instruction.

CULTURAL PLURALISM: NOT THERE YET

At one time, the United States was considered a "melting pot" of many different kinds of people. Immigrants were expected to give up the language and customs of their homelands and adopt the language and customs of their new country. During the nineteenth and early twentieth centuries, schools contributed to the melting-pot concept by socializing and acculturating immigrant children to American ways while discouraging them from maintaining the ways of their homelands. Some states even passed laws forbidding instruction in any language but English. The basic idea was to produce a society with one dominant culture. This process of incorporating an immigrant group into the mainstream culture is often referred to as *enculturation* or **assimilation**. Many European immigrant groups were easily assimilated into the dominant American culture, but people of color were often prevented from doing so.

The concept of the melting pot has generally been replaced by the notion of **cultural pluralism**, which calls for an understanding and appreciation of the cultural differences and languages among U.S. citizens. The goal is to create a sense of society's wholeness based on the unique strengths of each of its parts. Cultural pluralism rejects both assimilation and separatism, a philosophy that suggests each cultural group should maintain its own identity without trying to fit into an overall American culture. Instead, it seeks a healthy interaction among the diverse groups in our society—that is, each subculture maintains its own individuality while contributing to the society as a whole. As some commentators put it, cultural pluralism argues for replacing the melting-pot metaphor with that of a "mosaic," "tapestry," or "salad bowl" in which the individual parts remain distinct yet combine to make a unique whole.

Many people have promulgated cultural pluralism as a desirable goal, but it does not currently exist in the United States. Although racial, ethnic, and cultural diversity do exist, equality among the various groups does not. In general, racial and ethnic minorities do not share equal political, economic, and educational opportunities with those of the dominant culture, even though our society espouses such equality. In addition, some people resist the notion of cultural pluralism as a desirable goal. Some opponents argue in favor of assimilation, contending that cultural pluralism will undermine the United States' common traditions, historically derived from Western European cultures. Others favor separatism. Unfortunately, U.S. schools have often failed to support cultural pluralism. Traditionally, public schools have been run for the benefit of those in the dominant cultural group, thereby excluding minority groups from receiving the full range of benefits.

Schools that embrace cultural pluralism seek to promote diversity and to avoid the dominance of a single culture. Their faculty and administration provide minority role models for the students to interact with. Their curricula are infused with the histories and contributions of diverse groups. These schools attempt to use the cultural patterns of the students to provide instruction and promote learning. They may use the multicultural education approaches described next. The goal is for students to be comfortable operating within their own cultures and in other cultures as well. Students from all racial, ethnic, and cultural groups are urged to participate in the school's various social, athletic, and governmental activities. These

> *[Folks] know that parents have to parent, that children can't achieve unless we raise their expectations and turn off the television sets and eradicate the slander that says a Black youth with a book is acting White.*
>
> —BARACK OBAMA,
> Keynote Address, Democratic
> National Convention, 2004

schools seek to raise students from all racial, ethnic and cultural groups to the highest academic standards. In short, the goal for schools that aim for cultural pluralism is that no particular cultural group either dominates or is excluded from those activities and accomplishments that schools value.

MULTICULTURAL EDUCATION

Multicultural education represents one approach to meeting the educational needs of an increasingly diverse student population. "Multicultural education is an idea, an educational reform movement, and a process whose major goal is to change the structure of educational institutions so that male and female students, exceptional students, and students who are members of diverse racial, ethnic, language, and cultural groups will have an equal chance to achieve academically in school."[3] Spurred by the civil rights movement of the 1960s, multicultural education is a response to economic inequality, racism, and sexism in American culture. Originally used in conjunction with the notion of improving the lot of "people of color," this term has since been broadened to include gender, disability, and other forms of diversity. Its goals include reducing prejudice and fostering tolerance, improving the academic achievement of minority students, building commitment to the American ideals of pluralism and democracy, and incorporating minority groups' perspectives into the curricula of our schools. Like the concept of cultural pluralism on which it is based, multicultural education rejects both the notion of the melting pot and separatist philosophies.

At least five different approaches to multicultural education have been identified, which helps explain why the term often has very different meanings for different people:

1. *Teaching the exceptional and culturally different,* which helps students achieve academically and socially within currently existing schools by building bridges between the students' backgrounds and the schools to make the curriculum more user friendly.

2. *Human relations,* which attempts to build positive relations among members of different racial/cultural groups and between males and females.

3. *Single-group studies,* which focus on programs that examine particular groups, such as African American studies or women's studies.

4. *Multicultural approaches,* which promote cultural pluralism by reconstructing the whole educational process around the perspectives of diverse racial, ethnic, cultural, and social classes.

5. *Multicultural social justice,* which teaches students to examine inequality and oppression in society and to take action to remediate these inequalities.[4]

Multicultural education is not just for members of minority racial or ethnic groups, but for all students, including those with Western European heritage. A major goal of multicultural education is to help students from diverse cultures learn to cross cultural borders and to participate in a diverse, democratic society. True multicultural education does not consist of only black history or women's history months. Instead of simply adding information about particular groups to the curriculum and leaving the rest of it untouched, real multicultural education presents multiple perspectives and viewpoints to help students understand how various groups can interpret events and facts differently.

In addition to valuing cultural diversity, multicultural education is based on the concept of *social justice,* which seeks to do away with social and economic inequalities for those who in the past have been denied these benefits of a democratic society. African Americans, American Indians, Asian Americans, Hispanic Americans, mixed-race individuals, women, individuals with disabilities, people with limited English proficiency, people with low incomes, members of particular religious groups, and individuals with different sexual orientations are among those groups that have at one time or another been denied social justice. Educators who support multicultural education see establishing social justice for all people—but particularly for those who have experienced discrimination—as a moral and ethical responsibility.

An Ongoing Debate

Many school districts are attempting to permeate their curricula with a multicultural emphasis, believing that attention to multicultural education is the best way to combat the prejudice and divisiveness among the many different subcultures found in the United States. By developing mutual respect for and appreciation of different lifestyles, languages, religious beliefs, and family structures, students may help shape a better future society for all its members.

Some educators, however, are concerned about what they believe are potential dangers of multicultural education in the schools:

- Multicultural education may destroy any sense of common traditions, values, purposes, and obligations, thereby leading to a more fragmented and contentious nation.
- It may divert schools' attention from their basic purpose of educating for civic, economic, and personal effectiveness.
- It attacks the problem of minority students' underachievement by emphasizing self-esteem rather than hard work.
- It substitutes "relevance" of subjects studied for instruction in solid academics.
- It may undermine a sense of a common morality because some advocates of multiculturalism claim there are no universal moral positions that the public schools can legitimately teach.

These critics do not argue against the need to preserve and value the achievements of the diverse ethnic and racial groups of the United States, but they reject the position that everything is of equal value, that the schools have a responsibility to teach every possible belief and value, and that behavior is moral if it is believed to be so by any group. They assert that there are limits to pluralism and that those limits must be articulated by schools and school leaders. In addition, these critics believe that those who lose most from multicultural education are the minorities and immigrants themselves. They argue that the special curricular accommodations associated with multicultural education (i.e., the focus on the history and culture of different nationalities or ethnicities) divert time and energy away from the subjects that students need to compete in the economic world dominated by the majority culture. Other critics of multiculturalism completely reject the concept of cultural pluralism, preferring an assimilationist perspective whereby schools are charged with forging one dominant American culture in which English is the only acceptable language.

Clearly, the notion of multicultural education is not without controversy. Multicultural education has often been cast as a reform movement, designed to address inequities and discrimination resulting from the race, religion, socioeconomic status, gender, age, exceptionality, or language of students.[5] As with any attempt to solve social problems, excesses and overexuberance can occur. Nevertheless, schools do need to accommodate larger minority populations in a way that removes barriers and enables those students to compete academically and economically while preserving the basic purposes of schooling. (See the box, Ethnic Studies Controversy in Arizona, for more on these issues.)

ethnic studies controversy in arizona

In 2010, the Superintendent of Public Instruction in Arizona, Thomas Horne, convinced the state legislature to approve a law, later signed by the governor, that bars all public schools across the state from offering courses designed for a particular ethnic group, that advocate ethnic solidarity or that promote resentment toward a race or group of people. The Tucson Unified School District (TUSD) is the only school district in Arizona that offers district-wide ethnic studies courses, so the law appears to be directed toward TUSD. Mr. Horne contends that the courses teach anti-American ideas and encourage Mexican Americans to think of themselves as victims.

In late summer 2010, Mr. Horne sent a letter to the interim superintendent of TUSD, stating that if the district continues to offer ethnic studies, the Arizona education department will withhold 10 percent of the district's funds. Although Mexican American studies have been the target of the critics, Tucson High School also offers a Native American literature and an African American literature course. Of the 386 students taking ethnic-studies classes at the high school, 332 are taking Mexican American studies and 54 are taking either African American or Native American studies.

Teachers in the Mexican American studies department plan on filing a constitutional challenge to the state law, arguing that it violates both the First and Fourteenth Amendments of the U.S. Constitution because it targets one school district and one group of people.

Students in the Mexican American studies program say that critics' claims that they're being taught to be victims is completely false. One student stated the difference between ethnic studies and regular high school courses: "We are more socially critical of a lot of things around us. We explore the other side of the story." Enrollment in Mexican American studies in TUSD's 14 high schools nearly doubled from 2009–2010 to 2010–2011, from 781 to 1,400 students

Arizona, while garnering great notoriety over this issue, is only one example of the culture wars that affect the curriculum of the public schools.

Source: Mary Ann Zehr, "Tucson Students Aren't Deterred by Ethnic-Studies Controversy," *Education Week* 30 (September 22, 2010), pp. 1, 16.

▶❙❙ TeachSource VIDEO CASE

Culturally Responsive Teaching

Go to the Education CourseMate website to watch the video clips, study the artifacts in the case, and reflect on the following questions:

1. Which of the approaches to multicultural education listed in this chapter does the class shown in the Video Case represent?

2. How might teachers plan meaningful multicultural instruction for other grade levels or subjects?

Teaching Implications

One preferred method for teachers who want to acknowledge and accommodate cultural diversity in the classroom is **culturally responsive teaching**. Many educators have documented how cultural identity, communication styles, and social expectations of students from minority cultural groups often conflict with the values, beliefs, and cultural assumptions of teachers.[6] (Study the Video Case *Culturally Responsive Teaching* to see how one teacher helps students develop their writing skills.)

The school's middle-class culture often places students from other cultures at a disadvantage in understanding the school's cultural codes and communication styles. Teachers who recognize this problem can implement an *equity pedagogy*, a style of teaching that uses instructional materials and practices that incorporate important aspects of their students' family and community culture.

> *One day our descendants will think it incredible that we paid so much attention to things like the amount of melanin in our skin or the shape of our eyes or our gender instead of the unique identities of each of us as complex human beings.*
>
> —FRANKLIN THOMAS,
> Former President of the Ford Foundation

For example, a teacher whose class contains mostly immigrant children from Central America can place maps of both Latin America and the United States around the room, provide magazines and games in both Spanish and English, and play salsa music as background for certain activities. This teacher might also recognize that, for many students from a Latin culture, establishing direct eye contact with an adult authority figure is a sign of disrespect, so she does not have that expectation of her students. Knowing and understanding your students' cultural backgrounds can help you make your classroom more inviting and can increase students' academic achievement.

PAUSE AND REFLECT

1. What are the pros and cons of living in a culturally pluralistic society?

2. In your opinion, is this preferable to a "melting pot" or assimilationist approach to diversity? Why or why not?

3. Does the idea of multicultural education make sense to you? Why or why not? If so, what version of multicultural education appeals to you most?

children of immigrants and english language learners

More than 5.3 million **limited English proficient (LEP)** students or, stated more positively, **English language learners (ELLs)** are enrolled in public elementary and secondary schools (almost 11 percent of the total enrollment), and this number has increased every year for the last decade.[7] The majority of ELL students are concentrated in the states of California, Texas, New York, Florida, and Illinois. Across the United States, ELL students speak more than 400 different languages. Spanish is the non-English background of the great majority of ELL students (77%), followed by Vietnamese (2.4%), Hmong (1.8%), Korean (1.2%), Arabic (1.2%), French (Haitian) Creole (1.1%), and Cantonese (1.0%).[8] All other language groups represent less than 1 percent of the ELL student population.

You might think that these non-English-speaking youngsters are new to the United States, and some of them are. However, 80 percent of the children of immigrants were born in the United States; and approximately three-fourths of the ELLs were born in the United States, are U.S. citizens, and began school in kindergarten and first grade, the same as their English-speaking peers.[9] The remaining one-quarter of the ELLs were immigrant children and youth born in a country other than the United States. These data indicate that the predominant need for English language development instruction in U.S. school systems is for a large native-born population that does not speak English proficiently.

Twenty-one percent of all U.S. 5- to 17-year-olds speak a language other than English at home, and 5 percent speak English with difficulty.[10] Many of them also lack basic skills in the language spoken at home, which makes it more difficult to teach them English at school.

(T) F

The majority of English language learners were born in the United States and are U.S. citizens.

About three of every four ELL students were born in the United States and are U.S. citizens.

THE GOVERNMENT RESPONSE

Students whose native language is not English constitute one of the most conspicuous failure groups in the U.S. educational system. Because of their difficulty in speaking, writing, and understanding English, many of these ELL students fall farther and farther behind in school, and overwhelming numbers drop out before finishing high school.

To cope with this problem, Congress passed the Bilingual Education Act in 1968 and subsequently amended it a number of times to provide federal funds to develop bilingual programs. Much of the expansion of bilingual programs in the 1970s can be attributed to a series of court cases—most notably the 1974 U.S. Supreme Court case of *Lau* v. *Nichols,* in which the Court found that "where inability to speak and understand the English language excludes national origin–minority group children from effective participation in the educational program offered by a school district, the district must take affirmative steps to rectify the language deficiency in order to open its instructional program to these students."[11] Basing its ruling on the Civil Rights Act of 1964, the Court held that the San Francisco school system unlawfully discriminated on the basis of national origin when it failed to cope with children's language problems.

As a result of the *Lau* case, the U.S. Office of Civil Rights suggested guidelines for school districts to follow, the so-called Lau Remedies. The guidelines specified that "language minority students should be taught academics in their primary home language until they could effectively benefit from English language instruction."[12]

BILINGUAL EDUCATION MODELS

Students with a native language other than English have two goals in school: learning English and mastering content. Language programs for ELLs are of two types: (1) those that focus on developing literacy in two languages (**bilingual education**), and (2) those that focus on developing literacy in only English (English immersion). Among the models that focus on developing literacy in two languages are the *transitional* and *maintenance* or *developmental models*.

The *transitional model* provides intensive English-language instruction, but students get some portion of their academic instruction in their native language. The goal is to prepare students for regular classes in English without letting them fall behind in subject areas. In theory, students should transition out of these programs within a few years.

Maintenance or *developmental* bilingual education aims to preserve and build on students' native-language skills as they continue to acquire English as a second language.

In the *English immersion model,* students learn everything in English. Teachers using immersion programs generally strive to deliver lessons in simple and understandable language that allows students to internalize English while learning academic subjects. The extreme case of immersion is called *submersion,* wherein students must "sink or swim" until they learn English. Sometimes students are pulled out for *English as a Second Language (ESL)* programs, which provide them with instruction in English geared toward language acquisition.

> *Our common language is … English. And our common task is to ensure that our non-English-speaking children learn this common language.*
>
> —WILLIAM BENNETT,
> Former U.S. Secretary of Education

BILINGUAL EDUCATION CONTROVERSIES

Choosing the best method for educating students who need to learn English has become a divisive political battle. In the early 1970s, language-minority speakers and their advocates fought for bilingual education as their right. Today, however, many of them are expressing doubts about the effectiveness of bilingual programs. Civil rights and cultural issues are giving way to concerns that non-native English speakers are just not sufficiently mastering the English language, which in turn is keeping them from fully participating in American life. Although many educators believe students who use English as a second language should be educated in their native language as well, critics insist such an approach doesn't work. The critics believe the best path to academic achievement for language-minority students in most cases is to learn English and learn it quickly. Too many bilingual programs, they say, place ELL students into slower learning tracks where they rarely learn sufficient English and from which they may never emerge. These critics basically support an immersion model of bilingual education, opposing the transitional and maintenance models.

In response, supporters of transitional and maintenance models argue that students can best keep up academically with their English-speaking peers if they are taught at least partly in their native languages while learning English. They also cite research indicating that instruction in the native language concurrent with English instruction actually enhances the acquisition of English.[13] These advocates say it is not fair to blame bilingual education for the slow progress some students are making: the true problem is that becoming proficient in any second language takes longer than just one or two years. They also point out the shortage of well-qualified, fully bilingual teachers, which in many cases means that the problem with bilingual classes is not the curriculum, but rather the quality of the instruction. Some school systems have used paraeducators who speak the child's language to help connect the child and the school. The use of bilingual peer tutors may also help provide a greater sense of stability.

The transitional and maintenance models of bilingual education are in growing jeopardy. First California, Arizona, and Massachusetts gutted their bilingual programs, and now other states are threatening to follow suit. In 1998, California voters passed Proposition 227, which called for ELL students to be taught in a special English-immersion program in which nearly all instruction is in English, in most cases for no more than a year, before moving into mainstream English classrooms. Proposition 227 basically ended transitional and maintenance models of bilingual education in California, except when sufficient numbers of parents specifically request that their children continue in them. Many parents, administrators, and teachers are concerned that all children, not just ELL students, will be affected as mainstream teachers grapple with students who may be unprepared to deal with grade-level work in English after one year in immersion. The legality of Proposition 227 was challenged in the courts, but in 2001 a federal appeals court upheld the law. ELL students in California elementary and middle schools have improved their overall scores on state standardized tests since the implementation of Proposition 227—an outcome that supporters of the measure argue is a result of the law being implemented. On the other side of the coin, bilingual education supporters point out that average scores have risen for all students in California but note that the rate of increase in scores for ELL students still lags behind the rate of increase for English-speaking students.

Although research on the effectiveness of bilingual education remains controversial, in a recent study in which English-language learners were followed for as long as five years, researchers found that Spanish-speaking children learn to read English equally well regardless of whether they are taught primarily in English or in both English and their native language.[14]

Despite the controversy over bilingual education, many school districts are in desperate need of bilingual teachers, particularly those who speak Spanish and Asian languages. If you speak a second language or still have time to include learning a language in your college program, you could help meet a serious educational need while greatly enhancing your employment opportunities. Speaking a foreign language, especially Spanish, is also an asset for the regular classroom teacher who may have Spanish-speaking students in class.

NO CHILD LEFT BEHIND AND ENGLISH LANGUAGE LEARNERS

Title III of the Elementary and Secondary Education Act (ESEA, reauthorized as the No Child Left Behind Act of 2001) provides for federal grant money to state education agencies for the purposes of helping to ensure that limited English proficient children develop high levels of academic attainment in English and meet the same student academic achievement standards as all children are expected to meet. Title III provides more than $750 million a year to states, distributed proportionally, based on the number of ELLs in each state.[15]

The No Child Left Behind legislation requires that ELL students be tested at least once a year, using the tests chosen by each state. Like other students, ELL students must meet targets for adequate yearly progress, or their schools will be labeled as failing. Students who have been in U.S. schools for at least three years must take language arts/reading tests written in English, although students who meet certain criteria can get waivers for two more years. States are allowed to test ELL students in their own languages, but most states elect not to do so because of cost and because of the fact that so many different languages are spoken within states.

Although the No Child Left Behind Act doesn't specify what kind of instruction schools should use for ELL students, many school districts have discontinued bilingual education in such cases for two reasons: accountability tests are typically in English, and more time is needed for English instruction than for instruction in the student's native language. As might be expected, ELL students do not do as well on the tests as native-English-speaking students.

PAUSE AND REFLECT

1. How can you help prepare yourself for the diversity you are likely to encounter in the classroom?

2. What experiences with diversity will you bring to the classroom? How do you think these experiences will help you as a teacher?

diverse abilities

In some ways, many U.S. schools are not structured to address students' diverse abilities. In this section, we look at the theory that students may have many abilities and talents not tapped by traditional schooling. We also explore learning styles to see how different students learn; this exploration might broaden your views on approaches to teaching. Finally, we briefly examine characteristics of students along a range of disabilities and talents. Schools and teachers must make special efforts to effectively educate students who vary from average either because they have learning problems or because they are academically gifted.

MULTIPLE INTELLIGENCES

Howard Gardner, a leading psychologist, proposes that we should move toward educating **multiple intelligences**, of which linguistic and analytic abilities are only two facets. In Gardner's books *Frames of Mind* and *Multiple Intelligences: The Theory in Practice,*[16] he explains that we all have strengths, weaknesses, and unique combinations of cognitive abilities. Gardner states that people have at least eight distinct intellectual capacities that they use to approach problems and create products. He has also tentatively identified a ninth intelligence (*existential*) that he is currently trying to validate. (*Existential intelligence* refers to the ability to pose and ponder questions about life, death, and ultimate realities.)

1. *Verbal–linguistic intelligence* draws on the individual's language skills, oral and written, to express what's on the person's mind and to understand other people.

2. *Logical–mathematical intelligence* is a person's ability to understand principles of some kind of causal system, like a scientist does, or to manipulate numbers, quantities, and operations, like a mathematician does.

3. *Spatial intelligence* refers to the ability to represent the spatial world internally in the mind, like a chess player or sculptor does.

4. *Bodily–kinesthetic intelligence* is the capacity to use your whole body or parts of your body to solve a problem, make something, or put on some kind of production, like that of an athlete or a performing artist.

5. *Musical intelligence* is the capacity to "think" in music and to be able to hear patterns and recognize, remember, and manipulate them.
6. *Interpersonal intelligence* is the ability to understand other people—an ability that we all need but that is particularly important for teachers, salespeople, and politicians.
7. *Intrapersonal intelligence* refers to having an understanding of yourself and knowing your preferences, capabilities, and deficiencies.
8. *Naturalist intelligence* refers to the ability to discriminate among living things (plants and animals) and to have sensitivity toward features of the natural world, such as rock formations and clouds.[17]

Many of our schools tend to emphasize a curriculum that specifically targets the predominantly linguistic and logical–mathematical abilities students need to do well on commonly used standardized tests and to deemphasize or exclude other possible intelligences. This constricted focus on a limited range of abilities results in an education system that teaches and reinforces only certain types of achievement. Children who are strong in linguistic and logical–mathematical tasks are likely to be successful in school and feel a great sense of achievement. Other children, even though they may be very competent or even gifted in nontraditional school tasks, may experience frustration or failure in school. In Gardner's theory, abilities in diverse areas would be valued as indicators of intelligence and be considered worthy of further nurturance and development in school.

Gardner's Five Minds

Howard Gardner's latest book, *Five Minds for the Future: Cultivating Thinking Skills*, argues that because the future is so unpredictable and changing, everyone needs to cultivate five different ways of thinking:

1. *The Disciplined Mind* has mastered at least one way of thinking—a distinctive mode of cognition that characterizes a specific scholarly discipline, craft, or profession.
2. *The Synthesizing Mind* takes information from disparate sources, understands and evaluates that information objectively, and puts it together in ways that make sense to the synthesizer and also to other persons.
3. *The Creating Mind* breaks new ground. It puts forth new ideas, poses unfamiliar questions, conjures up fresh ways of thinking, and arrives at unexpected answers.
4. *The Respectful Mind* notes and welcomes differences among human individuals and groups, tries to understand these "others," and seeks to work effectively with them.
5. *The Ethical Mind* ponders the nature of one's work and the needs and desires of the society in which one lives. This mind conceptualizes how workers can serve purposes beyond self-interest and how citizens can work unselfishly to improve the lot of all.[18]

These five minds are different from the eight or nine intelligences Gardner identified. He thinks of them as broad uses of the mind that can be cultivated in school, the workplace, or in professions. To be certain, Gardner asserts, these five minds make use of the intelligences. For instance, to cultivate the respectful mind, one would have to exercise interpersonal intelligence. Or to cultivate the disciplined mind, logical-mathematical intelligence would likely be used.

Teaching Implications

Acknowledging and fostering individual abilities in a variety of areas is one way teachers can help students. To address varied intelligences, Gardner emphasizes learning in context, particularly through apprenticeships. Student development in an area like music should be fostered through hands-on practice and experiences.

Even traditional subjects should be taught in a variety of ways, such as those listed in the Multiple Intelligences Menu in Table 3.2, to address the varied intelligences of both students and teachers. For example, history might be taught through a number of media and methods, ranging from art and architecture to biographies and dramatic reenactments of events. Assessments should also be tailored to different abilities and should take place in a learning context as much as possible.

Although the theory of multiple intelligences is very popular with many educators and resonates with their own experiences, it should be noted that a number of psychologists have criticized it based on the lack of scientific measures for Gardner's various intelligences. Some critics argue that what Gardner calls "intelligences" are merely talents, personality traits, or cognitive styles. Others worry that schools, in attempting to address a range of abilities, may not adequately stress the importance of verbal and mathematical abilities, which they say are critical to success in our society. In particular, some critics worry that Gardner's theories will lead to the end of ability grouping in schools.[19]

Nevertheless, multiple intelligences theory offers teachers some ideas for expanding instructional repertoires and infusing variety into lessons. It provides a framework for enhancing instruction and a language to describe the efforts. Currently a number of schools across the United States are applying this theory in the classroom on a day-to-day basis. These efforts should contribute to our knowledge and skills in this area. Whether, or how, schools will address Gardner's Five Minds remains to be seen.

DIFFERING LEARNING STYLES

Another approach to individual abilities and differences is the theory of learning styles. A **learning styles** approach to teaching and learning is based on the idea that all students have strengths and abilities, but each student may have a preferred way of using these abilities. Whereas Gardner's theory of multiple intelligences centers on the *content* and *products* of learning and has its roots in an effort to rethink the theory of measurable intelligence, learning styles theory addresses differences in the *process* of learning and the different ways people think and feel as they solve problems, create products, and interact.

A number of theories and models of learning styles exist. One approach looks at four modalities for learning: visual (seeing), auditory (hearing), kinesthetic (moving), and tactile (touching). This approach is based on the idea that different people prefer different modes of learning. For example, some people learn better by reading (visual), whereas others prefer learning by doing (kinesthetic or tactile). Other models look at learning styles for processing information. For example, some learners absorb information concretely and in a sequential manner; others focus more on ideas and abstractions; and still others like to learn socially.

A learning styles approach to teaching is currently receiving considerable attention in education. Although few schools adhere strictly to any one model, the approach is being applied in varying

> *If students do not learn the way we teach, then let us teach the way they learn.*
>
> —KENNETH DUNN,
> Expert on Learning Styles

TABLE 3.2 **Multiple Intelligences Menu**

Linguistic Menu

Use storytelling to explain ___.

Conduct a debate on ___.

Write a poem, myth, legend, short play, or news article about ___.

Create a talk-show radio program about ___.

Conduct an interview of ___ on ___.

Logical–Mathematical Menu

Translate a ___ into a mathematical formula ___.

Design and conduct an experiment on ___.

Make up syllogisms to demonstrate ___, ___, and ___.

Make up analogies to explain ___.

Describe the patterns of symmetry in ___.

Bodily–Kinesthetic Menu

Create a movement or sequence of movements to explain ___.

Make task or puzzle cards for ___.

Build or construct a ___.

Plan and attend a field trip that will ___.

Bring hands-on materials to demonstrate ___.

Visual Menu

Chart, map, cluster, or graph ___.

Create a slide show, videotape, or photo album of ___.

Create a piece of art that demonstrates ___.

Invent a board or card game to demonstrate ___.

Illustrate, draw, paint, sketch, or sculpt ___.

Musical Menu

Give a presentation with appropriate musical accompaniment on ___.

Sing a rap or song that explains ___.

Indicate the rhythmical patterns in ___.

Explain how the music of a song is similar to ___.

Make an instrument and use it to demonstrate ___.

Interpersonal Menu

Conduct a meeting to address ___.

Intentionally use ___ social skills to learn about ___.

Participate in a service project to ___.

Teach someone about ___.

Practice giving and receiving feedback on ___.

Use technology to ___.

Intrapersonal Menu

Describe qualities you possess that will help you to successfully complete ___.

Set and pursue a goal to ___.

Describe one of your personal values about ___.

Write a journal entry on ___.

Assess your own work in ___.

Naturalist Menu

Create observation notebooks of ___.

Describe changes in local or global environment ___.

Care for pets, wildlife, gardens, or parks ___.

Use binoculars, telescopes, microscopes, or magnifiers to ___.

Draw or photograph natural objects ___.

Source: Reprinted with permission from Linda Campbell, "How Teachers Interpret MI Theory," *Educational Leadership* 44 (September 1997), p. 18.

forms and intensities in many schools. Key advocates and researchers of a learning styles approach to education agree that individual strengths and abilities should be emphasized, but they disagree on how to put the theory into practice. Some educators call for a formal assessment of each student's learning style and then a prescription for appropriate teaching methods for that individual. Others believe that students should be assessed and matched with teachers having similar learning styles. Still others warn that current tests are not yet technically adequate and that using these tests may actually harm students because they may result in improper labeling of individuals and their so-called learning styles.

Teaching Implications

Rather than label students as having a particular learning style, many educators argue that curricula and instruction should offer varied lessons that appeal to a range of strengths, abilities, and learning preferences over time. Teachers need to accommodate different learning styles by systematically varying their teaching and assessment methods to reach all students. Flexibility and variety are the keys: don't assume that all students learn the way you do, and don't undervalue students just because their learning styles differ from yours.

Differentiated instruction, as described in "What Is Taught?" (Chapter 5), is a powerful way to address academic diversity. Technology can also help teachers effectively vary their instruction and assessment methods. As teachers become more familiar with new technology, many are making use of wikis and blogs, probes and sensors, concept mapping tools, podcasts, Internet sites, and other multimedia tools that offer students varied ways to access materials and learning experiences.

PAUSE AND REFLECT

1. Looking at Howard Gardner's list of intelligences, which are your strongest intelligences? How do you know?

2. Should teachers and schools focus on fostering a variety of abilities such as those identified by Gardner, or should they concentrate on developing verbal and mathematical abilities? Explain your position.

3. What are the general characteristics of your learning style? If you don't know, visit one of the websites on learning styles and take an inventory to discover your preferred ways of learning.

4. How will you account for various learning styles in your students?

STUDENTS WITH DISABILITIES

Within the range of diversity your students will display, some will have disabilities. You may encounter many types of disabilities. For example, you may have students with mental retardation, emotional disturbance, learning disabilities, attention-deficit disorders, speech or language impairments, multiple handicaps, autism, traumatic brain injuries, orthopedic impairments, visual impairments or blindness, and hearing impairments or deafness.

Table 3.3 shows the percentage and number of students in each of the officially recognized categories. With over 6 million students, ages 6 to 21, receiving federal aid for their disabilities, these students represent about 9.2 percent of the total 6- to 21-year-old population. Almost 700,000 additional children, ages 3 to 5, also

TABLE 3.3	Specific Disabilities among Children Ages 6–21: Percentage for Each Category for the 50 States, and District of Columbia		
Disability			**Percentage***
Specific learning disabilities (otherwise mentally fit students who have disorders in one or more basic psychological processes)	2,727,802		45.3%
Speech or language impairments (problems in communication, including inability to use or understand language)	1,143,195		18.9%
Mental retardation (limitations in mental functioning, causing a child to learn and develop more slowly than a typical child)	533,426		9.2%
Emotional disturbance (includes inappropriate behavior, pervasive mood of unhappiness, or depression)	471,306		7.8%
Other health impairments (includes such disabilities as cerebral palsy, spina bifida, and epilepsy)	557,121		9.3%
Multiple disabilities (includes severe mental retardation along with movement difficulty or sensory loss)	132,595		2.2%
Autism (neurological disorder affecting ability to play, communicate, and relate to others)	192,643		3.2%
Orthopedic impairments (motor difficulty affecting a child's educational performance)	62,618		1.0%
Hearing impairments (impairment in hearing that affects a child's educational performance)	71,484		1.2%
Developmental delay (any condition or disorder that interferes with a child's normal development when compared to children of the same age)	78,915		1.3%
Visual impairments (partially sighted, low vision, legally blind, and totally blind)	25,369		0.4%
Traumatic brain injury (an injury to the brain caused by the head being hit or shaken)	23,449		0.4%
Deaf–blindness (children suffering from both hearing and vision loss)	1,539		0.03%
All Disabilities	6,021,462		100%

*Percentages may not add up to 100 percent due to rounding.

Source: 29th Annual Report to Congress on the Implementation of the Individuals with Disabilities Education Act, 2007, vol. 2 (Washington, DC: U.S. Department of Education, 2010), Table 1-3.

received federal aid for their disabilities.[20] In fiscal year 2010, the federal government distributed more than $11.5 billion to the states for students with disabilities.[21]

Special Education

The term **special education** is often used as a designation for services designed for students with disabilities. In 1975, the *Education for All Handicapped Children Act (PL 94–142)* established the right of all students with disabilities to a "free appropriate public education" (FAPE). The law specified that each such student must be provided with an **individualized education program (IEP)** outlining both long-range and short-range goals for the child. Since that time, a number of other federal laws have reinforced and extended the commitment to special education.

Preschool Legislation

The Education of the Handicapped Act Amendments (PL 99–457), passed in 1986, provided for early intervention for children from birth to age 2 who are developmentally delayed. For states that choose to participate, programs must include a multidisciplinary assessment of the child's needs, a written **individualized family services plan (IFSP)**, and case management. Services may draw from a variety of areas, such as special education, speech and language pathology, occupational or physical therapy, or family training and counseling, depending on the developmental needs of the child.

PL 99–457 also stated that FAPE must be extended to children with disabilities ages 3 to 5 years. Although state and local education agencies administer these programs, they may contract with other programs, agencies, or providers to supply a range of services, such as programs that are home based for part of the day. Families play a particularly important role in preschool education, and instruction for parents is to be included in the IFSP whenever it is appropriate and the parents desire it. When students reach school age, they are covered by the provisions of the Individuals with Disabilities Education Act (IDEA), as discussed in the next section.

IDEA and ADA

In 1990, Congress passed two significant federal laws relating to persons with disabilities: the *Individuals with Disabilities Education Act (IDEA)*, subsequently re-authorized in 1997 and again in 2004, and the *Americans with Disabilities Act (ADA)*. IDEA amended the Education for All Handicapped Children Act of 1975. ADA ensures the right of individuals with disabilities to nondiscriminatory treatment in aspects of their lives other than education.

Seven principles provide the framework of IDEA, around which education services are designed and provided to students with disabilities:

- Fair and appropriate education (FAPE)
- Appropriate evaluation
- An individualized education program (IEP)
- Least restrictive environment (LRE)
- Parent and student participation in decision making
- Procedural safeguards
- Response to Intervention (RTI)

Because of the wide variety of disabilities and infinite degrees of severity in which these conditions may be found in individual students, IDEA mandates that a "free appropriate public education" be defined on an individual basis, using the written IEP. The IEP identifies the child's current levels of educational performance, short-term objectives and annual goals, services to be provided, and criteria and schedules for evaluation of progress. In this way, it helps ensure that the educational goals designed for the child are appropriate to his or her individual learning needs and that these plans are actually delivered as intended. Provisions in the IEP must be reviewed and revised annually—or more often, if necessary. Teachers, parents or guardians, special educators, other professionals, and the child (whenever appropriate) are all involved in the development and approval of the IEP. IDEA also requires that all older students with a disability (usually ages 14–16) have an individualized plan for making the transition from school to work or additional education beyond high school through age 21.

Like the original act of 1975, IDEA further stipulates that services for students with disabilities be provided in a **least restrictive environment (LRE)**, meaning students with disabilities should be educated with children without disabilities to the greatest extent appropriate. Determination of what constitutes the LRE has been controversial. The social and academic benefits of the regular classroom must be weighed against the unique educational needs and individual circumstances for each child.

In the past, the term **mainstreaming** was used to describe the practice of placing special education students in general education classes for at least part of the school day, with additional services, programs, or classes being provided to these students as needed. More recently, the term **inclusion** has been used to mean the commitment to educate each child, to the maximum extent appropriate, in the regular school and classroom. Compared with mainstreaming, inclusion—and particularly *full inclusion,* as it is sometimes called—indicates an even greater commitment to keeping students with disabilities in regular classrooms. It usually involves bringing the support services to the child rather than moving the child to services located in separate rooms or buildings. One special education teacher describes her experiences as a co-teacher in this chapter's Voices from the Classroom.

Controversy over Inclusion In recent years, full inclusion has become a civil rights issue. Advocates of full inclusion argue that segregated education for students with disabilities is inherently unequal (much like the earlier practice of racial segregation) and therefore violates the rights of these children. They also argue that traditional special education programs have resulted in a costly special education bureaucracy that has not shown the expected benefits in terms of academic, social, or vocational skills. Among the benefits of full inclusion for children with disabilities, they say, are higher expectations and better socialization, as well as greater acceptance of human differences by children without disabilities. The "Breaking Out" feature describes how one student with autism has benefited from inclusion.

Critics of full inclusion say that both teachers and students are being hurt in the rush to embrace this teaching approach:

- Parents of children without disabilities often worry that the curriculum standards will be lowered by the inclusion of students with learning disabilities and that those students with attention-deficit/hyperactivity disorder (ADHD) or emotional problems can be a disruption to their classmates and teachers.

- Some special educators voice concerns that full inclusion may result in diminished or inadequate specialized services for students who have special needs. They point out that the regular classroom may not be the best setting for every child. Violent or emotionally disordered children, for example, may pose a threat

VOICES from the classroom

Reflections on Teacher Collaboration

Paula Hoffman has been teaching for more than 28 years, including 20 years in Albemarle County, Virginia. For the past five years, she has been the lead special education teacher and a contributing member of her school's School-Based Intervention Team (SBIT). Hoffman has a B.S. in mental retardation/elementary education, an M.Ed. in learning and behavioral disorders, and a J.D. in law. For the past 10 years, she has also been a clinical instructor for the Curry School of Education at the University of Virginia.

Collaboration is like a dance—two partners in sync with each other. It's been about 10 years since I first walked into an eighth-grade language arts class as the collaborating special education teacher. With the widespread inclusion of students with disabilities into regular education classrooms, special education teachers have collaborated with regular education teachers to ensure a positive learning environment for all students. I've since stopped calling myself a collaborating teacher, however, and now refer to myself as a co-teacher. I've been fortunate in that I've always worked with regular education teachers who have always treated me with the same respect as I treat them. This relationship reflects in great part my willingness to work hard and do my share in the planning and delivery of instruction.

Even after so many years of collaborating, I still have that anxious feeling the first day of school when I physically have to go into another person's classroom to teach. That feeling subsides quickly. Sometimes getting through a class block with two adults in the room can be challenging because of differences in classroom management styles and approaches to instruction. To the kids, my message is very clear, which in turn has helped the adults equally: *Don't talk to one teacher when the other teacher is teaching.* Furthermore, I'm careful to use words like *our* and *we*, and to sign e-mails with both my name and my colleague's name. The best part— so have my colleagues.

Perhaps the main reason why I have such strong and positive relationships with my regular education colleagues is that I view all the students in the classes I co-teach as "my kids" and not just those identified as special education kids. In turn, my colleagues do the same. It's a win–win situation, both for the kids and for us.

to themselves and to their classmates. These educators are wary of eliminating the range of service delivery options currently available in favor of a pure inclusion model. They argue that little evidence shows that inclusion programs strengthen students' academic achievement. (The same criticism could be made of many special education programs.)

- Overworked classroom teachers have complained that they are given inadequate resources and training to deal with students with disabilities. Ideally, when students with disabilities are included in regular classrooms, their teachers receive special training and help from a special education teacher who serves as either a co-teacher or a consultant. In some cases, however, teachers have been given sole responsibility for a class of 30 students, with as many as 10 having disabilities. True collaboration between general education and special education teachers is essential for inclusion to work effectively.

In too many instances, critics say, when children with disabilities are moved from resource rooms and self-contained classrooms into regular classrooms, the necessary supports do not follow them on their journey. One reason for this trend is that some school districts use the cover of inclusion as a way to cut costs for special education services. With voters reluctant to increase school taxes, and many school districts facing budget cuts as a result, some school boards and administrators see the inclusion movement as a way to save money by reducing funding for special education.

The 2004 reauthorization of IDEA committed the federal government in principle to paying 40 percent of the average per-pupil cost of educating a special education student by 2011. With more than 6 million students served under IDEA, schools are qualified to receive $18 billion in federal funds. Unfortunately, in 2010 the federal government provided approximately 17 percent of its commitment rather than the 40 percent specified by law.[22] This development is especially important because the 2001 No Child Left Behind Act requires that special education students take the same achievement tests that regular education students take, albeit sometimes with accommodations. Without additional funding or appropriate alternative assessments, many special education students will not pass these tests, and their schools will fail to meet the provisions of the law. For more on the No Child Left Behind law, see Chapter 11, "How Are Schools Governed, Influenced, and Financed?" and Chapter 12, "How Should Education Be Reformed?"

Despite the criticisms of the inclusion movement, one thing is certain: inclusion of children with disabilities has become accepted practice in U.S. schools. The majority of students with disabilities are taking part in regular classroom and school life alongside their peers. Inclusion seems to thrive in schools that have a shared vision of the school's purposes; strong lines of communication among teachers, administrators, and parents; and a culture of innovation and reform. In many schools with successful inclusion programs, the presence of students with disabilities has sparked other reform initiatives such as cooperative learning, peer teaching, team teaching, authentic assessment, and interdisciplinary instruction.

T (F)

Most children receiving special education services do so in separate classrooms with special education teachers.

Most students receiving special education services do so in the regular classroom in an effort to provide as normal an experience as possible.

In addition to students receiving special education services, a number of children in elementary and secondary schools have "504 plans." The "504" in "504 plan" refers to Section 504 of the Rehabilitation Act and the Americans with Disabilities Act, which specifies that no one with a disability can be excluded from participating in federally funded programs or activities, including elementary, secondary or postsecondary schooling. *Disability* in this context refers to a "physical or mental impairment which substantially limits one or more major life activities." This can include physical impairments; illnesses or injuries; communicable diseases; chronic conditions like asthma, allergies and diabetes; and learning problems. A 504 plan spells out the accommodations that will be needed for these students to have an opportunity to perform at the same level as their peers, and might include such things as wheelchair ramps, blood sugar monitoring, an extra set of textbooks, a peanut-free lunch environment, home instruction, or a tape recorder or keyboard for taking notes.

Response to Intervention (RTI)

In the 2004 reauthorization of IDEA, a new term and concept, **Response to Intervention (RTI)**, was introduced. The purpose of RTI is to catch struggling children early, provide appropriate instruction, and prevent the need to refer the child for special education. The U.S. Department of Education permits school districts to use up to 15 percent of their IDEA funding for early intervention services in regular education.

RTI is a tiered process of instruction that permits schools to identify struggling students early and to provide appropriate instructional interventions. By intervening early, students will experience a greater chance for success and less need for special education services. Although there are several models of intervention, typically a

breaking out: one school system's success with autistic children

Robert Goodfellow, age 6, has Asperger's syndrome, a mild form of autism that combines uncanny knowledge and awkward social skills. Students with Asperger's syndrome may be masters in mathematics, science, or computers, for example, but require daily drilling on such basics as how to make eye contact or maintaining appropriate distance from other children.

Before he joined a special program in the Seattle school system, Robert would sit alone in his yard, peeling bark off sticks he would find. He seemed fascinated by the process of removing the bark, often singing songs over and over again as he worked on the sticks. He also refused to bathe, clip his nails, or comb his hair.

Robert has benefited greatly from a new program in the Seattle school district. With his teachers' encouragement, Robert has channeled his obsessiveness in more socially accepted ways. He has become an expert on the Seattle Mariners baseball team and has learned to juggle extremely well. His new knowledge about the batting averages and other minutia of the Mariners, plus his juggling, has enabled Robert to relate better socially with his peers. They now admire his new knowledge and skills.

Students with Asperger's syndrome tend to excel in subjects that interest them, but other aspects of school may be difficult for them. For example, the hustle and bustle of recess or lunch can be extremely stressful. The Seattle program aims to help children like Robert function in their world without alienating others by their eccentric behavior. Robert and other Asperger's

students attend mainstream classes as much as possible, sometimes with a school aide, and only go to small special education classes when they need to work on a particular skill. The special education teachers function as case managers for the children, monitoring their schedules, serving as their advocates, and teaching them lessons on behavior, social skills, and life skills. Students in grades 1–4 are given visual cue cards to remind them of appropriate classroom behavior, such as raising their hands before speaking, and sitting still.

There is no cure for autism disorders, but "high-functioning" people with autism can make useful—even outstanding—contributions to society. The Seattle school district began its program in 1997 with a single elementary school pilot class for such high-functioning autistic children. Two years later, the program was expanded districtwide, and 12 classes are now offered in elementary, middle, and high schools. There are plans to add even more classes in upcoming school years.

Because autism is one of the fastest-growing categories of disability in special education, it presents new challenges to school districts. The Seattle program has attracted considerable attention, and educators from around the United States (and even from Japan and Korea) have visited to learn more about how to help high-functioning autistic children succeed in school.

Source: Lisa Fine, "Cracking the Shell," *Education Week* (November 21, 2001), pp. 22–29. Excerpted by permission of Editorial Projects in Education.

child would move from Tier 1 general education (classwide intervention) to a Tier 2 (more targeted small group interventions) and, if necessary, to a Tier 3, where the student would receive additional support and individualized attention. RTI is designed to increase the percentage of children who can pass the NCLB state tests in reading and mathematics.

Assistive Technology

Just as many students use contact lenses or glasses to help them compensate for poor eyesight, so students with disabilities may rely on a variety of technology-based innovations to help them learn better. The term **assistive technology** refers to the array of devices and services that help people with disabilities perform better in their daily

FOR BETTER OR WORSE

lives. Devices such as motorized chairs, remote control units to turn on appliances, voice recognition systems, ramps to enter and exit buildings, and computers can all assist people with severe disabilities. Computers are especially important in allowing many students with a range of disabilities to participate in normal classroom activities that would otherwise be impossible; we discuss their use more in Chapter 7, "What Should Teachers Know about Technology and Its Impact on Schools?"

Congress incorporated definitions of assistive technology into IDEA, declaring that such technology must be provided whenever necessary as an element of free and appropriate public education. Assistive technology must be considered a potential component of the IEP for each student with disabilities.[23] As a new teacher, you should be prepared to encounter situations in which a child uses technology as a medium for interaction and engagement within your classroom.

Teaching Implications

If you are a regular education teacher, students with disabilities will likely be in your classroom for varying portions of the school day, depending on the types and

Teachers are likely to have students in their classrooms with different kinds of disabilities, including such disabilities as cerebral palsy or spinal bifida.

▶❚❚ **TeachSource VIDEO CASE**

Inclusion: Classroom Implications for the General and Special Educator

Go to the Education CourseMate website to watch the video clips, study the artifacts in the case, and reflect on the following questions:

1. What are some of the strategies that the general teacher and the specialists use to keep the entire class functioning smoothly? Have you seen other successful strategies throughout your own education?

2. Do you find the work of the general teacher or that of one or more of the specialists more interesting as a potential teaching position for you?

3. What information from this Video Case do you believe will be most helpful to you in your career as a teacher?

amount of support services they are receiving. How will you deal with the different needs of these children?

It is most important that you do not stereotype these students. Certainly, different disabilities will have different implications for student learning. For example, a student with mental retardation may require repetition and practice to master simple concepts, whereas a student who uses a wheelchair may learn even the most difficult material quickly. Even within the parameters of each type of disability, however, you will probably encounter a wide range of differences. Consider two students identified as having learning disabilities: one may display a low–average intelligence quotient (IQ) and have extreme difficulty in mathematics; the other may have an extremely high IQ and have difficulty in reading. Although both of these students have a learning disability, you would not provide the same instruction or have the same expectations for both children.

You should approach instruction for children with disabilities just as you would for other students in the classroom: expect diversity, anticipate a range of abilities, and look for the particular strengths and learning profiles of each student. A helpful resource for recognizing student abilities and suggesting instructional strategies will be the special education teachers in your school. The more you and a special education teacher can coordinate instruction and services for your students with disabilities, the better the students' educational experiences are likely to be. (The Video Case *Inclusion: Classroom Implications for the General and Special Educator* introduces an elementary school teacher who has several special-needs students in her classes, and shows some of the specialists and adaptations that can help those students succeed in an inclusion setting.)

Here are a few other suggestions about how you as a regular education teacher can be effective in teaching children with disabilities in your classroom:

1. Be open to the idea of including students with disabilities in your classroom.

2. Learn about each child's limitations and potential and about available curriculum methodologies and technologies to help the child learn.

3. Insist that any needed services be provided.

4. Use a variety of teaching strategies, including hands-on activities, peer tutoring, and cooperative learning strategies.

5. Avail yourself of opportunities for co-teaching with a special education teacher.[24]

PAUSE AND REFLECT

1. Have you had any contact with individuals with disabilities (e.g., a relative or neighbor)? What did you learn from this relationship that might be helpful in your teaching?

2. What is your position on "full inclusion"? What reservations, if any, do you have about this strategy?

3. Do you have any concerns about your ability to work with students who have disabilities? What do you think will be the most rewarding aspects of working with these students?

gifted and talented students

One of the most challenging types of students is the gifted or talented child. The term *talented* most often refers to an ability or skill (e.g., musical or artistic talent) that may not be matched by the child's more general abilities, whereas the term *gifted* usually includes intellectual ability. The gifted child is extremely bright, quickly grasping the ideas and concepts you are teaching and making interpretations or extrapolations that you may not even have considered. Gifted children may also have a creativity that shows itself in original thinking or artistic creations.

Students who are gifted and/or talented are sometimes overlooked when educators talk about students with special needs. Although special educational care and services for students with disabilities have long been recognized and accepted, American education has been slow to accept the notion that gifted children require special adaptations in both curricula and teaching methods. Because the idea of giftedness implies an elitism to many Americans, it seems undemocratic to provide special services to children who already enjoy an intellectual advantage. However, as one educator says, "Highly gifted children are as far from the norm in the direction of giftedness as the severely retarded are in the other direction."[25]

When their special needs are neglected, gifted and talented students drop out of school at rates far exceeding the dropout rates for those not identified as gifted. Many of those students who stay in school feel unchallenged and become bored and apathetic. As a result, many of our brightest and most talented minds are being turned off or underdeveloped. However, many school districts have made serious efforts to identify gifted children and develop special programs for them.

Identifying Gifted and Talented Students

The areas in which states identify gifted and talented students can range from intellectual to psychomotor to artistic, with many variations. Through its evolution, the study of giftedness has moved increasingly toward more *inclusive* definitions and away from more *exclusive* ones. As we described earlier in the chapter, some people now think intelligence is composed of multiple factors. Consequently, in many schools, the definition of giftedness is shifting away from an emphasis on general intellectual ability (IQ) and toward the recognition that giftedness occurs in a variety of areas, such as mathematics, language, spatial ability, and kinesthetics.

In the past, school districts have tended to rely heavily on general intelligence and achievement tests in their assessment of students' intellectual abilities, as well as on teacher recommendations and grades earned in school. There is a danger of letting these assessment tools become synonymous with the *definition* of gifted and talented. To avoid this danger, teachers and administrators must study and interpret the data the tools provide rather than take the data at face value and use them for hard-and-fast cutoff points. Whether to recommend a child for a special program is a decision that should be made by the responsible teacher and other professional educators on the basis of their objective and subjective appraisals of the student, the nature of the gifted program or activity, and the atmosphere in which the student lives and goes to school. Parents should be a significant part of these discussions. The point is that the complexity of the variables involved requires that individual decisions be made by professionals using their best judgments rather than according to arbitrary, predetermined cutoff points on tests.

A major concern in the identification of gifted and talented students centers on the underrepresentation of economically disadvantaged students, learning-disabled students, and certain minority students. Asian American students are well represented in gifted and talented programs, whereas African American and Hispanic students are underrepresented in terms of their proportion in the total school population. Given this disparity, educators and parents are concerned that the measures being used to identify gifted and talented youngsters may work to the disadvantage of African Americans, Hispanics, and children from low-income families. Conversely, African American students are overrepresented in special education services, leading many educators and parents to wonder whether some form of cultural or racial bias is at work. The problem of identification is especially acute for bilingual children and children adjusting to a new culture.

Programs for Gifted and Talented Students

Programs for gifted and talented students exist in every state and in many school districts. The federal government reports that 3.2 million students were identified as gifted and talented in public elementary and secondary schools, representing about 6.7 percent of the total enrollment.[26]

The two main strategies for serving gifted children are **acceleration** and **enrichment**. With an accelerated curriculum, gifted children can learn at a pace commensurate with their abilities, allowing them to progress to advanced materials faster than their age norms or grade levels. By contrast, enrichment activities provide gifted students with opportunities to go beyond the regular curriculum in greater depth and breadth, to engage in independent or collaborative inquiry that develops their problem-solving abilities, research skills, and creativity.

Current educational programs for gifted and talented students are quite varied. Some programs establish special schools that are designated only for gifted or talented students and have special admission requirements. In such schools, stimulating courses can be devised and taught without concern for students who might be unable to keep pace, and teachers and students can be recruited on the basis of their talents.

Other programs adapt and enrich the regular school curriculum for gifted and talented children by grouping these students together for all or part of their instruction. This option normally is more flexible and practical than establishing special schools. Classes can be established on a continuing or short-term basis, in any subject area, with the intention of either enriching or accelerating the student.

In the United States, most gifted and talented students are likely to receive all, or nearly all, of their education in regular classrooms. In many school districts, in fact, separate programs for gifted students are being curtailed or phased out. The primary reasons for this trend are the spread of a philosophy that favors mixed-ability grouping, the cessation of tracking, and a lack of funds for separate gifted programs. In fact, only some $800 million per year is spent on gifted education, compared to over $11 billion federal dollars on special education.[27] The trend toward meeting gifted students' needs within the regular classroom parallels the inclusion movement in special education. Some advocates for gifted education programs are disturbed by this trend and suggest that gifted students will be shortchanged in the regular classroom. They fear that teachers will concentrate their efforts on struggling students or that gifted students will be drafted to serve as tutors for these students rather than working to fulfill their own potential. Supporters of the current trend, however, believe that most gifted students' needs can be met in the regular classroom if teachers can differentiate curricula and instruction for them and increase the level of challenge.

Still others argue that it is important to keep a continuum of programs and services available for gifted students if for no other reason than that they represent a valuable resource to the United States. Along with instruction in the regular classroom, these educators argue, the options for such students should include pullout programs, special classes, grade skipping, and separate centers and schools. A range of giftedness exists, such that some students will do just fine in a regular classroom, whereas others can benefit from different programs.

Teaching Implications

If you want to focus on teaching gifted students, find out whether your state is one of the 20 or so that requires teachers to obtain a gifted endorsement to their teaching license. More likely, you will discover certain students in your regular education class to be gifted or talented and, lacking any special program, you will be responsible for teaching these students as part of your normal duties. If your school or school district has special programs for gifted and talented students, you may be expected to work with resource teachers to help prepare individualized education plans for these students. What do you need to know?

1. Recognize that gifted pupils generally learn the standard curricular skills and content quickly and easily. They need teaching that does not tie them to a limited range, that is not preoccupied with filling them with facts and information, but rather allows them to use the regular class as a forum for research, inquiry, and projects that are meaningful to them.

2. Realize that these students are persistently curious. They need teachers who encourage them to maintain confidence in their own ideas, even when those ideas differ from the norm.

3. Teach these pupils to be efficient and effective at independent study so that they can develop the skills required for self-directed learning and for analyzing and solving problems independently. Allow students of varying abilities to work together in areas of high interest, such as social action research projects.

4. Help students apply complex cognitive processes such as creative thinking, critiques, and pro and con analyses.

5. Expand your ideas concerning which instructional materials are available. Consider businesses, religious groups, national parks, and resource people as sources of potential instructional materials in addition to the textbooks and reference books available in the school. Be sure to investigate any technological resources that are available, including websites and other electronic links to information and knowledgeable people outside the school.

6. Use differentiated instructional strategies such as flexible grouping, "tiered" assignments (in which all students explore the same topic but the level of questions or products produced varies depending on students' abilities), learning centers, student contracts, and mentorships. (See Chapter 5, "What Is Taught?" for more on differentiated instruction.)

7. Implement *curriculum compacting*, in which teachers test students on what they already know on upcoming units. Students who demonstrate mastery in advance are allowed to accelerate through the material or pursue enrichment activities while the unit is being taught to the rest of the class.

> *If 2 + 3 is always going to be 5, why do they keep teaching it to us?*
>
> —A GIFTED FIRST-GRADE STUDENT

8. Match students with mentors to help develop talent and engage students in relevant and applied problem solving. Mentoring programs encourage independent growth, increased self-confidence, and a willingness to reach out into new, untried areas.

diverse needs

In addition to the diversity of racial, ethnic, and cultural backgrounds, as well as ability levels, another element of diversity occurs within each individual. We all have basic physical and psychological needs, including needs for belonging, safety, and self-esteem. Of course, those needs may vary in their prominence and expression because of individual circumstances. Your students bring their own individual histories and backgrounds, as well as conditions that have influenced how and whether certain needs have been satisfied. For example, a child from a stable, secure home may have different needs than a child who has not enjoyed this kind of security. One way to understand the diverse needs of students is to see how one prominent psychiatrist and educator, William Glasser, has conceptualized the basic needs of all individuals.

GLASSER'S CHOICE THEORY

Glasser begins with the premise that each of us is born with fundamental needs for survival, love and belonging, power, freedom, and fun.[28] Throughout our lives, our motivations, actions, and behaviors are attempts to satisfy these needs. Glasser's **choice theory** states that if we understand and identify these needs within ourselves, we can make conscious choices about how best to meet them. The recognition of our ability to make choices results in personal empowerment: we have control over how we choose to react to external events and information.

Schools help students meet social, as well as academic, needs.

(© Charles Gupton)

▶❚❚ **TeachSource VIDEO CASE**

Motivating Adolescent Learners: Curriculum Based on Real Life

Go to the Education CourseMate website to watch the video clips, study the artifacts in the case, and reflect on the following questions:

1. Which of the student needs described by Glasser are met by working in the school store?

2. What are some other ways that teachers might help students meet their needs for power and belonging?

Glasser believes that teachers should empower their students through the use of choice theory—that is, by combining the needs of students with classroom assignments or activities. The more students are convinced that their schoolwork satisfies their needs, the harder they will try and the better the work they will produce. For example, when asked what is the best part of school, many students respond, "My friends." According to Glasser, this answer expresses the students' built-in need for friendship, love, and belonging. Rather than structure classroom settings to suppress this need, such as by emphasizing independent seatwork or teacher lectures, teachers should find ways to let students associate with others in class as a planned part of learning. Glasser refers to this kind of cooperative grouping as the use of *learning teams.*

Teaching students in cooperative learning teams also meets students' needs for power. Using the term *power* synonymously with *self-esteem* or *sense of importance,* Glasser explains that to fulfill this need students must have the sense that someone they respect listens to them. (The Video Case *Motivating Adolescent Learners: Curriculum Based on Real Life* shows how one middle school mathematics teacher helps students meet some of the needs Glasser describes.)

Unfulfilled needs for power often result in a number of undesirable attention-getting behaviors. Glasser believes these misguided efforts to achieve power are the source of 95 percent of discipline-related problems in school. In accordance with choice theory, he suggests that teachers structure opportunities for students to fulfill their needs for power appropriately during the school day. In addition to learning teams, in which students interact and listen to one another as part of the learning process, Glasser suggests that teachers provide opportunities for student input and a forum for students to be heard. He also recommends self-evaluation of homework, classwork, and tests. Glasser believes that students need to be encouraged to set their own standards for quality work and to evaluate whether they are meeting those standards. This helps them to satisfy their need for power and instills an internal standard for achievement in education and work.

Glasser proposes that students' needs for freedom and fun, although important, are not at the core of problems in schools. Students generally understand the need for some structure in dealing with large groups of people, and they realize that rules and regulations must govern behavior in school, even though they limit individual freedom. Although fun is an essential need, students who have a sense of belonging in school and a forum for personal power are already likely to be experiencing fun.

Glasser's theory of personal empowerment provides one interesting way of viewing and identifying a wide variety of student needs. Other approaches, such as Abraham Maslow's hierarchy of needs theory, may also be useful. (See Maslow's Hierarchy of Needs at www.businessballs.com/maslow.htm for an explanation of his theory.) The most important point is that teachers must be aware of their students' varying needs and respond accordingly in the classroom.

ADOLESCENT SUBCULTURES

Teenagers often satisfy their needs for belonging, power, and fun by forming cliques, or groups that share common characteristics and reflect status among their peers. Most schools have cliques of elites, average students, and outcasts, which are labeled with terms such as *jocks, preppies, skaters, emos, rockers, brains, punks, freaks, kickers, gangstas, nerds/geeks/dweebs,* and *goths.* Elite groups, such as the jocks and preppies, are the "leading crowd," whose members enthusiastically participate in, and receive the endorsement of, the school. The outcasts, such as the punks or the goths, tend to have an adversarial (rather than cooperative) relationship with the high school because they believe school doesn't serve their needs well.

Each clique has attitudes, behaviors, or dress characteristics that distinguish it from all other cliques. Clothing and adornment are probably the most powerful symbolic indicators of category membership, although each group also tends to stake out particular territories of the school as its own. As members of these adolescent subcultures, teenagers can express their own attitudes, explore personal relationships, and test themselves against others. For example, a high school we know cancelled its fall dance because the student body could not agree on the genre of music to be played. There were six contenders, each with a solid group of supporters. After weeks of controversy and amid angry talk of boycotts, school authorities gave up in frustration and called off the event.

Membership in teenage subcultures begins to form in the middle and junior high schools, as cliques develop around particular interests such as athletics, academics, student government, drugs, and tastes in cars and music. Often, teens don't even select a group as much as they are placed into one because of their image among their peers. The bonds between members of these groups strengthen as the teenagers begin to move away from their families, and peer membership becomes a type of new family where youngsters find comfort and support. By senior year, however, the hold of the subcultures on students has weakened. Students develop more self-confidence, and they seek greater personal freedom. At this point, the friendship group becomes a drag on their autonomy. Until that happens, however, the teen subcultures exert a strong influence on the values of their members.

Most high schools have done a reasonably good job of making academically and socially oriented students an integral part of school life. They have been less successful with other subcultures such as the various outcast groups. In fact, because groups such as the punks or goths reject the schools' values, the schools may be reinforcing their alienation. Finding ways to bring members of alienated subcultures into participation in their schools, bring the loners or outsiders into greater contact with their peers, and channel peer influence as a positive force is a major challenge for high school and middle school educators.

PAUSE AND REFLECT

1. Are you comfortable with the idea of sharing power with students through such techniques as having them evaluate their own homework? Why or why not? What other ways can you think of to empower your students or help them meet their social needs?

2. What kinds of school activities might be appealing to members of traditionally outcast groups?

gender

Earlier in this chapter, we made the point that some racial and ethnic groups have been denied equal educational opportunities throughout our country's history. Another group, women, has also suffered discrimination and denial of equal

Gender Equity in the Classroom: Girls and Science

Go to the Education CourseMate website to watch the video clips, study the artifacts in the case, and reflect on the following questions:

1. This section of the chapter describes several ways in which boys and girls are treated differently in school. Which of these problems does this teacher avoid? How?

2. Did your own teachers treat male and female students differently? If so, give some examples. What do you think was the result of this differing treatment?

3. In addition to the strategies listed in this chapter, what are some ways that you, as a teacher, can be fair to boys and girls in your classes?

T Ⓕ
After lagging men for many years, women now hold a similar number of jobs in science and mathematics fields.
Although women have caught up with men in terms of mathematics and science achievement, many fewer women than men tend to choose jobs in engineering and the sciences.

educational opportunities; historically, women in our society have been denied educational and employment opportunities routinely extended to men. In recent years, considerable progress has been made to address these inequities. For example, women now constitute the majority of college students and have gained admittance into and success within many professions from which they were previously excluded. Teachers must be alert to avoid unfairness in their treatment of either girls or boys. (The Video Case *Gender Equity in the Classroom: Girls and Science* shows how one middle school science teacher tries to meet the needs of all his students: boys *and* girls.)

Fairness and equality may be difficult to achieve, however, because by the time they get to school, boys and girls are already used to being treated differently. From very young ages through adulthood, society holds different expectations for males and females. These expectations, in turn, generate different patterns of behavior toward boys and girls. Whether it is pink or blue clothes, G.I. Joe or Barbie dolls, video games or drawing kits, or football helmets or ballet slippers, boys and girls get different messages from society about what is expected of them. Society tolerates aggressive behavior more in boys than in girls. Boys are encouraged to be independent, whereas girls often are expected to conform to accepted norms.

GENDER GAPS, SCHOOL ACHIEVEMENT, AND CAREER SELECTION

During the 1980s and 1990s, a number of research studies alleged that girls were being shortchanged in schools and classrooms. Numerous observational studies concluded that teachers often treated boys differently than girls, frequently to the girls' detriment, although teachers were generally unaware of their behaviors that favor boys.[29] These research studies suggested that in subtle and not-so-subtle ways, female students received the message that boys were more important than girls because teachers pay more attention to boys.

Studies during the 1970s and 1980s also found considerable gender stereotyping in textbooks and other reading materials. Great strides have been made to purge these gender stereotypes by publishers and authors, but stories that children read still focus on boys more often than on girls.[30]

Historically, girls shied away from science and mathematics courses, but girls have now closed the gap in mathematics and science, where girls' achievement in these subjects is comparable to that of boys. Girls also take calculus at the same rate as boys, though they lag a bit in physics.[31] However, girls are much less likely to enroll in computer science classes in high school than are boys.

In spite of comparable achievement levels in mathematics and science among boys and girls, recent studies on gender differences in **STEM (science, technology, engineering, and mathematics)** careers show that women lag men in choosing careers in those areas. In 2006, women received 30 percent of the doctoral degrees in the physical sciences, 32 percent of the mathematics doctorates, and

Unless teachers take precautionary steps, boys often dominate access to classroom computers.

(© Vicki Kerr/Getty Images)

17 percent of the doctorates in engineering.[32] The gender gap concerns many experts who fear that the United States may be losing its competitive edge over the rest of the world in science and engineering fields. Because countries like China and India have so many more people in science and engineering fields, the United States needs women to enter STEM fields so the United States can expand its pipeline for math and science talent.

Multiple explanations for this gender gap in STEM fields exist. Some say that girls aren't exposed to career opportunities in STEM fields while in middle and senior high school, while others say that women look for careers where they can combine work and family and that STEM fields seem less compatible with this goal. And, still another explanation is that girls may be choosing health- and environmental-related fields because they see them as being more compassionate professions. In all probability, each of these explanations is valid for some portion of the female population.

Some observers, while acknowledging the historic education discrimination and bias against girls, believe that schools are now failing boys more than girls. One clinical psychologist researcher at Harvard University argues that schools don't accommodate boys' learning styles and classroom needs. Boys perform best, he reports, when they have frequent recess breaks and are able to roam around the classroom. Boys are also more likely to enjoy argument and lively classroom debate, which is often discouraged.[33]

Researchers also cite the fact that the large gaps between the education levels of women and men that were evident in the early 1970s have essentially disappeared for the younger generation. High school females on average outperform males in reading and writing; take more credits in academic subjects; take more advanced placement (AP) courses in English, biology, and foreign languages; are more likely to be inducted into the National Honor Society; are more likely to attend college after high school; and are as likely to graduate with a postsecondary degree. Furthermore, two-thirds of all students receiving special education services are boys. Boys are much more likely to drop out of school than are girls.[34] If schools were really so biased against females, they argue, why are women doing so well academically?

> "Gender equality is more than a goal in itself. It is a precondition for meeting the challenge of reducing poverty, promoting sustainable development and building good governance.
>
> —KOFI ANNAN,
> Former Secretary General of the United Nations

Certainly women have made tremendous progress in educational attainment. What remains to be seen is how these attainments will be rewarded in the marketplace. The average earnings of female high school graduates, aged 25–34, are 85 percent of what their male counterparts receive. Even worse, female college graduates in the same age bracket earn salaries that are only 80 percent of what their male counterparts receive, although females in their twenties who work in urban areas are now reported to be making more than their male counterparts.[35] Whether these salary differences are attributable to workplace gender bias or to other factors, such as women's choice of occupations, leaving the workplace to raise families, or other reasons, remains an area of great debate.

Teaching Implications

What can you do to make sure that you are being fair to both male and female students in your classroom? To ensure sex-equitable learning environments in classrooms, teachers should consider the following steps:

- Have high expectations for all students.
- Examine instructional materials to be certain that sex role stereotyping or bias does not occur. If it does, try to find alternative materials.

urban prep charter school: single-sex education success story

One single-sex school that reports great success is the Urban Prep charter school in Chicago, Illinois. In Chicago, the high school graduation rate for African American boys is about 40 percent, and only about half of these graduates are accepted into some kind of college. Urban Prep, located in a poor neighborhood, reports a very different story. In March 2010, the school announced that 100 percent of its 104 young African American seniors had been accepted to four-year colleges, even though only 4 percent of those seniors had been reading at grade level as ninth graders.

How was Urban Prep able to achieve this remarkable feat, and is it replicable elsewhere? The school operates on an extended school day, which provides an additional 1,200 hours of school time each year, and as part of that additional time, a double period of English and extracurricular activities and public service projects are required.

More than this, the school's founder, Tim King, attributes success to the four R's: ritual, respect, responsibility, and relationships. Students are addressed formally, using their last names, and they wear coats and ties. Faculty members develop close, personal relationships with the students and are available by phone on evenings and weekends. For many of the young men, the teachers and administrators are the first positive male role models they've had. Every adult in the building knows and believes in the school's mission: to get students to college. They also know that admission to college is a milestone, and graduation from college is the real goal.

Are these results replicable at other schools? Pedro Noguera, a professor at New York University, who has been researching single-sex black schools, believes so. The key to the school's success, Noguera asserts, isn't that it's all male, but that it's the attention the teachers pay to teaching. However, the head of the Urban Prep English department admits that while teaching there is tremendously rewarding, it isn't for everyone. Teaching there requires enormous time and emotional commitments from the teachers. "There is an emotional cost," he said. "We're now surrogate [family] to almost 500 young men. It's hard finding a balance."

Source: Amanda Paulson, "All-Boys Charter Sending Whole Class to College," *Education Week* (April 28, 2010), p. 12.

- Examine and address, if needed, the frequency with which students are called on and the kind of responses that they provide the students to ensure that gender biases are not occurring. This can be done by audiotaping teacher–student interactions and listening to unintended patterns of interaction.
- Look at who uses or is encouraged to use computer technology in the classroom. Often, boys tend to monopolize computers and other technology.
- Eliminate the assignment of sex-stereotyped tasks.
- Organize classes so that students don't segregate themselves by sex.
- Model sex-equitable behavior.
- Choose your words carefully (e.g., *not* saying, "Boys will be boys"), and correct students' speech or actions when it borders on discrimination or bias.
- Pair learning with movement to increase brain activity and offset boredom.

Some school districts are attempting to address gender differences by offering single-gender schools or classrooms. Advocates of this approach argue that by separating the sexes, more attention can be given to the particular needs of boys or girls. Opponents argue that discrimination might still occur and suggest that keeping boys and girls together means that they learn to work with one another. At this point, insufficient research has been carried out to support either claim, but anecdotal reports claim successes for some single-sex classes. (See box Urban Prep Charter School about a Chicago school for one such report.)

sexual orientation

People kept coming up to me and making fun of me. They would call me horrible names and I would cry all the time. Letters were put in my locker saying things about AIDS and how my parents shouldn't have had me and how I should just die. Kids would threaten me after school and follow me home yelling things at me. No one should have to go through what I went through in school.

This statement by a lesbian student reflects what many **lesbian, gay, bisexual, and transgendered (LGBT)** students experience in school. According to a 2009 survey of 7,261 middle and high school students, nearly 9 out of 10 LGBT students experienced harassment at school in the previous year, and nearly two-thirds felt unsafe because of their sexual orientation. Nearly a third of LGBT students skipped at least one day of school in the previous month because of safety concerns.[36]

You are likely to have LGBT students in your classroom, especially if you teach at the middle or high school level, and you are apt to encounter LGBT parents of students at any level.

Considerable evidence indicates that school is often a hostile environment for young LGBT students. Teenagers tend to ridicule differences in general and differences in sexual orientation in particular. LGBT students have often experienced taunting, harassment, and even violence because of their sexual orientation. Teachers and administrators who condone such name calling as "dyke" or "faggot," while prohibiting profanity or racial slurs, are also promoters of hostility toward homosexual youth. In fact, LGBT students have won lawsuits against school officials who failed to maintain a safe school environment and to discipline students who regularly tormented them.

The hostility that LGBT youth encounter in school is mirrored in the larger society, which bombards them with messages that they are outcasts. This hostility leaves many of them isolated, frightened, and uncertain about their own worth. As a result, gay students are a high-risk population. Many run away from home or are thrown out by parents, abuse drugs and alcohol, suffer from depression, or attempt suicide.

The National Education Association, the American Federation of Teachers, and other leading education associations have all passed resolutions calling on their members and school districts to acknowledge the special needs of LGBT students, provide supportive services such as counseling and support groups, and implement anti-harassment measures. Fifteen states and the District of Columbia prohibit anti-gay harassment or discrimination in schools over and above the protection afforded by the U.S. Constitution and Title IX, and the U.S. Department of Education has issued guidelines spelling out that "gay or lesbian students" are covered by federal prohibitions against sexual harassment.[37]

Nevertheless, the issue of sexual orientation remains extremely controversial, and actions urged by gay and lesbian organizations are certain to provoke opposition by some community members who believe such steps would signal that the schools are condoning homosexual behavior. Some people believe that while touting tolerance, LGBT organizations are actually seeking to promote homosexuality among students at a developmental period in their lives when the sexual identity of many is not fully developed.

All students—regardless of their sexual orientation—have the right to a safe and supportive learning environment. As educators, we also have the responsibility to promote and protect the emotional well-being of all of our students.

Teaching Implications

There are many things that schools and educators can do to make school safer for all students as well as those who are gay, lesbian, bisexual, or transgendered:

- Establish classroom guidelines about name-calling. Challenge homophobic remarks everywhere and all the time.
- Respect different points of view.
- Make no assumptions about students' families or their sexual orientations. Use the words *gay, lesbian,* and *bisexual.* Use inclusive language, such as *partner* or *spouse* instead of *husband* or *wife.*
- Be role models for how all students should be treated with respect and dignity.

PAUSE AND REFLECT

1. Do schools treat boys and girls equally? What examples can you cite to support your response?

2. Do you have any beliefs or attitudes that would inhibit you from treating LGBT students fairly in your classroom? If so, what, if anything, do you intend to do about it?

the teacher's response to diversity

So far in this chapter, we have presented a great deal of information about the diversity of the children you will be teaching. Ultimately, how these children are educated will come down to you and your daily interactions with them in your classroom. How will you deal with diversity?

TEACHER–STUDENT DISPARITY

Consider what we know about the typical teacher today. Women and whites predominate in the teacher force; 76 percent of all public school teachers are women, and 84 percent of those teaching in public schools are white.[38] Despite efforts to increase the number of minority teachers (see Chapter 13, "What Are Your Job Options in Education?"), this gap between teachers and students is likely to persist for some time. Profiles of preservice and beginning teachers show similar gender, racial, and ethnic patterns. Most of these teachers come from relatively stable family backgrounds. The majority of teachers and future teachers in our classrooms, then, come from very different backgrounds than many of the students they teach.

As we mentioned in Chapter 2, "What Is a School and What Is It For?" the more alike students and teachers are in social and cultural characteristics, the more they share tacit expectations about behavior and academic performance. As gaps in those social and cultural characteristics widen, teachers need to rely on solid pedagogical training to overcome these differences. Too often white educators have been reluctant to recognize that their own backgrounds and the culture of the school have an effect on learning. As an incoming teacher, you will need to know about the commonalities and differences among students, and you will need to learn specific methods and techniques for addressing the plurality of culture and learning styles you will encounter.

DIVERSITY: A COMPLEX PHENOMENON

The school programs described in this chapter have been designed to address student diversity and create a more equal educational opportunity for children in our school systems. An inherent danger in these approaches to addressing diversity, however, is the tendency to label children and form stereotypic images of who they are. Student performance in school is affected by many factors, including social and cultural trends. The educational groupings we have been discussing are an administrative convenience, not a naturally occurring segmentation of children. Within each of these groups, each child will vary along a number of dimensions and have a very different learning profile of strengths and weaknesses.

Rather than thinking of minority students as having a culture that is valid—albeit different—from theirs, teachers sometimes think of these students as deficient. We encourage you, as a teacher, to remember that we are talking about *differences* in students, not necessarily deficits. Teachers are challenged to recognize the diversity of cultures represented by their students and to address these cultures in their teaching.

IMPLICATIONS FOR TEACHERS

Given this profile of the cultural discrepancy between students and teachers, and the complex diversity of today's student body, how can prospective teachers best prepare? Here are some steps you can take now:

- Seek out experiences to broaden your understanding of societal and cultural commonalities and differences (e.g., travel to foreign countries).

- Spend time in communities whose residents differ from you in terms of ethnicity, culture, or language.

- Volunteer in schools that differ from those you attended.

Once you have your own classroom, what can you do to address diversity there? Here are some guidelines:

- Learn about and appreciate the values and backgrounds of your students.

- Teach to your students' strengths rather than making them feel incapable or deficient.

- Provide a variety of educational experiences, and find ways for all students to achieve recognition from you and their peers for being good at something.

- Coordinate expertise and support with your students' parents or caregivers and other professional staff at the school so that students get a consistent message.

- Without lowering standards, recognize that the schools' traditional emphasis on middle-class values such as individual learning and competition may clash with the values represented by their students' cultures. Teachers can provide opportunities for students to learn ways to succeed in today's dominant culture, but they must also respect the value systems in students' home lives and help them, in positive ways, to bridge the gap between the two worlds.

OUR FINAL WORD

At one time, the only business of schools was to educate students. Now, however, because of the increasing complexity and diversity of our students' lives, other needs are being addressed and incorporated into the way schools are approaching "education." A major goal of this chapter has been to make you aware of the complexity of issues that directly affect many children's lives and their ability to get an adequate education.

You may be getting concerned about whether you can handle the breadth of diversities you may face in your classroom. Be assured that you do not face this challenge alone: numerous assistance systems have been devised to help teachers respond to the range of student needs. Besides having other teachers and administrators to help you, most schools have specialists, such as nurses, school psychologists, and counselors, who often can give you valuable advice or direct help to your students. A growing number of parent councils involve parents in giving advice and helping to deal with challenges. Teacher aides may be community members who speak the language of substantial minorities in the schools. Interns or students from the local college may help as well, providing another adult in the classroom.

You will need to use all the resources available to you, including parents and other professionals. Some teachers may initially feel threatened by this involvement or have a sense that the classroom is their "turf." As we have seen throughout this chapter, however, our students need the coordinated expertise and support of all school professionals and the crucial link with parents, to be given a fair shot at acquiring the good education that is their due.

WHY TEACH? YOUR FINAL WORD

In your journal or online at this textbook's website, respond to the following questions:

1. After reading this chapter, what questions or concerns do you have that you want to discuss with your colleagues or instructor?

2. What forms of diversity among students do you believe will present you with the greatest

challenges? What ideas do you have for meeting these challenges?

3. Describe your ethnic heritage and the influence of ethnicity on your family's past and present. Share your family history with your classmates.

KEY TERMS

acceleration (80)
assimilation (58)
assistive technology (76)
bilingual education (64)
choice theory (82)
cultural pluralism (58)
culturally responsive teaching (61)
English language learners (ELLs) (63)
enrichment (80)
inclusion (73)
individualized education program (IEP) (72)
individualized family services plan (IFSP) (72)

LGBT (lesbian, gay, bisexual, or transgendered) (88)
learning styles (68)
least restrictive environment (LRE) (73)
limited English proficient (LEP) (63)
mainstreaming (73)
multicultural education (59)
multiple intelligences (66)
Response to Intervention (RTI) (75)
special education (72)
STEM (science, technology, engineering, mathematics) (85)

FOR FURTHER INFORMATION

TEACHSOURCE VIDEOS

Benefits of a Multicultural History Curriculum

This video examines the benefits of including multiple perspectives in exploring history issues.

Learning Disabilities

This video looks at one family whose three children have learning disabilities.

WEB RESOURCES

University of Virginia, Office of Special Education: A Web Resource for Special Education. Available at http://special.edschool.virginia.edu/.

This website at the Curry School of Education at the University of Virginia contains much information

about special education, including the history of the field and types of disabilities. It also offers discussion groups, electronic addresses of special educators, and much more.

National Clearinghouse for English Language Acquisition. Available at www.ncela.gwu.edu.

Funded by the U.S. Department of Education, this site contains hundreds of articles, links, databases, and online assistance in the area of English language acquisition.

Learning Style Inventory. Available at www.learning-styles-online.com.

This website contains a free test of learning style preferences.

PRINT RESOURCES

James A. Banks and Cherry A. McGee Banks (eds.), *Multicultural Education: Issues and Perspectives*, 7th ed. (Somerset, NJ: John Wiley & Sons, 2010).

Various well-known educators explore the research, concepts, and debates about the education of students from both genders and from different cultural, racial, ethnic, and language groups.

Stephen Cary, *Working with English Language Learners: Answers to Teachers' Top Ten Questions*, 2nd ed. (Portsmouth, NH: Heinemann, 2007).

Responding to teachers' 10 most frequent and problematic questions about teaching ELL students, the author provides essential information, ready-to-use ideas, and helpful professional development supports.

Joe L. Kincheloe and Kecia Hayes (eds.), *Teaching City Kids* (New York: Peter Lang, 2007).

This book examines how urban youth are often misunderstood, and suggests ways of teaching based on an understanding and appreciation of them.

Judy W. Kugelmass, *The Inclusive School* (New York: Teachers College Press, 2005).

Looking at a public elementary school, the author shows how committed educators can collaborate to maintain a creative, inclusive educational environment and still rise to the demands of state-imposed standards.

Johnnie McKinley, *Raising Black Students' Achievement Through Culturally Responsive Teaching*, (Alexandria, VA: ASCD, 2010).

The author offers many excellent suggestions to raise African American student achievement through culturally responsive teaching, including how to make classroom management fit black student culture.

The Education CourseMate website for this text offers many helpful resources. Go to www.cengagebrain.com to access the TeachSource Video Cases and other TeachSource videos, flashcards, interactive quizzes, the eBook, reflection and enrichment activities, a state standards resource center, and other study aids.

4 what social problems affect today's students?

(© SCPhotos/Alamy)

FOCUS POINTS

- Many school-age children are affected by critical problems that directly influence their lives and often have negative repercussions in the classroom. Among these problems are severe poverty, homelessness, teenage parenting, child abuse, alcohol and drug abuse, and adolescent suicide.

- Violence, vandalism, bullying, and cheating are not confined to urban schools; they are widespread throughout the nation's schools.

- School dropout rates reflect disparities among various groups and foreshadow future societal problems.

- Sex education remains as controversial as ever, although concern about acquired immune deficiency syndrome (AIDS) has strengthened the argument for proponents of sex education.

Rarely a day goes by when the American public is not assaulted by news of some heartbreaking event or newly revealed problem involving the nation's young. Because formal education is so much a part of their lives, many of the youth-related issues and problems spill over and affect our schools and classrooms. This chapter explores some of the most sensitive and controversial issues in American education. In such a small space we can treat each topic only briefly, but we urge you to pursue additional reading on each issue.

Truth or Fiction?

T F Three-fourths of today's children live in families where either both parents or the only parent works full time.

T F The United States has a higher percentage of children living in poverty than any other industrialized country.

T F Almost half the children living in a household headed by a female live in poverty.

T F Teachers who suspect that a student in his or her class has suffered child abuse must use discretion in deciding whether to file a report.

T F Although cheating in school has received much media attention, it only occurs with moderate frequency.

The children who stream into a teacher's classroom each August or September bring their own personal histories. Although they may wish to start afresh with the beginning of the new school year, much of who they are is wrapped up in their past and their current out-of-school lives. It is likely that some of these students bear deep scars from their past experiences and that some are currently caught up in desperate widespread social problems. We wish to make you more fully aware of and more deeply sensitive to the sorts of problems your students may bring to your classroom.

Although many of the troubles and pathologies discussed in this chapter, such as drug use, teenage pregnancies, and school violence, appear typically among secondary school students, almost all have their roots in the lives of elementary school students. All teachers, therefore, need to be alert to these problems. We are not suggesting that you should be Mr. or Ms. Fix-It, taking in troubled children and, with a few quick adjustments to their psyches, sending them out into the world cured. We do, however, want you to recognize the healing power of education, which gives structure, purpose, and hope to youngsters whose daily lives often lack these stabilizing and motivating influences.

recognizing risk factors

Chapter 3, "Who Are Today's Students in a Diverse Society?" profiled changes in our society that are resulting in increased diversity among today's students. These conditions affect many students' lives, but they do not necessarily prevent them from getting an education. Other changes or trends in society do pose a more direct threat to the performance of students in school. Many teachers may have difficulty recognizing and adapting to differences that contribute to the problems some children bring to the classroom, because—unlike many of their students—most teachers come from relatively stable backgrounds. Although a teacher's stable background can be a source of strength, it means that students often inhabit different worlds than their teachers. Often there are striking gaps between teachers' and students' social class and their personal exposure to major social problems.

In our discussion here, we deal with several difficult conditions and problems, including poverty, homelessness, child abuse, alcohol and drug use, teenage parenting, sexually transmitted diseases, adolescent suicide, violence, cheating, and school dropout rates. These pervasive societal problems do not occur in isolation, but rather tend to cluster or overlap. In real life, it is difficult to separate out discrete sources of social problems. The compounding of risk factors contributes to the incredible scope of these problems and places a number of students at risk for not completing or succeeding in school. For such **at-risk students**, as they are often called, the chances are great that they will have difficulty getting an adequate education.

What are some of these risk factors? Here are six major ones:

- The child is not living with two parents.
- The head of the household is a high school dropout.

FIGURE 4.1

Percentage of Children, Ages 0–17, by Race, with Selected Risk Factors

Source: America's Children: Key National Indicators of Well-Being 2009 (Washington, DC: Forum on Child and Family Statistics, 2009). Available at http://childstats.ed.gov/americaschildren/famsoc1.asp

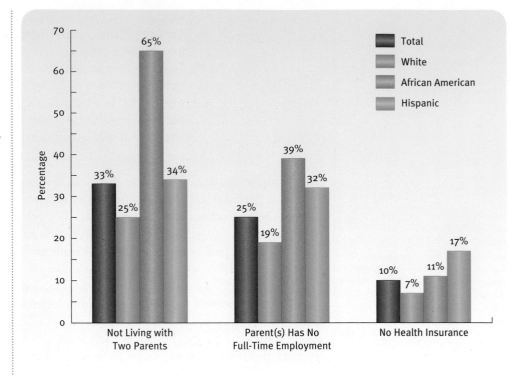

- Family income is below the poverty line.
- The child is living with a parent or parents who do not have steady, full-time employment.
- The family is receiving welfare benefits.
- The child does not have health insurance.

We know that these family variables do not necessarily compromise children. Many children from families with these risks overcome the odds to succeed in school and in life. Research indicates, however, that when several of these risk factors are present, fewer children make it. As one prominent author states, "The research . . . shows that the more risk factors are present, the greater the damaging impact of each. But the impact is not just additive—risk factors multiply each other's destructive effects."[1] Compounding the problem is the fact that multiple-risk families are often concentrated in economically and socially isolated communities that have limited job opportunities, poor schools, low-quality public services, and higher levels of crime and drug use. Figure 4.1 shows the percentage of children with some of these risk factors.

Let's examine some of these risk factors in more detail, starting with the changing patterns of the American family.

new american family patterns

In recent decades, our society has experienced dramatic changes in how families are structured. The once common image of the "breadwinner" father, a housewife mother, and two children of public school age now accurately describes only a very small percentage of households in the United States. So what is the typical family of our students like today? Actually, there is no longer one "typical" family pattern.

Rather, a number of economic and societal trends have resulted in families that come in many forms and, in turn, have a pervasive influence on children in school.

FAMILY COMPOSITION

An increasing number of children are being raised by single parents. Only 70 percent of all children younger than 18 in the United States live with two married parents, 23 percent live with only their mothers, 3.4 percent live with only their fathers, and 4 percent live with neither parent.[2] A breakdown of the figures by racial group reveals that 24 percent of white children, 61 percent of black children, and 31 percent of Hispanic children live in arrangements other than two-parent families.[3]

The high rate of divorce in the United States has also influenced the composition of families, particularly among couples who have children. More than half of today's new marriages will end in divorce. In addition to divorce, factors such as births to single parents, separation, and death of a parent contribute to the number of children living in single-parent households or possibly with grandparents or aunts and uncles.

Being a child in a family in which the parents' marriage is conflict ridden and unhappy may be less preferable in some ways than living in a single-parent family. Nevertheless, single-parent families have one major disadvantage relative to two-parent households: lower incomes. Over four times as many children who live with only their mothers live in poverty, compared to children living in married-couple households.[4] Single-mother families have been called the *new poor*. It is not just the absence of one parent, but the loss of a two-parent income, that puts a special burden on these families. More difficult to pin down is the effect of only one parent bearing the daily chores of monitoring, supporting, and guiding the school-age children.

Another result of high divorce rates is the increasing number of children living in blended families with stepparents, stepsiblings, and/or half-siblings. In some cases, divorced parents share physical custody of the children, with the result that children

In many American families, children are being raised by single mothers, which often results in children being raised in poverty.

(© Htuller/Dreamstime.com)

must split their time between parental households. As we discussed in Chapter 3, "Who Are Today's Students in a Diverse Society?" you may also have students whose parents are of the same gender.

Changes in American family patterns will likely influence your interactions with students and their parents in a number of ways. For example, in divorce situations it may be difficult to keep both parents informed of their child's progress, or a single parent may have a very heavy workload and may be unable to attend parent–teacher conferences at the usual times. Varied family patterns will also require more sensitivity in daily interactions, such as avoiding asking students to bring a note from "your mother." It would perhaps be better to say "your parent" or "the person who takes care of you." In the Voices from the Classroom feature, Christa Compton shares some of the ways she tries to create a supportive community within her classes.

FAMILY RELATIONSHIPS

Family composition affects the amount of time children and their parents have to spend with one another and can also affect the quality of that "together time." For a single parent, the combination of job demands and the necessities of maintaining a family, such as cooking, cleaning, and grocery shopping, does not allow for a great deal of leisure time to spend supervising and enjoying the children. Many single parents do a fine job of raising their children, but the hardships are considerable.

VOICES from the classroom

Families and School

Christa Compton taught high school English in Columbia, South Carolina, for nine years. She was South Carolina's Teacher of the Year in 2001. She recently completed her Ph.D. at Stanford University.

My students show up with hearts burdened by terrible losses. Angela's father was murdered when she was very young, and she still grieves for a man she only vaguely remembers. Marcus was put up for adoption at birth by his teenage mother, and his adoptive mother died of cancer two years ago. Peter is angry because his mother recently moved out of the house, and he blames her for breaking up their family. Many other families have been torn apart by divorce, and fathers are increasingly absent in their children's lives.

All of this means I have to work hard to earn students' trust, an especially difficult task with those who have been disappointed by other people they have trusted. If students don't find a sense of belonging at home, it becomes even more important to find it at school, so I try to create a supportive community within the class. I uncover the story of each kid's life and design activities that build relationships among the students. Throughout the year, we write sympathy cards when one of us is grieving, applaud the students who make the honor roll, welcome back the students who return from an absence, and do whatever we can to express concern for each class member.

It helps to observe the students' behavior and moods from day to day. Sometimes just a quiet comment can reassure them that someone cares. At other times, students reveal their anxieties in a written assignment, so I write notes on their papers to let them know that I am there to support them.

They desperately want someone to pay attention—to praise their successes, to notice when they are sad, to share the daily torments and victories that are the hallmarks of adolescent life. When they feel dismissed, I can provide encouragement. When their lives are chaotic and unpredictable, I can offer safety and consistency. I might be the one person they can count on, and I refuse to let them down.

> "
> *America's future will be determined
> by the home and the school. The child
> becomes largely what it is taught, hence
> we must watch what we teach it, how we
> live before it.*
>
> —JANE ADDAMS,
> Cofounder of Hull House and Nobel Peace Prize Winner

Even two-parent families can face challenges. Many mothers now go to work or return to work when their children are very young. In 31 percent of two-parent families, both the mother and father worked all year, full time.[5] Two-career families must balance the needs of childrearing and family life with the demands of two work environments. Neither Mom nor Dad is as available as she or he used to be to attend daily to children's social, intellectual, and moral development.

Seventy-five percent of today's students live in families in which either both parents or the only parent works full time.[6] When many children return home from school, they watch television rather than talk with their parents. Coming home to an empty house or apartment after school is standard for an estimated 4 million "latch-key" children in our country.

For parents of younger children not yet in school, working outside the home raises the issue of adequate child care. If both parents or the only parent goes to work full time, who is taking care of the children? Grandparents and extended family used to pitch in and help, but today it is less common for a family to settle in one location near relatives for extended periods. Parents who have to work—and especially single parents—can easily be caught in a bind, and they often must settle for whatever child care they can find or afford. The expenses of child care often create an additional hardship on the family's resources.

PAUSE AND REFLECT

1. Does your own family background reflect traditional or emerging family patterns? How do you think your upbringing will affect your ability to teach students from different family situations?

2. How can you prepare to work effectively with a variety of parents and caregivers?

SCHOOL AND TEACHER RESPONSES

In addition to limiting the amount of time children spend in close contact with their parents, the trend toward two-career and single-parent families has a direct impact on the schools. In the past, teachers could count on more support from families; now teachers often find it difficult to even get in contact with many parents. In the past, young people were actively involved outside of school in family and community. Today, however, the school is being urged to play a larger role in expanding and guiding the limited experiences of children.

In this situation, the more dramatic social problems, such as poverty and homelessness, take on even greater urgency for the schools. Schools are being asked to deal with the new problems that reflect the facts of modern family life and our changed economy. Many schools have responded to child care needs by offering both before- and after-school programs. For example, schools may offer enrichment and recreational programs or on-site day care before and after school to address student and parental needs. Some schools even stagger their bus schedules to accommodate students who stay for after-school programs. Many schools provide both breakfast and lunch programs. Some schools, such as those following the model developed by

LEADERS in education

James Comer (1934–)

(Photo by Diana Walker/Time Life Pictures/Getty Images)

James Comer is a public health physician and psychiatrist who, through his work with low-income schools in New Haven, Connecticut, has shown that it is possible for low-income African American children to achieve at high academic and social levels.

After receiving his M.D. from Howard University in 1960, Comer entered the public health service. He became interested in the study of how policies and institutions interact with families and children, and began to see the school as the place to improve the life chances for children from difficult home situations. Comer decided that a career in psychiatry would enable him to address the social problems that plagued the people with whom he worked, and in 1964 he began his psychiatric training at Yale University.

At Yale, Comer worked with the inner-city New Haven schools to find out why they were not helping African American children and how they could be made to do so. He wanted to give these children the same opportunities in life that education had given him. The more he worked with children, the more he came to believe that schools were the only places where children trapped in poverty and failure could receive the support their families could not give them.

With the help of a Ford Foundation grant, Comer became the director of the School Development Program with the New Haven public schools. A team of educational and mental health professionals consisting of Comer, school administrators and teachers, a social worker, a psychologist, a special education teacher, and other support staff worked to involve parents in developing a social skills curriculum that integrated academic disciplines. The curriculum included four major areas: politics and government, business and economics, health and nutrition, and spiritual and leisure time—all areas in which the students would need proficiency to succeed in school and to lead productive lives. Through the curriculum, the students became more aware of their community and of how their involvement in it could make a difference.

By adopting the findings of child development and behavioral science research, the team concentrated on problem solving rather than blame fixing and made decisions based on consensus. This consensus process gave each team member a sense of participation and ownership of decisions. The project was a great success: students' standardized test scores rose dramatically, project schools had higher attendance rates than other New Haven schools, and students graduated to become school leaders in their later schooling.

Comer's model emphasizes the social context of teaching and learning. No academic learning is possible, Comer asserts, unless a positive environment exists at the school such that teachers, students, parents, and administrators like one another and work together for the good of all children. Built around three elements—a school governance team, a mental health team, and parental participation—Comer's model seeks to create schools that offer children stable support and positive role models. With the school and parents working successfully together, no conflict arises between home and school. The students learn desirable values, disruptions at school are reduced, and both teachers and students have more time and energy to focus on academic and social skills learning.

Among the many sites that have successfully implemented Comer's approach, now known as the School Development Program, are Washington, D.C.; Dade County, Florida; Dallas; Chicago; Detroit; San Diego; and New Orleans. Many school districts have chosen this program's structure and processes as a way to implement site-based management.

James Comer—described in the Leaders in Education feature—have responded in a very different way, by redesigning the whole school to make effective teamwork with families a priority.

Interagency Cooperation

In addition to developing their own responses, many schools work with other agencies to meet the changing needs of students and their families. These schools offer nontraditional programs that coordinate agencies dealing with health, social, and recreational services. The interagency programs enable the schools to deliver needed social and health services to students and their families, to promote success in school.

For example, the coordinated school health initiative responds to the risk factors that threaten children and youth by providing student health services. It assesses the health problems in particular school communities, builds consensus on which services should be provided, and puts together a comprehensive approach to improving children's health using agencies that address health, mental health, dental health, social services, recreation, and youth development. The guiding principle for the coordinated school health initiative is that schools and communities can do much more with their current resources if they work together in partnership rather than as separate, isolated agencies. At least 1,800 of these school-based health centers are now operating in the United States.[7]

poverty

The rich are getting richer and the poor are getting poorer. This aphorism describes the extremes of different socioeconomic levels in our society today. **Socioeconomic status (SES)** is the term used by the U.S. Bureau of the Census to classify economic conditions of people using a family's occupational status, income, and educational attainment as measures of status. Individuals high in income, occupational prestige, and amount of education are considered to be high in socioeconomic status and are usually seen by others to be upper-class people who are influential in their communities. In contrast, people low in socioeconomic status are seen as being lower-class people who have little prestige or power.

WHO ARE THE POOR?

The poorest 40 percent of U.S. citizens receive 12 percent of the national income, whereas the wealthiest 20 percent receive 50 percent.[8] In 2009, the number of impoverished Americans was estimated to be 43.6 million, or 14.3 percent of the total U.S. population.[9]

In terms of sheer numbers, the majority of poor Americans are white; however, the *rate* of poverty is higher among minorities. Over 9 percent of whites, 26 percent of blacks, 25 percent of Hispanic Americans, and 12.5 percent of Asian Americans live below the poverty line (22,350 for a family of four in 2011).[10]

Poverty rates have increased over the last few years as a result of the 2007–2009 recession. The problem of poverty is now pervasive, and the prospects for breaking its grip on children are particularly bleak. As Figure 4.2 shows, 20.7 percent (15.5 million) of U.S. children live in poverty, the highest rate among all age groups

(T) F

The United States has a higher percentage of children living in poverty than any other industrialized country.

Even though the United States is one of the richest countries in the world, about 20 percent of all children live in poverty.

FIGURE 4.2

Percentage of Children Younger Than Age 18 Living in Poverty, by Race/Ethnicity, 2009

Source: Carmen DeNavas-Walt, Bernadette D. Proctor, and Jessica Smith, U.S. Bureau of the Census, *Income, Poverty, and Health Insurance Coverage in the United States: 2009.* Current Population Reports P60-238 (Washington, DC: U.S. Government Printing Office, 2010), Table B.2. Available at www.census.gov/prod/2010pubs/p60-238.pdf.

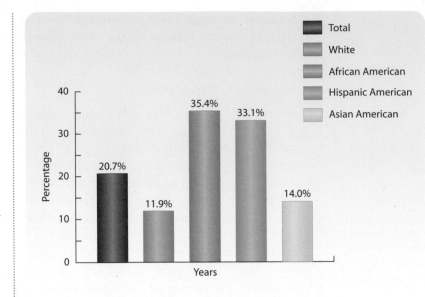

> *America is losing sight of its children. In decisions made every day we are placing them at the bottom of the agenda, with grave consequences for the future of the nation.*
>
> —ERNEST BOYER,
> Former U.S. Commissioner of Education

and the highest rate in any industrialized country. Children make up about one-fourth of the total U.S. population, but they constitute 34 percent of the poor. More than 43.5 percent of the children in families headed by females are poor, as compared to slightly less than 10 percent for married-couple families.[11]

In the past, poverty was assumed to be the result of unemployment, and for many this remains true. Twenty-seven percent of American children are growing up in households in which no parent has a full-time, year-round job.[12] Many other people hold regular jobs yet still find themselves in poverty: 31 percent of children living in poverty have at least one parent working full-time all year.[13] After World War II, many high school graduates could get manufacturing jobs that required minimal education but paid quite well. A high school graduate could support a family of four, buy a house, own two cars, and live comfortably. The U.S. job market has now changed. Many manufacturing jobs can now be done more efficiently and effectively by machines, and many of those jobs that are still done by people have been moved, or "outsourced," to countries with low-wage workers. The U.S. job market for unskilled workers today is found mostly in fast-food establishments and service jobs that typically pay minimum wage and offer no benefits. Full-time employment at the current minimum wage is not enough to support a family above the poverty line.

HOMELESSNESS

For families in or close to poverty, the threat of homelessness is very real. Poor families often pay more than one-half of their annual incomes in rent. With such a large percentage of income consumed by rent payments, a single incident or emergency in the family can disrupt this tenuous equilibrium and jeopardize the family's ability to maintain a home. Imagine, for example, the domino effect that could occur from mechanical difficulties with the one family car. Even minor repairs costing $50 to $100 may be beyond the family's budget. Without a car, the family breadwinner may be unable to get to work and the children unable to get to day care. It does not take long in such a situation to lose a job or a long-awaited slot in a child care center. If the main earner cannot work, paying rent can soon become impossible. It is easy to see why housing, which consumes so much of annual income, is a particular source of vulnerability for families in poverty.

Approximately 1.5 million children and youth in the United States are homeless at some point each year.[14] Imagine the obstacles for homeless children trying to get an education. Uprooted from their homes, many live in shelters or other locations in distant parts of town. Attending school may require extensive transportation, which parents are not likely to be able to afford. Enrolling children in a school near a shelter may be a difficult and intimidating process for parents struggling with daily survival. Many parents, believing they will be homeless only for a short time, may not even try to transfer their child's enrollment. As days turn into weeks and months, the child may miss a great deal of school. If the child is fortunate enough to attend school, other difficulties may arise, such as the stigma of wearing dirty and ragged clothes, being unwelcome by other children or school officials, or being unable to stay awake in class.

Some homeless children are on their own, having run away from home or been thrown out by their families. Many of these chronically homeless youth have been physically or sexually abused, and many suffer from drug or alcohol abuse, poor nutrition, inadequate sleep, exposure to the elements, and lack of health care. School can be a stabilizing force in the lives of these children, but it can also exacerbate their problems.

In 1987, Congress passed the Stewart B. McKinney Homeless Assistance Act, which is intended to provide protection for the educational needs of homeless children and youth. This legislation provides grants to states to make available money for the educational needs of homeless children. It also requires states to ensure that these children are educated with the rest of the youth in their area and are not isolated and stigmatized.[15]

You may have homeless children in your classroom; if so, they are likely to require support and understanding from you. Some may be malnourished or physically dirty because they lack access to shower or tub facilities. They may show emotional needs. Other children may make fun of them. Your support and caring could provide these children with hope and be crucial in improving their chances for success.

Homelessness, an outcome of poverty, affects many families in the United States, with serious consequences for the children's education.

More than anything else, homeless children need homes. As their teacher, you cannot be expected to provide the homes they need, but hundreds of local and federal programs serve runaway and homeless youth, and these agencies will help you work with these youngsters. Through them, some may find shelter.

SCHOOL AND TEACHER RESPONSES

Many people have thought that we could eliminate poverty through education and that, through schooling, it would be relatively easy to free people from the chains of impoverishment. The resulting efforts have been well intentioned but often too little, too late and, in retrospect, sometimes naïve. With poverty so prevalent, schools face a challenging problem, partly because they are not designed to serve poor children. The schools in the United States were created and continue to be supported by the middle class to perpetuate the middle-class way of life. There is nothing particularly startling about this bias. Middle-class people want their children to be like themselves or possibly somewhat better, so they have built and continue to pay for a school system that reflects their values and supports the way of life with which they feel comfortable.

Some critics see the middle-class bias of our schools in a more sinister light, as part of an enslavement system. They claim that schools do not help develop the individual talents and strengths of poor children, and that they make these children believe they are losers. After 8 to 11 years of schooling, many of these young people see themselves as unable to fit into the middle class and as people who, at best, will do society's menial work.

Although some of these critics see this system as a conscious plan of our society, we do not. Such a cynical view suggests that the teachers who are toiling in the poor urban and rural areas are either people of evil intentions or simply dupes. In our view, many of the most heroic teachers are those struggling to aid children trapped in and oppressed by poverty.

Our past and present inadequacies in educating the children of the poor have tempted some to turn away and devote their energies to more solvable problems. Our nation cannot follow this path. Ours is an evolving society; as a people, we are not finished with our own development. Eradicating the ravages of poverty and its withering effect on children should be at the top of our agenda as citizens of this nation and as educators. Although there are many important and solvable problems to work on, we cannot afford—in justice—to ignore this one.

One educator, Ruby Payne, has written extensively about issues of poverty and how schools can understand better the unique needs of children of poverty.[16] Payne describes *hidden rules,* unspoken clues that people in different socioeconomic groups use in decision making. Among the middle class, work and achievement are driving forces in decision making. In contrast, in **generational poverty** (being in poverty for two generations or longer), the driving forces are survival, entertainment, and relationships. According to Payne, the hidden rules guiding people who live in poverty mean that relationships and entertainment are more important than achievement.

Payne's major point is that unless educators understand these hidden rules that govern the behavior of those from generational poverty, they are unlikely to respond in appropriate ways. Schools tend to reflect middle-class values, which is why children from poverty backgrounds, who don't know the middle-class hidden rules, often feel out of place. Payne suggests that for students from

> *We need to permanently abandon the belief that race and poverty determine how much students can and will learn.*
>
> —KATI HAYCOCK,
> Director of The Education Trust

generational poverty to value academic learning, a significant relationship must be present, and academic tasks must be referenced in terms of relationships. This significant relationship can be with the teacher or with other students and friends.

Payne cites an example of how a teacher, while working with a 17-year-old student who did not do his homework on positive and negative numbers, suggested that it would be acceptable if his friends cheated him at cards. The student was furious at the idea. The teacher insisted that the student wouldn't know whether they were cheating him because he didn't know positive and negative numbers. The student grabbed a deck of cards to show the teacher that he did know how to keep score. After this display, the teacher said, "Then you do know positive and negative numbers. I expect you to do your homework." From then on, the student did his homework regularly.

Payne's work has generated considerable criticism from some in higher education for its lack of scientific evidence-based practice. Even so, many teachers and administrators find her perspectives compelling and useful.

PAUSE AND REFLECT

1. What are the challenges in teaching poor children?

2. Are you interested in teaching children from poverty situations? Why or why not?

3. What decisions of yours have been based on hidden rules related to your social class? How can you prepare to adjust or reveal hidden rules to meet the expectations of students you teach?

4. Why do you think it is so difficult for schools to overcome the effects of poverty on the academic achievement for poor children?

---

teenage parenting

The bad news: each year approximately 750,000 American teenagers get pregnant and give birth to some 435,000 children—by far the highest teenage birthrate among the world's developed countries. The good news: between 1990 and 2006, the birthrate among girls ages 15 to 19 declined from 60 to 42 births per 1,000.[17] Despite this trend, public funds expended for teenage pregnancies in the United States are estimated to exceed $9 billion per year.[18]

The consequences of early parenthood for teen fathers are generally not as severe as those for teen mothers. Almost 80 percent of teenage mothers are not married, which leaves them particularly vulnerable to poverty.[19] When we combine the difficulties of single parenthood with the likelihood that teenagers will have poor work skills and limited employment experience and, if they find work, will receive low wages, we gain some understanding of why more than 43 percent of the children from households headed by a female live in poverty. In fact, the poverty rate for children born to a teenage mother who has never married and who did not graduate from high school is 78 percent. Also, many young fathers do not provide financial assistance and support for these children. Because about four-fifths of teenage births occur out of wedlock, male parents often feel little responsibility for their

(T) F

Almost half the children living in a household headed by a female live in poverty. Over 43 percent of children living in a household headed by a female live in poverty. Single mothers often are undereducated, have poor work skills, and limited experience, leading to low wages.

children. Only 30 percent of mothers ages 15 to 17 receive child support payments, and most of those receive only a portion of the payments that are due to them.[20]

Not only do teenage parents face the enormous task of juggling childrearing and employment or school, but often they must care for a premature baby who is more likely to have health problems and possibly learning difficulties. Moreover, poverty often correlates with worse nutrition, less health care, more homelessness, and less education as compared to more advantaged families. To lessen this problem, many schools are working with local health officials to ensure that pregnant teenagers receive prenatal care and parenting advice. They are also encouraging these young women to stay in school and graduate. In many cases, the schools are permitting young mothers to bring their babies with them to school.

If you are planning on teaching in secondary schools, you may work with some of these young parents and should keep in mind the challenges they face. You should also give some thought to what you would do if one of your female students informs you that she is pregnant or one of your male students tells you that he has gotten his girlfriend pregnant. Know both your legal and ethical responsibilities in these cases. If you plan to teach in an elementary school, be prepared to work with very young parents, including some who may be your own age.

To prevent teenage pregnancies, many schools have established sex education programs, and some operate clinics where students can obtain birth-control devices. Both of these steps, while increasingly common, remain controversial.

SEX EDUCATION

Issues and questions of sexual behavior and sexual attitudes cut deep into the heart of their spiritual and social views for most Americans. It is hardly surprising, then, that our schools' efforts to educate young people frequently stir up strong passions and inspire heated debates. Although most people agree that children should be given information about sex, the controversy centers on three issues:

As pregnant teenagers struggle with the decision of whether to drop out of school, educators are finding ways to encourage pregnant teenagers and young mothers to stay in school and graduate.

(© Topham/The Image Works)

- Is the school the appropriate institution to offer such instruction?
- If so, should it limit instruction to strictly factual information, or should the psychological, social, health, religious, and moral aspects of sex also be included in the curriculum?
- Should the school emphasize "abstinence-only" sex education programs, or offer "comprehensive" sex education programs?

Many people argue that because sex is such an intimate topic and is closely related to religious and moral beliefs, sex education is the responsibility of the home and the church and should take place there. Advocates of sex education in the schools respond that they would agree with that position if parents did, in fact, provide adequate sex information for their children. In reality, they contend, the majority of parents fail to carry through on their responsibility to teach their children about sex. According to these advocates of sex education, the public school is the only institution that has access to most children over an extended period, and the responsibility must fall to the school because of the demonstrated failure of the home, church, library, and medical profession to provide effective sex education. Courts have also supported the right of state boards of education and local school boards to offer sex education in the curriculum.

Goals of Sex Education

Preventing teenage pregnancies is a major goal of any sex education program. Besides endangering babies, early pregnancies place the future lives of great numbers of teenage girls in serious jeopardy, interrupting and often terminating their education. Despite the availability of special counseling and accommodations intended to help teenage mothers stay in school, the majority drop out, drastically diminishing their job and career opportunities as adults.

Another goal of sex education is to reduce the incidence of sexually transmitted diseases (STDs). This aspect of sex education is also controversial, particularly regarding the use of condoms. An estimated 9 million Americans ages 15 to 24 are newly infected with an STD each year, with chlamydia and gonorrhea being the most commonly acquired diseases.[21] Although not the most common of the STDs, AIDS is a serious killer, and preventive measures to curtail its spread have become a matter of life and death. It is estimated that 5 percent of all new cases of human immunodeficiency virus (HIV) infection occur in people ages 13 to 24, and the majority of these infections are sexually transmitted. Approximately two-thirds of HIV infections occur in males.[22]

About 48 percent of high school students report that before graduating they have engaged in sexual intercourse (50% of males and 46% of females). However, only 62 percent of the teenagers report using condoms the last time they had sex; condoms, although clearly not as effective as abstinence, do provide some protection against AIDS and other STDs when used correctly.[23] Unfortunately, many teenagers—especially if they are using alcohol or drugs—neglect to use condoms, or use them incorrectly.

In addition to preventing pregnancies and STDs, sex education seeks to help teenagers become sexually healthy adults. Sexual health encompasses sexual development and reproductive health, and such characteristics as the ability to develop and maintain meaningful personal relationships, appreciation of one's own body, interaction with both genders in respectful and appropriate ways, and responsible decision-making skills.

Students need not only scientific information about human sexuality and prevention of pregnancy and disease, but also help to gain the self-control and strength of character needed to avoid risky and irresponsible behavior. One important form of prevention—abstinence—depends on developing the necessary self-control to handle sexual situations and feelings. Likewise, developing true respect for one's partner is an important character-related aspect of sex education.

Types of Sex Education

Arguments over the kind of sex education the schools should offer are even more heated than the controversy about whether to offer it at all. Some support comprehensive sex education programs (also called "abstinence plus") that, while advocating abstinence from sex outside of marriage, also provide information on contraception and disease prevention for those teens who elect to become sexually active.

The comprehensive sex education approach stands in sharp contrast to the moral or religious beliefs of other participants in the debate; they would recommend an abstinence-based curriculum that teaches students to abstain from sex outside of marriage and that neither advocates nor teaches about condom use. Advocates of the abstinence approach argue that when sex education programs teach both abstinence and the use of contraceptives, students receive a mixed message. According to these proponents, the only appropriate position for the public schools is to teach and to advocate abstinence, leaving the controversial sex education to others, such as parents, churches, and medical professionals. They argue that much of the mass media (i.e., films, TV, popular music) have so sexualized the world of young people that schools may be perceived as legitimizing teenage sex through advocating condoms and other devices, which sends the wrong message to students.

Others believe that the spread of STDs, especially AIDS, has strengthened the position of those who argue for comprehensive sex education programs. They stand behind the view that schools should provide children with the sex education that will help them understand the risks they face and how to prevent or minimize those risks.

Although President George W. Bush's administration weighed in on the side of abstinence-only programs and primarily supported these kinds of programs, President Obama's administration has taken a different direction. In 2010, his administration launched a $110 million campaign that funds a range of programs, including both abstinence-only and comprehensive sex education programs.[24]

Like few other issues in education, the "what's and when's and how's" of sex education are matters of deep and serious controversy in our public schools and in our culture. Rational people of good will have come to very different conclusions about what is best for students. As a teacher, you may have students in your class or school who are known to have HIV and other STDs. It is important for you and your colleagues to know how school district policy deals with these students and the ways in which the disease can be transmitted. Safeguarding other students while also attending to the rights and needs of the student with an STD requires knowledge, care, and understanding.

PAUSE AND REFLECT

1. What kinds of support do pregnant and parenting teenagers need from their teachers?

2. Do you think that you will be comfortable and well prepared to deal with your students' questions or remarks about sexuality? If not, how can you prepare now?

abused and neglected children

The education of the young brings us into contact with humanity's best impulses. Occasionally, however, we see the wreckage of its darkest and most vicious urges. For many years, the phenomenon of child abuse was known only to a small percentage of social workers and law enforcement people. More recently, we have become aware of the magnitude of this problem and the variety of forms abuse can take, including physical or mental injury, sexual abuse, negligent treatment, and maltreatment.

Because of the hidden nature of much child abuse and neglect, reliable data on it are somewhat difficult to obtain. Professionals in the field strongly suspect that most cases go unreported. Nevertheless, 3.7 million incidents of child abuse or neglect were reported to U.S. child-service agencies in 2008. Over 772,000 of these reported cases were substantiated. Over two-thirds of the victims of maltreatment suffered from neglect, one-sixth experienced physical abuse, and one-tenth were victims of sexual abuse.[25] Parental substance abuse was reported as a major contributing factor in child abuse cases.

The toll that abuse and neglect take on children's physical, emotional, and psychological development is difficult to assess. Children subjected to violent treatment may sustain injuries that cause serious learning problems in school. Abused children may be withdrawn or have trouble concentrating. They suffer enormous stress, and their self-esteem is low. They sometimes have excessive needs for control because they have experienced such helplessness. Also, they may be more likely to abuse their own children in the future.

The classroom teacher will not directly encounter the problem of abuse very often. However, in all 50 states, educators are legally responsible for reporting suspected cases of child abuse. Teachers must be aware of potential signs of abuse and know school policy and procedures for reporting suspected abuse. (See Chapter 8, "What Are the Ethical and Legal Issues Facing Teachers?" for a discussion of teachers' legal obligations regarding suspected child abuse.) Potential signs of abuse include the following:

- Repeated injuries such as bruises to the head or abdomen, welts, and burns
- Neglected appearance, stealing food, difficulty staying awake, or poor hygiene
- Sudden fall-off in academic performance
- Disruptive or passive, withdrawn behavior
- Secret or furtive behavior when using the Internet[26]

T (F)

Teachers who suspect that a student in his or her class has suffered child abuse must use discretion in deciding whether to file a report. Laws in all 50 states require teachers to report suspected child abuse to authorities, and protect them legally in case of lawsuits.

Teachers need to realize that even after an abusive situation has been reported and perhaps disclosed, these children's problems in school will not suddenly end. Children who have been abused have a continuing need for emotional safety and stability, including trustworthy praise, concrete rewards, and constructive ways to control their classroom environment. They need capable adult role models who can provide varied but predictable activities and measurable classroom achievement.

PAUSE AND REFLECT

What can schools, teachers, and other social agencies do to help parents and children avoid abuse?

Physical or emotional abuse of children may affect them in many ways, including emotional withdrawal, acting out, or aggressiveness toward other children.

(Zurijeta/Shutterstock.com)

alcohol and drug abuse

Many of the trends mentioned in this chapter can severely stress the functioning of families, provoking self-destructive responses in children. Substance abuse—involving the use of alcohol or various other drugs—is a particularly destructive response. It may be the act of either parents or children. Unfortunately, when one family member becomes entangled in substance abuse, the entire family is usually a victim.

Alcohol is the most commonly abused substance, and the first use of alcohol may occur at a young age, sometimes in elementary school. Historically, the greatest number of alcoholic teenagers have been male students, especially those with low grades, but the gap between males and females seems to be closing. The problem of alcohol abuse among high school students is widespread. In one 2010 survey, 7 percent of eighth-graders, 16 percent of tenth-graders, and 23 percent of twelfth-graders reported consuming five or more drinks in a row at least once in the past two weeks.[27] Alcohol use and premarital sex are also related. Specifically, teenagers who drink are much more likely to engage in sex than those who do not drink. Such behavior can lead to unprotected sex, which increases the risk of transmission of AIDS or other STDs.

In 2010, 0.5 percent of eighth-graders, 18 percent of tenth-graders, and 24 percent of twelfth-graders reported using an illicit

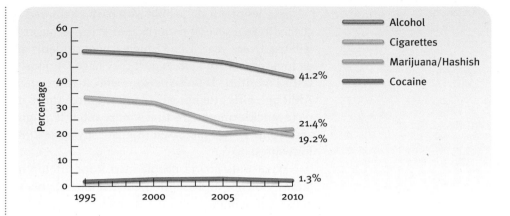

FIGURE 4.3

Student Drug and Alcohol Use: Percentage of Seniors Reporting Use in the Previous 30 Days, by Year and Substance

Source: Monitoring the Future: National Results on Adolescent Drug Use: Overview of Key Findings, 2010 (Ann Arbor: University of Michigan, Institute for Social Research), Table 7. Available at http://monitoringthefuture.org.

drug during the past 30 days.[28] See Figure 4.3 for more information on drug and alcohol use by high school seniors. Although these are the lowest rates reported since 1993, student drug and alcohol abuse remain serious problems. As mentioned earlier, many child abuse and neglect cases involve parental substance abuse, which has devastating results for children. (Studys the Video Case *Social and Emotional Development: The Influence of Peer Groups* to give you some ideas about how students experience peer pressure.)

Every public school in the United States is subject to the Safe and Drug Free Schools and Communities Act, which is now part of the No Child Left Behind Act of 2001. The basic purpose of these laws is to provide safe, disciplined, and drug-free environments conducive to learning by eliminating violence in and around schools and preventing illegal drug use on school property.

What should you do if you suspect one of your students is using drugs or binge drinking? The most important step is to talk with the school counselor about the situation. He or she has been trained to deal with these problems and can offer you advice on both the legal aspects of the situation and ways to assist the student. Students want some level of consistency in actions, not just in words. It is quite distressing to students when educators do nothing to address drug or alcohol abuse. Schools need clear-cut policies about how to handle alcohol and other drugs in the classroom and at school.

PAUSE AND REFLECT

1. Which elements of school culture serve to condone or even encourage student drinking and drug use? Which elements could be used to discourage substance abuse?

2. What can you, as a teacher, do to encourage responsible student substance use behavior?

adolescent suicide

Suicide is third only to motor vehicle accidents and homicide as a leading cause of adolescent death in the United States. Each year over 4,100 people ages 15 to 24 take their own lives.

Studies of young people who have attempted suicide and those who have succeeded reveal several patterns. For every teenager who commits suicide, 100 more will try. Every year, 1 in 12 high school students attempts suicide, and one-fifth of all high school students report they have "seriously considered" suicide within the last 12 months. Of those persons who attempt suicide, the vast majority are female. Although girls attempt suicide about three times more often than boys, boys complete suicide about five times more often than girls.[29] The suicide rate for blacks ages 15 to 19 has increased dramatically since 1980 but is still lower than the rate for whites.

What puts young people at risk for attempting suicide? Risk factors include family violence or disruption, mental illness, unemployment, a history of substance abuse, being bullied, and stress in school or social life. To add to the tragedy, young people sometimes engage in copycat suicides. In such a "cluster" syndrome, a wave of adolescent suicides plagues an area. In response, hundreds of school districts now offer programs in suicide prevention.

Despite the high prevalence of suicide among youth, most schools don't have a plan to prevent these deaths. Educators often have the opportunity to recognize children and youths who are suicide risks and to help them get the advice and support they need. Although suicidal behaviors are complex and the warning signs can be ambiguous or misleading, it is important to realize that most young people who commit suicide give warning signs first, signaling their need for help:

- Presence of a psychiatric disorder (e.g., depression, drug or alcohol, behavior disorders, conduct disorder [e.g., runs away or has been incarcerated])

whom you will teach

1. Percentage of high school students who admit carrying a weapon to school: 6

2. Percentage of students ages 12 to 18 who reported being victimized at school during the previous six months: 4

3. Percentage of high school students who report having been in a physical fight in the previous year at school: 12

4. The percentage of children read to by a family member three or more times per week: 86

5. Percentage of high school seniors who report having used an illegal drug in the previous 30 days: 23

6. Percentage of students whose parents report having attended a parent–teacher conference that year: 78

7. Percentage of seniors who spend three or more hours per weekday watching television/DVDs or playing video or computer games: 34

8. Number of hours the average high school student works per week: 20

9. Percentage of children younger than age 18 living with two married parents: 67

10. Percentage of children who are overweight: 17

11. Percentage of students who have disabilities and are served by federal programs: 12

12. Percentage of youths ages 16 to 19 who have ever been retained in a grade in their school career: 10

Sources: America's Children: Key National Indicators of Well-Being, 2009 (Washington, DC: Federal Interagency Forum on Child and Family Statistics, 2009); *Digest of Education Statistics 2009* (Washington, DC: National Center for Education Statistics, 2010); and *Indicators of School Crime and Safety: 2010* (Washington, DC: National Center for Education Statistics, 2010).

- The expression/communication of thoughts of suicide, death, dying or the after-life (in a context of sadness, boredom, hopelessness or negative feelings)
- Impulsive and aggressive behavior; frequent expressions of rage
- Increasing use of alcohol or drugs
- Exposure to another's suicidal behavior
- Recent severe stressor (e.g., difficulties in dealing with sexual orientation; un-planned pregnancy; significant, real, or anticipated loss, etc.)
- Family instability; significant family conflict.[30]

If you observe such potential indicators of suicidal tendencies, do not try to handle the burden alone. Seek a support network of the guidance counselor, the school social worker, and/or the school psychologist. Recognizing symptoms and getting professional help for students who behave in this way may prevent their suicides and help them develop effective coping skills so that they can deal with their problems.

school violence and vandalism

Massacre at Columbine High School in Littleton, Colorado—15 Die

Gunman Shoots Eighth-Grader in L.A.

Sixth-Graders Plot to Kill Their Teacher

Shooting Rampage by Student Leaves 10 Dead on Reservation

Teen Slashes Five Classmates in Knife Attack

These headlines suggest that the United States has become a dangerous place for children. In urban areas, crime and violence from surrounding neighborhoods have spilled over into the schools, affecting children, staff, and teachers alike. In the suburbs, communities have seen some horrible examples of students killing other students.

Costs resulting from vandalism or violence include expenditures for building repairs, skyrocketing premiums for liability insurance, human costs in terms of injuries to students and teachers, and, in extreme cases, even deaths. Many teachers are injured while attempting to break up student fights or to halt robberies. Student–teacher disagreements also sometimes provoke attacks. Still other teachers are injured not by students, but rather by intruders who may be dealing drugs or who see the elementary schools as buildings with little security, populated by women and children.

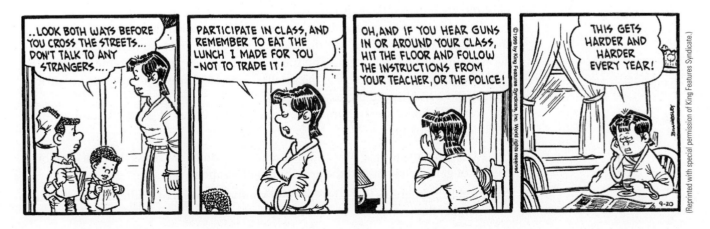

(Reprinted with special permission of King Features Syndicate.)

How extensive is the problem of school violence and crime? Despite the ominous headlines, serious violent crime constitutes a small percentage of the total amount of school crime, and homicide is extremely rare. Although the number of multiple-homicide events at U.S. schools has increased, and they receive national media coverage when they do occur, the chance of suffering a school-associated violent death is less than one in 1 million. Between 2000 and 2008, school-associated deaths (including deaths that happened while going to and from school), have ranged from a low of 33 to a high of 58.[31] Although school-related deaths are relatively few and have declined since 2006, many students still fear going to school because of threatened violence. Factors such as weapon carrying, fights, the presence of gangs, and bullying create an atmosphere of fear for many students, such that many high school students report not going to school at some point because of safety concerns.

In 2007, 8 percent of all students in grades 9–12 reported being threatened or injured with a weapon, such as a gun, knife, or club during the previous 12 months while on school property. For the same year, 7 percent of all teachers (elementary, middle, and high school) reported being threatened with injury by a student at their school, and 4 percent of teachers reported being physically attacked by a student at their school.[32]

GANGS

Severe violence is often associated with gangs. In 2007, 23 percent of students reported the presence of gangs in their schools.[33] The proportion of young people who actually join gangs is quite small, however. Approximately 774,000 gang members and 27,900 gangs are estimated to have been active in the United States in 2008. The number of gangs increased by 28 percent, and the number of gang members increased by 6 percent from 2002 to 2008.[34]

Although gang members are often stereotyped as belonging to the lower class, some are children of middle-class, suburban families who commit acts of vandalism, robbery, and drug dealing out of boredom or feelings of alienation from family and friends. Although most gang members are male, the number of females who are gang members, in either all-female or mixed-gender gangs, has grown in recent years. Gangs often display clothing, jewelry, tattoos, or graffiti that distinguish and identify their members.

Children and teenagers join gangs for a variety of reasons: the excitement of gang activity, peer pressure, physical protection, attention, financial gain, a sense of belonging, and sometimes because they feel ignored by the people they should be close to—usually one or both parents. In many cases, youths are not actively discouraged from gang involvement by their parents. Often parents are unaware that their children are engaged in gang activity.

The character of gang activity has grown more violent as gangs have become increasingly more involved in drug dealing and other criminal activities. The easy accessibility and spread of guns and the greater tendency to use extreme violence to settle disputes or to avenge even the smallest acts of "disrespect" have also contributed to the trend toward increased violence.

How can educators minimize the negative influences of gangs? Useful actions include the following:

- Establish and enforce clear codes of school conduct that stress the unacceptability of gang behavior and the prohibition of weapons.
- Establish programs that stress positive youth involvement as alternatives to gang membership.

- Assimilate gang-oriented students into the mainstream—academically, socially, and through extracurricular activities.
- Create school programs that focus on nonviolent conflict resolution and gang prevention.
- Take quick, decisive actions when instances of gang activity occur on school grounds.
- Prohibit gang "colors," insignia, and other signs of gang membership.

BULLYING

Everyone who has attended school most likely has memories of themselves or friends of theirs being frightened by a bully. Once dismissed as "kids will be kids" behavior, chronic teasing and bullying are now being viewed by educators as dangerous social acts. In 2007, about 32 percent of 12- to 18-year-old students reported having been bullied at school during the school year. Twenty-one percent of students said that they had experienced bullying that consisted of being made fun of; 18 percent reported being the subject of rumors; 11 percent said that they were pushed, shoved, tripped, or spit on; 6 percent said they were threatened with harm; 5 percent said they were excluded from activities on purpose; and 4 percent said that someone tried to make them do things they did not want to do and that their property was destroyed on purpose.[35] As a result of being threatened, many students skip school for fear of being bullied.

A relatively new form of bullying, **cyberbullying**, is of growing concern. Cyberbullying refers to bullying through information and communication technologies such as mobile phone text messages, e-mail messages, Internet chat rooms, and social networking websites such as Facebook, MySpace, and Bebo. Estimates of the number of youth who experience cyberbullying vary widely depending on the age of the group studied and how cyberbullying is defined. One study found that about 20 percent of the 4,400 11- to 18-year-old students studied had been repeatedly made fun of or harassed via text messages, e-mail, or online venues. About the same percentage admitted to cyberbullying themselves.[36] The results of such cyberbullying can cause shame, embarrassment, depression, anger, withdrawal, and even suicide. In 2010, several incidents of teenagers committing suicide after having been cyberbullied occurred, drawing national attention to this problem.

Preventing cyberbullying is primarily a matter of education and awareness. Parents and teachers need to understand the problem and the technologies involved. Becoming aware of the problem is the first step in the process of discussing with children the issues involved and bringing the problem out into the open.

Bullying takes a terrible toll on children. Their schoolwork suffers, as do their physical and mental health. Physical and psychological bullying is often reported to be a contributing cause in adolescent suicide attempts. Bullying is also bad for bullies, who rarely learn the consequences of their actions.

A nationwide program, Bully-Proofing Your School, teaches children to recognize bullying and to develop ways to protect themselves, such as humor and avoidance. As part of this program, teachers and other school workers also receive training. Civility training is another popular way to reduce bullying; it focuses on teaching children how to be kind and compassionate to all people. An evaluation of several anti-bullying programs found that reductions in bullying were associated with parent training, increased playground supervision, disciplinary methods, home–school communication, classroom rules, classroom management, and use of training videos.[38] When a bullying problem persists, some schools have implemented

Bullying is common in schools, producing consequences detrimental to both the bullies and the victims. Schools are responding with a variety of programs to reduce the incidents of bullying.

(© Rawdon Wyatt/Alamy)

zero-tolerance policies for aggressive behavior, under which they automatically suspend any student who harasses another student. By developing a heightened awareness of bullying and its negative consequences, teachers can take actions to make the school environment more hospitable and inviting for all students.

STEPS TO REDUCE SCHOOL VIOLENCE

Concern over school crime and violence has prompted many public schools to take measures to reduce and prevent violence and to ensure safety in schools. In particular, concerns about keeping schools secure from outsiders have increased since a 2004 incident in Russia, where Chechen terrorists forced their way into an elementary school, killing more than 300 people, including 250 young students. Measures adopted by schools include the following steps:

- Enacting zero-tolerance policies regarding weapons—that is, carrying a weapon to school will automatically result in expulsion
- Creating alternative schools for students with a history of violence
- Requiring students to wear uniforms
- Employing security measures such as visitor sign-in requirements and use of metal detectors
- Having police or other law enforcement officials stationed at the school
- Offering students and staff various types of violence prevention programs

The Video Case *Social and Emotional Development: Understanding Adolescents* shows a group of middle-school boys discussing productive ways to handle stress and anger.

> ▶❙❙ **TeachSource VIDEO CASE**
>
> **Social and Emotional Development: Understanding Adolescents**
>
> Go to the Education CourseMate website to watch the video clips, study the artifacts in the case, and reflect on the following questions:
>
> 1. What are your concerns, as a teacher, about violence in the schools?
> 2. Which of the strategies for teachers and schools listed in this chapter is represented in this case?
> 3. Can you think of additional techniques that you, as a teacher, could use to defuse potentially dangerous situations in school?

Several aspects of school organization can contribute to student aggression, including high numbers of students occupying a small space, imposition of routines and conformity that may anger some students, and poor building designs that may contribute to the commission of violent acts. Most incidents of violence occur during "transition times"—that is, at the start of school, during lunch periods, or at the end of the school day. Reducing crowding, increasing supervision, and instituting policies for handling disputes during these intervals can reduce the likelihood of conflicts and their resulting injuries. Students who enjoy positive interactions with faculty and staff, are academically successful, or participate productively in school activities are less likely to commit acts of violence. In most cases of school violence, warning signs are apparent—for example, notes, threats, journal entries, arguments, or physical fights. Teachers who are able to develop close relationships with students may be in a good position to spot these signals of impending violence. Developing mechanisms for reporting threats and other warning signs of potential violence can also help schools curb these incidents.

What else can schools—specifically, principals—do to reduce school violence?

- Establish common goals for the school and elicit commitment to these goals from teachers, students, and parents.
- Establish a firm, fair, and consistent system for running the school.
- Establish high expectations for the behavior and performance of students and staff.
- Create a curriculum that supports the values of honesty, integrity, kindness, and respect for others.
- Use a variety of security measures to keep intruders and weapons off school grounds.
- Establish the school as neutral territory for students, control rumors, and squelch loitering and tardiness.
- Create alternative schools for serious offenders.
- Provide students and teachers with training in effective communication.

What can teachers themselves do to prevent violence and vandalism?

- Establish a classroom environment centered on respect and kindness, where put-downs, ridicule, and sarcasm are not tolerated.
- Learn how to defuse conflict in ways that save face for both students and teachers.
- Develop intensive skills in classroom management.
- Use peer counseling or peer mediation to train students to handle problems before they become serious.
- Involve students in decision-making processes in areas such as finding methods to handle offenders.

The encouraging news is that although school violence and vandalism are serious problems, they affect a relatively small percentage of teachers and students in the public schools. Viewed from a broader perspective, this problem probably reflects as much a societal malaise as any particular flaw of schools. Boredom, frustration, alienation, despair, and low self-concept are characteristics that teenagers may experience in their homes and in society in general, as well as in school. The disintegration of the traditional family and the widespread depiction of violence in the media and in popular music are cited as two major causes of violence in the public schools. As long as violence prevails in society, schools will likely be affected.

PAUSE AND REFLECT

1. Have you ever been afraid to go to school? Why?

2. Were you aware of the problem of school violence and vandalism before you read this chapter? Will it be a major factor in your decision regarding whether or where to teach?

---

student cheating

Many educators express concern with what they see as increased incidence of cheating among students. Cheating takes many forms, including text messaging test answers to another student, plagiarizing by downloading information or entire papers from the Internet, copying from another student, or getting test questions and answers from a student in a previous period. How widespread is cheating? In a Duke University study, 75 percent of high school students admitted to cheating; if copying another student's homework is included in the definition of cheating, that number climbs to 90 percent.[38]

In the past, cheating was largely done by a few academically weak students who couldn't get good grades on their own. Today, however, more cheating is being done by academically sound students who are capable of doing good work without cheating. In fact, the Duke study found that 80 percent of honors and advanced placement (AP) students cheat on a regular basis. One explanation for this change in who cheats is that these students experience intense pressure to succeed. As one student stated, "There's so much pressure to get a good job; and to get a good job you have to get into a good school; and to get into a good school, you have to get good grades; and to get good grades you have to cheat."[39]

T (F)

Although cheating in school has received much media attention, it only occurs with moderate frequency.
One survey found that 75 to 90 percent of high school students admitted to having cheated by sharing test answers, copying from the Internet, plagiarizing, or copying homework.

Given that less than 2 percent of all academic cheaters are caught, and only half of those students receive punishment for their crime, students have an almost 99 percent chance of being successful.[40] Undoubtedly contributing to this attitude are the pop-culture role models who seem to get away with various immoral acts.

Another group of students who are likely to cheat are athletes. Because athletes must maintain a minimum grade-point average (GPA) to stay on the team and because they face great pressure related to their use of time, cheating is rampant among these students. In high school athletes who were interviewed in another study, a "win at any cost" attitude seemed to carry over into the classroom.

What can schools and teachers do to discourage cheating? Here are a few steps:

- Don't give the same test over and over again.
- Separate students so they can't see one another's papers.
- Make it clear to students that cheating is unacceptable behavior, and define in clear terms what constitutes cheating.
- Establish an honor system using student input so that students will be invested in the system.
- Require students to sign a pledge that they have not received or given unauthorized aid on tests, papers, and assignments.

- Forbid students from carrying electronic devices, including personal digital assistants (PDAs) and cell phones, when taking tests.
- Most importantly, institute character education programs that can help students to establish a moral compass.

high school graduation and dropout rates

There are significant disagreements among scholars about how to calculate dropout and graduation rates from public high schools and which data sources to use. Estimates of high school graduation rates range from 68 percent to 82 percent. Whites and Asian Americans have higher graduate rates (estimated to be between 75% and 82%) than do blacks and Hispanic Americans (estimated to be between 52% and 74%). Over 1 million of the students who enter ninth grade each year fail to graduate with their peers four years later, which means that 7,000 high school students drop out of school each day.[41]

Approximately 1750 chronically underperforming high schools (about 10% of American high schools) are responsible for more than one-half of the nation's dropouts. The majority of these high schools are located in northern and western cities and throughout southern states. These high schools produce 58 percent of all African American dropouts and 50 percent of all Hispanic dropouts, compared to 22 percent of all white dropouts.[42] In 2010, President Obama announced plans for a $900 million "Schools Turnaround Grants" program that would be available to states and school districts to target these "dropout factories."

Dropout rates are strongly related to income levels. Youth from low-income families are three times more likely to drop out than are students from high-income families.[43] Dropout rates are highest in schools with a larger proportion of students from low-income families.

Besides poverty, what contributes to high dropout rates? Students report poor grades, dislike for school, alienation from peers, marriage or pregnancy, and employment as common causes for leaving school. The most commonly reported factor is poor academic performance. Ninth grade serves as a bottleneck for many students who discover that their academic skills are lacking for high school–level work. Another cause of dropping out is unrealistic expectations about the world of work. Many students with high hopes for the imagined luxury of a regular income fail to realize that wages in the service sector of employment are low. Other teenagers may envision starting at the bottom of the work hierarchy and, through hard work, eventually climbing the ladder of success. Unfortunately, many of them lack job search skills and end up in jobs with limited potential for advancement. Despite this reality, the strong motivation to work often proves too powerful an incentive and results in a student leaving school. The immediate rewards of the workplace lure some students away from the more remote incentives of staying in school and attaining an education.

Students often give warning signs that they are at risk for dropping out—for example, increased absences, lethargy in completing work, and preoccupation with matters outside of school. Teachers can discourage students from dropping out by showing interest and care in their students and by talking to and encouraging them. Knowing your students well can help you detect changes in their attitudes and work habits.

> *I am often asked whether I approve of compulsory education, and I usually reply that I do and that I wish we had it; we only have compulsory attendance.*
>
> —JOHN BREMER,
> Former Superintendent of Philadelphia Public Schools

> ## PAUSE AND REFLECT
>
> 1. Can a secondary-level teacher, who may see 150 students each day, get to know them all well?
>
> 2. When you were in high school, did you know any students who dropped out? If so, what were their reasons for doing so?

OUR FINAL WORD

Given the range of social problems that we have discussed in this chapter and in the preceding chapter, it is not surprising to find that schools bear an ever-growing burden to guide young people's decision making. How well equipped are the schools to handle this task? Creating schools that are safe, healthy, and conducive to learning doesn't happen automatically. The climate in a school is a product of laws, rules, regulations, and, most importantly, attitudes and values held by those who work and study in school. When problems threaten the safety, health, or well-being of students, whether within the school or outside its boundaries, educators must intervene in productive ways to maintain a school climate that protects students and promotes learning.

WHY TEACH? YOUR FINAL WORD

In your journal or online at this textbook's website, respond to the following questions:

1. Which of the social problems discussed in this chapter do you consider to be the most serious? Why?

2. What experiences have you had that would assist you in meeting the challenges of these problems in our schools and society?

3. How do you think technology contributes to, or helps alleviate, some of the social problems discussed in this chapter?

KEY TERMS

at-risk students (95)
cyberbullying (115)
generational poverty (104)

socioeconomic status (101)
zero-tolerance policies (116)

FOR FURTHER INFORMATION

WEB RESOURCES

Children's Defense Fund. Available at **www .childrensdefense.org/**.

The Children's Defense Fund is a private nonprofit organization that advocates for children's needs. The website contains key facts about the condition of children in the United States, relevant legislation, and connections to other organizations advocating for children.

Striving to Reduce Youth Violence Everywhere (STRYVE). Available at **www.safeyouth.gov/Pages/ Home.aspx**.

This national initiative, led by the Center for Disease Control, takes a public health approach to preventing youth violence before it starts.

Safe and Drug Free Schools Program. Available at **www.ed.gov/about/offices/list/osdfs/index.html**.

A program of the U.S. Department of Education, the site contains descriptions of model programs, research findings, grant opportunities, and links to related sites.

PRINT RESOURCES

Lois Brown Easton, *Engaging the Disengaged* (Thousand Oaks, CA: Corwin Press, 2007).

With the goal of helping educators make positive connections with kids of all ages who are at risk of failing or dropping out, this book focuses on teacher–student relationships and teaching strategies for struggling learners.

Shane R. Jimerson and Michael J. Furlong, *The Handbook of School Violence and School Safety: From Research to Practice* (Mahwah, NJ: Lawrence Erlbaum Associates, 2006).

This 41-chapter handbook maps the full range of school violence issues, from bullying to serious physical assault. It reviews existing school violence prevention programs and the theories and research that guide them.

Walter B. Roberts, Jr., *Working with Parents of Bullies and Victims* (Thousand Oaks, CA: Corwin Press, 2007).

The author explores common concerns about bullying, provides sample dialogues written by parents of bullies and victims, and presents an eight-point plan for communicating with parents.

The Education CourseMate website for this text offers many helpful resources. Go to www.cengagebrain.com to access the TeachSource Video Cases and other TeachSource videos, flashcards, interactive quizzes, the eBook, reflection and enrichment activities, a state standards resource center, and other study aids.

5 what is taught?

(© Laura Dwight)

What knowledge is most worth knowing? What should be taught in the schools? The answers to these questions take the form of curricula, and they are often a source of tension among teachers, school boards, education professors, textbook publishers, policymakers, and parents. Currently, these groups are seeking to raise academic standards through common curricular emphases while also accommodating various cultural and ethnic groups' demands for representation in the curriculum.

Truth or Fiction?

T F More than four-fifths of the states have adopted a common core of academic standards in mathematics and language arts.

T F About two-thirds of American eighth-grade students score at the proficient or advanced level on the National Assessment of Educational Progress in mathematics and science.

FOCUS POINTS

- The school curriculum, which has evolved over time as a result of shifting purposes, consists of all organized and intended experiences of the student for which the school accepts responsibility.

- The present curriculum in most subject areas has been greatly influenced by the recent standards-based reform movement that identifies what students should know and be able to do in each subject area.

- The Common Core State Standards in English language arts and mathematics represents a major step in equalizing expectations about what children in the United States should know in these two subject areas.

- Textbooks have such a strong influence on what is taught in the classrooms that some people argue that such texts represent a national curriculum.

- Major innovative instructional approaches used across the curriculum include interdisciplinary teaching, cooperative learning, critical thinking and problem solving, writing across the curriculum, differentiated instruction, and block scheduling.

- The relevance of the schools' curricula to individual and societal problems is a continually debated issue.

T F Compared to other industrialized countries, the United States scores below average in tests of mathematics and science.

T F Differentiating instruction means assigning students of different abilities to classes with other students of comparable abilities.

T F Research studies indicate that the practice of tracking students into different ability-level groups is detrimental to low-ability students.

Baseball, debating, reading, and biology are all learned in school, along with love and tolerance, independence and frustration, mathematics and dramatics, values and ceramics, woodshop and poise, history and boredom, and computer science and leadership! Some are learned intentionally and others incidentally.

what is a curriculum?

We define the **curriculum** as all organized and intended experiences of the student for which the school accepts responsibility. In other words, the curriculum is not just the intellectual content of the subjects taught but also the methods used to teach them, the interactions that occur among people, and the school-sponsored activities that contribute to the "life experience." Educational theorists have identified several different kinds of curricula, including formal, extra, and hidden curricula. Let's briefly examine these different kinds of curricula.

The planned content and objectives of language arts, mathematics, science, and all other subject areas available to students constitute the *formal* or explicit curriculum. The states and the local school boards are responsible for determining the subjects that will be taught in this formal curriculum. Later in this chapter, we will examine the formal curriculum of the schools, including trends and controversies in each of the major content areas.

What students learn in the environment of the school extends beyond the planned curriculum of courses or subjects they will take, or the extracurricular activities in which they participate. That is, schools also teach a *hidden* or informal curriculum through which the classroom and school, as learning environments, socialize children to the values that are acceptable to the institution and society at large. The messages of the hidden curriculum are usually conveyed indirectly and deal with attitudes, values, beliefs, and behavior. These messages can either support or undermine the formal curriculum. When the hidden and formal curricula conflict, many observers believe the hidden curriculum carries more weight.

What are these attitudes and values, and how are they communicated to students? A major purpose of the hidden curriculum in schools has been to teach students the routines and values for getting along in school and in the larger society. Thus it tends to have a conservative bent, focusing on preserving the status quo. In the eyes of some critics, the hidden curriculum of the schools works against diversity, equity, and social justice.[1]

One researcher suggests that schools value several specific ways of thinking and behaving.[2] For example, schools emphasize compliant behavior as opposed to personal initiative. Students soon learn to give the teacher what she or he wants or expects. Reward systems used by schools teach students to "read" both the teacher and the system to determine just what is expected to get the grade, the teacher's attention, or the sticker with the smiling face. Similarly, competitiveness is learned through the examples of athletics, grading systems that compare students to one another, and ability grouping to separate students into classes according to their achievement. The many ways in which students learn what a school values include how the school allocates time to subjects of study, the rules established for the school, and even the architecture and furnishings of the school.

As a future teacher, you should be able to identify which rules of behavior, rituals and ceremonies, and accepted patterns of teacher and student interaction are communicated to students at schools you visit. Does the "climate" of the classroom and the school suggest warmth, support for diversity, and nurturing of individuals, or does it convey a mood of disinterest, regimentation, and antipathy among staff and students? Most important, what is the school's deeper message about the stance its students should take toward the current society?

PAUSE AND REFLECT

1. How can you determine the hidden curriculum of a school? Which clues would you look for?

2. Thinking back on your own schooling, can you identify some of the messages that you received from the hidden curriculum?

STANDARDS-BASED REFORM MOVEMENT

In this chapter, we examine the formal curriculum—those subjects that are taught in schools and some of the forces and instructional approaches that influence how they are taught. The typical school curriculum is a **subject-matter curriculum**, organized according to subject-matter divisions, and most of the efforts that go into curriculum development are still concentrated around traditional subject matter.

In Chapter 2, "What Is a School and What Is It For?" we discussed how the current curriculum is a *social bet* on which knowledge, skills, and attitudes the older generation thinks the young need to know to prosper, personally, and economically, in the twenty-first century. There is, by no means, a consensus among the parties involved in placing this social bet. In fact, curriculum decision making can resemble a battlefield in which conservatives and liberals, religious groups and agnostics, whites and people of color, and many other groups grapple to ensure that their beliefs and perspectives are represented in the school's curriculum. These curriculum battles at both state and local levels can be heated because those engaged believe there is a lot at stake—in essence, the future of the United States.

> *All that is taught is a commitment to what is thought valuable.*
>
> —R. S. PETERS,
> Expert on Moral Education

The strongest influence on a subject-matter curriculum over the last decade has been the *standards-based reform movement,* which is designed to promote academic excellence and equity. **Content standards** are statements of the subject-specific knowledge and skills that schools are expected to teach and that students are expected to learn.

In contrast to many other countries, the United States has traditionally had a decentralized system of state and local curricula. The national government has had little influence on what is taught in the nation's schools. During the 1980s and 1990s, however, spurred by concern about the United States' ability to compete with other countries in economic terms, a strong movement emerged toward national curriculum standards, national testing and assessment, and the establishment of national goals. A 1994 law, the Goals 2000: Educate America Act, codified eight national goals to guide future educational initiatives and funded different academic groups to develop national standards in the various subject-matter fields. The National Council of Teachers of Mathematics led the way in 1989 by publishing its mathematics standards; a decade later, most subject-specific teacher organizations had followed suit.

By 1996, these centralization efforts had lost steam, giving way to a growing consensus that the setting of standards and curriculum should remain the prerogative of individual states. Interestingly, many states continued to use the national standards developed by different academic groups in formulating their own state standards. (For examples of current common core and state standards in different subject matter and grade levels, see Table 5.1.) By the beginning of the twenty-first century, every state had developed its own standards for student learning, and most states backed up their new standards with rigorous accountability measures for both students and educators. The national No Child Left Behind Act of 2001 promoted accountability measures even more strongly, requiring states to administer annual, statewide assessments in reading and mathematics to all students in grades 3–8. For more on this law, see Chapter 11, "How Are Schools Governed, Influenced, and Financed?" and Chapter 12, "How Should Education Be Reformed?"

The standards movement was immediately surrounded by controversy. Some critics objected to the attention and money lavished on the development and assessment of standards instead of other pressing educational needs, such as habitable school buildings. Other critics were concerned with the testing that accompanied the state standards. Many state legislatures linked student passage of standards-based tests with "high-stakes" outcomes, including graduation from high school or school accreditation. Some legislatures made educators accountable for students' learning the standards and passing the assessment tests. Teachers' jobs and students' future education were suddenly at risk if students failed the tests, and educators and students alike felt much more pressure to succeed.

In spite of these criticisms, numerous polls show the public overwhelmingly supports the idea of high standards. Chapter 12, "How Should Education Be Reformed?" discusses the current status of national education standards and assessment in more detail.

Common Core State Standards

In 2010, led by the National Governors Association and the Council of Chief State School Officers, a set of common core standards was developed in English language arts and mathematics. The **Common Core State Standards** intend to define the knowledge and skills students should have within their K–12 education careers so that they will graduate high school able to succeed in entry-level, credit-bearing academic college courses and in workforce training programs. These standards addressed a weakness of the system of individual state standards, that is, the difficulty level of the standards and the tests used to assess them varied greatly. As a result, some states had high standards with lower pass rates, while other states had lower standards with higher pass rates. Many people believed that what students should

TABLE 5.1 Examples of Content Standards from the Common Core State Standards and Several States

Language Arts

Grade Level

3	Recount stories, including fables, folktales, and myths from diverse cultures; determine the central message, lesson, or moral and explain how it is conveyed through key details in the text. (CCSS-reading)
5	With some guidance and support from adults, use technology, including the Internet, to produce and publish writing as well as to interact and collaborate with others; demonstrate sufficient command of keyboarding skills to type a minimum of two pages in a single sitting. (CCSS-writing)
8	Analyze how particular lines of dialogue or incidents in a story or drama propel the action, reveal aspects of a character, or provoke a decision. (CCSS-literature)
11–12	Gather relevant information from multiple authoritative print and digital sources, using advanced searches effectively; assess the strengths and limitations of each source in terms of the task, purpose, and audience; integrate information into the text selectively to maintain the flow of ideas, avoiding plagiarism and overreliance on any one source and following a standard format for citation. (CCSS-writing)

Mathematics

Grade Level

2	Solve word problems involving dollar bills, quarters, dimes, nickels, and pennies, using \$ and ¢ symbols appropriately. Example: If you have 2 dimes and 3 pennies, how many cents do you have? (CCSS)
5	Find whole-number quotients of whole numbers with up to four-digit dividends and two-digit divisors, using strategies based on place value, the properties of operations, and/or the relationship between multiplication and division. Illustrate and explain the calculation by using equations, rectangular arrays, and/or area models. (CCSS)
7	Write verbal expressions as algebraic expressions and sentences as equations. (Virginia)
Algebra	Create equations in two or more variables to represent relationships between quantities; graph equations on coordinate axes with labels and scales. (CCSS)
9–11	Recognize the purposes of and differences among sample surveys, experiments, and observational studies; explain how randomization relates to each. (CCSS)

(Continued)

TABLE 5.1	Examples of Content Standards from the Common Core State Standards and Several States (Continued)

Science

Grade Level

2	Distinguish human body parts (brain, heart, lungs, stomach, muscles, and skeleton) and their basic functions. (Florida)
6–8	Explain how cells function as "building blocks" of organisms and describe the requirements for cells to live. (Illinois)
9–12	Build an understanding of the hydrosphere and its interactions and influences on the lithosphere, the atmosphere, and environmental quality. (North Carolina)
11	Identify the independent variables, dependent variables, and controls in an experiment. (Oklahoma)

Social Studies

Grade Level

4	Use different types of maps to solve problems (i.e., road maps—distance, resource maps—products, historical maps—boundaries, thematic maps—climates). (Arizona)
7	Describe the money and banking systems in various countries in the contemporary world. (Maryland)
9–12	Compare and contrast the experiences of different ethnic, national, and religious groups, including Native American Indians, in the United States, explaining their contributions to American society and culture. (New York)

Sources: Common Core State Standards Initiative and Education World. Available at www.corestandards.org/ and www.education-world.com/standards/.

learn in English language arts and mathematics shouldn't differ depending on the state they lived in. As a result, these Common Core State Standards were developed, and as of June 2011, four-fifths of the states had voluntarily adopted the standards. The plan is to have assessment tests and curricular materials, such as textbooks, aligned with the standards.

(T) F

More than four-fifths of the states have adopted a common core of academic standards in mathematics and language arts. States have adopted the Common Core State Standards in mathematics and language arts in order to have a common benchmark for achievement in these subject areas.

PAUSE AND REFLECT

1. Study the standards for a discipline area in which you are interested. (You can find standards websites listed at the end of this chapter.) Do you believe they are appropriate for the level of students you would like to teach? Why or why not?

2. Do you support the use of high-stakes tests to determine graduation from high school? Why or why not?

what is the present curriculum?

In looking at the courses of study prescribed by the 50 states, we will see that their similarities far outweigh their differences. Parts of this chapter discuss some reasons for this phenomenon, such as the influence of standards-based reform movements in the various states and the uniformity of available textbooks.

For now, we examine what is presently taught in elementary and secondary schools across the country. At both levels the curriculum is organized into subject-matter areas, which ordinarily are English language arts, mathematics, science, social studies, foreign languages, the arts, physical education and health, electives, and career and technical education. Most of the national organizations representing teachers of these various subject areas have developed content standards describing what elementary and secondary students should know and be able to do in each content area. The websites for these organizations and their respective content standards can be found in the For Further Information section at the end of the chapter.

> *I have often reflected upon the new vistas that reading opened to me....As I see it today, the ability to read awoke inside me some long dormant craving to be mentally alive.*
>
> —MALCOLM X (1925–1965),
> Political Sctivist

ENGLISH LANGUAGE ARTS

The *language arts* program seeks to develop in children the skills of reading, writing, speaking, and listening, as well as a knowledge of culture as represented in literature. The importance of language arts cannot be overemphasized because no subject can be successfully studied without adequate language skills. In elementary schools, most language arts programs focus on helping students develop written and oral communication skills, comprehension and problem-solving strategies, creativity, and appreciation for language and literature. At the secondary level, English courses focus on integration of the language arts using literature as the prime motivator.

Issues and Trends

Teachers today are selecting literature that is relevant to student interests yet representative of an accepted literary tradition; balancing classic literature selections with works by and about minority groups; instructing students in critical thinking; encouraging writing across the curriculum (discussed later in this chapter); integrating the various language arts by, for example, linking reading and writing together

or speaking, listening, and reading; composing and creating in new media forms such as video or online presentations; and maintaining a balance between composition and literature in the curriculum. Many English educators are chafing under the pressure to prepare students for state standards-based proficiency examinations that emphasize grammar, spelling, and basic skills, often to the exclusion of becoming involved with literature at a personal level. Adjusting the curriculum and use of standards for children from multiple language and cultural backgrounds constitutes a major challenge for language arts and English teachers.

Major disagreements exist in the field of reading education. The basic debate is whether reading instruction should emphasize the integration of language arts skills and knowledge in a literature-based approach, commonly known as the **whole language approach,** or whether it should focus on **phonics** instruction, an approach to reading that teaches the reader to "decode" words by sounding out letters and combinations of letters. The whole language approach to reading stresses that children should use language in ways that relate to their own lives and culture. Advocates of this approach tolerate the use of "invented spelling" by children because it is seen as part of a child's reading development and because it is feared that correcting a child's every spelling error will discourage the child from enjoying writing. Whole language teaching uses such common techniques as daily journal and letter writing, a great deal of silent and oral reading of real literature, and student cooperation. (The Video Case *Elementary Reading Instruction: A Balanced Literacy Program* provides a detailed example of a teacher who balances phonics and whole language approaches for teaching reading.)

During the 1970s and 1980s, whole language approaches to reading displaced the phonics approach in many schools. Eventually, discontent with declining reading scores in states that emphasized a whole language approach (notably California) spurred a renewed interest in phonics. In fact, the issue has become politically charged, with many conservatives supporting phonics and many liberals supporting whole language approaches. Although both the whole language and phonics camps have their strong believers, recent research concludes that it is important to teach explicit, systematic phonics within a context of meaningful literature.[3] *Phonemic awareness*—the understanding that sounds make up language—seems to be crucial in the development of good readers. Thus a balanced use of both approaches, rather than abandonment of one approach in favor of the other, seems to be the key to reading instruction. Many major publishers are now including both approaches in their reading series.

> ▶❚❚ **TeachSource VIDEO CASE**
>
> **Elementary Reading Instruction: A Balanced Literacy Program**
>
> Go to the Education CourseMate website to watch the video clips, study the artifacts in the case, and reflect on the following question:
>
> Which aspects of the language arts curriculum, as discussed in this chapter, are most likely to apply to the grade levels or subjects you would like to teach?

MATHEMATICS

Before the 1950s, schools emphasized student mastery of basic computational skills. In the 1960s, a new type of mathematics curriculum, known as the *new math,* emerged. It saw mathematics as a language that both communicates ideas about numbers and describes the quantitative aspects of ideas and objects. As a result, the new math stressed *structure* rather than drill and computational skills. The new math tended to be abstract, and for the average student its conceptual theories were of little practical use.

Today the traditional approach featuring drill and practice, computation, and memorization tends to be used in courses for non-college-bound students. College-bound students, after studying algebra and geometry, often take optional fourth-year courses that place strong emphasis on structure, learning by discovery, definitions, properties, sets, rigor, statistics, calculus, trigonometry, and other abstract concepts.

Issues and Trends

Mathematics at the elementary level emphasizes the use of hands-on manipulatives to aid students in learning about patterns in mathematics and the base-10 system. Mathematical reasoning and problem solving are emphasized. Experts in mathematics education are urging teachers to introduce multiple approaches for solving real-world problems. These emphases are consistent with the popular constructivist approach to learning, which is based on psychological theories suggesting that people must construct knowledge and meaning for themselves, rather than receiving knowledge passively from teachers or textbooks. (Constructivist approaches to learning are discussed further in Chapter 9, "What Are the Philosophical Foundations of American Education?" and Chapter 12, "How Should Education Be Reformed?") Teachers are being urged to focus on conceptual mathematics understanding before introducing procedural rules. This ordering reflects the growing body of research that suggests if students learn procedural rules before they learn mathematical concepts, they will score significantly lower than do students who learn concepts first.[4]

Calculators and computers have become common in the classroom, even at the elementary level, as mathematics education focuses less on computational skills and more on developing concepts, relationships, structures, and problem-solving skills. Moreover, the use of computers and computer programming in mathematics classes enhances the practical utility of mathematics instruction for many students. Not only do computers create interest in the curriculum, but students also receive valuable experience that may prove useful as they seek jobs. As described in Chapter 7, "What Should Teachers Know about Technology and Its Impact on Schools?" graphing calculators are seen as important tools to help students understand complex mathematical relationships.

Young children particularly benefit from the use of hands-on manipulatives to build basic understanding in mathematics.

(© BananaStock/Jupiterimages)

In addition to using technology and emphasizing problem solving, mathematics programs have been moving away from the traditional compartmentalization of arithmetic, algebra, geometry, calculus, and so on. As newer topics, such as probability, statistics, and computer science, are emphasized, course designers have begun to integrate a variety of mathematics skills and topics in one course or across several courses. The blending of mathematics with other subject areas, including consumer economics and personal finance, will continue as part of the trend toward broadening students' applications of their mathematical understanding and skills.

SCIENCE

Science in the elementary grades takes advantage of children's natural curiosity about the world around them—plants, seasons, color, light, sound, and animals. In the upper elementary and middle school grades, the curriculum expands to include weather and climate, the solar system, electricity, and health-related topics. The secondary school science curriculum is still centered on yearlong courses—general science, biology, chemistry, and physics—despite the efforts of some science educators to foster an integrated approach in which each of these science subjects is taught each year.

Issues and Trends

Two major questions drive science education reform: "Where will the next generation of scientists come from?" and "How can all students be prepared to make informed judgments about such critical and science-based issues as environmental pollution, energy sources, and biotechnology?"

For reformers, there has been both good news and bad news concerning science education in the United States. The bad news is that American youth do not know much science. The good news is that the country is reaching consensus about how to remedy the problem. The science curriculum has been undergoing dramatic redirection as a result of Project 2061 (named for the year in which Halley's comet is expected to return), an initiative of the American Association for the Advancement

Field trips to naturalist sites, such as aquariums, can both spur student interest in and enhance their knowledge of science.

(Image Source/Jupiterimages)

of Science. Inquiry-based learning and a hands-on approach are strong elements in these science reform efforts. Addressing both elementary and secondary science, the association's recommendations include the following:

- Reduce the boundaries between academic disciplines.

- Emphasize ideas and thinking skills rather than specialized vocabulary and memorization.

- Help students develop a cogent view of the world by including such key concepts and principles as the structure and evolution of the universe; basic concepts related to matter, energy, force, and motion; the human life cycle; medical techniques; social change and conflict; and the mathematics of symbols.[5]

> "
> *It is important for scientists to be aware of what our discoveries mean, socially and politically. It's a noble goal that science should be apolitical, acultural, and asocial, but it can't be, because it's done by people who are all those things.*
>
> —MAE JEMISON,
> Former NASA Astronaut

The work of Project 2061 appears to have had a strong effect on both the national standards for science education and many state curriculum frameworks, but it has been slow to change how science is actually taught in the schools. The No Child Left Behind legislation may also promote retention of the status quo because it required testing of students in science by 2007. The specter of these tests may influence teachers to use direct methods of instruction instead of the hands-on inquiries emphasized by Project 2061.

SOCIAL STUDIES

Social studies—the study of people and their ideas, actions, and relationships—is not a discipline in the same sense as mathematics or physics, although it draws on the various social sciences disciplines (history, geography, political science, economics, psychology, sociology, and anthropology), as well as on religion, literature, and the arts, for its content and methods of inquiry. (A *discipline* has been defined as an area of inquiry containing a distinctive body of concepts and principles, with techniques for exploring the area and for correcting and expanding the body of knowledge.)[6]

History has traditionally been the leading discipline of social studies at both the elementary and secondary levels. Although other disciplines have made some inroads in recent years, history remains the dominant focus in these schools. Recently, efforts have been made to restore geography to the social studies curriculum, following assessments that pointed out students' inability to locate countries on maps. Government is also a staple of the social studies curriculum. Ultimately, the social studies curriculum at both the elementary and secondary levels encompasses a hodgepodge of approaches. In many elementary schools in particular, social studies has been neglected in favor of efforts to meet the reading and mathematics testing requirements set out by the No Child Left Behind legislation.

Issues and Trends

A major debate is raging over whether the social studies curriculum overemphasizes European history and culture at the expense of Asian, African, and Latin American history and culture. We discuss this issue later in the chapter.

Civic learning, or **civic education**, is another issue gaining the attention of social studies educators. Advocates of this new focus call for courses that will acquaint a racially and culturally diverse student population with the heritage common to the American democratic tradition. These new courses would extend the basic study of American law and government to include trends in history, issues in contemporary society, and questions of character and values. Through critical study of case histories and current news reports, students would learn to apply principles of democracy to the everyday concerns they will face as citizens. Practical experiences in civic, cultural, and volunteer activities are also strongly recommended. The "new civics" courses may help unify educators who currently favor many different approaches to the teaching of social studies, including issues-centered, traditional, historical, critical thought, and character education approaches.

Standards have been developed by the various national organizations representing history, geography, economics, civics, and social studies. Unfortunately, these subject standards were developed independently of one another and do not relate to one another. The National Council for the Social Studies (NCSS) has articulated a framework that seeks to foster academic and civic competence by integrating the national standards across various social sciences. Ten themes are highlighted in the framework: (1) culture; (2) people, places, and environments; (3) individuals, groups, and institutions; (4) production, distribution, and consumption; (5) global connections; (6) time, continuity, and change; (7) individual development and identity; (8) power, authority, and governance; (9) science, technology, and society; and (10) civic ideals and practices.[7]

FOREIGN LANGUAGES

Compared with citizens in other nations, Americans are woefully unprepared to speak foreign languages. Approximately 44 percent of all students in U.S. public high schools are enrolled in a foreign language course, with Spanish and French being the most popular languages taken.[8] On the bright side, more elementary schools are offering foreign language programs in recognition of the ease with which young children learn foreign languages.

Issues and Trends

Foreign language departments in the public schools are trying to make the study of foreign languages more attractive by expanding their course offerings and integrating language study with concerns for international and multicultural education. Leaders in the field emphasize the cultural foundations of language, asserting that language study increases linguistic competence and cultural sensitivity. CD-ROMs and the Internet can assist students and teachers in gaining access to current materials from other countries and interacting with key-pals from other countries, thereby facilitating teaching and learning.

Early introduction of foreign languages continues to gain support, and concern about U.S. competitiveness in a global economy has led many business leaders and politicians to urge greater emphasis on foreign language instruction. For example, schools are seeing increased demand for instruction in Arabic and Chinese owing to U.S. involvement in the Middle East and the emergence of new trade opportunities in China.

Techniques used in elementary bilingual education—immersion, partial immersion, or the Foreign Languages in the Elementary Schools Program—have focused instruction on developing fluency in speaking, writing, and comprehension. Proficiency-oriented instruction, which focuses on what the learner can do with the language (rather than what the learner knows about the language), marks modern-day language teaching.

THE ARTS

The arts include visual arts, music, dance, and theater. Art and music in elementary schools are ordinarily taught by regular classroom teachers, although some schools hire specialist teachers in one or both areas. Dance and theater are largely ignored

Young children with musical interests typically receive instruction from private tutors and have opportunities to participate in recitals.

(iStockphoto.com/Joanne Green)

in elementary schools, despite the fact that children of this age are less inhibited and seem to enjoy these activities more than do secondary school students. The small amount of instruction provided in the arts for elementary students contrasts with high school offerings such as drama clubs, orchestras, bands, and dance groups. In most instances, instruction in music or dance during a child's elementary school years takes the form of private instruction outside the public school.

Issues and Trends

Programs in the arts have traditionally tended to emphasize the creation of an art object or the development of a performance. More recently, newer programs have emphasized aesthetic education and art as a way of knowing and perceiving the world.

Curriculum specialists have suggested integrating the arts with other subject matter to show the usefulness of the arts and to appeal to a broader range of intelligences. (See Chapter 3, "Who Are Today's Students in a Diverse Society?" for more on Howard Gardner's theory of multiple intelligences.) There is little doubt that the arts play a crucial role in the development of cultured, educated people and that they respond to a deep instinct in humanity. Even so, the arts remain an "endangered species," subject to extinction whenever budget cuts occur and when high-stakes assessments of standards in language arts, mathematics, and science dictate what teachers should emphasize in their classrooms.

> *The arts are the rainforests of society. They produce the oxygen of freedom, and they are the early warning system when freedom is in danger.*
>
> —JUNE WAYNE,
> Artist

PHYSICAL EDUCATION AND HEALTH

Physical education—education by and through human movement—contributes to physical fitness, skill and knowledge development, and social and psychological development. Currently, physical education curricula are designed to respond to four needs: (1) the need to develop aerobic capacity to maintain acceptable

Arts advocates support integrating the arts with the rest of the curriculum. These girls, for example, are studying *Macbeth.*

(© Bob Daemmrich)

cardiorespiratory efficiency, (2) the need to achieve appropriate levels of body fat, (3) the need to acquire strength to perform expected tasks of living, and (4) the need to achieve flexibility and abdominal strength to avoid lower back injuries. To address these needs, sports skills are alternated with fitness development through such activities as swimming, jogging, bicycling, yoga, and cross-country skiing. Students are given information on exercise and nutrition so they can understand how to balance caloric intake and maintain an appropriate body fat level. Physical education teachers are typically licensed for both elementary and secondary school teaching, but teachers usually seek out the age levels in which they are most interested. Physical education teachers are also trained to adapt activities for children with disabilities.

The health curriculum addresses such topics as injury prevention and safety, prevention and control of disease (including acquired immune deficiency syndrome [AIDS]), substance abuse, nutrition, family life (sexuality), consumer health, and mental and emotional health. More than most academic subjects, health education strives to change students' attitudes and behaviors to get them to take fewer risks and use more preventive measures. Concerns over childhood obesity have focused renewed attention on the school's role in helping to prevent obesity. In spite of this recent attention, many health educators express frustration that health is not identified as a critical component of the K–12 curriculum and that questions about health do not appear on high-stakes tests. Because health is not tested, it is not stressed in schools as much as health educators would like.

ELECTIVE COURSES

Most high schools today offer their students a number of options regarding the courses they take. Whereas the average high school student graduates with about 20 units (one yearlong course represents one unit), large high schools may offer as many as a hundred courses. The average student, then, will probably choose among optional courses according to individual interests and academic or career ambitions.

Examples of elective courses might include personal finance, art history, introduction to computers and applications, psychology, and anthropology.

Issues and Trends

Although college preparation has been the major goal of many high schools, efforts have increased recently to provide comprehensive programs for students not planning to attend college. This trend is especially evident in rural areas, where small, local high schools have often been replaced by comprehensive regional high schools. Some of the courses involved—such as technology education, distributive education, home economics, business education, and agriculture—are specifically vocational.

> *A liberal education is the only practical form of vocational education.*
>
> —JOHN HENRY CARDINAL NEWMAN (1801–1890),
> Roman Catholic Cardinal

Others—such as driver education and consumer education—have been added to the curriculum because of an obvious societal need or in response to student interest.

A disturbing trend for those who teach elective courses is the increase in requirements for graduation from high schools, which leaves less time for elective courses. Some argue that a common general education provides the best foundation for future work or academic study; others hope to maintain a large percentage of the curriculum as electives. These issues, when raised by teachers of elective courses, focus attention on the purpose of comprehensive schooling and on definitions of what is "basic."

CAREER AND TECHNICAL EDUCATION

The purpose of career and technical education (formerly called "vocational education") is to provide a foundation of skills that allow high school students to be gainfully employed after graduation. The subject areas most commonly associated with career and technical education are business, trade and industrial education, health occupations, agriculture, family and consumer sciences, marketing, and technology.

In recent decades, career and technical education has come under fire from those who note its inadequacy in preparing students for careers in high-technology fields or in the country's now-dominant service economy. Reformers urge teachers to help students see the relationships between the topics that they study and their applications in real-world contexts and to emphasize real-life problem solving.

Many School-to-Work programs, designed to help students develop skills and understandings that will prepare them to adapt to the changing needs of the workplace, have been developed. Such programs take many different forms, ranging from career academies that feature specialized career-oriented curricula in such areas as health professions, business, or law, to paid internships and co-op experiences. Schools work with local businesses to design courses and experiences that will prepare high school students for particular kinds of jobs that meet local business needs. Hundreds of thousands of businesses nationwide now participate in School-to-Work partnerships.

Issues and Trends

The emphasis on high-stakes academic assessments has contributed to a decline in the number of students who are enrolled in career and technical education, with 7.6 million secondary students in 2007–2008, a drop of 7 percent from the previous year.[10] In spite of this decline, in fiscal year 2007 the federal government distributed $1.29 billion dollars to the states to promote secondary and postsecondary career and technical education.[9] Some educators and labor officials urge that the line between academic and career and technical education be blurred and that all youngsters be provided with skills in traditionally "academic" subject areas, including mathematics, science, and English, as well as more applied learning experiences. Some states, such as Oregon, require all graduating high school students to have work experience and a career plan.

One form of work experience is apprenticeship programming, in which students receive on-the-job training with a company for four days a week and participate in classroom instruction on the fifth day. Such programs are designed to help youth make an easy transition from school to work.

Another promising trend is the development of "tech-prep" programs that link high school and postsecondary study. Tech-prep programs typically encompass the last two years of high school and the first two years of college (usually at a community college). They provide an attractive alternative for students who do not plan to attend a four-year college.

PAUSE AND REFLECT

1. What is your view of the issues and trends in your favorite subject field?

2. Are there any other developments that you would like to see?

---

assessing student academic performance

Both supporters and critics of contemporary curricula often focus on the results—that is, what students actually learn from their studies of language arts, math, science, and so forth. The methods of assessing results are themselves highly controversial and will be discussed further in Chapter 12, "How Should Education Be Reformed?" In this section, we look at the results of both national and international studies that attempt to judge the academic performance of U.S. students.

NATIONAL ASSESSMENT OF EDUCATIONAL PROGRESS

Since their introduction more than 30 years ago, National Assessment of Educational Progress (NAEP) assessments have been conducted periodically in reading, mathematics, science, writing, history, geography, and other fields. Administered to a representative national sample of students, the NAEP assessments are the primary source on educational achievement in the United States, and they have become known as "the nation's report card." Although almost all the states assess their students' progress on content standards, they do not use the same standards or the same tests, so until the Common Core State Standards in English language arts and mathematics, discussed earlier in the chapter, become operational, comparisons across states are mainly limited to the NAEP data. Assessment occurs at three grade levels fourth, eighth, and twelfth. Achievement levels are defined as *basic* (denoting partial mastery of knowledge and skills fundamental for proficient work), *proficient* (representing solid academic performance relative to challenging subject matter for the grade level), and *advanced* (signifying superior performance).

So how are American students doing? Figure 5.1 presents recent NAEP data on students' skills in mathematics, science,

T (F)

About two-thirds of American eighth-grade students score at the proficient or advanced level on the National Assessment of Educational Progress in mathematics and science.

Only 30 percent of eighth-graders scored at the proficient level in science, and 34 percent in mathematics.

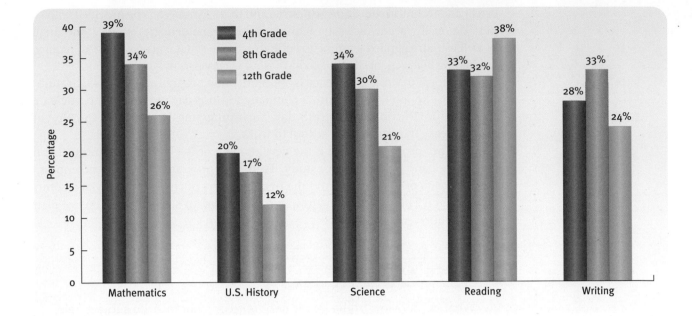

FIGURE 5.1 Percentage of Students Scoring at the Proficient or Advanced Level on NAEP Assessments in Various Subject Fields

Source: The Nation's Report Card. Available at http:nces.ed.gov/nationsreportcard.

reading, writing, and U.S. history. Thirty-four percent of fourth-graders, 30 percent of eighth-graders, and 21 percent of twelfth-graders scored at or above the proficient level in science.

Over the past decade, student achievement on the NAEP mathematics tests has improved significantly for all ages and all racial and ethnic groups, representing improvements of as much as one year's worth of mathematics knowledge since 1990 for fourth, eighth, and twelfth grades. However, for both fourth- and eighth-graders, less than 40 percent scored at or above the proficient level.

Reading scores, by contrast, have increased only slightly since 1994. The 2009 reading assessment of fourth-graders indicated that 67 percent of the students were at or above the basic level, whereas 33 percent were at or above the proficient level. For eighth-graders, the comparable figures were 75 percent and 32 percent.[11]

Further NAEP assessments reveal that despite improvements, U.S. students are still lacking in knowledge of history, geography, and civics. The 2010 history assessment showed a slight improvement in the basic scores for 4th and 8th graders, but not much change in the percentage of students scoring at the proficient or advanced level. Seventy-three percent of fourth-graders, sixty-nine percent of eighth-graders, and 45 percent of twelfth-graders achieved at the basic level. By comparison, 20 percent of fourth-graders, 17 percent of eighth-graders, and 12 percent of twelfth-graders reached the proficient or advanced level.[12] In the most recent geography tests, 21 percent of fourth-graders, 30 percent of eighth-graders, and 25 percent of twelfth-graders reached the proficient or advanced level. As these data indicate, in every subject field, a large majority of American students are failing to achieve the proficient level in the NAEP assessments.

Many of those students are members of minority groups. Black, Hispanic, and Native American students continue to score significantly lower than white and Asian American students on the NAEP assessments, although the gap between black and white students has been narrowing slightly. Males continue to outperform females to a slight extent on mathematics and science tests, whereas females significantly outperform males on the reading and writing tests.[13]

INTERNATIONAL COMPARISONS

Compared with the academic performances of students from other developed countries, U.S. students have tended to have average or below-average results. The **Trends in International Mathematics and Science Study (TIMSS)** tested the mathematics and science knowledge of students at three grade levels—fourth, eighth, and twelfth—in 1995, 1999, 2003, and 2007. Fourth-grade students from 36 countries and eighth-grade students from 48 countries were tested in 2007. TIMSS was the largest, most comprehensive, and most rigorous international comparison of education ever done.

T (F)

Compared to other industrialized countries, the United States scores below average in tests of mathematics and science.

According to the 2007 Trends in International Mathematics and Science Study (TIMSS), fourth- and eighth-grade U.S. students scored in the top third of all students in mathematics and science.

What were the results? In the 2007 mathematics testing, U.S. fourth-graders were outscored by students from 8 countries, while they outscored students from 24 countries, and were essentially the same as students from 4 other countries. The average mathematics score of U.S. eighth-graders was higher than those in 37 of the 47 other countries, lower than in 5 countries (all of them in Asia), and not measurably different from the average scores of students in the remaining 5 countries. The average U.S. fourth-grade science score was higher than those in 25 of the 35 other countries, lower than in 4 countries (all of them in Asia), and not measurably different from 6 countries. The average U.S. eighth-grade science score was higher than those in 35 of the 47 other countries, lower than in 9 countries (all of them in Asia or Europe), and not measurably different from 3 countries. Neither U.S. fourth- nor eighth-graders showed any detectable change in science achievement in 2007 compared to 1995, whereas both fourth- and eighth-graders showed improvement in mathematics over the same time period.[14]

Drawing achievement comparisons across different countries comes with many warnings. Countries participating in the TIMSS studies differ in many ways. Some have well-organized national curricula, complete with standard textbooks, whereas others have decentralized systems of education. Some of the countries are rich, whereas others are poor. Some have relatively uniform ethnicities, whereas others are very diverse. With these caveats, it is clear that compared to its performances in earlier TIMSS assessments, the United States has made some progress. Another international standardized assessment is the **Program for International Student Assessment (PISA),** which is administered every three years to 15-year-old students and tests knowledge in mathematics, science, and reading literacy. Administered in 2000, 2003, 2006, and 2009, the latest PISA assessment shows U.S. students scoring below average in mathematics and about average in reading and science literacy relative to their counterparts in other industrialized countries.[15]

A number of explanations have been proposed to explain the differences in mathematics and science achievement test scores between U.S. students and those from high-scoring countries, including cultural differences that result in greater value being placed on education in some countries than in the United States, lower expectations for U.S. students, and more U.S. students holding jobs. Moreover, the TIMSS studies revealed that the content of U.S. mathematics and science classes is not as challenging or focused as that of other countries. Many middle school students in the United States are still doing elementary arithmetic and introductory science while their international counterparts are studying algebra, geometry, physics, and chemistry. By the senior year of high school, many U.S. students have stopped taking math and science altogether. A large number of students never study algebra (37%), geometry (17%), trigonometry (92%), chemistry (34%), or physics (67%).[16]

Another factor may be the way that mathematics and science are taught in U.S. schools. TIMSS researchers have characterized the U.S. mathematics and science curricula as being "a mile wide and an inch deep"—that is, they cover many topics

Unlike these students, many American high school students spend little time in science laboratories conducting experiments.

(Monkey Business Images/Shutterstock.com)

but devote little time to any one topic. The United States is number one in the world in one category—the size of the textbooks, which tend to be encyclopedic rather than focused! U.S. teachers, supported by the textbooks they use, teach more topics but in less detail than teachers from high-scoring countries. Furthermore, compared with Japanese teachers, they focus much more on procedures and skills and much less on concepts, deductive reasoning, and understanding. Perhaps surprisingly, U.S. teachers assign more homework and spend more class time discussing it than do teachers from Japan and Germany.[17]

National and international assessments show that by high school, students often fall behind in learning sciences and mathematics. Unfortunately, most standardized assessments don't measure actual performances, such as these students conducting a science experiment, which can foster a deep understanding of key scientific concepts and methods.

The total amount of time students spend on academic pursuits also likely has an effect on their performance. At the high school level, U.S. students spend much of their school day in such nonacademic activities as counseling, gym, homeroom, driver training, pep rallies, and education about personal safety, AIDS, consumer affairs, and family life. An average of only 41 percent of secondary school time has to be devoted to core academic work to earn a high school diploma,[18] and that's probably the way most American parents want it. Both parents and students disavow a "nerdish" emphasis on strong academics in favor of preparing "well-rounded" individuals, making it difficult for schools to strengthen their academic requirements beyond a certain point. As long as a majority of Americans feel this way, it seems unlikely that we will see a radical restructuring of schools to emphasize strong academics.

There are several lessons to be learned from TIMSS and PISA. First, we need to continue setting clear, high standards for what students should know and be able to do in mathematics and science. Second, we need to align everything else we do with those standards: initial preparation of teachers, selection of texts and other curriculum materials, design of assessments, and continuing professional development of teachers. The difficulty is that, unlike most of the other countries participating in the TIMSS, the United States is highly decentralized in its educational decision making, which makes it extremely difficult to align the various educational components with the standards. Perhaps, the adoption of the Common Core State Standards in English language arts and mathematics by so many states will lead to a more unified approach to the teaching and study of these subjects.

PAUSE AND REFLECT

1. In your opinion, what would be the best ways to improve the performance of U.S. students in mathematics and science?

2. Do you think the United States should have a national curriculum, as do so many other industrialized nations? Why or why not?

additional influences on the curriculum

Although we can examine what is taught in the schools in terms of the subjects offered, the curriculum as students experience it is affected by a number of other factors. The individual teacher, of course, is a major variable in what students actually learn. This whole book is about you as that teacher. The classroom and school context also affect the delivery of the curriculum, as does the academic track to which the student is assigned. In this section, we will focus on two other major influences on the curriculum that is actually delivered to students: textbooks and innovative instructional approaches.

TEXTBOOKS

Education in the United States is constitutionally the domain of the various individual states—that is, the states are empowered to establish curricula and to organize and finance school systems. Unlike in many other countries, there is no national curriculum established by the federal government and implemented throughout the country. Even so, some educational observers assert that we do have a national curriculum of sorts, called *textbooks*. Several studies have concluded that most of what teachers and students do in classrooms reflects the specific textbooks used in those settings. For example, the objectives and goals for student learning are defined by the textbook (even the text you are now reading); learning activities and materials are provided to teachers as part of the textbook package; and tests geared to the textbook's objectives are usually prepared by the textbook publisher for the teacher's use.

States do exert some influence on the content of textbooks. Put bluntly, they cast their votes on that content through their decisions on whether to use a particular book. Critics, however, have noted the shortcomings of many adoption systems that allow too little time and too little money to support the selection of excellent texts by qualified personnel.

More than 20 states (mainly in the Sunbelt) have a textbook adoption process that involves reviewing textbooks according to state guidelines and then mandating either specific books that schools must use or lists of approved textbooks from which schools must choose. As part of this process, citizens have the opportunity to examine textbooks being considered for statewide adoption and to express their objections to particular books. Because textbook adoption is a multimillion-dollar business, publishing companies must be careful not to include material that influential groups and factions might find offensive and that might jeopardize their books' chances of adoption.

With the implementation of content standards in the various states, school boards and faculty responsible for adopting textbooks now examine how well textbooks address their state's standards. At one point in time, textbook publishers rarely customized their books for each state. Instead, they organized the books to meet the standards of those states that have a lot of children and that buy a lot of books. Publishers relied on the similarity of standards between states to assure that books geared toward the larger states' standards would meet at least some standards in nearly every state. As a consequence, standards set by large-population states such as Texas, California, and Florida greatly influenced the content of textbooks produced by commercial publishers. Today, however, textbook companies are more able to customize textbooks for each state. With the adoption of the Common Core State Standards in English language arts and mathematics by many states, a common set of textbooks are likely to be developed to address the standards in these two subject areas.

A wave of educational reform is directing attention to the quality of the textbooks that determine the curriculum. Some critics claim that texts are "dumbed down" to meet readability requirements; the writing style, designed to meet arbitrary criteria for lengths of words and sentences, can be awkward and stiff. Others believe that textbooks try to include too much material and so lack depth of coverage, a criticism certainly supported by findings from the TIMSS. Critics also complain about typical textbook emphases on skills development instead of stimulation of students' interest and intellect; these emphases, they say, create texts that are dry, barren of ideas, devoid of concepts, and lacking in the vigorous writing style that stirs students to comprehend and retain what they read. Many educational commentators suggest that teachers and curriculum developers rely too much on textbooks and not enough on primary sources.

Because what is taught in public schools touches people's hearts and minds, the content of the textbooks arouses political passions. One such controversy arose in Texas in 2010 when the elected Texas Board of Education voted (10–5 along Republican/Democratic lines) to make over 100 changes in the state's history and economic textbooks that will put a conservative stamp on the textbooks. The changes stress the superiority of American capitalism, question the Founding Fathers' commitment to a purely secular government, and present Republican political philosophies in a more positive light. One of the changes included downgrading the role Thomas Jefferson played in our nation's founding, apparently because his secular views (he coined the phrase, "separation between church and state") conflicted with the more Christian-oriented views of a majority of the Texas board. Conservative members of the board believed that the history textbooks being used in Texas classrooms reflected a liberal bias by promoting multiculturalism, secular values, and a negative interpretation of American history, at the expense of Christian values, the importance of free enterprise, and a belief in the exceptionality of America. The actions by the board provoked much criticism and discussion around the United States. What is clear is that what states choose to include in their textbooks can be very controversial and influenced by political and religious perspectives.

A recent modification of the traditional textbook involves the use of electronic materials. For example, the University of California–Berkeley developed the Full Option Science System (FOSS) for K–8 science, which incorporates CD-ROMs and online interactive activities both at school and at home. (See the FOSS website at www.fossweb.com/). Several states have adopted this system as an option for school districts to use in their science curriculum. The online software is available in both Spanish and English. Besides keeping information current, the technology provides access to rich materials and interesting projects such as using interactive and video elements to engage in or observe scientific experiments that would be impractical to conduct in the classroom. The technology also provides alternative assessments by permitting students to answer questions and follow directions on the disk or online.

Whether electronic media will make major inroads into textbook adoptions in other subjects remains to be seen. Conventional textbooks, although they lack technological pizzazz and become outdated more quickly, have some distinct advantages over their electronic rivals: books are more portable and they do not break down. One thing appears certain: textbooks, whether in paper or electronic form, are one of the major determinants of U.S. elementary and secondary school curricula, and that situation does not appear likely to change in the near future.

▶❚❚ TeachSource VIDEO CASE

Reading in the Content Areas: An Interdisciplinary Unit on the 1920s

Go to the Education CourseMate website to watch the video clips, study the artifacts in the case, and reflect on the following questions:

1. How do these teachers achieve the advantages associated with interdisciplinary instruction, such as making subject matter less fragmented? Do they succeed in making the students feel that learning about the 1920s is relevant to their lives?

2. For you as a teacher, what would be the advantages and challenges of planning and implementing an interdisciplinary curriculum or project?

3. Which kind of arrangements or support would help with implementing interdisciplinary curricula? For example, would you prefer working with another teacher or working alone to prepare interdisciplinary projects?

INNOVATIVE INSTRUCTIONAL APPROACHES

Curriculum and instruction are intimately related, and the instructional approaches that teachers use clearly shape how students experience the curriculum. Although these approaches have remained amazingly constant since the 1890s, especially at the secondary level, some alterations to traditional teacher-centered instruction have taken hold.[19] Educators are constantly searching for new ways to deliver the curriculum more effectively. All of the trends discussed here can be used in a variety of subject areas with students of many age and ability levels. We will look at six nontraditional instructional influences on the curriculum: interdisciplinary curriculum, cooperative learning, critical thinking and problem solving, writing across the curriculum, differentiated instruction, and block scheduling.

Interdisciplinary Curriculum

Students—and particularly secondary students—are often critical of the traditional curriculum, which seems irrelevant to their lives outside of school. They often fail to see how English, history, mathematics, and science relate to them. The curriculum they experience is fragmented and isolated. In one language arts class, the teacher gave the dates of a famous author's birth and death, and asked the students to figure out how old the author was when she died. Silence fell over the room as students pondered the question. Finally, one student said, "It's hard to do math in English class." Students have learned to segment and separate their knowledge into compartments because of the way we teach content.

Many teachers agree. Noting that the real world is not organized by disciplines but contains situations and problems that cut across disciplinary boundaries, these teachers are returning to an old idea of organizing and teaching the curriculum in an integrated and interdisciplinary fashion. Although numerous definitions of **interdisciplinary curriculum**, or **integrated curriculum**, exist, both terms are often used synonymously to mean a curriculum that cuts across subject-matter lines to focus on comprehensive life problems or broad-based areas of study that bring together the various segments of the curriculum in meaningful association.

Many approaches to developing integrated, interdisciplinary curricula are possible. One of the simplest is for two or more teachers from different disciplinary backgrounds to plan and teach their respective subjects together, seeking different disciplinary perspectives on a particular unit of study. For example, an English teacher and a social studies teacher might team together to integrate the study of the nineteenth century by examining the history and literature of that period. (The Video Case on page 143, *Reading in the Content Areas: An Interdisciplinary Unit on the 1920s,* shows how two high school teachers combine social studies and literature instruction.)

Another approach is *thematic* in nature. In this case, a cross-departmental team chooses themes as overlays to the different subjects. "Inventions," for example, is a theme that could combine science and mathematics in the study of machines and their mechanics, reading and writing about inventors in language arts, and designing and building models in industrial arts. Another example, "health," would permit a number of different subjects to be addressed in an effort to better understand specific health topics (Figure 5.2). Yet another thematic approach

FIGURE 5.2
Sample Interdisciplinary Approach

Source: Joan Palmer, "Planning Wheels Turn Curriculum Around," *Educational Leadership* 49 (October 1991), p. 58. © 1991 by ASCD. Used with permission.

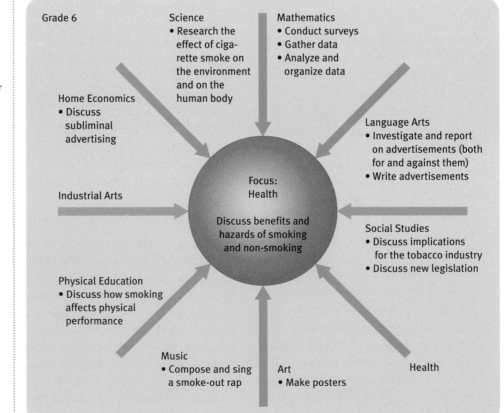

is to identify concepts that apply in different subjects, such as examining how symmetry, patterns, evidence, and proof apply in mathematics, art, science, social studies, and language arts.

Proponents of the interdisciplinary curriculum argue that its merits far outweigh the extra expenditure of time and effort required to implement this approach. Students benefit by experiencing coherence in the curriculum and connections to real-world situations. Critical thinking and problem-solving skills are developed within specific contexts rather than in isolation. Teachers benefit by having students who enjoy learning and by working collaboratively with other teachers.

Although interdisciplinary teaching is enjoying a resurgence of popularity, particularly in middle schools, the disciplinary approach to curriculum in the secondary schools is well entrenched and is being reinforced by the development of national standards within each discipline rather than across disciplines. The tension between the disciplinary and interdisciplinary approaches to curriculum development will likely persist for some time. For more on interdisciplinary curricula, see the For Further Information section at the end of the chapter.

Cooperative Learning

Cooperative learning in classrooms is another trend influencing what is taught in the schools. Those who have analyzed the "hidden" curriculum (i.e., the implicit teachings that schools communicate to their students) have observed that U.S. schools tend to reward competitive or individual accomplishment more than cooperative effort.[20] Arguing for cooperative learning techniques, some educators maintain that such techniques can change the ways students learn, their attitudes toward what they are taught, and their perceptions of themselves and others.

What is cooperative learning? (See the Video Case *Cooperative Learning at the Elementary Level: Jigsaw Model* for one model of cooperative learning.) It takes many different forms, but all involve students working in small groups or teams to help one another learn academic material. Cooperative learning strategies are organized, highly structured methods that usually involve formal presentation of information, student practice and coaching in learning teams, individual assessment of mastery, and public recognition of team success. Table 5.2 summarizes several such strategies.

By their structure and individual assignments, cooperative learning strategies avoid the problem of letting the hard-working students in the group do all the work while the other students get a free ride. Such strategies have proven successful across grade levels and in different subjects. Although the effectiveness of cooperative learning—particularly for achievement outcomes—depends on the particular approach used, overall positive effects have been found on such diverse outcomes as self-esteem, intergroup relations, acceptance of academically slower students, attitudes toward school, and ability to work cooperatively.[21]

▶❚❚ TeachSource VIDEO CASE

Cooperative Learning at the Elementary Level: Jigsaw Model

Go to the Education CourseMate website to watch the video clips, study the artifacts in the case, and reflect on the following questions:

1. How does the structure of the jigsaw method help avoid the problem of letting some students in a group "coast" while others do the hard work?

2. View the bonus video of a student from an expert group teaching his home group. How could the teacher encourage student "experts" to vary their techniques, perhaps using some of the options included in the "Ways to Teach" list shown among the Classroom Artifacts with the case?

3. Which of the outcomes listed in this chapter (achievement, self-esteem, and so on) seems most likely to be enhanced by this project? Why?

TABLE 5.2 Selected Cooperative Learning Strategies

	Name	Brief Description	Function
1. Student team learning	a. Student Teams Achievement Divisions (STAD)	Four-member mixed learning teams. Teacher presents lesson; students work within teams to make certain all team members have mastered the objectives. Students take individual quizzes. Points awarded based on improvement over previous quizzes.	Four-member mixed learning teams. Teacher presents lesson; students work within teams to make certain all team members have mastered the objectives. Students take individual quizzes. Points awarded based on improvement over previous quizzes.
	b. Teams–Games–Tournament (TGT)	Uses same teacher presentations and teamwork as in STAD but replaces quizzes with weekly tournaments.	Same as STAD.
2. Jigsaw		Each student on team becomes an "expert" on one topic by working with members from other teams assigned the same topic. Upon returning to the home team, each expert teaches the group, and students are all assessed on all aspects of the topic.	Acquisition and presentation of new material, review, informed debate. Promotes interdependence, status equalization. Used in social studies and other subjects where learning from text is important.
3. Jigsaw 2		Same as Jigsaw, except instead of each student being assigned a particular section of text, all students read a common narrative. Each student receives a topic on which to become expert.	Same as Jigsaw.

(Continued)

	Name	Brief Description	Function
4.	Group investigation	Students work in small groups using cooperative inquiry, group discussion, and projects. Students form two- to six-member groups. Groups choose subtopics from a unit, break subtopics into individual tasks, and prepare group reports.	Development of planning, investigating, and reporting skills.
5.	Think–pair–share	Students think by themselves on a topic provided by the teacher, then pair with another student to discuss it, after which they share their thoughts with the class.	Generation and revision of hypotheses, inductive reasoning, deductive reasoning. Fosters participation and involvement.

TABLE 5.2 Selected Cooperative Learning Strategies (Continued)

(© Cengage Learning 2013)

The success of cooperative learning strategies comes from three important characteristics: group goals, individual accountability, and equal opportunity for success. (Watch the Video Case *Cooperative Learning: High School History Lesson* on p. 148 to see how a high school teacher uses an informal model of cooperative learning.)

- *Group goals* usually take the form of rewards based on team success in academic tasks. To achieve team success, each member of the group must coordinate the completion of his or her assigned task with the work of the other group members; each team member is indispensable.

- *Individual accountability* involves assessing each student's mastery of the content, with the results usually given back to the group and the individual. Teammates practice together and support and coach one another, but people are assessed in the usual ways. The team's success is often judged by how much each team member improves relative to the earlier assessment. Even the lowest-achieving student can contribute to the team's success by improving over the first assessment.

- *Equal opportunities for success* are ensured by team scoring systems that are based on individual improvement over prior performance. This feature reinforces the perception that student effort—not just innate ability—counts.

Cooperative learning has been found to be a particularly effective instructional tool in teaching at-risk students who benefit from immediate feedback for their learning attempts. It works well because it offers students more involvement in and control over their learning activities. As many schools attempt to do away with tracking (discussed later in this chapter) and to encourage heterogeneous grouping, cooperative learning provides a means to make all students feel they are essential to the classroom learning process. It enables students to recognize that all of them, when given a chance, have something to contribute to everyone's learning. Cooperative learning has quickly become a major instructional method in the United States, particularly in elementary and middle schools.

Critical Thinking and Problem Solving

A growing interest in helping students become better thinkers and problem solvers is evidenced by the multitude of publications, workshops, curriculum study institutes, journal articles, and course requirements addressing the topics of thinking and problem solving. Although many people favor teaching it, definitions of **critical thinking** vary widely. At the heart of all these definitions, however, is the intent to help students evaluate the worth of ideas, opinions, or evidence before making a decision or judgment.

Some educators favor approaches that help students detect bias or identify a wide range of propaganda strategies. The teaching of philosophy is also proposed as a way to provide criteria by which students can judge others' thinking. Still other approaches identify component skills (e.g., making inferences, testing hypotheses, and identifying assumptions) within the realm of critical thinking and advocate direct instruction in each skill. Socratic questioning (a style of questioning that elicits a clear expression of truth that was implicitly known by the person being questioned) is also suggested as a way to teach the art of thinking.

Problem solving is an element of critical thinking that has attracted increased attention and seen increased use in recent decades. **Problem solving** generally refers to the process of either presenting students with a problem or helping them identify a problem and then observing and helping them become aware of the conditions, procedures, or steps needed to solve it. The problems may range from putting puzzles together, to solving simple science or mathematics problems, to solving more complex mental, logical, or social dilemmas. A problem may be presented as an individual activity, such as when independently predicting outcomes in a reading passage, or may be used with a group, such as when simulating wilderness "survival" activities that require group cooperation.

Despite the many possible ways of teaching problem solving, the emphasis in each case is on the *process* of reaching a solution. Proponents of problem-solving instruction point out that if students become more aware of their mental processes, they will be able to exercise greater control over their own learning and thinking in future situations. In group problem-solving activities, students may also benefit from interacting with one another and from being exposed to the variety of approaches used by peers in solving the same problem.

What is the role of critical thought in the curriculum? At one time, educators debated whether students could best learn effective thinking through separate courses or as an integrated part of every course. There is now widespread agreement that while students do benefit from stand-alone courses in critical thinking, they must also learn to think within the context of each discipline. The integration of critical thinking into subject areas appears to be the direction in which teaching is heading, especially given that the curricula of the schools are already so crowded. As

Many highly intelligent people are poor thinkers. Many people of average intelligence are skilled thinkers. The power of a car is separate from the way the car is driven.

—EDWARD DE BONO,
British Physician and Author

VOICES from the classroom

Triumphs and Setbacks

Judy Boch graduated from the University of Arizona and obtained a master's degree in educational leadership at Northern Arizona University. She has spent a total of 22 years as a classroom teacher and 11 years working as an instructional coach. Judy is currently an Instructional Coach at Dysart Unified School District in Surprise, Arizona.

Up until the time he came to me as a second-grader, Raul's content education had been conducted in Spanish. Only in the latter part of first grade did he begin to learn in English. My second-grade classroom was labeled "English as a Second Language" (ESL), but I spoke no Spanish. The only Spanish that Raul heard in the classroom was from a one-hour Spanish aide and from the other children.

I wondered how I was going to reach this obviously bright and talented boy. This was soon made clear during one of our first math lessons. Having been trained in cognitively guided instruction, I gave the children a story problem and asked them to solve it with their own invented strategies. Although Raul couldn't, at first, read the problem, another child translated for him. Raul came alive! He drew pictures and used numbers to model his strategy to the problem. I knew I was taking a risk that day when I asked Raul to share his strategy with the other students. I wondered whether I had made a mistake when he grasped for words to explain. But explain he did! He drew his picture on the board, labeled it with numbers, and wrote a number sentence to match the problem. In short phrases, he shared his thinking sequentially.

Raul blossomed after that day. His English began to improve as he continually volunteered to share his thinking in mathematics. In his math journal, Raul wrote: "Math is my favrit becuz I get to be the techer. It makes me feel prowd."

Unfortunately, Raul's excitement has not continued. This year, as a lead teacher on my campus, I visit Raul's classroom once a week. He is learning math through more conventional methods using the traditional algorithms. It is painful to see him using traditional methods that he really doesn't understand and that take him so much longer than his invented strategies. His teacher says he is becoming unfocused and having discipline problems. Although his English has improved considerably, math is no longer his great equalizer or passion. My only hope is that Raul rediscovers his love and enthusiasm for mathematics. For if he does not, we have failed him.

the Voices from the Classroom feature suggests, most students, including those who do not speak English as a first language, can benefit from instruction that emphasizes critical thinking and problem solving.

Writing Across the Curriculum

The **writing across the curriculum** movement has been a center of curricular interest for a growing number of educators since the 1960s. Also called *writing to learn* or *writing to learn in the content areas*, this instructional approach emphasizes writing as a tool for students' learning, not only in English classes but in all subject areas.

How can teachers use the act of writing as the medium through which subject-matter learning takes place? Students in social studies classes may be asked to take a written stand on school issues, moral questions, or political problems. Music students may write their own ballads. Students in science classes may work together to predict the future in story form or to write futuristic headlines and news features. Children in math classes can create their own word problems and keep records of what they have learned, their questions, and their observations. Art classes can write scripts for slide shows and cartoon strips or create illustrated guides and storybooks. Teachers at many grade levels and in many subject areas can ask students to keep informal journals or "learning logs." In these journals, students record their responses to what they have read and studied and can then interact both with text material and with the teacher's responses to their queries and remarks. These are just a few examples of the many ways teachers use writing as a thinking tool for students to use and apply their knowledge in the content areas.

Differentiated Instruction

The term **differentiated instruction** is relatively new on the educational scene, though its practice has been around for a long time. In its simplest form, differentiated instruction tries to respond to student variance rather than adopting a standardized approach to teaching that assumes all learners in a class are essentially alike. The academic diversity of students in today's classrooms is growing, and one instructional approach won't work for all students. (See Chapter 3, "Who Are Today's Students in a Diverse Society?" for more discussion of the various kinds of diversity found in modern-day U.S. schools.) As schools try to ensure that all students learn what is expected of them, teachers recognize that they need to customize their instruction techniques to meet individual student needs. That is, teachers are trying to tailor their instruction to provide appropriate challenges for gifted students, students who lag behind, and students who fall in between the two extremes. (See the Video Case *Academic Diversity: Differentiated Instruction* to see how one teacher adapts a writing workshop to the needs and interests of her students.)

Differentiated instruction is a teaching philosophy based on the premise that teachers should adapt instruction to student differences in reading readiness, learning preferences, and interests. According to Carol Tomlinson, a national expert on differentiated instruction, teachers can differentiate three aspects of the curriculum: content, process, and products.[22]

- *Content* refers to the concepts, principles, and skills that teachers want students to learn. All students should be given access to the same core content, but teachers can provide different means (e.g., texts, lectures, and demonstrations) to give students access to skills and knowledge.

- *Process* refers to the activities that help students make sense of and own the knowledge being taught. Teachers can vary the activities to provide some students with access to more complexity and others with more support, depending on their readiness levels, interests, or learning preferences.

- *Product* refers to culminating projects that students develop to demonstrate and extend what they have learned. The products assigned can vary depending on students' interests or learning preferences. For example, some students might prefer to work

T (F)

Differentiating instruction means assigning students of different abilities to classes with other students of comparable abilities. Differentiating instruction means adapting instruction to accommodate difference in student reading levels, interests, and learning preferences.

▶❚❚ TeachSource VIDEO CASE

Academic Diversity: Differentiated Instruction

Go to the Education CourseMate website to watch the video clips, study the artifacts in the case, and reflect on the following questions:

1. As noted in the video and viewing questions, one key to differentiating instruction effectively is getting to know your students well. How will you, as a teacher, do this?

2. How do posters and handouts, like the artifacts included in this case, help provide "access points" to a lesson for students who need extra help?

3. In addition to those strategies listed in this chapter and shown in the Video Case, what might be some other strategies for differentiating instruction?

> *Any subject can be taught effectively in some intellectually honest form to any child at any stage of development.*
>
> —JEROME BRUNER,
> Psychologist

as members of a group while producing a play about the topic being studied, whereas others might prefer to work alone while writing a term paper.

Differentiating content, process, and product for students requires teachers to know their students, their subject, and their materials. (See Table 5.3 for some strategies for differentiating instruction.) There is no formula for differentiation—no single

TABLE 5.3 Strategies for Differentiating Instruction

Many teachers accept the desirability of differentiating instruction but don't know how to go about doing it. Here are some of the many strategies that teachers can use to avoid lockstep instruction.

Stations	The teacher sets up different spots in the classroom where students work on different tasks at the same time. This strategy encourages flexible grouping because not all students have to go to all stations all the time.
Compacting	The teacher assesses students before beginning a unit of study so they won't have to waste time learning something they already know.
Complex Instruction	This approach uses challenging materials, open-ended tasks, and small instructional groups. Teachers circulate among the groups as they work, asking questions and probing student thinking.
Choice	The teacher writes work assignments on cards that are placed in Boards hanging pockets. The teacher asks a student to select a card from a particular row of pockets, which gives the student some choice within circumscribed options. Each row represents work at different levels of complexity.
Problem-Based Learning	This approach places students in an active role of solving problems.
Entry Points	Using some of the multiple intelligences identified by Howard Gardner (see Chapter 3, "Who Are Today's Students in a Diverse Society?"), students explore a given topic through as many as five avenues: narrational (presenting a story), logical–quantitative (using numbers or deduction), foundational (examining philosophy and vocabulary), aesthetic (focusing on sensory features), and experiential (hands-on).
Orbital Studies	Students conduct independent investigations, generally lasting several weeks, around some aspect of the curriculum. Students select their own topics and work with the guidance of the teacher.
4MAT	Teachers plan some lessons for each of four learning preferences (mastery, understanding, personal involvement, and synthesis) over the course of several days on a given topic. Each learner can approach the topic through his or her preferred modes of learning. (See Chapter 3, "Who Are Today's Students in a Diverse Society?" for more information about learning preferences.)

Source: Carol Ann Tomlinson, *The Differentiated Classroom: Responding to the Needs of All Learners* (Alexandria, VA: Association for Supervision and Curriculum Development, 1999).

best way to address all possible student differences. Rather, teachers must make a commitment to start with students and to make a match between learner and the material to be learned. The goal, however, is always the same: to maximize the capacities of each student.

One popular way of providing differentiation at the early childhood or elementary school level is through the **project approach**, which entails an in-depth investigation of a real-world topic worthy of children's attention and effort. The project approach uses a set of teaching strategies to guide children through their investigation. The project may involve a whole class or a subgroup of students.

Phase one of the project approach starts with an opening event (story, video, unusual object) designed to capture the students' attention. The teacher then gets the children to map out what they already know about the event and generate questions that they would like to investigate during the project.

In phase two, children participate in some type of field trip to investigate the topic and to try to answer their questions. A debriefing takes place after the field trip, and sometimes an outside expert is invited to share his or her knowledge about the topic.

In phase three, a culminating event takes place, to which parents, other classes, and other interested parties may be invited. Children also have the opportunity to personalize their knowledge through differentiated imaginative activities such as dramatic renditions or story writing.

Block Scheduling

A report by the National Education Commission on Time and Learning, an independent panel temporarily convened by the U.S. Congress, stated that time is "the missing element in the school-reform debate." The report urged that the traditional six-hour school day and 180-day year "be relegated to museums as an exhibit of our education past." Advising schools to be less rigid in how they use time, the report also recommended use of block scheduling and extension of the school year.[23] As the accompanying feature describes, in another innovative twist on the traditional school year, some schools are trying out **looping**, a practice that lets teachers stay with the same students for more than a single year.

Block scheduling is a "less is more" approach in which students take fewer classes each school day but spend more time in each class. In theory, block scheduling carves out more time for instruction by reducing the amount of time students spend going from class to class and the time teachers spend taking roll and settling down classes. This strategy was relatively rare two decades ago, but its popularity grew dramatically during the 1990s. Although block scheduling is not really an instructional approach, it does allow and encourage teachers to use cooperative learning, interdisciplinary teaching, critical thinking and problem solving, writing across the curriculum, differentiated instruction, and other innovative instructional strategies.

In the trimester approach to block scheduling, classes last 80 minutes; instead of students taking the traditional six classes per semester, they take four classes each trimester. Courses that once lasted a semester now last a trimester, and courses that once lasted a year now run for two trimesters. In the 4 × 4 plan, students take four 90-minute classes each day and complete them in a semester rather than a full year. In the A/B plan, students take eight 90-minute classes each semester, but classes meet every other day—four on day A and four on day B. Other models of block scheduling are also possible.

Research on block scheduling is relatively scarce, and the few findings that do exist are often contradictory. Anecdotal evidence indicates that students like the new schedule if teachers are good and keep students' interest piqued through various

looping (multiyear teaching)

Suppose someone offered you an educational innovation with the following benefits: better teacher–student relationships, improved teacher job satisfaction, extra teaching time, a richer curriculum, increased student attendance, increased student development in social skills and a sense of community, and easy implementation at very little cost. Sound good? Proponents of an old but increasingly common practice called looping claim these outcomes as being among its benefits.

Looping (also known as multiyear teaching) is a simple concept in which the teacher is promoted with his or her students to the next grade level and stays with the group for several years, typically two years but sometimes as long as five years. Although not much quantitative research exists on the benefits of looping, qualitative research supports the benefits just mentioned. By keeping the same group of students together with the same teacher, everyone gets to know one another well and feel comfortable in the group. Teachers get to know their students' strengths, weaknesses, and interests. Forging bonds of trust and understanding between teachers and students is at the heart of looping. Teachers who loop have fewer transitions to make at the beginning of the school year and can introduce curriculum topics right away at the start of the second year. They don't have to spend precious instructional time at the beginning of the new school year to establish classroom routines and expectations. Instead, teachers can spend the gained time exploring curriculum topics in greater detail.

Administrators argue that looping isn't for everyone, so implementation should be on a voluntary basis. Some administrators urge teaming teachers to implement looping. In that way, students can benefit from different teacher strengths, and if a student has a problem with one particular teacher, another teacher can compensate.

Sources: "Looping—Discovering the Benefits of Multiyear Teaching," *Education Update* 40, (March 1998), pp. 1, 3–4; *Looping: Supporting Student Learning through Long-Term Relationships*, Themes in Education (Brown University: LAB–Northeast and Islands Regional Educational Laboratory, 1997); Cheryl A. Franklin and Mary S. Holm, "Looping," in James W. Guthrie, ed., *Encyclopedia of Education*, 2nd ed. (New York: Macmillan Reference USA, 2003), pp. 1520–1522.

learning activities. Conversely, if teachers rely primarily on lectures, which are longer under block scheduling, students tend to complain. The key to success seems to be for teachers to change their teaching models so as to make better use of the additional time they have each day the class meets.

Many teachers seem to like the block schedules because they have fewer students each term (e.g., 90 instead of 150); as a result, they get to know those students better. In addition, block scheduling allows teachers more in-school preparation time. Teachers of certain disciplines such as music and foreign languages tend to dislike models of block scheduling that don't allow students to work each day on those subjects, arguing that developing skills in their subjects requires daily practice. By contrast, science teachers tend to like block schedules that allow for longer laboratory periods. Some parents and students are concerned about the problems linked to student absences (such as for illness), which in some forms of block scheduling mean they miss more material and find it difficult to make it up.

> **PAUSE AND REFLECT**

Have you had personal experience with any of the instructional approaches described in this section? If so, were they positive or negative? What made them so?

current curriculum controversies

Given the highly pluralistic society and many different educational philosophies represented in the United States today, it is little wonder that the questions of how and what schools should teach generate much controversy and debate. In this section, we briefly touch on two of the most highly charged curriculum issues: the question of whether the curriculum should strive to promote American unity or to recognize the diversity of the nation, and the issue of placing students in different "tracks" of study.

CORE VERSUS MULTICULTURAL CURRICULUM

American schools have traditionally played a central role in instilling the ideas and attitudes that maintain our pluralistic society as "one nation." They have helped weave the many ethnic and religious strands together to make a seamless national garment—at least that's the theory. Questions are now being raised about whether schools today provide a shared understanding of our culture, history, and traditions. Does the current curriculum of U.S. schools reflect our national diversity to the exclusion of our national unity? Or is the reverse true?

Proponents of a **multicultural curriculum** argue that minority students, whose representation in U.S. public schools exceeds 40 percent and is increasing every year, experience a Eurocentric (i.e., Europe-centered) curriculum that gives short shrift to the literary and historical contributions made by people from other parts of the world and to minorities within the United States. As a result, the proponents of multiculturalism argue, youngsters of color see the schools' curricula as being less relevant to them—and certainly not reflective of their own cultures or backgrounds. Some multicultural advocates take the position that the current school curriculum needs to be broadened to better reflect the contributions of people of color. Cultural pluralism, as a fact of our society, needs to be a fact of our school curriculum, they assert. (See Chapter 3, "Who Are Today's Students in a Diverse Society" for more on multicultural education and cultural pluralism.)

> *Humanity's survival does not depend on reducing differences to a common identity, but on learning to live creatively with differences.*
>
> —ANONYMOUS

A more extreme position is taken by those who demand that the whole curriculum be oriented to a particular ethnicity. For example, some advocates of an Afrocentric curriculum claim that African-American schoolchildren can learn effectively only in an environment that recognizes and amplifies their African heritage. The theory is that if students learn of the accomplishments of those who share their ethnic identities, their self-esteem will improve, which will in turn promote learning. When schools emphasize the achievements of African cultures, especially ancient Egyptian culture, and of persons of African descent, students will have a greater sense of pride and be more motivated to learn, thus raising their test scores. Although they were more popular in the 1990s, Afrocentric curricula are still being used in some large-city school districts.

In contrast, proponents of a **core curriculum**—that is, a course of study every student would be required to take—argue that ever since the 1970s schools have focused on celebrating national diversity and pluralism but have failed to help students develop a shared national identity and common cultural framework. As described in Chapter 9, "What Are the Philosophical Foundations of American Education?" some advocates of a core curriculum, such as Mortimer Adler,[24] have promoted the great literary works that have endured over the years as the basic elements of a core curriculum.

E. D. Hirsch, Jr., also endorses education based on the great literary works, but goes beyond them in his push for **cultural literacy** (now called **core knowledge**).[25] Hirsch sees a culturally literate person as someone who is aware of the central ideas, stories, scientific knowledge, events, and personalities of a culture. Cultural literacy is important, says Hirsch, because authors and speakers make allusions and references in their writing and speaking, assuming that the audience understands these references. If a person doesn't understand the reference, he or she will miss the point and not understand the message. If an author writes, for example, of the "Midas touch," and the reader doesn't know the story of King Midas, then the point is lost and the knowledge meaningless.

Hirsch does not restrict his idea of a core curriculum to the great works of "dead white males," a criticism leveled at many traditional core curricula; rather, he sees American culture as incorporating the contributions of many ethnicities and subcultures. Hirsch believes that privileged youth gain much of their cultural literacy at home. Unfortunately, many poor, minority, and immigrant children do not receive cultural literacy at home, so it is especially important that they receive it in school. If they do not, Hirsch argues, poor children and the increasing numbers of immigrant children will not learn those aspects of our common heritage that are necessary to succeed in American society. Hirsch and his colleagues, through the Core Knowledge Foundation, have developed grade-by-grade guidelines for a core knowledge sequence for grades K–8, as well as a series of books entitled *What Your First-Grader Needs to Know* (or second-grader, third-grader, etc.). Currently, several hundred schools across the country have adopted all or part of the core knowledge sequence.

In a society as large and pluralistic as the United States, many philosophies and notions of school purpose have committed supporters. How can the schools incorporate in their curricula such highly divergent ideas of what a school should do? If a certain philosophy is dominant within a given community, the curriculum of that community's schools is likely to reflect that set of beliefs, and those who don't agree will remain dissatisfied. Some communities are responding to the diverse philosophical conceptions of the curriculum by providing choices among alternative schools, each with a different curricular emphasis. The debate between those who advocate a common curriculum to ensure that all students learn what society has determined is important and those who favor state, local, and individual choice in what is learned will likely continue indefinitely. The adoption of the Common Core State Standards in English language arts and mathematics would seem to indicate that the pendulum is swinging toward a common curriculum.

© 1996 Randy Glasbergen.
www.glasbergen.com

"I can suck pudding up my nose and blow it out the corner of my eye, but they *still* won't put me in the gifted class at school!"

© Randy Glasbergen, www.glasbergen.com

TRACKING

The curriculum that a student receives is influenced by many factors, including aspirations for further schooling, academic ability, motivation, and vocational interests. Based on these and other factors, students are often sorted by ability and placed into academic program *tracks* that determine what courses they take; this process is called **tracking**. The track in which a student is placed can open or close future academic and vocational options. The three most common tracks are academic (stressing the traditional subjects of English, science, mathematics, and foreign languages), general (allowing more electives and less rigorous versions of the traditional subjects), and career and technical (preparing students for the world of work with a combination of academic and job-related courses). Each track has variations in courses required and different standards for student achievement. Within the academic track, further options exist, including advanced placement (AP), International Baccalaureate, and honors courses. (See Chapter 12, "How Should Education Be Reformed?" for more on the International Baccalaureate program.)

During the 1970s and 1980s, tracking came under attack. Several prominent educational researchers produced studies showing that students placed in the lower tracks received an inferior curriculum and less stimulating instruction than students in the academic tracks. Studies also showed that poor and minority students were disproportionately placed in the lower tracks, where they had less qualified teachers, less rigorous curricula, and poorer instruction than students in the upper tracks.[26] Tracking became a dirty word, and detracking efforts ensued.

Other educational studies found conflicting evidence about the detracking movement itself: although detracking does help the educational performance of low-achieving students, high-achieving students are hurt academically by elimination of tracking.[27] Parents of these high-achieving students often exert considerable pressure to ensure that their children have access to honors and AP classes, resisting efforts to detrack the schools. Tracking proponents argue that it is easier to teach relatively homogeneous classes and unrealistic to expect everyone to master the same curriculum. They say students feel more comfortable and learn better when they're grouped with peers of similar abilities. And they say tracking enables teachers to tailor instruction to the needs of respective groups of students. One study of Massachusetts middle schools found that more top scorers in mathematics came from tracked schools than from detracked schools.[29] Furthermore, teachers who teach the high-track students often resist efforts to detrack because they enjoy the intellectual challenge and prestige that come from teaching these students. The general sense is that tracking benefits high-ability students but hurts low-ability students, whereas the reverse is true of detracking.

(T) F

Research studies indicate that the practice of tracking students into different ability-level groups is detrimental to low-ability students.

A number of research studies indicate that students placed in lower tracks receive a less stimulating curriculum and inferior instruction, compared to students placed in middle or upper-level tracks.

PAUSE AND REFLECT

1. Have the curricula you experienced tended to be more like the multicultural curriculum or the core curriculum described in this chapter? What were the strengths and weaknesses of the curriculum you were taught?

2. Where do you stand on the tracking issue? Has your own educational background included tracking? How does your background affect where you stand on this issue?

is the existing curriculum relevant to today's society?

Today, the world community is confronted with staggering problems. There are over 6 billion people on our globe and forecasters project that the world population will reach 10 billion by 2050. Those people will need food, shelter, and an education that will allow them to lead fulfilled lives. The twentieth century saw great advances in manufacturing, agriculture, technology, and the growth of information, but these advances did not come without costs. Acid rain, for example, polluted our vegetation, wildlife, and the very bodies of millions of people. Together, the United States and the rest of the world need to stop the systemic despoiling of our planet. Diseases such as AIDS have weakened whole continents. Weaponry, such as nuclear devices and improvised explosive devices, daily threaten the world's peace and progress. Religious fanaticism, hunger, and poverty have bred a desperate terrorism in many corners of the world. It is no overstatement to say that we are in a race for global survival.

Schools and teachers will play a vital role in determining the outcome of this race. In Chapter 2, "What Is a School and What Is It For?" we described the curriculum as a social bet. The stakes of that bet are high. In fact, the most basic function of all education is to increase the survival chances of the human community.

Before anyone can determine whether a particular curriculum is relevant to today's urgent needs, some difficult issues must be addressed. In Chapter 2, "What Is a School and What Is It For?" we discuss the purposes of schools and different models of schooling, particularly the school as a transmitter of culture and the school as an agent of social reconstruction. In Chapter 9, "What Are the Philosophical Foundations of American Education?" we discuss four schools of educational philosophy: perennialism, progressivism, essentialism, and romanticism. In judging curriculum relevance, all of these matters come into play because the relevance of a curriculum strongly depends on one's basic beliefs about what people need and what is most worth knowing.

What you consider to be a relevant curriculum ultimately depends on your philosophical position. Conflicting trends have emerged in relation to the academic curriculum, each representing a different philosophy. For example, if one considers the school's primary objective to be the intellectual development of students, any curriculum that does not emphasize the mastery of certain subject matter and the training of the mind will be judged as irrelevant or wrong-headed. Conversely, if one believes the school should emphasize the development of the "whole child"—that is, the entirety of the child's emotional, social, and intellectual growth—a curriculum devoted exclusively to English, history, the sciences, mathematics, and foreign languages will be considered inappropriate for many students and thus inadequate. Those who take the view that education must equip students with necessary work and survival skills may consider a flexible curriculum that includes career and technical courses to be most relevant. "The Saber-Tooth Curriculum" (see the feature below) uses a humorous approach to demarcate the conflicts among different educational approaches.

> " *One looks back with appreciation to the brilliant teachers, but with gratitude to those who touched our human feeling. The curriculum is so much necessary raw material, but warmth is the vital element for the growing plant and for the soul of the child.*
>
> —CARL JUNG (1875–1961), Psychologist

the saber-tooth curriculum

In his classic satire on curriculum irrelevance, Harold Benjamin (writing under the pseudonym J. Abner Peddiwell) describes how the first school curriculum was developed in the Stone Age. The earliest theorist, according to Benjamin's book, was a man named New Fist, who hit on the idea of deliberate, systematic education.

Watching children at play, New Fist wondered how he could get them to do the things that would gain them more and better food, shelter, clothing, and security. He analyzed the activities that adults engaged in to maintain life and came up with three subjects for his curriculum: (1) fish-grabbing-with-the-bare-hands, (2) woolly-horse-clubbing, and (3) saber-tooth-tiger-scaring-with-fire. Although the children trained in these subjects enjoyed obvious material benefits as a result, some conservative members of the tribe resisted the introduction of these new subjects on religious grounds. But in due time, many people began to train their children in New Fist's curriculum, and the tribe grew increasingly prosperous and secure.

Then conditions changed. An ice age began, and a glacier crept down over the land. The glacier brought with it dirt and gravel that muddied the creeks, and the waters became so dirty that no one could see the fish well enough to grab them. The melting waters from the approaching ice sheet also made the country wetter, and the little woolly horses migrated to drier land. They were replaced by antelopes, which were so shy and speedy that no one could get close enough to club them. Finally, the new dampness in the air caused the saber-tooth tigers to catch pneumonia and die. And the ferocious glacial bears that came down with the advancing ice sheet were not afraid of fire.

The thinkers of the tribe, descendants of New Fist, found a way out of the dilemma. One figured out how to catch fish with a net made from vines. Another invented traps for the antelopes, and a third discovered how to dig pits to catch the bears.

Some thoughtful people began to wonder why these new activities couldn't be taught in the schools. But the elders who controlled the schools claimed that the new skills did not qualify as *education*—they were merely a matter of *training*. Besides, the curriculum was too full of the standard cultural subjects—fish-grabbing, horse-clubbing, and tiger-scaring—to admit new ones. When some radicals argued that the traditional subjects were foolish, the elders said that they taught fish-grabbing not to catch fish but to develop agility, horse-clubbing to develop strength, and tiger-scaring to develop courage. "The essence of true education is timelessness," they announced. "It is something that endures through changing conditions like a solid rock standing squarely and firmly in the middle of a raging torrent. You must know that there are some eternal verities and the saber-tooth curriculum is one of them!" (pp. 43–44).

The Saber-Tooth Curriculum was written in 1939, but its continuing applicability seems to be one of the "eternal verities."

Sources: J. Abner Peddiwell (Harold Benjamin), *The Saber-Tooth Curriculum.* Copyright © 1959 by the McGraw-Hill Companies. Reproduced by permission of the McGraw-Hill Companies. (*Note:* One chapter of this book is reproduced in *Kaleidoscope: Readings in Education*, the companion volume to this text.)

PAUSE AND REFLECT

Which goals and knowledge do you believe are most relevant or important for schools to include in their curricula?

OUR FINAL WORD

The rather innocuous word *curriculum* and the simple question "What is taught?" contain within them nothing less than the keys to our future. Inevitably, schools will have a curriculum and students will learn it, but the actual *stuff* of the curriculum and the ways in which students are encouraged to learn it constitute the key issue. Which knowledge from our past should be represented? Which deposits in our vast storehouse of scientific and cultural knowledge will they need? Which learnings from our moral heritage will they need to guide themselves and the nation to make the right choices? Which form of classroom and school life will encourage the habits of heart and mind that students will need to take up and meet the challenges they face in the world?

Our collective response will lead to either a prosperous and noble future or a future filled with disappointment and decline. What we select for students to learn in our schools will have a profound effect on their individual futures and on the future of our nation. Indeed, given the power and influence of the United States, the impact of our choices will be global.

What does this have to do with you as a future teacher? Plenty! What should be taught? What do students need to know? These questions are, and will continue to be, debated globally at the highest levels of governments, and here in the United States at national, state, and local school board levels. The person who brings the curriculum into the classroom—who makes thousands of decisions every week about every detail of what and how to teach—is the teacher. Curriculum questions, for this reason, are the special responsibility of teachers, of those who have dedicated their lives to the education of the youth. No small responsibility!

WHY TEACH? YOUR FINAL WORD

In your journal or online at this textbook's website, respond to the following questions:

1. In your opinion, has the standards movement improved or weakened the quality of education that most U.S. students receive? Why do you think so?

2. Are you decided or undecided as to the subject matter and/or grade levels that you want to teach? If undecided, what can you do to help make your decision?

3. After watching either the elementary or high school Video Cases on cooperative learning, what impressions are you left with regarding this teaching technique? Are you likely to use cooperative learning in your teaching? Why or why not?

KEY TERMS

block scheduling (152)
civic learning (civic education) (132)
Common Core State Standards (125)
content standards (124)
cooperative learning (145)
core curriculum (154)
critical thinking (148)
cultural literacy (core knowledge) (155)
curriculum (123)
differentiated instruction (149)
interdisciplinary (integrated) curriculum (144)
looping (152)

multicultural curriculum (154)
phonics (129)
Program for International Student
    Assessment (PISA) (139)
problem solving (148)
project approach (152)
subject-matter curriculum (124)
Trends in International Mathematics and
    Science Study (TIMSS) (139)
tracking (156)
whole language approach (129)
writing across the curriculum (149)

FOR FURTHER INFORMATION

WEB RESOURCES

American Council on the Teaching of Foreign Languages. Available at **www.actfl.org**.

An executive summary of the national standards for foreign languages can be found at this website.

Council for Exceptional Children (Special Education and Gifted Education). Available at **http://www.cec.sped.org**.

This site contains many resources for teaching students with disabilities.

Mid-Continent Research for Education and Learning. Available at **http://mcrel.org**.

One of 10 regional educational laboratories, this lab has a great set of materials in different subject areas, as well as research reports on effective practice. The website also offers links to other useful sites.

The following journals and websites contain many interesting and helpful items for teachers in the respective subject-matter fields. To find both national and state-by-state content standards in the various subject-matter fields, go to *Education World* at **www.education-world.com/standards/**.

Art: *Art Education, Arts and Activities, School Arts;* ArtsEdge at the Kennedy Center website, available at **http://artsedge.kennedy-center.org/**.

Career and technical education: *Industrial Education, Journal of Home Economics; Business Education Forum; Business Education Review;* Association for Career and Technical Education website, available at **www.acteonline.org**.

Elementary and early childhood: *Young Children, Teaching Young Children;* National Association for the Education of Young Children, available at **www.naeyc.org/**.

English: *English Journal;* National Council of Teachers of English website, available at **www.ncte.org**. Includes national standards in English and language arts.

Foreign languages: *Modern Language Journal, Foreign Language Annals;* American Council on the Teaching of Foreign Languages website, available at **www.actfl.org/**.

Mathematics: *The Mathematics Teacher;* National Council of Teachers of Mathematics website, available at **www.nctm.org**. Includes national standards in mathematics; Math Forum website, particularly

"Ask Dr. Math," available at **http://mathforum.org/dr.math**.

Music: *Music Educators' Journal;* MENC: The National Association for Music Education, available at www.menc.org. Includes a section for future teachers.

Physical education: *Journal of Health, Physical Education and Recreation;* American Alliance for Health, Physical Education, Recreation and Dance website, available at **www.aahperd.org/**. Includes national standards in physical education.

Reading and language arts: *Language Arts, The Reading Teacher;* The Children's Literature Web Guide, available at **www.ucalgary.ca/~dkbrown/**; and the International Reading Association, available at **www.reading.org/**.

Science: *The Science Teacher, School Science and Mathematics;* National Science Teachers Association, available at **http://nsta.org**; *Blueprints for Reform: Science, Mathematics, and Technology Education*, available at **http://project2061.org**. Includes national science standards.

Social studies: *Social Studies, Social Education;* National Council for the Social Studies, available at **www.socialstudies.org**. Includes national standards in social studies.

PRINT RESOURCES

Susan M. Drake and Rebecca Crawford Burns, *Meeting Standards through Integrated Curriculum* (Alexandria, VA: Association for Supervision and Curriculum Development, 2004).

This is an excellent book on how to develop interdisciplinary curricula while still incorporating state standards.

Robyn M. Gillies, *Cooperative Learning: Integrating Theory and Practice* (Thousand Oaks, CA: Sage, 2007).

This text highlights the strategies teachers can use to challenge student thinking and scaffold their learning as well as the strategies students can be taught to promote discourse, problem solving, and learning during cooperative learning. It also situates cooperative learning within the climate of the No Child Left Behind legislation and high-stakes testing.

E. D. Hirsch, Jr., *The Knowledge Deficit: Closing the Shocking Education Gap for American Children* (Boston: Houghton Mifflin, 2007).

Hirsch proposes ways to close the knowledge gap between poor children and those from more privileged backgrounds by focusing on a content-rich curriculum. (See the Core Knowledge Foundation website at **www.coreknowledge.org**.)

Allan C. Ornstein, Edward F. Pajak, and Stacey B. Ornstein, *Contemporary Issues in Curriculum*, 5th ed. (Boston: Allyn and Bacon, 2011).

A compilation of articles, written by different authors, that addresses the emerging trends and controversial issues in elementary and secondary curricula.

The Education CourseMate website for this text offers many helpful resources. Go to www.cengagebrain.com to access the TeachSource Video Cases and other TeachSource videos, flashcards, interactive quizzes, the eBook, reflection and enrichment activities, a state standards resource center, and other study aids.

6 what makes a teacher effective?

(© Corbis)

InTASC Standards 1, 2, 3, 4, 5, 6, 7, 8, 9, and 10

FOCUS POINTS

- Teachers are required to make many decisions as they plan for instruction, implement teaching strategies, and evaluate the outcomes of their planning and strategies.

- Four major types of attitudes affect teachers' behavior: attitude toward self, attitude toward children, attitude toward peers and parents, and attitude toward the subject matter.

- A teacher should have an intimate knowledge of the subject matter being taught, including both the instructional content and the discipline from which it derives.

- To be able to recognize and interpret classroom events appropriately, a teacher should be familiar with theoretical knowledge and research about learning and human behavior.

- Effective teachers demonstrate a repertoire of teaching skills that enable them to meet the differing

Effective teaching is much more than an intuitive process. A teacher must continually make decisions and act on those decisions. To do this effectively, the teacher must have *knowledge*—both theoretical knowledge about learning and human behavior and specific knowledge about the subject matter to be taught. A teacher also must demonstrate a repertoire of teaching *skills* that are believed to facilitate student learning and must display *attitudes* that foster learning and genuine human relationships.

Truth or Fiction?

T F   A primary difference between novice and expert teachers is the expert's ability to gather information in a short time and use it in multiple ways.

T F   The most important aspect of a teacher's effectiveness is his or her personality.

needs of their students. Research has identified a number of these skills in classroom management, effective questioning, and planning techniques, to name a few areas.

T　F　A teacher's expectation that all students can succeed greatly affects students' achievement.

T　F　Efficient teachers can provide students with as much as 180 hours a year more of engaged learning time than inefficient teachers.

T　F　Elementary and secondary school teachers plan their lessons in a similar fashion.

We once knew a teacher who was described as having not 20 years of experience but one year's experience 20 times. The message was that this teacher had stopped growing and developing as a professional after the first year. As someone just starting in your teaching career, this kind of problem may seem like a remote possibility. After all, there's so much that you know you don't know, and you're eager to learn as much as you can. Unfortunately, it is all too easy to fall into comfortable patterns of teaching, especially after you have gained a few years of experience.

How can you avoid this complacency and stagnation? One strategy is to maintain your curiosity and develop habits of inquiry and reflection. More educators are coming to believe that, although it is important to prepare beginning teachers for initial practice, it is even more important to help them develop the attitudes and skills that will enable them to become lifelong students of teaching. Ideally, rather than relying on authority, impulse, or unexamined previous practice, teachers will continually examine and evaluate their attitudes, practices, effectiveness, and accomplishments. This process of examination and evaluation is often called **reflective teaching**, which was introduced in Chapter 1, "Why Teach?" Reflective teaching is a major theme running throughout this book. Reflective teachers ask themselves questions such as these:

- "What am I doing and why?"
- "How can I better meet my students' needs?"
- "What are some alternative learning activities to achieve these objectives?"
- "How could I have encouraged more involvement or learning on the part of the students?"

Even when lessons go well, reflective teachers analyze the lesson to determine what went well and why, and how else things might have been done.

Developing the habits of inquiry and reflection should begin now, in your teacher education program. Your experiences with schools, teachers, and students along this path will give you many opportunities to reflect on what has occurred. You can use journal writing, observation instruments, simulations, or video recording to help you examine teaching, learning, and the contexts in which they occur. Comparing your perspectives with those of classmates, professors, and school personnel will broaden your interpretations and give you new insights. As you reflect on your experiences, you will come to distrust simplistic answers and explanations. Nuances and subtleties will start to become clear, and situations that once seemed simple will reveal their complexities. Viewing the Video Cases associated with this textbook and considering carefully the actions of the teachers can bring you additional insights into what constitutes effective teaching.

As you reflect, you are likely to encounter and think about moral and ethical issues. Teachers make moral and ethical decisions every day when they decide how they will treat students and others, and when they elect to create a classroom climate that fosters trust, safety, and cooperation. When they select certain examples from history or literature for study, teachers also make ethical decisions. Clearly, you cannot teach without making ethical decisions. Chapter 8, "What Are the Ethical and Legal Issues Facing Teachers?" discusses this topic in greater detail, but we hope you will study and reflect on the cases we present throughout this book, as well as the Video Cases, that deal with moral or ethical issues. By practicing reflective teaching, you will grow and develop as an effective, professional teacher.

framework for professional practice

> *The mediocre teacher tells. The good teacher explains. The superior teacher demonstrates. The great teacher inspires.*
>
> —WILLIAM ARTHUR WARD (1921–1994),
> American Author, Pastor, and Teacher

In recent years, several groups have attempted to identify what effective teachers should know and be able to do. The Interstate Teachers Assessment and Support Consortium (InTASC) (which is discussed in more detail in Chapter 15, "What Does It Mean to Be a Professional?") has identified the knowledge, dispositions, and performances that all teachers should possess. Many states are working in concert with InTASC to implement the standards as part of the states' own teacher licensing requirements. The website for the InTASC standards is listed at the end of the chapter, and the core standards are listed inside the back cover of this book, along with the appropriate pages in this text where these standards are addressed.

differences between expert and novice teachers

A number of educational researchers have tried to identify expert and experienced teachers and compare them with novice teachers. But before you read what researchers have found out about expert teachers, stop and reflect on a teacher of your experience whom you consider to be truly an expert teacher. Not necessarily your favorite teacher, but the most skillful. What made this teacher so expert?

We can think of an expert teacher as being similar to an expert chess player. Expert chess players quickly spot trouble areas in any chessboard pattern; likewise, expert teachers quickly recognize trouble spots in a classroom setting. Experts in chess or teaching draw on their hours of experience to build a repertoire of recognizable patterns. In one experiment, expert and novice teachers were asked to look at a photograph of a classroom and identify the class activity. Experts were better able to "read" the classroom, making inferences about what was happening in the picture. When observed in action, expert teachers also show greater ability to gather information in a short time for multiple purposes. For example, an expert teacher may be able to accomplish many tasks in an opening review session: gather attendance information, identify who did or did not do the homework, and locate students needing help with the next lesson.

In comparison, novice teachers described the surface characteristics of the classroom pictures they saw. When presented with descriptions of

(continued)

(T) F

A primary difference between novice and expert teachers is the expert's ability to gather information in a short time and use it in multiple ways.

Expert teachers can accomplish several tasks at once, e.g., take attendance, collect homework, and identify students needing help, whereas novice teachers focus on one task at a time.

student problems, they relied again on the literal features of the problems to suggest solutions. Their analyses did not correspond with the higher-order classifications used by expert teachers.

Experts differed from novices in their approaches to planning as well. In a simulated task of planning, experts focused on learning what students already knew about the subject matter to be learned, whereas novices planned to ask students where they were in their textbooks and then present a review of important concepts. In other words, experts planned to gather information from the students, whereas novices planned to give information to them.

The research suggests that experts in any field demonstrate skill in planning and in classifying problems and formulating solutions. This is no less true for teachers: the expert teacher shows problem-solving skills like those of other experts, whether in chess, bridge, or physics. The studies also indicate that the process of evolving from novice to expert teacher takes considerable time because extensive experience is necessary to develop enough episodic knowledge to interpret information about classrooms.

Sources: David C. Berliner, "Expertise: The Wonder of Exemplary Performances," in J. N. Mangiere and C. C. Block, eds., *Creating Powerful Thinking in Teachers and Students* (Fort Worth, TX: Harcourt Brace College Publishers, 1994), pp. 161–186; Greta Morine-Dershimer, "Instructional Planning," in J. M. Cooper, ed., *Classroom Teaching Skills*, 9th ed. (Belmont, CA: Wadsworth, Cengage Learning, 2011), pp. 57–65.

Visit the State Standards Resource Center on our Education CourseMate website.

In the following case study of a new teacher who faces problems that many classroom veterans will find familiar, we take a critical look at the many teaching decisions that she had to make.

The rapport that effective teachers establish with their students often goes beyond the classroom learning environment.

from PRESERVICE to PRACTICE

Carol Landis: A Case of Classroom Decision Making

As an example of how ordinary teaching situations can lead to useful reflection about effective teaching, consider the case of Carol Landis. Carol is beginning her first year of teaching. She prepared to be a high school social studies teacher, graduated, and accepted a job in her own community, a small city in the Northwest. Most of her students come from solidly blue-collar, working-class backgrounds.

Carol has been assigned three periods of world geography and two periods of American history. We join her as she prepares the first lesson of a new unit in world geography.

Carol plans to require her ninth-graders to work in groups to prepare panel discussions about a country of their choice. She wants the groups to research the relationships among the geography, political history, and culture of a country and share what they find in panel discussions with the rest of the class. Carol sets two goals for her students: that they work together in groups and that they make effective oral presentations of their research.

When planning how to present the assignment to her classes, Carol has many questions. Do these students know how to use the library? If not, will she need to provide directions for using reference materials? Maybe the librarian has already taken care of this step, and Carol's students will just need a review. Do these students know what "culture" means or understand general concepts that will help them look for relationships among culture, history, and geography? What background information do they need before they start researching a specific country? Also, do these students know how to work in groups? Have they ever participated in a panel discussion? In planning how to help her students complete this assignment, Carol bases her decisions on what she thinks she knows about them as learners.

Although Carol has already planned this assignment to meet her state's curriculum standards in social studies, she is concerned about whether the books in her room and the library will provide the information her students need. Which other resources are available? Carol knows that other teachers have back issues of *National Geographic*, for example. Maybe she could help students use the Internet in ways that tie together the geography, political history, and culture for their respective countries.

In addition to the panel discussions, Carol has considered having each student submit a written report. For this first research assignment, however, she decides that an oral presentation by the group is appropriate. Later, she will work with the classes on report writing. In the beginning, she wants her students to enjoy her classes, feel a part of a group, and get to know one another. Carol prefers listening to her students to grading written reports anyway, so this assignment fits her style of teaching.

Despite her planning, when Carol reflects on her second-period class after the first day of library research, she wonders what went wrong. One group argued the whole period and never did select a country. Maybe she should have assigned groups and not let students choose their own partners. She tried to ignore this group, believing they should work out their own differences and come to a group decision. But what if they never work together? She noticed that another group was completely dominated by one of the top students. He decided which country they would research, assigned the topics, and told the others where to look for information. When Carol urged the other members to share equally in the group decisions, they asserted, "Tom always gets A's. We don't mind if he tells us what to do." Carol didn't know how to respond to their concern for grades without insulting Tom, so she said nothing.

Later in the period, Tom asked her which religion predominated in Indonesia. Carol wasn't sure but was afraid to admit her lack of information, so she told him, "Just look it up." Tom responded, "So you don't know either?" Carol testily told Tom that she was not his personal encyclopedia. Now she wonders if she overreacted. Maybe she should have admitted she didn't know. Was Tom challenging her authority, or was he just reacting to the sharp tone in her order to look it up? Did she turn Tom and his group against her?

(continued)

Carol also wonders whether the other groups worked productively. She spent so much time watching the arguing group and Tom's group that she didn't have time to notice whether the chatter from the other groups was work or play. Maybe it didn't hurt to let the other groups have some fun today, anyway. She can direct her attention to them tomorrow.

There is so much to watch and monitor when students work in groups, Carol realizes. Many questions arise, such as "Where do I find this?" "Mr. Shaw won't lend me his magazines—what do I do now?" "This library stinks. Why do we have to do this assignment anyway?" and even "Miss Landis, what did you do this weekend?" Carol wonders if she will ever learn to field all her students' questions and comments and to distinguish the words on the surface from the real messages. She also worries about what to do about Ron, who has started reading a novel about life in Siberian concentration camps. Carol thinks it is the only book she has ever seen him read—but it won't help his group do their project on Kenya.

Maybe this assignment wasn't such a good idea in the first place, Carol thinks, or maybe she just wasn't up to working with her classes in groups. The stares from the librarian and the study hall teacher indicated that they didn't think she could handle her classes, and Carol hasn't even thought about how she will grade her students' panel discussions. Just thinking about it all exhausts her. How will she ever get through another day with that second-period class?

CASE QUESTIONS

1. If you were to teach the lesson Carol had planned, which changes would you make? Why?

2. What theoretical knowledge would have helped Carol to carry out a more successful lesson? Be as specific as you can.

the teacher as a reflective decision maker

Indecision becomes decision with time.

—AUTHOR UNKNOWN

We present Carol's case to illustrate that the teacher's role can be described as one of a *reflective decision maker*. Indeed, some educational researchers have identified skill in decision making as the most important teaching skill. Some decisions are made as teachers quietly deliberate curricular and instructional goals; many more must be made almost instantaneously as teachers and students interact. Let's look at some of the particular decisions that Carol made or will make, dividing them into three basic stages: planning, implementing, and evaluating.

PLANNING DECISIONS

Carol wants her students to understand the relationships among geography, history, and culture. But what exactly does she want them to know about these relationships? She must decide the particular kinds of understanding she wants her students to achieve, and this decision affects her choice of teaching techniques.

From a variety of possible techniques, she has chosen independent group work and has also decided that a panel discussion will provide evidence of her students' learning. These decisions reflect Carol's personal preferences, her goals for her students' learning, and her skills in methods of evaluating their learning. In addition, her decisions are based on a series of judgments about her students' ability to do research, work in groups, and present panel discussions, as well as on judgments about how long they will need to work together and which resources they will need. Carol might have also made some plans for what to do in case her judgments turned out to be wrong and she needed to adapt her lesson.

IMPLEMENTING DECISIONS

Carol, like most teachers, must make many of her decisions almost instantly, as she adapts her teaching to changing classroom conditions. As Carol teaches this lesson or series of lessons, she has to decide when and how to intervene with some of her groups, whether to allow Ron to continue reading a novel, and how to respond to students' questions.

EVALUATING DECISIONS

After the first day's library work, Carol reflects on her interactions with the students, facing decisions about how she has to adjust her strategies for the next day. As the groups continue to work, she will also face decisions about how to evaluate the impact of her planning and instruction on her students' learning.

In each of these planning, implementing, and evaluating stages of instructional decision making, Carol chooses among alternative concepts her students could learn, approaches to help them learn the concepts, ways to manage the classroom to encourage their learning, and ways to measure their learning. Could her decisions improve with more adequate knowledge, skills, and attitudes?

Factors Influencing Instructional Decisions

Teachers do not make instructional decisions in a vacuum; many factors influence the process. First and foremost are your students. Knowing and understanding your students and their backgrounds is imperative if your decisions are to be effective. Students differ in many ways, all of which affect how they learn.

Poverty. Some students come from backgrounds in poverty, which can influence their readiness to learn. Many students from poverty backgrounds are more likely to suffer from the effects of poor nutrition and inadequate health care, which can affect their abilities to attend school regularly, concentrate on learning, and do homework. School also tends to be oriented more toward serving middle-class children. Making the curriculum and instructional experiences germane to poor children constitutes a major challenge that our schools and teachers must meet.

Racial, ethnic, and cultural diversity. As our schools become more diverse— currently 44 percent of school-age children are minorities—many students' native language will not be English, presenting a serious challenge to schools and teachers. (See Chapter 3, "Who Are Today's Students in a Diverse Society?" for more on this issue.)

Gender. Students' gender influences how we think of them and what we expect of them. Treating boys and girls equitably as individuals rather than as stereotypes is a challenge for both male and female teachers.

Special needs. You will undoubtedly have children with special needs in your classroom. Differentiating instruction to meet both their needs and the needs of your other students will be a challenge. (See Chapter 3, "Who Are Today's Students in a Diverse Society?" for more on this issue.)

Other factors. Students differ in terms of their needs for belonging, safety, and self-esteem. Children coming from secure home situations will likely have different needs than children who have not had this kind of stability. Your students will all have different abilities, achievements, and learning styles, and your challenge will be to provide a variety of learning experiences to accommodate the diversity that your students will bring to your classroom.

aspects of reflective decision making

Next, we explore the areas of competence that help teachers make more effective decisions. Many educators believe that to be effective decision makers, elementary and secondary school teachers must have attitudes, knowledge, and skills essential to the teaching profession. Teachers should ask themselves not only, "What am I going to teach?" but also "What should my students be learning?" "How can I help them learn it?" and "Why is it important?" To answer these questions, teachers must be familiar with children and their developmental stages. They must know something about events occurring outside the classroom and the expectations that the society has for its young. In addition, teachers must have enough command of the subject they teach to be able to distinguish what is peripheral from what is central. They must have a philosophy of education that guides them in their role as teacher, and they must know how human beings learn and how to create environments that promote learning.

What are the specialized skills and attributes of the effective instructional decision maker? We consider five areas of competence to be essential for a teacher:

1. Attitudes that foster learning and genuine human relationships
2. Knowledge of the subject matter to be taught
3. Theoretical knowledge about learning and human behavior
4. Personal practical knowledge
5. Skills of teaching that promote student learning

Teachers draw on their competence in these five areas to inform the many decisions they make both as they plan instruction and as they spontaneously interact with the students in their classes. Figure 6.1 indicates the relationship of these

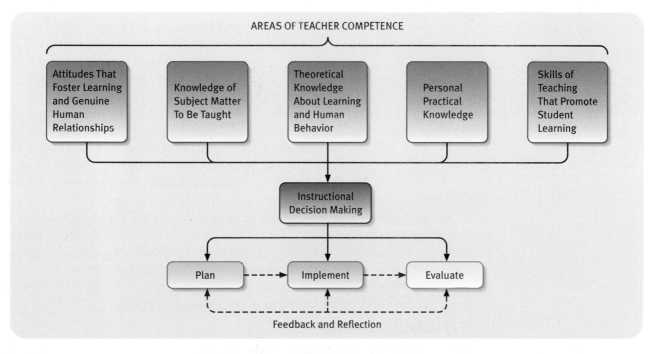

FIGURE 6.1 **Relationship of Teacher-Competence Areas to Process of Instructional Decision Making**

Source: James M. Cooper, ed., "The Teacher as a Reflective Decision Maker," in *Classroom Teaching Skills,* 8th ed. Copyright © 2006 by Houghton Mifflin Company. Reprinted with permission.

areas of competence to the process of instructional decision making. Next, we examine these areas of competence, now and then referring to the instructional decisions that Carol made and the attitudes, knowledge, and skills influencing her decisions.

what attitudes does the effective teacher possess?

Many people believe that the teacher's personality is the most critical factor in successful teaching. If teachers have warmth, empathy, sensitivity, enthusiasm, and humor, they are much more likely to be successful than if they lack these characteristics. In fact, many people argue that without these attributes, an individual is unlikely to be a good teacher. The Leaders in Education feature portrays one teacher known for her positive attitude—Helen Keller's famous tutor, Anne Mansfield Sullivan.

For years, educational researchers sought to isolate the characteristics essential to good teachers. General information about a teacher's personality, attitude, experience, achievement, and aptitude were all examined in an effort to predict a teacher's classroom behavior. Unfortunately, these characteristics were often unrelated to the teacher's work in the classroom, and they ignored the most important measures of effective teaching: the interactions of the teacher with the learners and the academic performance of the students being taught. Two researchers, summarizing 50 years of research on teachers' personalities and characteristics, conclude, "Despite the critical importance of the problem and a half-century of prodigious research effort, very little is known for certain about the nature and measurement of teacher personality, about the relation between teacher personality and teaching effectiveness."[1]

A person's *attitudes*—that is, his or her predispositions to act in a positive or negative way toward people, ideas, and events—are a fundamental dimension of that individual's personality. Although the relationship between general personality traits and teacher effectiveness has proven elusive, almost all educators are convinced of the importance of teacher attitudes in the teaching process. Attitudes have a direct but often unrecognized effect on our behavior in that they determine the ways we view ourselves and interact with others.

We believe four major categories of attitudes affect teaching behavior: (1) the teacher's attitude toward self, (2) the teacher's attitude toward children and the relationship between self and children, (3) the teacher's attitudes toward peers and pupils' parents, and (4) the teacher's attitude toward the subject matter.

TEACHERS' ATTITUDES TOWARD THEMSELVES: SELF-UNDERSTANDING

There is evidence from psychology that people who deny or cannot cope with their own emotions are likely to be incapable of respecting and coping with the feelings of others. If teachers are to understand and sympathize with their students' feelings, they must recognize and understand their own feelings. Many colleges are responding to this need

---

T (F)

The most important aspect of a teacher's effectiveness is his or her personality. Teachers with very different personalities can be equally effective in getting students to learn. Teacher attitudes, on the other hand, greatly affect a teacher's effectiveness.

❝

How we think shows through in how we act. Attitudes are mirrors of the mind.

—**DAVID JOSEPH SCHWARTZ,**
Authority on Human Motivation

LEADERS in education

Anne Mansfield Sullivan (1866–1936)

The proof is in the pupil. In this case, Helen Keller, a blind and deaf pupil, was a terror. Wily and mean, Helen was also animal-like. Nevertheless, her teacher, Anne Sullivan, enabled her to become an international celebrity.

Sullivan pioneered the teaching of individuals without sight and without hearing. Today we speak of a *deaf culture*, but this term was not used in the era of Anne Sullivan. "Teacher," as Helen always called her, is credited with making it possible to reach students who were thought to have mental retardation.

(©Bettmann/Corbis)

The daughter of Irish immigrants, Sullivan was born in Feeding Hills, Massachusetts, on April 14, 1866, and entered the almshouse at eight when her mother died and her father abandoned her and her brother. Half-blind herself, she went to the Perkins School for the Blind in Boston at age 14, without a toothbrush, hat, or coat; her only possessions were a shirt and stockings tied in a bundle.

At age 21, Sullivan took a job offered by the Keller family in Tuscumbia, Alabama, to teach the Kellers' daughter, Helen. Helen Keller was an angry and frustrated child, but she was not stupid. Sullivan quickly realized this fact and began her assault on Helen's locked mind. Within a month, she had made contact with Helen in the now-famous pump story, immortalized in the drama *The Miracle Worker.* Sullivan fingerspelled words into Helen's hand, each word suiting an action. Finally, Helen, feeling water over her hand, realized the connection between word and object. She had broken the code and realized that everything had a name.

Sullivan's methods were practical. She taught Helen to play through games and exercises, stimulating her to ask the names of the motions. She kept a menagerie of animals for Helen to help her understand movement. She progressed to abstractions like peace and God as soon as her pupil was ready.

Sullivan wanted to make Helen as normal as possible, giving her every experience she could. She worked at teaching her to sit, stand, and walk properly. As soon as Helen could distinguish between right and wrong, "Teacher" sent her to bed for misdeeds. Laziness, carelessness, untidiness, and procrastination were dealt with by ingenuity, humor, and light sarcasm.

Helen used the manual alphabet for three years before she began to speak. When Helen was 9, Sullivan was rewarded with the words "I am not dumb now." It was one of the most dramatic achievements in the history of teaching.

Sullivan's great discovery was that a child should not be taught each word separately by a separate definition but instead should be given endless repetition of language he or she does not understand all day long. Sullivan continually spelled words into Helen's hand to mimic the way a hearing child in the cradle absorbs words. This method had never before been put into practice in the education of a deaf child, especially a deaf-blind one.

When Helen attended a school for deaf pupils in New York, Anne Sullivan went along. At Cambridge School and Radcliffe College, Sullivan attended classes, interpreting instruction and looking up words for Helen. She made herself into Helen's eyes and ears and supplied knowledge to a starving mind as she fired her pupil's drive to study hard. After college, Sullivan accompanied Helen on worldwide lecture tours as Helen became a famous author and personality.

Extraordinarily close, teacher and pupil spent much of their lives together. The name "Teacher" has been enriched by Anne Sullivan's dedicated life, persistent high standards, and creative instruction.

Source: Marilyn Ryan.

by including counseling sessions, reflective thinking, and awareness experiences as part of their teacher education programs. These experiences emphasize introspection, self-evaluation, and feedback from other participants. The goal is to help prospective teachers learn more about themselves, their attitudes, and how other people perceive them.

TEACHERS' ATTITUDES TOWARD CHILDREN

(T) F

A teacher's expectation that all students can succeed greatly affects students' achievement. A teacher's attitude toward students can affect how the student reacts and how hard a student will try to succeed.

In general, a teacher's expectation that *all* students can succeed seems to make a difference in students' achievement. As a teacher, you need to believe that all of your students are capable of high academic achievement and adjust your beliefs and behavior based on the needs, abilities, and aspirations of each individual student.

Most teachers occasionally harbor attitudes or feelings toward some of their students that are detrimental to being an effective teacher. Strong likes and dislikes of particular pupils, biases toward or against particular ethnic groups, low learning expectations for children from poverty backgrounds, and biases in favor of or against certain kinds of student behavior—all can reduce teaching effectiveness. Self-awareness of such attitudes toward individual pupils or classes of children is necessary if teachers are to cope with their own feelings and beliefs. If teachers possess empathy for their students and value them as unique individuals, these teachers will be more effective and will derive more satisfaction from their teaching.

If a teacher expects a student or group of students to behave in a certain way, the teacher's attitude may serve as a **self-fulfilling prophecy**[2]—that is, the students may conform to the teacher's low expectations, thus confirming the teacher's original expectations. On the other hand, when teachers hold high expectations for students and communicate these high expectations, students will often act in ways to live up to the teacher's expectations. A teacher's attitude toward and expectation of students are powerful influences on whether or not students learn.

> *I touch the future. I teach.*
>
> —CHRISTA MCAULIFFE (1948–1986),
> First Teacher in Space

TEACHERS' ATTITUDES TOWARD PEERS AND PUPILS' PARENTS

Teachers do not exist in isolated classrooms. They interact with fellow teachers and administrators and often have sensitive dealings with parents. Sometimes teachers can be effective in dealing with children, but not work well with fellow educators and their students' parents. For example, some teachers may resent persons in authority and resist their suggestions for improvement. Other teachers may yield too easily to suggestions from persons in authority, only to later feel guilty about complying instead of sticking up for their own convictions. Or some teachers may feel the need to compete with other teachers for administrative or student approval. Many of the comments already made regarding teachers' attitudes toward themselves and children also apply to their attitudes toward peers and parents. Some teachers may harbor feelings of superiority or prejudice toward students' parents. Others simply have little tolerance for people who differ from them in values, cultural background, or economic status, and, as a result, they treat parents with disdain and contempt rather than patience and respect. By contrast, effective teachers—those who work well with colleagues and parents to empower children to achieve—show attitudes of acceptance. In their dealings with other teachers and parents, teachers should be real and genuine, value other people as worthy in their own right, and show empathy.

> *Treat people as if they were what they ought to be and you help them to become what they are capable of being.*
>
> —JOHANN W. VON GOETHE (1749–1832),
> German Poet and Philosopher

When teachers and parents respect one another and work together, children are certain to benefit.

(Stephanie Horrocks/iStockphoto.com)

TEACHERS' ATTITUDES TOWARD THE SUBJECT MATTER

The message, in one word, is ENTHUSIASM! Just as students are perceptive in discovering the teacher's attitude toward them, they are also sensitive to the teacher's attitude toward the subject matter. Teachers who are not enthusiastic about what they teach can hardly hope to instill enthusiasm in their pupils. After all, if you don't care about the subject matter, how can you ever hope to motivate your students into learning about it? (The Video Case *Elementary Writing Instruction: Process Writing* shows a teacher and a literary specialist who both demonstrate their enthusiasm for writing and their respect for their students.)

Some teachers find it difficult to feel enthusiasm for a curriculum they haven't constructed themselves, don't identify with, or don't want to teach. Unfortunately, as states have adopted learning standards geared toward mandatory testing for students, the latitude that teachers once had to choose content is being greatly curtailed. States expect teachers to teach to the standards, and the high-stakes assessment tests given to students exert considerable pressure on teachers to be certain they "cover the content" contained on the assessments.

Teacher enthusiasm is usually contagious.

(© Elizabeth Crews)

If you have to teach something you would rather not, try to develop a positive attitude toward the subject. Enthusiasm is key to teaching success: if the teacher has it, life in the classroom can be exciting; if it is missing, there is little hope that students will learn much of significance.

what would you do?

1. You are a woman, a beginning teacher in a ninth-grade English course. As the first semester proceeds, you realize that one of your students, Fred, has a crush on you. He is always volunteering to help you pass out papers, and he lingers after class each day to talk to you. He finds out your home address and comes to visit you one Saturday morning. His actions are becoming obvious to the other students, who are starting to kid him about his infatuation. *What would you do?*

2. You are generally recognized as one of the most popular teachers in your high school. The students look on you as a friend who can be trusted, and you have told them that if they ever have problems, whether school related or personal, they should feel free to come to you. One day, Maryanne, a junior in one of your classes, seeks you out. Close to hysteria, she tells you she is 10 weeks pregnant. You are the first per-

son she has told. She begs you for advice but insists that you not tell her parents. *What would you do?*

3. You are a fourth-grade teacher. Until recently, you have been quite comfortable in your class of 23 children. About three weeks ago, you had to speak to Debbie. Although she is your brightest student, she was continually talking when you were trying to address the class. Since your conversation, Debbie has been as cool as ice to you, and you recently discovered a nasty drawing in your desk drawer that was supposed to be you. *What would you do?*

4. You are a white teacher in a somewhat racially tense school. There are seven African American students in one of your classes. Because you fear alienating the African American students and being accused of prejudice, you make special efforts to treat them fairly. One

(continued)

day, three of your white students come to see you and accuse you of coddling the African American students and discriminating against whites. *What would you do?*

5. You teach in a school that uses a letter grading system. You have assigned your students a term paper. You know that one student has spent hours and hours on his report, but its quality is quite poor. The student has already expressed his hope that you will take effort into account when grading the reports. *What would you do?*

how do teachers treat low achievers?

Researchers have not definitely established why some teachers treat students they perceive as high achievers ("highs") and low achievers ("lows") differently, but observations of many classroom teachers reveal that they often behave differently toward these two groups of students. Good and Brophy (2008) have summarized these differences:

1. Teachers wait less time for lows to answer a question.
2. Teachers give lows answers or call on someone else for the answer instead of giving clues or providing additional opportunities to respond.
3. Teachers reward lows for inappropriate behaviors or incorrect answers.
4. Lows are more often criticized for failure than are highs.
5. Lows are praised less frequently for success than are highs.
6. Generally, teachers interact less often with lows, paying less attention to them.

> *High expectations are the key to everything.*
>
> —SAM WALTON,
> Founder of Walmart

7. Teachers call on lows less often for answers to questions.
8. Teachers seat lows farther from the teacher.
9. Less is demanded from lows.
10. When teachers grade tests and assignments, they give highs—but not lows—the benefit of the doubt in borderline cases.
11. Lows experience fewer friendly interactions, including fewer smiles and other nonverbal signs of support.
12. Teachers make less eye contact and respond less attentively to lows.
13. Teachers demonstrate less acceptance and use of lows' ideas.
14. Lows are exposed to an impoverished curriculum.

As a teacher, you should make it a point to reflect on your own behavior toward low and high achievers, making sure that you are treating all your students fairly.

Source: From Thomas L. Good and Jere E. Brophy, *Looking in Classrooms*, 10th ed. © 2008. Reproduced by permission of Pearson Education, Inc., Upper Saddle River, New Jersey.

PAUSE AND REFLECT

1. Can you think of any examples of where a teacher's expectations of you or another student led to a self-fulfilling prophecy? Describe the circumstances.

2. Which attitudes do you possess that you think will have either positive or potentially negative effects on student learning?

3. Do you have negative feelings or expectations about any group or type of people? Can you identify the basis of those feelings? Do you want to change them? If so, how might you try?

PAUSE AND REFLECT

1. Do you have any concerns about your attitudes toward students' parents, school administrators, or other teachers? If you do, what can you do now to improve your attitudes?

2. Can you think of any ways that you, as a teacher, might be able to work up more enthusiasm for a topic that does not at first seem very interesting?

3. If you begin to lose your enthusiasm about a certain subject after you have taught it for a few years, what steps could you take to rekindle your interest?

> *Enthusiasm is contagious. Be a carrier.*
>
> —SUSAN RABIN,
> Author and Communications Consultant

what subject-matter knowledge does the effective teacher need?

Very simply, prospective teachers need to understand the content of the subjects they teach as well as the methods of teaching the specific content. Three important components contribute to a teacher's content knowledge.

First, teachers need to understand the subjects they teach well enough to analyze and convey their elements, logic, possible uses, and social biases—that is, teachers need to understand the structure of the subjects they teach. Second, the teacher must understand the content of the school curriculum that pupils are expected to know. Unfortunately, most college courses in the specific disciplines don't prepare prospective teachers to actually teach the knowledge that students are expected to learn. Much of what prospective teachers learn from their study of the academic disciplines is not taught to children and so is not directly applicable to teaching. This is particularly true for elementary school teachers, who are called on to teach content that is rarely taught in universities. For example, a mathematics major who is preparing to teach elementary school may never have occasion to use differential equations or calculus in the content she or he teaches to elementary-age children. Thus, although studying and understanding specific disciplines is crucial, it is not sufficient for effective teaching. A teacher must also study the actual curriculum taught in his or her school, as well as the state learning standards for the particular grade. Carol Landis, for example, designed her group project so that it would contribute to her students' ability to meet their district's standards in social studies.

A third type of knowledge shown by effective teachers is **pedagogical content knowledge**, the knowledge that bridges content knowledge and pedagogy. Pedagogical content knowledge represents the "blending of content and pedagogy into an understanding of how particular topics, problems, or issues are organized, represented, and adapted to the diverse interests and abilities of learners, and presented for instruction."[3] The skilled teacher draws on the most powerful analogies, illustrations, examples, explanations, and demonstrations to represent and transform the subject so that students can understand it. For example, a physics teacher who possesses pedagogical content knowledge might use the analogy of water flowing through a pipe to explain how electricity flows through a circuit, but he or she would also know the limitations of such an analogy. Pedagogical content knowledge enables the teacher to recognize common misunderstandings that students may make in learning new concepts and to know how to overcome those errors in thinking.

These three types of knowledge—of discipline content (including the structure of the discipline), of curriculum content, and of pedagogical content—are, we believe, essential for effective teachers. Did Carol Landis have such knowledge? We suspect not, at least not to the degree that she could communicate information and concepts to her class with the authority and expertise required for effective teaching. In the next section, we examine more closely another area of the effective teacher's knowledge: theoretical knowledge about learning and human behavior.

PAUSE AND REFLECT

1. Which parts of the discipline content you are learning in college do you expect to teach to your own students? Which parts are you likely not to teach to them?

2. Do you recall any teachers from your own schooling who demonstrated especially strong or weak content knowledge? How did they demonstrate their level of knowledge?

---

what theoretical knowledge does the effective teacher need?

Theoretical knowledge about learning and human behavior equips the teacher to draw on concepts from psychology, anthropology, sociology, and related disciplines to interpret the complex reality of the classroom. The teacher who lacks a theoretical background will have to interpret classroom events according to commonly held

beliefs or common sense—much of which is based on erroneous notions of human behavior.

THEORIES-IN-USE

Carol Landis operated on the basis of certain ideas that are called *theories-in-use*, which differ from pure theories in important ways.[4] A theory is an unproved explanation of why something happens the way it does. In its simplest form, a theory is a hypothesis designed to bring generalizable facts, concepts, or scientific laws into systematic connection. By contrast, a theory-in-use is something people have in their heads and apply in their dealings with people and the world. Theories-in-use are often unexamined.

We all have our own theories-in-use, which guide us as we make our way through our daily lives. For example, you may eat certain foods because you have an idea that they have a healthy effect on the body. You may also decide to take a summer job in a public playground, believing that you will get to know children better and that future prospective employers might be pleased or impressed when they discover your experience.

Carol Landis has several theories-in-use. For example, she has the theory-in-use that groups should operate democratically and not be dominated by one student. She also has a theory-in-use that some children will perform better in school than others; as a result, Carol expects certain behavior from certain kinds of students. She also has a classroom management theory-in-use that she should give students some leeway before she resorts to firm discipline when they exceed her level of tolerance. Some of Carol's theories-in-use are clearly questionable. A few may have contributed to her problems that day in the library, and some may cause her more problems further down the line. Carol was not worried about her theories-in-use, however: she was worried about what she did and what she will do. In other words, Carol didn't question some of her conceptions. Theories-in-use were the last things she had in mind, even though they actually caused some of her problems.

PAUSE AND REFLECT

Has reading about Carol Landis and her theories-in-use helped you identify any of your own theories-in-use or those of teachers you have known? If so, what are some of those theories-in-use?

WHY STUDY EDUCATIONAL THEORY?

The fact that Carol did not reflect on the validity of her theories-in-use or try to recall some theories she had learned during her teacher education is not unusual. Indeed, many teachers question the basic usefulness of theory. Many a beginning teacher has been told by a senior colleague, "Forget all that theory they've been giving you in college. Here's what works in the real world." Further, preservice teachers often complain that courses are too theoretical. They want to get out to schools, where the real action is. This desire (perhaps it is your own desire) for things that work and ways to cope with real situations is vital, and we certainly do not want to diminish it. As a teacher, you will need practical techniques and solutions to real problems. Even so, it does not make educational theory any less important.

The case of Carol Landis illustrates how a lack of theoretical knowledge of classroom management can lead to inappropriate behavior on the teacher's part. Both theory and empirical research support the notion of being consistent in your expectations of student behavior. Carol, however, thought it was acceptable to let students behave as they wished until they crossed her tolerance threshold, at which point she came down hard on them. Carol probably would not have encountered such trouble if more of her theories-in-use had been challenged and adjusted.

Like Carol, you may have your own theories-in-use, and they need to be challenged and tested. The best way to do so is to pit them against other theories and ideas. We believe that theoretical information *is* practical. The problem is not that theory is always wrong or unworkable, but rather that many teacher education programs offer students few opportunities to apply theory to practical situations. As the great American philosopher John Dewey said, "Nothing is so practical as a good theory."* By giving attention to theoretical knowledge now, we are also looking ahead to the future: at a later stage of your development, you will encounter theories that will undoubtedly enlighten and enrich your work with the young.

HOW CAN THEORETICAL KNOWLEDGE BE USED?

A teacher's theoretical knowledge can be used in two ways: to interpret new or ambiguous situations and to solve problems.[5] (Conversely, personal practical knowledge is more limited in applicability and is used primarily to respond to familiar situations; we discuss personal practical knowledge shortly.) As the "Teaching: Art or Science?" feature describes, the "art" of teaching is knowing how and when to apply research and theory in the fast-paced classroom.

An Example of Using Theoretical Knowledge

Let's consider an example of how theoretical knowledge can help a teacher interpret classroom events and solve the problems arising from them. Educational psychology includes the concept known as the **zone of proximal development,** meaning a range of tasks that a child cannot yet do alone but can accomplish when assisted by a more skilled partner. In other words, the child is on the verge of being able to solve a problem but just needs some structure, clues, help with remembering certain steps or procedures, or encouragement to try. (This assistance, called **scaffolding,** allows students to complete tasks they can't complete independently.) This zone is where instruction can succeed and where real learning is possible. The concept of the zone of proximal development derives from the work of Russian psychologist Lev Vygotsky, who theorized that a child's culture shapes cognitive development by determining what and how the child will learn about the world.

Now suppose that a student, John, is experiencing difficulty doing some percentage problems in math. You, as the teacher, understand that the zone of proximal development is influenced by reasoning ability, background knowledge, and motivation. Armed with this theoretical background, you assess John's ability to

*For the moment we downplay the fact that John Dewey was primarily an educational theorist.

teaching: art or science?

One of the pioneers of research on teaching, the late N. L. Gage, of Stanford University, and Robert Marzano, a contemporary educational researcher, both believe teaching cannot be reduced to formulas or recipes for action, but see it as a blend of art and science. Teaching can be considered an art because teachers must improvise and spontaneously handle a tremendous number of factors that interact in often unpredictable and nonsystematic ways in classroom settings.

At the same time, both contend that teaching is also a science. Although science cannot offer absolute guidance for teachers as they plan and implement instructional strategies, research can provide a scientific basis for the art of teaching. For example, the research on academic engaged time has demonstrated the importance of keeping pupils on task with intellectually challenging, but not too difficult, subject matter.

These two components of teaching—art and science—interact in exciting ways. Empirically derived knowledge of the relationships among teacher behavior, pupil behavior, material to be learned, and desired student learning can guide teachers as they make artistic decisions about their teaching—that is, teachers use their knowledge of the research on these relationships to accomplish the artistry of moving a unique classroom filled with unique students toward the intended learning.

Is teaching an art or a science? The answer is "yes."

Sources: N. L. Gage, *Hard Gains in the Soft Sciences: The Case of Pedagogy* (Bloomington, IN: Phi Delta Kappa, 1985), pp. 4–11; Robert J. Marzano, *The Art and Science of Teaching* (Alexandria, VA: Association for Supervision and Curriculum Development, 2007), pp. 2, 4–5.

understand the problems by watching him try to solve one of them. You ask him to explain to you what he is thinking as he attempts the solutions. Is he missing some important understanding, or is he making some procedural error? Are the problems too difficult, or should he be able to solve them with some assistance? If the latter, what kind of assistance does he need? Who should give him the assistance—you or another student?

You decide that John is not lacking any fundamental knowledge and is very close to understanding the correct procedures. You ask Mary, a student who understands percentage problems pretty well, to come over and think aloud as she works on one of the problems. By thinking aloud and having John follow along, Mary provides John with insight into how she goes about solving the problem. You encourage John to ask Mary questions as she goes over her solution. You now ask John to work a similar problem, also thinking aloud as he tries to solve it. This time, he gets the problem correct. You ask him to do a couple more problems and to raise his hand when he finishes so you can check whether his understanding carried over to the new problems.

How did the theoretical knowledge about the zone of proximal development assist you in helping John? First, you had to determine whether John was close to understanding or was missing some fundamental knowledge. Was he in the zone of proximal development where additional coaching or assistance would help him, or would you have to reteach some important knowledge that he didn't have? Second, you had to decide which sort of scaffolding would benefit John. By having both Mary and John think aloud as they solved the problem, mistakes or errors could be easily determined and, if solved correctly, would provide a model for John. An understanding of the zone of proximal development and its related scaffolding strategies represents the kind of theoretical knowledge that can help you interpret and solve classroom problems.

This example helps show that a teacher needs much more than a common-sense understanding of human behavior. The capable and effective teacher uses theoretical knowledge drawn from various education-related disciplines to formulate and test hypotheses about human behavior in the classroom. The translation of theory into practice cannot be left to chance; however, you must constantly take advantage of opportunities that allow you to apply theoretical concepts to classroom situations and to receive guidance and feedback from your instructors about the application of these concepts. The field of cognitive psychology, in particular, has provided a treasure trove of research findings and theoretical concepts for teachers.

> *Education must bring the practice as nearly as possible to the theory.*
>
> —HORACE MANN (1796–1859),
> Nineteenth-Century American Educational Reformer

personal practical knowledge

Personal practical knowledge is the set of understandings teachers have of the practical circumstances in which they work. Personal practical knowledge includes the beliefs, insights, and habits that allow teachers to do their jobs in schools. This type of knowledge tends to be time bound and situation specific, personally compelling, and oriented toward action. Teachers use their personal practical knowledge to solve dilemmas, resolve tensions, and simplify the complexities of their work. For example, the personal practical knowledge that Carol Landis must develop ranges from learning whether another teacher will loan his collection of *National Geographic* magazines to other classes, to clarifying her beliefs about whether assigning students to groups is better than letting them choose their own groups. Because teachers' personal practical knowledge is so intertwined with their identities as individuals, researchers have not been able to summarize this knowledge into a codified body of teaching knowledge. Case studies of teachers have, however, provided us with rich images of how teachers use their knowledge to make sense of the complex, ill-structured environment that characterizes most classrooms.

Teachers' personal practical knowledge definitely influences the decisions they make. Some researchers argue that a well-informed belief system is the most credible basis for rational teacher decisions. They assert that teachers should become aware of the assumptions that comprise their belief systems. Over time, as they develop attitudes and habits of practice, teachers should reflect on these beliefs to ensure that they conform to accepted educational principles.[6] Carol Landis, for example, is already reflecting on the educational soundness of her belief that students work well in groups with their friends. As you plan instruction, interact in classrooms, and evaluate instructional outcomes, continually testing your attitudes and habits of practice against sound educational principles can help protect you against poor educational decision making.

which teaching skills are required of an effective teacher?

Simply knowing something does not guarantee the ability to act on that knowledge. There is a profound difference between *knowing* and *doing*. Teachers may know, for example, that they should provide prompt feedback to their students on written assignments, but they are not always able to act on that knowledge. Teachers may also know that certain kinds of questions stimulate higher cognitive levels of thinking, but they may not be able to ask those types of questions during a discussion. No teacher education program can afford to focus only on theoretical knowledge at the expense of the practice—that is, the "doing"—dimension of teaching, just as no individual teacher can rely solely on knowledge of subject matter. All prospective teachers need to develop a repertoire of *teaching skills* to use as they see fit in varying classroom situations.

Among the skills that many educators believe are essential to effective teaching are the following:

- Asking different kinds of questions, each requiring different types of thought processes from the student
- Providing effective feedback
- Planning instruction and student learning activities
- Diagnosing student needs and learning difficulties
- Varying the learning situation to keep students involved
- Recognizing when students are paying attention and using this information to vary behavior and, possibly, the direction of the lesson
- Using technological equipment, such as computers, to enhance student learning
- Assessing student learning
- Differentiating instruction based on the students' experiences, interests, and academic abilities
- Using students' cultures to make learning experiences relevant and effective for them

Although far from complete, this list does suggest that teachers need a large repertoire of skills to work effectively with students with varying backgrounds and different educational experiences. (Look at the list of InTASC standards on the inside cover of this book to see how many of these standards require particular teaching skills.) Using a variety of approaches is essential to meet the many different needs of students. As Figure 6.1 illustrates, effective use of teaching skills, along with appropriate attitudes, knowledge of subject matter, theoretical knowledge, and personal practical knowledge, leads to better instructional decision making.

Next, we focus on the skills preservice teachers need in three areas that are often of special concern: classroom management, effective questioning, and planning techniques. No other dimension of teaching causes more concern for beginning teachers than managing the classroom and maintaining discipline. "Will I be able to manage and control my class(es) so I can teach effectively?" is a question most beginning teachers ask themselves. Because this aspect of teaching generates so much anxiety, we have chosen to spend some time on this skill area first, before turning, somewhat more briefly, to questioning and planning skills.

CLASSROOM MANAGEMENT SKILLS

Classroom management refers to "the actions teachers take to create an environment that is respectful, caring, orderly, and productive. Classroom management supports and facilitates both academic and socioemotional learning."[7] Developing teacher–student rapport, arranging the physical environment, establishing rules and procedures, and maintaining students' attention to lessons and engagement in activities are examples of classroom managerial behavior. Managerial behavior also includes housekeeping duties such as record keeping, and managing time, facilities, and resources in the classroom. Effective classroom management focuses on how to prevent misbehavior, as well as how to handle misbehavior when it occurs.

There are a number of factors that contribute to beginning teachers' concerns about classroom management. First, classrooms are complex, diverse, and crowded environments that challenge teachers to meet the different needs of each individual student. Second, classes are more culturally diverse than ever, and the norms of what constitutes acceptable and desirable behavior often vary among different cultures. Third, many children with disabilities are now educated in general education classrooms, presenting regular education teachers with considerable challenge to meet the needs of all the students. Fourth, many students come from circumstances (e.g., poverty, broken families, abuse) that create psychological and emotional problems that teachers must cope with. (See Chapter 3, "Who Are Today's Students in a Diverse Society?" and Chapter 4, "What Social Problems Affect Today's Students?" for more on these topics.) And finally, beginning teachers often report that their teacher education programs did not adequately prepare them to address the factors mentioned above.

The last 40 years or so have produced significant new knowledge about effective classroom management practices. The following sections describe some of those findings.

Visit the website to link to more advice on classroom management.

Academic Engaged Time

Research that focuses on student behaviors, such as academic engaged time, reveals some interesting insights into effective teaching skills.* **Academic engaged time**, also known as *engaged learning time*, is the time a student spends being successfully engaged with academically relevant activities or materials. Several research studies indicate that academic engaged time is strongly related to achievement in those subjects.[8] Simply put, the more time elementary students spend working on reading or mathematics activities that provide them with successful experiences, the more likely they are to achieve in those areas. Although this finding may not seem very startling, observations indicate that tremendous differences exist in the amount of time individual students spend engaged in academic activities, both across classrooms and within the same classroom.

The research on academic engaged time clearly indicates that a primary goal of elementary teachers (and probably secondary teachers, although the research has been limited mostly to elementary schools) should be to keep students on task. Classes that are poorly managed usually have little academic learning time, so a major task of teachers is to learn how to manage their classes so that students are productively engaged.

Numerous studies indicate that the most efficient teachers are able to engage their students about 30 minutes a day longer than the "average" teacher. If the most efficient

---

* On-task behavior, time on task, and academic engaged time are related concepts. *On-task behavior* is student activity that is appropriate to the teacher's goals. *Time on task* refers to the amount of time students spend engaged in on-task behavior. *Academic engaged time* adds the dimensions of a high success rate and academically relevant activities or materials to the concept of time on task.

TABLE 6.1	Different Approaches to Classroom Management	
Name	**Major Developers**	**Characteristics**
Behavior modification	B. F. Skinner	Originates from behavioral psychology. Modify student behaviour by consistently and systematically rewarding (reinforcing) appropriate student behavior and removing rewards for, or punishing, inappropriate student behavior.
Socioemotional climate	Carl Rogers William Glasser Haim Ginott	Originates in counseling and clinical psychology. Emphasis on building positive interpersonal relationships between students and teachers.
Group process	Richard Schmuck and Patricia Schmuck Lois Johnson and Mary Bany	Originates in social psychology and group dynamics research. Emphasis on teacher establishing and maintaining effective, productive classroom group. Unity and cooperation, as well as group problem solving, are key elements.
Ecological	Jacob Kounin and Paul Gump	Emphasis is on *habitat*. Physical context has elements that must be established and managed to maintain order, such as planning and organizing lessons, monitoring activities, and explaining rules.
Authority	Lee Canter and Marlene Canter	Views classroom management as a process of controlling student behavior, primarily by using discipline. Emphasizes establishing and enforcing rules, using soft reprimands and orders to desist. Assertive *discipline is a popular* manifestation of this approach.

(© Cengage Learning 2013)

(T) F

Efficient teachers can provide students with as much as 180 hours a year more of engaged learning time than inefficient teachers. Research studies have shown that teachers vary greatly in their abilities to keep student on task and academically engaged, even as much as an hour a day difference.

teachers are compared with the least efficient, daily differences of one hour in academic engaged time appear. When this difference is extrapolated over 180 days, students of efficient teachers get 90 hours more of academic engaged time than students of average teachers and 180 hours more than students of inefficient teachers! Differences of this magnitude may help explain why students in some classes learn more than students in others. The feature on characteristic behaviors of effective teachers (below) describes some of the skills these teachers use to keep their students engaged so much of the time.

Kounin's Research

Jacob Kounin's research on classroom management in the elementary school grades explains which skills can help teachers improve their classroom management and keep pupils on task.[9] Kounin discovered that effective managers keep students involved in academic tasks, minimize the frequency with which students become

what are some characteristic behaviors of effective teachers?

In a review of research on teacher behaviors that relate to desirable student performance, Gary Borich identified five key behaviors that are consistently supported by research, and five helping behaviors that have some support and appear logically related to effective teaching.

Key Behaviors

1. *Lesson clarity.* Effective teachers speak directly and audibly to all students, and they explain concepts in a way that students can follow in a logical step-by-step order.
2. *Instructional variety.* Effective teachers vary their modes of presentation, use attention-getting devices, demonstrate enthusiasm, and vary the types of questions asked.
3. *Teacher task orientation.* Effective teachers spend more classroom time teaching academic subjects as opposed to procedural matters such as distributing handouts, collecting homework, or taking attendance.
4. *Engaged learning time.* Effective teachers' students spend more time actively engaged in learning the material being taught.
5. *Student success rate.* Effective teachers peg the academic work so students have a moderate-to-high success rate, which results in increased academic performance.

Helping Behaviors

1. *Using student ideas and contributions.* Effective teachers use student ideas and contributions to drive the learning process, which increases student engagement in the learning process.
2. *Structuring.* Effective teachers make comments for the purpose of organizing upcoming learning activities or summarizing what has occurred.
3. *Questioning.* Effective teachers ask a variety of questions about the content to be learned, tapping a range of thinking processes, from simple to more complex.
4. *Probing.* Effective teachers probe student responses to get students to elaborate on their own or other students' answers, thereby prompting students to think more deeply than their initial response.
5. *Teacher affect.* Effective teachers establish positive teacher–student relationships through their enthusiasm for their subjects and their students.

Source: Gary D. Borich, *Effective Teaching Methods: Research-Based Practice,* 7th ed. © 2011. Reproduced by permission of Pearson Education, Inc., Upper Saddle River, New Jersey.

disruptive, and resolve minor disruptions before they escalate into major ones. Of the concepts Kounin identified to describe teacher classroom management behavior, three seem particularly useful.

The first concept Kounin termed *withitness*. Teachers who are "with it" are those who communicate to pupils and so, by their behavior, appear that they know what is going on. Teachers who are "with it" pick up on the first sign of misbehavior, deal with the proper pupil, ignore a minor misbehavior to stop a major infraction, and so forth. Students are often convinced that these teachers have "eyes in the back of their heads."

The second and third concepts concern the problems of lesson flow and time management. *Smoothness* involves the absence of teacher behaviors that interfere with the flow of academic events. Examples of teacher behavior that do not reflect smoothness occur when a teacher bursts in on children's activities with an order, statement, or question; when a teacher starts or is engaged in some activity and then

leaves it "hanging," only to resume it after an interval; and when a teacher terminates one activity, starts another, and then initiates a return to the terminated activity.

The third concept, *momentum,* concerns the absence of teacher behaviors that slow down the pace of the lesson. Kounin conceptualized two types of slow-down behaviors:

- *Overdwelling*—when a teacher dwells too much on pupil behavior, on a subpoint rather than the main point, on physical props rather than substance, or on instructions or details to the point of boredom
- *Fragmentation*—when a teacher deals with individual pupils one at a time rather than with the group, or unnecessarily breaks a task into smaller parts when the task could have been accomplished in a single step

Kounin discovered that teachers who are effective classroom managers emphasize the prevention of disruptions rather than having to deal with them after they occur. Good managers do so by keeping the students engaged in lessons and assignments through effective application of the skills related to withitness, smoothness, and momentum.

Other Research Findings

Many researchers have replicated and extended Kounin's work on classroom management. Two key principles emerge from this research: (1) Good management is preventive rather than reactive, and (2) teachers create well-managed classrooms by teaching their students desired behavior.[10] Here are a few other important recommendations arising from the research:

1. *Establish clearly defined rules and routines.* Clear rules and routines decrease the complexity of the classroom, minimize confusion, and prevent loss of instructional time. Having students help make the rules increases their commitment to abide by them.

2. *Ensure students' compliance with rules and demands.* To encourage students to comply willingly with the rules and routines, teachers must gain students' cooperation by establishing positive relationships, sharing responsibilities, and using rewards. This is accomplished more effectively by establishing and maintaining effective learning environments than by relying on authority or the teacher's role as a disciplinarian. Nevertheless, teachers must be willing to enforce the consequences for repeated misconduct and be able to administer those outcomes in a way that is not threatening, punitive, or perceived as unfair.

3. *Involve families.* When families understand what the teacher is trying to achieve, they can provide valuable support and assistance, including helping develop and carry out successful behavior management plans.

One school of thought rejects the notion of effective classroom management as a system of rewards and punishments, arguing that these outcomes are seen as instruments for controlling people. In this approach, instead of teachers seeing themselves as being in charge and taking steps to maintain that control, they should give up some of the control and help students work together to decide how to be respectful and fair; that is, teachers should help students develop an internal sense of how to work together in a community.[11] The approach may sometimes engender chaos and uncertainty, but advocates believe that students will learn ethics and democracy in action. One of your responsibilities as a teacher will be to develop a philosophy and ways of operating in the classroom that make sense to you and that accomplish what you value. Your attitude toward the use of rewards and punishments will be part of that development.

As a result of researchers' work, we are learning more about what constitutes effective classroom management behavior. Understanding the related theories and research and practicing the skills that this body of knowledge has identified as effective will help you establish and maintain the conditions that promote student learning. Effective classroom management is a skill that can be taught and learned. (See the feature Kevin and Jim's Suggestions for Classroom Management Problems.)

kevin and jim's suggestions for classroom management problems

1. *When students misbehave, check your instruction.* Many behavior problems result from problems with instruction. Students may be bored or confused, in which case their response may be to get off task and into trouble.

2. *Take the time to ensure that students fully understand your classroom's rules and procedures.* As the old adage has it, "You have to keep school before you can teach school." At the beginning of the year, and again if and when things begin to break down, teachers need to fix in the minds of their students how the class is to be ordered.

3. *Regularly monitor the entire class.* Successful classroom managers frequently scan the class, noticing what each student is doing. Although the teacher need not react to every sign of off-task behavior or deviation from the established procedure, students should know that what they are doing is being noted.

4. *Move in on repeated or flagrant breaches of conduct quickly and directly.* Do not let things drift. Students will think you are afraid to confront them, and they may end up confronting you!

5. *Correct in private.* As much as possible, deal with student misconduct in private. Don't disturb the rest of the students and get them off task simply to get one or two students back to work. Also, public reprimands may backfire and get you involved in a game of escalating remarks with a student.

6. *Don't make empty threats.* Do not say you are going to "do" something to a student or the class unless you have thought it over carefully and are really ready to do it. For instance, do not threaten to call the parents of every child in the room and tell them what rotten children they have unless you have a good deal of time—and alternative plans for next year.

(continued)

7. *Don't put a hand on a student in anger or even annoyance.* Do not even think of striking a student, no matter how much you are tempted. When a situation is emotionally charged, even your well-intended gesture can be misinterpreted. If students are fighting, however, you may need to restrain them physically for their own good.

8. *Think through behavior problems.* When your class or an individual student is not behaving up to your expectations, treat the event as a problem-solving activity. Do not flail around or get panicky or discouraged. Coolly identify exactly what the problem is, consider possible causes, and test some possible solutions.

9. *Get help.* If management problems persist and you cannot solve them on your own, get help from a colleague or an administrator. Do not let things fester. Do not be shy about asking for help, particularly in relation to discipline problems, which are so common for many beginning teachers.

10. *Be sure there is a back-up system.* If you need to remove a student from your room, you need to know that a system is in place to back you up.

11. *Be sure your rules are in accord with school-wide expectations.* For example, if the school has decided that chewing gum is tolerable and you crack down on it, you can expect to have more trouble than the issue is probably worth.

PAUSE AND REFLECT

1. Do the research findings on academic engaged time surprise you, or do they seem obvious? If you think the findings reflect common sense, why do you suppose teachers vary so much in their ability to keep students engaged?

2. Are you concerned about your ability to establish and maintain a productive classroom environment? If so, what particularly concerns you?

3. We have included a number of suggestions for managing a classroom. Which seem most useful to you, and why? Which do you believe you would find most difficult to use, and why?

QUESTIONING SKILLS

The questioning process is a central feature of most classrooms. Teachers ask questions not only to monitor student comprehension but also to stimulate students to engage with the content, relate it to their prior knowledge, and to think about its applications. Studies indicate that teachers may ask hundreds of questions in a day's lessons, but they often fail to ask questions that require students to process and analyze information, and many of their questions require only a rote response of memorized facts. Teachers also tend to rush students' responses, not giving them adequate time to provide varied and thoughtful answers. Some teachers do not direct as many questions to certain groups of students, such as minority students, girls or boys, or "slower" learners, thereby depriving them of the opportunity to be active participants in classroom learning.[12] Mastery of questioning skills contributes to students' learning and therefore is important for effective teaching.

Wait-Time

Good questioning behavior requires that the teacher provide students with sufficient time to think about and respond to questions. What do you think is the average amount of time a teacher waits for a student to respond to a question she or he has asked? Mary Budd Rowe, a science educator, determined in a series of studies that the teachers she observed waited less than one second before calling on a student to respond. Furthermore, after calling on a student, they waited only about a second for the student to answer before calling on someone else, rephrasing the question, giving a clue, or answering it themselves! How can students think carefully or deeply when they have only one second to respond to a teacher's question?

Rowe followed up these observations with studies designed to train teachers to increase their **wait-time** after questions from one second to three to five seconds. She reported amazing results: (1) an increase in the average length of student responses, (2) an increase in unsolicited but appropriate student responses, (3) an increase in student-initiated questions, (4) a decrease in failures to respond, (5) an increase in student-to-student interaction, and (6) an increase in speculative responses. In short, she found that longer wait-times led to more active participation on the part of more students and an increase in the quality of their participation.

> *A prudent question is one-half of wisdom.*
>
> —SIR FRANCIS BACON (1561–1626),
> Seventeenth-Century English Philosopher

Subsequent research by others replicated Rowe's findings. If questions require students to think about material or generate original responses, they need a longer time to think about their answers than if they are being asked only to recall information from memory.[13]

Effective Questioning Techniques

In addition to longer wait-times, those who have studied the relationship between questioning strategies and student achievement have identified a number of other techniques as signs of effective teaching. This research suggests that teachers use the following strategies:

1. Phrase questions clearly. Avoid vague questions.
2. Ask questions that are purposeful in achieving the lesson's intent.
3. Ask brief questions, because long ones are often unclear.
4. Ask questions that are thought-provoking and demand original and evaluative thinking.
5. Encourage students to respond in some way to each question asked.
6. Distribute questions to a range of students, and balance responses from volunteering and nonvolunteering students.
7. Avoid asking "yes/no" and "leading" questions.
8. To stimulate thinking, probe students' responses or demand support for their answers.
9. Provide students with feedback about their responses, both to motivate them and to let them know how they are doing.[14]

With knowledge and practice, teachers can learn questioning strategies that engage all students in the verbal interaction that supports learning.

PLANNING SKILLS

Another skill related to a teacher's effectiveness is skill in planning. The plans teachers make for lessons influence the opportunities students have to learn because plans determine the content students will experience in a lesson and the focus of the teaching processes. Effective teachers base their plans on a rich store of perceptions of classroom events and of their students' progress toward educational objectives and

> *Failing to plan is planning to fail.*
>
> —EFFIE JONES (1919–2002),
> Twentieth-Century Teacher and School Administrator

Through effective questioning techniques, teachers can encourage and promote student attention and participation in discussions.

(© Laura Dwight)

content standards. This store of perceptions (ways of looking at students and classroom activities) also helps the teacher make adjustments during instruction when plans must be adapted to the immediate situation.

Teachers do four basic types of planning—yearly, unit, weekly, and daily—and all are important for effective instruction.[15] Research shows that experienced teachers don't plan the way curriculum experts recommend—that is, by beginning with instructional objectives and then selecting instructional activities to meet those objectives. Instead, many elementary school teachers begin by considering the context in which teaching will occur (e.g., the materials and time available); then they think about activities that students will find interesting and that will involve them; finally, they ponder the purposes these activities will serve. Secondary school teachers, by comparison, focus almost entirely on the content and preparation of an interesting presentation.[16] This discrepancy from the recommended approach doesn't mean experienced teachers don't have goals, especially in these days of content standards; rather, it suggests that the interest and involvement of their students are paramount. Because research shows that student achievement is related to academic engaged time, planning should include consideration of how to involve students.

T (F)

Elementary and secondary school teachers plan their lessons in a similar fashion. Elementary school teachers tend to think of the context (time and materials available) and plan activities that they think will interest students. Secondary school teachers, on the other hand, tend to focus on the content and how to make an interesting presentation.

In this section, we have looked at three skill areas—classroom management, questioning, and planning—that researchers have identified as competencies demonstrated by effective teachers. (Another important skill relates to the use of technology, to which we devote a whole chapter.) Principals and other school evaluators assess beginning teachers' competence in these and other skills areas as part of their observations of beginning teachers. Standards for new teachers, such as those created by InTASC (discussed earlier in this chapter), also emphasize these skills. As a consequence, developing classroom management, questioning, and planning skills should be an important concern for those preparing to teach.

OUR FINAL WORD

This chapter is an important one because it provides an overview of what a truly effective teacher should know and be able to do. It may have been a frustrating chapter if you concluded that there is no way you can achieve the ideal we describe. We share that frustration because we have not attained this ideal in our own teaching, and we're not certain that we ever will. Nevertheless, we continue to aspire to be the type of teacher described here. If you can fix your sights on this conceptualization of an effective teacher and continually work toward this ideal, you are certain to observe positive and rewarding results in your own classroom.

Although we can detail the various proficiencies teachers need, noted educational author Jonathan

Kozol cuts to the chase in his description of what he would look for in a teacher:

> [O]bviously we want people who can teach [their subjects]. . . . But if I had to narrow it down to one characteristic, I would always hire teachers whom I wouldn't mind getting stuck with on a long plane flight to California. I would look for people who are capable of making the world seem joyful, people who are a delight to be with, people who are contagiously amusing human beings. To me, that's more important than almost anything else. I would put the emphasis on the capability to create contagious enthusiasm for life. There are a lot of teachers like that, but not enough.[17]

WHY TEACH? YOUR FINAL WORD

In your journal or online at this textbook's website, respond to the following questions:

1. We have maintained that decision-making skills are important for teachers. What can you do to improve your ability to make good decisions as you plan and deliver instruction?

2. Can you think of any ways that you, as a new teacher, could speed up the process of gaining personal practical knowledge?

3. Which of the classroom skills listed in this chapter seem most important to you? Which skills would you add to the list? Which skills would you subtract from it?

KEY TERMS

academic engaged time (183)
classroom management (183)
pedagogical content knowledge (177)
personal practical knowledge (181)
reflective teaching (163)

scaffolding (179)
self-fulfilling prophecy (172)
wait-time (189)
zone of proximal development (179)

FOR FURTHER INFORMATION

WEB RESOURCES

Education World. Available at: **www.education-world. com/a_curr/archives/shore.shtml.**

Education World presents a range of information concerning classroom management, including many tips for how to handle certain management problems.

Interstate Teacher Assessment and Support Consortium (InTASC). Available at **www.ccsso.org/resources/ programs/interstate_teacher_assessment_ consortium_(intasc).html and www.ncpublicschools. org/pbl/pblintasc.htm.**

A consortium of state education agencies, higher education institutions, and national educational organizations dedicated to the reform of the education, licensing, and ongoing professional development of teachers. Its core standards for beginning teachers can be located at either of these two sites.

The New York Times. Available at **www.nytimes.com/ learning/teachers/index.html.**

This newspaper website has daily lesson plans for grades 6–8 and 9–12, as well as daily news "snapshot" activities that can be developed into lesson plans for grades 3–5. This site can be a valuable resource for exemplary lessons and activities, especially by allowing users to access related academic standards for many individual states.

Teachers.Net. Available at **www.teachers.net/.**

This excellent site has an online reference desk, an active chat board, and a lesson plan exchange.

PRINT RESOURCES

James M. Cooper, ed., *Classroom Teaching Skills,* 9th ed. (Belmont, CA: Wadsworth, Cengage Learning, 2011).

This self-instructional book is designed to help teachers acquire basic teaching skills such as writing objectives, evaluation skills, classroom management skills, questioning skills, and differentiating instruction skills.

Charlotte Danielson, *Enhancing Professional Practice: A Framework for Teaching,* 2nd ed. (Alexandria, VA: ASCD, 2007).

This useful book, organized around a framework of professional practice, is based on the PRAXIS III criteria, including planning and preparation, classroom environment, instruction, and professional responsibilities.

Thomas L. Good and Jere E. Brophy, *Looking in Classrooms,* 10th ed. (Boston: Allyn and Bacon, 2008).

This excellent book provides teachers with concrete skills that will enable them to observe and interpret the classroom behavior of both teacher and students.

Robert J. Marzano, *The Art and Science of Teaching* (Alexandria, VA: Association of Supervision and Curriculum Development, 2007).

This highly readable text presents a framework for effective teaching based on research findings.

Carol Simon Weinstein and Andrew J. Mignano, Jr., *Elementary Classroom Management: Lessons from Research and Practice,* 4th ed. (New York: McGraw-Hill, 2007).

This practical book, based on sound research findings, addresses the major issues in establishing and maintaining effective learning environments. Weinstein has a secondary school version entitled *Middle and Secondary Classroom Management* (2007), also published by McGraw-Hill.

The Education CourseMate website for this text offers many helpful resources. Go to www.cengagebrain.com to access the TeachSource Video Cases and other TeachSource videos, flashcards, interactive quizzes, the eBook, reflection and enrichment activities, a state standards resource center, and other study aids.

7 what should teachers know about technology and its impact on schools?

InTASC standards 1, 2, 3, 4, 5, 6, 7, 8, and 10

FOCUS POINTS

- Technology and technological change are not new to the field of education.

- Schools are being pressured from many sides to incorporate contemporary technologies into instruction.

- Students can use computers not just for drill purposes but also in ways that promote creativity, collaboration, and higher-order thinking.

- Technologies can help teachers change their role from dispensers of information to facilitators of students' learning.

- Teachers can benefit from the productivity of computers in areas ranging from record keeping to staff development.

- The placement of technology within the educational setting affects how it can be used.

- Issues involving equity, teacher education, infrastructure, and budgeting will need careful consideration as technological tools become more integrated into classroom instruction.

(© Susie Fitzhugh)

The use of technology in the classroom has gained attention as an issue in education. As our society continues to embrace new forms of communication, networking, and computer technologies, our schools are scrambling to keep up. In this chapter, we explore what teachers should know about technology and its use in the educational setting, which roles technology may fulfill in education, and how those roles may change what students and teachers do in the classroom.

Truth or Fiction?

T F One of the main pressures on schools to use technology comes from the business sector.

T F Drill-and-practice programs increase fluency of a skill.

T F Technology produces a generation of rote learners.

T F The best way for students to get computer access is for every school to have a computer lab.

from PRESERVICE to PRACTICE

Patricia Gonzalez: Using Technology to Innovate in Her Classroom

Patricia Gonzalez issues a challenge to her eighth-grade class: "Where should the next landfill be built in our state?" The students are interested in this topic, which they have heard their parents discuss. To find a solution, Patricia's class works with local city officials, who coach them on the mechanics of using a geographic information system (GIS). A GIS, in simple terms, is a collection of electronic tools that translate data into a digital map. The power of a GIS comes from its ability to display several layers of maps on the computer screen at a single time. For example, students can look at a map showing population density and then at another map that depicts distance from urban areas. They can also view these two maps together as they deliberate the site of their landfill. The GIS tools allow students to zoom in and out on an area as they begin to narrow down their choices for the site. They can then search the GIS database to make sure they will not disturb any known historic or archaeological sites.[1]

After two weeks of investigation, Patricia's class divides into teams to present their choices. Three sites are offered, and a different group presents the case for each location. The culminating activity requires students to role-play a city council meeting, assuming such roles as city councilor, mayor, geologist, and angry citizen.

Two years later, the same students are still using GIS, but now they are in the field collecting water samples near the landfill that was actually built. Students meticulously record data, which are transferred to a GIS database. They still work with municipal officials, this time to monitor the safety of the landfill.

CASE QUESTIONS

1. How does the fact that students in Ms. Gonzalez's class have access to the Internet and GIS facilitate the problem she has given the students to solve?

2. How would the students attack this problem without the technology?

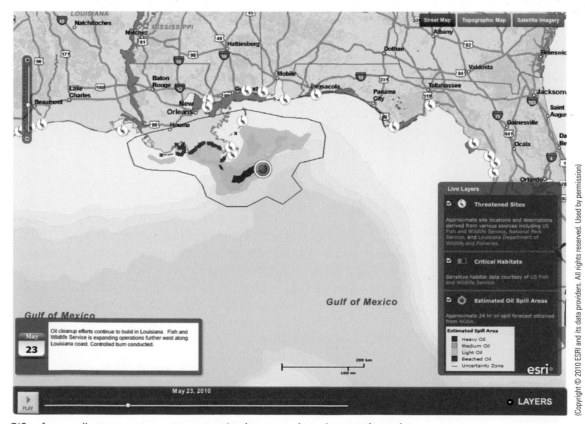

GIS software allows users to create customized maps such as the one shown here.

Patricia Gonzalez's role in the classroom is far from the traditional view of the teacher as sole dispenser of information. Instead, Patricia functions as a facilitator. She allows her classroom to become an active laboratory where students take charge of their own learning and hypothesize about solutions to problems posed by Patricia. As she circulates around the room, she challenges her students to consider what evidence they will need to convince an area's citizens that their backyards are the best place for the landfill. Patricia is just one reference point that her students must consult, along with the GIS data, municipal officials, and other students.

As this example demonstrates, computers are not replacing teachers. In fact, teachers have an expanded role in this technologically enriched environment, though this role differs from the traditional one associated with teaching. Later in the chapter, we explore in more detail how teachers can use computer technologies to change the roles of both students and teachers. To put contemporary changes in perspective, let's first look at the way technology has affected American schools in the past.

a brief look at education's technological past

Today people usually equate educational technology with computers. But technology in a more general sense is by no means new to education. In the early 1800s, a technological innovation was introduced to classrooms and had a profound impact on teaching. Although advocates called this new tool "invaluable" and it was installed in classrooms throughout the country, many teachers ignored it at first. Schools had to encourage use of this new technology by preparing training manuals with step-by-step instructions to help teachers integrate the device into their lessons. What was this technological wonder? The chalkboard!

In the old one-room schoolhouses, where students of different ages worked on their own individual lessons, the function of a chalkboard was not immediately apparent. During the nineteenth century, however, classroom structure began to evolve from a one-room orientation to the graded classrooms we know today. When teachers began to teach the same lesson to an entire group of students, the chalkboard came into its own.[2]

The twentieth century brought a variety of technological devices into the classroom, including the filmstrip projector, the overhead projector, the motion picture, and educational television.[3] Such changes were viewed as so significant that in 1913 technological proponent Thomas Edison stated, "Books will soon be obsolete in the schools. Scholars will soon be instructed through the eye. It is possible to teach every branch of human knowledge with the motion picture. Our school system will be completely changed in ten years."[4]

Similarly, when microcomputers became affordable in the 1980s, many software products were introduced to drill students on basic skills, and some educational visionaries predicted the end of classroom instruction and the end of the teaching profession as we know it. Of course, this forecast turned out to be no more correct than Edison's overstatement.

Today, educational technology is viewed as just another tool that teachers can use, rather than as something that can or should replace the teacher. Technology supports and extends what teachers and students can do in the classroom—whether it's an Internet archive enriching a research project or a GIS allowing students to engage in real-world problem solving. The key idea is that, from the chalkboard to the microcomputer, the needs of teachers and students shape the uses of technology in the classroom, not the other way around.

Once a technology enters the classroom, the uses to which it is put are affected by what we might call the technology's level of maturity. In education, as in other fields, new technologies tend to go through three stages of application:

1. In the first stage, the technology is applied to things we already do. For instance, when most teachers begin to use slideware (such as *PowerPoint* or *Keynote*), they initially use it to show text and pictures, which is exactly what previous technologies, such as slide projectors and overheads, have done in classrooms for decades.

2. In the second stage, the technology is used to improve upon existing tasks. To continue the previous example, many teachers now use *PowerPoint* or *Keynote* to link to websites, videos, or other slides as part of the presentation. Instead of delivering a linear march through information, these innovative teachers use the technology to branch out in different directions as the topic and the discussion suggest. Ambitious teachers can even use these tools to produce games, quizzes, tutorials, or branching narrative activities.[5]

3. In the third stage of maturity, the technology is used to do things that were not possible in the past. An excellent example is the geographic information system software that Patricia Gonzalez used in our opening case study. In addition to helping them solve the problem, students can use GIS to present their findings by displaying and manipulating the data in real time. In this way, the technology opens up new possibilities for the classroom rather than just allowing teachers and students to do old things in new ways.

In keeping with this pattern, the role of any technology in the classroom will tend naturally to change as the technology matures. In addition, teachers follow a similar progression as they become more comfortable with various technologies. Teachers who are just beginning to use technology may start with applications such as slideware that are similar to something they already do. As they begin to learn about technology's possibilities, they will move on to applications, such as GIS, that allow them to innovate. As we examine different technologies, ask yourself at which stage they can be applied and at which stage you would feel comfortable using them.

PAUSE AND REFLECT

1. How have recent developments in technology affected you and your family?

2. When you were in high school, which types of technology were your teachers using? At what stage was the technology applied?

how are schools being pressured to change?

Computer and networking technologies are an integral part of our society. It is hard to imagine a world without ATMs, e-mail, pay-at-the-pump gas stations, and cellular phones. Now imagine a classroom with no TV, no DVD player or VCR, no phone, and no computer. This classroom scenario is easily imagined because we have all experienced it. Most people agree that schools should prepare students for life in our society. If pervasive use of technology is a fact of life, should the classroom be

▶❚❚ **TeachSource VIDEO CASE**

An Expanded Definition of Literacy: Meaningful Ways to Integrate Technology

Go to the Education CourseMate website to watch the video clips, study the artifacts in the case, and reflect on the following questions:

1. Which of the pressures to use technology described in this chapter are evident in the comments of the teachers in this case?

2. What roles do these teachers seem to take when their classes use technology?

3. Which advice from this case about integrating technology do you believe will be most useful to you as a teacher?

Ⓣ F

One of the main pressures on schools to use technology comes from the business sector.

Businesses want their future employees to be technologically literate, so they have influenced the governors and legislatures of many states to require digital literacy as a requirement for high school graduation.

❝

We are currently preparing students for jobs and technologies that do not yet exist ... using technologies that have not been invented yet in order to solve problems we do not even know are problems yet."

—KARL FISCH,
Director of Technology at Arapahoe High School,
Centennial, Colorado

an exception? (In the Video Case *An Expanded Definition of Literacy: Meaningful Ways to Integrate Technology*, three teachers talk about the importance of using technology as well as the benefits and challenges of doing so.)

No wonder, then, that schools are feeling pressure to increase their use of technological tools. This pressure is coming from many sources:

1. Parents are placing pressure on schools to use technologies in the classroom. They see a discrepancy between what is taught to their children and which kinds of real-world activities they perform every day at work. Parents are concerned not only that their children have access to technology in the classroom but also that the students learn technology skills that will allow them to compete in a job market increasingly powered by technology. Patricia Gonzalez's students, for example, are learning the marketable skills of using technology to collect and analyze data as they solve the landfill problem.

2. Students are placing pressure on schools by knowing more about which technologies are currently available and how to use them than do many of the teachers.[6]

3. Teachers are placing pressure on schools because they need both access to technology in their classrooms and training to use the technology effectively. In particular, new teachers who have used technological tools in college and at home also want to use these tools in their classrooms.

4. Businesses are placing pressure on schools and governmental agencies to adequately prepare future employees. A report on the "21st Century Skills" needed by today's students identifies digital literacy as a requirement for high school graduates.[7] Computer-based information processing power is doubling every 18 months,[8] and the pace of change in technology is significantly faster than even the pace of change in business, let alone that in education. The pressure on schools to keep up with this frantic rate of change is intense.

5. The perception that the United States is falling behind the world in educational attainment has increased the pressure on schools and teachers to bridge this gap. Business and governmental agencies march to the drum of global competition: "If America is to compete with the world, America's schools must be the best!" Regardless of their truth, such rallying calls add to the pressure on schools to use technology.

6. Governmental agencies have moved to support federal, state, and local initiatives to ensure access to technology for K–12 students. Many state departments of education have written "technology skills" into teacher licensure requirements, and national organizations are moving toward establishing specific subject-area technology standards for K–12 students.*

*For one example, see ISTE's National Educational Technology Standards (NETS) (**http://cnets.iste.org/**).

> *But technology is a tool, not a virtue.*
>
> —EMILY G. BALCH,
> Social Reformer and Peace Activist

Within each of these groups are voices calling for schools to help close the digital divide—that is, the gap between those who are able to benefit from technology and those who are not. Several types of gaps are evident, including those that divide along such lines as socioeconomic status, race, gender, ability, or geographic location. Citizens are concerned that technology is further deepening all sorts of cleavages between the haves and have-nots of American society.

Although we have been speaking of "pressures" for change, these forces can also be seen as opportunities. Many educators welcome the chance to try new curriculum materials and methods in their classrooms or to help bridge the digital divide. The evolution of teaching has also opened up new opportunities for teachers with skills in technology, which are seen as giving candidates an important competitive edge in the job market. Most importantly, the drive to incorporate new technologies into the classroom presents tremendous opportunities for students, as the next section describes.

PAUSE AND REFLECT

1. What other pressures can you add to the list presented in this section?

2. As a teacher, from where do you expect to feel the most pressure to incorporate technology into the classroom?

3. Which pressures on schools might encourage them to *avoid* adopting technology?

---

how are technologies affecting student learning?

As the example of GIS software shows, many new technologies have been introduced into the educational setting in the last decade. To discuss technologies for education, we must take several different approaches to this topic. First, we touch upon technologies you probably use in your personal life, contrasting these applications with what teachers seek to do in the classroom. Second, we organize technologies around specific tasks that teachers and students might undertake (see Table 7.1). Third, we group technologies into content-specific categories.

You are probably familiar with many computer applications already. You use word processors to write papers and e-mail programs to communicate, and you may use a spreadsheet to keep track of your personal finances. When used in these ways, these applications are called **productivity tools:** they let you accomplish tasks more efficiently than if you had to use a typewriter, a calculator, or postal mail. Teachers certainly use productivity tools, but teaching with technology encompasses far more.

Some computer applications can be classified as **cognitive tools** when they are used to engage and enhance thinking.[9] For example, a math student can use a spreadsheet to dynamically generate and manipulate graphs to understand concepts such as slope and *y*-intercept. Cognitive tools manage information

> *During my eighty-seven years I have witnessed a whole succession of technological revolutions. But none of them has done away with the need for character in the individual or the ability to think.*
>
> —BERNARD MANNES BARUCH,
> American Financier and Presidential Adviser

TABLE 7.1 **Tasks and Technology Tools for Teachers and Students**

Task	Technology Tools	Example	Educational Benefits
Research	• Search engines • Online archives • Databases	The *Valley of the Shadow* online archive offers students access to a variety of searchable documents from two communities during the Civil War.	Online archives provide users with a tremendous variety of information, whether material designed for young learners or data sets used by professionals.
Collaboration	• Blogs • Wikis • Online social software Online productivity software	The *GLOBE** program supports a project that uses data on acid rain and waste disposal collected and submitted by students around the world.	Through projects such as GLOBE's database, users can interact with other learners around the world or within the same classroom.
Communication	• Blogs • Listserv • Wikis • Text chat, voice chat, and video conference tools • Podcasts	*H-NET is a free online community* of humanities and social science educators. Teachers can browse archived discussion logs or subscribe to a listserv to receive new postings in their e-mail.	Participants in discussions on H-NET and other listservs can ask questions, provide advice, share resources, and enrich one another's professional practice.
Composing	• Word processors • Image editors • Video editors • Audio editors • Three-dimensional modeling tools	*AlphaSmart, a portable and user-friendly word processor*, is especially popular with teachers who work with younger writers.	AlphaSmart and other word processing tools allow easy cut-and-paste, multiple versions of documents, and built-in supports such as spell checkers and dictionaries. These supports can encourage reluctant writers.
Presenting	• Slideware • Alternate, zooming presenters • Concept-mapping tools	Teachers looking for alternatives to slideware are turning to other web-based products such as	Well-designed, media-rich presentations can stimulate student interest and enhance *(Continued)*

*To learn more, visit the GLOBE website (www.globe.gov).

TABLE 7.1   Tasks and Technology Tools for Teachers and Students (Continued)

Task	Technology Tools	Example	Educational Benefits
	• Geographic information systems	Prezi. *Prezi uses one large canvas to display the whole presentation* and users can zoom in on certain parts of the presentation. It is a different style of presentation than the linear form of slideware.	understanding. Teachers may also want students to create their own presentations.
Collecting data	• Probes and sensors • Digital still cameras and video cameras • Digital audio recorders • Handheld computers	Students can quickly and easily gather motion data with collection devices. The data are then sent to a computer or graphing calculator for analysis.	Data collection tools easily capture real-world phenomena in a digital format. Collecting the same information by hand, in many cases, is tedious if not impossible.
Analyzing data	• Spreadsheets • Data display programs • Geographic information systems • Graphing calculator	Students can use the Excel spreadsheet program to view and analyze census data to determine demographic trends and forecast future population levels.	Spreadsheets and other analysis tools provide students with multiple ways to view and think about data: as individual entries, as aggregated categories, or as graphs.
Acquiring and practicing skills	• Self-contained tutorials • Drill-and-practice software • Educational games	The *Fundamental Math* tutorial allows teachers to individualize students' instruction in mathematics.	These tools enable teachers to efficiently differentiate instruction. They often contain built-in automated assessments.
Assessing	• Classroom response systems • Online survey and quiz tools	Web-based products such as *Poll Everywhere*, an assessment application that allows for multiple choice and text	Assessment tools allow teachers to build formative feedback into their instruction. With these automated tools, assessing-to-

(Continued)

TABLE 7.1	Tasks and Technology Tools for Teachers and Students (Continued)		
Task	Technology Tools	Example	Educational Benefits
		answers. Students respond through multiple methods such as SMS and the web. Teachers can embed the polls into slideware and watch it update in real time.	learn, rather than assessing-to-grade, becomes more feasible.
Publishing	• Personal or class-room websites, wikis, or blogs Specific-interest forums	*21 Classes is a blogging tool* built specifically for teachers and students.	By bringing students' work to the Web, teachers encourage students to engage with a wider audience. As a result students may be more motivated to do their best work

Source: Adapted from Thomas C. Hammond, "A Task-Oriented Framework for Stand-Alone Technology Integration Classes," *Journal of Computing in Teacher Education* 23 (Summer 2007), pp. 119–124.

in ways that allow users to think more clearly, creatively, and critically. Teachers can structure students' use of cognitive tools by providing scaffolds for their thinking. To extend the spreadsheet example, the teacher might ask the student to complete the example on a partially constructed spreadsheet and then observe the resulting slope and y-intercept. In an English class, the teacher might provide students with a blank concept map and ask them to fill in information drawn from a reading selection.

Cognitive tools are not necessarily meant to make learning easier. They do allow users to organize information in new ways, to evaluate it, and to construct new, personally meaningful representations of the information. At the same time, using cognitive tools often requires students to think harder, more critically, or more creatively than they might without the tool.[10] Patricia Gonzalez's students, for example, were thinking hard and working collaboratively to solve the problem of where to locate the landfill.

Another useful way to discuss technologies for education is to consider the tasks that teachers and students engage in while teaching and learning. This task-oriented approach helps teachers concentrate on what it is they want to do with the tool rather than focus on the tool itself. Table 7.1 presents a partial list of these tasks and the tools that can help you undertake them. Note that in some instances tools may be used merely as productivity tools, whereas in other circumstances they are used as cognitive tools.

As a teacher, you may also want to think about technologies in terms of how they apply to specific content areas. Some technologies, such as sensors and probes, are more appropriate for math or science than for English or social studies. Other technologies, such as GIS, can cross disciplines and interweave subjects, such as social studies and math. As you prepare instruction for a particular content area, you will want to consider both how certain technologies add depth to students' engagement with the content and how these technologies may be able to bridge content areas and engage students in multidisciplinary thinking.

ENGLISH/LANGUAGE ARTS EDUCATION

Teachers of many disciplines will find the tools for developing literacy useful. In this section, we examine word processors, software applications to develop reading skills, multimedia presentation and communication tools (including digital video), and ways to combine technologies across disciplines.

Writing with Word Processors

Although technology has vastly broadened the avenues of expression available to students, writing ability is still highly valued in our culture. Today many students write using **word processors**. These tools offer many advantages over paper and pencil. For example, editing is less tedious when you don't have to laboriously erase several lines of text, or even start over. Using a word processor, students can easily experiment with different sequences for their paragraphs. In fact, students who learn to write using word processors are more likely to revise their work and make more substantial revisions than are students who learn to write without the tool.[11] Built-in spelling and grammar checks in most word processing software help struggling students focus on their ideas, and the keyboard itself avoids the handwriting obstacle many students face. These aids are controversial, however: they are not foolproof, and some educators believe they are often a crutch. Nonetheless, the more students edit their writing, the more they learn about the writing process. In this respect, the word processor engages students and enhances thinking, making it a cognitive tool.

SALLY FORTH   *BY STEVE ALANIZ & FRANCESCO MARCIULIANO*

The addition of an **LCD projector** enables teachers to project a writing example and, by either using the "track changes" feature of the word processor or writing directly onto an interactive whiteboard, model the process of editing for students. Online word processors, such as *Google* documents **www.docs.google.com**, may allow students to work on compositions whether in class or in the library. They also make it easy for multiple students to collaborate on a draft.

▶❚❚ TeachSource VIDEO CASE

Multimedia Literacy: Integrating Technology into the Middle School Curriculum

Go to the Education CourseMate website to watch the video clips, study the artifacts in the case, and reflect on the following questions:

1. In what ways are the students using technology in this case? What is the role of the teacher?

2. This chapter mentions that the use of particular technological tools is not limited to specific disciplines. How could these students use their new ability to create slide shows in another subject area, such as mathematics or science?

3. What are some ways that teachers can balance content instruction with technology-skills instruction, a concern mentioned by the teacher in this case?

Communicating in Multimedia

The spread of technology has required an expanded definition of literacy. Students are now becoming literate not just in the written word but also in video, audio, and multimedia* productions. In Chapter 3,"Who Are Today's Students in a Diverse Society?" when we discussed Howard Gardner's theory of multiple intelligences and the concept of learning styles, we emphasized that different individuals learn best in different ways. Students who struggle with written expression may enjoy the chance to publish a webpage or create a multimedia presentation instead of submitting a traditional five-page essay. Presentation tools, such as *PowerPoint* and *Prezi*, can combine text, graphics, audio, and video to communicate complex ideas. Students can use multimedia-authoring programs like *HyperStudio* or *Kid Pix* to create their own interactive presentations or illustrate and present stories.[†] (The Video Case *Multimedia Literacy: Integrating Technology into the Middle School Curriculum* shows one language-arts class making slide shows to present their research findings.) The current generation of students is the first to have widespread capability of authoring compelling multimedia works using digital tools. Programs such as *Movie Maker* and *iMovie*, which are included with the operating systems sold by Microsoft and Apple, allow students to shift from the role of passive observer to active creator of digital media. Students can use their strengths in expressing themselves while they develop visual literacy, become familiar with valuable tools for the future, and strengthen their ability to analyze and synthesize information.

Digital storytelling is a project that can engage even the most reticent students. In digital storytelling, students create images, often by taking digital photos, then pair these images with narratives they write and record in their own voice. For students who are having trouble beginning to write, the pictures they choose can serve as prompts to engage them in the writing step. Because students have chosen and edited the images to accompany the narrative, they have greater ownership and connection to their stories.[‡] With the introduction of increasingly affordable digital video cameras and user-friendly software, students can even research, direct, and produce their own digital documentaries. For example, a student might film a Native American elder telling an important story from his or her tribal culture as the culminating project for a unit on storytelling.

---

*Multimedia productions combine various media such as text, graphics, video, music, and voice narration.

[†]*PowerPoint* is a product of Microsoft (**www.microsoft.com/**; telephone: 425-882-8080). For *HyperStudio*, contact Knowledge Adventure **www.mackiev.com/hyperstudio/**. For *KidPix*, contact The Learning Company **www.learningcompany.com/**.

[‡]For more information on digital storytelling, consult the Center for Digital Storytelling webpage at **http://storycenter.org/**.

It is relatively easy to publish student work on the Internet, and the knowledge that their work may end up publicly available motivates students to care more about their creations.[12] Many students enjoy publishing and reading Web logs, more commonly known as **blogs**. A blog is basically a journal that is available on the Web. Another more current approach to a blog is a Video log, or a **vlog**, where the students create video journals; a common form of this is through You Tube. Blog and vlog software requires little technical expertise and is no more complex to learn to use than most e-mail programs.

Learning to Read

Drill-and-practice programs were the earliest form of educational software or educational games. First used as an interactive worksheet, the software provided feedback to the user, usually by labeling an answer as right or wrong, and then presented the next task. Now, many programs monitor the students' progress so they do not move on until they have mastered the current concept. As described in the accompanying box, many of today's drill-and-practice programs also feature a motivational, game-like design. Drill-and-practice programs generally increase the fluency of a skill rather than actually teaching it.[13] For example, products such as the *Reader Rabbit**series are popular choices for reinforcing young children's reading skills, such as letter recognition, rhyming words, and word families. Teachers also use drill-and-practice programs such as *Reader Rabbit* to diagnose students' ability in reading and other subjects, and to assign students to the appropriate group.

One interesting tool for integrating individualized drill-and-practice with whole-class discussion is student response systems (also known as "clickers"). These handheld devices are distributed to individual students or to small groups, and the teacher prompts students to use the clickers to answer questions posed to the whole class. Students' responses are then automatically compiled and displayed for the teacher to use as a discussion point or to shape further instruction. This form of assessment can be accomplished online using tools such as Poll Everywhere, as described in Table 7.1; students can then use laptops and other handheld devices such as the cell phone and the iPod Touch to respond.

(T) F

Drill-and-practice programs increase fluency of a skill.

Drill-and-practice computer programs are better at increasing the fluency of a skill, rather than teaching the skill initially.

"edutainment" software

A software application that is both entertaining and educational is referred to as "edutainment." Ordinary drill-and-practice software is repetitive by nature, and children can easily lose interest in such mundane tasks. To overcome this problem, software developers added game-like characteristics to their applications in the hope of motivating users to complete the task. These features also helped to sell the products to students and parents looking for educational activities for the home.

Reader Rabbit is a product of the Learning Company **www.learningcompany.com/**, which was bought by Brøderbund **www.broderbund.com/**.

Making Mind Maps and Webs

Students and teachers often create graphical representations, known as **mind maps** or **webs,** to demonstrate their understanding of a story or concept. Software such as *Inspiration* or *Kidspiration** uses these visual learning techniques to teach students to clarify, organize, and prioritize their thoughts. Mind maps can serve as an alternative assessment tool for teachers, who can examine the thinking patterns, interrelationships, and even misconceptions revealed by students' diagrams. *Inspiration* can also be used as a prewriting activity to help students brainstorm, draft, and revise their writing.

Combining Technology and Crossing Disciplines

Technology can facilitate interdisciplinary connections in a powerful way. Like word processors, multimedia tools are used across the disciplines—from a presentation on the Depression that includes music of the era and clips from President Franklin D. Roosevelt's "fireside chats" to a hurricane project with graphs, images, video clips, and links to the National Weather Service website.

An example combining several types of technologies and crossing content areas is the *I Lost My Tooth project.*[14] First-grade students around the world use e-mail to share stories and myths about losing their teeth. Using these rich and diverse stories, teachers develop interdisciplinary activities that can make use of a variety of educational tools, both technological and traditional. For example, students study maps, either on computer or on paper, to locate the countries where other children live, and ask their "e-pals" about the weather and local heroes of their regions. Students can use drawing software, or basic crayons, to illustrate their tooth fairy stories. They use their math skills, and perhaps graphing software, to chart the number of teeth lost. In this project, technology is functioning at the second stage we described: facilitating and enhancing what teachers can do.

SCIENCE EDUCATION

As the case study at the beginning of this chapter showed, technology can allow students to do legitimate scientific investigations on a scale that would otherwise be impossible. Technology enabled Patricia Gonzalez to use a constructivist approach to education that encouraged her students to build their own knowledge on the basis of their experiences. (See "Cognitive Tools and Constructivist Teaching" in this section. See also "The Influence of Psychological Theories" in Chapter 9, "What Are the Philosophical Foundations of American Education?"; and "What Ought to Be the Elements of Educational Reform?" in Chapter 12, "How Should Education Be Reformed?") Through the Internet, students can find images from a professional observatory in Australia to learn about how supernovae form or monitor the regularity of Old Faithful's eruptions through a live Web camera. Putting these technologies in students' hands allows learning to become an active process in which they do the experiments, draw conclusions, and engage in problem solving, rather than merely reading about an investigation and memorizing the results.

> *The important thing in science is not so much to obtain new facts as to discover new ways of thinking about them.*
> —SIR WILLIAM HENRY BRAGG (1862–1942), British Physicist

*Inspiration and Kidspiration are both products of Inspiration Software, Inc. (http://inspiration.com/; telephone: 800-877-4292).

cognitive tools and constructivist teaching

In the constructivist approach to teaching, learning is recognized as an active process. Students engage in constructing their own knowledge on the basis of their previous experiences instead of passively absorbing knowledge as presented by the teacher. This approach to instruction celebrates the differences among students instead of continually emphasizing their similarities.

Constructivist teachers can find cognitive tools especially helpful. Because cognitive tools do not try to instruct, they do not assume any particular learning style or methodology. Using *Movie Maker* or *iMovie* to create a digital story is a good example

demonstrating these tools' flexibility. The student must bring the goals—and the content to achieve them—to the tool, and then the tool will facilitate the student's discovery of knowledge and construction of meaning.

Note that it is *how* the tool is used that makes it constructivist, rather than *what* the tool is. Although cognitive tools are an excellent match for constructivist methods, many other applications can be used in a similar manner. As so often is true in teaching, only the student's and teacher's ingenuity, creativity, and experience set the limits for a tool's educational use, not the tool itself.

Although the equipment to conduct many of these experiments is costly, there are ways around these financial obstacles. For example, most city governments own GIS software, and many are interested in partnering with a local school to share their expertise, as government workers did with Patricia Gonzalez's class. Many organizations support collaboration between scientists and schools; for a reasonable membership fee, schools receive the technical support they need and an opportunity to work with experts. Such partnerships let students see how people in the "real world" do their jobs, as well as allowing them to participate in interesting projects. This section discusses some of these opportunities, ranging from conducting sophisticated local research that contributes to an organized database, to collaborating with NASA scientists via conferencing technology.

Scientific Hardware

Imagine conducting class beside a stream behind your classroom and having the technology to collect a water sample; instantly and accurately find the pH, temperature, and amount of dissolved oxygen in it; and graph the data on the spot. Revolutionary technology in the form of affordable handheld computing devices, such as the Palm,* and accompanying probes, thermometers, and sensors, allow this scenario to become reality. No longer are teachers forced to demonstrate stale experiments in the sterile environment of a lab. Instead, schools are moving toward **ubiquitous computing**, in which each student has access to some type of mobile computing device to use inside the classroom, in the field, and at home. Students can access rich data sets, perform calculations, and test their hypotheses themselves. Science students today do things like measure ozone and sulfur dioxide levels from the air near their schools, or use GPS (global positioning systems) to be "environmental detectives"† in a simulation to discover the source of groundwater contamination. (See the Video Case *Integrating Technology to Improve Student Learning:*

*Palms are produced by Palm, Inc (**www.palm.com**/; telephone: 800-881-7256).

†The MIT "Environmental Detectives" website can be accessed at **http://education.mit.edu/content/environmental-detectives**.

▶❚❚ TeachSource VIDEO CASE

Integrating Technology to Improve Student Learning: A High School Science Simulation

Go to the Education CourseMate website to watch the video clips, study the artifacts in the case, and reflect on the following questions:

1. Does the technology that the students are using in this case fit this chapter's description of a cognitive tool? Why or why not?

2. What is the role of the teacher in this case? How do you feel about taking this role as a teacher?

A High School Science Simulation for a demonstration of how a high school science class uses a computer simulation to understand and solve questions related to genetic inheritance.)

Digital Imagery

Much of science education is based on the skill of observation, and resources that allow students to visualize concepts lead to greater understanding. The use of both still images and video in the science classroom has been greatly enhanced by digital tools. Teachers and students can go online and download images or video clips of processes such as amoeba reproduction or a lunar eclipse. As the prices of digital cameras and digital microscopes have declined in recent years, students themselves have gained the ability to capture still or moving images that can be analyzed later or, with the use of an LCD projector, by the entire class. Processes that are too fast to observe, such as dropping a ball, can be slowed down, and students can use time-lapse capabilities to capture processes that are too slow to see, such as the growth of a plant.[15] Document cameras provide an opportunity for all the students to clearly watch an experiment without having to all fit around a small table. A document camera captures a real time image, which can be a 2D document or a 3D item such as a science experiment, that is then projected onto a screen or a Smartboard for the larger audience to view.

Tools for Analysis

Having collected data, students will need to organize and analyze the information. **Spreadsheets**, such as *Excel* and *Google* spreadsheets, are widely used tools for organizing data sets, conducting numerical analyses, and creating graphs. Spreadsheets allow users to perform multiple calculations. The user can see all numbers and formulas at once, and any change is immediately reflected in the entire sheet.

Other tools extend the capabilities of basic spreadsheets to offer more powerful opportunities for analyzing and visualizing data. *Fathom* and *InspireData* are two

An elementary school girl is using a science experiment's projected image on a Smartboard to solve a problem.

(UPI Photo/Bill Greenblatt /Landov)

software applications that provide a flexible, drag-and-drop interface for combining data, graphs, and formulas. These tools are adaptable enough that teachers can, with the aid of a projector, work with data sets live as a whole-class activity. Geographic information systems allow geographically referenced spreadsheet data, such as information collected with a GPS, to be displayed and manipulated as an interactive map.

Enhancing Problem Solving

Teachers often wonder what their students are thinking, and technology is providing some ways to discover and understand the cognitive processes students use as they solve problems. At Cedar Way High School, students use the *True Roots* program* to play the role of forensic scientists trying to determine whether a girl is correct in asserting that she was switched at birth in the hospital. Using genetic data, students must try to deduce whether the girl is related to the parents who have raised her. The program tracks students' decisions so that the teacher can later analyze their problem-solving strategy. Teachers instruct students not to guess or proceed randomly, but rather to follow a systematic plan. To reinforce the idea that problem solving should be a logical exercise, classes often use the program two times over three days. Teachers take the middle day to show students the graphs of their problem-solving strategies. Students try again and are graded on their improvement.[16] Here, technology is functioning at the third stage of progress: offering teachers unique insight into their students' cognitive processes, which they would find difficult or impossible to get otherwise.

SOCIAL STUDIES EDUCATION

Digital resources can be used to promote historical thinking and inquiry-based learning in social studies classrooms. Social studies teachers can make use of a variety of technological tools, including online archives, electronic simulations, virtual fieldtrips, and spreadsheets.

Accessing Information

Research skills are an integral part of social studies education. Much of the information students will work with in the social studies disciplines is not neatly packaged in the textbook, but rather is located in the library, in archives, online, and elsewhere. Accordingly, social studies educators should make research skills an explicit part of their classroom instruction.

You are undoubtedly familiar with online search engines such as *Google* and *Yahoo!* For classroom use, you should also familiarize yourself with search tools designed for use by young learners, such as *Factmonster* (www.factmonster.com) and the *Yahoo! Kids Directory* (www.kids.yahoo.com/directory). In addition to knowing how to use these tools, you should know how to teach about them (e.g., how to use Boolean logic to conduct a search) and how to manage them (e.g., how to set the content filters to keep out inappropriate material).

Besides taking advantage of general-use information-searching tools, you will want to explore information sources specific to the social sciences. Social scientists are digitizing† immense archives and publishing them on the Internet. Without the computer to help organize and manage such large amounts of information, a teacher might be limited to using several photocopied diary entries to expose students to

---

*True Roots is produced by IMMEX (Interactive Multimedia Exercises) at UCLA (**http://www.immex.ucla.edu**; telephone: 310-649-6568)

†The digitizing process stores documents in an electronic format that allows them to be viewed on the Web and archived in a more permanent form.

primary sources.* Giving students access to a rich online or CD-ROM archive allows them to broaden their understanding of history and the work of historians.

For example, the *Valley of the Shadow* website† contains detailed databases of Civil War–era census results, church records, newspaper articles, military records, and letters about two communities, one Southern and one Northern. Users can investigate the answers to questions such as "What was the average number of slaves people held?" or "How did occupations differ in the North and South?" The role of the teacher changes from dispenser of knowledge to that of a guide through the archives, helping students learn to ask the right questions and examine the sources critically. In this way, students and teachers construct their understanding of history together.

Simulations

A **simulation**, a representation of an activity or environment, is a time-honored and effective teaching technique. A simulation can be a fun way to explore an environment or a concept that would be too expensive, or possibly dangerous, to handle in reality. For this reason, simulations have proven to be a fertile field for educational software developers. A large variety of computerized simulations are available for classroom use in practically every field.

Decisions, Decisions: Local Government‡ is a simulation game in which users assume the role of the mayor of a community facing a dilemma. The program can be used by the class as a whole, with only one computer, or it can accommodate multiple small groups working at separate computers. After students input their decisions, the software reacts and presents them with the results. For example, if the mayor raises taxes, she or he must accept some public dissatisfaction. The software frees the teacher to be more involved with the students and to mediate instruction.

The teacher helps a student find information on the Internet.

(Diego Cervo/Shutterstock.com)

*A primary source is a firsthand account. For example, a soldier who fought at the battle of Gettysburg and described it in his diary provides a firsthand account or primary source.

†To learn more, visit the University of Virginia's *Valley of the Shadow* website (**http://valley.vcdh.virginia.edu/**).

‡The *Decisions, Decisions* series of software titles is available from Tom Snyder Productions (**www.tomsnyder.com/**; telephone: 800-342-0236).

Virtual Fieldtrips

Virtual fieldtrips provide a wealth of opportunities to extend learning. Not limited to social studies, virtual fieldtrips can be used to provide information about a site that students are unable to visit.[17] It is unlikely you will manage a class outing to the Amazon rainforest, for example, but National Geographic's Jason Project* can send students on a "fieldtrip" through the computer. Teachers, agencies, governments, and students themselves have produced hundreds of such sites.

Student-produced virtual fieldtrips are often used in connection with local history. Students may, for example, conduct interviews and use digital cameras to take pictures of important sites and people in their community. By using photo-editing software such as *Photoshop*,† they can manipulate these images or enhance them on the computer screen. Students can also put their images of local sites into a multimedia presentation program such as *HyperStudio* or *PowerPoint* and add descriptions. These presentations can then be published on the Internet and viewed by others. In this way, students can act as historians who are contributing to the preservation of their community's story.

WebQuests

A **WebQuest**‡ is an inquiry-based learning activity that directs learners in using information from the Web. In a WebQuest, the appropriate tasks and websites are provided so that the students can focus on the analysis of information rather than losing time by searching for it. For example, in the "King Tutankhamen: Was It Murder?" WebQuest,§ middle school students take on the roles of medical examiner, reporter, archaeologist, professor, or historian, and explore information about the death of King Tut. Using the provided links, students visit websites and then use what they learn to develop a persuasive essay presenting their verdict on whether King Tut was murdered.

Using Spreadsheets to Connect Disciplines

Technology helps facilitate interdisciplinary relationships. Social studies and math, for example, are not subjects that people naturally connect, but they are combined when students access and study rich data sets available on the Internet. The National Center for Health Statistics website§ provides data on a range of demographic topics, such as the number of live births in the United States. Students can use spreadsheets and data manipulation software (described more fully in the "Science Education" section) to mathematically analyze and display the information. Did live births increase or decrease over time? What periods of time show deviations from the overall pattern? The trends observed in the data can be connected with students' knowledge of U.S. history.[18]

MATHEMATICS EDUCATION

From slide rules to calculators, math teachers have relied on technology for years. This section deals with some of the newer uses of technology in math education.

---

*To learn more, visit The Jason Project website (**www.jasonproject.org/**).

†*Photoshop* is available from Adobe (**www.adobe.com/**; telephone: 800-833-6687).

‡The WebQuest model was developed in 1995 by Bernie Dodge with Tom March. Information about WebQuest can be accessed at the San Diego State University WebQuest site at **http://webquest.sdsu.edu/**.

§**www.pekin.net/pekin108/wash/webquest/**

§To learn more, visit The National Center for Health Statistics website (**www.cdc.gov/nchs**).

Tutorial Software

Tutorials are educational software applications designed to provide the initial instruction on a given topic. They are used in most disciplines. Unlike drill-and-practice exercises, tutorials present the skill or concept, check for understanding throughout the process, and evaluate the learner's grasp of the topic once the program is completed. More narrative in nature than the drill-and-practice programs, tutorial software often has the feel of a book placed on a computer.

Tutorial software is somewhat controversial because many tutorials are intended to replace the teacher as the primary agent of instruction for a particular topic. To achieve this goal, the software is self-contained and self-paced. Small chunks of information are delivered to the learner in a careful sequence of instruction designed to adjust to students' needs, allowing them to achieve success. One such tutorial program is *CornerStone Mathematics*.* With this software, users move through concepts such as fractions and decimals at their own pace; topics are explained, reinforced, and tested. The learner's progress through the material is saved from one session to the next. Generally more flexible than drill-and-practice applications, tutorials give teachers a powerful tool for individualizing instruction and monitoring student progress.

Other Math Software

Certain mathematics-specific software enhances what teachers can do. For example, *The Geometer's Sketchpad*† allows students to explore the relationships among points, lines, planes, and angles in an environment conducive to experimentation. Users are offered a palette of tools for drawing and deriving geometric concepts. This cognitive tool enables the user to explore, question, learn, theorize, fail, succeed, and grow.[19]

Calculators and Graphing Calculators

Schools are trying to heed the message inherent in the National Council of Teachers of Mathematics' statement that "Electronic technologies—calculators and computers—are essential tools for teaching, learning, and doing mathematics. They furnish visual images of mathematical ideas, they facilitate organizing and analyzing data, and they compute efficiently and accurately."[20] These electronic technologies help teachers and students with some of the same tasks that were conducted without these aids. Many students find it difficult to make connections among the graphical, numerical, and algebraic representations of mathematical functions, for example, but the speed and ease with which graphs can be generated and manipulated using graphing calculators can help students to better understand those relationships.

Experts state that once students have mastered the basic computation of a problem, they can use calculators to bypass this to move onto higher order concepts that they have not yet mastered.[21] Others point out that students who are struggling to develop the basic concepts of a math problem can compensate for these skills when they use technology to gain access to the higher-level skills.[22]

Technology also enhances what teachers and students are able to do. Students can use data collection devices)‡ connected to their calculators, such as various types of sensors or temperature probes, to gather their own data as the basis of their investigations

---

CornerStone Mathematics is available from Achievement Technologies. (**www.achievementtech.com**; telephone: 888-391-3245).

†Key Curriculum Press produces *The Geometer's Sketchpad* (**www.keypress.com/x24119.xml**).

‡To find out more about data collection devices, visit the Texas Instruments website (**http://education.ti.com/us/product/tech/datacollection/features/features.html**; telephone: 800-842-2737).

into mathematical phenomena. Learning becomes more meaningful and authentic with these approaches, as students consult with both technology and the teacher.[23]

FOREIGN LANGUAGE AND ESL EDUCATION

The Internet and other communications tools open up vast opportunities in foreign language education. Years ago, foreign language teachers struggled to collect current materials in the target language. Now students can view authentic materials over the Internet or even use it to communicate with students in other classrooms in a foreign country. Compare assigning a sterile textbook article about French food to connecting your students with e-pals in French-speaking Africa so they can ask about the cuisine themselves: the advantages of the latter approach are obvious.

Technology supporting instruction

There are a number of technologies that can be used by foreign language students and English Language Learners to develop their proficiency in English. Podcasts are of great value as correct pronunciation can be modeled through teacher-created podcasts, and also practiced as the students create their own podcasts.[24] There are a number of free programs on the Internet that are very simple to use to create the podcasts, *Audacity** is one such free program, providing a user-friendly interface with the option to convert to other file formats such as MP3, which allows the recording to be played on other devices such as the iPod or other MP3 players.

Learning through the Home Language

As teachers are supporting their English Language Learners, they also need to follow the standard curriculum teaching math, science, and other subjects. This can be very difficult as the students are trying to decipher the language while perhaps learning a new mathematical formula. Classrooms are not always equipped with a translator to support that student. There are a number of programs on the market that enable students to learn concepts in their home language. Education City[†] is one such program for students ages 3 to 12 and covers language arts, math, and science. The web-based program provides highly interactive games with visual and audible reinforcement. In the math component, the curriculum content, text, and audio can be fully presented in neutral Spanish if that option is chosen. This is very useful as students can focus on mathematical understanding and not be obstructed by language barriers that may be inhibiting their learning.

Connecting with People

A **news group** is a feature of the Internet that can be compared with a large wall full of messages in chronological order. When you subscribe to a news group, you join an online discussion that occurs as people post messages and reply to one another. Teachers nationwide log on to these resources to share ideas, find e-pals for their students, and converse with other professionals in their field. For example, ESPAN-L[‡] is a news group for teachers of Spanish, whose discussion ranges from cultural notes to grammatical points.

*www.audacity.sourceforge.net

[†]http://us.educationcity.com/

[‡]To learn more about ESPAN-L and other mailing lists for teachers, visit **www.theteachersguide.com/listservs. html**.

Students can connect with speakers of other languages both through news groups and other emerging formats, such as text chat and voice-over-Internet tools. For example, Dickinson College hosts Mixxer, a language exchange community (www.language-exchanges.org). Mixxer allows language learners to find one another; a classroom of English-speakers learning Spanish can be connected with a classroom of Spanish-speakers using English. Individuals or groups from these classes then connect with tools such as *Skype* (www.skype.com), a free downloadable application that supports text, voice, and video chat. As they participate in the discussion, students put their communication skills to the test. These engaging ways of learning foreign languages are changing the way we teach, and they encourage learners to be creative and flexible and to take risks—all of which are indispensable to learning any new language.

Both ESL and foreign language teachers can take advantage of numerous websites designed for language learners and teachers. Among the most famous are "Tennessee Bob's Famous French Links"* and "Dave's ESL Café."† These sites offer numerous links to websites with lesson plans, interactive activities, vocabulary and grammar resources, and virtual tourism sites. The Internet is rich with resources for learners of almost any language.

DISTANCE EDUCATION

School districts vary greatly in location, size, budget, composition of populations, and graduation requirements. Such differences often create educational inequities, particularly when a school district simply cannot afford to provide the quality and variety of courses offered by larger or more affluent districts. **Distance education** is a fast-growing alternative for schools that are trying to overcome such constraints.

Distance education involves using technology to link students and instructors in separate locations. Whereas two-way audio and video allow live interaction between individuals who are hundreds or thousands of miles apart, the Internet allows the rapid exchange of data over distances. Using such technology, schools can increase their educational opportunities by offering courses otherwise prohibited by cost or other constraints.

Distance education is playing an ever-increasing role in the education of rural students. The United States has experienced a long-term population shift from rural to metropolitan areas. This population loss has caused many districts to close or consolidate schools, forcing many rural students to travel long distances to reach schools.[25] At the same time, the decline of rural populations has often been accompanied by state educational reforms that pressure schools to broaden programs and offer more courses. In response, more rural schools have begun to offer online courses—even more so than urban schools.[26] All told, a half-million U.S. students now take classes online.[27] An example of intensive use of online learning is the Virtual High School (VHS).‡ The school first offered courses in 1997–98; by 2010, it had expanded its operations and offered 336 courses to almost 13,000 students. Students from around the country use their VHS courses' websites as their starting point. From there, they obtain readings and assignments. Students then log on to a daily discussion group in which the teacher conducts a *netseminar*. This flexible arrangement accommodates a variety of school schedules as well as time zone differences. The convenience and additional time for reflection that come from logging on at any point make the netseminar particularly appealing. Students

*Tennessee Bob's Famous French Links can be found at **www.utm.edu/departments/french/french.html**.

†Dave's ESL Café can be found at **www.daveseslcafe.com/**.

‡To learn more, visit the Virtual High School website (**www.govhs.org/website.nsf**).

complete collaborative projects for the course by exchanging information over the Internet.

TECHNOLOGY FOR STUDENTS WITH SPECIAL NEEDS

Technology tools can also assist students with special needs. For students with learning disabilities, such tools can help level the playing field by presenting information in a manner best suited to the student's preferred learning style and unique needs. Although using a software program does not replicate the experience of learning from a teacher, the computer is not constrained by the human variables of limited patience and classroom distractions. Using the right software, an alternative, individualized curriculum can be created for students with special needs, paralleling the standard school curriculum.

In addition to its direct instructional uses, technology plays a second, very important role for special-needs students. Assistive technology describes the array of devices and services that help people with disabilities perform better in their daily lives. (See Chapter 3, "Who Are Today's Students in a Diverse Society?" for a further discussion of assistive technology and special education.) Students with disabilities may rely on a variety of innovations to help them achieve successful inclusion in regular classrooms.[28]

Computers are especially helpful in allowing students to participate in normal classroom activities that would otherwise be impossible. User-friendly keyboard enhancements simplify typing, and assistive technology can be used to control most basic computer applications. ERICA (Eyegaze Response Interface Computer Aid) is one revolutionary technology that opens up opportunities for special-needs students. ERICA tracks and records the user's eye movements and pupil dilation across a computer display, so that the mouse can be controlled with eye movement alone; this technology allows even extremely immobile students to communicate with teachers and classmates.*

Assistive technology helps some students with disabilities participate in regular classrooms with their nondisabled peers.

(Elizabeth Crews / The Image Works)

*To explore ERICA-derived products, see **www.enablemart.com/Catalog/Head-Eye-Controlled-Input**.

The variety of tools to help special-needs students fully participate in school is constantly expanding. One option includes a word-predictor feature* that facilitates keyboarding. After the student types a letter or two, the computer presents a list of likely words, and the student simply selects the correct word rather than typing it out completely. Other aids, such as voice recognition software, which translate a student's spoken words into text on the computer screen, or programs that will read text aloud,† can make writing a satisfying experience for students who struggle in this area.[29] Blind students and their teachers can use Braille software, which provides easy-to-use, sophisticated print-to-Braille and Braille-to-print translations.‡

As discussed in Chapter 3, "Who Are Today's Students in a Diverse Society?" assistive technology must be considered a potential component of the Individualized Education Program (IEP) required under law for each child with a disability. Regular classrooms now often include students with disabilities and other students with special needs, and you should be prepared to work with children who use assistive technology in your classroom. This process may be easier than you realize because many features developed for special-needs users have been incorporated into general-use software. For example, *Adobe Acrobat* can read documents aloud; *Microsoft Word* includes a voice recognition feature; and the *OpenOffice* word processor uses word prediction technology.

PAUSE AND REFLECT

1. To which technologies should students have access?

2. Pick the technology that most interests you in this section, and think about how you might use it in your classroom. Would the technology allow you to improve on something you already did? Would you be innovating with the technology?

3. Do you have any educational concerns about the use of these technologies in schools?

---

how are technologies affecting teaching?

As a teacher, you can expect that your students will have to meet some standards relating to technology. Some states give technology only a brief mention in their standards, whereas others have separate standards exclusively for technology. In line with the current nationwide move toward standards-based learning (see "What Ought to Be the Elements of Educational Reform" in Chapter 12, "How Should Education Be Reformed?"), the International Society for Technology in Education (ISTE) has produced national technology standards. For example, before completing eighth grade, students should "design, develop, publish, and present products (e.g., webpages, videos) using technology resources that demonstrate and communicate curriculun concepts to audiences inside and outside the classroom."[30] ISTE encourages teachers to

---

*One such product is *Co-Writer* by Don Johnston Inc. (**www.donjohnston.com/**; telephone: 800-999-4660).

†DragonDictate is a popular voice-input program available from Software Maintenance, Inc. (**www.ddwin.com/dictate.htm**; telephone: 888-343-3773). *IntelliTalk II* is a talking word processor from IntelliTools (**http://intellitools.com/**; telephone: 800-899-6687).

‡Kurzweil Educational Systems offers software for visually impaired students (**www.kurzweiledu.com/**; telephone: 800-894-5374).

teach these skills within the context of their academic curriculum. To this end, ISTE has worked with content specialists to provide resources for incorporating the ISTE technology standards into subject standards for the rest of the curriculum.

Although this trend is encouraging, for technology to be truly integrated as an important part of classroom instruction, current practices and attitudes must change in several other ways. The impact of technology on learning depends more on the ways in which teachers use the technology than on the characteristics of the technology itself.

A DIFFERENT ROLE FOR THE TEACHER

Technology is just a tool. In terms of getting the kids working together and motivating them, the teacher is the most important.

—BILL GATES,,
Founder of Microsoft

Integrating technology into your teaching can change the way you deliver content to your classes. Many schools and teachers have been slow to discover the true potential of new technologies, but some new trends are emerging. Technology can be more effective in a teaching environment where computers help to facilitate instruction and foster a constructivist approach to learning, as discussed in "The Influence of Psychological Theories" in Chapter 9, "What Are the Philosophical Foundations of American Education?" As we have mentioned throughout this chapter, a constructivist approach to infusing technology is related to several other classroom characteristics, including the following:

- *Teacher as Facilitator.* Think back to the scenario at the beginning of this chapter. Patricia Gonzalez was *facilitating* instruction as needed to bring a deeper understanding of the topics and their relevance to students. Because of the technology the students employed, she was no longer the sole source of information for her class. By using technology to present basic factual and historical information, the teacher is freed to become much more involved in higher-level evaluation of performance. Teachers can monitor students' projects, guiding their efforts and providing feedback. Instead of being a teller and a tester, the teacher can be a leader and a co-learner. In such environments, teachers must view themselves as "coaches" or "facilitators" who guide students as they use technology to discover facts and concepts.

- *Embedding Technology in the Curriculum.* With the encouragement of groups such as ISTE, the idea of teaching technology skills in isolation is giving way to a new model of embedding technology skills within the context of the content.[31] For example, a social studies teacher might teach the mechanics of a program such as *HyperStudio* as part of a unit on the local community that asks students to create a virtual fieldtrip. In this model, the subject matter drives the technology, rather than the reverse. In the words of one team of researchers, "We learn best 'with' technology rather than 'from' it."[32]

- *Small-Group Instruction.* To better use some technologies, teachers must move from whole-class instruction toward smaller group projects and activities that are more conducive to active, engaged learning and student interactions. This shift is not one that all teachers warmly embrace. Smaller group work may mean that students learn different things at different times rather than an entire class learning the same material together. In many ways, this scenario resembles the days before chalkboards and full-class instruction. Classrooms that effectively use technologies such as **wikis** (websites developed collaboratively by a community of users) and blogs may evolve into cooperative rather than competitive social structures, and student assessment should shift away from just pencil-and-paper testing and toward the evaluation of products and progress in meeting established criteria under such models.[33]

- *Importance of Formative Assessment.* In traditional, teacher-centered instruction, teachers use formative assessments to monitor and redirect students' understanding as a lesson unfolds. When teaching with technology, this feedback process becomes even more important: teachers need to confirm not just students' understanding of the concept, but also their understanding of the technology tools they are using and the connection between the use of the tool and the content-learning goals of the lesson. Furthermore, because student use of technology often requires critical thinking skills, teacher feedback during the working process can be a catalyst for students to achieve a deeper level of understanding.

T (F)

Technology produces a generation of rote learners.
Furthermore, because student use of technology often requires critical thinking skills, teacher feedback during the working process can be a catalyst for students to achieve a deeper level of understanding.

"
It is not the strongest of the species that survives, nor the most intelligent; it is the one that is most adaptable to change.

—CHARLES DARWIN (1809–1882),
English Naturalist

The connection between technology and constructivism is not clear, but some researchers are beginning to understand certain elements of it. We know that teachers who have changed to a more constructivist approach in their classrooms are the same teachers who have used computers consistently and in meaningful ways in their classrooms. These teachers are more willing to discuss subjects in which they are not experts and tend to assign longer, more complex projects. It appears that technology does not make teachers change; rather, technology facilitates changes that teachers already wanted to make.[34]

Of course, change in education is rarely swift. Even highly motivated teachers who regularly used technology take a while to become comfortable with new technology and fit it into their classroom goals. Given the increasing pressure on schools to incorporate up-to-date technology, and with other supporting factors present, such as sufficient funding and on-site technical support, we can expect to see changes in teachers' pedagogy as they become more comfortable with the power and teaching opportunities technology provides.

Florida's Project CHILD (Computers Helping Instruction and Learning Development)* demonstrates some of the changes in common teaching practices and attitudes toward learning classrooms that help teachers effectively incorporate technology in teaching. In this program, elementary school teachers work together in teams of three, clustered by grade level (K–2 or 3–5). Each teacher focuses on one of three subject areas: reading, writing, or math. After direct instruction from the teacher, students complete independent work while rotating through three stations: a computer station for technology work, a textbook station for paper-and-pencil work, and activity stations for hands-on work. The teacher also has a teacher station for small-group tutorials or individual assistance. The students rotate among the three subject-area classrooms, working with the same three teachers for three years. This systematic approach ensures equitable computer time for all, and teachers can individualize instruction by specifying where students begin working each day. Children often work together to complete group projects and to have maximum computer time, learning from one another and from the computer and other materials in each room.

Project CHILD combines both traditional and constructivist views of instruction. Although teachers offer some traditional direct instruction, one of the aims of

*For more information, visit Project CHILD's website at **www.ifsi.org/**.

the project is to help teachers shift from being the single source of knowledge in their classroom to being a facilitator and coach. While students are using their station time, teachers circulate to facilitate learning.

How effective is this program? Students who participated in the CHILD project for a full three-year cycle scored better on standardized tests than their peers in conventional classrooms with similar computer–student ratios.[33] These results suggest that an important variable is not simply how many computers students have access to but rather how those computers are used.

PROFESSIONAL RESOURCES AND COMMUNICATION

In the past decade, we have witnessed a boom in communications. Cellular phones with digital cameras and Web capabilities, satellite and Internet broadcasting, and powerful handheld computers have been shrinking our world. With these tools, a teacher can communicate with colleagues and community members anywhere in the world, both quickly and cheaply.

E-mail

E-mail is an excellent medium for teachers to use in sharing ideas, materials, and resources. Besides being fast and cheap, e-mail can be sent with attachments, allowing correspondents to share anything from documents to digital video files. E-mail can also be sent to large groups of recipients just as easily as to one person, making it much more efficient than the telephone or mailings. Teachers can communicate with parents via e-mail, and vice versa, without the disruption of ringing phones and the need to play "telephone tag" with answering machines or voicemail. Within the school setting itself, e-mail has streamlined the work environment, reduced staff meetings, and decreased the mounds of accumulated paper.

The Internet

The Internet connects teachers to professional organizations in their field and to vast databases of lesson plans and teaching materials throughout the world. The list of websites at the end of this chapter is just a small sample of the vast possibilities available on this incredibly large and growing resource.

The Internet also provides teachers with opportunities to belong to communities of practice to communicate and share ideas. For example, Tapped In* has a free program through which teachers can set up a virtual office and up to two group rooms or classrooms. These spaces allow for synchronous (real-time) chat and asynchronous discussions with other teachers, as well as places to post files, links, and notes. Tapped In hosts virtual groups on a wide variety of subjects, with events posted each month for online forums.[36]

In the last couple of years, Twitter has begun to offer an alternative community for teacher discussion. Twitter is a microblog where the user posts text up to 140 characters in length. To follow and respond to other teacher posts, Twitter users can now join Twibes,† which filters the many posts to provide the user with only those relevant to the topic of interest. There are many Twibes to choose from, such as EdTech twibe‡ for teachers interested in technology and education.

*Tapped In, a project of SRI International's Center for Technology in Learning, is available at **http://tappedin.org/**.

†Twibes. For more information visit **www.eztweet.com/downloads/Twibes-FAQ-2010-01-19.pdf**.

‡This twibe and other education twibes can be found at **www.twibes.com/category/education**.

CLASSROOM MANAGEMENT

Teaching involves many complex tasks. Organizing learning activities, creating or gathering the materials needed, keeping records, managing conduct, and delivering instruction—all of these together add up to a big job. A teacher may have from 25 to 150 or more students every day, with attendance records to be kept and grades recorded for each one. Technology can both complicate and streamline this job. The introduction of technology can affect the dynamics of a classroom, as students are in control of the equipment; this shift in power can pose a challenge for some teachers who are not used to constructivist learning activities. Technology lessons require careful planning, rearrangement of room configurations, and creation of an alternate plan for when equipment malfunctions. Additionally, teachers have to monitor the appropriateness of language in online communications and the appropriateness of websites viewed. Teachers who are new to technology may find that it can be time-consuming at first but improves over time.[37]

Although integrating technology into the curriculum can take time, teachers can also make use of technology to save them time in other areas of their daily work. As both the sizes and price of handheld computers shrinks, some teachers have begun using them for tasks such as grade input, schedule coordination, file sharing, organization of students' data, and webpage downloading in a portable form. Such tools allow teachers to spend more time at the art of teaching and less time dealing with paperwork, organization, and materials management. In addition, a variety of software, referred to collectively as teacher productivity tools, can save teachers time by speeding up other management tasks. Popular teacher productivity tools include these:

- A *software gradebook*, also referred to as an *electronic gradebook*, is a hybrid application of a spreadsheet and a database. The database functions keep records of student and parent information such as mailing addresses, phone numbers, locker numbers, book numbers, and other details. The spreadsheet functions calculate grades and provide the teacher with statistical information regarding assignments, tests, and performance of students over time. In addition to saving teachers hours of work in doing calculations and retrieving student information, gradebook software gives teachers new ways to identify students' strengths and weaknesses. Some programs, for example, allow the teacher to print charts of a student's academic performance over time (quarters or semesters) for the student or parent to inspect. On the downside, the increased quantitative output of electronic gradebooks, such as averages and graphs, can discourage the use of other effective assessment techniques, such as written comments.

- *Test generators and question bank software* allow teachers to create a database of questions and then construct tests from them. The teacher can easily create two or three versions of the same test with the questions in a different order or with slightly different questions. This capability is particularly useful for pre- and post-assessments or for giving a different test to students who were absent on test day.

- *IEP software* helps manage the paperwork involved in the individualized programs required in special education.

- *Time management tools* can be used for both personal and academic purposes. Academically, teachers can use schedule or calendar software to track their progress through a curriculum map. More conventionally, these tools can help teachers keep track of appointments and schedules. Most of these tools can maintain both public and private information; public events such as a back-to-school night can be displayed to everyone, whereas private information such as a student conference remains viewable only by the teacher. Some packages even allow viewers to request a meeting. When these tools are used across an entire school, they can help groups, such as a curriculum committee, find a common meeting time.

- Keeping students' grades and personal information safe is an issue under revision in many schools. This revision is due to the appearance of technologies such as the mobile technologies, which allow the teacher to take work home. Students' grades and personal information are being taken out of school on teacher laptops, flash drives, and other such portable devices, which can be a privacy issue if the technologies are lost or stolen. One way to protect against private information getting into the wrong hands is to encrypt the files. Both Word and Excel have a very simple feature in which the file with be encrypted with a password.

PAUSE AND REFLECT

1. To which technologies should teachers regularly have access?

2. Do you envision yourself as a teacher who would be comfortable using technology in a constructivist way, such as Patricia Gonzalez did?

3. What do you see as the pros and cons of such an approach?

how are computer technologies organized for student use?

Computer technologies generally operate in several different arrangements within the school setting, and it is useful to think of these arrangements as ranging across a continuum from concentrated to infused, as shown in Figure 7.1. When technology is *concentrated*, students are given intense exposure to computers from time to time. Technology that is integrated smoothly into the daily classroom experience is described as *infused*. Several common computer setups exist along this continuum.

COMPUTER LABS

Computer labs offer a concentrated arrangement in which all the students use computers at the same time. This setup is ideal for technology education—teaching about the computer or how to employ a particular application. In many labs, a large display

FIGURE 7.1
Arrangements for Computer Technologies

One way to think about the different ways of arranging computer technologies within a school is to consider where each arrangement fits along a continuum, from concentrated to infused. If the arrangement is concentrated, students are exposed to computers in an intense way from time to time, whereas technology that is integrated smoothly into the daily classroom experience is considered infused. (© Cengage Learning 2013)

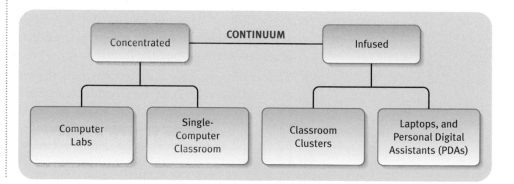

station for the teacher facilitates the demonstration of skills for more effective whole-class instruction. Labs may also feature specialized equipment such as interactive whiteboards. Forty-three percent of computers in U.S. schools are found in computer labs, and 48 percent are found in classrooms, according to one national survey.[38]

Most computer labs do not lend themselves to interdisciplinary or cooperative group projects because of a lack of open table space, although some teachers foster collaboration by having two chairs around one computer. Access to computer labs is another key factor in their use by teachers. If many classrooms must share a single computer facility, there may be little lab time for each class, and visits to the lab must always be planned. For these reasons, computer labs tend to foster technology education rather than what we might call education *with* technology—that is, education that uses technology to facilitate learning about other subjects. Computer labs do not always allow teachers to provide the best access to technology. There are other options that should be kept in mind.

SINGLE-COMPUTER CLASSROOMS

In a slightly more infused arrangement, the single-computer classroom might have the computer that is kept on the teacher's desk or rolled into the room on a mobile cart. Until classrooms reach a 1:1 student–computing device ratio, teachers will need to find instructional uses for one or just a handful of computers.

Although a single computer makes it difficult to use the technology for active instructional tasks, with the addition of a projection system teachers can make the rich resources of the Internet available for the entire class. For example, teachers might demonstrate complex mathematical or scientific concepts by using dynamic visualization programs such as *The Geometer's Sketchpad* or *Starry Night*; when used properly, this strategy can support student learning and inquiry.[39] Unfortunately, projection systems are all too frequently misused, with students being subjected to endless and wordy *PowerPoint* slides in darkened rooms, where they become passive consumers of the digitally rendered information rather than active learners.

CLASSROOM CLUSTERS

In a more infused situation, a cluster is usually a table or an area of a classroom where three to five computers are available for use at any time by the students in that class. Clusters provide convenient access to computer technologies for a variety of tasks. For example, a teacher might use two of the computers to allow cooperative groups access to cognitive and communication tools and reserve the other computers for use as learning stations for specific subjects.

Providing a cluster of computers in each classroom generally requires more of an investment in technology than the other arrangements we have described. A single computer lab of 25 computers can serve 10 classrooms, whereas the same number of classrooms might require 30 to 50 computers in a cluster arrangement. If a school can afford them, clusters offer a very flexible use of technology in the classroom setting. Teachers can plan to use them in instruction and can set up each computer to fit their needs. This arrangement genuinely fosters education *with* technology. It is not particularly good for technology education, however, because not every student has access to the technology simultaneously.

LAPTOPS AND HANDHELD COMPUTING DEVICES

Wireless laptop carts (carts of laptops that can connect to the Internet wirelessly and can be rolled into a classroom) provide a good solution to the issue of computer access in the classroom. This is a useful option as laptops are usually cheaper and take up less space than desktop computers, and there is not a wait time for the students to access the handful of computers the room may have. Some middle and high schools are moving to a policy of one laptop for every student, providing equitable access throughout the school. This arrangement facilitates deep, flexible use of technology by the students and encourages the teacher to assume the role of facilitator.

Handheld computing devices, such as the iPod Touch and Smart phones, offer the benefit of achieving a 1:1 ratio at a fraction of the cost of laptops, but such a device is still primarily a business tool and, as with the majority of technologies, these were not created for classroom use. A growing trend in many classrooms is to adapt these business tools for instructional uses.

There are hundreds of **apps** (an abbreviation for an application that runs on mobile devices) and websites now being developed for handheld devices such as the iPod Touch. Students in K–8 can use the Tales 2Go app, which offers a wide range of books with an auditory feature that can be switched on if the student requires that form of scaffolding. Middle and high school students can use web-based products such as Wolfram Alpha,* which enables students to find statistical information and data-related charts and visuals for a number of mathematical concepts. IEAR.org[†] (I Educational Apps Review) is a useful site for teachers to begin looking for appropriate apps. The site provides a review and description of the apps, which are easily accessible through a clearly labeled index.

In addition, a few affordable educational handhelds, such as AlphaSmart's Dana Wireless, are currently available, and more are likely to be developed in the coming years. See this chapter's Voices from the Classroom feature for an example of how an elementary teacher uses technology to enhance her teaching and student learning.

As handheld computing devices become more powerful and cheaper, they are increasingly finding their way into elementary and secondary school classrooms.

(Tom Grill/Getty Images)

*www.wolframalpha.com/examples/Math.html
[†]www.iear.org/

> **PAUSE AND REFLECT**
>
> 1. Envision yourself teaching with each of these computer arrangements. What would you and your students be able to do in a computer lab?
>
> 2. How would that be different if each of your students were able to use a handheld device in school?
>
> 3. How would your instruction change if you were assigned to a classroom with a single computer?

what are the key issues in educational technology?

You probably realize by now that many features of educational technology have given rise to serious debate among educators, policymakers, and the general public. To achieve the best use of available technology, schools must reach some consensus

VOICES from the classroom

Technology

Helen Crompton has worked in schools for 16 years, teaching students ages 5 to 16 in both mainstream and special needs schools.

When I first started using digital technology, I began with the basic computer operating system. The students seemed somewhat interested, and I could see that they could do some drill and practice activities. As technology has progressed, I find that it is making my busy life as a teacher so much easier, in so many ways. As I have used various technologies in my teaching, I keep in mind that it is not the technology that helps students learn, but the way that tool is used that makes a difference.

For the last few years I have taught fifth grade at a school in Chapel Hill, North Carolina. I was fortunate that I have had either a computer projector or a Smartboard. This was helpful as I have been able to do many things such as modeling letter writing in Language Arts classes and taking virtual field trips to many places around the world, using tools such as Google Earth. My mathematics lessons were transformed. I used to teach the students how to use a protractor by holding up a plastic protractor and describing what the students needed to do. I would usually have to follow this up with a trip around each table to demonstrate it in person.

Now I am able to use a large interactive protractor that I can manipulate for the whole class to see as I take my time demonstrating how to use it correctly.

During science and mathematics, I have been able to create podcasts with the students. I have found that this is useful as the students feel proud; not only do they listen to their own learning podcasts on a regular basis, but they also get all their friends in the class to listen as well. Podcasts have been valuable to the English Language Learners in my class; they are able to listen to their peers model the language and are also able to listen to their own developing language as they record themselves.

I am still careful with the technologies I use in the classroom as I do not want to use technology just for the sake of using technology. I will not let each child come up one by one to come and answer a question on the Whiteboard. When you have 27 students in the class, this can take a great deal of time and produce a great many disinterested students as they wait their turn. Before I integrate technology into my teaching, I make sure that I am using it for the benefit of the students, not just for novelty value.

on several key issues, including questions about infrastructure, budgeting, teacher education, parent support, equity for students, and how to infuse technology into the curriculum.

EDUCATION OF TEACHERS

Because of the excitement and demands generated by new technology, there is increasing pressure to improve both the preparation of new teachers and the staff development options for in-service teachers.

Teacher Preparation

When you graduate, you can count on having to demonstrate your skills in technology. In addition to National Educational Technology Standards for Teachers (NETS-T),* most states have included technology components as part of their licensure requirements. Schools of education, much like elementary and secondary schools, are grappling with the challenge of developing competent teachers who will meet these goals. Many instructors indicate that, even with the recent emphasis on computer literacy, instructional technology is not adequately modeled for future teachers.[40] Schools of education are continuing to rethink their programs and are gradually using modern technology to enhance what they offer. To this end, education students often develop electronic portfolios of their work, create computer-based assessments, and use digital video to capture and reflect on their student teaching. Visit the State Standards Resource Center on our Education CourseMate website.

The University of Virginia's Curry School of Education operates the Technology Infusion Project (TIP), which pairs each preservice teacher enrolled in the Applied Teaching with Technology course with a local classroom teacher who has an interest in learning more about using technology in the classroom. During their collaboration, the classroom teacher provides insight into curriculum and classroom practices, while the preservice teacher shares the new skills learned in the TIP program, such as use of multimedia applications or skills in constructivist uses of technology. As both teachers become more familiar with new technologies, they jointly explore instructional possibilities, culminating in a long-term project that they teach together in the classroom. In this way, preservice teachers gain a valuable classroom perspective from veterans in the field and ground their technology learning in classroom practice, and the classroom teachers gain professional development in technology. Whereas introducing technology into a classroom can be intimidating for some teachers, TIP's collaborative nature makes it a more comfortable experience and provides an extra set of hands to assist with the process.

Staff Development

Some states are adding more stringent technology requirements that teachers must meet to renew their licenses. Several states also offer incentives for teachers to develop technology skills, with the incentives ranging from paying for classes, to buying hardware and software. Teachers report, however, that one of the greatest obstacles to their use of computers is lack of release time to learn how to use technology. Experts do not agree exactly how training should be offered. Some believe training should be an ongoing process that is accessed at the teacher's convenience, whereas others advocate for an intensive, off-site course with follow-up seminars to allow teachers a chance to learn with undivided attention. With the advent of widespread

*ISTE's NETS-T can be viewed at http://cnets.iste.org/teachers/.

telecommunications networks, many professional development courses are now offered online.* Teachers who cannot be released during the school day can log on at night or during the summer to work through self-paced lessons. Accompanying discussion groups allow time for reflection.

PAUSE AND REFLECT

1. Which skills in using media and technology do you think teachers should have?

2. How can you prepare yourself to use technology in your classroom?

3. What are your concerns about using technology in the classroom?

4. What kinds of support systems do the teachers you know have for using technology in instruction? Whom do they ask when they have questions?

PARENTS

Teachers need to develop good lines of communication between the school and home in order to foster a trusting relationship and greater parental involvement. There are many ways in which technology can now be used to keep your students' parents connected with what is happening in the classroom. Cell phones, e-mail, and websites are just a few of the technologies being used in schools, which are often welcomed by parents who do not have the time for many face-to-face meetings.[41] These have the added bonus that they are much more likely to get directly into the hands of parents; notebooks are often lost at the bottom of book bags, especially if there is bad news.

Many parents want to know what is happening at school, and websites provide a great way to post photographs, text, and even video to provide a window into your classroom community. School districts often provide class websites that can be easily manipulated through a template system. If you do not have access to a class website through the school, you can always take advantage of the many good free website options available, such as Google sites.† Edmodo is another free Web resource where the teacher can gain a secure place for posting homework, grades, school notices, and other resources that ensure parents can follow what is happening in the classroom.

Technology can be either a "hook" to get parents involved or a quick deterrent to send them running. Parents who are not familiar with technology may be intimidated by or fearful of their child's computer use. Technology can become an obstacle between you and your students' parents. If you have a class website that gives pertinent information to the parents, also ensure that you provide paper copies to those parents who do not have Internet access.

EQUITY

Students who use a computer at home have opportunities to develop skills and explore technology's potential that are not available to students without these resources. Students with Internet access from home, and particularly broadband access, may have opportunities that others do not. Although the divide is closing between those with Internet access, and those without, there is still a large discrepancy between the

---

*To learn more, visit the Buddy Project website (www.buddyproject.org/).

†https://sites.google.com/

two. Reports dated 2009 show that while 55 percent of urban homes have Internet access, only 41 percent of rural households have access,[42] and rural Internet users are also far more likely to be limited to dial-up access.[43] However, simple access is not the only barrier. One technology expert argues that students from poorer families are more likely to use computers for games, whereas children from middle-class families are more likely to use the computer for online research.[44]

Some critics also argue that current patterns of technology use in schools contribute to disparities in educational quality. At school, data indicate that poorer students are at a disadvantage. Although the presence of computers in schools in wealthier and poorer areas has almost equalized, the digital divide still exists in terms of quality of equipment and type of instruction. For example, underprivileged children are more likely to use computers in a rigid drill-and-practice format rather than in more flexible formats, such as doing online research, that build higher-level cognitive skills. The impoverished city of Camden, New Jersey, spent $8 million on computers and software offered by a software vendor to boost students' scores on math and reading tests to meet the mandatory performance levels set by the 2001 No Child Left Behind law. Elementary and middle school students are in the computer labs up to five times a week, drilling to pass the annual tests. Critics of Camden's approach point to the loss of constructivist activities time and the resulting lack of higher-order thinking skills. These critics believe that drilling software can lead to an achievement gap.[45] Besides the basic question of fairness, these inequalities will have implications when these students graduate and look for jobs, as they will in many cases lack the skills of their more affluent peers. Visit the Education CourseMate website to link to more information about the digital divide.

Technology access and use divides along racial—as well as income—lines. A 2010 study by the Kaiser Family Foundation showed a difference in Internet access in regards to race; out of 8- to 18-year-olds living in America, 88 percent of white students, 78 percent of black students, and 74 percent of Hispanic students, had Internet access at home.[46] This information was gained from taking a large sample of 2,000 students across America. As computers become more commonplace in schools, teachers must consider students' access to technology outside of school, particularly when they are assigning homework.

Gender differences also have emerged as a factor in the effective use of technology in education. Researchers argue that certain types of technologies aggravate the differences (whether inborn or socialized) between boys and girls. For example, many commonly used applications value speed, aggression, and efficiency[47]—qualities that boys tend to display. For girls, technology appears to be more interesting when it's used for a relevant problem-solving exercise or collaboration rather than as an end in itself.[48] Blogging is one example of a technology that girls have adopted more rapidly than boys.[49] The key to engaging girls in technology appears to be *how* technology is used in the classroom. Tasks that require versatility and collaboration in classrooms (and businesses) that move to a more integrated approach to technology may invite more girls to participate.

Teachers can take steps to dispel technology-related inequities within their own classrooms. For example, students with little computer experience can be teamed with more experienced users. Classrooms and computer labs can be made available to students before and after school, and teachers can promote gender equity through modeling, attitude, and expectations. Technology need not become a wedge widening the gap between the "haves" and the "have-nots"; but without awareness of the problem, the potential for increased inequity is very real.

> ### PAUSE AND REFLECT

1. Where do you see evidence of the digital divide in the world outside of the K–12 classroom?

2. How will the digital divide affect you and your classroom?

INTEGRATION INTO THE CURRICULUM

> *We need to recognize that it is one thing to use technology in isolated classrooms and quite another to make technology a potent force in transforming an entire school or an entire education system.*
>
> —BARBARA MEANS,
> American Educational Psychologist

For computer technology to become a genuine part of school life, as it has in the business world, the tools of technology must be *integrated* into school behaviors. Integrating technology means bringing the tools of technology into daily learning and teaching activities, just as teachers already do with chalkboards and books. This is not an easy task. Much of this chapter has focused on how computer technologies can be used as tools for student learning, but we have also seen that many support systems must be in place.

Which conditions must be present in a school "to create learning environments conducive to powerful uses of technology"?[50] Among other conditions, schools must have the following:

- Student-centered approaches to learning
- Access to contemporary technologies, software, and communications networks
- Educators skilled in the use of the technology for learning
- Technical assistance for maintaining and using technology resources
- Ongoing financial support for sustained technology use
- Content standards and curriculum resources
- Community partners who provide expertise, support, and real-life interactions
- Vision with support and proactive leadership from the education system
- Assessment of the effectiveness of technology for learning*

> *We must adjust to changing times and still hold to unchanging principles.*
>
> —JIMMY CARTER,
> 39th President of the United States

As this list indicates, real change in education and technology cannot be the job of a lone teacher who is a whiz on the Internet or a single school board member who votes for new software. It must be a systemic change coming from a critical mass of individuals who are committed to the integration of education *with* technology.

*International Society for Technology in Education, *National Educational Technology Standards—Connecting Curriculum and Technology* (telephone: 800-336-6191 [United States and Canada] or 541-302-3777 [international]; e-mail: cust_svc@iste.org; **www.iste.org**). Copyright 2000. Reprinted with permission.

OUR FINAL WORD

The final word on the role of technology in education must belong to the teacher. Are we spending billions of dollars on fancy hardware, remodeling schools to accommodate wireless networks, and asking veteran teachers to change their ways without reason? What do we lose when we incorporate technology into our teaching? With increased access to vast amounts of up-to-date information and powerful new technologies, are students learning "the basics" as well as they do in more traditional classrooms?

(iStockphoto.com/kristian sekulic)

One view of the mission of schools is that they serve as work force preparation. According to this view, equipping students with "twenty-first-century skills" includes preparing them to use technology.[51] Teachers, by comparison, tend to have a broader focus: they want to develop healthy bonds with their students that will lead to intellectual growth. Teachers hope to develop responsible, educated citizens who have every opportunity open to them. When teachers see the rapidly changing world of technology in which machines sometimes break, certain applications take a long time to learn, and some programs are not flexible enough to meet their needs, they hesitate to take part in it.[52] Although policymakers might rush to shove schools into the information age, teachers make up a crucial part of the integration question. To reach some consensus, the dialogue should begin not with the goals of technology, but rather with the goals of schooling. When agreement is found, educators should raise the question of how technology can help reach those goals.

Certainly new technologies are no panacea for the classroom, but they offer tools that can help change the classroom from a teacher-centered to a more cooperative and student-centered environment. Students can use technological devices as tools—not toys—in the same ways that they will likely use technology in their future lives. We believe that all teachers should have the opportunity to gain skill in educational technologies; in particular, it would behoove new teachers to develop these skills in the context of their preservice work. Most important, we want you to consider how technology will affect your future classroom. Ask yourself where technology can enhance what you do and where it can allow you to innovate. If it is not accomplishing these goals, ask yourself why you are using it.[53]

WHY TEACH? YOUR FINAL WORD

In your journal or online at this textbook's website, respond to the following questions:

1. Do you think parents should be concerned about the role—or lack of it—that technological tools play in the education of their children? At what age do you think children should be taught to use computers?

2. Should governments spend billions of dollars on technology for schools, or should the money be spent differently?

3. What do you see as the goals of schooling? Are there ways you can use technology to reach those goals?

KEY TERMS

app (222)
vlog (204)
blog (204)
cognitive tools (198)
digital storytelling (203)
distance education (213)
drill-and-practice (204)
LCD projector (203)
mind maps (webs) (205)
news group (212)

productivity tools (198)
simulation (209)
spreadsheet (207)
tutorials (211)
ubiquitous computing (206)
virtual fieldtrips (210)
WebQuest (210)
webs (205)
wiki (216)
word processor (202)

FOR FURTHER INFORMATION

WEB RESOURCES

EdTechTalk: Educational Technology That Talks. Available at http://edtechtalk.com/.

This site is a portal to a range of podcasts about educational technology in the classroom, often by classroom teachers themselves. Audience members can either listen to archived podcasts or interact with the podcasters live during new sessions.

International Society for Technology in Education (ISTE), *Resources for Educational Technology Professionals*. Available at www.iste.org/resources/.

A superb list of links that covers a wide range of issues including standards, the digital divide, professional development, and technology integration.

ISTE, *Learning and Leading with Technology*. Available at www.iste.org/LL.

A monthly journal available online that offers great suggestions from teachers for teachers on how to use technology effectively in the K–12 classroom.

PRINT RESOURCES

David H. Jonassen, *Modeling with Technology: Mindtools for Conceptual Change*, 3rd ed. (Englewood Cliffs, NJ: Prentice Hall, 2006).

Centering on the use of computer applications to foster constructivist, higher-order thinking skills, this is a useful book for learning how to integrate "mindtools" into instruction.

Maggie Niess, Sara Kajder, and John Lee, *Guiding Learning with Technology* (New York: John Wiley and Sons, 2008).

This text is designed to help teachers guide their students in learning with multiple information and communication technologies, both existing and emerging.

Sharon E. Smaldino, Deborah L. Lowther, and James D. Russell, *Instructional Technology and Media for learning*, 9th ed. (Upper Saddle River, NJ: Prentice Hall, 2008).

Now in its ninth edition, this is one of the seminal books on the "how to" of using media in the classroom. For one example, see ISTE's National Educational Technology Standards (NETS) (http://cnets.iste.org/).

 The Education CourseMate website for this text offers many helpful resources. Go to www.cengagebrain.com to access the TeachSource Video Cases and other TeachSource videos, flashcards, interactive quizzes, the eBook, reflection and enrichment activities, a state standards resource center, and other study aids.

8 what are the ethical and legal issues facing teachers?

© Park Street/PhotoEdit

FOCUS POINTS

- Ethics and the law are closely related, but they also differ.

- Ethical teaching has six specific characteristics.

- In addition to teaching's everyday ethical dimensions, teachers can and should formulate their own codes of professional ethics.

- Teachers have to understand fully how two basic legal terms, *due process* and *liability*, relate to their work.

- Broad areas of the law—from contracts to copyright, from self-defense to religion in the classroom—permeate school life.

- Students have rights under the law, such as the rights to due process and privacy, and teachers need to understand and respect these rights.

This chapter aims to sharpen your sense of the ethical dimension of teaching and your understanding of the legal underpinnings of many aspects of school life. We examine several common ethical problems faced by teachers, along with legal issues and recent court rulings that have affected them.

Truth or Fiction?

T F Unlike medical doctors who have the Hippocratic Oath, there is no single, universally accepted code of ethics for teachers.

T F It is legal in American public school classrooms to study religious books, such as the Bible, the Talmud and the Koran.

T F After many years of delay, recently the Supreme Court has made corporal punishment in our schools unconstitutional and therefore illegal.

If each of us were the only person on the face of the earth, we could behave exactly as we chose. We would not have to worry about the rights or feelings of anyone else. We would be free of the constraints and demands imposed by others as we went about doing our own will. Of course, this is simply not the case. Everyone who walks the earth is bound by real—if unseen—connections with his or her fellow humans. The English poet John Donne said it most succinctly: "No man is an island."

Our systems of ethics and laws are a major part of these invisible connecting fibers. Together they make civilized society in a neighborhood and coexistence on a planet possible. Ethics, as we say in Chapter 9, "What Are the Philosophical Foundations of American Education?" brings us into the realm of what is the right way to act. **Ethics** refers to a system or a code of morality embraced by a particular person or group. Law is related to, but different from, ethics. A **law** is a written rule that members of a given community must follow. The law is a system of such rules that governs the general conduct of a particular community's citizens.

laws and our ethics

Whereas ethics may be invisible obligations that we perceive, laws typically are statements that have been hammered out by the legitimate authority of a particular community, state, or nation, and are used in court as standards by which to judge, and often penalize, the actual behavior of individuals. What someone might refer to as an *unstated law* is not a law at all, however: it is an ethical statement.

Laws are concrete, made by people, and usually written down for the public to see; ethics, by contrast, consists of ideas that are less tangible and observable. Most of our laws are simply the codification of what we see as our moral or ethical obligations to one another. For example, we have laws against excessive speeding that follow from our ethical beliefs that we ought not endanger the lives of others. Sometimes, however, laws are unethical, such as the racial segregation laws that existed in this country only a few decades ago. Also, ethical obligations may not always be codified as laws, such as the ethical obligation to help the weak, the poor, and the sick.

the teacher's responsibility

What does all this have to do with teachers? First, it is the responsibility of teachers to convey to the young the fundamental moral message that we are all legally and ethically bound to one another. Much of this moral message is incorporated into the content of our curricula, from our great stories to our history as a people. Second, a unique set of ethical relationships and legal obligations is embedded in teachers' work. As a consequence, teachers carry a special ethical and legal burden. This second issue is the subject of this chapter.

At the heart of the teacher's unique ethical and legal relationship with students is *power*. Like it or not, power resides in the "office" of teacher. Compared with a corporate executive or a military officer, it may not appear that a teacher has a great deal of power. In reality, the teacher has a special type of power. This power arises from the fact that the teacher has an impact on people when they are still at a very malleable stage. The teacher is in command of the classroom insofar as he or she has the responsibility for what goes on. Teachers evaluate their students. They not only "mark" them with tangible symbols that become part of students' official records, but they also "mark" their minds and hearts. Many careers are open to you, but few offer such truly awe-inspiring power.

If you wish to know who a man is, place him in authority.

—YUGOSLAV PROVERB

Because of the potential for abuse of this power, codes of ethics have been established to guide the teacher, and a body of laws governs the work of teaching. Ignorance of the law (and ethics) is no excuse to violate it, so we urge you to take the material in this chapter quite seriously.

PAUSE AND REFLECT

1. When you think about some of your favorite teachers, can you recall ways in which they exhibited ethical habits or principles?

2. Do you have memories of teachers behaving unethically? How?

3. What would you say is the greatest ethical obligation of a teacher?

---

the ethics of teaching

Being an ethical teacher means having a special relationship with your students and the other people with whom you work. Consider the following situation, as told to educator Kenneth Howe by a practicing teacher.[1]

from PRESERVICE to PRACTICE

The Characteristics of Ethical Teaching

Marilyn Henderson is a fifth-grade language arts teacher at Willoughby Elementary in South Lake, a medium-size city with a population of roughly 150,000. Marilyn is troubled to learn that Connie Severns, a fifth-grade social studies teacher with whom Marilyn worked previously in another school in the South Lake system, will be transferred to Willoughby. Marilyn believes Connie to be incompetent and is uncomfortable with this knowledge, especially in light of the fact that her students will be moving through Connie's class. As Marilyn recalls, "Connie didn't teach anything; she couldn't teach anything." Others in the district share Marilyn's assessment of Connie as a teacher and apparently with good reason. Connie seems totally to lack control. Children cry and complain about the chaos, some steal things from her purse, and on one occasion another teacher discovered a child chasing Connie around the room.

Marilyn had previously tried to do something about Connie's incompetence but met with little success. The teachers' union advised her that they would have to stand behind a tenured teacher, and the school administration claimed to have to follow procedures that could take years, according to Marilyn. At this point in time (before Connie's transfer), the principal of Willoughby called the affected teachers together. He too was concerned about Connie's transfer and proposed that they discreetly and surreptitiously "write things down" to build a case that they could use to have Connie fired. Marilyn is asked to be a part of this effort. What should she do?

From Kenneth R. Howe, "A Conceptual Basis for Ethics in Teacher Education," *Journal of Teacher Education* 37 (May–June 1986), p. 6. Reprinted with permission.

CASE QUESTIONS

1. As a colleague of Connie's, what should Marilyn do?

2. As a member of the teaching profession, what should Marilyn do?

THE CHARACTERISTICS OF ETHICAL TEACHING

This story provides just a peek into the teacher's ethically complex world. Howe suggests that in dealing with issues involving ethical judgment, we as teachers need to exhibit six characteristics: appreciation for moral deliberation, empathy, knowledge, reasoning, courage, and interpersonal skills.[2]

Appreciation for Moral Deliberation

We need to see an ethical dilemma such as Marilyn's as a situation characterized by conflicting and competing moral interests—in this case, Connie's need for a job, the students' need for a competent teacher, and the other teachers' need to be fair in what they say to and about Connie. We must see the complex moral dimensions of the problem and appreciate that care must be taken to protect the rights of all parties.

Empathy

Empathy is the ability to mentally "get inside the skin" of another person. We need to feel what the others in an ethically troublesome situation are feeling. In the case described, we would need to empathize with everyone who is affected by the burden of a questionable teacher—the students and their parents, Connie, and Marilyn and the other teachers.

Knowledge

One of the most valuable tools of a teacher who is able to deal effectively with ethical issues is knowledge. We must remember the facts that will enable us to put an issue in context. What does Connie actually do in the classroom? Which formal procedures are in place to deal with ineffective or incompetent teachers? We have to be able to formulate reasonable approaches to the problem and then, from experience, anticipate the consequences of each approach. In Marilyn's case, she has to be able to think clearly about the alternatives—such as participating in the principal's questionable plan or perhaps directly confronting Connie—and she must think through, with some degree of accuracy, what the likely consequences of such actions would be. This process requires knowledge of the context in which she and Connie are working.

Reasoning

To reason is to reflect systematically on an issue. When we reason about an issue, we move through it step by step and draw conclusions, or we compare a particular event or action with some moral principle and come to some conclusion. For instance, Marilyn may hold as moral principles the notions that people should not deceive others and that spying is deception. Through reasoning, she may come to the conclusion that what the principal has asked her to do is spying. Of course, this line of reasoning leaves Marilyn with another problem: how to tell her principal that his plan is unethical.

Courage

> *It is easy to be brave from a safe distance.*
>
> —AESOP

To feel, to know, and to reason are not enough. To be ethical, we must act—and action sometimes takes courage. To be ethically correct often requires the willpower to act in what we perceive to be the right way rather than in the comfortable way. Frequently, when confronted with a seemingly no-win dilemma like Marilyn's, we tend to ignore it in the hope that it will simply go away. However, as the theologian Harvey Cox sees it, "Not to decide is to decide." Among other things, Marilyn must find a way to tell her principal that she simply cannot be a part of his secret reporting network. Besides courage, this act will require tact.

Interpersonal Skills

Acting on ethical principles demands sensitivity and courage. In addition, teachers need the communications skills to deal sensitively with issues that demand great tact. They have to be able to call up the right words, with the right feeling and tone, and address the issue at hand openly and honestly.

NEEDED: A GUIDING CODE OF ETHICS

Behind this six-part process of dealing with ethical issues is something rather intangible, but nevertheless quite real: a personal code of ethics. Each of us has one, although some are beacons and others are dim lights in a dark room. For example, in Marilyn's response to her principal's request that she spy on Connie, what she does will be influenced by her personal code of ethics. That is, Marilyn's own answer to the question, "What is the right thing to do here?" is what will come into play.

When individuals enter the classroom as teachers, they are not always able to act in a manner that they find most satisfying. For instance, a student's rude remark to you may cry out for a sarcastic comeback, and you may have the perfect one on the tip of your tongue. The actions of a student—even a very small child—may provoke a rush of anger. An athletic coach, a good friend, may ask you to raise the grade of one of your students who has become ineligible to play on the coach's team. Whatever you would like to do or what you might have done before as a "civilian" is of little importance in these situations: you must respond as a professional, as a teacher. You need to be ready and act from a well-formed code of ethics.

As mentioned earlier, ethics deals with "the right thing to do." Everyone is expected to do the right thing, but the teacher's *responsibility* and *power* ratchet up the demand for solid and sound ethical decisions on his or her part. In addition, teachers often must be able to make ethical decisions on the spot. Telling the athletic coach, "I'll think about it," won't do.

Our personal answers to questions about what is the right thing to do represent our code of ethics. Unlike the formal codes of ethics that govern doctors (i.e., the Hippocratic Oath) and established teachers' organizations, such as the National Education Association, our personal codes are not written down. Nevertheless, they are quite real and serve as our daily guide in moral matters large and small.

Scholars often argue about whether humans are born with an imprinted sense of what is morally correct. Few would suggest that we are born with a full-blown, guiding moral philosophy of life. Instead, developing a strong, guiding code of ethics is one of our primary responsibilities as members of society. As part of this evolution, we can draw on a variety of sources, including human examples, spiritual and religious wisdom, secular guides, reason, and our moral compass.

Human Example

Humans are imitative creatures. First, we copy our parents and siblings, and then, as we move out into the world, we copy various people who cross our paths. Most of the important things we learn—such as language, physical skills, and ways to treat others—we learn from the example of others. Like Marilyn, when we are confronted with a "What should I do?" question, the human examples we admire play a strong role in helping us come up with a positive response. We recall the vision of a revered grandfather, parent, or friend to guide us. "What would Grandpa do in a situation like this? What would he expect me to do?"

Many people regularly rely on the examples set by people they have never met, such as individuals from history or literature. For example, some people wear "WWJD" bracelets, standing for "What would Jesus do?"; the bracelets are meant to be a regular reminder of how to respond to ethical situations. Others draw on the examples of staunchly moral Americans, such as George Washington, Abraham Lincoln, Martin Luther King, Jr., and Eleanor Roosevelt. This is one reason why these figures are studied in our schools.

Parents want their children to be taught by ethical people because they want their children to be influenced by good examples. Conversely, attentive parents often shield their children from "bad companions" and violent TV and movie characters out of concern that their children will acquire those behaviors.

Spiritual and Religious Codes

For many people, one of the primary sources of ethical guidance is the spiritual and religious domain. Holy books, such as the Bible, the Torah, and the Koran, are rich in moral precepts and stories. Some of this ethical guidance is quite direct and pointed. For instance, the Old Testament's Ten Commandments are hardly the "Ten Suggestions to Christians and Jews," and the eight Beatitudes of the New Testament are not simply a collection of nice ideas. Instead, these precepts are meant to be strong guides to practice and to become life habits. The ethical precepts of many other traditions serve much the same role.

Secular Guides

A large part of our ethical guidance comes from everyday life. A parent regularly repeats an aphorism, such as "A stitch in time saves nine." We see a Nike commercial that urges us to "Just do it!" At a red light, we read a bumper sticker imploring us to "Question Authority." These everyday adages and maxims are guides to behavior. Many, in turn, are richly ethical, such as the message conveyed by the bumper sticker "Perform random acts of kindness."

In recent years, there has been an explosion of self-help books on topics ranging from how to succeed in business to how to be a good spouse. Much of this content is intended to provide ethical guidance to the reader. For instance, most of the self-help parenting books direct parents on issues such as how to raise "good" children—that is, children who will be considerate of others and know right from wrong. In reality, these books are helping parents instill a code of ethics in their children.

Reason

As we discuss in Chapter 9, "What Are the Philosophical Foundations of Education?" ethics is a branch of the discipline of philosophy that aids us intellectually to examine issues of right and wrong. Through the use of our reasoning abilities, we can sort out whether an issue has an ethical component and think through the consequences of various courses of action. In the case of Marilyn, she can think through what might happen if she decides to help the principal build a case against her colleague, Connie. A significant aspect of being a *reflective practitioner,* as we urge throughout this book, is the capacity to bring reason to bear on the ethical issues you confront as a teacher.

Moral Compass

The factors that contribute to our personal codes of ethics do not operate in isolation from one another. Ideally, they work together to help us sort out a problem and act properly. As occurs with acquiring a good golf swing or achieving fluency in a foreign language, many small elements come together in a smooth, coordinated way. With our personal code of ethics, each factor contributes to our moral compass—the ethical "mental magnet" that quickly enlightens us about what we ought to do. The four elements that make up our code of ethics provide us with a moral North Pole. Someone with a strong moral compass doesn't have to tell the athletic coach that he or she will "get back to him"; instead, the teacher immediately rejects the proposal. When the principal makes an unethical request or the teacher sees a favorite student cheating, the teacher knows immediately what he or she must do.

ETHICAL DILEMMAS IN TEACHING

As with golf or speaking a foreign language, the skillful application of a code of ethics takes practice. Throughout this book, we have sprinkled many teaching cases that are explicitly ethical in nature or have an ethical component. We urge you to take these opportunities to practice sharpening your ability to apply your personal code of ethics to professional situations. As you read each case, take time to reflect carefully on it. Keep in mind the six characteristics described by Kenneth Howe. Also, bring your own moral compass to bear on the cases. Discuss them with other people. We often see much more in a situation involving ethics and recognize many other possible courses of action once we have talked to other people about it.

from PRESERVICE to PRACTICE

A Big Deal or a Little Fudge?

Recently, drugs have plagued your community, and increasingly they are coming into the schools. You are a sixth-grade teacher, and there has been only sporadic evidence of drugs in your building. Your principal has been making what seems to you a big deal out of very little in his crusade to stamp out drugs in "his" middle school. He has threatened the student body, first-graders through sixth-graders, in a special assembly about what will happen to them if they are caught with drugs of any kind. Most of your in-service training time this year has been taken up with the subject of drugs. You are concerned about the misuse of drugs in our society, but, like most of the other teachers, you find the principal's preoccupation with drugs overzealous and slightly laughable—and you are afraid of what will happen to the first offender he catches.

Coming from lunch, you see Alan, one of your sixth-graders, showing two of his friends a plastic bag containing what appears to be three or four marijuana joints. You are startled, but unsure that you have actually seen what he has. Alan shoves the bag into his pants pocket, and you act as if nothing has happened and usher the boys into class. To gain time to think, you set the students to work on a composition.

Alan is a kid with a spotty record in the school. His family life is rumored to be rather chaotic, but he has behaved well in your class. You have never seen the slightest evidence that he has been high in school. Knowing Alan, you guess he got the dope from one of his brothers and brought it to school to impress his friends. But you could be wrong, and the situation could be much more serious. You are sure of one thing: if you report what you saw to the principal, as you are expected to, he will move in on Alan like a crazed SWAT team.

As you mull all this over, Alan and his friends are nervously watching you and anxiously looking back and forth at one another. Suddenly, Alan gets up,

(continued)

comes to your desk, and asks if he can go to the boys' room. What do you do?

Righting Wrongs?

Donald Mitchell is a veteran history teacher in your high school, and he has "ruled the roost" in the department for the past 15 years. Many current and former advanced placement (AP) and honors students adore him. They find him exceedingly challenging, and they claim that his teaching prepares them for the rigors of college.

Apart from his senior AP classes, Mr. Mitchell teaches two sections of American government to tenth-grade students. A number of the students in those two classes have individualized education programs (IEPs). Mr. Mitchell publicly claims skepticism about many of these students' learning disabilities, doing only grudgingly what he has to do to comply with the IEPs. (Learn more about learning disabilities and IEPs in Chapter 3, "Who Are Today's Students in a Diverse Society?")

You have often heard Mr. Mitchell complain about "lowering standards of educational excellence" when he sits with his cronies in the school lunchroom. He does not hesitate to announce to the others about what he sees as being wrong with the school administration, the student body, and on occasion even faculty from other departments. His latest pet peeve is the "laxness" with which the English department teaches writing, so he has designed a strict procedure for writing his history papers. You have often found Mr. Mitchell to be boorish, but you reasoned that his behavior and opinions are his own prerogative. After all, you think to yourself, his teaching approaches are really a matter of academic freedom.

One afternoon, one of your students comes to class visibly upset. Janelle is one of your more challenging students. She has had a few minor run-ins with the vice-principal, and she does not demonstrate much interest in academics. You often have been frustrated by what you see as Janelle's lack of motivation and effort. Privately, you ask her what is wrong. She tells you that she has just left Mr. Mitchell's class, where she received a paper that was given a D–. You listen to her, reluctant to talk about the grading policies of another teacher.

After calming down, Janelle tells you that it wasn't the grade itself that made her so upset, but how the teacher returned the papers. She claims that Mr. Mitchell stood at the front of the class, stating that some of the students' papers followed the proper format. Others, he sneered, were so riddled with errors and so poorly written that the only use for any of them would be to line a kitty litter bin. He added that he designed his format so that some students would learn to write correctly, but that many of them apparently could not or would not even follow his simple format. With that statement, he scattered those papers on the floor. He passed the satisfactory papers to the rest of the students. When the rest of the students—all inclusion students—were left without their papers, he glanced at them and said, "Well, go on. They're right there if you want them." And he pointed to the floor.

Janelle tells you that she waited until class was dismissed to pick up her paper from the floor. You excuse Janelle so that she can go to the girls' room, and then you ask to speak to another student who is in that same class. When you ask him—again privately—if anything unusual happened in his history class, the student replies it was a regular class. You're still curious, so you ask him how Mr. Mitchell returned the papers. The student looks at you quizzically and says, "How'd he return the papers? The same way you do. He walked around the room and handed them back to us."

You're very disturbed by the story Janelle told you, and you want to do something to intervene. Yet, the other student's report makes you hesitant. What if nothing unusual did occur? Making an enemy of Mr. Mitchell would not be the politically savvy thing to do, and Janelle can certainly be difficult at times. Maybe she was just angry at the teacher for some reason and wanted to cause trouble, but what if that story was true? What should you do?

CASE QUESTIONS

1. What are the ethical issues in these two cases? Are there complexities that cause ethical conflicts? If so, what are they?

2. How did your moral compass react to these situations? To the case of Alan? To Janelle's situation?

3. In each case, what would you do? Who needs to be considered as you try to decide on your course of action?

THE EVERYDAY ETHICS OF TEACHING

As we hope the preceding case studies make clear, serious ethical issues strongly influence the lives of teachers. Few teachers get very far into their careers without having to deal with ethical dilemmas like these. Of course, these cases hardly exhaust the ethical responsibilities of the teacher. A much larger area of ethical responsibility exists that we call the *everyday ethics of teaching*.

Although it is clear that parents have the primary responsibility for the ethical training of their children, schools do influence the character and moral lives of students. (We discuss character education in Chapter 12, "How Should Education Be Reformed?") Classrooms and schoolyards overflow with issues of right and wrong: A student submits a report that is downloaded from an Internet site; a group of girls starts a rumor that another girl is pregnant; a teacher continually and harshly picks on the same student. Events like these send strong ethical messages to students. In particular, teachers ethically influence students in three ways: by their personal example, by the classroom climate they create, and by the dialogue they establish.

> *Living up to basic ethical standards in the classroom—discipline, tolerance, honesty—is one of the important ways children learn how to function in society at large.*
>
> —ELOISE SALHOLZ

First, teachers can set a good *personal example*. An old adage states that "who you are speaks louder than what you say." The way in which teachers do their work, the care and seriousness of their teaching, and the manner with which they treat students are perhaps their most powerful ethical messages to students.

Second, teachers can establish a beneficial *classroom climate* by creating an environment of safety and trust where students are free from fear and ridicule, where a spirit of cooperation and friendly competition prevails, and where students are working hard and feeling the satisfaction of learning.

Third, teachers can establish an *ethical dialogue* in their classrooms by discussing with students the core ethical values, such as honesty, respect for others, and responsibility, that come into play not only in the study of literature and history but especially in the real life events of the school.

The everyday ethics of teaching, then, means *doing the job as it ought to be done*. It means realizing the preciousness of the minutes and hours that you spend with students and making sure they do not waste their time with you.

CODES OF PROFESSIONAL ETHICS

Teachers do not struggle alone when they face ethical issues. Besides their own understanding, reasoning, and moral compass, they have the support of a professional group. Professional groups, such as those composed of doctors, architects, and teachers, have special obligations to their clients.

Whereas some entire professions have formulated their own universal code of ethics (like the Hippocratic Oath taken by all medical doctors), there is no single, universally accepted code of ethics for teachers. Nevertheless, several codes of ethics for teachers have been published. The best known is the code of the National Education Association (NEA). (You can link to the NEA code from the website for this book.) In recent years, a number of states' departments of education have also developed codes of ethics to govern the work of their teachers. Among the more specific codes is the one in the accompanying box, which was developed by the Alaska Professional Teaching Practices Commission.

(T) F

Unlike medical doctors who have the Hippocratic Oath, there is no single, universally accepted code of ethics for teachers. Whereas some entire professions have formulated their own universal code of ethics (like the Hippocratic Oath taken by all medical doctors), there is no single, universally accepted code of ethics for teachers.

code of ethics and teaching standards

In fulfilling obligations to students, an educator:

- May not deliberately distort, suppress, or deny access to curricular materials or educational information to promote the personal view, interest, or goal of the educator.
- Shall make reasonable effort to protect students from conditions harmful to learning or to health and safety.
- May not engage in physical abuse of a student or sexual conduct with a student and shall report to the commission knowledge of such an act by an educator.
- May not expose a student to unnecessary embarrassment or disparagement.
- May not harass, discriminate against, or grant a discriminatory advantage to a student on the grounds of race, color, creed, sex, national origin, marital status, or political or religious beliefs; physical or mental conditions; family, social, or cultural background; or sexual orientation; shall make reasonable effort to assure that a student is protected from harassment or discrimination on these grounds; and may not engage in a course of conduct that would encourage a reasonable student to develop a prejudice on these grounds.
- May not use professional relationships with students for private advantage or gain.
- Shall keep in confidence information that has been obtained in the course of providing professional service, unless disclosure serves a compelling professional purpose or is required by law.
- Shall accord just and equitable treatment to all students as they exercise their educational rights and responsibilities.

In fulfilling obligations to the public, an educator:

- Shall take reasonable precautions to distinguish between the educator's personal views and those of any educational institution or organization with which the educator is affiliated.
- Shall cooperate in the statewide student assessment system by safeguarding and maintaining the confidentiality of test materials and information.
- May not use institutional privileges for private gain, to promote political candidates, or for partisan political activities.
- May not accept a gratuity, gift, or favor that might influence or appear to influence professional judgment, and may not offer a gratuity, gift, or favor to obtain special advantage.
- May not knowingly withhold or misrepresent material information in communicating with the school board regarding a matter before the board for its decision.
- May not use or allow the use of district resources for private purposes not related to the district programs and operation.

In fulfilling obligations to the profession, an educator:

- May not, on the basis of race, color, creed, sex, age, national origin, marital status, or political or religious beliefs; physical condition; family, social, or cultural background; or sexual orientation, deny to a colleague a professional benefit, advantage, or participation in any professional organization, and may not discriminate in employment practice, assignment, or personnel evaluation.
- Shall accord just and equitable treatment of all members of the profession in the exercise of their professional rights and responsibilities.
- May not use coercive means or promise special treatment to influence professional decisions of colleagues.
- May not sexually harass a fellow employee.
- Shall withhold and safeguard information acquired about colleagues in the course of employment, unless disclosure serves a compelling professional purpose.
- Shall provide, upon the request of the affected party, a written statement of specific reasons for recommendations that led to the denial of increments, significant changes in employment, or termination of employment.

(continued)

- May not deliberately misrepresent the educator's or another's professional qualifications.
- May not falsify a document, or make a misrepresentation on a matter related to licensure, employment evaluation, test results, or professional duties.
- May not intentionally make a false or malicious statement about a colleague's professional performance or conduct.
- May not intentionally file a false or malicious complaint with the commission.
- May not seek reprisal against any individual who has filed a complaint, provided testimony, or given other assistance in support of a complaint filed with the commission.
- Shall cooperate fully and honestly in investigations and hearings of the commission.

- May not unlawfully breach a professional employment contract.
- Shall conduct professional business through appropriate channels.
- May not assign tasks to unqualified personnel.
- May not continue in or seek professional employment while unfit due to (1) use of drugs or alcohol that impairs the educator's competence or the safety of students or colleagues, or (2) physical or mental disability that impairs the educator's competence or the safety of students or colleagues.
- May not interfere with a colleague's exercise of political or citizenship rights and responsibilities.*

*The authors slightly modified the form of this code of ethics for the purpose of clarity.

Another, shorter example is the Boston University Educator's Affirmation, which is taken voluntarily in a special and quite popular ceremony, during or after student teaching. Run by the education students, the ritual marks their commitment to the high ideals and standards of the profession. In this sense, this affirmation is similar to the Hippocratic Oath taken by physicians.

BOSTON UNIVERSITY EDUCATOR'S AFFIRMATION

I dedicate myself to the life of an educator, to laying the living foundations upon which successor generations must continue to build their lives.

I dedicate myself to the advancement of learning, for I know that without it our successors will lack both the vision and the power to build well.

I dedicate myself to the cultivation of character, for I know that humanity cannot flourish without courage, compassion, honesty, and trust.

I dedicate myself to the advancement of my own learning and to the cultivation of my own character, for I know that I must bear witness in my own life to the ideals that I have dedicated myself to promote in others.

In the presence of this gathering, I bind myself to this affirmation.[3]

the teacher and the law

Once upon a time, teachers were like the kings and queens of small kingdoms. Their authority was wide, and their decisions were rarely questioned. Students who would not or could not do the work were "held back" or told not to come back. Students who did not conform to the teacher's standards of behavior were expelled. Education was something of a "scarce commodity," and students and their parents tended to view education as a special opportunity that put definite responsibilities on the student's shoulders. In fact, much of the legal authority of teachers was based on the principle of *in loco parentis*, meaning "in the place of parents." In other words, it was generally

▶❙❙ **TeachSource VIDEO CASE**

Legal and Ethical Dimensions of Teaching: Reflections from Today's Educators

Go to the Education CourseMate website to watch the video clips, study the artifacts in the case, and reflect on the following questions:

1. Which of the legal issues listed in this chapter and discussed in this case are you most concerned that you might face as a teacher?

2. How did this video help you feel more prepared to cope with the legal issues involved in teaching?

agreed that teachers acted as parental figures while students were in their care. For that reason, teachers' leeway in treating students was fairly broad, and they could make decisions about students based on what they thought was in the best interest of the student or students.

In the last few decades, however, the attitude toward schooling in the United States has changed. The authority of the adults in general, and of teachers in particular, has eroded noticeably, and many students are often more fixated on their rights than on their responsibilities. Many reasons for this change exist, but suffice it to say that we are a very litigious society. The United States has more lawyers per capita than any other nation in the world—and our increasing tendency to use the courts to settle differences and conflicts has had its impact on the work of the teacher. (The Video Case *Legal and Ethical Dimensions of Teaching: Reflections from Today's Educators* shows a roundtable discussion among real teachers about the legal situations they face.)

Our elementary and secondary schools have always been governed by school law. In recent years, however, the presence of the law in educational matters has grown dramatically. Like many societal changes, this trend has been a mixed bag. On the one hand, teachers are often cautioned to remember that students are autonomous, with individual rights that continue to exist even when students pass through schoolhouse doors and are under the supervision of teachers. As a result, teachers are required to be much more deliberate and cautious in their dealings with students to prevent an infringement of students' rights than they were in earlier decades. On the other hand, our new consciousness of the teacher's legal responsibilities and our heightened sense of students' rights have helped schools eliminate problems such as dictatorial practices by teachers and administrators, the systematic denial of certain rights to students, and the abusive use of corporal punishment.

Woodrow Wilson once said, "The law that will work is merely the summing up in legislative form of the moral judgment that the community has already reached." In other words, our laws represent our collective social judgments and decisions about what is fair. Laws differ from codes of ethics, though, because they apply to all the people, not to a particular group like doctors or teachers. Laws are public, whereas ethics can reflect one's private standards. And laws have judicial teeth, whereas codes of ethics do not. Rarely is a teacher suspended, or expelled, or even sanctioned by the teaching profession for violating general codes of ethics. Conversely, teachers are regularly affected by the law and are occasionally brought to court. The next sections examine some specific areas of law that can affect your work as a teacher.

One other issue complicates the legal front for teachers. The laws governing schools are part of a complex and overlapping system of federal, state, and local laws. Most of the cases discussed in this chapter started out as local school district disputes, only to travel to state courts, then to federal courts, and finally to the U.S. Supreme Court. Some caused the Supreme Court to reinterpret past rulings, leading to new legal guidelines. Because of their broad impact, the majority of the cases we deal with in this chapter are Supreme Court cases.

School law, like many other facets of our society, is dynamic and open to change. Although the Supreme Court justices are supposed to dispassionately interpret cases in light of the U.S. Constitution, it is said that "justices read the newspapers," meaning they are conscious of and sensitive to issues which are on peoples' minds, and this affects the cases they select to adjudicate. Therefore, cases involving contentious issues, such as school choice, are difficult for the Court to avoid.

THE TEACHER AND DUE PROCESS

- A young junior high teacher, on a lark, changes his "image." He comes to school one Monday morning sporting a shaved head and a diamond stud earring. He is fired on Tuesday.

- A teacher gives a speech at a meeting of the local gay and lesbian alliance. The newspaper runs a story on the event, and the superintendent asks her to resign quietly.

- A business education teacher who has been teaching for three years has been visited by administrators only twice during that period. He loves teaching and was recently told by his principal that he was a "shoo-in for tenure." Instead of getting the expected letter from the superintendent outlining the upcoming tenure review process, he receives a dismissal notice in May, claiming that his teaching is not up to the district's standards.

All three of these examples represent violations of the teachers' rights to due process. Due process is one of the most important principles embedded in our nation's laws. The essential meaning of **due process** in education is that fairness should be rendered and teachers' rights as individuals should not be violated. Many of the most influential court decisions concerning education, teachers, and the law concern fundamental issues of due process.

Due process protections come directly from two amendments to the U.S. Constitution. The Fifth Amendment states, "No person shall … be deprived of life, liberty, or property, without due process of law." The Fourteenth Amendment adds, "Nor shall any State deprive any person of life, liberty, or property, without due process of law."

The Fourteenth Amendment goes on to stipulate that no person should be denied "the equal protection of the law." Legal rulings related to due process in education often reflect the requirement that individuals be treated equally in their education or by school officials.

Two Types of Due Process

When judging the fairness of an action, there are two due process concerns:

- *Substantive due process* has to do with the issue itself.
- *Procedural due process* concerns the fairness of the process followed.[4]

For example, if a teacher is fired because he wears a nose ring, it raises an issue of substantive due process. Is this matter substantive enough in this particular circumstance to deny a teacher employment? What is a fair decision in this matter? Procedural due process would involve how the case is handled. Suppose the teacher, after hearing several rumors that the nose ring is irking the superintendent, gets a curt letter saying his "services are no longer needed." Is this process fair? Has the teacher had a fair chance to defend himself?

The precise meaning of procedural due process varies from state to state, but the Supreme Court decision in *Goldberg* v. *Kelly* (1970) indicated that "the minimum procedural safeguards … demanded by rudimentary due process" would include the following:

- Procedural safeguards
- The opportunity to be heard at a reasonable time and place
- Timely and adequate notice, giving details of the reasons for the proposed suspension or dismissal
- An effective opportunity to defend oneself, including oral presentation of evidence and arguments
- An opportunity to confront and cross-examine witnesses

- The right to retain an attorney
- A decision resting solely on the legal rules and evidence adduced at the hearing
- A statement of the reasons for the determination and the evidence relied on
- An impartial decision maker[5]

Procedural due process exists so that individual teachers and students are protected from arbitrary actions against them. The principle of due process and these guidelines reach into many corners of the teacher's life, as will be discussed.

CONTRACTS, TENURE, AND DISMISSAL

Some of the most fundamental legal issues have to do with the legalities of employment. When, for instance, is a teacher actually hired? How does a teacher know he or she has an actual teaching position? What does having tenure mean for a teacher?

Teachers are not self-employed: they are employees of a school board or, in the case of a private school, of a board of trustees. As employees of a governing body, teachers must be familiar with and abide by the stipulations of the contract issued to them by the school board. If teachers do not fulfill the requirements of the contract, they are at risk of losing their jobs.

Contracts to Teach

Imagine the following situation: You are a recent college graduate, newly licensed to teach, and you are actively interviewing for teaching positions. Your interview at the Long Meadow school district goes extremely well, and the superintendent tells you

A future teacher takes her first look at her first contract.

(Ersler Dmitry/Shutterstock.com)

she would like you to join the faculty. She says that she plans to recommend your hiring to the school board, telling you that for all intents and purposes, you should consider that you have a teaching position, because the board usually votes to approve the superintendent's recommendations. You tell her that you would like to join the faculty, accepting her verbal offer.

Several weeks go by, and you hear nothing from the school district. In the meantime, you are invited to interview at the Centerville school district. When you interview there, you realize it is *the* ideal school district for you. The school administrators seem equally impressed with you, and in several days the superintendent calls and offers you the position. Although you want to accept immediately, you ask the superintendent for a day to think over the offer. In fact, what you really want to do is find out your status at the Long Meadow school district. Do you really have a job there? If you accept the offer at Centerville, are you violating some legal obligations to the Long Meadow school district?

The answers to these questions depend on whether you have a legal contract for employment. A **contract** is a binding agreement between two or more persons or parties. It indicates the rights and responsibilities of each party to the agreement, and all teachers, new or old, sign a contract with their board of education or trustees. Contracts differ from district to district and from state to state, but they generally specify the teacher's salary; course, teaching assignments, or instructional areas; the maximum class size, length of school day and school year; and grievance procedures. A **grievance** is the formal expression of a complaint about an unsatisfactory working condition. Grievances typically concern disputes over working conditions; when a person files a grievance, he or she usually argues that the working condition was in violation of the teacher's contract. Additionally, contracts generally indicate whether the local teachers' association or union is the official bargaining agent for teachers.

Contracts cover a set period of time. Most new teachers work on a contract that has to be renewed annually if the teacher is to stay employed by the school district. Even teachers on tenure (to be discussed shortly) sign a yearly contract stipulating the terms of employment. Occasionally teachers may work under a **continuing contract**, which states that its terms will remain in force until the teacher is given notice that the contract will be terminated on a particular date.

To be considered a legally enforceable document, a contract must do the following:

- Have a lawful subject matter
- Represent a meeting of the minds of both parties
- Include an exchange of something of value (*called a consideration*)
- Be entered into by parties who are competent to do so
- Be written in proper form (instead of in vague terms such as "pay the teacher what he or she is worth")

In addition, the school board must act officially to ratify a teacher's contract. Many people assume that contracts must be written. In fact, unless state law requires a written contract, an oral contract that includes all legal requirements can also be legally binding.[6]

In the previously described scenario, unless all of the conditions were included in your discussion with the Long Meadow superintendent and the school board acted upon, or *ratified*, the superintendent's recommendation to hire you, you did not have a legally binding offer. Therefore, you could accept the Centerville offer without hesitation.

Now suppose that scenario were altered slightly. What if you had signed a contract for the Long Meadow school district and then accepted the Centerville offer?

In that instance, you could be held liable for **breach of contract**. A legal contract is binding on both sides—that is, on both the school district and the teacher. If either party violates conditions of the contract, the contract itself is said to have been breached, and the other party can sue for damages.

When an injured party successfully sues the other party for breach of contract, the court may order that the contract be fulfilled, that the injured party receive monetary damages, or both. For instance, the district may have to rehire a fired teacher and pay damages, or a teacher who walks away from a job may have to pay the district's cost of finding a replacement. In addition, whenever a teacher breaches a contract, his or her professional reputation is in danger of being tarnished.

Given these concerns, before you accept any position, you should study the contract carefully and ask about anything unclear to you. That contract will govern many of the important details of your life as a teacher.

Tenure

Imagine a few years have passed since you accepted the Centerville position. At what point are you granted **tenure** (or what some states call *continuing contract status*)? New teachers are hired on a probationary basis, with the probationary period often lasting three years, so the school district can ensure that the nontenured teacher can teach well enough to be granted permanent faculty status. State law determines when a teacher is eligible for tenure and outlines the requirements for earning tenure or continuing contract status. Some states require that the school board take some positive action to grant the teacher tenure status; in other states, the teacher is granted tenure automatically when he or she successfully completes the probationary period.

What does possessing tenure actually mean for a teacher? The word *tenure* comes from the Latin root meaning "to hold," as in "hold that job." Thus, if you become a tenured teacher in the Centerville school district, you are entitled to contract renewal every year. The general purpose of tenure was nicely stated by the Supreme Court of Pennsylvania in 1957: tenure helps to maintain "an adequate and competent teaching staff, free from political or arbitrary interference." In addition, tenure allows "capable and competent teachers" to feel secure and to perform their duties efficiently.[7]

Tenure guarantees your position as a teacher in the school district, but it does *not* mean that you are guaranteed to have the exact same teaching assignment every year. A teacher can be reassigned to teach second grade after being a fourth-grade teacher for years, or a school district can reassign a tenured teacher to another school in the district.

Tenure is an issue about which both the general public and teachers often hold strong views and, just as often, are greatly misinformed. Contrary to the views of many, poorly performing tenured teachers *can* be fired. There are clear sets of procedures administrators can follow to provide the evidence necessary for dismissal. Of course, following the procedures takes a good deal of time and energy if a solid case is to be made. Recently, there has been a growing chorus of complaints about what many in the public believe is the failure of the nation's schools to get rid of ineffective teachers. In 2010, the popular documentary film *Waiting for "Superman"* appeared to blame tenure for much of the ills of American public schools. One of the facts the film presented was that in Illinois 1 in 57 doctors loses his or her medical license; 1 in 97 lawyers loses his or her license to practice law; and 1 in 2,500 teachers loses his or her teaching credentials. This failure to dismiss poorly performing teachers is laid at the feet of tenure and the strong legal protections of teachers' unions.[8] For this reason, some education critics and school reformers advocate the elimination of tenure, though it is doubtful that this will happen in the foreseeable future.

In fact, teacher tenure is no more than a guarantee of procedural due process. Nevertheless, a school district needs to follow a strict set of guidelines for disciplining or dismissing a teacher. These guidelines are somewhat different for tenured teachers than for teachers who have not yet earned tenure.

Dismissal

Sometimes teachers fail. Perhaps they simply cannot handle the job, or perhaps they make a big mistake, such as striking a child in anger. Occasionally, teachers have "philosophical differences" with administrators, sometimes further complicated by mild or severe cases of "personality conflict." These situations and many more may result in an attempt to dismiss a teacher. Dismissal procedures are covered by the laws in each state, and those procedures must follow due process.

If a school district decides in the middle of a school year (and therefore in the middle of a contract) to dismiss an untenured teacher, the teacher always has a right to a full hearing and due process. By contrast, if the district decides not to extend a second- or third-year contract to a new teacher, as in the example given earlier in this chapter, the situation is less clear. Although in some states an untenured teacher who is not being rehired can demand a hearing, in most states the school district does not have to justify its reasons for not rehiring a teacher on probationary status.

For tenured teachers, the legal situation is different. Tenure is protected under the Fourteenth Amendment and is considered part of the teacher's "property." Tenured teachers have the expectation that they will have continued employment, which is considered a "property interest." In a sense, the tenured teacher has "earned" and "owns" the job, and he or she can be separated from it only under very special circumstances. In light of that fact, a teacher can call on the full protection of the law, just as she or he would if someone were trying to take away a home or a car. To justify dismissal, the school district must prove that the tenured teacher has violated some provision of the tenure law.

In most states, a tenured teacher can be dismissed only "for cause." States vary concerning what they consider due cause for dismissal, but most require a good reason that will withstand the scrutiny of the courts, such as sexually molesting a student, gross negligence, or clear incompetence. In some states, the law stipulates that a tenured teacher cannot be dismissed without being given an opportunity to correct his or her deficiencies. In those instances, the courts usually determine what is "remediable," or faults that could be corrected by the teacher. For example, if a teacher demonstrates poor classroom management, that failure can be seen as something correctable, and most courts would not allow a tenured teacher to be dismissed before he or she was warned about the management problems and given a chance to correct them. Certain actions, however, are so unprofessional that the damage is "irremediable." Being convicted of a crime and engaging in sexual relations with a student are both considered irremediable.[9] In those instances, the school district is under no legal requirement to help the teacher correct his or her behavior and dismissal procedures can begin immediately.

The most common reasons for dismissal include immorality, insubordination, incompetence, and "conduct unbecoming a teacher." The last reason is a fairly vague term that allows schools some leeway in dismissing a teacher whose behavior is unethical but may not be classified under the other, more specific causes such as insubordination or incompetence. For example, sometimes "conduct unbecoming" means a teacher has used the classroom for purposes other than teaching. One teacher was dismissed because he used class time to advocate that the students, their families, and their friends vote for a particular candidate running for superintendent of schools.[10] In another case, a teacher was dismissed for tampering with the school telephone system and eavesdropping on telephone conversations. It is the responsibility of the courts to weigh the individual situation, review the law on the subject, and determine whether the case justifies dismissal.

Reduction in Force

In most instances, a tenured teacher can only be dismissed for wrong behavior or incompetent teaching. The one exception to that occurs when the school district needs to eliminate some teaching positions for economic reasons. Sometimes the courts allow schools to dismiss teachers as a result of curricular reorganization. For example, a school board might decide to drop its classical languages department. Most commonly, however, reductions occur when the school district has a drop in student enrollment and does not need all the teachers that it employs or when it experiences a budgetary shortfall that requires teacher dismissals. Under those conditions, a school district can lay off tenured teachers, and the decision about which tenured teachers to dismiss is usually made on the basis of seniority. Called **reduction in force**, or "riffing" in slang, this practice was common in the 1970s and 1980s, when student enrollments were shrinking. More recently, as an effect of the economic recession of 2008 and 2009, school districts across the country resorted once again to riffing because of budget curtailments. In the spring of 2009, more than 2,000 teachers in over half the districts in Washington State were riffed. Federal stimulus money was made available to many public sector workers and in the case of Washington State, 87 percent of the "riffed" teachers regained their positions.[11]

TEACHERS' LIABILITY

Liability means blame, as in "The teacher should accept liability for the student's dislocated shoulder," and other accidents and mistakes. It implies that the teacher behaved negligently or intentionally in a way that allowed an injury to happen. See the feature "The Teacher and Liability" below.

from PRESERVICE to PRACTICE

The Teacher and Liability

Lori Spinelli, a middle school Spanish teacher, often employed cooperative learning activities in her lessons so students would have more opportunities to practice speaking and listening to each other. Although the students worked together, Lori often circulated around the room to converse with each small group, using the week's vocabulary words in her brief conversations with them.

One afternoon, while she was working with a small group in the front of the classroom, Lori heard a scream from the back. One of her students, Jared, was writhing in pain on the floor. He had tried to show his group members a certain dance move and had dislocated his shoulder.

Later that afternoon, Lori replayed that class in her mind, feeling more and more dread, worrying and wondering about whether she would be held liable for Jared's injury. True, she had been in the classroom, but Lori realized that while she was talking to the group in the front of the room, her back had been turned to most of the students in the room, including Jared. What if Jared's parents held her and the school district liable for their son's injury?

CASE QUESTIONS

1. What teaching mistake, if any, did Lori make?
2. In your judgment, is Lori liable for Jared's injury?

Teachers are responsible for ensuring the safety and well-being of their students in their own classrooms and work spaces and in the activities they oversee. This includes fieldtrips and after-school clubs and activities, such as band, sports, and play rehearsals. Teachers are also liable if they do nothing when they observe a student in some potentially dangerous act that eventually turns out to be harmful. Turning one's back on misbehavior in no way lessens this responsibility. Teachers can be held liable for acts of omission.

Lori has good reason to be concerned. A court trying to determine whether her supervision was adequate would focus on whether Lori could have reasonably prevented Jared from getting injured or whether his injury was something that could not have been reasonably anticipated by her.

Two court cases help shed light on the extent of a teacher's liability. In one case (*Sheehan* v. *St. Peter's Catholic School,* 1971), an eighth-grader was injured when her teacher took a group of students outside to watch a baseball game and then went back inside the school. In the teacher's absence, a group of students began throwing pebbles at the spectators, and Margaret Sheehan was hit in the eye with a pebble, sustaining a serious eye injury. In that case, the court ruled that the school did not take reasonable precaution to prevent student injury. It is impossible, after all, for a teacher to monitor students if the teacher is inside while the students are outside. The teacher should have anticipated that in leaving the group of students alone and unsupervised, a dangerous situation could develop.[11]

Does that mean teachers need to be in a position of directly observing students at all times? Does it mean that a teacher like Lori would be considered liable for her student's dislocated shoulder? Maybe not.

In another case concerning liability, teachers took a group of junior high and high school students to visit Chicago's Natural History Museum (*Mancha* v. *Field Museum of Natural History,* 1971). When the group arrived at the museum, the teachers allowed students to visit the exhibition halls on their own. One student, while in an exhibition hall apart from the teachers, was approached and beaten up by a group of teenagers who did not attend the same school. In this case, the court ruled that the risk of student injury in a museum usually would be "minimal," so it was an unreasonable expectation that teachers should have been able to foresee and prevent the student's beating. Furthermore, the court indicated that expecting teachers to supervise directly every student on the fieldtrip would place such an unreasonable expectation on teachers that few would plan fieldtrips or other educationally valuable activities for their students.[12]

Thus, even though teachers are required to exercise prudence and foresight in their supervision of students, the courts expect *reasonable* prudence and foresight. Some student injuries are accidents or unforeseen injuries, and in those cases the teacher is not held responsible.

Liability Precautions

Indeed, when teachers can demonstrate they have taken reasonable precautions to prevent student injury, courts have not found teachers liable for student injuries. To show that they have been "reasonably prudent," teachers need to be able to demonstrate that their actions met the following criteria:

- They made a reasonable attempt to anticipate dangerous situations.
- They provided proper supervision.
- They took precautions.

Certain school activities can be dangerous—and constitute an area of potential teacher liability.

(© Image Source/Jupiterimages)

- They established rules.
- They gave a warning to minimize the chances of students getting hurt.

Because teachers are vulnerable to legal suit, it is important that they be covered by some form of liability insurance. In recent years, many teachers have been scared into buying more insurance than they need or, more commonly, into buying insurance when they are already covered by school district insurance policies. Every new teacher should check his or her on-the-job coverage with the district's personnel director before beginning work.

One area in which experts suggest teachers are particularly at risk is automobile liability. Often teachers volunteer to take students in their own cars to sports games or on fieldtrips. Even if teachers have personal insurance, they often do not have enough to cover liability claims if a serious accident happens. Before taking students in a private car, the teacher should be sure that the district's insurance policy covers such cases or that his or her own policy is adequate.

To Lori Spinelli's great relief, no charges were brought against her. Lori had established an orderly classroom, and she was in the room when Jared was injured. Other students indicated that Ms. Spinelli had taught them rules of behavior and of courtesy, especially given that they would often be working in small groups. Jared was, in general, a well-behaved student, so there would be no reason for Lori to expect that he would decide to jump up and show a dance move to his group members. Finally, her lesson for the class, which covered presenting and practicing written dialogues for their partners, would not be considered a dangerous situation for students. The mere fact that her back was turned to Jared's group wouldn't be grounds to hold her liable—after all, no teacher can face all of the students all of the time. Lori's established good teaching practices and her sound judgment demonstrated her competence. In another situation, in which just a few of those factors were different, a teacher may have been held responsible.

In all these issues of liability, it is important for the teacher to use good judgment. Accidents often "just happen," and there may be no liability involved. If a school injury does result in a lawsuit, the courts will try to determine whether the teacher was providing reasonable care and, in general, was acting in a prudent and careful manner.

Teachers must be vigilant about possible abuse of their students.

REPORTING CHILD ABUSE

In addition to preventing harm to students under their supervision, teachers have a legal responsibility to safeguard students from abuse and neglect at the hands of their parents and other adults. Teachers in every state are required by law to report suspected child abuse or neglect. The laws vary somewhat from state to state, but they all include two or more of the following elements in their definition of abuse and neglect: physical injury, mental or emotional injury, and sexual molestation or exploitation.[13] If teachers suspect that a student has experienced *any* of those injuries, they are legally obligated to report their suspicions of child abuse and neglect to the appropriate authorities. Schools typically have detailed instructions in their faculty handbooks about how to report such suspicions. Additionally, principals or other administrators will often remind teachers of those procedures so that all teachers understand explicitly the necessary reporting protocol.

A teacher does not have to be *certain* that a child is being abused before he or she makes a report to the principal. Child abuse is clearly one of those areas where it is better to act and be wrong. If a teacher has a reasonable cause to suspect that a child is being abused, that is sufficient grounds for making a report. To protect a teacher from reaction to an incorrect report or from the anger of an offending parent, the reporting is kept confidential. Further, teachers in all 50 states are granted immunity from accusations of slander or any possible libel suit.[14] Without such protection, many teachers would hesitate to report their suspicions. (For a more detailed discussion of child abuse, see Chapter 4, "What Social Problems Affect Today's Students?")

SELF-DEFENSE

Schools are very crowded places, and they are crowded, by definition, with immature individuals. Thus it is not surprising that conflicts sometimes erupt and teachers find themselves encountering hostile behavior. For instance, a teacher may have to break up a playground fight or stop some students from vandalizing another student's locker, or a student may strike a teacher in anger.

Self-defense is defined broadly here to take in all these situations. In the first two cases, fighting and vandalism, the teacher is expected to intercede in the interest of safety. In a fight, for instance, the teacher must act to stop the students from hurting one another. Strong and loud words usually are effective, but sometimes the teacher must become physically involved. The operating principle here is "reasonable force." If a teacher uses reasonable force and if, in the process of stopping the fight and separating the students, a student suffers an injury (say, a strained wrist or dislocated arm), the courts typically will find that the teacher is not liable. If the same injuries resulted from a fight the teacher did not act to stop, he or she may be held liable.

In more obvious cases of self-defense, a student threatens or actually strikes a teacher. The principle of reasonable force applies here too. What constitutes reasonable force is generally a matter of common sense, but the heat of the moment can make good judgment difficult. In one case, a male seventh-grader who weighed 110 pounds struck a 220-pound coach. The coach grabbed the boy, lifted him off the ground, and threw him against a wall, breaking the child's back. When the case was brought to court, the teacher-coach claimed self-defense. He lost—big time. In the court's view, the teacher's responsibility is to keep a level head.

Assault and Battery

A teacher's recourse against an abusive student is governed by assault and battery laws. In legal terms, *assault* has come to mean a threat to do harm. Threats should always be taken seriously and reported to the principal, but their legal status depends very much on the student's ability to carry through on the threat. An angry fourth-grader's threat to "do something terrible to you" does not have the same status as a high school junior's threat to blow up your classroom.

Battery means a willful attack on another person that results in harm. Being unintentionally knocked to the hall floor by a rushing student is not battery (although it may call for some disciplinary action by the school). Being intentionally pushed by a student or a parent is an entirely different matter, however, and makes the pusher immediately liable.

Incidents of assault or battery should be promptly reported and disciplinary action demanded or legal charges filed. Often teachers, particularly new teachers, are hesitant about making a fuss or turning offending students in to the proper school authorities. They should not equivocate: verbal abuse and physical violence have no place in our elementary and secondary schools.[15]

FREEDOM OF EXPRESSION

One of the most treasured rights of American citizens is the freedom of expression. Freedom of expression includes symbolic expression and verbal or written expression. For teachers, freedom of expression also subsumes **academic freedom**, the freedom of a teacher to select course materials and to teach in a way he or she thinks fit. Before we go on, take a moment to consider your ideas about freedom of expression.

Until about 40 years ago, teachers who publicly criticized administrators' decisions or school board policies received little sympathy from judges. The attitude

> ### PAUSE AND REFLECT
>
> 1. Is the freedom of expression limitless? Can a teacher say anything or teach anything, claiming it is his or her right to free expression?
>
> 2. To what degree do you think that you, as a potential teacher, should have the right to select your own course materials or to provide information to students?
>
> 3. Are there any instances in which you think a teacher's freedom of expression should be limited?

of the courts was that judges had no business interfering in the legitimate affairs of the schools. Things changed, though, as a result of Marvin Pickering.

Pickering, a high school English teacher, wrote a long and sarcastic letter in the local newspaper about his superintendent and school board. He accused them of, among other things, taking the local taxpayers "to the cleaners," devoting excessive expenditures to athletics, and forcing teachers to live in an atmosphere of totalitarianism. It was later shown that Pickering's information on a number of issues was wrong.

Pickering was fired. He sued for his job, but the original court verdicts upheld the firing. Pickering's case was appealed before the U.S. Supreme Court in 1968. Because Pickering, an English teacher, made erroneous statements about athletic expenditures and those expenditures were matters of public record, the Court indicated that Pickering did not speak with any greater authority on the matter than any other taxpayer. The Court also found that his comments did not impede his proper performance in the classroom or otherwise interfere with the regular operation of the schools, so the judges reversed the lower courts' ruling and ordered Pickering reinstated and compensated.[16]

In effect, the Court said in the *Pickering* decision that society needs to balance the interests of a teacher, as a citizen commenting on issues of public concern, and the interests of the state, as the teacher's employer trying to promote smoothly running schools. Although the Court affirmed the teacher's right to free expression, it pointed out that this First Amendment protection is not an absolute right. A teacher cannot expect to say absolutely anything and then cry out for protection under "freedom of expression." As a U.S. Court of Appeals stated in the 1970s *Scoville* v. *Board of Education* case, "Freedom of speech includes the right to criticize and protest school policies in a nondisruptive manner, but it does not include the use of 'fighting' words or the abuse of superiors with profane and vulgar speech."[17] If teachers become disruptive forces in a school or make irresponsible statements, for example, the courts will not support their expression of their views. For instance, in 1981 the courts ruled against a teacher who had claimed that the racially derogatory comments he made to his principal and assistant principal were constitutionally protected.[18]

The Supreme Court also ruled against teacher John Stroman (*Stroman* v. *Colleton County School District,* 1992) after he circulated a letter harshly critical of school administration. In it, he urged fellow faculty members to stage a "sickout" to show the administrators just how unified the faculty was in their discontent. In its ruling, the Court indicated that urging a "sickout" when individuals were healthy was an appeal for dishonest behavior and conduct unprofessional for teachers.[19]

Symbolic Expression

Personal expression is not limited to spoken and written words. Dress styles, armbands, and buttons have been used in recent years to "make a statement." Typically

the courts support teachers (and students) in these cases of free symbolic expression. A key issue here involves the potential of this type of expression to lead to "substantial disruption" within the school. A school might forbid such symbolic clothing as a teacher's Ku Klux Klan button in a high school with many African-American students or students' gang "colors" or jacket insignias if they provoke fighting. These judgments cannot, however, be a matter of a teacher's or an administrator's "taste." Bans on symbolic expression of one's views or preferences must be based on clear indications that the efficiency or safety of the school is endangered.

CyperSpace Expression

The popularity of the new electronic communication, particularly e-mail and social networking, has brought with it many benefits and some hazards. Used in schools, it can maximize communication among teachers, students, administrators and parents in way unimaginable just a decade earlier. Among the hazards, however, is the fact that e-mail messages, which a writer thought were personal and "deletable," can be retrieved and subpoenaed by the courts in legal conflicts.

Social networking can present a particular danger to teachers, particular young teachers who have grown up using them for personally revealing exchanges with friends. A 2008 federal court case in Connecticut illustrates the problem. A second-year teacher heard about MySpace from his students and soon opened his own MySpace account. So far, so good. The teacher, however, allowed students access to the account, and various exchanges ensued involving lewd inquires and responses about his sex life. Also, he posted the picture of a nude man, plus comments, on his site. Word got out, administrators investigated, and the young teacher was let go. Believing he had been badly treated, he filed suit in federal court, claiming the school system had violated his Fourteenth Amendment rights of procedural due process, substantive due process, and equal protection and his First Amendment freedoms of expression and association. The Court made rather short work of his defense primarily because *he was a teacher* and this type of communication was inappropriate. Commenting on the issues behind this case, education legal specialist, Perry A. Zirkel wrote [in a nicely titled piece, "MySpace?"] that it is

> not surprising that teachers, like students, would get ensnared in the web of new technological issues. . . . However, at a time when the Supreme Court and the rest of the judiciary is leaning away from individual rights under the Constitution, including the cited First and Fourteenth Amendment decisions in the public employment context, the new technologies—including but not limited to e-mail, MySpace, Facebook, YouTube, and electronic surveillance

tools—present traps for the unwary. The problem of establishing an effective relationship with students, close enough for internal trust but distant enough for external trust, is an age-old problem that is as tricky as distinguishing between the pertinent definitions of "confidence."[20]

Academic Freedom

A subcategory of freedom of expression, academic freedom, deals largely with issues in the classroom and the teachers' (and students') rights to discuss ideas and read material of their choosing. Academic freedom allows teachers to speak freely about their subject matter, to select reading assignments, and to choose teaching methodologies based on their professional judgment. It is designed to allow experimentation with ideas and to foster an open spirit of inquiry.

Academic freedom can meet with opposition when teachers want to discuss controversial or unpopular ideas such as sexual mores, gun control, or abortion. If such issues are a part of the school's curriculum, problems rarely arise. When a teacher "adds" them to the curriculum, however, he or she needs to make a reasonable case that they are relevant to the curriculum. Dismissal for teaching controversial issues may or may not be upheld by the courts. Teaching about volatile issues that may disrupt a particular school, such as homosexuality or the alleged characteristics of different races, is frowned on by the courts. So too is teaching controversial material considered unsuitable for the age of the students. In addition, courts have not allowed teachers to use controversial teaching methods that are unsupported by professional opinion or prohibited by reasonable school policy.

Political issues, both local and national, are also points of tension. In the classroom, teachers may discuss current political controversies, but they must deal with them neutrally and in a balanced way. Away from work, advocating a particular cause or political party is fine, but a teacher may not behave as a partisan supporter in the classroom.

Particular essays and books that contain sexually explicit material or even words that are offensive to certain members of a community have been a major source of legal controversy in schools. In one important case, *Keefe* v. *Geanakos* (1969), a Massachusetts English teacher, Robert Keefe, assigned his students an article from the well-respected *Atlantic Monthly* that contained offensive language. Keefe's assignment kicked up a firestorm of protest, and he was eventually fired for refusing to agree not to assign the article again. Subsequently, he was reinstated by a circuit court decision because the offending language existed in a number of books already in the school library; the school board had not notified him that such material was prohibited; and that court believed the word in question was not all that shocking to the students. As the decision stated, "With the greatest respect to such parents, their sensibilities are not the full measure of what is proper education."[21]

The Court ruled similarly in another often-cited case concerning academic freedom (*Parducci* v. *Rutland*, 1970). Marilyn Parducci, a high school English teacher, had assigned *Welcome to the Monkey House*, by Kurt Vonnegut, to her eleventh-grade English class. Ms. Parducci was called down to the principal's office the next morning and told not to teach that story in any of her classes. Parducci disagreed, contending that the short story had merit as a literary work, despite the principal's remark that it was "literary garbage." Parducci indicated to the principal and assistant superintendent that she would continue to teach her eleventh-grade English class using whatever material she wanted and in whatever way she thought best. Parducci was fired from her job, with the explanation that she was "insubordinate" and the course reading had a "disruptive" effect on students. The Court found that the Vonnegut story was not inappropriate reading for eleventh-graders. The finding added that the short story was met with "apathy" by most of the students, so the reading itself could not have created an undue distraction.[22]

Absolute academic freedom at the K–12 level does not exist, however, and some court decisions have limited teachers' perceived academic freedom. The decision in a more recent case (*Boring* v. *Buncombe County Board of Education,* 1998) stands in contrast to the rulings in the Keefe and Parducci cases. Margaret Boring chose *Independence,* a play containing mature subject matter, for her advanced acting class to perform in a statewide competition. After reading the script, the school principal informed Boring that the class would not be allowed to perform it at the state competition. Boring, along with parents of the actors, met with the principal, requesting that he not cancel their performance. He agreed that they could perform the play, but only after certain portions were deleted. The students performed the play, with portions deleted, and won second place at the competition.

At the end of that school year, the principal requested the transfer of Boring from the high school, citing "personal conflicts resulting from actions she initiated during the course of the school year."[23] Boring argued that her transfer was in "retaliation" for expression of unpopular views through the production of the play and therefore violated her right to freedom of speech.

The Supreme Court ruled in the school board's favor. In its decision, the Court stated that this was nothing more than an ordinary employment dispute, not a matter of public concern. For that reason, it found that the dispute did not constitute protected speech. The Court also wrote that school administrators have a "legitimate pedagogical interest in the makeup of the curriculum of the school," and that the "school, not the teacher, has the right to fix the curriculum."[24]

Issues of academic freedom often generate a great deal of heat. When they reach the courts, the following considerations, among others, are brought to bear:

- The teacher's purpose
- The educational relevance of the controversial publication
- The age of the students involved
- The quality of the disputed teaching material and its effects on the class[25]

These considerations are critical guidelines to remember when one teaches.[26] Perhaps the most important point to remember is that academic freedom is limited: it cannot be used to protect the incompetent teacher or the indoctrinating zealot.

COPYRIGHT LAWS

Good teachers are always on the hunt for effective teaching materials: a story that carries a special message, a poem that captures an idea with beauty and economy, an article that contains the latest information about an issue students are studying. Having found the "perfect" piece, it is difficult to resist the temptation simply to copy it and share it with the class, and the wide availability of photocopying equipment makes this practice all too easy.

Printed matter is the product of someone's labor, the same way that a painting or a piece of furniture is. Under the law, it is considered intellectual property, and the creator or author has a legal right to receive a reward for his or her labor. Without such payment, few people could afford to write books, plays, or articles. For this reason, first in 1909 and more recently in 1976, the U.S. Congress passed copyright laws to protect writers and publishers from the unauthorized use of their material.

For teachers, the heart of the current copyright law is its **fair use** guidelines, which specify which printed materials teachers may photocopy and under which conditions they may do so. The general principle behind fair use is "not to impair the value of the owner's copyright by diminishing the demand for that work, thereby reducing potential income for the owner."[27] In other words, if people simply copy print materials whenever they want, they will not buy the books, and publishers and authors will suffer. Some copying is allowed, of course, and it is important for teachers to know what they may and may not do.

Teachers may copy materials under the following circumstances:

- Make a single copy for class preparation of a chapter from a book; a newspaper or magazine article, short story, essay, or poem; or a diagram, chart, picture, or cartoon from a book or magazine.

- Make a copy for each of their students of a poem if it is fewer than 250 words and printed on not more than two pages; and one copy for each student of an article or short story if it is fewer than 2,500 words.

Teachers may not copy materials in the following situations:

- Make copies of a work for their classes if another teacher in the same building already has copied that same material for his or her class.

- Make copies of the same author's work more than once a semester or make copies from the same anthology, text, or periodical issue more than three times a semester.

- Create a class anthology by copying material from several sources (a favorite trick of many teachers!)

- Make multiple copies of weekly newspapers or magazines specifically designed for classrooms, or of consumable materials, such as copyrighted games, exercises, and particularly worksheets from workbooks

- Charge more for legally permissible copies than it cost to copy them

These guidelines may seem overly restrictive and technical, but teachers actually have more liberal guidelines for copying than the average citizen does.

Videotapes, Software, and the Internet

There is a great temptation for teachers to tape material "off the air" and to build tape libraries of material to use in instruction. Although this tactic may be effective pedagogy, it may not be legal. Commercially produced videos are **intellectual property** and, like printed materials, are covered by U.S. copyright laws. Copyrighted television programs (and most of them *are* copyrighted) can be kept for only 45 days, after which they must be erased or taped over. Also, during the first 10 days after the taping, the teacher may show the tape only twice: once for initial presentation and once when "instructional reinforcement" is called for. Finally, schools cannot routinely record material for potential later use by a teacher; such recording can be done only at a teacher's request.

The personal computer has helped to revolutionize American life in general and American education in particular. Since 1976, a huge new source of intellectual property has burst on the scene and opened up a plethora of new opportunities—the Internet being the most dramatic example. Today it is possible to copy information from government agencies, libraries, legal systems, commercial sites, and other schools with the click of a mouse.

Given the ready accessibility of websites, you may be tempted to copy a research report from an online news information service and make copies for all students in your class. However, contrary to what many believe, the Internet is *not* in the public domain. Most webpages—including the information on them and the code used to create them—are protected by copyright law. Because the Internet is global, it is regulated by an international treaty, the Berne Convention for the Protection of Literary and Artistic Works, to which the United States and most English-speaking nations are signatories. The law in this area is still evolving and until it settles, we suggest you follow the fair use guidelines cited earlier. Also, many teachers find that their school's media specialist can help them keep up with changes in copyright laws regarding digital, as well as print and video, materials.

Computer software programs are not treated in the same way as text, video clips, or still pictures. Commercially sold software differs from material "taken off" the Internet. Software should not be passed around and copied. In some cases, the software publisher may allow the purchaser to make one backup copy of the software, but making any other copies is a violation of the copyright laws.

Although all of this may seem like overkill, it is important for teachers to follow the rules—not simply because it is the law, but because students will follow their example.

lifestyle and the teacher

Teachers bring into their classrooms more than their minds and their lesson plans: they bring their attitudes and values. Elementary and secondary teachers traditionally have been considered extensions of the family in passing on to the young the community's positive values. In past generations, teachers who behaved in ways counter to the community's values were dismissed. Teachers were summarily fired for homosexuality, being pregnant and single, living with someone of the opposite sex, using illegal drugs, being publicly drunk, or committing a crime. However, the late 1960s saw a shift in the balance between the community's right to require certain standards of behavior and the rights of individuals to pursue their own lifestyles and values. Although the law in some areas has not yet been settled, on many questions judicial opinion (the way judges are tending to rule) is clear.

PAUSE AND REFLECT

1. To what degree do you believe that a teacher's personal life should be truly private? Should what the teacher does on his or her own time always be off-limits for school authorities and protected by the law? Is the teacher completely free to live his or her life in whatever way he or she decides?

2. Were there teachers in your elementary or high school experience whose behavior "pushed the envelope" and were in conflict with your community's standards? If so, how did the school district respond? Do you believe justice was served? Was the cause of education served?

PERSONAL APPEARANCE: HAIR, CLOTHES, AND WEIGHT

In the late 1960s and early 1970s, the courts tended to rule in favor of teachers' rights to do what they wished with their hair. More recently, the courts have often sided with school districts' rights to impose reasonable grooming codes for teachers. Teachers, according to the current view, do not have a *constitutional* right concerning their "style of plumage."[28]

The situation is similar for clothing. Courts have upheld districts' judgments on skirts that are considered too short and requirements (in some districts) that male teachers wear neckties. Courts are asserting that the First Amendment does not extend to "sartorial choice."

For health reasons, obesity may be its own punishment. But does a school district have a right to fire a teacher because it decides she or he is too fat? A California school district released a 42-year-old female physical education teacher because, at 5 feet 7 inches and 225 pounds, the district felt she was "unfit for service." Her principal argued that she "did not serve as a model of health and vigor" and was restricted in her ability to perform on the trampoline, in gymnastics and modern dance, and in other aspects of the program.[29] In this case, the court sided with the teacher, claiming that the district had not proved that her girth had impaired her performance.

PRIVATE SEXUAL BEHAVIOR

In the past, sexual behavior was considered an area in which a community had a complete right to impose its standards on people selected to teach its children. More recently, the courts have increasingly viewed teachers' private sexual habits or preferences as separate from their public, professional lives as teachers.

One landmark case involved Marc Morrison, who was fired after his former lover, another male teacher, reported their brief relationship to the superintendent. The school district believed it was on solid ground in dismissing Morrison for several reasons. The district's representatives argued that California's law requiring teachers to be models of good conduct applied to the case that teachers are required to impress on their charges "principles of morality," and that homosexual behavior is contrary to the moral standards of the people of California.

In 1969, the California Supreme Court ruled in Morrison's favor. It acknowledged that homosexuality is, for many people, an uncertain or controversial area of morality. Nevertheless, the court made an important distinction between a teacher's private life and his or her professional performance. As there was no evidence that Morrison's sexual orientation had ever been part of his relationship with his students, or in any way affected the performance of his teaching duties, or affected his relationship with his fellow teachers, he was reinstated.[30]

Similarly, cases involving pregnancy out of wedlock and unmarried couples living together have been settled in favor of the individual teacher. To win such a case, however, the conditions just cited are required. Specifically, the behavior must not intrude into the classroom or seriously affect the teacher's professional performance.

A teacher would be misguided to think that his or her behavior after school hours is *always* protected under the law. For example, a tenured California teacher was fired after she was arrested by an undercover policeman for engaging in sexual activity at a swingers' club. California state courts ruled that her behavior at this semi-public party showed "a total lack of concern for . . . decorum or preservation of her dignity and reputation" and that she demonstrated a serious lack of "normal prudence and good common sense."[31] Flaunting one's deviation from the community's standard tends to increase the chances that the courts will uphold dismissal. In all these cases, however, circumstances play a crucial role in the courts' final opinion.

CONDUCT WITH STUDENTS

Whereas the courts have become increasingly lenient on issues of private sexual behavior, the line is being held firm with regard to socially unacceptable behavior that spills over into the classroom. One sure way to lose one's teaching position is to make a sexual advance or engage in any kind of sexual relationship with a student. Usually, even a single incident is enough to sustain a dismissal. The same goes for smoking marijuana, taking other drugs, public drinking to the point of drunkenness, or even using excessively obscene language in the presence of students. In this area, the teacher bears the full weight of the responsibility to be a role model.

Teachers should also realize that they can become "overinvolved" with students, even when no sexual impropriety has occurred. A fourth-grade teacher, Drew Kerin, was dismissed from his job when he became so involved with one of his students that he sued the boy's mother for custody. The child had been allowed to live with the teacher for nine months, but when the mother wanted her son to return home, Kerin filed suit for custody. The custody battle generated so much publicity that the district fired him. Kerin was found to have "exploited his position as a teacher," which provided "just cause for termination."[32]

In general, except in matters of personal appearance, the courts are allowing teachers a good degree of freedom in their private and personal lifestyles as long as their choices and their behavior do not adversely affect their performance as teachers. Table 8.1 summarizes the court cases and rulings discussed in this and the previous sections.

TABLE 8.1   Selected Court Cases Dealing with Teachers' Rights and Responsibilities

Issue	Case	Ruling
A teacher's liability for student's injury	*Sheehan* v. *St. Peter's Catholic School* (1971)	A teacher is liable for student injuries (i.e., eye injury) if he or she leaves students unsupervised.
	Mancha v. *Field Museum of Natural History* (1971)	A teacher is not liable for student injuries under unusual circumstances (i.e., a fight in a museum) if he or she has taken appropriate precautions.
A teacher's right to free speech (such as criticizing the school authorities)	*Pickering* v. *Board of Education* (1968)	A teacher can criticize the operation of a school as long as his or her criticism does not interfere with the normal running of the school.
	Scoville v. *Board of Education* (1970)	Freedom of speech does not include the use of "fighting words" or the abuse of superiors with profane and vulgar speech.
A teacher and academic freedom	*Keefe* v. *Geanakos* (1969)	A teacher may not be dismissed only for selecting reading assignments with offensive words.
A teacher and his or her private life	*Morrison* v. *State Board of Education* (*California*, 1969)	A teacher's sexual orientation is not grounds for revocation of licensure, particularly when it in no way affects the performance of professional tasks.

© Cengage Learning 2013

law, religion, and the school

According to the First Amendment to the Constitution, "Congress shall make no law respecting an establishment of religion, or prohibiting the free exercise thereof." During the past two centuries, the U.S. judicial system has interpreted this amendment inconsistently with respect to the place of religion in public schools—a topic of high controversy and the cause of much public unrest in recent years. This controversy is not a new one: the role of religion has been a bone of contention since the beginning of public education in the United States.

Among the questions currently being asked are the following:

- Which religious observances, if any, are permitted in public school classrooms?
- Is all prayer, public and private, illegal in public schools?
- Are extracurricular religious clubs allowed in public schools?
- May parents insist that schools provide alternative textbooks consistent with their religious beliefs?

PRAYER AND SCRIPTURE IN THE SCHOOL

Until the mid-twentieth century, religious observances, including Bible reading and prayers, were common in the public schools. In fact, Bible reading and the recitation of the Lord's Prayer were required by constitutions or by statutes in a number of states. In *Abington School District* v. *Schempp* (1963), however, the Supreme Court ruled both to be unconstitutional.

In a 1962 decision (*Engel* v. *Vitale*), the Court had already ruled against the recitation of a nondenominational prayer, holding that Bible reading and prayer violate both clauses of the First Amendment. The Court recognized that the schools involved did not compel a child to join in religious activities if his or her parents objected; nevertheless, it held that the social pressures exerted on pupils to participate were excessive. In essence, no distinction was believed to exist between voluntary and compulsory participation in religious activities.

The Court did note that the study of comparative religion, the history of religion, and the relationship of religion to civilization were not prohibited by this decision. It would also appear that, although the Bible may not be used to teach religion, it might, if objectively presented, be used in such areas of study as history, civics, and literature. Indeed, most thoughtful people would agree that failure to be conversant with the Old and New Testaments makes understanding of Western history and literature impossible. In the same way, if a student set out to learn about Chinese culture and was not permitted to read Confucius, he or she would be doomed to a very limited understanding.

The Court has also affirmed the right of individual public school pupils who so desire to say prayers and read scriptures of their choice in the morning before school starts or after the regular school day has ended. As discussed in the next section, many students join clubs or groups for these activities. If prayers are said during lunch period, they must be silent. Many students who are

Ⓣ F

It is legal in American public school classrooms to study religious books, such as the Bible, the Talmud, and the Koran.
Although the Bible may not be used to teach religion, it might, if objectively presented, be used in such areas of study as history, civics, and literature.

" *Teaching about religion is not the same as teaching someone to be religious. In our multicultural, multiethnic society, understanding another person's faith will foster tolerance and harmony, a goal common to all religions.*

—MARGARET BARTLEY,
Author and Historian

religious continue to seek avenues for expressions of beliefs within the public school day, whereas other students and their families campaign to avoid mixing religious expression with school activities.

The daily recitation of the Pledge of Allegiance has been controversial in some quarters for several decades. Originally challenged on the ground that the compulsory recitation of the Pledge is unconstitutionally coerced allegiance to the country, courts allowed students to opt out of reciting it. This was not enough for a California atheist father who did not want his third-grade daughter to have to listen to the Pledge's phrase "under God." In an extremely controversial ruling in June 2002, the 9th U.S. Circuit Court of Appeals, which has the nine Western states under its jurisdiction, banned the teacher-led pledge for the nearly 10 million public schoolchildren. Two years later, in 2004, the Supreme Court rejected the father's case on a technicality. The ban imposed by the 9th Circuit Court has been lifted until the Supreme Court issues a final ruling. The Supreme Court has also determined that the recitation of prayers at a public school function is unconstitutional. In the *Lee* v. *Weisman* case (1992), the principal of a public middle school, Robert Lee, had invited a rabbi to say a benediction and invocation at the middle school graduation exercises, instructing the rabbi to offer nonsectarian prayers. Student Deborah Weisman and her father filed a suit in court seeking a permanent injunction against including prayers in graduation ceremonies. The Court used the following facts to reach its decision: (1) public school officials directed the performance of formal religious exercises at the graduation ceremonies, and (2) although such exercises do not require attendance, they are in a real sense obligatory for all students, even those who object. As a result, the Court upheld the decision of the lower court, ruling that it is unconstitutional to include clergy members who offer prayers as part of school graduation ceremonies.[33]

What if the students themselves select the prayer or the person delivering the prayer at after-school events? In 2000, the Court ruled that student-led, student-initiated prayer at football games violates the First Amendment, in part because attending school football games is mandatory for some students, such as athletes,

"Meeting at the flag" for morning prayer is one way students integrate their religious beliefs with their schooling.

(© Rob Crandall/The Image Works)

cheerleaders, and band members and other students who might object to the prayers feel social pressure and/or genuine desire to participate in high school football.[34] Nevertheless, students who are religious continue to seek avenues for expressions of beliefs within the public school day.

RELIGIOUS CLUBS AND PRAYER GROUPS

Are extracurricular religious clubs legal in public schools? Court decisions provide no clear guidelines here. In at least one case, a district judge ruled in favor of such clubs based on students' right to free speech. A U.S. Circuit Court of Appeals later overturned the decision, maintaining that such clubs violate the First Amendment's "establishment of religion" clause. The U.S. Supreme Court did not clear the waters: the five-justice majority upheld the district court opinion on a technical point but declined to comment on the constitutional issues raised.[35]

In yet another case, *Board of Education of Westside Community Schools* v. *Mergens* (1990), the Court ruled that extracurricular religious group meetings held on public school grounds do not necessarily violate the U.S. Constitution. The Court stated that if the school provides a limited public access for other noncurriculum student groups, then, under the Equal Access Act, a student religious group may also use the school building for its meetings. Under these circumstances, a student religious group meeting in the cafeteria after school does not violate the constitutional separation of church and state.[36]

Subsequent court rulings have supported students' rights to use school facilities for religious club meetings, even if the club is directed by adults. The Supreme Court ruled that a school district could not prohibit the Good News Club, a private Christian organization for children 6 to 12 years old, from meeting in a school building after school hours. The Court stated that the school district had already adopted a policy of broad community access to its schools and, in doing so, had created an open forum. Prohibiting the club from meeting violated the club's First Amendment right of free speech (*Good News Club* v. *Milford Central School District,* 2001). Although a key point in the *Good News Club* decision was that teachers do not participate in such meetings, the 8th Circuit Court of Appeals in St. Louis later ruled that a teacher may *on his or her own time* lead such religious meetings after school.[37]

RELIGION AND SECULAR HUMANISM

The many court cases dealing with prayer in school, extracurricular clubs, and the presence of the Bible in schools, as well as the publicity surrounding them, have had a chilling effect on teachers and administrators. Rather than get involved with what is clearly a controversial set of issues, many public educators have tended to discourage any expression or even mention of religious issues or topics. This, in turn, has caused a reaction from parents and others who think that by ignoring the religious dimension of life, the public schools create a distorted, and ultimately dangerous, view of humankind—a view labeled *secular humanism*. Secular humanism asserts the dignity of human beings, but ignores the idea of God and the spiritual.

Objecting to what they see as the prevailing secular humanism of the schools, some parents contend that such fundamental questions as "What is a person's true nature?" can be treated in schools from every perspective except the religious view. They claim that this presentation is not only intellectually unbalanced, but also poses a danger to their children. Speaking to this issue, one legal scholar has written, "When government imposes the content of school, it becomes the same deadening agent of repression from which the framers of the Constitution sought to free themselves."[38] Many parents are voting not only with their pocketbooks, by turning down school budgets and tax requests for public schooling, but also with their feet, by walking away from the public school system. This trend has fueled a dramatic growth in religious schools and particularly in home schooling in recent years.

Specific objections to secular humanism in the schools have taken a number of forms. Two examples are the controversies over teaching about the origins of the human race and the debates over the use of certain textbooks.

The Creationism versus Evolution Controversy

Major concern over the teaching of evolution dates to the famous 1925 Scopes trial in Tennessee, in which a high school biology teacher, John Scopes, was accused of illegally teaching the theory of evolution. Scopes was found guilty and fined $100, but the verdict was later overturned on a technicality. Although the trial came to national attention at the time (and again decades later with the award-winning play and film, *Inherit the Wind,* based on that trial), it did not set any legal precedent.

The issue returned to the public eye later in the century, when citizens asked for equal time for the biblical account of creation. In 1982, the Louisiana legislature passed the Balanced Treatment for Creation-Science and Evolution-Science Act, which quickly came to be known as the Balanced Treatment Act. The act defined *scientific creationism* as "the belief that the origins of the elements, the galaxy, the solar system, of life, of all the species of plants and animals, the origin of man, and the origin of all things and their processes and relationships were created ex nihilo (from nothing) and fixed by God."[39] In addition to requiring that scientific creationism be taught whenever evolution was taught, the act required the development of curriculum guides and research services for teaching creationism. At the same time, the act provided none of these resources or protections for those teaching evolution.

After several challenges and lower court rulings, a case testing this act, *Edwards* v. *Aguillard,* reached the U.S. Supreme Court. In 1987, the justices ruled seven to two against the Balanced Treatment Act. According to the Court, the Balanced Treatment Act was, in fact, not balanced because its provisions favored the teaching of creationism over evolution. Further, the Court asserted, the Balanced Treatment Act was motivated by the legislature's desire to promote a particular religious viewpoint, which violated the Constitution's provision against the establishment of a state-sponsored religion.

Despite the Court's ruling, few observers think this controversy has been fully settled. In 1999, for example, the Kansas Board of Education voted to drop the requirement in the state's academic standards that evolution be taught in public schools.[40] Within days, suits were filed challenging the decision.

For several years, the creationism-versus-evolution clash has been the battleground between those who believe the public schools have become antireligious and are promoting secularism and those who are opposed to the schools teaching a religious point of view. Recently, this controversy has taken a somewhat different turn with the introduction of **intelligent design theory**. This theory suggests that some biological structures and other aspects of nature are so complex and so highly interdependent that they could not have developed through Darwinian evolution, or "undirected natural causes." Intelligent design theorists believe there is evidence that "an intelligence" either created or somehow guided their development.

Although this theory differs from creationism on several points, it is quite compatible with a belief in God and is frequently explicitly linked with such a belief. Many in the scientific community have criticized intelligent design as mere speculation and a violation of scientific principles because it relies on preexisting causes to explain natural phenomena. Whatever its merits, intelligent design theory has pumped new life into the arguments put forth by those who believe the public school curriculum, and science curriculum in particular, have been de facto antireligious.

The Textbook Controversy

Recent court cases have been launched by fundamentalist Christian parents who argue that texts used in their children's public school classes are anti-Christian and therefore a violation of their children's constitutional rights. In a 1986 Tennessee case, a U.S. district judge agreed that students' constitutional rights were violated when they were expelled after they refused to read certain texts. The following year, a U.S. Court of Appeals reversed the decision of the lower court, ruling that the texts in question did not promote or require a person to accept any religion.[41]

Shortly thereafter, another challenge to the public schools' choice of textbooks was made in Alabama by fundamentalist parents, students, and teachers. Forty-four textbooks used in history, social studies, and home economics courses were cited as advancing secular humanism. In this case (*Smith* v. *Board of School Commissioners of Mobile County,* 1987), the court rulings followed a pattern similar to that of the Tennessee case just described. Initially, the district court ruled that secular humanism is a religion and that some of the textbooks in question did discriminate against theistic religion. On appeal, this decision was reversed, and the court ruled that the textbooks promoted neither secularism nor any other religion.[42]

GUIDELINES FOR RELIGIOUS NEUTRALITY

Table 8.2 summarizes the court rulings on religion and the public schools. When all the cases are considered together, teachers may very well be confused about what

TABLE 8.2 **Selected U.S. Court Cases Dealing with Religion and the Schools**

Issue	Case	Ruling
Teaching evolution and/or creationism		
Teaching evolution in public schools	*Scopes* v. *State of Tennessee* (1925)	The court upheld the state law disallowing the teaching of evolution as an explanation of the origins of the universe. The law was eventually struck down in 1996 by the state legislature.
Balancing the teaching of creationism and evolution in public school curricula	*Edwards* v. *Aguillard* (1987)	Schools teaching the biblical explanation of creation violate the Constitution's provision against teaching a particular religious viewpoint.

TABLE 8.2	Selected U.S. Court Cases Dealing with Religion and the Schools (Continued)	
Issue	**Case**	**Ruling**
Public schooling, prayer, and the Bible		
The inclusion of Bible reading and prayer	*Engel* v. *Vitale* (1962)	Bible reading and teacher-led prayer in schools are violations of the First Amendment; because of the social pressures involved, there is no difference between voluntary and compulsory prayer in school. Private prayer and Bible reading are protected.
	Abington School District v. *Schempp* (1963)	Reading the Bible and reciting the Lord's Prayer in public schools are violations of the First and Fourteenth Amendments; however, the Bible may be studied for historical, cultural, or other general educational purposes.
Reciting nondenominational prayers at public school ceremonies	*Lee* v. *Weisman* (1992)	It is unconstitutional to include adult-led prayers at public school ceremonies because all students are virtually obligated to attend ceremonies such as graduations, including those students who object to the practice.
Students reciting nondenominational prayer at extracurricular events	*Santa Fe Independent School District* v. *Doe* (2000)	Schools cannot allow student-led prayer at extracurricular events (e.g., sporting events) because attendance is not completely voluntary.
Public schools and extracurricular religious groups		
Extracurricular religious clubs meeting on public school property	*Board of Education of Westside Community Schools* v. *Mergens* (1990)	If a public school allows a limited public forum for other extracurricular groups, the Equal Access Act indicates that extracurricular religious groups may meet in public school buildings without violating the Constitution.

they can and cannot do. Thankfully, some attempts have been made to establish guidelines for the teacher and the school.

Thomas McDaniel recommends a *religious neutrality principle* in the classroom and offers four guidelines for putting it into practice:

1. Students may not be required to salute the flag or to stand for the flag salute if this behavior conflicts with their religious beliefs.

2. Bible reading, even without comment, may not be practiced in a public school when the intent is to promote worship.

3. Prayer is an act of worship and as such cannot be a regular part of opening exercises or other aspects of the regular school day.

4. Worship services, such as prayer and Bible reading, are not constitutional, even if voluntary rather than compulsory. Consensus, majority vote, or excusing objectors from class or participation does not make these practices legal.[43] This principle of religious neutrality does not mean that the public school must completely ignore religion. On the contrary, teachers in public schools are free to study the history and contributions (pro and con) of individual religions with their students, to have them read the Bible as literature, and in general to expose students to our culture's religious heritage. It is only when teachers cross the line by advocating a particular religion or involving students in prayer that they become vulnerable to legal action.

A few years ago, as debate over such issues continued, the White House asked the Department of Education to issue a directive on religion in the public schools. The resulting guidelines are an attempt to find a new common ground between religious expression and religious freedom and to correct the perception (or the fact) that schools are hostile to religion. Among the specific points listed in the guidelines are the following:

- Public schools should not interfere with or intrude on a family's religious beliefs.

- Public education should be respectful of religion, open to appropriate religious expression, and should teach about religion because it is so very much a part of our nation's history.

- Advocacy of religion by teachers and administrators has no place in public education.

- Students' religious clubs and groups are entitled to hold meetings, to have common prayer, to read scriptures, and to have their meetings publicized through school bulletin boards, newspapers, and public address systems.

- Although school-sponsored prayer should not be permitted, it is appropriate to begin the school day with a moment of silence.[44]

A U.S. Department of Education directive gained teeth after the passage of the No Child Left Behind legislation; the directive contains a provision that federal funds will not be provided to a school district unless it stipulates in writing that "it has no policy that prevents or otherwise denies participation in constitutionally protected prayer in public schools." Although this directive and the federal legislative support have been well received by many parents and educators, they have yet to be tested in the courts, nor do they address all of the conflicting issues surrounding religion in public schools.

> **PAUSE AND REFLECT**
>
> 1. Do you believe that the textbooks you used as a student or that you have seen in your fieldwork promote secular humanism? What can you do, as a teacher, if your assigned curriculum materials seem to you to promote or denigrate a particular religious viewpoint?
>
> 2. Do you believe that controversies about religion in the schools will have a chilling effect on your own willingness as a teacher to have students read religious literature or study the contributions of religions?

students and the law

Many of the most important legal issues that affect the lives of teachers relate directly to students and their rights. Students—and particularly public school students—have a special status under the law. In this section, we touch on a few of the more significant student-related issues that can affect the teacher.

THE STUDENT AND DUE PROCESS

As described earlier in this chapter, for many years the courts used the legal principle of *in loco parentis* in cases involving students. Teachers following this principle are expected to treat their students in a caring and informal manner instead of in the formal and legalistic manner that governs relationships "out in the world." By the same reasoning, because we do not require due process in the home, for a long time it was not valued in the schools.

Gradually, through decisions made in court cases such as *Tinker*[45] and others described in upcoming sections, the *in loco parentis* principle has been eroded, and the courts have come to appreciate that students often need to be protected from the arbitrary use of authority. As a direct result, many schools have developed clear statements governing procedures for expulsion, suspension, student privacy, freedom of speech and publication, and various breaches of discipline. Informing students of the rules, procedures, and consequences of violations in these areas is a major step toward providing due process rights. Even so, the most important aspect of due process remains the spirit of fair and even-handed justice with which teachers respond to the daily events of the classroom.

In terms of disciplinary matters relating to students, schools can operate on a continuum with regard to student due process. For trivial matters or emergencies, schools may act without due process. For matters that may result in a short suspension (one or two days) or some entry on the student's record, schools must use some measure of due process; for disciplinary matters that may result in a long-term suspension or expulsion, they must demonstrate careful due process.[46]

SUSPENSION AND EXPULSION

Ever since schools began, individual students have had difficulty following the rules and staying out of trouble. In recent decades, as schools have tried harder to keep older youth from dropping out, and as use of drugs and violence have increased in society as a whole, disciplinary problems within schools have escalated. Two of the most dramatic and horrible examples are the massacres that happened at Columbine High School in Colorado in 1999 and at Virginia Tech (college) in 2007.

Educators need to keep in mind that some students are severely troubled or deeply unhappy (or both). Some, having been compelled to stay in school, find little to capture their imaginations and to motivate them. For these students, school is a place of failure and frustration, and trouble is often close behind. Some of the more common forms of school infractions today are stealing; vandalizing school property or someone's private property; bringing a weapon to school; possessing, using, or selling drugs or alcohol; fighting (or encouraging others to fight); and repeatedly disobeying the reasonable directives of teachers and other school personnel.[47]

School districts are not powerless in the face of these kinds of disciplinary breaches. For maintaining a safe and effective academic environment, schools have three disciplinary alternatives at their disposal: in-school suspension, out-of-school suspension, and expulsion. Typically, in-school suspension is for minor offenses and is brief in duration. Out-of-school suspension and expulsion are more serious and last for longer periods, with expulsion meaning complete separation from the school. This school district power must be wielded in a manner that ensures that students' constitutional rights to due process are protected. Recently, the U.S. Department of Education sent to U.S. schools a useful publication, entitled "Early Warning, Timely Response: A Guide to Safe Schools,"[48] that stresses prevention but also offers helpful strategies for building good relationships with students. Nevertheless, it is in these areas—in the prevention of disruptions and violence and in the administration of suspension and expulsion—that school administrators have frequently become entangled in lawsuits.

Major Court Cases

One of the most important dismissal cases was *Goss* v. *Lopez,* a 1975 suspension case involving Dwight Lopez, a high school sophomore from Columbus, Ohio.[49] Lopez was suspended for 10 days for allegedly becoming involved in a cafeteria disturbance. This suspension occurred without a hearing and without any prior notification. Although a suspension of this length and without a hearing or prior notice was in accord with the Ohio statutes, a suit was filed stating that Lopez's constitutional rights had been violated because he was not given any notice or hearing. The case went to the U.S. Supreme Court, which ruled in favor of Lopez on the grounds that students facing suspension from a public school have property and liberty interests and therefore are protected by due process. In addition, the Court stated that "longer suspensions (longer than 10 days) or expulsions for the remainder of the school term, or permanently, may require more formal procedures."

Lopez Suspension Case

In a 1988 lawsuit with some similar elements, *Honig* v. *Doe,* the Court ruled against California school officials.[50] In this case, a school district had suspended indefinitely two emotionally disturbed students on the grounds that they were dangerous. The Court ruled that this suspension was a violation of PL 94-142 [later called the Individuals with Disabilities Education Act (IDEA)], which allows school authorities to suspend dangerous students with disabilities for a maximum of 10 days. Longer suspensions require either the permission of parents or the consent of a federal judge.

Because of the fear of school violence, which was exacerbated by the Columbine and Virginia Tech school tragedies, a number of school districts have adopted zero-tolerance policies toward weapons, drugs, and school fights, calling for automatic suspension or dismissal of student violators. Court cases involving "zero tolerance" have yet to be heard by the Supreme Court, although lower courts have already heard cases in which zero-tolerance policies have played a part. (The issues surrounding "zero tolerance" are discussed further in Chapter 4, "What Social Problems Affect Today's Students?") It would appear, however, from the 2008 federal court case of Murakowski versus the University of Delaware, that the law is shifting toward supporting the school's responsibility to maintaining a safe and constructive learning environment. The case involved a college student who built a website and posted his own essays, such as his personal "guide to sex" and a graphic piece on how to skin a cat. In addition, his essays were filled with racist, anti-gay and anti-Semitic comments. Dorm mates, claiming to be frightened by his behavior, complained to university officials. After a hearing, he was banned from the campus and required to undergo a mental health assessment. Murakowski insisted that his writings were satire and humor and that the university was violating his constitutionally protected rights. He sued, hoping to receive $59,000 in damages. He won, but the Court, considering the university's action amid the recent climate of fear on campuses, awarded him $10.

A 2000 court case in Illinois, *Fuller* v. *Decatur Public School Board of Education School District 61,* highlighted the zero-tolerance approach as well as the volatile issue of racial profiling.[51] This school district, in accordance with its zero-tolerance policy on fighting, expelled a group of students for two years for starting a fight in the bleachers at a home football game. The fight, from all accounts (including a videotape), was brief but violent; seven spectators were injured. The students argued that the expulsion was because of racial profiling; they were unfairly singled out, they argued, because they were stereotyped as gang members. Further, they argued, because no guns, knives, or drugs were involved, their behavior did not merit an expulsion. The Court ruled that the students failed to present any evidence that their expulsion was in any way based on their race.[52] Thus, although that court case found no evidence of racial profiling in the school's application of its zero-tolerance policy, it seems likely that future cases will involve both issues in school disciplinary actions.

School dress codes are another area where students' rights and strict (sometimes zero-tolerance) policies are clashing. In response to provocative and immodest student dress, these codes are being revised. Among the recent additions: no tank tops or tube tops; no low-riding, hip-hugging pants; no exposed midriffs; no capri pants; no overalls; no pajama tops or bottoms; no sweat pants; no shirts with slogans or offensive illustrations; no athletic jerseys; no hats; no hooded sweatshirts; belts are required unless the pants or skirt lack belt loops; shirts and blouses should be tucked in at all times—and should be long enough to stay tucked.[53] Although such a policy is difficult to enforce, as the Voices from the Classroom feature attests, increasingly educators are recognizing that there is a connection between edgy or over-the-line clothes and a school's poor learning environment.

Freedom of speech issues related to dress codes cut two ways. In response to the problems of students' overdressing and underdressing, some schools have gone beyond dress codes and now require school uniforms. These policies are particularly popular in large cities. Currently, New York, Chicago, Houston, Philadelphia, Miami, and Los Angeles have uniform policies. Not surprisingly, many parents and students are suing their districts over these policies, claiming having to wear a uniform is an abridgement of their First Amendment rights to free expression.[54]

Zero-tolerance policies, though hailed by many as tools to bring greater order and discipline to schools, are not without their detractors. In recent years, there have been a number of highly publicized incidents, such as the suspension of a third-grader for bringing a butter knife to school, that have made this policy rather controversial. Collectively, these incidents have proved a key point: no school policy can substitute for an educator's common sense.

Teachers: Pregnancy, Parenthood, and Marriage

Not many years ago, unmarried teachers who became pregnant were routinely dismissed from their teaching positions. Similarly, once a student was discovered to be either married, pregnant, or both, she was dismissed. Pregnant students were considered to be morally corrupting influences on other students, and their presence in school was seen as legitimizing premature sexual activity and early marriage. Although many people still hold these views, the courts have tended in recent years to see such dismissals as discriminatory to young women and as a denial of their rights to an education. As a consequence, most school districts now make arrangements for the education of pregnant students. Nevertheless, vexing issues keep coming up, such as "Should an obviously pregnant cheerleader be allowed to continue cheering?"

Guidelines for Educators

Overall, the pendulum of judicial decisions seems to be moving away from an emphasis on student rights and back toward positions favoring the authority of the

VOICES from the classroom

Dress Codes

Rob Famularo, a former sixth-grade teacher, is now the principal of the Calvin Coolidge School in Wyckoff, New Jersey.

In my very first year as a teacher, I quickly realized the numerous and varied job responsibilities that undoubtedly come with the profession. On any given day, a teacher may be asked to be a coach, friend, counselor, helping hand, disciplinarian, or facilitator, to name just a few possible roles. What I did not realize quite so quickly, however, was the number of important decisions I would make on a regular basis. Many of these decisions carry moral, ethical, or legal implications. Consider, for example, the decisions involved in enforcing my public school's dress code.

Although the U.S. Supreme Court has stated that students relinquish some of their First Amendment rights in school, teachers nonetheless often struggle with the legal and ethical ramifications of controlling student dress and deeming what is "appropriate or inappropriate" attire for school. There are, of course, lots of theoretical, legal, and ethical questions surrounding dress codes, such as these: "Is it the responsibility of a public school

to determine which attire is appropriate dress for school?" "Can a school still make this determination even if a parent objects or disagrees?" "How can a teacher make an objective and consistent decision for every student?" These questions, which have deep moral, legal, and ethical significance, are worthy of thoughtful reflection and consideration by anyone entering the teaching profession.

The situation becomes quite real, however, when the administration sets a specific dress code that I am expected to enforce when students enter my classroom first period in the morning. Can (or should) I tell a female high school student that her skirt is too short or that her shorts are more appropriate for the beach than for school? Or should I simply turn a blind eye to the situation, saving both the girl and me the embarrassment? Am I really doing my job by ignoring the situation? This is when teachers get the chance to truly define their own personal meanings for what seem like abstract legal and ethical questions.

schools. Nevertheless, when dealing with matters that might lead to suspension or expulsion, teachers and administrators should follow these guidelines:

- *Documentation.* Before suspension and expulsion can take place, students must be notified (either in writing or orally) of the nature of their offense and the intended punishment.
- *Explanation.* The school must give students a clear explanation of the evidence on which the disciplinary charges rest.
- *Opportunity to defend oneself.* The school must give students an opportunity to refute the charges before a fair and impartial individual with decision-making authority.

CORPORAL PUNISHMENT

Although few educational theorists living today advocate it, corporal (i.e., physical) punishment is alive and well in American schools. The Supreme Court has regularly refused to rule on corporal punishment, leaving the issue up to the states. The trend among the states is clearly in favor of banning it. In 1979, only 2 states had banned corporal punishment in public schools, but currently 30 states prohibit it[55] (see Figure 8.1) A number of other states currently have legislation pending that would abolish corporal punishment. Still, many states leave the decision up to local school districts. In the 2005–06 school year, 223,190 students were reported to have been spanked in U.S. schools.[56]

What does this situation mean for teachers from a legal point of view? First, they must know the rules established by their state and school district. Second, they must be aware that the courts have ruled that corporal punishment can be administered only under certain conditions. Thus teachers must be sure they use only "moderate" and "reasonable" corporal punishment and use it only to establish discipline. A teacher who severely punishes a child, especially if that punishment results in any permanent disability or disfigurement, is highly liable to a lawsuit. Also,

T (F)

After many years of delay, recently the Supreme Courts has made corporal punishment in our schools unconstitutional and therefore illegal.

The Supreme Court has regularly refused to rule on corporal punishment, leaving the issue up to the states.

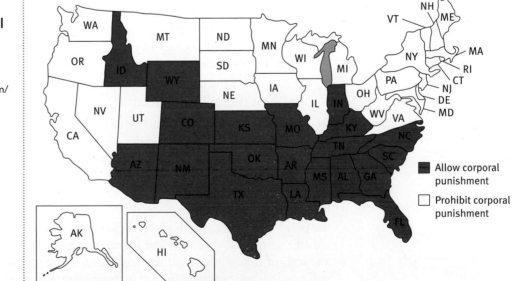

FIGURE 8.1

States Banning Corporal Punishment

Source: Discipline in Schools. Center for Effective Discipline. Available at www.stophitting.com/index.php?page=statesbanning.

Allow corporal punishment

Prohibit corporal punishment

punishment cannot be administered out of spite, revenge, or anger. In ruling on cases of excessive corporal punishment, the courts scrutinize the teacher's state of mind and motivation.

The instruments of corporal punishment and the locations on the body they can be administered are also matters of concern to the courts. Fists are totally inappropriate; so are switches and canes. Blows must not strike parts of the body where the risk of injury is high. Also, the punishment must be in scale with the crime—no horse whipping for whispering, for instance. Apparently the days of the principal's dictum, "The beatings will continue until the morale improves," are over.

Corporal punishment, of course, also entails important ethical considerations. Is it better to paddle a schoolyard bully and keep him in school or to have legal hearings and separate him from the possibility of further education? One major problem with corporal punishment is that a ruler on the palm of the hand may provoke terror in one student, but it is essentially meaningless for the next student. Conversely, non-corporal punishment, such as the prolonged separation of an offending student from classmates, may cause true psychic pain for some children. The entire area of dealing with disruptive and offending students needs careful thought and even more careful actions. Until these issues are settled definitively, it is imperative for new teachers to become thoroughly conversant with their district's policies concerning punishment for student offenses.

SEARCH AND SEIZURE

Many students—even students of junior high and elementary ages—possess and sell illegal drugs. Schools have drug problems because American youth culture is inundated with images of drug use. Drugs are only one problem that poses questions relating to search and seizure in schools, however. Despite the risks of suspension or expulsion resulting from many schools' zero-tolerance policies, students also bring alcohol, pornography, and even dangerous weapons to school. As a result, school administrators may be urged to step up their searches of students for possession of drugs, alcohol, weapons, or other illegal items.

A student's locker may be searched by an appropriate school official, usually an administrator, *if there are reasonable grounds* to suspect that the locker contains something illegal or dangerous. The New York State courts have gone further in stating that "not only have the school authorities the right to inspect, but the right becomes a duty when suspicion arises that something of an illegal nature may be secreted there."[57] At the same time, courts have found that policies under which school personnel systematically spot-check lockers in hunts for drugs, weapons, or other illicit materials violate students' rights under the Fourth Amendment and therefore are illegal.

Reasonableness and Probable Cause

In the world outside school, authorities must have "probable cause"—that is, a substantial reason for believing that the person is in possession of something illegal—to conduct any kind of search of a person or possessions. Yet because schools are specifically designed for the education and supervision of minors, courts have often allowed schools to use greater latitude in their searches. These decisions have been in keeping with the principle of *in loco parentis,* the notion that schools act in place of the parents during the school day. Schools may merely need to demonstrate a "reasonable suspicion" that a student was in possession of an illegal substance to conduct a search of that student, rather than demonstrating the "probable cause" that law enforcement officials would need to demonstrate under similar circumstances.[58]

A law enforcement team with drug-sniffing dogs is now a common sight in schools in the United States.

(© Mikael Karlsson/Alamy)

The importance of *reasonableness* in cases of search and seizure was shown by the 1985 U.S. Supreme Court ruling in *New Jersey* v. *T.L.O.*[59] In this case, a teacher found two high school girls smoking in the bathroom and immediately brought them to the assistant vice-principal's office. One girl admitted to smoking, but the second denied not only smoking on this occasion, but even being a smoker. The administrator asked the second student to come to his office, where he opened her purse and discovered a pack of cigarettes, cigarette-rolling papers, marijuana, a pipe, empty plastic bags, a wad of bills, and a list of names entitled "People who owe me money." Enter the police. The student was turned over to the juvenile court, where she was judged to be delinquent. She appealed on the basis that the search of her purse had violated her constitutional rights, and therefore the evidence against her had been obtained illegally.

This case eventually made its way to the U.S. Supreme Court, where the student lost. The Court stated, "The legality of a search of a student should depend simply on the reasonableness, under all the circumstances, of the search." Reasonableness appears to be determined, first, by whether the search has been initiated by a "reasonable" suspicion. In this case, having seen rolling papers, it was reasonable for the school administrator to look for marijuana, given that the two are so often closely related. The second criterion of reasonableness is that the search's scope and conduct must be "reasonably" related to the circumstances that gave rise to the search. Further, school officials must take into consideration the age and gender of the student and the nature of the offense.

The distinction between "reasonable suspicion" and "probable cause" is a fine line that is not always crystal clear. The prudent guideline for schools when conducting searches is that any invasive search (e.g., body searches) would require "probable cause," whereas less invasive searches (student lockers) would not require as rigorous a standard; in the latter cases, "reasonable suspicion" would suffice. Mistakes here, particularly in the case of unwarranted strip searches, can be not only painfully embarrassing to the students but also very expensive for the school district.

In 2009, the Supreme Court released a ruling in the rather sensational case of a 13-year-old middle school student who was strip searched by school authorities. The girl, who was alleged to be selling prescription-strength Ibuprofen pills, first had her backpack and outer garments searched. Finding no pills, and even in the face of the girl's assertion of innocence, the school assistant principal was convinced she had pills hidden on her person, He therefore directed two female school employees to search her in the nurse's office. The search of her bra and her panties exposed her breasts and to some degree her pelvic area. No pills where found and the girl sued. The Court's ruling was a split decision. Yes, the girl's rights had been violated, not by the first searches, but by the intrusive body search. However, in this case, the school district received a pass. The school and the assistant principal were given immunity because their motives were impelled by a desire to protect students from the dangers of drugs.[60]

The police, on the other hand, do not have the same *custodial relationship*—the same kinds of responsibility toward students—that school officials do. Therefore, as a general rule, police need a warrant and the consent of school officials to search individual students or their lockers.

PAUSE AND REFLECT

1. If school authorities hear rumors that there are drugs in students' lockers, do you believe they should be allowed to search students' lockers without their permission?

2. Do you believe it is fair for school officials to use drug-sniffing dogs to search for drugs in students' lockers?

Drug Tests as Searches

Most people have heard of potential employees or Olympic athletes taking tests to see whether they have any illegal drugs in their systems. Can schools decide to administer such kinds of drug testing for those who go out for sports teams?

In the late 1980s, the Vernonia School District of Oregon noted a surge in students' use of drugs. Athletes, in particular, were leaders in this drug culture. In response, the school decided to institute random urinalysis to spot-check for drug use among the athletes. All students who signed up for a team were required to provide their own and their parents' written consent for testing.

In 1991, a seventh-grader, James Acton, signed up to play football, but was denied participation on the team because he and his parents refused to provide the test consent forms. The family sued, claiming that the drug testing was an invasion of student privacy and an illegal search. The case eventually was decided in the Supreme Court, which ruled in favor of the Vernonia School District. The justices took into consideration several of the district's arguments, including observations that athletes participate in any number of activities, from "suiting up" in the locker room to preseason physical exams, that reasonably decrease their expectations of privacy, and that the drug test was relatively unobtrusive. The Court also considered the severity of the need, based on the widespread student drug use, and ruled that the policy was reasonable and constitutional. In its ruling, however, the Court cautioned against assuming that suspicionless drug testing would be constitutional in all other situations. It indicated that in this case, the most salient factor was that the school district was enacting its governmental responsibilities in monitoring and supervising schoolchildren entrusted to its care.[61] In 2002, the Court significantly broadened its ruling to include not just athletes, but all students engaged in "competitive" extracurricular activities, be they football or debating. The ruling reaffirmed and stressed the school's "custodial responsibility." Because search and seizure touches upon such fundamental American rights, schools will probably always need to be vigilant about how school policies and practices align with constitutional rights.

FREEDOM OF SPEECH

The right to say what we want, where we want, is the cornerstone of a free society, and as such it is near and dear to Americans. As Justice William O. Douglas stated, "Restriction of free thought and free speech is the most dangerous of all subversions. It is the one un-American act that could most easily defeat us."[62] Despite U.S. courts' vigilant protection of this right, however, it is not an absolute right. The great Supreme Court Justice Oliver Wendell Holmes wrote that freedom of speech does not give a person the right to yell "Fire!" in a crowded theater or to knowingly and maliciously say or write lies that damage the reputation of another. In schools, freedom of expression must be balanced with the school's responsibility to maintain a safe and orderly environment and to protect people's feelings and reputations.

Students' First Amendment Rights

During the 1960s and early 1970s, many social protests and antiwar demonstrations spilled over into the schools, and particularly into high schools. In one case, *Tinker* v. *Des Moines Independent Community School District* (1969), students who had been suspended for wearing antiwar armbands took the issue to court, claiming that the school had interfered with their right to freedom of expression. The Supreme Court ruled in favor of the students, stating that their black armbands were a form of symbolic speech in protest of the Vietnam War and should not be prohibited. A key point in this affirmation of students' First Amendment rights was the passive and nondisruptive nature of the students' protest. According to the Court, there was no evidence that the wearing of armbands would "materially and substantially interfere with the requirements of appropriate discipline in the operation of the schools."[63]

A Shift in Legal Direction: Restricting Student Speech

During the 1970s and 1980s, the *Tinker* case was often cited, but the tide of court opinion in favor of students' right to free speech soon began to turn. In the 1986 case of *Bethel School District No. 403* v. *Fraser*[64], Matthew Fraser, a high school student in Bethel, Washington, nominated another student for vice president of the student government in a formal speech at an assembly before 600 students. Despite the warning of two teachers, Fraser built his speech on an elaborate, graphic, and explicit sexual metaphor comparing the nominee to a sexual organ. The court records of this case fail to tell us the outcome of the election, but Fraser got the ax. He was suspended for three days and removed from the list of candidates to speak at graduation. Fraser sued and won initially, but when the case went to the Supreme Court, he lost by a seven-to-two decision. The Court affirmed the school's right to "establish standards of civic and mature conduct" and to enforce them.

The definition of students' right to free speech was further refined in the 2007 Supreme Court ruling in *Morse* v. *Frederick* (No. 06-278). Joseph Frederick, a high school student in Juneau, Alaska, was suspended from school for 10 days when he unfurled a large banner ("Bong Hits 4 Jesus") across the street from the school when the Olympic torch parade went through Juneau en route to the 2002 Winter Games in Salt Lake City. Frederick claimed that it was a prank, a stunt to ensure that he and his mates got on television. As a public relations event, the act was a resounding success. The school principal, and eventually the majority of the Supreme Court, saw the banner as advocating—or at least celebrating—illegal drug use. Chief Justice John Roberts wrote, "The First Amendment does not require schools to tolerate at school events student expression that contributes to those dangers."[65] Although something of a worrisome ruling for high school pranksters across the land, this ruling reaffirmed the authority of school officials in these matters.

School Newspapers and Freedom of the Press

School newspapers have long been the arena for struggles over freedom of speech and freedom of the press. Often the very best efforts to make the paper "vital" and "relevant" draw the newspaper staff into controversies. That is what happened at Hazelwood East High School in the spring of 1983.[66] Attempting to make their paper, *The Spectrum,* speak more directly to the real issues confronting their fellow students, the staff submitted two controversial articles, one dealing with the personal accounts of three Hazelwood students who had become pregnant and one focusing on divorce and its effect on students.

In line with standard practice, the advisor and teacher of the journalism class that produced the paper passed the issue on to the principal for his approval. The principal eliminated the two pages containing the offending stories and sent the other four pages to the printer. In response, Kathy Kuhlmeier and the six other journalism students sued, contending that their freedom of speech rights had been violated. Eventually, in 1988, the Supreme Court ruled in favor of the school district. Although dissenting justices complained about the potential for "thought control" and the "denuding of high school students of much of the First Amendment protection that *Tinker* in itself prescribed," the majority supported the principal's actions as legal and responsible. As stated in the majority opinion: A school may in its capacity as publisher of a school newspaper or producer of a school newspaper or producer of a school play disassociate itself not only from speech that would substantially interfere with its work or impinge on the rights of other students but also from speech that is, for example, ungrammatical, poorly written, inadequately researched, biased, prejudiced, vulgar or profane, or unsuitable for immature audiences. . . . A school need not tolerate student speech that is inconsistent with its basic educational mission even though the government could not censor similar speech outside the school.[67]

Implications of the Court Cases

Taken together, the three cases we have just discussed—*Tinker/Des Moines, Bethel/ Fraser,* and *Hazelwood/Kuhlmeier*—suggest that freedom of speech and expression in schools is hardly absolute. Students may be punished for offensive or disruptive speech or publications. Schools, then, are something like Justice Holmes's crowded theaters, and students' freedom of speech is somewhat limited. Students can and should express themselves, but in an orderly and nonviolent way. For its part, the school has the right and responsibility to ensure that language is not used to hurt or scandalize the students in its charge.

One cutting-edge freedom-of-speech issue involves the Internet. As discussed in Chapter 7, "What Should Teachers Know about Technology and Its Impact on Schools?" the Internet can be a marvelous educational tool, opening up almost infinite intellectual resources to students. At the same time, it can expose students to written and visual pornography, obscenity through e-mail, electronic bullying, and chat-room predators. Many school districts have been struggling to respond to these dangers without unduly restricting students' exploration of the electronic world beyond the school. Among the responses currently in place are orientation programs on appropriate use of the Internet, more careful supervision of computer stations, and special software designed to block forbidden sites. Many districts have **acceptable use policies** that provide rules of the road for students using this technology.

SEXUAL HARASSMENT

A major study by the American Association of University Women (AAUW) in 1993, entitled *Hostile Hallways,* reported that 81 percent of U.S. students acknowledged that they were the subjects of sexual harassment at some time during their school lives. Only 11 percent reported the incident to a teacher. One-fourth of the girls and one-tenth of the boys reported being harassed by a school employee. Most harassment, however, was of the student-to-student variety. Teenage girls responded to the survey with stories of pervasive and overt sexual harassment. Girls described sexual jokes and taunts; attempts to snap their bras, lift their skirts, and grope their bodies; and other unwanted physical attention. Boys and girls get the message that girls are not worthy of respect and that it is okay for boys to exert power over girls. Spreading sexual rumors and calling a person "gay" or "lesbian" were often-reported verbal forms of harassment. Most of the harassment occurred in plain view of others—in hallways, lunchrooms, classrooms, assemblies, and playgrounds, and on school buses.[68]

Since the study first appeared, schools have attempted to address this abuse, focusing in particular on student-to-student harassment. The study's definition of **sexual harassment** is "unwanted and unwelcome sexual behavior which interferes with your life." Of course, what constitutes sexual harassment in a particular situation can be a thorny issue. For instance, in 1996, a North Carolina school suspended a *six-year-old* boy who had kissed a female classmate on the cheek, claiming that he committed sexual harassment. Conversely, many readers may know of truly serious and frightening harassment incidents from their own school experience. One such incident was the subject of a Supreme Court ruling in *Davis* v. *Monroe County Board of Education.*[69]

When LaShonda Davis was in fifth grade in Forsyth, Georgia, her harassment nightmare began. A fellow student began groping her, grinding up against her, and declaring that he was "going to get in bed with her." The girl and her parents made repeated complaints to her teacher and the school principal. After five months, the teacher finally agreed to move the boy's desk to the other side of the room. But the sexual taunting and lewd overtures continued until finally the family sought legal counsel. Six years after the initial incident, and with much legal work, the suit finally made its way to the Supreme Court. The Court, in a controversial five-to-four decision, ruled for the Davises and against the school district.

What has made this case legally controversial is the perceived danger of our courts being flooded with cases ranging from innocuous flirtations to true, hard-core harassment. Further, judges worry that the budgets of school districts will be drained by the legal expenses involved in fighting frivolous suits. In the prevailing opinion, the *Davis* decision stresses that school districts are liable only if they were "deliberately indifferent" to information about "severe, pervasive, and objectively offensive" harassment among students.[70] It appears that although the Court has come to the defense of harassed students, the criteria for what actually constitutes an offense have been set quite high.

Nevertheless, the problem of sexual harassment in our schools appears to be growing. In particular, whether it is a response to the new societal openness to same-gender sexuality or some other reason, the harassment of gay and lesbian students has increased significantly in recent years. Schools that formerly had taken this issue casually are now working to respond to it more seriously. Schools can work to avoid the problem by drafting a sexual harassment policy; requiring training programs for administrators, teachers, and students; acting quickly when confronted with sexual harassment; enlisting the support of parents; and instituting disciplinary actions against repeat harassers.

Many schools now have sexual harassment policies that they distribute to students and staff. However, as the AAUW study revealed, neither boys nor girls are likely to report actual incidents to adults for fear of being labeled a "snitch" or suffering repercussions. The challenge for educators is to change the culture of harassment in schools and to encourage the use of existing resources to address the problem. All our students—boys and girls—have the right to attend schools whose environments are free from such harassment. As a teacher, you cannot ignore such instances when you see them occur. Choose to make such times "teachable moments" by helping students learn to appreciate the dignity of others and ensuring that the classroom is a welcoming environment for all students.

Table 8.3 summarizes the *Davis* case, along with other major students' rights cases discussed in preceding sections.

TABLE 8.3 Selected Court Cases Related to Students' Rights

Issue	Case	Ruling
Students' right to free speech		
Students' right to make a symbolic protest	*Tinker* v. *Des Moines Independent Community School District* (1969)	Students have the right to symbolic protest, if that protest does not interfere with the school's operation.
Students' right to use lewd language for a school speech	*Bethel School District No. 403* v. *Fraser* (1986)	Schools have the right to establish and enforce standards of civic conduct.
Student newspapers and freedom of the press	*Hazelwood School District* v. *Kuhlmeier* (1988)	Because public schools are not public forums, school officials have the right not to publish student articles that may violate the sensibilities of other students.
Students' right to expression supporting drug use	*Morse* v. *Frederick, No. 06-278* (2007)	Schools have the right to discipline students even in cases involving playful expression of drug use.
Students' right to education		
Disabled students with behavior problems	*Honig* v. *Doe* (1988)	Dangerous students with disabilities may not be suspended for more than 10 days without parental consent or permission of a federal judge.

TABLE 8.3 | Selected Court Cases Related to Students' Rights (Continued)

Issue	Case	Ruling
Students' school suspension for fighting at a game	*Fuller* v. *Decatur Public School Board of Education School District 61* (2000)	The school's policy of zero tolerance for fighting was upheld by courts.
Students' right to freedom from sexual harassment	*Davis* v. *Monroe County Board of Education* (1999)	The school can be held liable if it ignores excessive sexual harassment of one student by another student.
Students' right to due process		
Students' right to notification and hearing before a suspension	*Goss* v. *Lopez* (1975)	Schools violate students' constitutional right to due process if they suspend students without a hearing.
Students' rights regarding search and seizure		
Students' protection from school searches of personal items	*New Jersey* v. *T.L.O.* (1985)	Schools can search students' lockers and other private items if there is reasonable cause.
Students' rights against intrusive body search.	*Safford* v. *Arizona* (2009)	School can perform body searches only under conditions of heightened suspicion.

RECORDS AND STUDENTS' RIGHT TO PRIVACY

In this information age, most of us probably have a digital history tucked away on some kind of computer disks. For students, this history may consist of school records, various test scores, and ratings by teachers on everything from citizenship to punctuality. Teachers and other staff members judge a student's character and potential, and others use those judgments to decide whether the student should go to this school or get that job. Certainly we need some system for exchanging information about one another; otherwise, we would hire only our friends or attend only those schools where enough people knew us to vouch for us. Unfortunately, the kind of information in school records may be highly imperfect, and the danger that it will be misinterpreted or fall into the wrong hands is great.

In the early 1970s, a series of situations came to light in which information was poorly used or in which parents and students were denied access to records (e.g., when a diagnosis was used to justify sending a child to a class for students with mental retardation). In response, the U.S. Congress passed the Family Educational Rights and Privacy Act in 1974. The act, also known as the **Buckley Amendment**, outlines who may and see a student's record and under what conditions. Parents, who previously were kept from many of the officially recorded judgments that affected their children's futures, are the clear winners as a result of this legislation. The Buckley

Amendment states that federal funds will be denied to a school if it prevents parents from exercising the right to inspect and review their children's educational records. Parents must receive an explanation or interpretation of the records if they so request.

However, the Buckley Amendment does not give parents the right to see a teacher's or an administrator's unofficial records. For instance, a teacher's private diary of a class's progress or private notes about a particular child may not be inspected without the teacher's consent.

Although the Buckley Amendment has undoubtedly reduced the potential for abuse of information, it has had a somewhat chilling effect on teachers' and others' willingness to be candid in their judgments when writing student recommendations for jobs or colleges. Because students may elect to see a teacher's letter of recommendation, some teachers choose to play it safe and write a vague, general letter that lacks discriminating judgments, pro or con, about the student. In effect, some faculty members and other recommenders have adopted the attitude, "Well, if a student doesn't trust me enough to let me write a confidential recommendation, I'll simply write an adequate, safe recommendation."

Nevertheless, the Buckley Amendment's impact, in our view, has largely been positive. In the past, many students lost opportunities for higher education and desirable jobs because of inaccurate statements in recommendations or in their school records. One professor reported to us an incident that occurred in his school in 1975, shortly after the Buckley Amendment came into being:

> Our counselors at the junior high school where I taught were "purging" the records of subjective comments with black markers. In one student's permanent record folder, a *Playboy* magazine fell out. It seems a grade school teacher took it from Carl and included it in his permanent record because she wanted future teachers to know what kind of kid Carl really was.

Despite the fact that the Buckley Amendment is more than 30 years old, its implications for what constitutes a violation of students' right to privacy concerning his or her educational records are not always apparent. That fact was made all too clear in the fall of 2001, when the Supreme Court agreed to hear a case involving student rights to privacy.

An Oklahoma mother, Kristja Falvo, brought suit against the Owasso Independent School District for violating the Family Educational Rights and Privacy Act. Her son's classroom teacher asked the students to grade one another's quizzes and to call out the grades so the teacher could record them. The mother argued that such a practice violated her son's right to privacy because the practice publicly disclosed educational information about him. Ms. Falvo was especially concerned that this practice would have a detrimental effect on his learning. In a 2002 decision, the Supreme Court ruled in favor of the school district, stating that peer grading is not in violation of the Buckley Amendment.[71]

◆ OUR FINAL WORD

This chapter marks the beginning of what we hope will be your ongoing probe of the important roles that two related issues, ethics and law, play in the life of the teacher. Together these issues increasingly permeate the school environment. Whereas ethical issues may raise timeless questions, some laws continually change, and even now the courts may be giving a different complexion to some of the decisions cited in this chapter. Also, this chapter touched on many issues only briefly and omitted others entirely because of lack of space. We urge you to move on from this introduction to investigate further the work of the teacher in its larger ethical and legal framework.

WHY TEACH? YOUR FINAL WORD

In your journal or online at this textbook's website, respond to the following questions:

1. Can you remember examples of the "everyday ethics" of teaching shown by the teachers you had in elementary and secondary schools? Can you remember examples in which your teachers' ethical behavior was clearly questionable?
2. What do you think about the current controversies over the place of religion in public schools? Of prayer? Of the Bible and other religious works? How would you solve the issues related to religion and public education?
3. Teachers are expected to be people of good character and to act as good role models to students. What are the limits of this expectation? What are some points at which the rights of the school district end and the rights of the teacher begin?

KEY TERMS

academic freedom (251)
acceptable use policy (277)
breach of contract (245)
Buckley Amendment (279)
continuing contract (244)
contract (244)
due process (242)
ethics (231)
fair use (255)

grievance (244)
in loco parentis (240)
intellectual property (256)
intelligent design theory (263)
law (231)
liability (247)
reduction in force (247)
sexual harassment (277)
tenure (245)

FOR FURTHER INFORMATION

TEACHSOURCE VIDEO

Legal and Ethical Dimensions of Teaching: Reflections from Today's Educators
This video shows a group of teachers, administrators and a lawyer-moderator discussing the legal implications of teaching.

WEB RESOURCES

Acceptable Use Policies: A Handbook. Available at **www.doe.virginia.gov/support/safety_crisis_management/internet_safety/acceptable_use_policy.shtml.**
This handbook, available on the Internet, is produced by the Virginia Department of Education and is a rich source of information on using the Internet in schools and developing acceptable use policies.

The Legal Information Institute's Supreme Court Collection. Available at **www.law.cornell.edu/supct/.**
This website gives you access to the most important Supreme Court school-related decisions.

LII Legal Information Institute: Supreme Court Decisions. Available at **www.law.cornell.edu/supct/cases/credits.htm.**
This website, the motto of which is "Democratizing Access to the High Court since 1994," is another fine source for following up on Supreme Court rulings.

PRINT RESOURCES

Nathan Essex, School Law and the Public Schools: A Practical Guide for Educational Leaders. 4th ed. (Boston: Addison Wesley, 2008).

This concise paperback provides contemporary and practical coverage of the relevant legal issues that affect teachers, prospective teachers, and policy-makers at all educational levels.

David Schimmel, Louis Fischer, and Leslie R. Stellman, *School Law: What Every Educator Should Know, A User-Friendly Guide*, (New York: Pearson Education, 2008).

This book, which was written by scholars who are lawyers and professors of education, bridges the worlds of the courts and the classroom with great detail and clarity.

Kenneth Strike and Jonas Soltis, *The Ethics of Teaching*, 5th ed. (New York: Teachers College Press, 2009).

This short book is an excellent source of ways to approach the topic of ethics in teaching. It contains a number of practice cases.

Perry Zirkel, "De Jure" column in *Phi Delta Kappan* (Bloomington, IN: Phi Beta Kappa International).

This recurring magazine column reports on important issues of school law and provides an excellent way to follow recent developments.

The Education CourseMate website for this text offers many helpful resources. Go to www.cengagebrain.com to access the TeachSource Video Cases and other TeachSource videos, flashcards, interactive quizzes, the eBook, reflection and enrichment activities, a state standards resource center, and other study aids.

9 what are the philosophical foundations of american education?

InTASC Standards 2 and 9

FOCUS POINTS

- Philosophical knowledge has a fundamental role in clarifying questions of education.

- Philosophical thought has distinct characteristics that contribute to the way we know the world. Four branches of philosophy—metaphysics, epistemology, axiology, and logic—relate rather directly to the work of the teacher.

- Four philosophies of education—perennialism, essentialism, romanticism, and progressivism—have many practical implications for the classroom teacher.

- Psychological theories—and particularly constructivism—influence modern educational thought.

- Teachers need to have a philosophy to guide their practice. Many develop eclectic personal philosophies that incorporate elements of several major philosophical views.

- Discovering your personal philosophy is a lifelong process, but it should begin now.

(© Michael Newman/PhotoEdit)

This chapter examines the role of philosophy, a key foundational discipline in the work of the teacher. First, we describe philosophy; then we discuss four different philosophies and analyze their applications to the classroom.

Truth or Fiction?

T F A teacher's religious views should have no influence on his or her philosophy of education.

T F Progressive educators view nature as being in flux, as ever changing. Therefore, teachers consider knowledge as something that must continually be redefined and redis-covered to keep up with that change.

T F A late-night, college bull session is, by definition, nonphilo-sophical.

A medical student who wants intensely to be a surgeon, has marvelous hands, and displays a high level of technical skill, but does not know how the body functions or what constitutes health can hardly be called a doctor.

An aspirant to the ministry who loves to work with people and possesses a marvelous gift of speaking, but has no opinion about humanity's relationship to God or about the purpose of religion, can hardly be suited for religious ministry.

And a person who has a great desire to be with young people, wants to live the life of a teacher, and possesses great technical skill, but lacks purpose and direction, is hardly a teacher.

These three individuals are like wind-up toys, moving along blindly without a plan or an intellectual compass. Although this image may be somewhat dramatic, there *are* people who prepare for professions without delving into the core meaning of what those professions are all about. Such directionless behavior can cause problems in any occupation or profession but is particularly vexing in teaching. What kind of a teacher can someone be who lacks a view of what people are and a vision of what they can become? Who cannot clearly define right and wrong in human behavior? Who doesn't recognize what is important and what is unimportant or can't distinguish clear thinking from sloppy thinking? The person who would take on the responsibility for educating the young without having seriously wrestled with these questions is, to say the least, dangerous because that individual is going against the very grain of what it means to be a teacher. In fact, it is safe to say that such a person is not a teacher, but a technician.

This chapter introduces you to philosophy, one of the foundational subjects in education. Philosophy, along with history and psychology (and, to some degree, economics, political science, sociology, anthropology, and the law), forms the intellectual underpinning on which the practice of education rests. The study of philosophy helps the teacher systematically reflect on issues that are central to education, including such basic concepts as *learning, teaching, being educated, knowledge,* and *the good life.*

what is philosophy?

The word **philosophy** is made up of two root words: "love" (*philo*) and "wisdom" (*sophos*). In its most basic sense, then, philosophy is the *love of wisdom.* Although not all people love wisdom in the same way or to the same degree, all humans are questioning beings—that is, seekers of answers. As children, we are preoccupied with such lofty questions as "How do I get fewer veggies and more dessert?" Then we progress to such questions as "How does the teacher always know to call on me when I don't have the answers?" and "What do I need to do to get a decent grade in geometry?" Ultimately, we may move to more fundamental levels of questioning: "Who am I?" "What is the purpose of life, and what am I doing here?" and "What does it mean to be a really good person?"

FUNDAMENTAL QUESTIONS OF EXISTENCE

Until approximately 100 years ago, most people relied on religion and philosophy for answers to such fundamental questions. Whereas religion is said to represent the revealed word of God, philosophy represents a human attempt to sort out by reason the fundamental questions of existence. Many of the great thinkers of Western civilization—Plato, Aristotle, St. Thomas Aquinas, René Descartes, Jean-Jacques Rousseau, Immanuel Kant, Friedrich Nietzsche, John Locke, John Stuart Mill, William James, Alfred North Whitehead, and John Dewey—have been philosophers.

Because education has always been a central human concern, philosophers have thought and written a great deal about education and the questions surrounding it. Twenty-three centuries ago in Ancient Greece, Aristotle puzzled over how to educate the young:

> In modern times there are opposing views about the practice of education. There is not general agreement about what the young should learn either in relation to virtue or in relation to the best life: nor is it clear whether their education ought to be directed more toward intellect than toward character of the should. . . . And it is not certain whether training should be directed at things useful in life, or as those conducive to virtue, or at nonessentials. . . . And there is no agreement as to what in fact does tend toward virtue. Men do not all prize most highly the same virtue, so naturally they differ also about the proper training for it.[1]

Aristotle then went on to offer some of the most profound answers to these questions in human history.

THE NATURE OF PHILOSOPHY

Only a few people in our society are professional philosophers who earn their daily bread (usually a rather meager fare) by pursuing answers to the fundamental questions of life. However, all of us who wrestle with such questions as "Who am I?" and "What am I doing with my life?" are engaged in philosophical activity. Although a distinction may be made between the few professional philosophers and the vast number of amateur philosophers, the questions we ask and the answers we glean usually have a major influence on the practical affairs of our lives and determine how we choose to spend our life force. For instance, the very practical decision of whether to become a teacher, a real estate broker, or a professional poker player almost always has its roots in a person's philosophy of life, whether that person knows it or not.

" HOW DO YOU EXPECT ME TO LEARN ANYTHING WHEN YOU'RE THE ONE WHO KEEPS ASKING ALL THE QUESTIONS ? "

T (F)

A teacher's religious views should have no influence on his or her philosophy of education.

In developing a philosophy, we draw on many influences: our experiences in life, our religious views, and our reading of literature, history, current events, and our culture.

In developing a philosophy, we draw on many influences: our experiences in life, our religious views, and our reading of literature, history, current events, and our culture. A major difference between professionals and amateurs, however, lies in the precision of their methods. Philosophy is an extremely pure and abstract science. Philosophers work with neither test tubes nor white rats, use neither telescopes nor microscopes, and do not fly off to remote societies to observe the natives. The method or process of philosophers is questioning and reasoning; their product is *thought*.

THE PHILOSOPHER'S METHOD AND LANGUAGE

Basically, philosophers are concerned with the meanings of things and the interpretation of those meanings. They have an intense interest in the real meanings of words, for example. Although some philosophical discussion and writing involves technical language, it generally uses "plain language," the ordinary language of people. At the same time, philosophers try to be extremely clear and careful about their use of terms. They do not want their ultimate goal (getting at the meaning of things) to become lost in a thicket of fuzzy language.

Although philosophy appears to deal with simple issues in simple language, behind the philosophers' questions are raging debates about profound issues that can have far-reaching implications. For example, the question "What is a human?" leads to other questions, such as "Is a fetus human?" and "When, if ever, can a fetus be aborted?" or questions such as "What rights do severely disabled persons have?" or "Should humans clone humans?"

PAUSE AND REFLECT

Before you go much further in this chapter, you should clarify where you stand today. What are your answers to these philosophical questions?

1. What are the fundamental life questions to which you are seeking answers?

2. What are the ends or goals of the education you hope to provide students?

3. Should a school lay out what is to be learned, or should students have the larger say in what and how they learn? Why?

the terrain of philosophy

Philosophy covers a large amount of intellectual turf. The terrain of philosophy is divided into several areas, including four that are particularly important to the teacher: metaphysics, epistemology, axiology, and logic. These four branches of philosophy are central to the educative process and speak directly to the work of the teacher.

METAPHYSICS

Metaphysics involves the attempt to explain the nature of the real world or the nature of existence. It attempts to answer the question "What is real?" without relying on revealed religion, such as the Bible. Most metaphysicians believe that it is not possible to address fundamental matters such as the nature of a human being or of the universe simply by collecting data and formulating statistically significant generalizations. From most metaphysical perspectives, the true nature of a person cannot be captured by measuring or counting alone—that is, a person is more than the sum of his or her height and weight, IQ (intelligence quotient) and SAT (Scholastic Aptitude Test) scores, and other "vital" statistics.

In probing the nature of reality, the metaphysician asks a whole array of questions: "Does life have meaning?" "Are human beings free or totally determined?" "Is there a purpose to life?" "Is there a set of enduring principles that guide the operation of the universe?" "Can these principles be known?" and "Is there such a thing as stability, or is our world ever-changing?

Metaphysics and the Curriculum

The abstract questions addressed by the metaphysician are ones that the educator cannot dismiss. Ultimately, the purpose of education is to explain reality to the young. The curriculum and the way in which we teach it represent our statement of what that reality is and which part of that reality we should teach. In other words, the curriculum of a school represents what the community believes is *most worth knowing*.

Although teachers may not actually be metaphysicians, they do take a stand on metaphysical questions. If a teacher decides to teach because he or she believes the most important thing in the universe is a human mind, that career decision is driven by a metaphysical view: the importance of an individual person. The people who serve on school boards also take stands on metaphysical issues. For example, whether a particular school system makes a major investment in educating individuals with severe mental disabilities or emphasizes vocational education depends very much on someone's metaphysical decision about the nature of the person and the place of work in a person's life.

EPISTEMOLOGY

Epistemology deals with questions regarding knowledge and knowing. The epistemologist, seeking the true nature of knowing, asks such questions as "What is true knowledge (as opposed to false ideas)?" and "Is truth elusive, always changing and always dependent on the truth seeker's particulars of time, place, and angle of vision?" Some people, whom we call *skeptics*, question our capacity to ever really know the truths of existence. Others, whom we call *agnostics*, are convinced that there are no "truths" and that seeking knowledge of ultimate realities is a wasted effort and an empty hope.

Epistemology deals not only with the nature of truth, but also with the ways in which we can know reality. Questions such as "How do we come to know the truth?" and "What are the sources for gaining knowledge?" are part of the conversation. There are a variety of ways by which we can know reality, each of which has its advocates and detractors. Among the ways of knowing are by divine revelation, by authority, through personal intuition, from our own five senses, from our own powers of reasoning, and through experimentation.

Teaching and Ways of Knowing

Questions concerning knowledge and knowing are, almost by definition, of great concern to the teacher. The epistemological question "How do you know that?" goes to the heart of teaching methodology. If a teacher wants her students to have a concept of democracy, how does she proceed? Does she explain the characteristics of different forms of government, such as monarchy and oligarchy, and then the characteristics of democracy? Or does she take a more hands-on approach and have the students do a role-playing exercise during which one student is appointed class dictator and the rest must obey the student-dictator's orders? The student who has only read about democracy "knows" it in an *epistemologically* different way than a student who has been bullied and harassed for several days by a teacher-appointed dictator.

Individuals clearly differ in their preferred methods of learning. As discussed more fully in Chapter 3, "Who Are Today's Students in a Diverse Society?" much of the teacher's work focuses on helping students find the most effective way of gaining new knowledge. This important, breakthrough work on students' learning styles grew essentially out of a philosophical quest—an epistemological question—"How do we know things?"[2]

Some people—for example, parents and community members—may have strong opinions regarding these epistemological questions. For instance, many people hold strong beliefs about what the true origin of humankind is and how one knows it. This issue, which is sometimes called the *creationist controversy*, reflects a sharp and fundamental argument over the questions "Who are we?" and "How did we get here?" One faction insists that the public schools should present the evidence of humans' origin that is given in the Book of Genesis, which we know by divine revelation. Others insist that the way to know the origin of the human race is through the scientific theory of evolution, grounded in the interpretation of artifactual evidence. As you see, behind this ongoing educational controversy is a fundamental question of epistemology.

AXIOLOGY

Axiology focuses on the nature of what we value and how we value it. As human beings, we naturally search for the correct and most effective way to live. In doing so, we inevitably encounter questions of values. Of course, when different people look at life, they often come up with very different sets of values. For instance, *hedonists* believe in seeking pleasure and living for the moment. By contrast, *stoics* have an austere way of looking at life and seek to be unaffected by pleasure or pain. Many people regard values from a religious perspective, asserting that unless God originally created humanity and the rest of the natural world, existence as we know it is just the meaningless coming together of cosmic dust and debris. According to this view, the only genuine values derive from God.

Most people would agree with Socrates (described in the Leaders in Education feature) that schools have a dual responsibility: to make people smart and to make them good. To the degree that teachers accept the second function—that is, to assist their students to become good people—they are grappling with an axiological issue. In fact, teachers are intimately involved with questions of moral values. Young people are seeking ways to live lives that are worthwhile, and teachers traditionally have been expected to help students establish moral values both as individuals and as contributing members of society. (See Chapter 12, "How Should Education Be Reformed?" and Chapter 8, "What Are the Ethical and Legal Issues Facing Teachers?" for more discussion of this issue.) Moral values such as honesty, respect for other people, and fairness are necessary if we are to live together in harmony. Although a majority of people agree on a large core of values, such as respecting others and avoiding violence in settling disputes, other value-related issues separate people. For example, certain sexual practices, capital punishment, gun control, and abortion are all contemporary social issues that evoke a wide range of viewpoints about the right or correct way for people to behave.

> *The function of education is to teach one to think intensively and to think critically. Intelligence plus character—that is the goal of true education.*
>
> —MARTIN LUTHER KING, JR. (1929–1968),
> Minister and Civil Rights Leader

LEADERS in education

Socrates (469–399 B.C.)

The ancient Greek philosopher Socrates was condemned to death for supposedly corrupting the youth of Athens. Today, we know him primarily through the written "dialogues" of his student Plato. How much Plato's portrayal resembled the actual man is open to debate. Nevertheless, the Socrates of Plato's dialogues has had a deep and lasting influence on both philosophy and education, as the source of terms such as "Socratic teaching," "Socratic questioning," and "the Socratic method." The following passage explains some of the basic tenets of Socrates' approach.

Socrates expressly denied that he was a teacher in the commonly accepted sense of that term. What he meant by this—at least in part—was that he was not a sophist, a professional pedagogue who, for a fee, would endeavor to transmit some knowledge that he possessed to someone who lacked it. Not only did Socrates charge no fees, he claimed not to have command of any such knowledge.

The learning that Socrates was concerned with simply didn't fit the information-transmission model of education implicit in the Athenian public mind and the teaching profession. Neither did his pioneering focus on virtue and wisdom square well with the popular attachment to honor, fame, and wealth. As he tries to explain at one point to Anytus in Plato's dialogue *Meno*, "[W]e are inquiring whether the good men of today and of the past knew how to pass on to another the virtue they themselves possessed, or whether a man cannot pass it on or

receive it from another." Because it was clear that wisdom and virtue could not simply be passed on from one person to another, Socrates sought an alternative way of conceptualizing how such excellences of mind and character were acquired. What was the teacher's role in that acquisition, if not simply being a supplier?

As an alternative to the receiving-knowledge-from-another model, Socrates proposed that learning was "recollection"—that is, a process akin to dredging up knowledge from one's own resources. "Teaching" on this model he later compared to acting as a "midwife"—assisting in the birth of knowledge *in* another person rather than serving as a supplier of it *to* another person. This was to be accomplished in conversation, mostly by skillful questioning and cross-examination ("Socratic teaching," "Socratic questioning," and "Socratic method").

Socrates admitted to behaving like a "gadfly" in this dialectical pursuit of truth, goading people into serious thinking about human living. And he also confessed to acting like a benumbing "sting ray" or "torpedo fish," referring to his ability to render people tongue-tied about matters that they thought they already knew perfectly well—but actually didn't. Not until people felt the sting of not really knowing about life's important matters could they be prompted to inquire into them seriously.

Source: Reprinted by permission of Steven S. Tigner.

Ethics and Aesthetics

Axiology has two subtopics: ethics and aesthetics. Ethics takes us into the realm of values that relate to "good" and "bad" behavior, examining morality and rules of conduct. At one time, teaching children how to deal with issues of good/bad and right/wrong was the primary purpose of schooling. In recent decades, the pendulum has swung the other way, and schools have become more concerned with transmitting factual and scientifically verifiable knowledge and skills than with instilling ethical knowledge in students. More recently, signs indicate that schools are being called back to their earlier mission of helping children deal with ethical issues.[3]

The subject of ethics not only teaches us how we can intellectually ascertain the "right" thing to do, but also is often used to help us establish a particular set of standards, such as a code of ethics. Chapter 8, "What Are the Ethical and Legal Issues Facing Teachers?" devotes particular attention to the issue of how to develop your own code of ethics.

The second subtopic of axiology, **aesthetics**, deals with questions of values regarding beauty and art. Many discussions about the value of a particular film, book, or work of art are attempts to reach some aesthetic judgment on the value of the work. Whether a person "has good taste" is an example of a common aesthetic judgment.

LOGIC

Logic is the branch of philosophy that deals with reasoning. One of the fundamental qualities that distinguishes human beings from animals is that humans can *think*. The pursuit of logic is an attempt to think clearly and avoid vagueness and contradictions. Certain rules of logic have been identified, and they constitute the core of this branch of philosophy. Logic focuses on reasoning and modes of arguing that bring us to valid conclusions. A primary task of the schools is to help children think clearly and communicate logically. Two types of reasoning are commonly taught in schools: deductive and inductive.

Deductive Reasoning

In **deductive reasoning**, the teacher presents a general proposition and then illustrates it with a series of particulars. The most highly developed form of this approach is the classic method of the syllogism. In a *syllogism*, one makes two statements, and then a third statement, a conclusion, is *deduced*, or drawn, from them. For instance:

> All human beings are mortal.
> I am a human being.
> Therefore, I am mortal.

In this kind of deductive reasoning, the general proposition—an abstract concept—is followed by a factual statement, which in turn leads to a new factual statement and the creation of new knowledge, at least for the learner.

As another example, imagine that in October, Mrs. Wells, a fifth-grade teacher, writes the following statement on the board:

> All trees that shed their leaves at the end of a growing season are deciduous trees.

As a two-week project, Mrs. Wells asks her class to observe and record data about the trees that surround their school. For two weeks, the students observe the three dozen maple trees shedding their leaves during the fall. The teacher then writes her earlier sentence on the board again:

> All trees that shed their leaves at the end of a growing season are deciduous trees.

Using their observational data (and with a little intellectual nudging from Mrs. Wells), the students complete the syllogism:

> Maple trees shed their leaves at the end of the growing season.
> Therefore, maple trees are deciduous.

Then the students try to identify other types of trees that fit the deciduous classification.

Much of what a teacher does in school focuses on helping children both acquire the intellectual habits of deductive thinking and expand their storehouse of knowledge through this process.

Inductive Reasoning

Inductive reasoning works in the opposite fashion. With this type of reasoning, the teacher sets forth particulars, from which a general proposition is derived, or *induced*. For instance, the teacher may wish to lead the students to the discovery that water is essential to plant growth. He gives each child two similar plants (a different type, from weeds to flowers, for each child) and then has each student daily feed one plant with water and leave the other plant without water. After 10 days, the teacher has the students report on the conditions of their plants. From all of these individual reports, he leads the students to generalize about the necessity of water to plant life. In fact, they have induced their answer.

Although the deductive and inductive forms of reasoning are opposites, both are essential to logical thought and therefore need to be developed in learners. Effective teachers design a variety of learning activities, some of which (like the tree example) help students think deductively, and others (like the plant example) that focus on inductive reasoning.

Logic is not confined to inductive and deductive reasoning. To think logically means to think clearly, in many different ways. Teachers need logic in many aspects of their work, from trying to understand the behavior of a child who seems to have an erratic learning pattern, to developing tests that accurately measure what has been taught in a course. Most of all, teachers need to model this clear, logical thinking for students.

Overall, the four branches of philosophy—metaphysics, epistemology, axiology, and logic—address some of the major concerns of the teacher. We now consider the answers they suggest to the teacher and the implications they have for actual classroom practice.

PAUSE AND REFLECT

1. Which of these four branches of philosophy do you think is of greatest importance to you as a future teacher?

2. Which of these four branches contains the questions and issues about which you are most comfortable? And least comfortable?

---

schools of educational philosophy

Answers to the philosophical questions that pepper the preceding section have almost infinite variety. Over the years, however, certain answers by particular philosophers have received more attention and allegiance than others. These more enduring sets of answers or world views represent schools of philosophy. Some started with the early Greek philosophers and have grown and evolved through the centuries. Other schools of thought are more recent developments and offer fresh, new formulations to ultimate questions.

In this section, we describe four philosophies that have had a major influence on American education and demonstrate the variety of ways in which teaching and learning can be conceived. Be aware that many important philosophies relevant to education are not included here. Among them are neo-Thomism; existentialism; and classical Eastern thought, such as Zen Buddhism and Confucianism. In addition, some major educational ideas do not quite qualify as "philosophies," but are nevertheless having a major impact on schools.

The four philosophies discussed at length in this chapter are perennialism, essentialism, romanticism, and progressivism. Behind these rather daunting words are very different ideas of what people are, how we should live our lives, and how we should conduct the education of children. We elected to cover these philosophies not because they are the "Top Four Philosophical Hits," but because each viewpoint has exerted a major influence on American educational thought and practice.

We have grouped these philosophies based on whether they are *subject centered* or *child centered*. For each philosophy, we present first a brief explanation of its origins and the core ideas it embodies, followed by its implications for teaching and learning, and then a "personal point of view" by a teacher (fictitious) who is committed to that particular philosophy. These positions are not just windy abstractions or the preoccupations of ivory tower thinkers; rather, they have practical implications for learning, shaping what people teach and how they teach it.

SUBJECT-CENTERED PHILOSOPHIES

The first two schools of philosophy, perennialism and essentialism, stress the importance of subject matter knowledge in education. Both schools of thought show a strong allegiance to the curriculum, and both argue that well-educated students should possess a defined body of knowledge. Also, both often get a "bum rap," being labeled as "teacher centered." The label "teacher centered" conjures up images of an authoritarian teacher turning himself or herself into the center of attention, making all the decisions, and attempting to control everything that goes on in a classroom. Clearly, authoritarianism and ego-tripping can hide behind each of the four philosophies we will explore. Although they are convinced of the importance of certain knowledge, subject-centered teachers can be passionately committed to student learning.

Perennialism

Perennialism, which is derived primarily from the writings of Plato, views truth and nature—in particular, human nature—as constant, objective, and unchanging. Beneath the superficial differences from one century or decade to the next, the rules that govern the world and the characteristics that make up human nature stay the same. The purpose of life, according to Plato, is the search for these constant and changeless truths, which reside in the nature of things. This search is achieved through the Socratic dialogue or dialectic, a process in which ideas are debated in a back-and-forth discussion until some recognizable clarity (the "light") is reached. Essential to undertaking such a pursuit is mental discipline and rational thought processes.

your philosophy of education self-inventory

Now that you know the philosophical "lay of the land," and before we explore the dominant philosophies of education that exist in our schools, it is time to pause and reflect. What are your deepest beliefs and attitudes about teaching, students, and what should be learned? This short inventory allows you to bring your current philosophy of education to the surface. (We say "current philosophy of education" because the philosophies of many educators go through change—and sometimes quite dramatic change—as a result of study, classroom experience, or both.)

Following are 20 statements about teaching, students, schools, and the curriculum. Using a five-point scale (where 5 = strongly agree; 4 = agree; 3 = neutral; 2 = disagree; and 1 = strongly disagree), indicate your beliefs and feelings about each of the following statements. To gain the greatest insight from this survey, you should try to have your "average" ranking be a "3."

___ 1 Essentially, children learn by doing and by discovering things on their own.

___ 2 The goal of schooling should be to rigorously prepare children to be productive and engaged members of society.

___ 3 The teacher's role is to respond to the learner's information needs, not to be a mere information dispenser.

___ 4 Teachers should be experts in content knowledge, ready to vigorously engage students in the culture's accumulated wisdom.

___ 5 Older students ought to be trained primarily to uncover key ideas and truths through Socratic questioning.

___ 6 The teacher's role is to stimulate students' interests and then to be an effective facilitator of those interests.

___ 7 The true purpose of an education is to make us strong enough to overcome the evils of society.

___ 8 Students are in school primarily to acquire the knowledge that has lighted the way for humankind from our earliest years.

___ 9 Because we live in a democracy, schools should be built around democratic principles, with a major focus on learning how to exist together in democratic harmony.

___10 Students are in school to listen and to learn the knowledge and skills that they will need to function and prosper in a modern economy.

___11 Education is serious business, so teachers should avoid methodological frills and focus on tried-and-true teaching strategies.

___12 Schools should aid students in becoming socially adept and politically literate so they can take up their responsibilities as democratic citizens.

___13 Instructionally, a teacher must focus on creating an interesting and productive learning environment and, whenever possible, on individualizing instruction.

___14 Elementary schools should concentrate on teaching basic skills, whereas secondary schools should focus students' learning on disciplined knowledge and scholastic achievement.

___15 Students are naturally good, and their self-esteem must be protected and fostered.

___16 During the elementary school years, teachers should ensure that students master the basics, which will enable older students to study materials reflecting universal themes containing humanity's enduring knowledge.

___17 Teachers have to be skilled in group processing strategies and be able to get students to work together on projects.

___18 The teacher's primary concern should be teaching a common body of useful knowledge rather than focusing on cultivating the intellect, self-esteem, or democratic living.

___19 The curriculum should be fluid, based on the interests of the learner, but students should not be forced to study.

___20 The schools should be devoted to a changeless vision of what is essential for human beings to know.

Find the answers to your self-inventory in the next section.

INTERPRETING YOUR SELF-INVENTORY

Each of the 20 questions to which you have responded represents one of the four philosophies of education covered in depth in this chapter. The four philosophies and the five statements primarily associated with them are listed here. Fill in the score you gave each statement and then add up the topic score for each philosophy. The maximum score for any philosophy is 25 and the minimum is 5. These numbers will give you an indication of your philosophy of education preferences as you begin a closer analysis of this topic.

Perennialism	Essentialism	Romanticism	Progressivism
___ 4	___ 2	___ 3	___ 1
___ 5	___ 10	___ 7	___ 6
___ 8	___ 11	___ 13	___ 9
___ 16	___ 14	___ 15	___ 12
___ 20	___ 18	___ 19	___ 17

> *Never mistake knowledge for wisdom. One helps you make a living; the other helps you make a life.*
>
> —SANDRA CAREY,
> Lawyer

▶❙❙ TeachSource VIDEO CASE

Middle School Reading Instruction: Integrating Technology

Go to the Education CourseMate website to watch the video clips, study the artifacts in the case, and reflect on the following questions:

1. Does this teacher's approach represent perennialism as it is described in this chapter? Why or why not?

2. Which of the other philosophies mentioned in this chapter might be included in this teacher's approach?

3. How well would this teacher's approach fit with your own developing philosophy of teaching?

Perennialists view education as crucial because it develops a person's mental discipline and rationality, which are necessary to the search for truths that will help humans avoid being dominated by the instinctual (i.e., animal-like) side of human nature.

Perennialism in the School

For the perennialist, the purpose of education is to find the changeless "truth," which is best revealed in the enduring classics of Western culture. According to this perspective, schools should emphasize classical thought as their subject matter. Perennialists believe that schools should teach disciplined knowledge through the traditional subjects of history, language, mathematics, science, and the arts. They place particular emphasis on literature and the humanities, believing that these subjects provide the greatest insight into the human condition.

Although this view of the curriculum is evident in many areas of education, in its most complete form it is known as the *Great Books approach*, as developed by Robert Maynard Hutchins, who was president and chancellor at the University of Chicago throughout the 1930s and 1940s, and the late Mortimer Adler, a professor at the University of Chicago during the same time period. The Great Books, which constitute a shelf of volumes stretching from Homer's *Iliad* to Albert Einstein's *On the Electrodynamics of Moving Bodies*, are a perennialist's ideal curriculum. In perennialist-oriented high school curricula, a broader and more modern selection of works is included, though the emphasis remains on the intellectual richness of the material. (See the Video Case *Middle School Reading Instruction: Integrating Technology* for an example of how one middle school teacher makes use of an ancient book in a thoroughly modern setting.)

> *One glance at a book and you hear the voice of another person, perhaps someone dead for 1,000 years. To read is to voyage through time.*
>
> —CARL SAGAN (1934–1996),
> Astronomer

For perennialists, in the early years of schooling the development of the intellect is best achieved through a teacher-directed instructional approach that develops the foundational skills needed for later learning. Socratic dialogue is then used to help mature learners question and examine their beliefs, enabling them to move closer to the truth.

Since the early 1990s, a controversy has arisen over the content of perennialist literature, history, and philosophy courses. Scholars and students have criticized colleges and high schools for promoting a "Eurocentric" view of knowledge and culture, one that ignores the contributions of everyone except "dead, white, male writers and thinkers." They urge adoption of a more inclusive curriculum—that is, one that gives greater attention to women, minorities, and members of Eastern, African, and Hispanic cultures. Also, since the events of September 11, 2001, many have begun insisting that we need to gain greater understanding of Islamic literature and culture. Although some perceive this movement to be a direct attack on the perennialist curriculum, others see it as a natural and useful extension of the perennialists' search for the best of the world's wisdom. One perennialist friend of ours, who welcomes this new approach, suggested, "Sure, students should know about Islamic literature and Eastern philosophy, but they should first get to know their own neighborhood, Western culture."

EDUCATION AS PREPARATION FOR LIFE

Education is of great importance to perennialists, but it is an education that is rigorous and demanding. Perennialists insist that education is preparation for life and, therefore, believe that it should not attempt to imitate life or be lifelike. Students should engage in a rigorous examination of the classics—mostly ancient, but some modern—to discover the timeless wisdom embodied in this literature, rather than focusing on knowledge that might seem personally meaningful.

In summary, the perennialists' view is that a person learns through disciplined study of the great works and ideas of human history. This view leans heavily on the authority of the collected wisdom of the past and looks to traditional thought to guide us in the present. As such, the curriculum is structured and clearly defined. Perennialists also see education as protecting and conserving the best thought from the past. In this sense, they favor a very traditional or conservative ("conservative" as in *conserving* the best of the past) view of education. The following case study presents the point of view of a more or less typical perennialist teacher.

> *The object of education is to prepare the young to educate themselves throughout their lives.*
>
> —ROBERT MAYNARD HUTCHINS (1899–1977),
> Educational Practitioner and Theorist

Essentialism

Essentialism is a uniquely American philosophy of education that began in the 1930s and 1940s as a reaction to what was seen as an overemphasis on a child-centered approach to education and a concern that students were not gaining appropriate and adequate knowledge in schools.

The Roots of Essentialism

Essentialism has its philosophical origins in two older philosophies and draws something from each. From Plato's *idealism*, it takes the view of the mind as the central

from PRESERVICE to PRACTICE

A Perennialist Teacher

I came into education 25 years ago for two reasons.

First, I was bothered by what I thought was all the nonsense in the curriculum and by all the time my friends and I wasted in school. We were allowed to take whatever courses we wanted, the majority of which were electives that seemed to be little more than the teacher's hobby. There were so many discussions—discussions that seemed to go nowhere and seemed only vaguely to touch on the supposed content of the course. I often felt as if we were simply sharing our ignorance.

My second reason for becoming a teacher is a more positive one. I am convinced that our society, our culture, has great ideas, ideas that have been behind our progress in the last 2,500 years. We need to share these ideas, to vigorously teach these ideas to the young. Essentially, I see my job as passing on to the next generation, as effectively and forcefully as I can, the important truths—for instance, about human dignity and the capacity of people to do both good and evil.

That has always been the teacher's role until recent times, when we seem to have lost our way. I am convinced that a society that doesn't make the great ideas and the great thoughts the foundation of education is bound to fail. Nations and societies do falter and fall. The last 50 years have seen several formerly prominent nations slip to the wayside while other younger, more vigorous countries, like Singapore and South Korea and most recently China, have risen. I am convinced that most of those failed countries fell because of the inadequate education they provided. I am dedicated to the goal of not letting that happen here.

I think students are just great. In fact, I've given my life to working with them. But I don't think it is fair to them or to me or to our country to allow them to set the rules, to decide what they want to learn, or to tell me how to teach it. Sure, I listen to them and try to find out where they are, but I make the decisions. My job is to teach; theirs is to learn. And in my classroom, those functions are quite clear. Really, students are too young to know what are the important things to learn. They simply don't know what they need to know. As a teacher, as a representative of the larger culture and of society, that's my responsibility. Turning that responsibility over to students or giving them a huge say in what is taught just strikes me as silly. Worse, it's wrong.

I also believe that students should be pushed. School should be very demanding, because life is very demanding. I'm not worried about students' so-called self-esteem. Self-esteem is empty unless it is earned. It will come when students discipline themselves. All of us are lazy when we are young. We would much rather play than work. All of this "trying to make school like play" is just making it more difficult for students to acquire the self-discipline needed to take control of their lives. What schools are turning out right now—and it pains me to say this—are a lot of self-important, self-indulgent kids. And it's not their fault. It's our fault as teachers and parents.

And the answer is so simple! We just need to go back to the great ideas and achievements of the past and make them the focal point of education. When we achieve this goal, the students don't mind working. The students and the other teachers kid me about being a slave driver. I don't really pay attention to that. But I do pay attention to the large number of students, both college-bound and non-college-bound, who come back two or three years out of high school and tell me how much they value having been pushed, how glad they are that I put them in contact with the very best!

CASE QUESTIONS

1. Have you seen elements of the perennialist view in your own educational background?

2. How much emphasis on classical enduring works do you hope to include in your own teaching?

tool for understanding an objective and unchanging reality, as well as for learning those *essential* ideas and knowledge that we need to live well. From Aristotle's *realism*, it takes the tenet that the mind learns through contact with the physical world; according to this view, to know reality, we must learn to observe and measure the physical world accurately. From our observations, we use our reasoning ability to gain new knowledge. This contrasts with the perennialist view that reasoning alone can lead to truth.

Essentialists believe that there exists a critical core of information and skills that an educated person must have. They are convinced that the overwhelming number of children can and should learn this core of essential material. According to this view, schools should be organized to transmit this knowledge and skill as effectively as possible. For essentialists, the methods used to transmit this knowledge and skill are not specifically prescribed. The focus is, instead, on the knowledge that is gained by the students.

In many ways, essentialism sounds a good deal like perennialism. Although these two views have much in common, some important differences exist between them. For instance, essentialists do not focus as intently on "truths" as do perennialists. They are less concerned with the classics as being the primary repository of worthwhile knowledge. Instead, essentialists search for what will help a person live a productive life today. If the current economic realities strongly suggest that students need to graduate from high school with computer literacy, for example, essentialists will find a place for this training in the curriculum.

Essentialists follow Aristotle's idea that students must experience the world around them, as these students are doing on a fieldtrip, to learn from it.

(Mike Watson Images/Jupiterimages)

In this regard, essentialists are very practical. Like perennialists, essentialists look upon the many elective courses in our high schools as "frills," distracting students from the core knowledge they will later need. At the same time, whereas perennialists will hold fast to the Great Books as the storehouse of critical knowledge, essentialists will make more room for scientific, technical, and even vocational emphases in the curriculum. Essentialists see themselves as valuing the past, but not being captured by it.

The philosophy behind the Core Knowledge program (discussed in Chapter 5, "What Is Taught?"), which speaks in detail about what students from kindergarten to eighth grade should know, is probably best categorized as essentialist. Based on the book *Cultural Literacy*, by E. D. Hirsch, Jr., this content-rich curriculum stresses academics and learning of specific knowledge. Although its emphasis on important ideas and great works of the past makes it attractive to perennialists, the curriculum's focus on current literature and emphasis on science point more to its alignment with the essentialist movement. Currently the Core Knowledge curriculum is being used in 694 U.S. schools.[4]

> *The ability to think straight, some knowledge of the past, some vision of the future, some skill to do useful service, some urge to fit that service into the well-being of the community—these are the most vital things education must try to produce.*
>
> —VIRGINIA CROCHERON GILDERSLEEVE (1877–1965), Stateswoman and Scholar

Essentialist Goals and Practices

For essentialists, the aim of education is to teach youth the essentials they need to live well in the modern world. To realize this goal, schools should focus on the established disciplines, which are the "containers" of organized knowledge. As captured in the educational slogan, "Back to the basics," the elementary years should concentrate on the basics such as the "three R's." These and other foundational tools are needed to gain access to the disciplined knowledge with which one begins to come in contact in high school.

Although some debate persists about what is "essential" in the curriculum, essentialists believe this is not a debate to which children can contribute fruitfully. Instead, they see the role of the student as simply that of learner; thus the individual child's interests, motivations, and psychological states are not given much attention. Nor do essentialists advocate a "romantic" view of children (discussed later in this chapter) as being naturally good. They see the students not as evil, but rather as deficient and needing discipline and pressure to keep learning. School is viewed as a place where children come to learn what they need to know. Teachers are not guides, but authorities. The student's job is to listen and learn. Given the imperfect state of the students, the teacher must be ingenious in finding ways to engage their imaginations and minds.

One notable essentialist was James Bryan Conant, a Harvard professor and president for much of the first half of the twentieth century. Concerned about disparities in the knowledge and skills that high school students brought with them to college, Conant argued for standardization of college requirements for high school students. He was also influential in the establishment of the SAT as a measure of essential knowledge a potential college student needs to possess. Although not purely an "essentialist movement," much of the thought and energy behind the drive for state standards, standardized testing, the No Child Left Behind Act (NCLB), and Race to the Top has a strong essentialist flavor.

The following case study offers the perspective of a representative essentialist teacher.

from PRESERVICE to PRACTICE

An Essentialist Teacher

In my view, the world is filled with real problems, and the young people who leave school have to be ready to take up the challenge of life and solve those problems. For me, the watchword in education is *usefulness*. I think everything that is taught has to pass the test of whether it is useful. My job as a teacher is to find out what is useful and then to make sure the students learn it.

I believe that school should be relevant to the young. However, my view of what is relevant is very different from the views of lots of other people. For me, relevance is not what is personally "meaningful" or a "do your own thing" approach; what is relevant is what helps the individual live well and what benefits humanity. For that, we need to look very carefully at the past and sort out the most valuable learning. That is what should be taught and what should be learned. I find the back-to-the-classics approach quite valuable. However, most advocates go too far in concentrating on classics. They also stress the humanities and the arts a little too much and tend to underplay science and technology. If children are going to function in today's world, and if our world is going to solve all the problems it's confronted with, we have to give more attention to science and technology than we have in the past. But clearly the past is the place to begin our search for the relevant curriculum.

It's not the most pleasing or satisfying image, but I think the concept of the student as an empty jug is the most accurate one.

Certainly kids come to school with lots of knowledge and lots of interests. However, the job of school is to teach them what they don't know and to teach these things in a systematic and organized way. It's not to fill their minds with isolated fragments of information but to fill them with systematic knowledge. They need tools to learn, and, as they get older, they need human insights and skills that come from the disciplines.

Given that there is so much to learn, an emphasis on student "interests" and "projects" and "problem solving" is quite wasteful. There is plenty of time for that outside of school or when school is over. Inside the school, the teachers are the authorities, and the students are there to learn what they don't know. The environment should be task oriented and disciplined. It doesn't have to be oppressive or unjust or any of that. I tell my students that learning is not necessarily going to be fun, but that at the end of the year they will have a great sense of accomplishment. I'd take accomplishment over fun anytime. By and large, most students do too.

CASE QUESTIONS

1. What knowledge do you believe will be essential for the students you teach to learn if they are to be effective members of their society?

2. In what ways do perennialist teachers differ from essentialist teachers?

CHILD-CENTERED PHILOSOPHIES

In contrast to perennialism and essentialism, the next two schools of philosophy—romanticism and progressivism—look first to the learner rather than to the curriculum. Both consider the development of the learner to be the main purpose of education. A well-educated person does not necessarily have a definite body of knowledge; rather, a well-educated person is able to function well in society and life.

> *Learning is not attained by chance; it must be sought for with ardor and attended to with diligence.*
>
> —ABIGAIL ADAMS (1744–1818),
> Wife of John Adams, Second President of the
> United States

Romanticism

Romanticism, also known as naturalism, is based on the writings of Jean-Jacques Rousseau, an eighteenth-century Swiss-French philosopher. In a condemnation of society and the educational system of the time, Rousseau wrote *Emile*, a novel that details

Rousseau's ideas about education through the example of a fictional young boy, Emile.

The Education of Emile

Rousseau believed that children are born good and pure. Once exposed to the evils of society, however, they become corrupted. To keep children good, they need to be isolated from society for as long as possible.

Rousseau describes a serene, yet well-controlled, bucolic environment for the ideal education of Emile; he is to be educated by a private tutor at the country manor where he lives. Emile's education begins with his exploration of the world of nature surrounding him. From his observations, he may ask questions about the natural world that the tutor answers. There are no formal lessons, no books to read or facts to memorize, no specific curriculum to learn. Emile decides what he learns about and when. As Emile matures, the tutor helps him develop rational thinking skills, but Emile continues to decide the topics of study. When Emile is around 15, he is slowly introduced to certain social situations until he is deemed "ready" by his tutor to resist the evils of society and live a productive life in the social world. By the time he is 20, Emile is ready to take a mate and make a life for himself.

Implications for Education

Unlike the perennialists and essentialists, who highlight the importance of educating the individual for society, the romantics consider the needs of the individual more important than the needs of society. For the romantics, the purpose of education is individual self-fulfillment—that is, education must help the students develop physically, intellectually, socially, and morally (usually in that order).

Romantics believe that education is a natural process, which grows out of children's innate curiosity. This curiosity is most obvious during the "why?" phase of young childhood, when nearly every utterance out of the child's mouth is another question: "Why is the dog barking?" "Why is the boy sad?" or "Why is the bird blue?" (Exhausted parents often want to ask in return, "Why do you ask so many questions?") Romantics argue that we must let children's interests and curiosity drive their learning. The teacher's job is to respond to the children's questions as they arise and not to impose the learning of subjects that are not of interest to the child. The learner's responsibility is to maintain his or her natural curiosity and desire to learn. Because they perceive learning to be guided by student interests, romantics do not advocate the establishment of a set or common curriculum of study. Some students may be interested in kayaking, while others want to study photography, and still others may be fascinated by how an iPod can do all it can do. As students pursue their own areas of study, the approach to teaching and learning likewise becomes individualized. Much of the learning is self-directed and self-guided by the students, with teachers serving as sources of information or resources to help the students satisfy their curiosity rather than functioning as taskmasters or authorities on knowledge.

Romanticism has been especially influential in the early childhood and elementary grades. Many early childhood educators, including such pioneers as Maria Montessori, Frederick Froebel, and Johann Pestalozzi, basically agreed with Rousseau's ideas about humans' innate curiosity and using the child's interests to define the curriculum. Although none proposed as radical a school setting as Rousseau's pastoral manor, they did adopt some of Rousseau's other ideas about education, such as providing young children with extensive opportunities to manipulate wooden blocks and

> "
> *A sense of curiosity is nature's original school of education.*
>
> —SMILEY BLANTON (1882–1966),
> Psychiatrist

clay and other real materials and establishing learning environments that provoke students' curiosity.

Today, schools such as Summerhill in Suffolk, England, and the Sudbury Valley School in Framingham, Massachusetts, embody many of the beliefs of the romantics. At these schools, there are no set curricula, no formal classes, and no tests. Students decide what they want to study and, in some cases, are expected to take responsibility for their learning.

The following case study represents the views of a romantic teacher.

from PRESERVICE to PRACTICE

A Romantic Teacher

Have you ever seen the thrill on a young child's face when he or she figures out how to make something work? What about their wonder as they ask another question about why there are rainbows or thunder and lightning? I see these young children, and then I look at some of the students in school today. Their faces are filled with so much dread or disinterest or boredom that I get disheartened. What happened to that enthusiasm, that excitement for learning, I wonder? That schools, which should be places of learning, can turn students off to learning so strongly is the reason I became a teacher. I want my classroom to be a place where students can explore their interests and satisfy their curiosities. I can't make them learn information if it's not something they're interested in.

In my classroom, students decide what they want to study and I help them find the resources. Sometimes we get books from the library, or find websites on the Internet. The Internet has been a wonderful resource for my students. Some of them have been able to have online conversations with professionals in fields like aerospace engineering and bioengineering. Sometimes, I set up face-to-face meetings with professionals in a particular field. Last week, we had a computer programmer in to talk to a couple of students who were interested in learning more about writing code. It's so exciting to see students enthusiastic about what they are learning.

What I call the Test Nazis really have trouble with my approach. Their view is that students have big holes in their knowledge; they don't learn "the hard stuff"; they can't pass standardized tests. My students may not do very well on standardized tests (what do they *really* measure, anyway?), but they do learn the hard stuff! I mean, computer programming, aerospace engineering, and bioengineering? Those are not easy topics to understand. It may be that my students don't know a lot of facts in the standardized subjects, but they know well what they learn because they have selected these topics themselves. They *want* to learn about them, so they do.

CASE QUESTIONS

1. How would teachers in public schools, who are held accountable for students' mastery of curriculum standards, be able to follow a romantic philosophy of letting student interest guide the curriculum?

2. Do you think you would be comfortable adopting the romantic approach? Why or why not?

Progressivism

Progressivism is a relatively young philosophy of education. It came to prominence in the 1920s, growing out of the progressive political and social movement of the time. This school of thought drew from some of the ideas of Rousseau and from the work of John Dewey, the most influential educational philosopher of the twentieth century (see the Leaders in Education feature in this section).

(T) F

Progressive educators views nature as being in flux, as ever changing. Therefore, teachers consider knowledge as something that must continually be redefined and rediscovered to keep up with that change.

Progressivism views nature as being in flux, as ever changing. Consequently, knowledge must continually be redefined and rediscovered to keep up with that change.

Progressivism views nature as being in flux, as ever changing. Consequently, knowledge must continually be redefined and rediscovered to keep up with that change. Whereas other philosophies see the mind as a jug to be filled with truth or as a muscle that needs to be exercised and conditioned, progressives view the mind as a marvelous mechanism for problem solving. Like the romantics, advocates of the progressive viewpoint believe that people are naturally exploring, inquiring entities. When faced with an obstacle, they will try to find a way to overcome it. When faced with a question, they will try to find an answer. For progressives, education aims to develop this problem-solving ability.

Progressive Education

Progressive educators believe that the place to begin an education is with the student rather than with the subject matter. When following this philosophy, the teacher identifies what each student's interests and concerns are and tries to shape problems around them. The teacher then helps the student develop strategies to solve the problems posed. Students' motivation to solve problems is the key to this educational model, and posing problems based on students' interests helps heighten their motivation.

Students should start with simple study projects and gradually learn more systematic ways to investigate until they finally master a variety of problem-solving strategies. Rather than being a presenter of knowledge or a taskmaster, the teacher is an intellectual guide, a *facilitator* in the problem-solving process. Students are encouraged to be imaginative and resourceful in solving problems. They are directed to a variety of learning methods, from reading books and studying the traditional disciplines, to performing experiments and analyzing data. (The Video Case *Middle School Science Instruction: Inquiry Learning* shows how one middle school teacher guides students as they develop and test hypotheses.)

Method is of great importance to advocates of the progressive philosophy. Conversely, knowledge—formal, traditional knowledge—is not given the same honored place. For progressives, there is really no special, sacrosanct knowledge or subject matter that all students must learn. Instead, the value of knowledge is seen as residing only in its ability to solve human problems.

Regarding the school curriculum, progressives believe that a student can learn problem-solving skills from electronics just as easily as from Latin, from agronomy just as well as from geometry. The focus for progressive educators is teaching students *how* to think rather than *what* to think. The slogan "Teacher as guide on the side rather than sage on the stage" captures the uniqueness of the progressive view. Progressive teachers often introduce traditional subject matter, but they use it differently from the way it is used in a traditional classroom. Because the problems students are trying to solve are of paramount importance, the subjects contribute primarily through providing contexts for problems students must solve. Subject matter knowledge may also provide information that leads to solutions.

▶❚❚ **TeachSource VIDEO CASE**

Middle School Science Instruction: Inquiry Learning

Go to the Education CourseMate website to watch the video clips, study the artifacts in the case, and reflect on the following questions:

1. Does this teacher's approach represent progressivism, as it is described in this chapter? Why or why not?

2. Which of the other philosophies or psychological influences mentioned in this chapter does this teacher's approach incorporate?

3. How well would this teacher's approach fit with your own developing philosophy of teaching?

LEADERS in education

John Dewey (1859-1952)

John Dewey, the founder of instrumentalism, is widely considered the single most influential figure in the history of American educational thought. At the same time, his ideas and beliefs have been frequently misunderstood and misinterpreted, leading to the misapplication of his theories.

Dewey grew up in Vermont, where he attended public schools and the University of Vermont. As a graduate student in philosophy at Johns Hopkins University, he was deeply influenced by the ideas of Charles S. Pierce and William James, the founders of pragmatist philosophy. Dewey recognized the implications for education of Pierce's argument that ideas, or propositions, have worth only if they make a difference in future thoughts or actions. Calling his own philosophy *instrumentalism* to emphasize the principle that ideas are instruments, Dewey argued that philosophy and education both involve a practical, experimental attempt to improve the human condition.

Dewey denounced the public school's classical curriculum in the nineteenth century as totally unsuited to the demands of newly industrialized society of the United States. He claimed that the schools were divorced from life and that they failed to teach children how to *use* knowledge. Defining education as a "continuous reconstruction of experience," Dewey said that schools should teach children not what to think, but how to think. In his 1916 treatise *Democracy and Education*, he claimed that the schools offered students—as future citizens—no preparation for assuming the responsibility of citizenship in a democracy. Dewey called for schools to provide a concentrated study of democratic processes and to reflect those processes in the organization of school life, going as far as advocating that students be given the power to make decisions affecting life in the school in a democratic way. He considered participation in life, rather than preparation for it, the hallmark of an effective education.

In 1896, Dewey established the University Laboratory School, an elementary school at the University of Chicago. It was experimental in two senses: in its use of experiment and inquiry as the method by which the children learned and in its role as a laboratory for the transformation of the schools. The activities and occupations of adult life served as the core of the curriculum and the model teaching method. Children began by studying and imitating simple domestic and industrial tasks. In later years, they studied the historical development of industry, invention, group living, and nature. Dewey wrote that we must "make each one of our schools an embryonic community life, active with types of occupations that reflect the life of the larger society and permeated with the spirit of art, history, and science."

The late 1920s to the early 1940s—the era of progressive education—saw a massive attempt to implement Dewey's ideas, but the rigid (and often inaccurate) manner in which they were interpreted led to remarkable extravagances in some progressive schools. For instance, some educators considered it useless to teach geography because maps changed so rapidly. The role of subject matter was gradually played down in progressive schools, replaced by a stress on method and process. The rationale was that it was more important to produce a "good citizen" than a person who was "educated" in the classical sense. Until he was well into his 90s, Dewey fought vehemently against these corruptions of his views.

The centrality of John Dewey's thought to U.S. education has waxed and waned over the years. Traditionally more popular in universities than in actual classroom practice, Dewey's work is often invoked by people who are attempting to make the schools more humanistic and the curriculum more relevant to the current world. Whether in favor or out, John Dewey represents the United States' most distinctive contributor to educational thought.

With the progressive viewpoint, the process—not the product—is viewed as the critical concern. Although both romantic and progressive educators start with students' interests, progressives have more structure behind their teaching. They also have goals for their students, as discussed next.

The School as Training Ground for Democracy

Unlike romantic educators, who may see society as a negative influence on the student, progressives see society as an integral aspect of the student's life. Progressives view schools as small societies in themselves, places where students are learning as they live life, not simply preparing for life. This gives the progressive school a unique atmosphere, different from that of the perennialist storehouse of wisdom or a place with the clearly defined roles and authority structures promoted by essentialists.

Progressive educators believe the school should be democratic in structure so that children can learn to live well in a democracy and become good citizens. They emphasize group activity and group problem solving so that students learn to work with others and help others. This is one reason many teachers who describe themselves as progressive educators are enthusiastic about cooperative learning strategies, such as those discussed in Chapter 5, "What Is Taught?"

> *Education makes people easy to lead, but difficult to drive; easy to govern, but impossible to enslave.*
>
> —HENRY BROOKS ADAMS (1838–1918),
> American Novelist and Historian

Implicit in the progressive approach is the belief that children must not only learn to solve their own problems but also help to solve the problems of their neighbors. For progressives, one of the main purposes of education is to make society better, which requires that people work together to solve problems. It is not uncommon for the problem-solving activities of the progressive school to spill out into the community and involve students in issues such as ecology and poverty. In this way, students learn an important principle of progressive education: knowledge should be used to redesign or improve the world.

One notable progressive educator was William Heard Kilpatrick (1871–1965), who was a professor of philosophy of education at Columbia University in New York. He was a follower of many of Dewey's ideas about education but differed on the importance of subject matter in a child's educational experience. Rejecting formal curriculum study, he developed the **project method** of education, in which students work in groups on a topic of interest to them. He believed that because students learn only what is of interest to them, they should be the ones to determine topics of study.

Both progressive and essentialist educators claim their particular approach is the true American philosophy of education. One can make a case that both match this description, but each reflects different aspects of the American personality. Progressivism represents our antiauthoritarian, experimental, and visionary side; essentialism speaks to our more practical, structured, and task-oriented side. In recent years, many of the tensions and public debates in U.S. education can be traced to struggles between these two philosophies of education. Clearly, essentialist educators gained ground on progressive educators in the 1980s and 1990s. Concerns over the country's global economic competitiveness and the perceived "softness" of our schools have created a receptive climate for essentialist views.

To judge your own sympathy for the progressive approach, see what you think of the following representative statement by a progressive educator.

from PRESERVICE to PRACTICE

A Progressive Educator

I'm a progressive educator and proud of it. I'm not ducking that label just because it is unpopular in many quarters these days, usually among people who don't really understand what it is. Quite honestly, for the life of me I cannot understand how a teacher can be anything *but* a progressive educator.

I'm dedicated to a few simple and, I believe, obvious principles. For one thing, children come into the world with a very plastic nature, capable of being molded one way or another. We should therefore work to surround them with activities and opportunities that bring them in contact with good things. Also, by their nature children are curious. Instead of rejecting their curiosities, I believe we should build on them. Schools should be exciting, involving places where students are caught up in interesting activities.

I think that I'm a progressive educator because I have looked at my own experiences. I know I learn best when I'm trying to solve a puzzle or a problem that really interests me. Somehow I've always been able to get much more interested in how we're going to solve the problems of our own society than in the affairs of the Athenians and Spartans. I can get much more involved in a research problem about which MP3 player gives the best value for the dollar than about some dry economic problem presented to me by a teacher. And I really don't think I'm different from the overwhelming majority of students.

I see many of my fellow teachers spending all their energy damming up student curiosity and imposing work on their students. And then the teachers wonder why they themselves are so tired or burned out. I'm sure it's quite tiring to try to convert children into file cabinets and to stuff facts into their heads all day.

One of the things that sets me apart is that I'm not so hung up as others are on what I call the "talky" curriculum. I am convinced that students learn most effectively by *doing*, by experiencing events and then reflecting on and making meaning out of what they have experienced. I think more science is learned on a nature walk than from the same time spent reading a textbook or hearing teacher explanations. I think students learn more abstract principles, such as democracy, from trying to set up and maintain a democratic society in their classroom than from a lot of learned lectures and dusty prose on the subject. I'm trying to get to their hearts and their heads. The traditional approach gets to neither place.

To me, life is a matter of solving problems. New times have new problems and demand new knowledge. I don't want my students to be ready for life in the eighteenth century. I want them to be effective, functioning, curious citizens of the twenty-first century. They are going to need to be able to develop solutions to fit new and unique problems. Although much knowledge is important, they need to realize that knowledge is only today's tentative explanation of how things work. Much of what we know now is incorrect and will have to be replaced.

It's not that I think that ideas and content and the traditional subjects are worthless—far from it. I teach much of the same material as other teachers. I just get there by a different route. I let the issues and problems emerge and then give the students a chance to get answers and to solve problems. As they quickly learn, they have to know a great deal to solve some of the problems. Often they get themselves involved with some very advanced material. The only difference is that now they want to. Now they have the energy. And, boy, once they get going, do they have energy! No, it doesn't always work. I have students who coast, and I've had projects that failed. But I'd put my track record against those of my more traditional colleagues any day.

CASE QUESTIONS

1. Did any of your teachers take a progressive approach to teaching? If so, how did you, as a student, respond?

2. Do you believe your students would respond well if you chose to implement a progressive approach? What difficulties, if any, do you think you might encounter?

the influence of psychological theories

Since early in the twentieth century, educational practice has been greatly influenced by the discipline of psychology. Psychology—the scientific study of the mind and human behavior—was a natural influence on the work of teachers, particularly given its focus on how we learn. Over the years, various schools of psychology have emerged, often having roots in particular philosophies. Some of these psychological theories have had a great deal to say to educators. Two in particular have strongly influenced our schools: behaviorism and cognitive psychology.

BEHAVIORISM: CONDITIONING STUDENTS OR SETTING THEM FREE?

The psychological theory of behavior modification, also known as **behaviorism**, is an educational approach that emerged directly from the pioneering research of B. F. Skinner (1904–1990), who himself was influenced by the social efficiency movement in education of the 1920s and 1930s. Skinner developed the theory called operant conditioning, which viewed learning as the learner's response to various stimuli (e.g., sounds, words, or the actions of people) present in the environment. Subscribing to the view that humans learn to act in specific ways based on the response they receive for their actions (generally reward or punishment), the behaviorist teacher believes that learners need incentives, both positive and negative, as motivators to learn.

In planning for teaching, the behaviorist (1) uses clear objectives, spelled out in terms of the behaviors to be learned; (2) establishes a learning environment, which will positively reinforce desired behaviors and eliminate undesirable behaviors; and (3) closely monitors and gives the learner feedback on progress until the goal is achieved. The curriculum is organized in sequenced, discrete segments. Because the same behaviors and knowledge are desirable for all students, standardization of the curriculum and of means to measure progress is important. Behaviorist teachers often use objective tests made up predominantly of multiple-choice questions to measure how well students have learned the curriculum and to give prompt feedback to students. In some behaviorist classrooms, students are expected to practice a specific skill until they show a certain level of mastery of the skill. At that point, they move on to the next skill or concept to be learned.

In the 1960s and 1970s, many educators made behaviorism their dominant, organizing educational theory. This educational movement has been criticized for being teacher dominated and causing teachers to treat students as passive objects to be conditioned and therefore manipulated. Nevertheless, behaviorism remains a dominant theoretical presence, particularly in the areas of special education and classroom discipline. The popular "Assertive Discipline," in which teachers are urged to "catch students doing good" and then reward that behavior, is based squarely on behaviorism.[5] Many teachers rely on behavior modification practices to get students to be quiet when they see or hear the teacher's signal or to get them to do their best work in order to receive a reward sticker.

Critics argue that behaviorist teachers exercise too much control over students' learning and focus on the learning of facts rather than deep conceptual knowledge. In response, behaviorist teachers insist that their goal is to eventually put control of learning in their students' hands once they have learned to respond appropriately to the teacher's prompts.

COGNITIVE PSYCHOLOGY: STUDENTS AS MAKERS OF MEANING?

Over the past 30 years, researchers in both medicine and psychology have been investigating the human brain to find out more about its role in human learning and memory. Cognitive psychologists, drawing heavily on the trail-blazing research of Swiss psychologist Jean Piaget (1896–1980), the Russian psychologist Lev Vygotsky (1896–1934), and the American psychologist Jerome Bruner (1915–), have discovered a great deal about how people learn to think and solve problems. Their discoveries have led to the development of new theories about learning and cognition that have tremendous implications for how teachers teach. One increasingly popular theory derived from the research findings states that for new information to be internalized by the learner, it must be integrated into the learner's preexisting knowledge base. This process of integration is referred to as **constructivism**.

> *What we want to see is the child in pursuit of knowledge, and not knowledge in pursuit of the child.*
>
> —GEORGE BERNARD SHAW (1856–1950),
> Irish Playwright

According to this theory, knowledge cannot be *transmitted* directly from the teacher to the learner, but rather is *constructed by the learner and later reconstructed* as new information becomes available. Instead of seeing students as partially full vessels waiting to be filled, as some essentialists do, constructivist teachers view them as actively engaged in *making meaning*.

Teachers, therefore, need to create learning situations where students can build their own knowledge rather than having students sit and listen to the teachers' lectures. One constructivist technique for helping students "make meaning" of a concept is called scaffolding, whereby the teacher provides support as the student attempts to understand that concept. (Scaffolding is also discussed in Chapter 6, "What Makes a Teacher Effective?") Although not without its critics,[6] constructivism has become so influential in education in recent years that we give it particular attention here.

Constructivists view individuals as having an aversion to disorder. They believe that we are all continually trying to sort things out, to find clues and patterns amid our impressions that will help us to make sense of the world around us. When we encounter something new—say, a strange sound in the night—we immediately attempt to fit it into the patterns or structures we already possess (e.g., "Don't worry. That's the midnight whistle of the Ole Ninety-Eight headin' down to New Orleans"). But sometimes we encounter new information that leads (or forces) us to realize that our knowledge base as it is currently "constructed" is incorrect or outdated ("Uh-oh! The railroad retired that train two years ago!"). We may respond in a number of ways: we may search for new input from our senses, seeking either to reconstruct the knowledge base or develop different patterns and structures so that the information "fits" ("Maybe that noise was from the hot water boiler and it's about to explode," or "Maybe that creepy guy from the apartment down below is on my fire escape," or "Maybe I shouldn't read Stephen King novels before going to bed!"). In some instances, we may be so convinced of our knowledge base that we refuse to make allowances for the new information. ("No, I'm sure that it was a train whistle. The railroad must have put that train back in service.") Students follow the same patterns as they try to make sense of new information they encounter in school.

VOICES from the classroom

Constructivist Philosophy

Susan Dougherty writes about her career as a fourth-grade teacher at Bayberry School in Watchung, New Jersey.

As I began my career in education, I held firm one belief about students: they must be active participants in the classroom. Twelve years later, I hold that same basic belief but have refined what it means for a learner to be active.

Early in my career, "active" meant that my students would not sit in rows and spend the day doing seatwork. My first position as a kindergarten teacher quickly revealed that I might strive for something greater than physical activity. Of course, kindergarten students are active—try and keep them from being anything but active! I came to recognize that while active bodies can be important, what I really wanted was to engage the minds of my students.

As I taught students at many elementary levels, I learned to ask probing questions that required my students to consider their learning carefully. How do you know to add these two numbers? What kind of person do you think the main character of this story is? How would you explain why oil floats on water to someone who didn't understand? Although my students were often physically active, acting out scenes from a novel we were reading, experimenting with magnets or prisms, or using pattern blocks to build models of math problems, they also spent time physically inert but inwardly engaged in active thought.

Soon, however, I was not satisfied with simply engaging the minds of my students. I wanted to reach their hearts. I wanted to awaken a passion for learning within each student. How might a teacher encourage the awakening of such passion? One key, I think, is to allow and encourage the students to ask and seek the answers to their own questions. In this way, students' minds and hearts become active, leading them on a lifelong journey of inquiry and self-motivated learning.

Cognitive psychologists also suggest that we organize our knowledge in ways that allow us easy access to knowledge we use regularly. These cognitive structures, which are called *schemas or schemata*, change constantly as new information is taken in, hypotheses are developed, and theories are tested. These processes of hypothesis development and testing can be done independently or in interaction with others. Thus real learning for constructivists involves moving from the Trivial Pursuit or *Jeopardy* type of factual or declarative knowledge to applicable knowledge—in other words, from "knowing what" to "knowing how." To achieve this transformation, learners must develop cognitive learning strategies for particular kinds of learning tasks; that is, they must learn how to think through or go about solving problems. One teacher describes how she puts her constructivist philosophy into action in the Voices from the Classroom feature.

your philosophy of education

At this point, you may be a little confused and possibly discouraged by all this heavy vocabulary and lofty thought. To expect to be able to understand and evaluate critically every aspect of each philosophy is to expect of yourself what few professional philosophers are able to do. What you have just finished reading is a précis of some of the major ideas of Western civilization (see Table 9.1 for a summary). Some of

TABLE 9.1 Four Philosophies and Their Applications to Education

	Perennialism	Essentialism	Romanticism	Progressivism
Metaphysics: What is real? Does it have meaning?	The meaning of life is the search for unchanging truth found in the collective wisdom of Western culture.	What is relevant is what helps an individual live well and what benefits humanity.	Reality is stable; the meaning of life is derived primarily through self-development away from society.	Reality is in flux and ever-changing, so meaning is in the context of the individual, who is a "problem solver."
Epistemology: Knowledge and knowing—what is truth?	Truth and knowledge are changeless, revealed through guided reflection and in classics of Western culture.	Truth exists in the classics *and* modern science. Students must learn process *and* content. Knowledge is gained through the interaction of experiences and rational thought.	Knowledge is gained through sensory experiences and interaction with one's environment.	Knowledge is gained via individual experience. Truth is individually defined so that emphasis is on learning *how* to learn.
Axiology: Values, ethics, aesthetics	Changeless. Determined by the very nature of reality.	Determined by the natural order of things. Values exist in the best of culture.	Determined by the individual.	Determined by each individual in interaction with his or her culture, based on the shared values of the community or culture.
Logic: How we think, deductive and inductive	Rationality, especially deductive thought, is developed by studying classics and through the Socratic dialectic.	Rationality is best developed through interplay of deductive and inductive thinking.	Emphasis is primarily on inductive thought, because learning starts with experiences and moves to hypotheses.	Emphasis is on inductive thinking and problem solving.
Purpose of Education/ Schooling	Educate the intellect; develop in learner rational thought and an understanding of the truths of humankind.	Prepare students to be productive, contributing members of society.	Make learner strong (physically, intellectually, morally) to resist the evils of society.	Help students become good citizens familiar with the workings of democracy and with good problem-solving skills.
The Teacher	Teacher is expert of content knowledge. Passes on to next generation the accumulated wisdom of the past.	Teacher is expert of content knowledge. Teaches essential knowledge. Maintains task-oriented focus.	Teacher responds to the learners' requests for knowledge; does not initiate learning in the learners.	Teacher is facilitator of student learning; provides resources for students' problem-solving abilities. Develops students' problem-solving abilities. Helps children do what they want to do.

(continued)

TABLE 9.1 **Four Philosophies and Their Applications to Education (Continued)**

	Perennialism	Essentialism	Romanticism	Progressivism
Teaching Strategies	Cultivates rational powers through contact with the culture's best and through imitation. For older students, Socratic dialogue is key to uncovering truths found in classics.	Avoids methodological frills and soft pedagogy and concentrates on sound, proven instructional methods.	Creates productive learning environment for learners; individualized approach to learning, depending on students' interests.	Stimulates students to plan and carry out activities and research projects using group processes and democratic procedures.
The Child	Is there to learn what is taught.	Is there to listen and learn.	Is naturally good and must be protected from the evils of society.	Learns by doing and by discovering.
Curriculum	In younger grades, focuses on basic skills to develop mental discipline and rational thought processes. Older learners study materials reflecting universal and recurring themes through which the truths of humanity can be revealed.	Strong emphasis on basic skills in elementary schools and on disciplined knowledge and scholastic achievement in secondary schools.	Depends on the interests of the learner. No set curriculum, no specific skills to be acquired.	Centered on the student's interest in real problems and interdisciplinary solution seeking.

Source: Adapted from a table suggested by James Hotchkiss. Used by permission of James Hotchkiss.

these ideas have been around for centuries, and some are the fruits of thinkers who are still with us.

How can you use the summary in Table 9.1 to help you develop your own philosophy of education? First, recognize that selecting the philosophy by which you will live and by which you will guide your professional activities takes much more investment of time, thought, and energy than reading our short chapter. Second, realize that you have already begun to uncover your philosophy of education—you started when you filled out the Philosophy of Education Self-Inventory. You can further your self-understanding by following the suggestions in the feature entitled "Identifying Your Own Philosophical Leanings." Third, realize that developing and refining one's philosophy of education is a lifelong endeavor, and commit yourself to making this journey.

Some teachers, like the teacher-philosophers discussed in this chapter, settle on one philosophical view, and that view then serves to structure all of their work. Other teachers lean strongly toward a particular philosophy, even if they may not be fully conscious of their position or able to give it a proper philosophical label. Typically they have a particular view of the learner, including how the learner should be approached and what is most worth knowing. Of course, few teachers are philosophical purists. Some teachers, recognizing that they draw ideas from various philosophies, label themselves *eclectics*. But what does it really mean to be an eclectic teacher in contemporary education?

identifying your own philosophical leanings

Think of your favorite teacher from elementary or secondary school, or a teacher you have admired during your teacher education. On a separate piece of paper, list some of that teacher's practices that you admire most. Include instructional techniques, classroom management strategies, ways of relating to the students—anything you think helped that person be an effective teacher.

Now, on the same piece of paper, write the philosophical outlook that you think may underlie each practice you admire. This exercise will take some reflection, and you may well find that no single philosophy matches all the teaching characteristics you listed. Use whatever philosophical labels seem most appropriate.

After completing both tasks, what general conclusions can you draw about the philosophy of this teacher you admire? Does the teacher's practice reflect the tenets of a single educational philosophy discussed in this chapter? Or does he or she take an eclectic approach [described below], drawing on different philosophical traditions? Are there ways in which this teacher is too unique to fit any category?

As a final step, reflect on what your conclusion tells you about your own philosophical leanings. If you hold this teacher in high regard, presumably you share at least some of his or her philosophical convictions. Does anything surprise you about the philosophical beliefs you have deduced? Do they suggest that you are more traditional or more progressive than you supposed? More child centered or subject matter centered? More nicely balanced or just more muddled? Which aspects of your own philosophical base do you need to think about further and clarify?

(© Susie Fitzhugh)

(© Laura Dwight)

Explore the two qualities of excellence in teaching: a focus on one's students and a passion for the subject matter.

PAUSE AND REFLECT

1. It is perhaps unfair of us to ask you so soon after having read descriptions of different philosophies and theories of education, but right now, which one holds the greatest intellectual appeal to you? Which one holds the least appeal? Why do you feel that way?

2. How has reading about these four philosophical alternatives changed your own philosophy of education? Consider retaking the Philosophy of Education Self-Inventory now that you have more knowledge about these philosophical underpinnings.

ECLECTICISM: NOT AN EXCUSE FOR SLOPPY THINKING

Eclecticism embodies the idea that truth can be found anywhere, and therefore people should select from various doctrines, systems, and sources. The eclectic teacher selects what he or she believes to be the most attractive features of several philosophies. For example, the teacher might take from romanticism the innate curiosity of the learner and from essentialism, a curricular viewpoint dominated by the criterion of usefulness.*

Eclecticism is quite popular, but often for the wrong reasons. It sometimes appears as the easy way out of philosophical uncertainty, just taking what you please from the philosophical cafeteria of ideas. ("Let's see now: I think I'll begin with a light vinaigrette salad of romantic individuality and follow that up with a main course of progressive problem-solving projects, but with some hearty perennialist classics as side dishes. And, oh, yes—let's finish with a popular and tasty dessert of essentialist vocational training.") One problem with this approach is the probability of inconsistency. To take one's view of society from the romantic, who gives primacy to individual freedom, and one's teaching methodology from the progressive, who stresses group membership and democratic process, is liable to make everyone confused. Selecting eclecticism must not be an excuse for lazy thinking.

Despite this warning, most teachers feel quite free and justified in borrowing teaching methodologies and strategies that are associated with various philosophies of education. The ardent perennialist teacher may choose to involve his or her sixth-grade students in a hands-on project that involves constructing a large topographical map of Odysseus's 10-year journey to his home after the fall of Troy. Conversely, the free-spirited romantic teacher may insist that each student memorize and be able to recite 50 lines of *The Odyssey*. Although this type of eclecticism may, in a narrow sense, seem philosophically inconsistent, at its heart is the recognition that no philosophy of education is able to dictate the ideal methodology or learning strategies for all situations or all students trying to learn all subject matter. Related to this notion is the growing realization (discussed in Chapter 3, "Who Are Today's Students in a Diverse Society?") that different students possess a great range of learning styles and that what works with one student may flop with another. In sum, eclecticism can be a serious philosophical position, and eclecticism in the selection of teaching strategies is quite justified. But, to reinforce our earlier statement, the choice to be "eclectic" should not be a substitute for sloppy thought.

PHILOSOPHY AND LIBERAL EDUCATION

We are not suggesting that you sit yourself down with a cup of coffee, think through all these issues, and come up with a tight set of philosophical answers that will last the rest of your lifetime. Rather, we hope that we have focused—or refocused—

T (F)

A late-night college bull session is, by definition, nonphilosophical.

The infamous college bull sessions may be where the real philosophical inquiry occurs. These debates are frequently thinly veiled discussions of what really counts in life and what one should try to do with one's life.

"

Never in my life have I been more convinced that it is our philosophy of life that dictates our philosophy of teaching, and that it is this "philosophical identity" (or lack of same) that we envelop ourselves in each day as we walk into our classroom that ultimately distinguishes those who find joy and passion in this profession from those who find drudgery and then just pick up a paycheck two weeks later.

—JOHN PERRICONE,
Author, From Zen and the
Art of Public School Teaching

*In the process of writing this chapter, we discovered that we are really traditional but progressive essentialists who are searching for a Great Books Club to join.

your attention on some of life's most critical questions and on some issues that reside at the very core of teaching.

One purpose of the general education component of teacher education programs (i.e., the courses in the arts and sciences required of the prospective teacher) is to provide a chance for future teachers to think through these fundamental questions of human nature and existence. A primary purpose of the college curriculum is to present the student with a wide range of society's best thinkers and their attempts to understand their own existence. Of course, the infamous college bull sessions may be where the real philosophical inquiry occurs. These debates are frequently thinly veiled discussions of what really counts in life and what one should try to do with one's life. In effect, then, both the formal apparatus of college and its curriculum and the informal opportunities to meet, talk, and test your ideas with a variety of people should help you discover where you stand on some of these essential human questions.

OUR FINAL WORD

The contemporary writer, Parker Palmer, has written about the need for teachers not merely to "understand" ideas, but to be ready to "stand under" certain ideas, letting them serve as the vital supports for what they do as educators.[7] This idea goes to the essence of this chapter. The teacher stands under a philosophy of education, a guide and support that has three components: (1) an expression of what the teacher values—what he or she esteems and believes to be important; (2) the individual's moral compass—what the teacher relies on to make critical ethical decisions; and (3) an engine of ideas—the knowledge that the teacher uses to respond to new and changing situations that life presents.[8] As we said at the beginning of this chapter, the teacher who will be more than a technician has an obligation to take philosophical issues and questions seriously. Teachers owe it to themselves and to their students to understand where they are going and to understand why they are going there.

As a wise teacher wrote, "A philosophy of education cannot be crammed down people's throats. They must feel it to be true in the marrow of their bones and look with trust and approval upon the leaders who attempt to give it expression. It must catch and reflect their temper, not arouse their distemper."[9] Teachers owe it to themselves to make sure that the schools in which they work are hospitable—and certainly not hostile—to their own philosophies of education. It is important that you be ready both to discuss your own philosophy of education with prospective employers and to inquire about the district's or school's philosophy of education. Do not, however, expect those interviewing you to be able to define their schools precisely according to the particular philosophies described in this chapter. Although educators live out a philosophy of education, we are not always able easily to capture it in words.

WHY TEACH? YOUR FINAL WORD

In your journal or online at this textbook's website, respond to the following questions:

1. At the present time, which beliefs do you hold about the following: the role of the teacher, the nature of the learner, the nature of the curriculum, and the ways in which people learn best? Explain your beliefs.

2. What role, if any, does religion or the spiritual realm play in your philosophy of education?

3. Why do you think that superintendents and principals often ask teaching candidates about their philosophy of education?

KEY TERMS

aesthetics (290)
axiology (288)
behaviorism (306)
constructivism (307)
deductive reasoning (290)
epistemology (287)
essentialism (295)
inductive reasoning (291)

logic (290)
metaphysics (286)
perennialism (292)
philosophy (284)
progressivism (301)
project method (304)
romanticism (299)

FOR FURTHER INFORMATION

TEACHSOURCE VIDEO

Philosophical Foundations of American Education: Four Philosophies in Action

This video provides an operational views of various philosophies of education as they occur in real life classrooms.

WEB RESOURCES

School Marm's Lil Red Schoolhouse. Available at: **http://schoolmarm.org/main/index.php?page=p_genphil**

This site, constructed by a classroom teachers, both expresses her teaching philosophy and also offers several resources to fellow teachers.

Materials on the Philosophy of Education. Available at **http://wilderdom.com/philosophy/SampleEducationPhilosophies.html**

This site is a fine collection of descriptions of important old and new philosophies of education. In addition, it includes substantial information on the philosophy behind outdoor education.

Society for Philosophical Inquiry (SPI). Available at **www.philosopher.org**

SPI is a grassroots nonprofit organization devoted to supporting philosophical inquirers of all ages and walks of life. It offers a number of ways to getting involved in the SPI's activities, such as its Socrates Café program.

PRINT RESOURCES

Gary D. Fenstermacher and Jonas F. Soltis, *Approaches to Teaching*, 4th ed. (New York: Teachers College Press, 2004.

This slim volume shows how two philosophers can unpack the term *teaching* and explain what is behind several different approaches to instruction.

Gerald Gutek, *Historical and Philosophical Foundations of Education: A Biographical Introduction*, 4th ed. (Upper Saddle River, NJ: Prentice-Hall/Merrill, 2005).

This textbook is a comprehensive and up-to-date account of the competing schools of educational philosophy and their application to schooling. It provides thumbnail sketches of key figures and leads the reader in investigating their thought.

John Perricone, *Zen and the Art of Public School Teaching* (Frederick, MD: PublishAmerica, 2005).

The author is a teacher and martial arts specialist who has written a witty, practical, and often inspiring book about how he puts his philosophy of education to work daily in his teaching.

The Education CourseMate website for this text offers many helpful resources. Go to www.cengagebrain.com to access the TeachSource Video Cases and other TeachSource videos, flashcards, interactive quizzes, the eBook, reflection and enrichment activities, a state standards resource center, and other study aids.

10 what is the history of america's struggle for educational opportunity?

(© Bettmann/CORBIS)

FOCUS POINTS

- Education in colonial America was originally religious in orientation but differed in form according to geographical area. Schooling in colonial America was not universal; it was intended primarily for white males.

- During the nineteenth century, influenced by the ideas of Thomas Jefferson and Benjamin Franklin and led by such reformers as Horace Mann, free public education became a reality. Common schools at the elementary level were supported by taxes and open to all children; their purpose was seen as cultivating a sense of American identity and loyalty.

- The nineteenth century also saw the development of public high schools that were designed to prepare young people, within a single institution, for either vocations or college; this goal of providing comprehensive educational opportunities was unique to American education.

To understand the present U.S. educational system, its successes and failures, and the problems it still faces, we must look to our past. There we can identify the forces that have affected and continue to affect the development of American education. This chapter reviews the history of schooling and education in the United States, pointing out seven important themes and examining the contributions that significant men and women have made.

Truth OR Fiction?

T F The Constitution of the United States guarantees a free system of public education to American children.

T F During colonial times, most students did not finish elementary school.

T F The great majority of private schools in the United States have a religious affiliation.

T F Efforts to desegregate the public schools during the 1960s through the 1980s came as a result of a Supreme Court ruling.

- Private education has always played an important role in America, particularly in the nation's early days. Even today, approximately 10 percent of elementary and secondary school-age children attend private schools. Most private schools have a religious affiliation and thus offer alternatives to the public schools' secular emphasis.

- Equal educational opportunities for minorities and women have not always existed in America. Ethnic groups such as African Americans, Hispanic Americans, American Indians, and Asian Americans, as well as women, have had to fight uphill battles to gain educational rights and treatment equal to those given to white males.

Rare is the college student who feels a burning urgency to answer the question "What is the history of American education?" Unless you are a history buff, you will probably ask yourself, "Why do I need to know this stuff? How will it help me do a better job in the classroom?"

First, understanding American educational history will give you a sense of perspective. As educators, we are sometimes accused of being faddist, which implies that we blindly follow each new approach or idea, thinking it is the greatest thing since the Internet. At the other extreme, we are sometimes accused of reinventing the wheel, spending a great deal of energy discovering something that has been in the educational literature for years or was a significant part of the education program of a different culture.

Second, studying the history of American education will enable you to better understand the culture and context in which you will work. It will help you see the "big picture"—that is, why things operate as they do in today's schools.

> *The farther backward you can look, the farther forward you are likely to see.*
>
> —WINSTON CHURCHILL (1874–1965),
> Prime Minister of Great Britain During World War II

Finally, studying the history of education will help you appreciate its truly noble heritage. Schools have been a progressive instrument in the lives of most people who have attended them. They have freed people from superstition and false information and given them new skills, positive values, and world-expanding visions of what each individual, as well as what we as a people, can become. Some of the greatest people who have walked the earth—Socrates, Jesus, and Gandhi, among others—saw themselves essentially as teachers. Teachers, then, are part of a long-lived, progressive, and inspirational human endeavor. Knowing our educational history and gaining a historical perspective will help you live up to and extend this tradition.

themes in american education

Kindergarten or nursery school led to elementary school, then to middle school or junior high school, then to high school, and now to college. You may have taken this progression for granted, assuming that's the way things have always been.

In reality, you are presently enjoying a level of education that was available only to the elite of earlier generations. You are already close to the top of an educational pyramid for which the foundation was laid almost 350 years ago. The growth of the pyramid has been shaped and energized by seven major themes in American educational history:

1. *Local control.* Originating in New England during colonial times, the concept of local control of schools spread during the nineteenth century with the formation of the school district system. Because of their fear of a too-strong federal government, the framers of the U.S. Constitution made no reference to

education. As a result, state governments assumed the role of educational authorities and then delegated substantial powers to local school boards. Not until the mid-twentieth century did the federal government become substantially involved in educational matters.

2. *Universal education.* Education for all children has been a developing theme in America. In the colonial period, education was reserved for a small minority—mainly white males. During the nineteenth and twentieth centuries, children from various groups previously omitted from educational opportunity (girls, minorities, immigrants, people with disabilities) gained access to elementary and secondary education. Today, a college education is generally available to all who actively seek it.

3. *Public education.* In the colonial period, education was generally private and primarily reserved for the middle and upper classes. Today private education remains a small and important part of the overall educational system, but nationhood for the United States brought the expansion of publicly supported education. By the early twentieth century, not only was public education widespread, but education became compulsory as well.

4. *Comprehensive education.* The basic abilities to read, write, and do arithmetic were once sufficient to prepare most children for fulfilling their adult roles in society. Eventually, the growth of urban, industrial life in America during the nineteenth and early twentieth centuries demanded that people be educated for work. The result was the comprehensive public high school, which includes both training for trades and preparation for college.

5. *Secular education.* In the earliest colonial times, the purpose of education was religious training. Beginning in the eighteenth century and progressing through the twentieth century, the function of American education became increasingly secular, concerned with producing socially responsible citizens. Religious study has remained mainly in the private sector.

6. *Changing ideas of the basics.* Literacy and classical learning were the main goals of colonial education, whereas practical skills for a pragmatic, democratic society were the aims of nineteenth-century schools. Technical and scientific literacy were added to the basics in the computer- and space-age late twentieth century. Today, preparing students to compete in a global marketplace seems to be the focus.

7. *Expanding definitions of educational access and equality.* In the nineteenth century, the goal for educational access was to build schools in places where children lived and to enroll as many of them as possible. Since then, the focus on **equality of educational opportunity** has expanded. By the beginning of the twentieth century, efforts to equalize education involved offering more curricular choices, including vocational training, to help prepare students for different economic and social roles. Throughout the middle of the twentieth century, the focus was on removing legal, racial, and economic barriers to schooling. From the 1960s through the 1970s, access and educational opportunity became redefined as they became increasingly tied to results. The removal of racial, linguistic, mental, and physical discrimination as the basis for expanded access was augmented by a focus on measuring learning outcomes among different groups as a test of whether improved access led to real educational opportunity. As one educational historian noted, "By the end of [the twentieth] century, . . . expectations had

shifted to an emphasis on academic achievement."[1] During the first decade of the twenty-first century, the emphasis on academic achievement has continued.

Many contemporary educational issues have their roots in these seven themes, which continue to shape the character of American schooling and education. Consider these examples of current issues:

- *Local control.* What should be the role of the federal government regarding education? Should federal legislation, such as the No Child Left Behind law, require states to test students in particular grades and on particular subjects?
- *Universal education.* How can we ensure the quality of education regardless of whether students live in wealthy or poor school districts?
- *Public education.* Should private and religious schools receive public tax support?
- *Comprehensive education.* Should the schools require all students—vocational and college prep—to follow a common curriculum?
- *Secular education.* How should public schools treat the presence of religion in American society and world culture?
- *Changing ideas of the basics.* Is technological literacy a new "basic" of education? If so, how will schools finance the programs that train students to use new technologies?
- *Expanding definitions of equal access and opportunity.* What should schools do about "achievement gaps" between poor and minority students and students from white or wealthier families?

These are just a few of the issues facing today's policymakers. As you read the rest of this chapter, look for links between historical forces and the key topics and debates in contemporary education. This chapter's tour through history is not intended to be a dead-end journey into the past. What happened in earlier generations has greatly influenced the schooling you received and the system you will enter as a teacher.

PAUSE AND REFLECT

Why is it important for teachers to know the history of American education? How might you use such knowledge?

---

elementary education

COLONIAL ORIGINS

In the 1600s, some girls received elementary instruction, but formal colonial education was intended mainly for boys, particularly those of the middle and upper classes. Both girls and boys might have had some preliminary training in the *four R's*—reading, 'riting, 'rithmetic, and religion—at home. Sometimes, for a small fee, a housewife offered to take in children, to whom she would teach a little reading and writing, basic prayers, and religious beliefs. In these **dame schools**, girls also learned basic household skills such as cooking and sewing. The dame schools often provided all the formal education some children, especially girls, ever received.

Throughout the colonies, poor children were often apprenticed or indentured to local tradesmen or housewives. Apprenticeships lasted 3 to 10 years, generally ending around age 21 for boys and age 18 for girls. During that time, an apprentice would learn the basic skills of a trade and might also be taught basic reading and writing and perhaps arithmetic as part of the contractual agreement.

Although the lines were not drawn hard and fast, the three geographic regions of the colonies—New England, the South, and the Middle Colonies—developed different types of educational systems, which were shaped by each region's particular settlement patterns.

New England Town and District Schools

In New England, the Puritans believed it was important that everyone be able to read the Bible and interpret its teachings. As early as 1642, Massachusetts passed a law requiring parents to educate their children. That law was strengthened in 1647 by the famous **Old Deluder Satan Act**. Because Satan assuredly would try to keep people from understanding the Scriptures, it was deemed important that all children be taught how to read. Therefore, every town of 50 or more families was obligated to pay a man to teach reading and writing. With these schools, known as **town schools**, New England set the precedent that if parents would not or could not educate their children, the government was obligated to take on that responsibility.

When settlers spread out, seeking better farmland, the town schools began to disappear. What emerged in their place was the so-called **moving school**, in which a schoolmaster traveled from village to village, holding sessions in each place for several months before moving on.

Discontent with this system of education eventually led to the development of the **district school**. Under this scheme, a township was divided into districts, each having its own school and teacher and being funded by the town treasury. The theme of local control over schooling developed in these various kinds of schools. The district school system soon entrenched itself in New England because it was inexpensive to finance and gave some measure of schooling to every child. Laws made attendance compulsory, but they were not very rigorously enforced.

Some towns allowed girls to have one or two hours of instruction between 5:00 and 7:00 A.M., when boys were not using the school building. For the most part, however, girls had no access to the town elementary schools until after the American Revolution.[2] If few girls went to school in the towns, even fewer did so in the outlying districts. The theme of universal education, which would include girls, was not to develop until the next century.

Students entered school around age 6 or 7 and stayed in school for only three or four years. They learned their ABCs, numerals, and the Lord's Prayer from a *hornbook*, which consisted of a page that was laminated with a transparent material made from boiled-down cows' horns and then attached to a flat piece of wood. Having learned the basics, students graduated to the **New England Primer**, an illustrated book composed of religious texts and other readings. Although other primers and catechisms existed, the *New England Primer* was the most famous and remained the basic school text for at least 100 years after the first edition was published in 1690.

The learning atmosphere of these colonial schools was repressive and grim. Students were under orders to keep quiet and do their work, and learning was characterized by an emphasis on memorization. If students did well, they were praised and given a new task. If they did poorly, they were criticized harshly and often

(T) F

During colonial times, most students did not finish elementary school.
Children were sent to school to learn to read and write just to get by. They then were expected to assist their parents or be hired out as apprentices.

> *Foolishness is bound up on the heart of the child; but the rod of correction shall drive it from him.*
>
> —NEW ENGLAND PRIMER

Discipline in colonial schools was often strict and harsh.

given a rap across the knuckles or on the seat of the pants. If children did not pay attention, their lack of focus was taken as a sign of how easily the devil could distract them from the path of righteousness. Such views continued to serve as a justification for severe classroom discipline throughout the first 250 years of American history.

Education in the South

Conditions in the South were quite different from those in New England. Many upper-class Englishmen emigrated to the South, where they established large estates. As opposed to the more centralized conditions in New England, the great distances between southern settlements encouraged plantation owners to educate their children with private tutors, who were often local ministers or itinerant scholars. As in England, education of the poor and orphans was often undertaken by the Anglican Church or by religious groups such as the Society for the Propagation of the Gospel in Foreign Parts. The Society's main mission was to convert natives and slaves to Christianity.

Most southern settlers were members of the Anglican Church and did not share the Puritan belief that everyone had a religious obligation to learn to read. The lack of concern for general education of the entire community caused public education in the South to lag behind that of other regions of the country for many generations. Town governments established schools, but their administration was usually delegated to a group or corporation, which could collect tuition, own property, hire and fire teachers, and decide curriculum content.

Education in the Middle Colonies

Unlike Puritan New England and the Anglican Southern Colonies, the Middle Colonies were composed of various religious and ethnic groups. Quakers, Catholics, Mennonites, Huguenots, Baptists, and others each wished to train their children in their respective faiths; Dutch, German, and Swedish settlers also wanted a separate education for their children. As a result, **private venture schools**, which were licensed by the civil government but not protected or financed by it, flourished, and the use of public funds to educate everyone's children did not become customary.

In these private schools, parents paid the teacher directly on a contractual basis. The instructor managed the school and curriculum, accepting or rejecting students as desired. The denominational schools in the Middle Colonies shared the New England concern for proper religious training as a primary goal, but they also began early to offer, in addition to the basics, practical subjects such as bookkeeping or navigation.

PAUSE AND REFLECT

Why did the educational development of colonial America differ among the New England, Middle, and Southern colonies? In what ways were the educational systems different? Can you see similarities to any of the colonial systems in today's schools?

THE COMMON SCHOOL

Before the American Revolution, the term **common school** referred to schools that provided education for the average person, albeit not necessarily at public expense or available to all. Even in colonial New England, parents had to pay for their children's schooling. In the first blush of the new republic, however, conditions began to favor **universal education**—the idea that some sort of elementary education should be provided free, at public expense and under public control, for everyone who could not afford or did not want private schooling.

Even though the Constitution had relegated control of education to the states, the impetus for such public schooling came from the federal government, in particular as a result of the enactment of the **Northwest Ordinances** of 1785 and 1787. Concerned with the sale of public lands in the Northwest Territory (which ranged from present-day Ohio to Minnesota), Congress passed the Northwest Ordinance of 1785. Every township was divided into 36 sections, of which one was set aside for the maintenance of public schools. In the Ordinance of 1787, Congress reaffirmed that "religion, morality, and knowledge, being necessary to good government and the happiness of mankind, schools and the means of education shall forever be encouraged."[3]

Arguments for the Common School

After the American Revolution, it was recognized that a democratic government would be only as strong as the people's ability to make intelligent choices, which in turn depended on a basic education for all. It was also argued that education was a natural right, just like the very rights for which the Revolution had been fought. During this period, Benjamin Franklin and Thomas Jefferson suggested educational plans, as did other leaders of the Revolution.

This early period of independence also saw an increased concern with citizenship and nationhood. Leaders perceived that a system of common schooling would strengthen the new nation's unity. An influx of immigrants in the 1840s and 1850s, following a period of upheaval in Europe, further stimulated demand for an educational system that would serve to "Americanize" the waves of foreigners and keep U.S. society stable.

In contrast to European social structure, class membership in America was rather fluid: wealth and social status in this country depended less on the social

> *If a nation expects to be ignorant and free, in a state of civilization, it expects what never was and will never be.*
>
> —THOMAS JEFFERSON (1743–1826),
> Third U.S. President and Author of the
> Declaration of Independence

class into which a person was born. Universal education, one of the key themes of American education, was thus seen by the newly evolving working class as a means of equalizing economic and social opportunities. As a result, another reason given for spreading educational opportunity was that better-educated people would increase productivity and enhance everyone's prosperity while diminishing crime and reducing poverty.

In fact, school materials of the time reflected this argument. Whereas the *New England Primer* reflected the religious orientation of much colonial education, the textbooks of the nineteenth century began a trend toward secular education (another of the seven major themes in the history of American education), emphasizing morality and Americanism. No other book was more popular than the six-volume series of **McGuffey Readers**, which sold more than 100 million copies between 1836 and 1906. Besides training students in (American) English language and grammar, these texts introduced poetry and the writings of statesmen, politicians, moralists, and religious leaders.

Although at this time universal education was meant only for whites, the same arguments advanced by its advocates were used later to extend equal opportunities for education to include racial and ethnic minorities and children with disabilities, to name just a few groups that have been denied equal educational opportunities in the past. The desegregation efforts of the 1960s and 1970s, for example, were based on these very arguments.

Arguments against the Common School

As proper as these thoughts may sound to the modern ear, they often encountered opposition. The arguments against the public common school were based on economics as much as on educational or political principles: Why should one family pay for the education of another family's children? Many people believed that schooling, especially for the poor, should be the responsibility of religious groups. Still others thought that a free public school would gradually weaken or dilute the particular culture or religion that they had sought to establish in America. If ethnic groups mingled together, what would be the fate of each group's native culture and language? Similar concerns are reflected in the current controversies about multicultural and bilingual education, discussed in Chapter 3, "Who Are Today's Students in a Diverse Society?"

Educators also struggled with another question: What was to be done about religious study? The ability of different religious groups to exist together in one school, as in democracy itself, demanded that no one religious group be favored over another. Although many competing proposals were advanced, the common schools finally settled on the teaching of basic moral values such as honesty and sincerity, as a substitute for direct religious instruction. As described in Chapter 8, "What Are the Ethical and Legal Issues Facing Teachers?" the same issues continue to inspire controversy today.

Victory of the Common School

Between 1820 and 1920, the establishment of common schools made steady progress across the United States. By the middle of the nineteenth century and certainly by the end of the Civil War, thanks in large part to the efforts of Horace Mann (who is profiled in the Leaders in Education feature) and other advocates of the common school, the ideal of universal elementary education was generally acknowledged, if not universally practiced. By 1930, 11 states and the District of Columbia had passed compulsory attendance laws in addition to making common schools generally available.

> *The Common School is the greatest discovery ever made by man.*
>
> —HORACE MANN (1796–1859),
> Nineteenth-Century Champion of the
> Common School

As a result of these efforts, between the Civil War and World War I, the number of students in schools grew enormously. In 1870, 57 percent of children between 5 and 18 years old were enrolled in some form of schooling. By 1918, more than 75 percent of all U.S. children in that age range were enrolled.[4] In 1870, average attendance was 45 days per year; in 1918, it had grown to more than 90 days. Thus the hundred years between 1820 and 1920 saw extraordinary growth in the commitment to free, publicly supported, universal education.

PAUSE AND REFLECT

How are the arguments for and against common schools reflected in today's controversies about using vouchers to pay for private or religious schooling?

OTHER DEVELOPMENTS IN ELEMENTARY EDUCATION

European Influences

From Europe came new ideas about education. One of the most far-reaching experiments was the **kindergarten**, or "children's garden," where pleasant children's activities such as songs and stories were used to lay a foundation before formal education began. Friedrich Froebel of Germany developed the first kindergarten in 1837. The first U.S. experiments with this sort of education were actually made before the Civil War, but it was not until 1873 that a public school kindergarten was established in St. Louis, and the idea spread rapidly. Elizabeth Peabody brought Froebel's ideas to the United States and was influential in instituting early childhood education in our country.

European influence also resulted in greater emphasis on the interests of the child in elementary education. Johann Pestalozzi modeled his educational doctrines on a Swiss experimental school at the beginning of the nineteenth century. Pestalozzi attempted to educate the heads, hearts, and hands of his pupils, relying on attitudes of acceptance and love of the individual student to reach large numbers of poor and handicapped children. Among his instructional techniques were *object lessons*, which focused on actual objects and pictures. Pestalozzi also emphasized learning through sense perceptions and sequencing of learning experiences from the known to the unknown. We can still see in American education the influence of many of Pestalozzi's ideas.

German educator Johann Friedrich Herbart, influenced by Pestalozzi's thinking, stressed that the primary purpose of education was moral development. Herbart also established a highly structured mode of teaching that strongly influenced American teachers during the early part of the twentieth century.

Many European thinkers, and American educators influenced by them, believed students could learn best by direct experience—that is, by using their senses and relating new learning to their previous knowledge. As a result, some schools incorporated more physical activity and manual training in their curricula. This innovation was designed not to train technical workers, but rather to complement and round out traditional intellectual instruction. Maria Montessori was particularly influential in developing a curriculum that emphasized learning through the senses for young children.

The theories espoused by Froebel, Pestalozzi, Herbart, and Montessori, among others, entered American education through their influence on issues of curriculum

LEADERS in education

Horace Mann (1796–1859)

(© CORBIS)

Horace Mann was the radical educational reformer of his day. Born in Franklin, Massachusetts, Mann received only the most rudimentary schooling until he was 15. Most of his education was self-acquired, a fact that profoundly influenced his philosophy of education. He studied hard to be admitted to Brown University, where he became a brilliant student.

In 1827, Mann was elected to the Massachusetts House of Representatives. Although a luminous political career was clearly within his grasp, he became committed instead to education and to the use of political methods to bring about educational reform. Asked why he had exchanged the practice of law for education, Mann answered that "the interests of a client are small compared with the interests of the next generation."

Mann strongly believed in the ideals of the common school and championed its cause throughout his career. He saw education as a tool of liberation by which the poor could raise themselves, African Americans could become emancipated, and children with disabilities could adjust to their handicaps. After all, Mann reasoned, education had brought him fame and position. Thus, more than 150 years ago, the idea of social mobility through education was born in America.

For education to be as powerful a force as Mann envisioned it, he thought the school term must be lengthened and teachers' salaries raised. To make learning more relevant and enjoyable, he helped introduce new textbooks designed to illustrate the relationship between knowledge and the practical problems of society. Mann organized libraries in many schools, making books readily available to students. He believed less in the formal curriculum than in individual learning—undoubtedly because of his own self-education.

Mann was intensely interested in teacher preparation, and he believed teachers should serve as intellectual, moral, and cultural models for their communities. He was responsible for the establishment of the Massachusetts Board of Education and for the founding in 1839 of the first public *normal school* (a two-year school chiefly for the training of elementary teachers) in Lexington, Massachusetts. Although the normal school opened with only three students, the concept spread and was widely imitated throughout the country.

Another goal of Mann's was to abolish the cruel floggings that were then routine in the public schools. Most schoolmasters of the day believed flogging was an aid to learning and that it was their duty to drive the "devil" out of their students. Many of them administered from 10 to 20 floggings per day.

Many of Mann's ideas were controversial, but he was most violently denounced for his position on religion in the schools. Although a religious man, he believed religious training belonged outside the schools, which should be run by the state. Because of his views, Mann was attacked from many Boston pulpits.

Mann was regarded as a dreamer and a visionary by many of his colleagues. When he took over the presidency of Antioch College in 1852, it opened its doors to members of all races and religious sects, and admitted women on an equal basis with men; some educators predicted that these measures would promote the collapse of higher education. Were he alive today, Mann might still be fighting for ideas he espoused more than a century ago, because many people have yet to accept these ideas.

and instruction. The emphasis on the child's interest and experience, which was advocated by the progressive educators (described in this chapter and in Chapter 9, "What Are the Philosophical Foundations of American Education?") and remains a strong force in American elementary education, owes much to these European thinkers.

Curriculum Changes

The movement toward comprehensive education that occurred during this time period exemplifies one of the key themes of the history of American education. During the colonial period, it was hardly necessary for a person to know anything beyond the four R's unless he was wealthy and wanted to go on to college. In the early and mid-nineteenth century, the common school curriculum simply expanded on the colonial curriculum. The primary concern, however, was less with religious training and more with the task of obtaining functional knowledge for life after school. Subjects such as spelling, geography, history, and government were added because they were considered important for good citizenship. Instruction in the natural sciences, physical training, and mechanical drawing were also included to provide a complete, well-rounded education.

Consolidation

Although the one-room school had served well in the days of the frontier, in the twentieth century it became clear that the smaller, poorer districts could not provide the educational opportunities available in larger, wealthier ones. As a result, the early 1900s saw a period of consolidation of smaller school districts into larger, unified systems. In 1910, more than half the states allowed such unification. By the 1920s, the growth of industry and the invention of the automobile (and the school bus) had helped consolidate the large number of one-room schools around the country into centrally located, modern facilities that could serve larger areas better than the old district schools did.

The Progressive Education Association

John Dewey (who is discussed more fully in Chapter 9, "What Are the Philosophical Foundations of American Education?") and other educators tried to create new, experimental, child-centered schools in the early 1900s. In 1919, the Progressive Education Association was established in a formalized attempt to reform education according to the following principles:

1. The child should have freedom to develop naturally.
2. Natural interest is the best motive for work.
3. The teacher is a guide, not a taskmaster.
4. A student's development must be measured scientifically, not just by grades.
5. Students' general health and physical development require attention.
6. The school and the home must work together to meet children's needs.
7. The progressive school should be a leader in trying new educational ideas.[5]

The progressive school movement eventually went in several different directions. Some educators argued for letting children do whatever they wanted; others tried to turn the school into a community center for recreation, adult education, and even social reform. Critics ranged from traditionalist advocates of the subject-centered curriculum to some progressives, including Dewey himself, who argued that the ties between society and the child would be broken if children were granted total freedom to do whatever they wanted.

The 1940s brought a rather conservative reaction to the progressivism of the previous generation. Even so, many ideas we take for granted now—such as teaching through student projects, fieldtrips, and non-lecture methods of instruction—were hotly debated innovations that were introduced by progressive educators and managed to survive the retrenchment of that era.

Since World War II

After World War II, the United States' role in world affairs expanded dramatically, thus broadening the scope of educational objectives for the nation's schools. The use of the single textbook was supplemented by a great variety of learning resources. Other major developments in elementary education included the rapid growth of kindergartens and an emphasis on providing special educational programs for children with disabilities.

During the period of the 1950s and 1960s, we were in what was called "the Cold War" with the Soviet Union. In response to the Soviet launch of the space satellite *Sputnik* in 1957, for example, national curriculum projects emphasizing mathematics, science, and social studies were developed and implemented in our elementary schools.

Also during this period, two types of students received major attention from elementary school educators: the gifted and the disadvantaged. (See Chapter 3, "Who Are Today's Students in a Diverse Society?" for more on gifted education and students from poverty backgrounds.) Gifted students received attention because of U.S. concern over the ongoing Cold War with the Soviet Union and the perceived need to produce scientific breakthroughs to ensure U.S. military superiority over the Soviets. As the movement for civil and human rights gained momentum, an increasing number of curriculum reform movements also focused on the "culturally disadvantaged" child. In response to judicial decisions and protests by minority groups, the federal government advanced significant financial aid in an effort to change schools to better address the needs of these children. Compensatory education programs, such as Head Start and Title I of the Elementary and Secondary Education Act, improved the learning of disadvantaged children. (See Chapter 11, "How Are Schools Governed, Influenced, and Financed?" for more details on compensatory education programs.)

As achievement test and Scholastic Aptitude Test (SAT) scores declined during the 1970s, many parents, politicians, and educators argued that the schools had tried to accomplish too much and had lost sight of their basic purposes. A return to the basics seemed to be the cry of the late 1970s and early 1980s. Today, academic rigor continues to be emphasized in the form of content standards, but more programs have been developed to meet the needs of students who are at risk for dropping out. (See Chapter 5, "What Is Taught?" and Chapter 12, "How Should Education Be Reformed?" for more discussion on standards.)

Although a public elementary school education is now available everywhere in the United States, the issues of what constitutes a proper education—how comprehensive it should be, how secular it should remain, and how basic learning should be defined—are far from finally settled. The changing nature of what constitutes the basics of education has been another key theme of the history of American education.

secondary education

Today's *public comprehensive high school* evolved from earlier forms of secondary education that included colonial *grammar schools*, which were designed to either prepare students for college or for particular careers, and private *academies*, which were popular throughout the nineteenth century.

EARLY FORMS

Latin Grammar Schools

In the colonial period, all secondary education—that is, all education beyond the elementary level—served the sole purpose of preparing for entrance to college. The earliest secondary institution was the **Latin grammar school**, whose name gradually came to mean "college preparatory school." The term *prep school* still carries that classical connotation today.

A boy entered a Latin grammar school around age 7 or 8 and spent the next seven years learning Latin and Greek from texts written by ancient Romans, Greeks, or medieval scholars. Much work was memorized, and over three or four years the student learned composition and writing of Latin verses. He also might have given some attention to the study of the Hebrew language and the New Testament.

The first Latin grammar school in the colonies is generally considered to have been the one established in 1635 in Boston. It was public and open to boys of all social classes. The Old Deluder Satan Act of 1647, which required communities of 50 or more families to establish elementary schools, also required communities of 100 or more families to establish Latin schools. At first, Latin grammar schools were found primarily in New England; a bit later, they emerged in the Middle Colonies.

English Grammar Schools

The growth of middle-class businesses in the 1700s led to the demand for a secondary education that would provide practical instruction in everything from navigation and engineering to bookkeeping and foreign languages. To meet this demand, private **English grammar schools** were established. These schools catered to the growing number of students who needed more than elementary instruction but were not interested in preparing for college. Classes were offered at various times and places, sometimes to both girls and boys. Commercial rather than religious subjects were taught. Some subjects, such as music, art, and dancing, were actually not practical, but were meant to train students for socializing in polite company.

Secondary Education for Females

In the 1700s, private venture English grammar schools were more flexible than the Latin grammar schools and, as a result, were the first secondary institutions to accept female students. Depending on the sophistication of the particular school and the preferences of its clientele, girls typically studied the three R's (reading, 'riting, and 'rithmetic), geography, and French, but they also sometimes learned English grammar, history, and Latin. Some practical vocational subjects, such as bookkeeping, were occasionally taught, along with such traditional and socially accepted skills as art and instrumental music.

Because of the somewhat larger number of private venture schools in the Middle Colonies, girls who lived there probably had greater educational opportunities than girls elsewhere. Quaker leaders, including William Penn and French-born Anthony Benezet, were concerned with and supported the education of several deprived groups, such as African Americans and American Indians—and women.

In the South, the daughters of wealthy landowners could receive traditional instruction in the various arts and letters, such as music, dancing, and French, which would give them the social skills appropriate for the lady of a household. By the end of the colonial period, separate class-based education tracks were developed for girls similar to those for boys in the English or Latin grammar schools.

THE ACADEMY

A new type of secondary school, known as an **academy**, emerged during the second half of the eighteenth century. The academy was an attempt to combine Latin and English grammar schools through separate Latin and English departments within one school. Academies were unlike the Latin grammar schools in that the primary language of the academy was English; they were unlike the English grammar schools in that they included classical subjects in the curriculum. Gradually, the academy took the place of both types of school.

Growth of Academies

The number of private academies grew rapidly after the American Revolution, in response to the growing need for practical business training. By 1850, approximately 6,000 academies were in operation.[6] Compared with the Latin grammar schools, the academies included instruction for a larger age range, which on the low end overlapped the curriculum of the common schools and on the upper end sometimes provided instruction that was as extensive as that of colleges. Although academies first focused on practical, useful studies rather than on college preparatory courses, over the years the emphasis shifted back to the classical languages and curriculum. Because they were private institutions, the academies were also at greater liberty to accept girls.

> *The ability to secure an independent livelihood and honorable employ suited to her education and capacities is the only true foundation of the social elevation of woman.*
>
> —CATHARINE BEECHER (1800–1878),
> Nineteenth-Century Champion of
> Female Academies

Female Academies

The real surge of development in education for girls and young women came in the first half of the 1800s, with the growth of academies and seminaries that were established especially for young women. Female academies were established by Emma Willard in Troy, New York (1821); by Catharine Beecher in Hartford, Connecticut (1828); and by Mary Lyon in South Hadley, Massachusetts (1837).

A secondary education acquired at one of these institutions was often the highest level of education women would ever receive. Eventually, some of these academies themselves became colleges, such as Mount Holyoke College and Wheaton College.

The availability of women teachers at low salaries during the late nineteenth century helped keep education costs down but, at the same time, contributed to the low-salary problem that persists even today.

(© CORBIS)

The female academies had to buck the established norms against formal education for women, who in many quarters were still considered intellectually inferior to men. The schools compromised somewhat by offering courses related to home economics in addition to more classical subjects.

In practical terms, the leaders of the women's education movement were committed to two goals. First, they sought to produce women who could handle the domestic chores and challenges of wives and mothers intelligently and wisely so as to "become companions rather than satellites of their husbands."[7] To meet this goal, the curriculum of female academies was designed to include subjects similar, but not identical, to those at men's institutions. Domestic skills were presented as practical applications of the more abstract traditional subjects. Second, women's education was intended to prepare women for life as teachers.

THE PUBLIC HIGH SCHOOL

Although the private academies reflected the democratic independence of the middle class, their tuition and fees effectively ruled out enrollment of members of the poorer working class. In the years following the American Revolution, the growing demand for free public elementary education understandably provided a basis on which to advocate for free secondary education. Such schooling at public expense was the educational system most appropriate for democracy, it was argued, and the only system that could maintain democracy.

> *The ladder was there, "from the gutter to the university," and for those stalwart enough to ascend it, the schools were a boon and a path out of poverty.*
>
> —DIANE RAVITCH,
> Educational Historian

Although by no means universally accepted, the argument for free public high schools was a logical one, based on the inequality of providing elementary schools for everyone but secondary schools only for those who could afford tuition. In 1821, Boston created the first public English high school; a second one, for girls, was established in 1826. Unlike the academies, high schools were governed by the public rather than by private school boards.

The number of public high schools throughout the states increased slowly but steadily as an extension of the common school system. Not everyone favored their spread. Opponents of the idea of public high schools did not dispute the need for common elementary schools, but did argue that secondary school was a luxury and was not within the domain of the taxing authorities. In 1874, in the famous **Kalamazoo** case (*Stuart and Others* v. *School District No. 1 of the Village of Kalamazoo and Others*), the Michigan courts finally ruled that the school district could tax the public to support both high schools and elementary schools. This court case set the precedent for financing public high schools.

Debate over the Secondary Curriculum

In the late nineteenth century, debate shifted from whether public secondary schools should be supported to what the content of the curriculum should be. As remains the case today, guidelines for the curriculum were derived largely from the goals expressed for the schools. One goal was to reduce social tensions and strengthen the democratic form of government by bringing together all social classes and ethnic groups.

Another goal was to provide better preparation for Americans to participate, on graduation, in the full range of industrial occupations. In addition, the high schools were to offer specialized vocational and technical training. At the beginning of the 1800s, the appeal of the academies had been to provide training in studies that prepared students for a practical livelihood and not necessarily for college. By the 1840s, the same goal was being applied to public high schools. Seen in retrospect, the academies were really a link between the earlier grammar school and the later high school. High schools were supposed to provide both a terminal educational experience for most students and a bridge to higher education for those who were capable and chose to pursue further studies.

The Comprehensive High School

To meet these varied purposes, the secondary curriculum underwent considerable revisions between the Civil War and World War I. The basic mathematics courses in arithmetic, geometry, and algebra tended to be taught in a more commercial and practical context. American literature began to compete with English literature, and commercial English was added to the study of literary English. The classical languages continued to give way to modern foreign languages. In the sciences, physiology, chemistry, physics, botany, and astronomy were joined by meteorology, zoology, forestry, agriculture, and geology. Physical education was added to the curriculum. In social studies, the number of courses in American history grew, although European history continued to be central. Civics and citizenship were added to history. Moral philosophy fell away completely and was replaced by purely commercial courses such as typing, stenography, commercial law, home economics, industrial arts, and manual training (wood and metal working).[8] The result was the institution known today as the **public comprehensive high school**, which embodies the notion of comprehensive education, another of the key themes of American education.

During the twentieth century, public comprehensive high schools continued to spread. Between 1890 and 2010, the number of students in public high schools increased as a percentage of all students attending public school, from 1.6 percent to 29 percent.[9]

GROWTH OF JUNIOR HIGH AND MIDDLE SCHOOLS

For some time, educators debated the best way to divide grade levels for elementary and secondary training. The main question was when to stop teaching basic skills and start teaching content: Should there be eight elementary grades and four secondary school grades, or six elementary grades and six secondary grades, or some other arrangement?

In an attempt to resolve these issues, educators began to experiment with various ways to reorganize the grades. Finally, in the school year 1909–10, in both Columbus, Ohio, and Berkeley, California, a separate program was established for the intermediate grades 7, 8, and 9. This new grouping was called **junior high school**. By 1926, more than 800 school systems had a six–three–three organization, and that pattern became the dominant one.[10]

Since the 1960s, the system of five elementary–three intermediate–four secondary grades has become increasingly popular, with a **middle school** being home to grades 6, 7, and 8 rather than a junior high school. Advocates argue that middle schools have significant advantages over junior high schools. For one thing, they offer a unique environment where 10- to 13-year-olds are free to grow up at their own rates and where attention is focused on the needs of this age group rather than on mimicking the high school's emphasis on academic and sports competition, as is often the case with junior high schools. Because of the earlier onset of puberty in today's children, sixth-graders may be better served in a school designed for early adolescents in grades 6, 7, and 8 than in an elementary school. Additionally, giving the ninth grade, which is still considered the first year in the college entrance sequence, to the high school frees middle schools to try new programs and new approaches without having to make them specifically applicable to college preparation.

Since the mid-1980s, the United States has made a deepening national commitment to improving the education of its early adolescents, with a strong emphasis on personal growth and development. To encourage this kind of personal growth, middle schools often use interdisciplinary team teaching, block scheduling, advisory homerooms, and exploratory activities and courses.

At least one report has questioned whether students of this age should be in separate schools.[11] A 2004 report from the RAND Corporation portrayed the middle school years as a time when American adolescents feel unsafe, socially isolated, and academically unchallenged, and it called for a reconsideration of stand-alone middle schools. The RAND report relied on research indicating that young teens do better in K–8 schools than in schools that require a transition to an intermediary school. Additionally, international comparison studies have revealed that the relative performance of U.S. students in mathematics and sciences declines from elementary school to middle school, and national tests of proficiency show that the majority of eighth-graders fail to reach proficiency in mathematics, reading, and science.

Teachers are the key to what goes on in the classroom. In the past, many states permitted teachers with either elementary or secondary teaching licenses to teach in middle school, but now more of them are upping the academic coursework required of elementary school teachers who want to teach in middle schools in an effort to refocus the middle school curriculum on academic subject matter. A number of states have broadened the licensure eligibility of secondary teachers to allow them to teach levels as low as the sixth grade. Thirty-three states also offer teacher licenses specifically for middle school that focus on both adolescent development and academic subject-matter preparation. The RAND study suggests that relatively few teachers obtain this type of licensure; only 12 to 25 percent of teachers have specialized training in middle-grades education.[12]

SECONDARY EDUCATION TODAY

Look at the pictures of the two secondary classrooms below, one taken in the late 1800s and the other from today. In what ways are they similar? How are they different? The most remarkable observation made about secondary education today is how little it has changed over the last 100 years. There have been changes, of course, but they have been small relative to the dramatic changes that have occurred in American living patterns, values, technologies, and careers. The curriculum revolves

(© Bettman/CORBIS)

(© Bob Daemmrich)

Compared to the changes that have occurred in most of society, the changes in high schools over the past 100 years have been small.

around subjects that are taught by specialists and are not very different from the subjects offered in schools during World War I.

The reason for this consistency relates to the basic structure of the high school. Its organizing framework, which was initially developed in the nineteenth century, persists today across all regions of the United States. High schools are complicated organizations, requiring considerable orchestration to work efficiently. A change in one part of the system means that other parts must change in tandem. As a result, relatively little change occurs. (Chapter 12, "How Should Education Be Reformed?" examines recent efforts at structural or system-wide reform.)

PAUSE AND REFLECT

1. What made the development of the American secondary school so unique in the history of the world?

2. How would you group the grade sequence from elementary to secondary school? Why?

---

private education

Private schools have always been part of American education. For more than 150 years, until the growth of the common school movement in the early 1800s, most education in America was private. Historically, private schools have served three major purposes, providing (1) instruction for various religious denominations, (2) an exclusive education for the wealthy, and (3) an alternative for any group that finds the available forms of education unsatisfactory.

Since the middle of the nineteenth century, by far the largest private school enrollments have been in parochial schools run by the Roman Catholic Church. The earliest Catholic schools existed primarily in the Spanish-speaking Southwest and in French-speaking Louisiana. After 1840, however, Irish and Italian immigration increased the support of Catholic institutions in the North and East. The total number of Catholic schools grew from about 100 in 1840 to about 3,000 in the 1880s, to 8,000 in 1920, and to more than 13,000 in the early 1960s. From that point, however, many Catholic schools have closed. Today, the number of Catholic schools is slightly less than 7100.[13]

In terms of enrollment, Catholic schools now have a total student membership of about 2.12 million, compared with an estimated 1.93 million students in other religious schools and an estimated 986,000 in nonsectarian private schools.[14] There are more than 33,700 private schools, with a total enrollment of about 5.1 million, or about 10 percent of all students in U.S. schools. About 80 percent of private schools have a religious orientation.[15]

Chapter 13, "What Are Your Job Options in Education?" offers more information about teaching opportunities in private schools.

The steady reduction in the percentage of private school students in the nineteenth and early twentieth centuries was not merely a sign of public school strength; it also reflected outright discrimination and pressure against those who wanted to be "different." In an extreme case following World War I, Nebraska

(T) F

The great majority of private schools in the United States have a religious affiliation. Nonsectarian private schools comprise only 20 percent of all private schools.

passed a law prohibiting the teaching of German in either public or private schools. However, in 1922, the U.S. Supreme Court ruled that a state could not interfere with the prerogative of parents to educate their children as they see fit—in this case, at a private school that taught the German language—simply on the grounds of desiring to "foster a more homogeneous people with American ideals."[16]

When, in 1925, an Oregon law required all children to attend public school, a Roman Catholic school and another private school successfully challenged the law on the grounds that their Fourteenth Amendment rights were being threatened. In a landmark decision in *Pierce* v. *The Society of Sisters*, the Supreme Court overturned the Oregon law, holding that the act "unreasonably interferes with the liberty of parents and guardians to direct the upbringing and education of children under their control."[17]As a consequence of this decision, nonpublic schools survived efforts to eliminate them.

Public schools have clearly become the principal mode of education in America. Nevertheless, private education has remained an important alternative for about 10 percent of the population. This fact reflects a paradox. On the one hand, from the early days private schools have represented the freedom of immigrant groups to pursue life in America and to educate their children as they choose. That privilege was essential to the young democracy and still represents a basic freedom of choice in America. On the other hand, some argue that private education supports a caste system that is, in principle, undemocratic. The very existence of private forms of education can be viewed as an implied criticism either of the quality of public education or of its availability on equal terms to all comers, irrespective of class, religion, or race. As discussed in detail in Chapter 12, "How Should Education Be Reformed?" this issue has become more prominent as school voucher plans expand to include private and religious school options.

The picture of American education that we have drawn up to now has been quite rosy because the educational achievements of this country over the past 350 years are clearly impressive. There is, however, a less pleasant side to the picture. The history of education provides insight into people's values in general, and the educational experience of minorities tends to reflect how a society relates to them. The somewhat idealized image of the melting pot begins to break down when we look at the experience of non-white groups.

PAUSE AND REFLECT

1. Do you believe the role of private education is likely to increase, decrease, or stay the same in the upcoming years? Why?

2. What are the advantages and disadvantages of private education versus public education?

education of minorities

The United States is a multiracial, multiethnic, and multiclass society. Indeed, many people consider it to be one of the most successful mixed societies the world has ever seen. Even so, it is far from perfect, and many children born into poor or minority-group families face severe disadvantages in their attempts to live decent lives and to climb the ladder of success. Schooling is intended to help individuals in this process.

Traditionally, however, ethnic minorities such as African Americans, Hispanic Americans, American Indians, and Asian Americans have not been given equal educational opportunity in America. Not until the late nineteenth century, for example, did the federal government make any serious effort to provide education for American Indians. Many groups struggled throughout the nineteenth and twentieth centuries to claim their share of the growing access to education that developed for the majority of white students in America. American society is still suffering today from the effects of educational neglect of various minority groups.

In our coverage of the education of minorities, we often discuss members of a minority group as though they were a homogeneous subgroup of Americans. In reality, the terms *African Americans, Asian Americans, Hispanic Americans,* and *American Indians* encompass many ethnic, national, and linguistic groups. Although it is convenient to use these broader terms, we should not forget that great diversity exists within each subgroup.

EDUCATION OF AFRICAN AMERICANS

For African Americans, the struggle for equal access to schooling and education paralleled the growth of education for the majority, beginning with efforts to simply provide schools. Efforts throughout the twentieth century focused next on offering a broader variety of curriculum options to African American students, and then on removing legal obstacles to equality of education.

Before the Civil War

As is true of colonial education generally, the earliest motivation to educate African Americans was religious. In New England, the Reverend Cotton Mather started an evening school for slaves as early as 1717. In the South, the first attempts to educate African Americans were carried out by clergy, particularly English representatives of the Society for the Propagation of the Gospel in Foreign Parts. To dubious slave owners, ministers defended the education of slaves not only as a religious duty to save their souls but also because conversion to Christianity, it was believed, would make them more docile.[18]

In the North, schools were established for free African Americans. In 1731, Anthony Benezet, a French-born Quaker, started a school for slave and free African American children in Philadelphia. In 1774, another school was begun by Benjamin Franklin, as president of the Abolitionist Society. In 1787, an African Free School was established in New York City, with an enrollment of 40 students, which grew to more than 500 by 1820. The city provided funds in 1824 and took over the school in 1834, thus providing education for African Americans before many white children were receiving it.

Yet conditions were not all bright in the North. In 1833, Prudence Crandall, a white schoolmistress in Canterbury, Connecticut, began to take in African American girls. The villagers boycotted the school, threw manure into its well, and tried to burn it down. Finally, a mob broke the windows, and the school was closed.[19]

In the South, following slave rebellions in the early 1800s, states gradually prohibited altogether the teaching of African American children, whether slave or free. Some slaves were taught to read by favorably disposed masters. More generally, slave owners reasoned that reading would lead to thinking, and thinking would lead to the desire for freedom. As the Civil War approached, abolitionist agitation often emerged from the few liberal colleges

> *Prejudices, it is well known, are most difficult to eradicate from the heart whose soil has never been loosened or fertilized by education; they grow there, firm as weeds among stones.*
>
> —CHARLOTTE BRONTË (1816–1855),
> Nineteenth-Century Novelist (from Jane Eyre)

that allowed the enrollment of African American students, such as Oberlin College in Ohio and Bowdoin College in Maine.

The Late Nineteenth Century

In the period following the Civil War, the seeds for the education of African Americans that had been sown before the war slowly began to sprout. During the period of Reconstruction, from 1865 into the 1870s, the federal government, through the Freedmen's Bureau and, in the former Confederacy, an occupying army, attempted to promote African American voting registration and schooling. Help also came from private and religious philanthropies in the North. Because it was hoped that whites also would benefit from these endeavors, schooling was advocated for the general public as well. Despite these efforts, the common school movement remained weakest in the South. At first, most whites there refused to participate not only in integrated schools but also in segregated schools, both of which they believed the northern carpetbaggers were forcing on them.

By the end of Reconstruction, southern whites began to allow the existence of separate schools for African Americans. African American enrollment in the schools, which had been only 2 percent of the school-age children in 1850, reached 10 percent by 1870 and 35 percent by 1890, although it dropped somewhat after that during a period of severe repression by the new white state governments.[20] During this period, "Jim Crow" laws were passed, separating African Americans from whites in all areas of life.

Into these conditions, a young African American teacher named Booker T. Washington (1856–1915) was called to start an African American normal school in Tuskegee, Alabama, in 1881. Originally named the Tuskegee Normal School for Colored Teachers, it was later renamed the Tuskegee Institute. In Tuskegee, Washington found only a few students, no buildings or classrooms, and a hostile white community. Washington, who had been born a slave, thought that the traditional curriculum of the classics would neither prepare his students

The Tuskegee Normal School was established in 1881 by Booker T. Washington.

to help other African Americans learn nor help ameliorate the tensions with the white community. Believing strongly in the idea of learning by doing, Washington instructed his students to build the school themselves. In this process, they learned practical skills, grew produce that could be sold to the white community, and in general showed the whites that African Americans could be productive members of society. Washington gradually came to be considered the outstanding African American leader of the time by the white establishment.

> *Education must not simply teach work— it must teach life.*
>
> —W. E. B. DU BOIS (1868–1963),
> African American Civil Rights Activist

Over time, a growing number of young African Americans who, unlike Washington, had not been born into slavery came to believe that Washington's conciliatory policy of training for menial positions in white society would not benefit African American people in the long run. They suggested that, although practical training was necessary, an intellectually sound and academically rich program of study must also be established for the "talented tenth" of the student body, who would form the African American intellectual leadership. This was the view of W. E. B. Du Bois (1868–1963), an African American intellectual and scholar who held a doctorate from Harvard.

In 1862, the U.S. Congress passed the **Morrill Act**. This legislation granted each state a minimum of 30,000 acres of federal land with the proviso that the income from the rent or sale of these lands must be used to establish colleges for the study of agriculture and mechanical arts. A total of 6 million acres of federal land were donated to the states. The resulting land-grant institutions, such as the University of Illinois, Texas A & M, and Michigan State University, became the great multipurpose state universities that now enroll hundreds of thousands of students from all segments of society.

In 1890, Congress enacted a second Morrill Act that increased the endowment of land to the original land-grant colleges but forbade the granting of money to a college with an admission policy that discriminated against non-whites unless a separate facility for African Americans existed nearby. This second Morrill Act provided federal support to states to create "separate but equal" colleges for African Americans. As a result of this legislation, a number of so-called **1890 institutions** were created for the higher education of African Americans. Many of these historically African American colleges, such as Florida A & M and North Carolina A & T, still exist today, albeit now as integrated institutions.

In 1896, in the case of ***Plessy v. Ferguson***, the U.S. Supreme Court upheld the constitutionality of "separate but equal" accommodations for African Americans. Although the ruling originally referred to seating in a railroad car, it was quickly extended to the schools. The practical significance of this ruling was its federal sanction of the legal separation of African American schoolchildren from white children, most notably in the South—a condition that would persist for the next 58 years.

The Twentieth Century

The fact that southern schools for African Americans were not equal to those for whites is woefully clear from looking at financial expenditures alone. In 1912, the southern states, as a group, paid white teachers slightly more than $10 per white child in school but paid African American teachers less than $3 per African American child. In the 1930s, in 10 southern states, African American children accounted for 34 percent of the school population but received only 3 percent of the funds available for school transportation. Discrimination also existed in the distribution of federal funds, particularly in vocational education, the largest and most important educational program subsidized by the federal government.[21]

VOICES from the classroom

Teaching in Segregated Schools

Mary Reese is retired and lives in Charlottesville, Virginia. She was an elementary school teacher for 11 years before becoming a principal. She later served as assistant superintendent of schools in Charlottesville, Virginia, and associate director of the American Association of School Administrators.

College diploma and job contract in hand, I headed to my first teaching job in a small, rural, segregated school. The advice, help, and insights provided by the experienced principal and teachers that first year convinced me that teaching was indeed a good career choice. It mattered not that the "new" books they were excited about receiving turned out to be the "used" books from the white school and that the children had to walk fairly long distances to get to school because there was no bus transportation provided for them. The belief that a new school year meant a new opportunity to help children created an unbelievable aura of new beginnings.

I later became a teacher in a segregated school in a large urban school district—a school serving students from three public housing units. Again, "new" books, except for newly adopted state textbooks, included used books from other schools. School repairs, if made at all, were taken care of after the needs of the white schools had been attended to.

One of the most powerful insights from both of these experiences was how important the teacher was to the life of the students and the community in which they lived. I taught more than the basic academic skills to students. I assumed the role of family social worker, financial advisor, and any other roles necessary to help students and their parents believe that the school was there for them. I had to convince the student and parent that getting a good education was the key to a better future. I took it as my responsibility to help them learn that segregation was only a barrier if we let it become one.

I became the principal of that urban school after 10 years of teaching in it. Shortly thereafter, the school was integrated, and we became a mix of low-income African American, and middle-class white students. It was bittersweet to see much of the maintenance work that had been requested, but never done, suddenly being taken care of without my having to submit work order requests. It was humiliating to have white parents come and give the woodwork and cafeteria equipment "the white-glove treatment." But it was as equally rewarding to know that their fears would be unfounded because of my belief that the school should be a clean and safe place for any student and staff member assigned there. Because we already had excellent teachers, a strong academic program, and a belief in and requirement of strong parental involvement, integration proceeded more smoothly than in some of the other schools.

Most northern states did not have **de jure school segregation**—that is, segregation by law. Nevertheless, the crowding of African Americans into isolated neighborhoods often resulted in **de facto** segregation—that is, segregation resulting primarily from residential patterns. Furthermore, large numbers of southern African American children who migrated with their parents to northern cities often had to be demoted because they had not mastered the same amount of material as their northern counterparts. Generally, even in the North, African American teachers taught African American children. For a vivid, firsthand description of one educator's experiences in segregated schools, read this chapter's Voices from the Classroom feature.

Although these conditions persisted in varying degrees through the 1940s, some gains were achieved. For example, the average daily attendance of African American children increased and approached that of white students. The salaries of African American teachers also increased, reducing the economic gap between African American and white teachers with equal training.

In the late 1940s, the National Association for the Advancement of Colored People (NAACP) began taking cases dealing with inequality in educational opportunities to the courts. Beginning with universities rather than elementary schools, the NAACP succeeded in having the courts rule that various law school facilities for African Americans were clearly unequal to those for whites.

The stage was then set for the precedent-shattering case of **Brown v. Board of Education of Topeka** (1954), in which the Supreme Court ruled that separate educational facilities are inherently unequal and that laws requiring white and non-white students to go to different schools were illegal. This decision held that segregated schools are inherently unequal because the effects of such schools are likely to differ. Thus a new component was introduced into the theme of educational opportunity: equality of educational opportunity became defined in terms of the effects—rather than the provision—of schooling. Before *Brown*, the community and educational institutions were expected only to provide equal resources such as teachers, facilities, and materials. Responsibility for the best use of those resources lay with the child and the child's family. In the *Brown* decision, the Supreme Court found that even if the facilities and teacher salaries provided were identical, "equality of educational opportunity" would not exist in segregated schools. In the decades since then, many people have come to consider it the responsibility of the educational institution, not the child, to create achievement.

Desegregation Efforts

In *Brown* v. *The Board of Education*, the Supreme Court concluded that *de jure* school segregation violated the Fourteenth Amendment of the Constitution. Early desegregation efforts, therefore, were aimed at eliminating *de jure* segregation. Throughout the 1960s and into the 1970s, many school systems, often in response to specific court orders, also attempted to reduce or eliminate *de facto* school segregation. As a result, many school districts underwent desegregation efforts. What have been the results of these efforts? Several researchers have concluded that desegregated schools have accomplished more than mere educational reform—that is, African American students who attended integrated schools experienced desegregation in several aspects of adult life, including attending predominantly white colleges and universities, working in desegregated settings, and living in desegregated neighborhoods.[22]

> (T) F
>
> Efforts to desegregate the public schools during the 1960s through the 1980s came as a result of a Supreme Court ruling.
>
> The Supreme Court's ruling in *Brown* v. *Board of Education* (1954) that *de jure* segregation violated the Fourteenth Amendment, paved the way to desegregate the schools.

Busing. Although these long-range findings are quite positive, desegregation efforts have produced some negative results. One major problem has concerned busing. Busing students to desegregated schools was one of the most inflammatory issues in education in the 1970s and 1980s. Emotions on the topic often ran very high—so high, in fact, that white parents sometimes slashed bus tires, burned buses, and physically prevented buses from running to avoid having their children bused to other schools.[23]

Busing to achieve desegregation has experienced mixed success. One of the most successful busing plans began in Berkeley, California, in 1968, without any disruptive incidents; standardized test scores subsequently indicated that white, African American, and Asian American students all made better progress after desegregation.[24] In many other communities, attempts to desegregate the schools by busing met with tremendous community resistance.

By the end of the 1980s, court-ordered busing was no longer the preferred method for integrating the schools. Busing, of course, was never an end in itself. It was merely one means of integrating society, and polls indicate that even opponents

Efforts to desegregate schools, especially busing white children to desegregated schools, met with stiff opposition from white parents in some communities, including those in the north.

(Barney Sellers/Commercial Appeal /Landov)

of involuntary busing agree that our society needs to be integrated. However, that goal remains elusive.

Big-City Desegregation. A major obstacle to desegregating big-city public schools is that the minority percentage of inner-city populations has increased dramatically during the past several decades. In part, this trend has been the result of "white flight"—the exodus of white residents as parents have chosen to move to the suburbs or place their children in private schools. (This term is somewhat misleading, however, as not only whites are fleeing the city schools; middle-class African Americans are also leaving to give their children a chance to be educated in better schools.) Today, cities such as New York, Los Angeles, Chicago, Detroit, Atlanta, Houston, and Dallas have school minority enrollments over 90 percent.[25] How can schools in major cities be desegregated when the percentage of racial minority students is growing and the percentage of white students is decreasing?

In addition, several Supreme Court decisions during the 1990s dramatically reversed school desegregation plans ordered by lower courts, thereby eliminating much of the pressure to desegregate schools. In these rulings, the Court essentially conceded that practical limits exist as to what a federal court can do to remedy prior discrimination; once school districts have corrected the initial racial imbalances, they are not required to remedy subsequent imbalances caused by demographic changes. In a 2007 ruling, the Supreme Court, by a five-to-four margin, further backed away from desegregation efforts by striking down plans in Seattle and Louisville that sought to maintain school-by-school diversity by identifying students by race and assigning them to schools based on that classification.

Recent Developments. Increasingly segregated residential patterns and the slackening of legal pressures to desegregate during the 1980s and 1990s have led to a phenomenon known as **resegregation**, in which schools are becoming more segregated again. Evidence suggests that resegregation of African Americans has reached the levels seen before 1970. The average white student now attends a school that is 77 percent white, whereas the average African American student attends a school that is 29 percent white.[26] In large urban centers, the percentage of African American students is much higher.

Although many political and educational leaders remain committed to desegregated schools, others are questioning whether integration is an idea whose time has passed. In many communities, these leaders, who are typically members of minority groups, call for shifting the emphasis from integrating schools to improving the quality of one-race neighborhood schools. They have lost faith in the idea that desegregation is the answer to calls for better schools. These supporters of resegregation argue that it demeans African American children to believe that they can learn only when they sit next to white children in desegregated schools. Some also think that resegregation will protect African American culture from the gradual eradication that would occur in an integrated setting. Further, they argue, resegregation would relieve African Americans of the disproportionate burden they have carried under most desegregation arrangements.

Supporters of desegregation counter with the argument that most parents are mainly interested in good schools for their own children, not for the children of others. Accordingly, they say, whites will support only African American students who happen to be in school with their own children. Thus, if African American children are to benefit educationally, they need to attend school with white children. Otherwise, resegregation forces poor, largely African American school districts in low-tax-base cities to continue their losing struggle to find educational money that they don't have. As one advocate for desegregation says, "[African Americans] who favor resegregation are doing whites the great favor of relieving both their guilty consciences and their pocketbooks."[27]

> "
> *Segregation was wrong when it was forced by white people, and I believe it is still wrong when it is requested by black people.*
>
> —CORETTA SCOTT KING (1927–2006),
> Wife of Martin Luther King and Civil Rights Leader

Desegregation versus Integration. Another point must be made before we close this discussion—namely, desegregation does not necessarily lead to integration. True integration is a very human process that can occur only after desegregation has gone into effect. It happens when people from different racial and ethnic backgrounds learn to be comfortable with one another and to get along together. Integration means ending racial prejudice and respecting ethnic differences. Anyone who has spent time in racially mixed schools, especially high schools, knows that African American and white students who attend the same school can still be extremely distant from one another. Just bringing together students from different racial groups, social classes, and neighborhood backgrounds will not automatically lead to friendship, understanding, and appreciation of one another. As long as the larger society remains segregated, efforts to integrate our schools are likely to produce tension, at least in the short run. Integrating individuals with increasingly diverse racial, cultural, and linguistic backgrounds remains one of the key themes and challenges to schools and society.

PAUSE AND REFLECT

1. Where do you stand on the issue of *de facto* resegregation of urban schools? What, if anything, should be done about it?

2. In what ways did desegregation of American schools work, and in what ways has it failed?

EDUCATION OF AMERICAN INDIANS

As early as 1622, in an ominous foreshadowing of future policies, one colonist wrote back to England that it was easier to conquer the Indians than to civilize them.[28] The education of American Indians traditionally received less public attention than that of African Americans because American Indians were considered an impediment to westward expansion; they were far from major population centers; and their dealings were largely with the federal government.

Initially the education of American Indians, like that of African Americans, had a religious purpose. Once they had been put on reservations, American Indians received schooling from missionaries, who attempted to "civilize" them through the three R's and, of course, the fourth R—religion. In the 1890s, these missionary schools were gradually replaced by government boarding schools, which tried to forcefully assimilate American Indians into the mainstream culture by prohibiting them from speaking their native language and teaching them skills associated with white society, such as farming and mechanical skills for boys and domestic chores for girls. Little emphasis was placed on academics.

The people who had been living on the North American continent for 20,000 years finally became American citizens in 1924—but that did not mean they controlled their own education. The federal government, through the Bureau of Indian Affairs (BIA), directed the education of American Indians until the mid-1970s. During this time, American Indian participation was virtually ignored, as was acknowledgment of their own culture in their educational programs.

By 1965, American Indians had begun to demand control of their schools, and a few demonstration sites for such tribal schools were funded. These schools were able to include much of the native culture in their curricula, but they remained financially dependent on the federal government, which meant limited instructional materials and lower-paid teachers than in many public schools.

Between 1972 and 1975, Congress enacted three bills that affected American Indian education and self-determination. These bills encouraged the establishment of community-run schools, offered grants to develop culturally relevant and bilingual curriculum materials, and established an advisory council made up of American Indians. The Department of the Interior's BIA is still actively involved in educational matters, though it now acts in a supportive rather than directive capacity. The federal government has shifted much responsibility for educating American Indians

> *My son, Wind Wolf, is not an empty glass coming into your class to be filled. He is a full basket coming into a different environment and society with something special to share. Please let him share his knowledge, heritage, and culture with you and his peers.*
>
> **—ROBERT LAKE-THOM,**
> Author and Native Healer in the
> Seneca and Cherokee Tribes

At the beginning of the twentieth century, special schools for American Indians, such as the Carlisle Indian School in Carlisle, Pennsylvania, taught basic skills, such as mending clothes, to students.

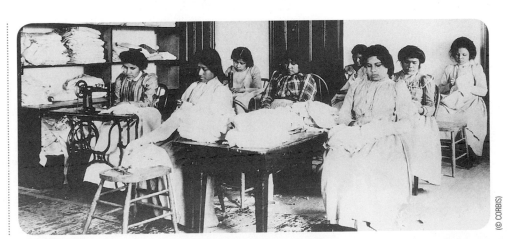

(© CORBIS)

from the BIA and tribal schools to public schools. The BIA runs 183 schools, primarily located in Arizona, New Mexico, North Dakota, and South Dakota. Approximately two-thirds of the schools are operated by Indian tribes or tribal organizations under grants or contracts with the BIA. The schools serve 42,000 students—about 8 percent of all American Indian students enrolled in K–12 schools in the United States.[29] The other 92 percent of American Indian students in grades K–12 attend public schools.

This trend may have helped reduce the isolation of American Indian students. However, because American Indian community involvement in public education is slight, the move toward public schooling has resulted in a loss of the limited control American Indians had begun to exercise over the education their children receive.

Today the education of the American Indian population in the United States, about 644,000 students, is still plagued by problems such as poverty, parental alcoholism, underachievement, absenteeism, overage students, and a high dropout rate. Indeed, American Indian students drop out of school more often than members of any other racial group except Hispanics.[30] Many American Indians believe that a culturally appropriate curriculum is needed to overcome these deficiencies and reduce the cultural discontinuities between home and school. Only a small percentage of American Indians students have teachers from their same tribe; most of their teachers are white females. One evaluation of American Indian schools concluded that they should integrate their programs into a whole-school, standards-based reform effort and increase the participation of the American Indian community.

The No Child Left Behind Act of 2001 poses challenges to American Indian students who have a long history of struggling on standardized tests, particularly because of their limited English proficiency. States can craft native-language versions of the tests, but that is unrealistic for many states because of the many dialects spoken. Many American Indian schools also face a tough time in meeting the law's mandate that all teachers be "highly qualified." In addition, educators worry about the federal law's call for "scientifically based" research in creating school curricula and instructional practices. Most of the methods of integrating native culture and language into classroom teaching have not undergone the same level of research scrutiny as those used with non-American Indian populations, creating concern among American Indian educators that these methods will wither away.

EDUCATION OF HISPANIC AMERICANS

As with American Indians, the first contact Spanish-speaking people had with the United States was often a result of annexation and warfare. Although they have lived in the continental United States for more than 400 years, Hispanic Americans came into substantial contact with whites about 200 years ago, and almost from the beginning there was a cultural clash. Hispanic American children first attended religious mission schools, which were gradually replaced by secular public schools. In the process, the Spanish language and Hispanic American culture were subjected to a type of discrimination that was perhaps less blatant than that against African Americans, but just as pervasive. The common school of the nineteenth and twentieth centuries, although it opened educational and social opportunities for some minority students, often sealed off those opportunities for Hispanic Americans. Hispanic children tended to receive lower scores than white children on English-language intelligence quotient (IQ) tests, which not only were written in a language that was not their own, but also reflected white middle-class values. All of these factors combined to reinforce an image of Hispanic American children as intellectually inferior to their white counterparts.

▶❚❚ **TeachSource VIDEO CASE**

Bilingual Education: An Elementary Two-Way Immersion Program

Go to the Education CourseMate website to watch the video clips, study the artifacts in the case, and reflect on the following questions:

1. How does the scenario depicted in this case compare with the historical treatment of Hispanic students described in this chapter?

2. How can you begin developing the skills you will need to work effectively with a diverse group of students?

Today, almost 70 percent of Hispanic American students speak Spanish at home.[31] These students are likely to have parents who have less education than those who speak mostly English at home. Children whose parents have not completed high school, and who do not speak English, are less likely to receive at home the background skills and knowledge to begin school successfully. Schools need to develop programs to address the needs of these students, particularly those with limited English proficiency.

Since the 1940s, the courts have acknowledged that *de facto* segregation exists between white and Hispanic American schoolchildren and have required corrective integration plans. The 1965 Elementary and Secondary Education Act provided new support to the education of Hispanic Americans, just as it did to the education of American Indians. Another response has been the establishment of bilingual education programs to provide students with instruction in their native tongue at the same time they learn English. The goal of such bilingual education programs is for students to enter the English-language curriculum at the appropriate age levels for their grades. However, as mentioned in Chapter 3, "Who Are Today's Students in a Diverse Society?" bilingual education programs have fallen out of favor in recent years and have been replaced with English immersion programs in such states as California and Arizona. (The Video Case *Bilingual Education: An Elementary Two-Way Immersion Program* shows one current approach to teaching children whose first language is Spanish, known as two-way bilingual education.)

Although significant progress has been made, much concern remains about the education of Hispanics in the United States. For example, the high school completion rate for Hispanic Americans over the age of 25 is only 62 percent, compared with 92 and 83 percent for whites and African Americans, respectively.[32] Approximately 13 percent of Hispanic adults have earned bachelor's degrees, compared with 33 and 20 percent for whites and African Americans, respectively.[33] Furthermore, reading and mathematics proficiencies are significantly lower for the Hispanic American population in comparison with the white population. The public schools have not served these students well, and the cost of this failure in human and economic terms is enormous.

Hispanic American youth represent the fastest-growing segment of the U.S. population; about one in five children in the public schools is Hispanic. Demographers project that increasingly higher percentages of Hispanic American students will be enrolled in public schools in the twenty-first century, so the schools' responses to these students' needs will have important consequences for society. The problem is made even more acute by the estimated 12 to 20 million illegal immigrants living in the United States. Without increased educational attainment, Hispanic Americans, both legal and illegal, will be relegated to low-skill jobs and locked into the lowest socioeconomic brackets, with negative consequences for all Americans.

EDUCATION OF ASIAN AMERICANS

The diversity of Asian Americans is evident from the historical beginnings of different groups of Asian Americans in the United States, and it persists in educational issues today. The three largest groups of Asian Americans are individuals of Chinese, Filipino, and Japanese heritage.

▶❙❙ **TeachSource VIDEO CASE**

Diversity: Teaching in a Multiethnic Classroom

Go to the Education CourseMate website to watch the video clips, study the artifacts in the case, and reflect on the following questions:

1. How does the scenario depicted in this case stand in contrast to the historical treatment of Asian Americans, both in schools and in the larger U.S. society, that is described in this chapter?

2. In one of the bonus videos, the two teachers talk about how to make the best use of the limited number of students with strong Japanese-language reading skills in the class. If a class had an even smaller percentage of students who shared a language other than English, could a teacher carry out a project like this one? How? In what other ways might a teacher incorporate the cultures of English-language learners into the curriculum in a way that was useful for all students?

Discrimination against early Asian Americans was rampant, especially in the West, where most Asian Americans originally settled. Although immigrants from China, the Philippines, and Japan often entered the United States to fill the need for hard-labor jobs, whites resented the competition for employment. Exclusionary laws limiting immigration of these groups were passed in the late 1800s and early 1900s.

School segregation of Chinese American children in California lasted until at least 1946. Japanese American children in California were forced to attend segregated schools up until World War II. With the outbreak of World War II, the "yellow peril," perceived as emanating from Japanese Americans, resulted in the imprisonment in detention camps of more than 110,000 Japanese Americans, most of whom were American-born citizens. With the end of World War II, discrimination against Asian Americans began to subside. Naturalization rights were eventually extended to resident Asian aliens. (The Video Case *Diversity: Teaching in a Multiethnic Classroom* shows how the teacher of an elementary school class with a large percentage of Japanese students works with the class today.)

Many Asian Americans benefited from greater job opportunities during the post–World War II expansion of the U.S. economy. Previously established immigration restrictions were lifted in 1965, and the influx of Asian immigrants greatly increased. Since the U.S. withdrawal from Vietnam in 1975, enormous numbers of Indochinese immigrants have also journeyed to the United States and entered our school systems.

Asian and Pacific Islanders currently account for approximately 4 percent of all students enrolled in public elementary and secondary schools, and this figure is expected to continue to rise for the foreseeable future. Current census estimates indicate that Asian and Pacific Islanders number roughly 14.5 million, or about 4.5 percent of the U.S. population. It is projected that by the year 2020 this group will reach about 19 million, representing 5.4 percent of the U.S. population.[34]

Owing to the higher educational achievement and income levels of some Asian Americans, this group has often been touted as a "model minority" that has overcome discrimination through hard work, perseverance, and industriousness. This rosy stereotype is misleading, however, and has sometimes contributed to misconceptions and complacency in meeting the educational needs and concerns of Asian American students. The success levels achieved by more recent Asian immigrants have varied because of the range of educational levels and previous socioeconomic circumstances associated with these new Americans.

Many recent Asian American immigrants to the United States have little or no knowledge of the English language. Sixty-four percent, or 1.3 million, Asian students spoke a language other than English at home.[35] This issue creates formidable language and cultural barriers for students entering the U.S. educational system, and it may lead to serious family–school discontinuities, alienation from school, and dropout problems. The Supreme Court established in *Lau* v. *Nichols* (1974) that schools must offer students sufficient special instruction to be afforded equal educational opportunity. (See Chapter 3, "Who Are Today's Students in a Diverse Society?" for more on *Lau* v. *Nichols*.)

Parental and community involvement of Asian Americans in the education process also should be fostered. In part because of the respect traditionally accorded to educators in their native countries, parents of Asian American students often hesitate to intervene when they are dissatisfied with their children's educational progress, instead deferring to the educational system's authority. Another deterrent to parental participation is the fact that a high proportion of Asian American families have two parents employed, a situation that makes attendance at traditional teacher conferences or parent–teacher organization (PTO) meetings difficult. Many communities are making efforts to organize and voice the needs of Asian American students.

As the number of Asian American students continues to grow, it will become increasingly important for teachers and administrators to be knowledgeable about and sensitive to the special problems and needs of Asian American students and their families. To serve these students adequately in our schools, educators must keep in mind that Asian Americans are a changing and complex group whose achievement, aspirations, and learning styles should not be relegated to a simplistic stereotype.

ACCESS AND EQUALITY OF EDUCATIONAL OPPORTUNITY

From our discussion of the education of minority students, it is clear that, even today, large numbers of minority-group students are leaving school without the academic and occupational skills necessary to function effectively in American society. The same is also true of poor students from all ethnic groups. Who—if anyone—is to blame for this situation? The schools? The students? The families? Teachers and administrators? Is the responsibility that of society as a whole, and are the schools merely being made a scapegoat? Talk to five different people, and you will probably hear five different opinions about where blame should be fixed.

At one extreme are those who think the problem resides in the so-called deficiencies of poor and minority children. Their impoverished home life, their particular cultural milieu, English language deficiencies, and even their mental capacities are cited as the sources of their unequal results in school.

At the other extreme are those who claim the problem lies with the schools. Some suggest that the problem is linked to the way schools are governed and financed. Numerous court cases have challenged the school finance systems in various states, charging that when educational spending in rich school districts exceeds that of poor districts by two or three times, students in the poor districts are not getting access to equal educational opportunities. In a number of cases, courts have ordered legislatures to redesign the school finance system. (See Chapter 11, "How Are Schools Governed, Influenced, and Financed?" for more on the topic of equitable school finance.)

Others believe that teaching must be improved, that teachers today neither stimulate nor instruct poor and minority children with the intensity that is needed. Teachers expect these children to do poorly, they claim, and this expectation becomes a self-fulfilling prophecy. As described in Chapter 3, "Who Are Today's Students in a Diverse Society?" this position assumes that it is the school's obligation to diagnose the learner's needs, concerns, and cognitive and affective styles and to adjust its program accordingly. In fact, the No Child Left Behind Act of 2001, which requires schools to report the academic performance of students in various racial and ethnic groups, is intended to close the academic achievement gaps between white and Asian American students on the one hand, and on the other hand among African American, Hispanic American, and American Indian students. Not everyone accepts this assertion, of course. In fact, many argue that the school should do its best to provide equal educational resources for all its students but cannot be held accountable for differences in student learning.

As with most controversies, the real answer probably lies somewhere in between these two extremes: many poor and minority students do come to school with certain deficiencies, but the schools need to learn how to overcome them.

PAUSE AND REFLECT

1. In what ways were the histories of the education of minority groups and of women similar? In what ways were they different?

2. Limited English proficiency seems to be a major problem in increasing educational attainment for several minority groups. What ideas do you have about how this problem should be addressed?

3. Do you agree that equality of educational opportunity should be defined by its effects rather than by its provisions? Why or why not?

TABLE 10.1 Key Events and Curriculum Trends in American Education

Time Period	Key Educational and National Events	Educational Trends/Emphases and Characteristics of Curriculum	Dominant Educational Philosophies
1620–Revolutionary War	1635: Establishment of the Boston Latin grammar school 1647: Massachusetts Old Deluder Satan Act 1687–1690: First edition of the *New England Primer*	Education limited by sex and socioeconomic class. Curriculum emphasized religious training (Bible), moral development, reading, writing, and arithmetic basics.	Perennialism
1770s–1820s	1775–1783: Revolutionary War 1783: Noah Webster publishes *American Spelling Book* 1785, 1787: Northwest Ordinances 1788: U.S. Constitution ratified	Education emphasized literacy to make democracy work. Curriculum emphases included moral development and either practical education for a career or university education.	Perennialism
1820s–1880s	1821: First U.S. public high school 1821: Emma Willard establishes first school for women's higher education 1839: First U.S. public normal school, Lexington, Massachusetts 1860: First U.S. English-language kindergarten 1861–1865: Civil War 1862: First Morrill Act establishes land-grant institutions	Education used to promote "melting pot" assimilation of immigrants and minorities. Curriculum emphases included basic tools of literacy, conservative moral values (*McGuffey Readers*), cultivation of American identity.	Perennialism
1880s–1950s	1890: Second Morrill Act calls for nondiscrimination in college admissions or "separate but equal" institutions 1896: U.S. Supreme Court ruling in *Plessy* v. *Ferguson* establishes separate schools for Whites and Blacks 1914–1918: World War I 1930s: Great Depression 1939–1945: World War II 1944: GI Bill funds higher education for veterans	Child-centered curriculum became popular, emphasizing activities and experiences rather than verbal and literacy skills; cooperative rather than individual learning activities; citizenship; and self-adjustment.	Progressivism Romanticism

TABLE 10.1   Key Events and Curriculum Trends in American Education (Continued)

Time Period	Key Educational and National Events	Educational Trends/Emphases and Characteristics of Curriculum	Dominant Educational Philosophies
1950s–1970s	1954: U.S. Supreme Court ruling in *Brown* v. *Board of Education of Topeka* requires desegregation of schools 1957: Soviet Union launches *Sputnik* 1965: Elementary and Secondary Education Act 1971: U.S. Supreme Court ruling in *Swann* v. *Charlotte–Mecklenberg County* states that busing may be used for desegregation 1972: Title IX 1975: Education for All Handicapped Children Act (Public Law 94–142) 1979: Department of Education established	Curriculum emphases in the 1950s and 1960s included structure of the discipline and the discovery method of teaching, teaching gifted and talented students. Emphases in the 1970s on mainstreaming, multicultural education, career education, and a flexible curriculum with many electives.	Essentialism
1980s	1983: A *Nation at Risk* published	Educational reform; reports issued leading to back-to-basics movement, core curriculum, stronger academic requirements. Inclusion and multicultural education grew.	Essentialism Perennialism
1990s	1990: Americans with Disabilities Act (ADA) 1990: Individuals with Disabilities Education Act (IDEA)	Growing teacher shortage. National Education Association (NEA) and American Federation of Teachers (AFT) merger talks fail. Growing standards movement leads to high-stakes testing. Strong technology emphasis. Growing rejection of bilingual education.	Essentialism
2000 and beyond	2001: No Child Left Behind Act (reauthorization of Elementary and Secondary Education Act) 2002: Supreme Court rules Cleveland's voucher plan does not violate U.S. Constitution 2004: Reauthorization of IDEA 2009: Race to the Top (federal program designed to spur reform in K–12 education)	Federal emphasis on "scientifically based" instructional practices in schools and "highly qualified" teachers.	Essentialism

OUR FINAL WORD

At the beginning of this chapter, we identified seven major themes that have shaped the history of American education and schooling: local control, universal education, public education, comprehensive education, secular education, changing ideas of the basics, and expanding definitions of access and equal opportunity. If you think about the issues raised in earlier chapters of this text, you can see the effect of these themes on contemporary education. For example, the universal and public nature of the educational system strikes at the issue of equal educational opportunity and questions of school finance and governance. Current controversies over the content of education—questions about the secular or sacred nature of the curriculum, debate about the need for standards of learning, and efforts to provide excellence in education without sacrificing equality of opportunity—relate to the concepts of secular, universal, and comprehensive education and the definition of what is "basic." Thus these seven themes continue to play themselves out in our evolving educational system. Table 10.1 lists important dates and events in American education, many of which relate to these seven themes.

WHY TEACH? YOUR FINAL WORD

In your journal or online at this textbook's website, respond to the following questions:

1. Which new piece of information about the history of education in the United States did you find most interesting or disturbing? Why?

2. Which educational legacies from the past are most likely to affect you in your teaching? In what ways?

3. Are you interested in teaching in an urban school district, as opposed to a suburban or rural school district? If you prefer one setting to another, why do you think that is?

KEY TERMS

1890 institutions (336)
academy (328)
Brown v. Board of Education of Topeka (338)
common school (321)
dame school (318)
de facto school segregation (337)
de jure school segregation (337)
district school (319)
English grammar school (327)
equality of educational opportunity (317)
junior high school (330)
Kalamazoo case (329)
kindergarten (323)
Latin grammar school (327)

McGuffey Readers (322)
middle school (330)
Morrill Act (336)
moving school (319)
New England Primer (319)
Northwest Ordinances (321)
Old Deluder Satan Act (319)
Plessy v. Ferguson (336)
private venture school (320)
public comprehensive high school (330)
resegregation (339)
town school (319)
universal education (321)

FOR FURTHER INFORMATION

WEB RESOURCES

Library of Congress. Available at **www.loc.gov**.

Users of this site will find easy access to THOMAS (legislative information), the Library of Congress catalog, and much more. Particularly relevant for the history of American education is the "Learning Page," found under the "Teachers" heading, which provides information on using materials in the American Memory historical collections, as well as lesson plans and links to related web pages.

School: The Story of American Public Education. Available at **www.pbs.org/kcet/publicschool**.

An interesting website, sponsored by PBS, which provides an excellent look at the history of the American public school.

PRINT RESOURCES

K. Tsianina Lomawaima and Teresa L. McCarty, *To Remain an Indian: Lessons in Democracy from a Century of Native American Education* (New York: Teachers College Press, 2006).

The authors critically evaluate U.S. educational policies and practices—from early twentieth-century federal incarnations of colonial education through the contemporary standards movement—in this fascinating portrait of American Indian education over the past century.

Vivian Gunn Morris and Curtis L. Morris, *The Price They Paid: Desegregation in an African American Community* (New York: Teachers College Press, 2007).

Focusing on an African American community in Alabama, the authors document not only the gains but also the significant losses experienced by students when their community school was closed and they were forced to attend a white desegregated school across town.

John Charles Boger and Gary Orfield, eds. *School Resegregation: Must the South Turn Back?* (Chapel Hill, NC: University of North Carolina Press, 2005).

In 13 essays, leading thinkers in the field of race and public education present not only the latest data and statistics on the trend toward resegregation but also legal and policy analysis of why these trends are accelerating, how they are harmful, and what can be done to counter them.

Joel Spring, *Deculturalization and the Struggle for Equality: A Brief History of the Education of Dominated Cultures in the United States*, 6th ed. (New York: McGraw-Hill, 2010).

Spring interprets American history in terms of Anglo-American racism and school policies affecting dominated groups in the United States. In the process, he gives voice to the perspectives of African Americans, Asian Americans, Hispanic/Latino Americans, and Native Americans.

Wayne J. Urban and Jennings L. Wagoner, *American Education: A History*, 4th ed. (New York: Routledge, 2009).

This book is a relatively brief overview of American education, written by well-known scholars.

The Education CourseMate website for this text offers many helpful resources. Go to www.cengagebrain.com to access the TeachSource Video Cases and other TeachSource videos, flashcards, interactive quizzes, the eBook, reflection and enrichment activities, a state standards resource center, and other study aids.

11 how are schools governed, influenced, and financed?

(© Jeff Greenberg / Alamy)

FOCUS POINTS

- Legal responsibility for school governance belongs to the state, though policy decisions and administration have traditionally been delegated to local school boards.

- In addition to local school boards and state governments, many other groups exercise some measure of influence on educational decisions, either through legal authority or through less formal means. These other groups include professional education organizations, parents, teachers, the business community, the federal government, and the courts.

- Court rulings in some states have shifted the responsibility for public school financing from dependence on local property taxes to greater reliance on state support.

- The federal government's role in education has increased with the passage of the No Child Left Behind Act, which places much more emphasis on accountability.

Few beginning teachers are concerned about issues related to school governance and finance. The topic seems remote to them; it is something administrators and representatives of teacher organizations care about, but it does not seem particularly vital for beginning teachers, who are more concerned with learning how to survive in the classroom. We feel differently. We believe beginning teachers must have some understanding of the way schools and school systems operate because they will be affected personally by governance and financial decisions. Not understanding how these decisions are made and how they might affect you as a teacher will reduce your effectiveness as a professional.

Truth or Fiction?

T F   The administration and operation of public education are primarily the responsibility of each state.

T F   Although women make up the vast majority of teachers, only one out of five school superintendents is a woman.

T F   Approximately half of public school financing comes from the federal government, with the rest coming from state and local governments.

T F   The United States spends about the same percentage of its resources on public schooling as the average of other industrialized nations.

T F   "No Child Left Behind" and "Head Start" are popular reading programs in the elementary schools of the United States.

How would you explain the following decisions?

- A very popular high school teacher was not given tenure.
- The sex education program being planned in your local school district was never implemented.
- A textbook with a fresh approach to the curriculum was removed from circulation after a year, even though the teachers favored its use.
- A coalition of superintendents from poor school districts in your state sued the state government for increased financial support.

It is quite possible that at least one of these decisions has been made in your local school district or state. All of them reflect the ongoing struggle for governance, control, and influence over the public schools. This chapter explores how the U.S. educational system is organized, governed, and financed. Although there are legal authorities for the schools and organizations established to exercise this authority, the educational system is strongly influenced by interest groups that do not appear on any organizational chart. We first examine the legal governing authority that exists in most states and then discuss special-interest groups that influence educational policy. Next, we look at how the U.S. educational system is financed and explore how disparities between rich and poor school districts are generating strong challenges to current financing policies. Finally, we examine the increased role of the federal government in education, particularly through the No Child Left Behind legislation and the economic stimulus money sent to the states.

who legally governs public education?

In most countries, the public schools are a branch of the central government, being federally financed and administered and highly uniform in curricula and procedures. In the United States, however, responsibility for the public schools evolved as a state function as a result of the Tenth Amendment to the U.S. Constitution, which reserves all powers to the states and the people that are not specifically designated to the federal government. Each of the 50 states has legal responsibility for the operation and administration of the public schools within its own boundaries. In most aspects of public education (we discuss certain exceptions later), the authority of federal, county, and city educational agencies is subject to the will of the state authorities.

Although legal responsibility for school governance belongs to the states, policy decisions and administration have traditionally been delegated to local school boards (see Figure 11.1). These school boards exist largely because Americans have come to insist on control of schools at the local level. Recently, however, states have been reasserting their policymaking prerogatives.

(T) F

The administration and operation of public education are primarily the responsibility of each state.
Because the U.S. Constitution says nothing about education and the Tenth Amendment reserves to the states and the people all powers not specifically designated to the federal government, education is the province of the states.

FIGURE 11.1

Organizational Structure of a Typical State School System

© Cengage Learning 2013

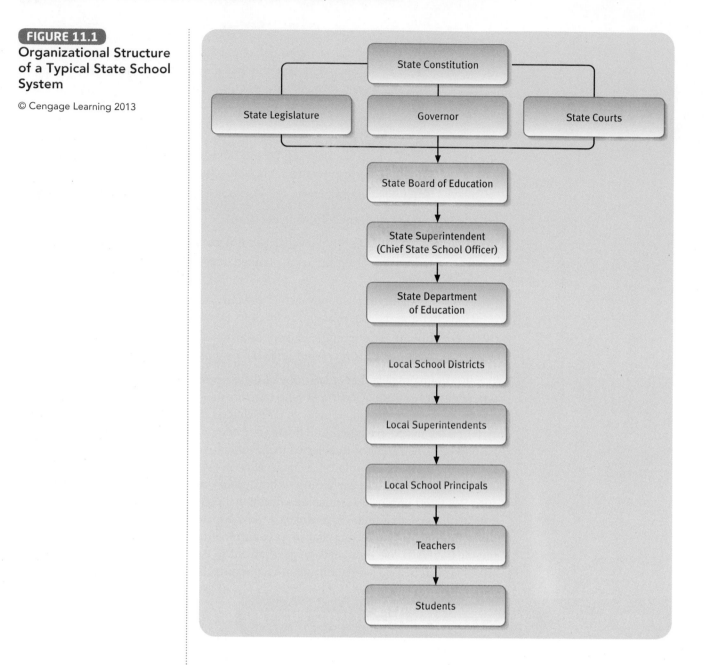

STATE OFFICES AND ADMINISTRATORS

At the state level, educational services can be influenced by a variety of actors, ranging from the governor to the many employees of the state's department of education.

The Governor and the State Legislature

Policy analysts agree that the state legislatures are the most influential actors in establishing educational policy. Legislatures wield such power because they make the laws that govern and affect education within their states, and they appropriate the money needed to fund state government. In recent years, because of the high profile of educational issues, legislatures' interest in educational policy has increased, particularly in the areas of school finance and the establishment of standards for student academic achievement.

Like legislatures, the governor's office has the power to affect educational policy but often chooses to do so only on limited issues. Many governors, however, have played more prominent roles, beginning with the educational reforms of the 1980s. Former President Bill Clinton and his education secretary, Richard Riley, for example, became nationally visible as governors through their educational leadership in Arkansas and South Carolina, respectively. Former President George W. Bush likewise pushed his education agenda as governor of Texas.

On financial issues, the roles of governor and legislature are especially obvious. Governors propose and legislatures act on budgets that contain funding for school districts. This is, as one wag has stated, the "Golden Rule: Whoever has the gold makes the rules." When state economies are strong, more tax revenues are available to invest in public education. Conversely, when recessions occur and state governments face a loss of tax revenues, they cut back on their educational commitments and initiatives, forcing school districts to make corresponding cuts in their budgets. In either scenario, governors and state legislatures have tremendous influence over educational policy and expenditures.

The State Board of Education

The state's legal responsibility for public education requires it to establish an organizational framework within which the local school districts can function. The result is the establishment of a **state board of education** to exercise general control and supervision of schools within the state. The state board of education is the state's educational policymaking body for elementary and secondary schools. It typically sets goals and priorities for education in the state; formulates education policy and curricular offerings, including establishing academic standards and their assessment; establishes and enforces rules and regulations for the operation of educational programs; represents the public in matters regarding the governance of education; reports to the public on accomplishments and needs; and makes recommendations to the governor and/or state legislature for the improvement of education. The state board of education also establishes and enforces minimum standards for the operation of all phases of elementary and secondary education from the state to the local school system level.

The procedure for selecting state board members varies from state to state. In most states, members are appointed by the governor; in about one-third of the states, however, members are elected by popular vote. The number of members on a state board of education varies from state to state, but a board of 9 to 15 members is typical.

The Chief State School Officer

The executive officer of the state board of education, the **chief state school officer**, usually is responsible for the administration of public education and reports to the state board of education. (The actual titles for this position, which vary from state to state, include *superintendent of education, commissioner of education, secretary of the state board of education,* and others.) The responsibilities normally involve serving as the chief administrator of the state department of education (discussed later in this chapter) and the state board of education; recommending improvements in educational legislation; arranging studies and creating task forces to identify problems and propose solutions; and reporting on the status of education within the state to the governor, legislature, state board of education, and the public. This officer exercises little direct administrative authority over local educational officials, but his or her indirect influence is widely felt at the local level. The officer is elected by the voters in 14 states, appointed by the governor in 12 states, and appointed by the state board of education in the remaining 24 states.

The State Department of Education

The **state department of education** (sometimes called the *state department of public instruction*) usually operates under the direction of the state board of education and is administered by the chief state school officer. The state department of education is responsible for carrying out the policies of the state board of education and the laws passed by the state legislature. It consists of a large bureaucracy of officials, often numbering in the hundreds of employees.

Originally organized to provide statistical reports, state departments of education have grown in size, power, and influence over the years. Their primary responsibilities usually include administering and distributing state and federal funds, licensing teachers and other educational personnel, providing schools with technical assistance in improving curriculum and teaching, providing educational data and analyses, providing administration for special programs, accrediting college and university educational licensure programs, evaluating existing programs, and issuing reports. Most schools, school districts, and colleges of education are strongly affected by the policies and actions of these state departments. School and college personnel, including public school teachers, serve on advisory committees and task forces to assist the chief state school officer and the state department of education in their decision-making processes.

THE LOCAL SCHOOL DISTRICT

To facilitate local control of education, the state creates local school districts for the purpose of carrying out education in a manner that conforms to state policy. Thus the school district is a unit of the state government and is usually distinct from the local municipal government.

The Local School Board

The policymaking body of the school district is the **local school board**, which represents the citizens of the district in setting up a school program, hiring personnel to operate the schools, determining organizational and administrative policy, and evaluating the results of the program and the performance of personnel. Many school boards are empowered to raise money through taxes. Although school board members are usually elected by the citizens of the local district, they are officially state officers (not simply local representatives), and they must follow the guidelines and policies established by the legislature, the state board of education, and the state department of education.

> *In the first place, God made idiots. That was for practice. Then he made school boards.*
>
> —MARK TWAIN,
> Nineteenth-Century American Author and Humorist

The tension between states' efforts to regulate educational policy and local districts' desire to determine their own policies has increased in recent years as states have taken the initiative in the educational reform movement.

Methods of selecting school board members are usually prescribed by state law. Approximately 96 percent of all U.S. school boards are elected by popular vote, and the rest are appointed, often by the local mayor or city council.

What does the composite profile of school board members look like? The majority of today's school board members are male, white, and between ages 40 and 59 — demographic characteristics that have changed little in recent years.[1] The proportion of women serving on boards has increased from 12 to around 44 percent since 1972, but representation of minorities remains small. Eighty-one percent of school board members are white. At least 86 percent of all school board members have annual family incomes exceeding $50,000. Three-fourths of them have at least bachelor's

Local school boards often come under pressure from many groups who want the schools to reflect their values and beliefs.

(© Bob Daemmerich/PhotoEdit)

degrees. Most are professionals, managers, or business owners; have children in the public schools; and consider themselves to be either moderates or conservatives. Thus, in many ways, school board members are not typical of the public they serve. Whether or how this difference influences their values and decisions is not known. Can you think of any ways in which it might?

The Superintendent of Schools

The **superintendent of schools** is typically a professional educator selected by the local school board to act as its executive officer and as the educational leader and administrator of the school district. In a few large urban areas, such as Chicago and Washington, D.C., the mayor of the city chooses the superintendent, giving the mayor more power and accountability over the schools. The superintendent is undeniably the most powerful officer in the local school organization. Given that the school board consists of laypeople who are usually not education experts, it often delegates many of its responsibilities to the superintendent and his or her staff.

One of the superintendent's most important functions is gathering and providing information to the local school board so its members can make informed decisions. Additionally, the superintendent must recruit, select, place, and promote personnel. Often, the superintendent plans the budget and supervises the maintenance, construction, and renovation of school buildings.

Decisions about how to improve educational opportunities, including all aspects of curriculum and instruction, may originate with the superintendent. The superintendent generally has responsibility for maintaining harmonious relations with the community by communicating the mission of the schools to the public and marshaling support for district programs.

Theoretically, the superintendent's role is administrative and executive—he or she (less than 22% of the nation's superintendents are female) keeps the schools functioning, whereas the local school board of education retains policymaking responsibilities. In practice, the superintendent has become the major policymaker in the school district.

(T) F

Although women make up the vast majority of teachers, only one out of five school superintendents is a woman.

Whether it is because school board members who select superintendents are primarily men; fewer women aspire to become superintendents; or some other reason, women make up only about 22 percent of the school superintendents.

Superintendents versus Local School Boards

The way a school board and superintendent operate together to govern a school district depends on their relationship. According to independent observers, this relationship is often characterized by conflict.

> *In building support for their initiatives and protecting their programs from attack, superintendents must discover their political allies and adversaries . . . no superintendent could hope to lead without acting politically.*
>
> —SUSAN MOORE JOHNSON,
> Professor at Harvard's Graduate School of Education

One observer, Larry Cuban, asserts that "conflict is—and always has been—the essence of the superintendency."[2] One measure of conflict between superintendents and school boards is the turnover rate—that is, how often superintendents change their jobs. The average tenure for superintendents in urban districts is slightly less than five years, and the national average among all superintendents is five and a half years.[3]

Cuban describes the conflict between the superintendent and the school board, or between the superintendent and local private groups, as one of seeming competitors seeking to achieve their goals at the expense of the other participants. Cuban maintains that the issues over which boards and administrators disagree may change as a result of shifting political concerns, changes in school funding or demography, or constantly changing coalitions of teachers or local constituencies. Whatever the particular issues, however, the relationship often remains tempestuous. Although school boards hire and fire them, superintendents are expected to lead the board. If they fail to do so, board members are likely to act independently, often with disastrous consequences.

School boards and superintendents search constantly for local constituencies to provide the funding and support for school programs, and with every school board election new points of view may be brought to the governance of the district. Superintendents must weather these changes in points of view and the emerging coalitions resulting from board member turnover. Sympathies with the schools' mission may be in a constant state of flux, requiring superintendents to exercise coalition-building skills. Their survival as nonelected public officials rests on their ability to mobilize support and manage conflict.

The School Principal

For the schools within a school district, the superintendent and the local school board of education select professional educators to serve as principals. High schools and middle schools may have a staff of administrators to assist the principal, including assistant or vice-principals with specific responsibilities for discipline or curriculum and instruction. At the elementary level, principals may be responsible for more than one school building or may serve part-time as teachers. Whatever the pattern of administrative assignments, those who act as principals are generally considered to be a part of the administrative organization, directly accountable to the superintendent and the local school board. (See Table 11.1 for a profile of school administrators.)

As administrators, principals usually interview prospective teachers and make teaching assignments, supervise and evaluate staff members, schedule students and classes, manage school budgets, administer district discipline policies, and procure and dispense supplies. Their tasks are many; to list them all would be impossible. Historically, the role of the principal has included management, supervision, and inspection duties. Most importantly, principals are expected to function as instructional leaders for their schools. In a number of states, principals and their teachers are being held accountable for increasing student learning on statewide assessments

TABLE 11.1 Profile of School Administrators (in Percent)

| | Secondary School | | Elementary School |
	Superintendents	Principals	Principals
Sex			
Male	78.3	71	41
Female	21.7	29	59
Ethnic Background			
White	94.9	84	80
Black	2.2	9.8	10.9
Hispanic American	1.4	4.5	7.6
Asian American	0.2	0.4	0.7
Native American	0.8	0.6	0.7
Other	0.5	0.7	0.6
Salary (12 Months)	$155,634	$91,500	$86,400

Note: Because of rounding, some totals may not add up to 100 percent.

Sources: Willa D. Cooke and Chris Licciardi, "Principals' Salaries, 2008–2009," *Principal* (May/June 2009), p. 27; *The Condition of Education 2010* (Washington, DC: National Center for Education Statistics, 2010), Indicator 29. Available at http://nces.ed.gov/programs/coe/2010/section4/indicator29.asp. *The State of the American School Superintendency: A Mid-Decade Study* (Alexandria, VA: American Association of School Administrators, 2007); *Education Vital Signs 2009* (Alexandria, VA: National School Boards Association, 2009), p. 11.

of achievement. However, as can be seen in the Voices from the Classroom feature, principals and teachers may not always be on the same page.

Effective principals serve as instructional leaders by promoting a productive working and learning environment. They do so by understanding the mission of the school, communicating it to the staff and students, and rewarding excellent performance. They also represent the school to parents and the community. Involving parents and community members in the school's activities and securing their support for these activities are important functions of the principal.

PAUSE AND REFLECT

1. From what you have read about the role of the superintendent, what impressions have you formed about the power of the superintendent and the constraints on that power?

2. The authors of this textbook believe that the hardest job in public education is that of a high school principal. Do you agree or disagree with this position? For what reasons?

3. In your opinion, should chief state school officers be elected or appointed? What reasons do you have for your position? What arguments can you muster for the opposite opinion?

VOICES from the classroom

Swimming against the Current

This testimonial is from an elementary school reading specialist in a small town in Virginia. The contributor wishes to remain anonymous.

Remember the cartoon where the "school" of fish swims along, sporting mortarboards? Well, I can carry the metaphor even further. Teaching with the support of the principal and local administration is like swimming downstream. When that support is missing, you're just bucking the current.

For several years, my colleagues and I taught an excellent comprehensive reading curriculum, with the support of principals and district administration. The curriculum's implementation produced dramatic effects among kindergartners and first-graders in the district's lowest-performing elementary school, Center City. This school was on its way, but it would take some time for the results to manifest themselves in the state tests, which were administered in third grade and later, and thereby gain Adequate Yearly Progress (AYP) status under the No Child Left Behind law.

Then the current changed. Our superintendent retired, and shortly thereafter we lost our assistant superintendent in charge of curriculum and our literacy coordinator. The new superintendent mandated that Center City replace our successful reading program with a basal program. Some teachers scrambled to find time to supplement the basal program with instruction they knew worked, but it was difficult, and progress slowed among the primary-grade students. However, those early gains in reading finally showed up on the spring state tests, and Center City made AYP.

In the spring of the next year, Center City became eligible to apply for a federal Reading First grant. The district and a new principal, without consulting the school's reading specialists or classroom teachers, decided to apply, assigning the grant-writing job to an employee of the basal publisher. Despite their strenuous efforts, the faculty ended up with minimal input. The application was accepted and a reading coach hired. Although enjoying the principal's support, the coach made decisions that negatively affected student instruction and alienated the teachers. The following spring, after three years of inadequate reading instruction, Center City failed to make AYP.

What are the lessons to be learned from this experience? First, when new players enter the game, they want to make their own impact and will initiate changes that may not be as effective as instruction already in place. Second, the people closest to the action (the teachers and reading specialists) may not be consulted in decisions that greatly affect them. And third, although in our work as teachers the students should present our primary challenge, this isn't always the case. Still, we can never stop bucking the current on their behalf.

who influences american public education?

In this chapter, we do not intend to examine in detail the authority and power that enable various groups to influence certain aspects of public education. However, even a brief look at the interplay of influence exercised by professional education organizations, parents, business, the courts, and the federal government yields some fascinating insights into how decisions about public education are actually made.

PROFESSIONAL EDUCATION ORGANIZATIONS

Among the most influential forces on the schools are professional education organizations—in particular, the National Education Association (NEA) and the American Federation of Teachers (AFT).

In recent years, the role of teacher organizations in determining educational policy has greatly increased. At the national level, the NEA and the AFT exert considerable influence on educational policy and legislation. Moreover, the state affiliates of both associations are among the most effective lobbying groups in their respective states. (See Chapter 15, "What Does It Mean to Be a Professional?" for more on these two teacher organizations.) State politicians pay attention to these organizations because of their power and influence. The NEA and AFT affiliates have well-articulated positions on selected issues, represent hundreds of thousands of teachers who can be mobilized to vote for or against particular legislators, and spend considerable amounts of money to make their positions known. At the local level—largely as a result of collective bargaining techniques, including work stoppages or the threat of them—teacher organizations have won more and more power over educational policy.

> *Just as war is too important to be left to the generals, education is too important to be left to the educators.*
>
> —PAUL WOODRING,
> Twentieth-Century American Education
> Author and Professor

Today many local teacher organizations, including NEA and AFT affiliates, have won recognition as the official bargaining representatives of their members. Such organizations are also demanding that issues previously considered the prerogatives of local school boards and superintendents be subject to collective bargaining. Among these areas of contention are teacher and paraprofessional salaries, clerical and secretarial assistance, curriculum development, fringe benefits, in-service training, class size, textbook selection, and even the appointment of department heads and other school administrators.

PARENTS

Ask educators who has the most influence in determining whether children succeed in school, and almost all of them will have the same response: *parents*. Parents are their children's first and primary teachers and the only ones who follow a child's progress from year to year. As the two major forces for educating and socializing children in society, parents and teachers should be natural allies. Too often, however, a wide chasm separates them. Some teachers fear that parents will interfere in their classrooms; others feel pressed for time and don't want to spend the extra effort to communicate with and effectively involve parents.

> *A parent is the most important teacher a child ever has.*
>
> —JOAN BECK,
> American Author on Child Raising

Some parents seem too consumed with the problems of work and raising a family to become involved in schools, whereas others actively participate in various school functions. Research is clear on this point: without effective parental interest and involvement in the schools, most students will not succeed academically. In a national survey of public school teachers, 22 percent identified a lack of parental involvement as a serious problem.[4]

The Parent Teacher Association (PTA) is a loosely knit national organization with almost 6 million members and more than 26,000 local units. The local parent–teacher group, sometimes called the **parent–teacher organization (PTO)**, may or may not be affiliated with the national PTA. Local groups devise their own organizations and activities to fit the needs of the local school community. Generally, they serve as a communications link between parents and the formal school organization, with teachers usually acting as representatives of the schools.

Most PTOs are comparatively impotent in achieving educational aims. This weakness of parent groups concerns educational reformers because they know that reforms will last only if parents become actively involved in the work of their schools. Some states have actually passed legislation mandating that schools involve parents in school governance and in the education of the students.

Family support and emphasis on the value of education are extremely important influences on a child's success in school.

(iofoto/Shutterstock.com)

Many strategies can be implemented to increase parental involvement and improve the partnership between parents and teachers: frequent parent–teacher conferences; homework hotlines, websites, or e-mails, through which parents can find out about homework assignments or communicate with teachers; workshops for parents that address a variety of topics; school volunteer programs; and school councils on which parents, teachers, and administrators discuss school policies and practices. Teachers and school administrators must be trained to overcome barriers to effective parental involvement and to create school environments where parents of all races, ethnicities, and social classes feel welcome.

BUSINESS

Throughout American history, concern about the quality of U.S. public education and its ability to produce workers with the knowledge and skills that business needs has prompted partnerships between educators and business executives. In particular, during the 1980s and 1990s and continuing into the twenty-first century, the business community has been at the forefront of efforts to restructure public education. Business leaders have been substantially involved in almost every educational reform report. As a result, they have become both the strongest critics and the staunchest advocates for public education. More than 100,000 business–school partnerships have been formed since 1983, and business has donated hundreds of millions of dollars to improve elementary and secondary schools.

Why should the business community show such interest in the field of education? Its initiatives to improve the quality of American education go beyond altruistic impulses. One source estimates that children between the ages of 4 and 19 spend $200 billion per year, and children younger than age 12 influence the spending of $500 billion each year.[5] With that kind of money involved, businesses would certainly like to make their presence known in the schools, where these potential consumers are a captive audience.

In addition, like the nation's governors, many business leaders are convinced that educational reform is essential to the health of the U.S. economy. Competition from Asian and European manufacturers in world markets, a massive U.S. trade deficit, and industry's perception that entry-level workers lack proper job skills have focused attention on educating the American workforce. In fact, U.S. companies spend billions of dollars annually on remedial education for their workers.

A recent coalition of businesses and educational organizations and government leaders, The Partnership for 21st Century Skills, seeks to make changes in our nation's schools by aligning classroom environments with what the organization believes are real-world environments. This alignment occurs by fusing the core subjects and four C's:

- The core subjects include English, reading or language arts; mathematics; science; foreign languages; civics; government; economics; arts; history; and geography.

- The four C's include: critical thinking and problem solving; communication, collaboration; and creativity and innovation.

- The P21 initiative has developed a framework outlining the knowledge and skills that students will need, and educators and business leaders are working hard to implement these outcomes in our schools.[6]

Purchasing Pressures?

Not everyone sees the greater business involvement in education as a totally positive trend. Some express concern that financial support from business will lead to business intrusion—that schools may be unduly shaped to meet business needs. Another concern centers on business's provision of free curriculum and instructional materials for teachers. Critics argue that corporate handouts are not simply supplementary gifts, but rather sophisticated marketing tools containing subtle and not-so-subtle messages to support the corporation's biases and promote brand identification and product loyalty. For example, Clairol distributes free bags of shampoo to students as they leave school, along with surveys asking whether they had "a good or bad hair day." In another example, a Nike program asks young people to devote a week of classroom time to learning the life cycle of a Nike shoe. Other opponents of corporate involvement in the schools object to exclusive marketing contracts that schools sign with such companies as Coca-Cola or Pepsi, agreeing to sell only products produced by the particular company in exchange for funding from the firm. Some people cynically view business's push for the expanded use of technology in schools as an attempt to create a new market for computers and other educational technology, and for digital marketing of businesses' products.

Many schools earn extra money from corporations by allowing exclusive marketing and sales rights of their products in the schools. However, more and more schools are trying to get rid of fattening or sugar products in favor of healthier snacks and drinks.

(Tim Boyle/Getty Images)

PAUSE AND REFLECT

1. Did the schools you attended work in partnership with business and industry?

2. Did your education prepare you for further education and entry into the workforce?

3. What, in your opinion, is an appropriate relationship between business and schools?

Privatization Efforts

Another way business influences education is through the recent movement toward private management of public schools, known as educational management organizations (EMOs), that has occurred in some urban areas. Private corporations such as the Edison Learning and Sylvan Learning, Inc., have contracted with some school districts to provide specific educational services, operate schools whose students have been performing poorly on academic tests, or begin new schools with promising designs. Advocates of this **privatization** movement argue that private corporations can operate these schools more effectively and less expensively than can public entities. Opponents of this trend—especially teachers' unions—claim that schools operated under a profit motive may shortchange students' welfare in the private firm's drive to make money. They do so, the critics claim, by hiring inexperienced teachers, using unlicensed staff, and eliminating high-cost special education programs. To date, private management of public schools has often led to cleaner buildings, greater access to computers, and more individualized instruction, but the verdict is still out on whether they lead to academic improvement.

> *The classroom is . . . a place in which the claims of various political, social, and economic interests are negotiated. The classroom is both a symbol and a product of deadly serious cultural bargaining.*
>
> —NEIL POSTMAN (1931–2003),
> American Professor, Media Theorist, and Cultural Critic

There is no question that the role of the business community in educational affairs has greatly expanded since the mid-1980s, and most people see this trend as a positive one. Businesses and corporations, which have a vested stake in the outcomes of public education, will undoubtedly continue to be major players in the reform of our educational system. The challenge for educators will be to walk the fine line between partnerships and cooperation on the one hand and exploitation for commercial purposes on the other.

THE FEDERAL GOVERNMENT

Although the federal government does not have formal authority over education, all three branches of the government exercise considerable influence over schools in the country through legislation, court rulings, and the activities of the U.S. Department of Education.

The Federal Courts

The history of education has been shaped by important court decisions on the duties and responsibilities of school officials in such areas as school desegregation, religion in the schools, student rights, and, especially at the state level, school finance. The U.S. Supreme Court has played a particularly important role in changing educational policy in this country. (See Chapter 8, "What Are the Ethical and Legal Issues Facing Teachers?" for a more detailed discussion of the impact of Supreme Court decisions on U.S. education.) Because its rulings have altered or reduced the power of state and local educational authorities, some of the Court's decisions have generated deep resentment among those who abhor this "federal intrusion" into states' rights. Other people applaud the Court's decisions as steps intended to make American education more responsive to broad democratic principles. Over the years, the Supreme Court has issued key rulings affecting such important educational policies as desegregation, public aid to private schools, rights of people with disabilities, gender equity, voucher plans, and sexual harassment.

Even as powerful as they are, the courts cannot do everything by themselves. Often judicial rulings must be supported by federal administrative and legislative action before they can alter educational practice. In the famous 1954 case of *Brown* v. *Board of Education of Topeka* (discussed in more detail in Chapter 10, "What Is the History of American Education and the Struggle for Educational Opportunities?"), for example, the U.S. Supreme Court ruled that the doctrine of "separate but equal" had no place in public education. But how was this momentous judgment to be implemented? The Court declared that "all deliberate speed" should be employed to abolish the dual school system for African Americans and whites, but no judicial guidelines were developed to steer this process. As a result, almost no changes

Federal legislation and federal court decisions have significantly affected education, including the education of children with disabilities, many of whom now engage in the same activities as their nondisabled peers as a result of the least restrictive environment requirements of the federal IDEA law.

(© Elizabeth Crews/The Image Works)

occurred for a decade, until a combination of new congressional laws on civil rights and education along with strong enforcement of desegregation by President Lyndon Johnson's administration took place in the 1960s.

The U.S. Department of Education

The Department of Education is a significant part of the federal government, with cabinet-level status and a budget of slightly less than $70 billion in fiscal year 2011.[7] The department administers a variety of programs passed by Congress, including programs concerned with elementary and secondary education, postsecondary education, educational research and development, vocational and adult education, special education, and civil rights. It also administers funds devoted to the collection of educational statistics. In addition, billions of additional federal dollars for education are administered by other federal agencies, such as the Department of Health and Human Services, the National Science Foundation, and the Department of Defense.

The federal government's level of involvement in education often fluctuates, depending on whether Republicans or Democrats control the White House and Congress, and on the particular ideology professed by the party in power. Republicans generally have sought to decrease the involvement of the federal government in education, even advocating abolition of the U.S. Department of Education, whereas Democrats tend to be more supportive of both the department and federal efforts to improve education. Bucking this trend, during the administration of President George W. Bush (a Republican), the federal government's share of costs for elementary and secondary education increased from 7 percent to slightly less than 9 percent by 2007. By 2010, the economic stimulus money, along with the regular education funding, had brought the federal share to about 10.5 percent, the highest in history.

T (F)

Approximately half of public school financing comes from the federal government, with the rest coming from state and local governments.

Only about 9 to 11 percent of public school funding comes from the federal government, with the rest coming from the states and local school districts.

PAUSE AND REFLECT

Which other groups, besides those listed in this chapter, influence education?

how are schools financed?

The total amount of money available to a school district for education is the sum of locally raised revenues, state aid, federal aid, and miscellaneous revenues. During much of the country's history, most of the money used to support public elementary and secondary schools came from local revenue sources, primarily property taxes. Beginning in the late 1970s, for the first time in U.S. history the states' share of support for public education exceeded the local share, and this situation continues today. Increased state revenues have helped offset the decreases in local funding of the schools. Currently, state governments contribute about 46 percent; local governments provide approximately 44 percent; and the federal government provides just over 10 percent of the financing of public schools.[8]

The percentages of educational expenditures funded by federal, state, and local sources vary considerably from state to state. Federal contributions for public education range from a high of 17 percent of educational spending for Alabama and Louisiana, to a low of about 3 percent for Rhode Island and New Jersey. Local

FIGURE 11.2
Expenditures per Pupil

*Source: Rankings and Estimates
2010–2011* (Washington, DC:
National Education Association,
2011).) Available at www.nea.org/
assets/docs/HE/NEA_Rankings_
and_Estimates010711.pdf

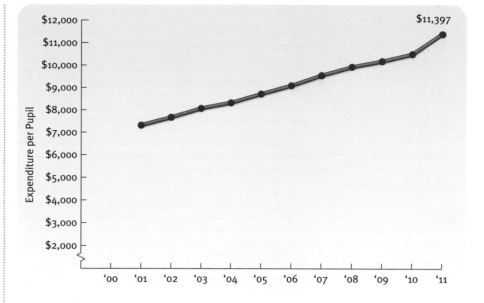

contributions range from a high of almost 70 percent of educational spending for Illinois, to a low of less than 2 percent for Vermont. The state receiving the highest proportion of revenues from state sources is Vermont, at 90 percent; the state with the lowest level of state funding is Illinois, at 17 percent of educational spending.[9] Let's look in more detail at state and local spending and funding patterns.

SCHOOL SPENDING

Figure 11.2 shows the upward trend in average expenditure per pupil in daily attendance. The nationwide average stood at $11,397 per pupil for 2010–2011. From state to state, however, the per-pupil expenditures vary widely (Figure 11.3), ranging from a high of over $22,000 (Vermont) per pupil each year to a low of $6,708 (Arizona).[10] The reason for these differences is primarily economic. A state's ability to pay for education depends on the income level of its residents and corporations and the willingness of its citizen to financially support public education. In general, the southwestern states fund education at lower levels than do the northeastern states, but the cost of living in the Southwest is generally less than the cost of living in the Northeast. As a result of the lower funding, are students who live in some of the Sunbelt states being deprived of a quality education? The connection between funding and excellence of education is often disputed, but a group of researchers from the University of Chicago, after reanalyzing 32 studies on this issue, concluded that higher per-pupil expenditures, better teacher salaries, more educated and experienced teachers, and smaller class and school sizes— all directly a result of higher funding—are strongly related to improved student learning. Conversely, some researchers assert that no such relationship exists between the amount of money spent on education and the achievements of the students in that district.[11]

STATE AND LOCAL FUNDING

State governments use a combination of sales, personal income, corporate income, and excise taxes to generate revenues. Some states fund their schools partly with income from state-run lotteries. State revenue systems are as diverse as school

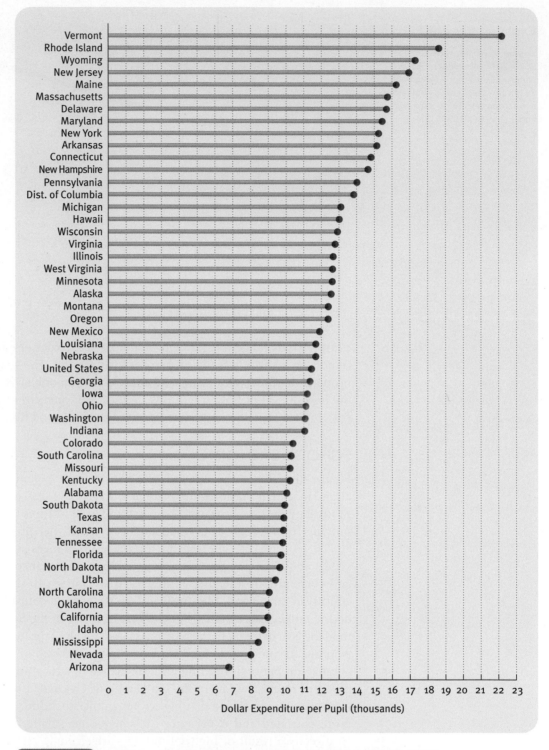

FIGURE 11.3 Average Expenditure per Pupil, by State, 2010–2011

Source: *Rankings and Estimates 2010–2011* (Washington, DC: National Education Association, 2010) , p. 96. Available at www.nea.org/assets/docs/HE/NEA_Rankings_and_Estimates010711.pdf

finance plans and reflect the socioeconomic makeup, the political climate, and the educational needs of each state.

Local governments, in contrast, rely primarily on property taxes for income. Most states require the citizens in a school district to vote either on the property tax

where does the united states stand on education funding?

Many politicians, arguing against the need for increased spending on education, assert that the United States already spends more on public education than do most comparable countries but gets worse results. "Money is not the answer," they claim. We can shed some light on the debate by comparing U.S. educational spending with that of some other countries. To allow for differences in size of the economies, we can consider public spending on education as a percentage of gross domestic product (GDP), the total value of a country's output. The United States spends 4.0 percent of its GDP on public elementary and secondary education, while the average for the 31 industrialized countries sampled was 3.6 percent. Countries that spend more than the United States include Iceland (5.1% of GDP), Denmark (4.3%), United Kingdon (4.2%), Belgium (4.1%), and Sweden (4.1%). Countries spending the same percentage as the United States include Korea, New Zealand, Switzerland, and Brazil., Countries spending less than the United States include Slovak Republic (2.5%), Japan (2.8%), Czech Republic (2.8%), Spain (2.9%), and Germany (3.0%).

Such figures indicate that the United States devotes a slightly higher percentage of its resources to public elementary and secondary education as the average of other industrialized nations (4.0% vs. 3.6%). However, the United States might be

(T) F

The United States spends about the same percentage of its resources on public schooling as the average of other industrialized nations. The United States spends about 4 percent of its gross domestic product (GDP), while the average of industrial nations is about 3.6 percent of GDP.

expected to spend proportionally more than other countries because of certain characteristics of its school system and society. The decentralized school system in the United States is more expensive than the single, centrally administered system found in many other industrialized nations. The U.S. population is more diverse than most countries', which presents unique educational challenges, and the very high number of U.S. children living in poverty creates additional demands for schools. Also, the United States, compared with the other countries, spends a much greater percentage of its public education funds (17%) on special education services. Given these factors, and compared to other industrialized nations, the percentage of U.S. GDP spent on elementary and secondary education does not seem extravagant.

Source: Organization of Economic Cooperation and Development, *Education at a Glance, 2010*, p. 7. Available at www.oecd.org/document/52/0,3343,en_2649_39263238_45897844_1_1_1_1,00.html.

rate to support education or on the school budget itself. Many states have begun to rely less on local property taxes to fund their schools.

Why would districts want to minimize their reliance on property taxes? Many knowledgeable educators and politicians argue that one of the major causes of unequal educational opportunities in this country is the method used to finance school systems. Because local districts rely heavily on property taxes, those districts where property values are high generate much more money to finance their schools than those districts where property values are low. Within the same state, for example, the average amount of money spent per child in one district may be more than three times the amount spent in a nearby district. Such spending differentials result in great educational disparities, as measured by pupil–teacher ratios, training and experience of staff, and availability of facilities, equipment, and counseling services.

SCHOOL FINANCE REFORM AND THE COURTS

As a result of numerous court decisions, efforts to equalize the disparities in funding within states have shifted some of the responsibility for funding from local school districts to the state level. A 1971 class action suit, *Serrano* v. *Priest,* charged that California's school-financing scheme was unconstitutional. The Supreme Court of California supported the parents' claim that the quality of a child's education must not be a function of wealth other than the wealth of the state as a whole. The court also held that the California system of financing schools on the basis of local property taxes violated the Fourteenth Amendment to the U.S. Constitution, which provides equal protection of the law for all citizens.

In 1973, however, the Supreme Court of the United States, by a five-to-four vote, reversed a similar decision (known as the *Rodriguez* case) involving the school finance system of the state of Texas. The Court found that the U.S. Constitution was not violated because the right to an education is not guaranteed explicitly or implicitly by the Constitution. Although *federal* law had not been violated, the Court did indicate that the finding should not be interpreted as a victory for the status quo. In effect, issues of inequity in school finance were returned to the province of the state courts and legislatures. Many state constitutions, unlike the U.S. Constitution, contain equal protection clauses that can be interpreted to include education as a protected right.

Since the *Rodriguez* case, other state courts have ruled that their school financing systems violate their state constitutions. In those states where the finance system has been ruled unconstitutional, the issue has centered on inadequacies in the level of educational opportunities offered to children in the poorer school districts. The courts in those states considered whether the poor children were receiving a sufficient education as required by the state constitution and as measured by contemporary education standards or by comparisons with the best or highest-spending districts. In contrast, in states where the system of school finance was upheld, the courts usually interpreted their state constitutions as guaranteeing only a basic minimum level of funding.[12] As a result of court challenges, more than 20 states have reformed their school finance laws since 1973, and some states continue to grapple with the issue. In the last few years, state courts seem to be backing away from making decisions about increasing K–12 funding, stating that education funding is a political question for the legislature, not the courts, to decide.

Educators, parents, and public officials are greatly concerned that the quality of a child's education should not depend on whether the child lives in a school district with high property values. Many of these concerned citizens are urging that state governments take responsibility for raising educational revenue and distributing all funding for local schools to the school districts. The school districts would continue to be in charge of the operation of the local schools but would no longer carry the burden of raising the money needed to do so.

PAUSE AND REFLECT

1. Of the various methods of school financing discussed in this chapter (local property taxes, state financing through statewide taxes, and state-run lotteries), which do you believe is most equitable? Why?

2. Do you believe state governments should redistribute money from rich to poor school districts through state taxing power? Why or why not?

FEDERAL FUNDING

Although the federal government typically provides much less money for public schools than do state or local governments, federal funds are strategically important and have a far greater impact than their proportion of school funding would suggest.

Funding in the Past

Much of federal aid to education traditionally has taken the form of **categorical grants**—that is, money that must be spent for designated purposes (or categories) stated generally in the legislation and more precisely by the federal agency administering the funds. As a result, the federal government has been able to influence school districts and institutions that have accepted or sought its aid.

For example, in an effort to stimulate the U.S. economy out of recession, the U.S. Congress passed the **American Recovery and Reinvestment Act (ARRA)** of 2009. This piece of legislation provided $787 billion in tax cuts and benefits; funds for education, healthcare, and jobless benefits; and federal contracts, grants, and loans. In 2010, Congress also passed legislation to provide an additional $20 billion "education jobs fund" to help school districts to keep from laying off thousands of teachers. Although much of the ARRA money earmarked for education went directly to the states for their cash-strapped education programs, the U.S. Department of Education kept $4.35 billion for its Race to the Top competition.

The **Race to the Top** competition was designed to encourage and reward states for education innovation and reform. States that wished to compete for Race to the Top funds had to submit proposals that showed how they would accomplish the following:

- Turn around their lowest-achieving schools.
- Recruit, develop, reward, and retain effective teachers and principals.
- Build data systems that measure student growth and success, and inform teachers and principals to improve instruction.
- Adopt standards and assessments that prepare students to succeed in college and the workplace and to compete in the global economy.

Although many states were appreciative of the opportunity to compete for these funds, other states elected not to submit proposals because they resisted the direction that the competition criteria would lead them.

Compensatory Education and Title I

Although the federal government provides money for a variety of educational programs, its most significant efforts have sought to address the needs of children from high-poverty areas who are at risk for educational failure. **Compensatory education** is an approach to creating more equal educational opportunities for disadvantaged children.

Compensatory education was formalized in a section of the original **Elementary and Secondary Education Act (ESEA)** of 1965, known as **Title I**. Congress continues to strongly support Title I: Improving the Academic Achievement of the Disadvantaged because the money reaches almost every school district and thus provides jobs and services in every congressional district. Few members of Congress will vote against providing these benefits to their districts. Under the 2001 reauthorization of ESEA—called the **No Child Left Behind (NCLB) Act**—Title I has

T (F)

No Child Left Behind and Head Start are popular reading programs in the elementary schools of the United States. The No Child Left Behind Act is the latest version of the Elementary and Secondary Education Act, the primary federal funding to education, whereas Head Start is a compensatory education program for economically disadvantaged children.

come to account for the largest portion of federal spending on public schools. (See Chapter 12, "How Should Education Be Reformed?" for more information on the No Child Left Behind Act.)

Title I was designed to do two things: (1) deliver federal funds to local school districts and schools for the education of students from low-income families and (2) supplement the educational services provided to low-achieving students in those districts. Subsequent reauthorizations of ESEA have changed the rules for schools that receive Title I funds. To receive money, states and school districts now must submit a state improvement plan that includes the adoption of challenging content standards and aligned assessments for Title I students. Schools are allowed to use their Title I funds on a schoolwide basis rather than only for the poorest students, and they can combine money from multiple federal programs. At the same time, school districts must rank their schools based on their percentages of poor students and distribute Title I funds accordingly, with the poorest schools receiving the most money per pupil.

Between 1965 and 2010, Title I provided more than $250 billion for educational services in almost all of the nation's school districts. This program now distributes more than $14.5 billion each year on behalf of more than 17 million children in more than 50,000 schools. Of these students, approximately 60 percent were in kindergarten through fifth grade, 21 percent in grades 6–8, 16 percent in grades 9–12, 3 percent in preschool, and less than 1 percent ungraded.[13]

Compensatory programs come in many forms. Some are preventive approaches, targeting children who are "at risk" for later school failure during their preschool or infant years. Such programs may help parents learn how to interact more effectively with their babies and young children in the areas of cognitive and psychosocial development. The most famous preschool initiative is **Head Start**, described in the accompanying box.

head start

Head Start is a federal program that aims to improve the learning skills, social skills, and health status of preschool-age, poor children so that they can begin schooling on an equal basis with their more advantaged peers. Since its inception in 1965, Head Start has served more than 26 million children in total, and it currently supports more than 900,000 children.[14]

Although Head Start is more than 40 years old, the program is not without its critics and, like other sectors of public education, is the target of reform. For the 2011 fiscal year, the federal government budgeted $8.2 billion for Head Start programs. Along with Congress's reauthorization of the Head Start program, however, came a call for a new focus on academics.

The proposed focus on academics has been strongly opposed by many early-childhood education experts, who fear that the increased attention to academic skills will dilute efforts to promote positive social and emotional development and that the health services Head Start currently provides will be abandoned. Others argue that there is no reason why Head Start programs cannot address all these goals satisfactorily. Certainly, the students served by Head Start programs need and deserve attention to academic, social, and health concerns so that they will be prepared to succeed in school.

Early intervention programs, such as Head Start, target children who are at risk of school failure by intervening in their early years to improve skills.

(© Laura Dwight)

Some compensatory programs are designed to intervene with even younger children, from birth to age 3, for example. Some programs target children with developmental delays, whereas others target older children and focus on basic skill instruction, tutoring, or remediation in a variety of academic areas. Success for All, described in the box on page 372, is an example of a program that is implemented in elementary schools. Dropout prevention programs, job training, and adult literacy instruction are all attempts to help older individuals improve the quality of their lives through education and to help prevent the cycle of educational disadvantage from being passed down through generations.

Evaluations of Title I and other compensatory education programs, such as Head Start, have yielded mixed results. A recent evaluation of Head Start showed modest gains for children in this programs in terms of their prereading, prewriting, and vocabulary skills, but no improvements were found in oral-comprehension or math skills. One researcher states that although children in Head Start make learning gains, they are "well behind middle-class kids" when they start the program, and that "making modest improvements doesn't close the gap in a major way."[15]

By contrast, long-range studies that have followed students from preschool to age 19, like the study of students in the very successful Perry Preschool Program in Ypsilanti, Michigan, provide other indicators of program success. Effective early childhood programs may result in fewer special education placements, more high school graduations, lower teen pregnancy rates, increased employment and earnings, fewer crimes committed, and greater commitment to marriage.[16] *Early intervention*—beginning the program early in the child's life—may provide the key to success in compensatory education programs.

Critics of Title I see little point in strengthening programs that they believe have failed to meet their original goals. Proponents of Title I argue that, considering the enormity of the problem, the expenditures devoted to such programs are a mere drop in the bucket. In spite of what seems like an enormous amount of money, only about 50 percent of all eligible children receive services from Title I funds. Because Title I has never been funded at a high enough level to meet the needs of low-income schools and because its resources are widely dispersed, even the recent funding increases have not checked the growing educational crisis in low-income areas.

success for all

One compensatory education program that has proved quite successful is the Success for All program developed by the Center for Research on Effective Schooling for Disadvantaged Students at Johns Hopkins University. The Success for All program restructures the elementary school with one goal in mind: to ensure that all students perform at grade level in reading, writing, and mathematics by the end of third grade.

Success for All schools start early, offering a half-day of preschool and a full day of kindergarten, both focused on providing a developmentally appropriate learning experience for children. The curriculum emphasizes the development and use of language and balances academic readiness with music, art, and movement activities.

The program also makes use of the center's research findings to implement one-to-one tutoring, regrouping for reading, family support teams, frequent assessments of learning with immediate help on problems, and an effective reading program. Two social workers and one parent liaison work full time in the schools to provide parenting education and to encourage parents to support their children's efforts. The program also includes tutors for children in grades K–3. Each tutor is a certified, experienced teacher or paraprofessional who works one-on-one with 11 students per day. First-graders get priority for tutoring.

The Success for All program includes 90 minutes of uninterrupted reading instruction each day, during which teachers are asked to follow a fast-paced script written by the Success for All researchers. In spite of its success in teaching students to read, many teachers dislike the reading program, because it tells them exactly what to do throughout their lessons. For some teachers, this process seems contrary to their beliefs about the importance of paying attention to the learning style of each child and varying their instruction accordingly.

Overall, evaluation results for students enrolled in Success for All have been outstanding—much higher than for any other intervention strategy ever tried with at-risk students. Starting with one Baltimore school in 1987, the Success for All program had spread to approximately 1,500 schools in 48 states, and it has produced dramatic gains in students' reading proficiency. Almost all Success for All programs are in high-poverty, Title I schools, and the costs of implementing the program are about the same as the costs for supporting students in other Title I schools.

The primary lesson learned, according to the major developer of Success for All, Robert Slavin, and his colleagues, is that disadvantaged children can routinely achieve substantially greater success in schools that are neither exceptional nor extraordinary. Rather than having to depend on the availability of an outstanding principal or charismatic teacher to ensure success, every child, regardless of background, has an excellent opportunity to succeed in school.

In 2010, Success for All received a $49 million grant from the U.S. Department of Education's Investing in Innovation competition, which is aimed at improving achievement for students at risk of academic failure.

Sources: Robert Slavin, "Success for All," in James W. Guthrie, ed., *Encyclopedia of Education*, 2nd ed. (New York: Macmillan Reference, U.S.A., 2003); Robert E. Slavin and Nancy A. Madden, eds., *Success for All: Research and Reform in Elementary Education* (Mahwah, NJ: Lawrence Erlbaum Associates, 2001); Success for All website available at http://successforall.com/about/index.htm; Debra Viadero, "In Whole School Reform, Staying True to Model Matters," *Education Week* (May 16, 2007), pp. 12–13.

Proponents can also point to recent gains in achievement. A 2007 national assessment of Title I showed that students whom Title I is intended to benefit (including low-income students, racial/ethnic minorities, English-language learners, migrant students, and students with disabilities) have made modest gains in meeting proficiency levels on state assessments in reading and mathematics, as well as on the National Assessment of Educational Progress (NAEP) tests in reading and mathematics (see Chapter 5, "What Is Taught?" for more on NAEP). Although the performance of students in high-poverty schools is improving, they continue to lag behind their higher-income peers in meeting basic standards of performance in both reading and mathematics.[17] As the centerpiece of the NCLB law, Title I will likely continue to receive funding increases in the years to come.

Both sides acknowledge that not all programs are equally effective. The best programs achieve desired results, whereas the less effective programs do not seem to have lasting effects on student performance. Likewise, both sides can agree that, in addition to education efforts, a simultaneous attack should be made on external factors that contribute to low achievement, such as poor housing, family instability, health and nutrition, and low income.

OUR FINAL WORD

What does the future hold in terms of school governance and financing? The federal government, through the NCLB law, has assumed a major role in education in the United States, much more than it played in the past. President George W. Bush made the NCLB legislation the key part of his educational agenda, and his administration supported increased funding for education to help finance educational reform, even in light of growing federal budget deficits. The strong accountability measures included in NCLB give the federal government influence over U.S. education that goes well beyond the actual dollars it spends. Although states continue to have the major say in educational matters, the federal government is no longer a "silent partner," and this trend is likely to continue in the future.

WHY TEACH? YOUR FINAL WORD

In your journal or online at this textbook's website, respond to the following questions:

1. What role, if any, do you think the federal government should play in compensating for educational disadvantages that result from living in poverty?
2. Do you believe you would like to become a school principal or local superintendent someday? Why or why not?
3. The National Education Association and the National Association of Secondary School Principals make this statement about successful secondary schools: "In good secondary schools, the principal and teachers develop and maintain a variety of cooperative links with the community. Family and community involvement and support complement the efforts of the school." Describe some of the cooperative links you would suggest at either the elementary or secondary level.

KEY TERMS

American Recovery and Reinvestment Act (369)
categorical grants (369)
chief state school officer (353)
compensatory education (369)
Elementary and Secondary Education Act (ESEA) (369)
Head Start (370)
local school board (354)
No Child Left Behind (NCLB) Act (369)

parent–teacher organization (PTO) (359)
privatization (362)
Race to the Top (369)
state board of education (353)
state department of education (354)
superintendent of schools (355)
Title I (369)

FOR FURTHER INFORMATION

TEACHSOURCE VIDEO

No Child Left Behind (NCLB): Good Intentions, Real Problems

Secretary of Education, Arne Duncan, and Jonathan Kozol, an education activist, discuss the No Child Left Behind law.

WEB RESOURCES

National Education Association. Available at **www. nea.org**.

The NEA website offers many resources, including an annual report (called "Rankings and Estimates") that features many statistics on the states, including average teacher salaries, per-pupil expenditures by state, per capita expenditures on education, and many other interesting statistics. To find the report, go to the Search function and enter "Rankings and Estimates."

U.S. Department of Education. Available at **www. ed.gov**.

This home page will keep you abreast of educational initiatives developed by the federal government. Clicking on the National Center for Education Statistics link will give you access to many government publications and statistics on education. For information on Head Start, visit **www.acf.hhs.gov/ progams/hsb**.

PRINT RESOURCES

Vern Brimley, Jr., and Rulon R. Garfield, *Financing Education in a Climate of Change,* 10th ed. (Boston: Allyn and Bacon, 2008).

This comprehensive text examines how schools are financed in the United States, the role of the federal government, and significant court cases affecting school finance.

Michael W. Kirst and Frederick M. Wirt, *The Political Dynamics of American Education,* 4th ed. (Berkeley, CA: McCutchan, 2009).

This text presents an analysis of the politics of education by two leaders in the field.

Theodore J. Kowalski, *The School Superintendent: Theory, Practice, and Cases* (Thousand Oaks, CA: Sage Publications, 2006).

A comprehensive examination of the school superintendency.

 The Education CourseMate website for this text offers many helpful resources. Go to www.cengagebrain.com to access the TeachSource Video Cases and other TeachSource videos, flashcards, interactive quizzes, the eBook, reflection and enrichment activities, a state standards resource center, and other study aids.

12 how should education be reformed?

FOCUS POINTS

- The current educational reform movement is being fueled by a widespread belief that U.S. schools are not educating many students adequately for the demands of the present, let alone the future.

- Although most people agree that schools should educate students to be good citizens, workers, and people, differing educational philosophies and beliefs about the purposes of schooling lead to a variety of approaches to schooling.

- Some key educational ideas *ought* to be at the heart of this current reform movement.

- Responsibility for school reform resides primarily with state and local educational agencies, with the federal government and national associations also making significant contributions.

- Teachers are the crucial element in meaningful reform.

(© Fancy / Alamy)   (© Ian Shaw / Alamy)

This chapter takes a concentrated look at the educational reform movement. For more than 30 years, politicians and educators have been working vigorously to alter the course of American elementary and secondary education. Although the results of their efforts have been mixed to date, certain patterns and key educational ideas are evident.

Truth or Fiction?

T F Currently in the United States, approximately 1.5 million students are educated at home.

T F Research clearly shows that charter schools are academically superior to regular public schools.

T F Although service-learning activities are popular with students, most believe it keeps them from working hard on academic chores.

It has been said that trying to change or reform our schools is like trying to change a flat tire on a speeding car—something that needs to be done but is nearly impossible to achieve. For nearly 100 years, attempts have been made to bring about change in American schools, with mixed results. Many of these reform efforts have been fueled by philosophical debates as to what the purpose of schools should be (see Chapter 2, "What Is a School and What Is It For?").

For example, in the early 1900s, with the development of factories, which were seen as a more efficient way of producing goods, some people argued that students could be more efficiently educated if schools looked and functioned like factories. They also thought that students would become better adult workers if their schools resembled factory assembly lines. Opponents of this view (including John Dewey, who is profiled in Chapter 9, "What Are the Philosophical Foundations of American Education?") thought that schools should educate students to be good thinkers and citizens who, as adults, would work to bring about a better, more equitable society. Thus our schools became more democratic.

The most recent movement to bring about change in U.S. schools grew out of an influential 1983 report by the National Commission on Excellence in Education, entitled *A Nation at Risk*. In clear and forceful language, the Commission described what it called a "rising tide of mediocrity" in the schools. The report demanded that this tide be stemmed through a greater focus on the academic achievement of students.

In the 30 years since this report was released, some progress has been made toward reforming schools. How much more can or must be made remains open to debate. Some educators and politicians argue that much more needs to be done to improve U.S. schools, given that the reforms implemented to date have not led to significant gains in academic achievement. Others disagree, stating that U.S. schools are a great social achievement, educating more children to higher levels than the schools supported by any other society in the world.

Skeptics believe that the schools—and particularly the public schools—are "broken" and incapable of being reformed. Other observers argue that schools, as institutions, are deeply resistant to change and that, unlike corporations, whose effectiveness can be judged by bottom-line profits or losses, the effectiveness of schools is all but impossible to measure, in part because their purposes remain vague and multiple. Without a single, clear definition of a well-educated person, schools cannot agree on how to reform themselves.

> *It is not the strongest of the species that survive, nor the most intelligent, but the one most responsive to change.*
>
> —CHARLES DARWIN (1809–1882),
> Nineteenth Century British Naturalist

PAUSE AND REFLECT

1. Based on your own personal school experiences, do you believe our schools need to be reformed and changed in any major ways? Why?

2. What do you believe are the most compelling reasons to reform U.S. schools?

current reform initiatives

The United States has historically been an education-oriented society. As a society, we have been proud of our schools and their accomplishments of providing an achievement ladder for anyone who took advantage of them. In recent decades, this faith has eroded, and more and more evidence piles up, first, about the achievement gap between our students and those of many nations, and, second, about the failure of so many schools to serve adequately children from poverty backgrounds and students of color.

Although the issue of school reform has been on the national agenda with healthcare and the environment, in 2010 it emerged to new prominence. Major television networks devoted time and resources to exploring what was wrong with our schools and what should be done. Independently and within months of one another, filmmakers released four powerful documentaries—*Waiting for "Superman," Race to Nowhere: The Dark Side of America's Achievement Culture, The Lottery*, and *The Cartel*—all of which are highly critical of our educational system. This intense media attention focused in particular on our urban schools and how they are educating African American and Latino students and newly arrived immigrants.

Two themes that have come to prominence both in the education literature and in the popular media are high-stakes testing and school choice. Testing, which 20 years ago was seen as the spearhead of the school reform movement, is increasingly being seen as overused and sucking the air out of what should be the joy of learning. The theme of parental choice of schools is hardly new but has gained in intensity as many parents seek educational alternatives for their children. These themes and the others to which we now turn have been intensified by the current economic demands and the realizations that our national future depends so on the quality of the education we are providing our children today.

Again, though, most educators agree that the modern reform effort started with the 1983 federal report *A Nation at Risk*. This strongly worded document declared that the United States was in serious danger because its schools had left the nation vulnerable to its military and economic competitors. The report called for longer school days, more homework and effort on the part of students, tougher grading policies, more testing, and more demanding textbooks. It arrived at a time of particularly widespread dissatisfaction with the public schools. The remainder of the 1980s saw a blizzard of national and state reports, most hitting many of the same themes and all calling for massive change.

The 1990s was a period of intense development of curricular, programmatic, and pedagogic initiatives aimed at bringing about change in schools and better student performance. Several different groups at the national, state, and local levels created proposals for reform. So what have been the results?

NATIONAL-LEVEL REFORM EFFORTS

Since the publication of *A Nation at Risk* in 1983, education has had a prime place in every presidential candidate's platform. After President Reagan, President George H. W. Bush launched an aggressive educational reform effort called **National Education Goals for the Year 2000**. With the support and cooperation of the 50 state governors, this program committed the nation to achieve six educational milestones by the arrival of the new millennium. The next president, Bill Clinton, added two more goals and recommitted the nation to achieve these goals by 2000.[1] Although well intentioned, in retrospect the National Education Goals for the Year 2000 effort seems somewhat naïve, promising more than the schools could reasonably deliver.

No Child Left Behind Act

The next major educational reform effort was the No Child Left Behind Act, which President George W. Bush signed into law in January 2002. This bill is the revised Elementary and Secondary Education Act (ESEA; originally passed in 1965), now known as the No Child Left Behind Act of 2001 (NCLB).[2] NCLB is the main federal law on K–12 education, and its revision greatly increases the federal role in education by putting into place requirements that reach into virtually every public school in the United States.

Still very much in effect, the main goal of NCLB is to close the "achievement gap" between students who perform well in schools and those who perform poorly. To do so, NCLB requires that all teachers be "highly qualified" and that every student be "proficient" in reading and mathematics by the 2013–2014 school year. It requires states to develop tests in reading and mathematics that will be administered every year to students in grades 3 to 8. Further, all students in every school district of the state should demonstrate progress toward academic proficiency. The law also puts pressure on school districts to turn around low-performing schools, with a series of negative consequences for schools that persistently fail to demonstrate adequate yearly progress toward having all students meet state standards.

key provisions of the no child left behind act

NCLB changed the federal government's role in K–12 education by asking U.S. schools to describe their success in terms of what each student accomplishes. The act focuses on President George W. Bush's four basic education reform principles: stronger accountability for results, increased flexibility and local control, expanded options for parents, and emphasis on teaching methods that have been proven to work. Major provisions of the law include the following areas.

Annual Testing
Starting in the 2005–2006 school year, states were required to begin administering annual statewide assessments in reading and mathematics to students in grades 3 through 8, and to test students at least once during grades 10 through 12. States may select and design their own assessments, but the tests must be aligned with their state's academic standards. Starting in the 2007–2008 school year, NCLB also called for states to administer science assessments once during each of the three levels of schooling: elementary, middle, and high school. Test results must include individual student scores and be reported by race, income, special education status, English proficiency, and other categories. The purpose is to identify not just overall trends but also gaps between, and progress of, various subgroups. Schools may need to report test results for as many as 30 subgroups of their students.

Academic Improvement
States must set a minimum performance threshold, and by the 2013–2014 school year all students must attain this level of proficiency. Each state must raise the level of proficiency gradually over time, leading to 100 percent proficiency. This criterion is known as adequate yearly progress (AYP). If a school fails to make AYP for two years in a row, the school receives technical assistance from the district and must provide its students with the option of transferring to another public school or asking for funds to pay for supplemental services such as tutoring. If inadequate progress continues, more drastic consequences ensue, including changing the teachers and administrators of the school.

Teacher and Paraprofessional Qualifications
By the end of the 2005–2006 school year, every public school teacher had to be highly qualified, which means that a teacher has been licensed (including through alternative routes) and has demonstrated a high level of competence in the subjects that he or she teaches.

Source: U.S. Department of Education, "Introduction: No Child Left Behind." Available at www.ed.gov/nclb/overview/intro/execsumm.html.

The passage of NCLB was accompanied by a 40 percent increase in the federal contribution to K–12 education, much of this going to urban school districts. Although the additional funds were welcomed by the cities and their schools, enthusiasm for NCLB has cooled somewhat. Many have applauded the requirement that children's scores must be reported by race, ethnicity, income, special education status, and English proficiency, which focuses attention on the academic achievement for groups of students who might otherwise go unnoticed. Many more cheered that the schools were seriously focusing on evaluation and accountability. Popular too was the idea that students in failing schools would be given a voucher to a school of their choice and be able to opt out. This last feature, the option to transfer to another school, has been particularly disappointing. Either through the underachieving school's failure to educate parents on this option or because of sheer inertia, "only a tiny percentage of eligible students asked to transfer to better schools.[3]

Support for NCLB has been eroded, particularly among teachers and their professional associations, because of what is seen as an overemphasis on testing and evaluation. NCLB's requirements for yearly testing in reading and mathematics, testing for a high school diploma, and the very real threats of negative consequences to teachers and administrators whose students show little improvement did, indeed, effectively change the behavior both of students and teachers. In what appears to be a classic example of "the law of unintended consequences," test preparation and the results of testing quickly became the focus of classrooms across the nation. The time and attention given to other subjects, such as history, science, geography, the arts, and even recess and sports, suffered. School superintendents told principals, and principals told teachers to "forget everything except test prep." In the words of historian and once-NCLB advocate, Diane Ravitch, "Testing became an obsession."[4] Critics too complain that this single-minded focus on testing and on such a narrow range of content has sucked all the joy out of education and turned it into mere training.[5] Further, many find unfair the NCLB provision that if one of the 20-plus subgroups of students fails to meet proficiency, the school is deemed to have failed.

One of the current features of the federal NCLB effort is that the 50 states have been allowed to rely on their own academic standards and goals. The legislation, further, allows each state to use its own tests, its own measuring rods, to gauge their students' progress. Although this unevenness has long been the case, the result is that a student can easily pass the tests in one state, only to find himself failing when he moves to a different state with higher standards. (We will address this problem, which the federal government is trying to solve with the next national reform effort.)

As educators and legislators prepare for the reauthorization of NCLB, a number of changes are being considered. Among them are these:

- Replace the law's unrealistic goal of 100 percent achievement by 2013–2014 with rates of success that can actually be achieved by the most effective public schools.

- Allow states to measure progress by using students' growth in achievement rather than by relying on a particular achievement score when determining levels of academic proficiency.

- Use multiple indicators of student achievement—for example, application of knowledge to real-world situations and performance-based demonstrations of knowledge—instead of relying solely on standardized tests.

- Use student achievement progress as a measure for determining teacher salaries; that is, implement performance pay.

- Fully fund Title I, the major provision of NCLB (see Chapter 11, "How Are Schools Governed, Influenced, and Financed?" for a discussion of Title I).

- Distinguish schools where only one or two student groups fail to make annual yearly progress (AYP) from those schools where more student groups fail to achieve this standard.
- Change the definition of "highly qualified teacher" based on paper qualifications to one based on performance in the classroom.

As Congress and the president grapple with the reauthorization of NCLB, it seems clear that the major intent of the legislation—to reduce the achievement gap between high-performing and low-performing students—will remain the centerpiece of the act. Time will tell whether NCLB's lofty goals substantially improve the education of the nation's children.

Race to the Top

In 2010, President Obama and Secretary of Education Arne Duncan presented what has been described as a "stick-and-carrot" program to jump-start what they consider to be exemplary educational ideas and practice, in hopes that other states will adopt similar practices. Called Race to the Top, the program's goals are to reward school reform efforts and provide educational exemplars to the nation's educational community. Using $4.35 billion of stimulus monies as awards (i.e., "carrots") and attaching various conditions (i.e., "sticks"), such as eliminating legal barriers to charter schools, the administration hopes to bring about specific changes. Among them are these:

- Expanding the number and quality of charter schools
- Updating the way school districts evaluate the effectiveness of teachers
- Improving student data-tracking systems to help educators know what students have learned and what must be retaught
- Turning around thousands of the lowest-performing schools.[6]

Eleven states declined to compete in Race to the Top, and the prize money was awarded to 12 states. The contest has left a somewhat sour taste in the mouths of many educators because all the winners except Hawaii were Eastern seaboard states and typically had significant urban populations.

National Standards

Some critics fear that NCLB is eroding the nation's cherished ideal of local control over education and the states' tradition of setting their own academic standards. There can be little doubt that complying with these federal mandates means that fewer educational decisions are made at the local level. The federal monies coming from Washington, D.C., arrive with strings attached, and those mandates shift decision making away from local teachers, administrators, and the school board. Still, because of the decentralized nature of U.S. education and the provisions of the NCLB legislation, each state educational agency (SEA) has the authority to decide what students in that state learn. For many years, these SEAs delegated curricular authority to the local educational agencies (LEAs) so that each school district could decide the most appropriate course of study for its students. Critics complained that these practices led to too much variation in what students were learning, raising concerns about both the quality of education received and equality of educational opportunity. These concerns led to a drive for **national curricular standards**. As discussed in Chapter 5, "What is Taught?" the Common Core State Standards initiative has currently been adopted by three-quarters of the states.

A National Curriculum

Although federal officials have been developing and mandating national standards, discipline-specific national groups of scholars and educators have come together as part of larger attempts to bring about reform of what is taught in American classrooms. These curricular reform projects identify not just what students all over the United States should learn at each grade level, but in some cases how students should be taught.

The various curriculum reform projects have come about through partnerships among scholars in the discipline, teacher educators, and classroom teachers. Today, ideas and suggestions flow across lines that were once rigid boundaries. University academics observe in elementary and secondary classrooms, and back on the campus, elementary and secondary school teachers instruct scholars on the realities of teaching their subjects to a wide variety of young students.

One advocate for a national curriculum is E. D. Hirsch Jr., who popularized the concept of "cultural literacy." He presents the equality argument, insisting that a national curriculum is needed because so many students move around from state to state and from school to school. With a national curriculum, relocated students would be able to integrate easily into their new school environment, with no time lost academically. Hirsch points to facts such as these: one-fifth of all Americans relocate every year; one-sixth of all third-graders attend at least three different schools between first and third grades; and a typical inner-city school has a 50 percent student turnover between September and May.[7] Others make the quality argument by citing the educational excellence attained by France, Germany, and Japan—all countries with national curricula, national standards and national exams. These proponents insist that a national curriculum will ensure that all students in the United States receive a high-quality education, no matter where they attend school.

Other educators strongly oppose national standards and an accompanying curriculum and testing program, fearing an educational power grab by the federal government. In their view, the idea of Washington bureaucrats, instead of locally accountable individuals, answering the questions "What should our children know?" and "How well should they know it?" seems both educationally flawed and politically dangerous. Opponents also believe that in a large nation with so many racial, religious, and ethnic groups and so many regional traditions, a national curriculum would trample on cultural diversity and promote a bland sterility. Further, many are convinced that a national curriculum would put disadvantaged students at an even greater disadvantage. It would appear that the current Common Core State Standards movement represents a compromise: national standards, but on a voluntary basis.

National Voluntary Networks

One of the most interesting recent educational developments is the appearance of networks of schools and school districts.[8] Among these loose, voluntary alliances are two: the Coalition of Essential Schools begun by the late Theodore Sizer, and the network of schools modeled after James Comer's New Haven School Development Project. Others include John Goodlad's National Network for Educational Reform, Robert Slavin's Success for All Schools, Henry Levin's Accelerated Schools, and a newly established network called Schools of Character, formed by the Character Education Partnership. Schools in these networks commit themselves to a common educational ideal or set of ideals rather than a prescribed course of study or

the partnership for 21st century skills

In many ways, the reform of American education is too important to be left to educators alone. Everyone has a stake particularly now as the health of the nation economy and position in the world has been so clearly related to the quality of our schools. The Partnership for 21st Century Skills (P21) is a national organization that has not only called attention to the need for K–12 educational reform, but and its members provide tools and resources to help schools, teachers, and pupils get ready for the demands of the 21st century.

Essentially, P21 is a catalyst organization, a partnership among leaders from education, business, the foundation world, and government, that calls attention to the profound gap between the knowledge and skills most students learn in school and the knowledge and skills they need in typical 21st century communities and workplaces. More than that, P21 is attempting to get our schools to take a fresh look at what and how they are teaching. To do this, P21 has created a well-developed model, one involving fusing the classic "three R's" and what it calls "the four C's "(critical thinking and problem solving, communication, collaboration, and creativity and innovation). (These "Four C's" are quite similar to The Tools for Learning we describe on p. 404.)

Although the three R's are necessary to master the core subjects (English, history, the arts, mathematics, science, foreign languages, geography, economics, civics and government), P21 insists that students need to move beyond basic mastery of these subjects. They must master them at a higher level, enabling them to weave them into what P21 calls **21st century interdisciplinary themes**, such as global awareness, financial, economic, business and entrepreneurial literacy, civic literacy, health literacy, and, finally, environmental literacy.

P21 presents educators with a fresh and challenging vision of our work which we can only touch on here. We urge you to follow up and check out the P21 website at www.p21.org/index.php.

approach to teaching and learning. For instance, the schools in the Coalition of Essential Schools try to put into practice the Ten Common Principles, which include the following points:

- Helping adolescents use their minds well
- Teaching for the mastery of essential skills and acceleration in certain areas of knowledge
- Recognizing the student as worker rather than the teacher as deliverer of information
- Provoking students to learn how to learn
- Reflecting values of trust, decency, tolerance, and generosity in the tone of the school
- Expecting much from students without threatening them[9]

High School Reform

Most of the reforms of the previous two decades, successful and otherwise, took place in elementary schools and, to a lesser extent, middle schools. However, in 2005, a long-overdue campaign to reform U.S. high schools was launched. The initiators of this transformational project are a coalition of state governors, foundation directors, and business leaders, including Microsoft's Bill Gates, himself a rather successful college dropout.

The group believes that the current American high school is an "obsolete" institution, out of touch with the global world of work and the demands of higher education. Its members are concerned that our trading partners around the world have more rigorous and productive high schools than those of the United States. In response to these concerns, they are dedicated to implementing several of the changes recommended in this chapter, especially higher academic standards accompanied by a more rigorous curriculum and a better testing and accountability system that measures students' readiness for work and for college.

Armed with strong financial support from businesses and foundations, plus fresh, compelling evidence of the inadequacies of many high school graduates, this coalition is seeking wider support to transform U.S. schools. For example, it has launched the American Diploma Project (ADP) Network, which is attempting to "bring value to the high school diploma by raising the rigor of high school standards, assessments, and curriculum, and aligning expectations with the demands of postsecondary education and work."[10] Specifically, the ADP Network is committed to four actions:[11]

1. Raising high school standards to the level needed for success in college or the workforce
2. Requiring all students to take a rigorous college- and work-ready curriculum
3. Developing a test of college and work readiness that all students will take in high school
4. Holding high schools accountable for making sure all students graduate ready for college and work, and holding colleges accountable for the success of the students they admit

Whether this unique partnership of businessmen, foundation directors, and governors has the energy and leverage to change the U.S. high school in fundamental ways will be one of the most important and closely watched educational questions of the second decade of the 21st century.

Implications of National-Level Reform Efforts

Overall, two things are clear about educational reforms at the national level. First, we are in the middle of a strong push toward national influence on education and, with the passage of the NCLB legislation and the Race to the Top competition, that push is getting stronger. Second, there has been a robust response from the states to improve their curricular standards and to hold local school districts accountable for these standards by imposing statewide testing with high-stakes consequences (graduation-dependent testing). The days of strong local control over schools in America appear to be waning.

STATE EDUCATIONAL REFORM

As education evolved into more of a national issue, reform also became a hot political topic on levels from the state house to the mayor's office. Statewide task forces were formed by governors, state legislatures, and state boards of education, and a large number were formed by citizens' groups and foundations. Some states had several task forces operating on the same issues at the same time. Numerous local school districts established their own blue-ribbon commissions to respond to what was increasingly called *the school crisis*. As the late Ernest Boyer said, "You could draw a 'Keystone Kops' image here of people charging off in different directions and bumping into each other and, in some instances, having a conflict with one another.

There is no overall sense of where the problem is and how we should work together to get there."[12] There was, however, one common theme: the **call for excellence** (discussed earlier in this chapter).

Throughout both American industry and education, mediocrity was the dominant criticism of the existing educational system, and excellence became the rallying cry of the reformers. Many of these recent state and local task force reports have *excellence* or *quality* in their titles. Because these task forces and reports were sponsored by state governmental agencies or well-connected citizens' groups or educational foundations, their recommendations were quickly turned into legislative proposals for school reform.

Common Elements in State Reform

At the state level, the "search for excellence" came down to specific proposals for change. The most widely adopted state reforms are described next.

An Increase in Graduation Requirements. Instead of mandating that students take only one or two years of English and history, states began requiring three and four years in core subjects. To be awarded academic high school diplomas, science and advanced mathematics courses were required. The idea of "social promotion" (i.e., moving students through the grades so that they could stay with their own age groups independently of their performance) came under great pressure and has been eliminated in many places, especially with the advent of mandated tests for graduation (see the section on standards-based education).

Spurred on by the United States' relatively poor performance on recent international studies of math and science proficiency, the majority of states have increased the number of academic credits needed for graduations, with particular increases in the number of years of English, science, and mathematics.[13]

More Academic Learning Time. Research has shown that *quality* instruction time, rather than time merely spent in class, is the key to quality schooling. Nevertheless, in the minds of many educators, the short school day and the long, academically fallow period between June and September are major causes of the poor performance of U.S. students. More time in school overall, they suggest, improves the chances of having more high-quality time.

In response to this notion, school days, which in many locales were only five and a half to six hours, were lengthened to six and a half to seven hours. The school year, which in many states was between 170 and 175 days or fewer, has been lengthened to an average of 180 days, although states still vary from between 174 days (North Dakota) to 182 days (Ohio) of school per year.[14] Though many of the reform reports recommended that U.S. schools follow the example of Japan (240 days) and Germany (216 to 240 days), no states and relatively few school districts have taken such a major step in lengthening the school year. One reason is that lengthening the amount of schooling is extremely costly.

In some states, the idea of **year-round education** has attracted the attention of educators. In most year-round schools, students go to school the same number of days as in traditional schools, but the school days are more evenly distributed throughout the school year. The most popular schedule is referred to as "45–15." Students attend school for 45 days, and then have 15 days vacation. In the summer, students have six weeks of vacation instead of the usual 8 to 10 weeks. According to the National Association for Year-Round Education, as of 2007 more than 2,700 public schools in 46 states, as well as many private schools, had adopted some kind of a year-round schedule.[15]

Critics of year-round education cite the strain such a schedule places on school finances when upgrades such as air conditioning are needed. They are also concerned about disrupting established family life patterns and summer opportunities for teachers' professional development. On the other hand, proponents insist that the long 10-week summer vacation is hardest on poor children, for whom camps and pricy recreational and enrichment programs are out of reach. They argue that the academic ground lost over the summer is a significant contributor to the achievement gap that separates high- and low-income children. President Obama, citing the fact that students in many other countries yearly spend at least a month longer in school than our students, urged that American students have a longer school year.[16]

Standards-Based Education. The "standards movement" has been at the core of educational reform. Proponents of standards-based education argue that, just as businesses have to meet certain quality standards of production, so schools should be held to certain standards in the education of students. By clearly and precisely identifying what students at each grade level are expected to know, state policymakers can more easily determine the quality and effectiveness of the schools throughout the state. Critics argue that similar reform efforts have already been tried and failed. They also express concern about possible *standardization* of education, which often ignores students' individual learning needs.[17]

Largely as a result of the NCLB financial incentives, all 50 states have adopted curriculum or content standards specifying the material that all students in that state are expected to know and the grade level at which they should know it. In many cases, these state standards are drawn from the voluntary national standards discussed earlier in this chapter. (Also see Chapter 5, "What Is Taught?" for examples of state content standards.) To make certain that the effort and monies going into their reform efforts pay off as expected, both federal and state legislatures are demanding *accountability,* generally in the form of state-mandated assessments. Nevertheless, as discussed above, critics of the standards movement and the extensive use of testing in American schools insist this form of accountability is having a negative impact.[18]

> *Ideas move fast when their time comes.*
> —CAROLYN HEILBRUN (1926–2003),
> Literary Scholar and Novelist

Increased graduation requirements and calls for more testing are part of many states' educational reforms.

Higher Expectations for Teachers. One of the major state-driven reform efforts of the 1980s and 1990s was the move to improve the quality of America's teaching force. Two initiatives were particularly notable in this regard: teacher competency testing and career ladder programs.

The first initiative, **teacher competency testing**, was not new, though it emerged with a vengeance during the last two decades of the twentieth century. Currently, all but three states (Montana, North Dakota, and Texas) have some form of teacher testing, which typically takes place when candidates are leaving their teacher education programs or before they receive state licensure.[19]

One vexing issue that has plagued the movement for teacher competency testing has been the definition of an appropriate and valid standard to which all teacher candidates should be held. In some states, cut-off scores have been set so low as to make them meaningless. In effect, teachers are supposed to demonstrate their proficiency by jumping over a hurdle, but the hurdle has been so low that anyone could jump it. In other states, the standard is considered too arbitrary, dissuading teachers from seeking licensure in those states. There is variation too regarding which competencies are being tested, such as general English and math proficiency, along with content knowledge. In some states, efforts are being made to test competencies beyond mere paper-and-pencil tests and to observe for competence in actual classrooms. The second teacher-related initiative involved **career ladders**. Critics have long complained about the "flatness" of the career structure in teaching. The criticism goes something like this: "Beginners have too much responsibility at the start of their careers and too little opportunity to make the most of their abilities once they really learn to teach. The only way to get promoted in education has been to be promoted *away from students*, by becoming a department chair, curriculum coordinator, or administrator." With the encouragement of state legislatures, a variety of teacher specialty programs, such as master teacher programs, differentiated staffing, and mentoring programs for new teachers, have now appeared on the scene. Typically, these programs give experienced teachers new roles, new responsibilities, and usually new rewards. Although these innovations have had somewhat limited adoption, the assumption that "a teacher is a teacher is a teacher" has been dispelled, and new roles, such as mentor teacher, lead teacher, and team leader, have been opened to teachers who want new challenges but also want to stay in the classroom, close to students.

Higher Salaries for Teachers. A key problem revealed by the blizzard of reports published in the 1980s and 1990s was the weak rewards system for teachers. Career ladders and other schemes that expand and enrich the teacher's role represented one way to reward teachers, but more was needed if teaching was to become an attractive professional option for talented students. Salaries were an obvious target. During the 1980s, the average teacher salary increased at a rate twice that of inflation. Since then, average salaries have generally kept pace with inflation.

Closely linked to this change has been a significant move to make teaching more attractive by increasing the starting salaries of teachers. In the late 1980s, beginning teachers earned $12,000 to $13,000. By the 2008–2009 school year, the national average for beginning teachers was $38,999.[20] (See Chapter 13, "What Are Your Job Options in Education?" for more information on current salary trends.) Meanwhile, various commissions and commentators continue to press for higher salaries both for teachers entering the field and for experienced teachers. All across the United States, the lock-step pay scale under which teachers were rewarded only for years of service and number of courses taken or degrees earned has been altered to allow for **performance pay (pay for performance)**, a form of recognition and reward for acquiring new knowledge or skills, or for increasing student achievement. In 2007, 28 nationally recognized, award-winning teachers came together and issued a widely hailed report, "Performance Pay for Teachers: Designing a System that Students Deserve," which forcefully calls for changes in the way the United States recognizes excellence in teaching.[21] Also, the Obama administration made pay for performance a strong plank in its Race to the Top school improvement plan. In 2010, however, supporters of merit pay plans, such as pay for performance, received a setback with the release of a study by the National Center on Performance Incentives. This large scale study concluded that students of teachers receiving performance pay achieved no better on tests than those taught by teachers not receiving such financial bonuses.[22] However, we doubt that this is the end of efforts to provide pay incentives to outstanding teachers.

SCHOOL CHOICE

As we stated at the beginning of this chapter, school choice (along with testing) is a major theme in efforts to provide better education for America's children. Implemented on both the local and state levels, the school choice reform aims to offer families more options about where their children will attend school. Technically, all parents have a choice as to where they wish to have their children educated. If they do not like the public, state-supported school to which their children are assigned, they can send them to a private or religious school (if one is available in their locale), or they can move to another community where the schools are more to their liking. Another increasingly popular option (as described in the accompanying feature) is for parents to teach their own children at home.

The only problem with this idea is that not everyone can put it into practice. For the large percentage of parents without the time and ability to conduct homeschooling or the resources to pay tuition at private or religious schools, there really is no choice at all. Therefore, many people are touting **school choice** as an

important aspect of access and educational opportunity. They argue that poor parents should have a choice in the schools their children attend, just as wealthier parents do. According to these people, being able to choose the school your children attend is, first, the right of parents and second, an important way to ensure access to educational opportunity. If the neighborhood public school isn't doing an adequate job, shouldn't parents have alternative choices of schools?

The advocates of school choice see the current system as monopolistic. The United States, they note, is recognized around the world as a consumer's paradise. Whether it is soft drinks in the supermarket, jeans in a clothing store, or sports cars at the auto dealer, the principle of choice rules—except in K–12 schooling. School choice advocates want to redesign the way we organize education, shifting the decision of where a child must go to school from the school system to the child's parents. In essence, they want *market forces* to regulate the schools, instead of the educational monopoly that they claim currently operates.

home-schooling

Hilary Tucker is a mother of four children who lives in Auburn, Alabama. She is one of a growing number of parents who have decided to educate their children themselves, most often in their homes. The U.S. Department of Education estimates that approximately 1,500,000 children are home-schooled in this country. Reasons cited for home-schooling range from concerns about the moral climate in public schools, to religious objections to the curriculum, to the absence of particular courses of study. In all cases, however, parents strongly believe that they can provide a better education for their children than the public schools can.

Regulations for home-schooling vary from state to state. In some states, parents have to submit an educational plan for their home-schooled children; in other states, they merely inform the school and/or the state education agency of their intention to home-school their children.

Home-schooling these days offers every child an opportunity for a world-class education. It doesn't have to cost a great deal, and it is adaptable to many circumstances and individuals.

In recent years, the opportunities for co-op classes, tutoring, and online courses have exploded. Home-schooling parents no longer have to do it all themselves. My 13-year-old takes Latin, theology, and humanities with an online academy. She also

Ⓣ F

Currently in the United States, approximately 1.5 million students are educated at home.
~~Approximately 1,500,000 children are home-schooled in this country.~~

takes Spanish and biology in local home-school classes, but she is most impassioned about the ideas presented in her online classes and reading assignments. Ten eager elementary students come to study Latin and Roman history with us on Wednesday mornings, providing the classroom experience of more formal schooling, tests, and competition. A friend with teaching experience teaches them English grammar, and the older students meet with a math tutor, who teaches them individually.

By having personally tailored curricula and individual attention, home-schooled students' time is rarely wasted. My children have their formal lessons during the morning hours, but in some way, the schooling never stops. There are many hours in the week for both directed and leisure reading, and the TV rarely comes on in this house. My preschooler is working through reading lessons, memorizing poetry, and otherwise engaging in creative activities.

(continued)

During the afternoons, once the assignments are done, the kids follow their own interests. The older children practice piano and violin and are involved in sports, dance, and other programs. The hobbies are fruitful too. At age 7, my daughter charted the birds that came to our yard. She's learned how to knit and sew (thanks to an obliging friend), has started her own blog, and is teaching herself web design. During their younger years, my children spent many an afternoon climbing trees and examining bugs. And they played. They worked out elaborate fantasies about knights and princesses, formed pioneer families, and discovered elves. They built forts and pressed flowers.

For home-schooling parents, offering each child (not just the brightest) the opportunity to become passionate about ideas is worth the sacrifice of having their children under their supervision for most of the day. Students develop the habit of learning, so they don't always have to depend on an instructor. They come to know what it means to master bodies of knowledge and how to reason. They can progress at their own rate. The advanced student is not held back and made to repeat exercises she has already learned. The slower student does not miss out on building foundational skills because other students are ready to move on. Where the student has weaknesses, he receives extra help. Where there are strengths, he has the opportunity to soar. As a teacher, I am able to teach my children a time-tested curriculum so the child is spared trendy new subjects that may not be around in 10 years.

Perhaps understandably, parents of home-schooled kids are often asked, "What about socialization?" It is true that home-schooled children do not spend their days in a classroom filled with 22 peers and are deprived of this particular group experience. Yet this freedom from the bustling crowd can be an advantage. The children learn to cooperate with other children of all ages, primarily and significantly their siblings, but friends and peers in the neighborhood and in community sports leagues and other activities too.

Home-schooling is not an insular experience for the children I know. Support networks are well developed and surprisingly diversified. Most days, tennis, music lessons, dance classes, and trips to the library get this family out of the house. The kids have played in city sports leagues and been in local theater programs. They also have more time with grandparents and neighbors. And, of course, their friends come over to play. With all this, the children divide their time between other children and the adult world. This is one reason why home-schooled students are so strikingly comfortable around people of all ages.

I believe I, and many other parents, can serve my children and society best by educating them in our home. And, besides the progress they are making, I am enjoying it immensely.

Parents as Educational Consumers

Advocates for school choice say that the current public schools have no real incentive to better serve students because educators' salaries and benefits are unaffected by either good or poor student results. The teacher who works 16 hours a day and gives heart and soul to the school is on the same salary scale as the teacher who is the first one out of the parking lot at 2:30 p.m. According to school choice advocates, if parents can act as consumers, schools will have real incentives to improve. Free-market principles suggest that "more choice equals more competition equals better products at lower prices." Here, the phrase "better products" means better-educated students. Supporters of school choice also suggest that the group getting the worst public education today—urban minorities—stands to benefit the most under such a plan.

The choice concept appears to be gaining support across the United States. In addition to home-schooling, at least three kinds of school choice exist. The least controversial kind, **within-district choice**, allows parents to choose from among the various public schools that a school district or state operates. Many school districts have created a variety of schools with different goals and purposes, and allow parents to select the one they want their child to attend. A more controversial and popular kind of school choice is the *charter school* concept, and the most controversial kind is *school voucher plans*. The major political parties have staked out positions on the choice issue, with Democrats typically favoring choice within the current public school system and Republicans tending to support voucher plans. Although the teachers unions usually give only token support to charter schools, they typically draw support from both Republicans and Democrats.

Public School Choice

Increasingly, public school systems are offering parents and students options, in addition to the traditional neighborhood school, as to which schools students attend. Some schools have a particular specialty such as mathematics or science. Others are "alternative" schools designed for youth who don't seem to fit well within traditional schools.

Several varieties of public school choice exist, most of which are fairly noncontroversial. Districtwide (intradistrict) choice allows parents to select among the schools within their home district. These school choice options are offered in numerous school districts, including Boston, Seattle, Minneapolis/St. Paul, and District 4 in New York City. Statewide (interdistrict) choice allows students to attend public schools outside their home school district.

Charter Schools

Forty years ago, a number of American cities adopted an early form of school choice, called **magnet schools**. These elementary, middle, and high schools specialized in a specific academic area, such as science or the arts, and in basic skills. Magnet schools were originally designed to stop white flight from urban schools and to attract (like a magnet) white students back to inner cities. Although still in existence in many cities, enthusiasm for magnet schools has been displaced by what has become the darling of choice advocates: charter schools.

Charter schools are public schools with special privileges. Recent years have seen a rapid growth in charter schools. In 2009, there were about 4,600 character schools in the country, with 1.4 million students.[23] Teachers, administrators, parents, and community representatives who wish to open a charter school in a district negotiate an agreement with the school district or other agency authorized to grant charters. As long as they meet the specifications of their charters, these schools are free to control their own budgets, hire their own consultants, design their own curriculum, and infuse the school with their own educational flavor. These schools are, in effect, *independent public schools*. Typically, students are chosen randomly from those who apply to attend the particular charter school.

Because they are independent, charter schools usually have a strong element of **site-based decision making** (also known as *site-based management* or *school-based management*), in which participatory decision making is the mode of operation. In theory, the charter school's site-based decision making provides everyone—teachers, parents, and students alike—with more say about what goes on in their school and with a great degree of ownership of and commitment to the decisions that are made. An example of a network of for-profit charter schools, the Knowledge is Power Program (KIPP) schools follow.

the kipp schools

One of the most successful of the new breed of alternative schools are the Knowledge Is Power Program schools or, as they are commonly referred to, the KIPP schools. Begun in 1994 by two teachers, in 2010 there were 99 KIPP schools in 20 states, serving over 26,000 students.[24] All of the KIPP schools are 5–8 middle schools, and the great bulk of them are charter schools serving a largely minority student body.

The success of the documentary film, *Waiting for "Superman,"* brought much greater awareness to the KIPP model. With a few exceptions, these schools are public schools under contract with their communities to provide educational service. Although initially supported heavily by foundations and donors, KIPP schools survive on budgets similar to their neighboring "regular" public middle schools. The similarities after that are few.

KIPP schools are called "no-excuses" schools because of their commitment to students' development of self-discipline and good behavior. And these qualities are seen as the keys to their impressive record of achievement. Over 90 percent of KIPP middle schoolers attended college prep high schools and over 85 percent have gone on to college. This from a population of students of whom 95 percent are either Latino or African American.

The schools achievement is based on a fierce commitment to excellence, which in turn rests on KIPP's five pillars:

- *High Expectations.* KIPP schools have clearly defined and measurable high expectations for academic achievement and conduct that make no excuses based on the students' backgrounds. Students, parents, teachers, and staff create and reinforce a culture of achievement and support through a range of formal and informal rewards and consequences for academic performance and behavior.

- *Choice and Commitment.* Students, their parents, and the faculty of each KIPP school choose to participate in the program. No one is assigned or forced to attend a KIPP school. Everyone must make and uphold a commitment to the school and to each other to put in the time and effort required to achieve success.

- *More Time.* KIPP schools know that there are no shortcuts when it comes to success in academics and life. With an extended school day, week, and year, students have more time in the classroom to acquire the academic knowledge and skills that will prepare them for competitive high schools and colleges, as well as more opportunities to engage in diverse extracurricular experiences.

- *Power to Lead.* The principals of KIPP schools are effective academic and organizational leaders who understand that great schools require great school leaders. They have control over their school budget and personnel. They are free to swiftly move dollars or make staffing changes, allowing them maximum effectiveness in helping students learn.

- *Focus on Results.* KIPP schools relentlessly focus on high student performance on standardized tests and other objective measures. Just as there are no shortcuts, there are no excuses. Students are expected to achieve a level of academic performance that will enable them to succeed at the nation's best high schools and colleges.[25]

Although KIPP schools have many of the advantages of charter schools, such as parents' selecting into the school and the capacity to expel poor performing or uncooperative students, still they have many features that are seen as quite compatible with regular pupil schools. This capacity to provide inspiration and competition is one of the major contributions of the school choice movement.

Charter schools are judged on how well they meet the student achievement goals established by their charter, or contract, and how well they manage their fiscal and operational responsibilities. Although charters generally allow schools to be run with substantial autonomy, the schools must operate lawfully and responsibly with the highest regard for equity and excellence, or their charters will be taken away. In the

T (F)

Research clearly shows that charter schools are academically superior to regular public schools.

Recent research indicates overall rather mediocre achievement gains by students in charter schools compared with a matched group of students who wanted to attend charter schools but could not be accommodated. Only 17 percent of the charter school students outperformed the others.

two decades charter schools have been around, many have failed due to financial mismanagement and occasionally because of embezzlement.

Even more disappointing to charter advocates has been recent research that indicates overall rather mediocre achievement gains by students in charter schools. In the fall of 2009, two studies emerged. One large study showed that only 17 percent of the students in charter schools outperformed their counterparts in regular public schools. The other study compared the achievement scores of students who had been accepted into charter schools with those for whom there was no room. Here the charter students outperformed the others.[26]

Evaluations of charter schools, however, is on-going, and their popularity with the media and the public remains high. One measure of their popularity is that as the 2010 school year began, 400,000 students were on waiting lists across the nation for charter schools.[27] In 2110, both political parties, Republican and Democrat, supported their expansion beyond the then 1,700 charter schools in the nation.[28] Often, however, evaluations have been carried out by individuals with vested interests in either proving the effectiveness of charter schools or showing that they are ineffective and lack accountability. More time will be needed to see whether charter schools will revolutionize public education or remain just a boutique innovation.

States vary greatly in the ease with which charter schools may be created and in the number of restrictions and amount of autonomy these schools are granted.

Many supporters see charter schools as a way to encourage innovation, provide parents with school choice, and still be supportive of the public school system. Opponents wonder why the charter schools should be exempt from regulations, whereas the rest of the public schools must abide by them. They also see charter schools as a form of "voucher lite"—that is, a foot in the door toward the creation of school vouchers, to which we now turn.

Vouchers

More controversial than charter schools are school **voucher plans**. In their typical form, vouchers give the parent-consumer the widest array of choices. In effect, this type of plan gives parents a piece of paper, a voucher worth a certain dollar amount, that they can use to help pay the costs for their child to attend the public or private school of their choice. The school collects a voucher from each student who chooses that school and then turns in its vouchers to the state government for real dollars with which to run the school.

The voucher idea came to public attention 1955 when Nobel Laureate economist, Milton Freidman wrote an article entitled "The Role of Government in Education," based on well-known free-market principles.[29] Friedman strongly questioned the appropriateness in a democracy of the government (national, state, and local) dictating what is taught in school. According to Freidman, in a "pure choice" system, all schools would be public schools, the way all department stores are public stores. Advocates of the voucher system believe it would release an enormous amount of competition-driven creativity in our schools. Teachers and administrators would join together to provide high-quality, unique educational programs that would attract students and parents. Educational institutions would be like most other American enterprises, competing to put out the best possible product—namely, students. Those that succeeded would prosper, attracting many students (and therefore voucher dollars). Those schools and teachers who failed to attract or hold "customers" would "go out of business," perhaps to start again with a better educational idea.

Voucher plans are still relatively novel, and no really thorough test has been conducted to see whether they can deliver on these heady promises. Two districts pioneering voucher plans are Milwaukee and Cleveland. Their plans, however, are limited to low-income, mostly minority families.

In Milwaukee, which initiated the voucher plan idea in 1990, nearly 15,000 students use vouchers. In effect, 26 percent of Milwaukee students receive public funding to attend schools outside the traditional Milwaukee public school system. In the 2008–2009 school year, 127 Milwaukee schools participated in the choice program, and nearly 20,000 students in the city attended the private schools on vouchers worth up to $6,607 per student. However, halfway through a five-year study, poor students going to private schools on vouchers show no more academic progress than those attending the Milwaukee Public Schools.[30]

Cleveland's voucher plan was quickly tested in the courts, because most of the students chose to use their vouchers for Catholic schools, which raised concerns about whether spending public dollars for students to attend religious schools violates the principle of church and state separation. In 2002, the U.S. Supreme Court ruled (in *Zelman* v. *Simmons-Harris*) in a five-to-four decision that Cleveland's voucher plan, which empowers parents to redeem tuition vouchers at either religious or nonreligious private schools, does not violate the constitutional prohibition against "establishment" of religion because government aid goes directly to parents, who then use it at their discretion. This decision is interpreted as giving a green light to states to implement school voucher plans to assist students attending "failing schools," and more school voucher plans are likely to be implemented. For example, a voucher plan is being established in New Orleans that is sponsored by the federal government. The plan was put into effect in response to the school crisis brought on by the city's devastation by Hurricane Katrina.[31]

In 2009, a year where state budgets were strained, the amount of public money allocated for vouchers increased by 5 percent, so that in the nation as a whole, 180,000 K–12 students received a voucher.[32] Some education critics see the voucher concept as the savior of education in the United States. Others see it as a plot to undermine both

Voucher programs that allow students to use public funding to attend private schools are quite controversial.

the public schools and their interpretation of the meaning of the separation of church and state. Many politicians who support charter schools oppose voucher plans. They see charter schools as providing choice opportunities to parents and encouraging school reform efforts while staying within the public education system, but view voucher plans as draining money from the public schools and delivering those funds to private and religious schools. Vouchers reduce funding indirectly by decreasing public school enrollment, which is one of the factors on which governments base their allocations of money to public schools. (Learn more about school finance in Chapter 11, "How Are Schools Governed, Influenced, and Financed?")

Opponents of voucher plans have voiced several other objections and concerns to these ventures:

- They argue that voucher plans bring false hopes of school choice because the private schools, not the parents, do the choosing through admissions decisions, and a private school is under no obligation to accept students with vouchers.

- In some proposals, the vouchers are worth only $1,000 to $2,500 per student, seriously limiting the choices of schools for which these amounts would pay the actual costs of tuition.

- Citing the fact that vouchers are being used to educate children in religious schools and in spite of the recent Supreme Court ruling, many still see this use of vouchers as breaching the wall of church–state separation.

- Many voucher opponents, including the two largest teacher unions, suggest that if voucher plans become widespread, the public schools will lose much-needed revenue and be forced to educate children with great needs, whom the private schools would not accept, while lacking the resources to do a good job.

- Voucher opponents contend that applying market forces to educational institutions doesn't make sense, arguing instead that schools should be driven by the need to serve the public good, not the desire of individuals and corporations to earn profits.

Those who support voucher plans offer counterarguments to many of these objections. For example, although funding private and religious schools with public money is very controversial in the United States, it is a less contentious issue in many other countries. The United States is one of the few developed nations with such strict limits on parental choice of schools. Many other Western democracies fund private or religious schools with public money, although if these schools accept public money, they usually have to meet certain conditions required by the government.

Voucher supporters also point out that although many people believe U.S. tax dollars fund only public schools, private and religious schools already benefit from public money. The major breakthrough for private and religious schools was the passage of the Elementary and Secondary Education Act of 1965, which funneled millions of dollars into private schools through federal Title I programs to support the education of poor children. In addition, private schools in many states have received public assistance ranging from pupil transportation, textbooks, health services, and general auxiliary services to salary supplements for teachers. In general, state assistance in areas other than transportation, milk, school lunch programs, and textbooks has been attacked in the courts. Both federal and state monies, however, have been used to provide scholarship aid to students attending religious universities and colleges.

Another argument cited in support of voucher plans notes that the private schools, which provide education for more than 5 million students each year, lighten the burden of the public schools. If, for example, the cash-strapped Catholic school system collapsed, more than 2.5 million new students would enroll in the public schools, creating a massive shortage of space, teachers, and money. Advocates of private school aid argue that by partially subsidizing private schools to keep them in operation, the public schools can avoid a deluge of students whom they would be unable to assimilate readily. If a substantial number of these schools were to shut down, the public schools would incur a substantial portion of these costs.

As is the case for charter schools, research on the success or failure of various voucher plans is limited and, in the eyes of many, driven by ideological issues. The issue of school choice is likely to remain a contentious one for some time to come.

FOR-PROFIT SCHOOLS

A small but growing element of the school choice picture is **for-profit schools**, also known as *educational maintenance organizations* (EMOs—modeled on health maintenance organizations [HMOs]). These financially driven businesses typically contract with a community or school district to provide educational services. Although school districts have long hired private companies to provide food services, transportation, and technological support, only recently have districts contracted for a total educational package: curriculum, teachers, administrators, buildings. Three of the best-known EMOs are the Edison Learning Schools, the Advantage Schools, and the KIPP. (Knowledge Is Power Program, described earlier) However, several other for-profit schools are now operating, and still others are on the drawing board.

Although many people criticize EMOs' underlying business model (i.e., making a profit from educating children), proponents of these schools believe that the imagination, drive, and rigor that has made U.S. business the envy of the world is just what has been lacking in our schools. If nothing else, the advent of these for-profit schools is testimony of the American public's hunger for quality education.

Like many of the other choice plans and alternatives, EMOs have generated a great deal of interest, but rigorous evaluations of their effectiveness have yet to appear. We will have to wait to see whether an educational Starbucks, Walmart, or Staples emerges on the scene soon.

PAUSE AND REFLECT

1. Which form of school choice appeals most to you? Why?

2. Do you support the use of school vouchers for students to attend private or parochial schools? Why or why not?

LOCAL-LEVEL SCHOOL REFORM

Former Speaker of the U.S. House of Representatives, the late Tip O'Neill, was fond of saying, "All politics are local." The same is true of education. Children are educated at their local schools, not at the state capitol or in Washington, D.C. Although some school reform efforts, such as the Coalition of Essential Schools Project, are national in scope, even those programs are implemented in local schools under the supervision of a school district.

At present, the great majority of changes being made in schools are coming at the direction of the various states' departments of education, and educational funds are often linked to how faithfully and quickly a school district implements the desired reform mandates. Locally initiated reform efforts, although in no way stopped, have slowed down, partly because of a shortage of local funds. Growing competition for fixed amounts of municipal tax dollars—from police and fire departments to agencies serving the poor and the elderly—and competing thoughts on the primary purpose of public education have made it difficult to secure monies for new, locally supported reform efforts. What we are witnessing is a classic shift in power, with the statehouse and the White House increasingly dictating to the localities not just *what* should be taught but *how* it should be taught.

Although the center of gravity may be elsewhere, the local school district is, nevertheless, deeply involved in the current reform movement. Furthermore, the overwhelming majority of reform ideas that have made their way onto the agendas of national and state reform groups first emerged at the local level. Put simply, they became statewide or national because they succeeded first at the local level. Even more innovative ideas, such as block scheduling, year-round education, service-learning requirements, single-sex schools, school uniforms, and site-based decision making, will undoubtedly continue to bubble up from our local schools in the future.

LEADERS in education

Michelle Rhee (1969–)

In 2007, the then mayor of Washington, D.C., made a bold decision. The schools over which he presided were among the very worst in the nation. Although the city had the third highest per-pupil costs in the country, student academic performance was dismal. In desperation, he hired a young woman only 15 years out of college and with only *three years of teaching experience.* The woman is Michelle Rhee.

Three turbulent years later, a new mayor was elected, and it was clear to Rhee that he wanted a new school leader, so she resigned. The fact that she chose the Oprah Show to announce her post-retirement plan is an indication of just how much attention Rhee's leadership in the D.C. schools attracted and how much controversy her actions caused.

Michelle Rhee is the child of Korean immigrants who came to this country in the 1960's. Born in 1969 in Ann Arbor, Michigan, Michelle's family moved to Toledo, Ohio, where she attended elementary and high school before going to Cornell University. Majoring in political science at Cornell, she was admitted to Harvard's Kennedy School of Government and in 1994 earned a Masters in Public Policy. Instead of pursuing a university career or going into government work, Michelle joined Teach

for America, a graduate program that trains and places college graduates in some of the nation's most challenging schools serving the poor.

Michelle's first and only teaching assignment was at the Harlem Park Elementary School in Baltimore, Maryland. She must have done something right, because she was able to move her students' scoring on average at the 13th percentile on national standardized tests to 9 out of 10 scoring at the 90th percentile or higher. She freely admits, though, that her first year was "the worst and in many ways definitely the toughest year of my entire life."

Like many first-year teachers, her problem was discipline. She claims her second-graders were notorious for how much noise they made while passing through the halls. One day, out of frustration, she had the students put masking tape over their mouths to keep them from talking on the way to lunch. It worked, until they arrived at the lunchroom and she told them, "Okay, take the tape off." Then she realized that she hadn't told the class to moisten their lips before applying the tape. As she recounts the incident, "The skin is coming off their lips and they're bleeding. Thirty-five kids were crying."

(UPI/Kevin Dietsch /Landov)

(continued)

It may have been incidents like this, plus her passion for the plight of new teachers, that lead to her next venture, founding The New Teacher Program (TNTP) in 1997. Since its inception, TNTP has trained or hired approximately 37,000 teachers, benefiting an estimated 6 million students nationwide in 31 states. Ten years later, Rhee was selected "as Chancellor," (i.e., Superintendent, or Chief School Officer) of the D.C. schools.

Michelle Rhee is known as an energetic, no-nonsense person and, as the leader of the Washington, D.C. schools, she hit the ground running. In short order, she came to the conclusion that there was too much waste in the system, from space to personnel and curriculum, and changes had to be made. She announced the closing of 24 schools and the removal of several principals. She also cut the central office by 50 percent. Besides her cuts and controversial school closings, Rhee institute extensive curricular changes, including art and music programs, early childhood education, and gifted and talented programs. During her three years, elementary reading scores increased by 6 percent, and math by 15 percent. The improvement among secondary students was 14 percent in reading and 17 percent in math.

Rhee's most innovative and controversial moves had to do with the district's teachers. Using the No Child Left Behind Act as justification, she fired 76 teachers for lack of proper licensure. Another group of teachers whose students were performing poorly were evaluated and then fired, too. All together, 241 teachers were dismissed and another 737 school employees were "put on notice."

Her most notorious move, and one that made her reputation as a top school reformer, was to take on teacher tenure. Rhee proposed to the local teacher's union that she would exchange high salaries (up to $140,000 per year) and bonuses ($20,000 to $30,000) for the elimination of tenure. After much pulling and pushing and some modification, Rhee's plan was accepted. On the other hand, she has burned many bridges, losing the support of local politicians, parents, and teachers. In retrospect, Rhee freely acknowledges that the speed of her actions frightened many effective teachers and that in her zeal to bring about reform she did not bring them along with her plans.

At her November 2010 appearance on Oprah, Michelle Rhee made it clear that although she left her job, she is not through with reforming American education. She took the occasion to launch StudentsFirst.org, a board-based lobbying group to focus on student achievement and bring the lagging U.S. schools back to the global forefront.

what ought to be the elements of educational reform?

We believe firmly that the most important player in educational reform is the teacher. Overwhelmingly, the changes and improvements in schooling have come from classroom teachers who were seeking a better way to serve students. Although millionaires, politicians, and foundations provide resources and support for educational change, it begins—and ends—with the teacher. It is essential, therefore, for teachers to see themselves as fundamental to the reform process. But every change agent needs goals, or what we call "educational oughts," that is, a menu of ideas to support and develop. With this in mind, we offer the following reform candidates.

HIGHER STANDARDS AND ACCOUNTABILITY

Behind the increase in testing and the academic standards movement described earlier is the belief that the great majority of students can and must reach high standards. Students must adopt a serious task orientation toward their studies and show mastery of content that is measured through rigorous tests.

In the past, teachers were often encouraged to focus first on raising students' self-esteem through positive reinforcement and gentle coaching. In a high-standards

"He has to write an essay without using the words 'cool,' 'like,' or 'awesome.'"

(© Nick Hobart)

environment, self-esteem is seen as the direct *byproduct* of student achievement. Instead of giving self-esteem to students, the teacher sets up learning situations so that students can be successful and earn self-esteem through their own devices. One elementary school we know captures the twin themes of setting high standards and earning self-esteem by challenging its students with the motto "Your best today. Better tomorrow."

Helping children achieve high standards is a challenge for the teacher too. It requires that teachers understand individual students by determining their weaknesses and strengths, interests, and talents. It demands that teachers not only know their subject matter but also know how to engage students of many different abilities, interest levels, and learning styles. (See Chapter 5, "What Is Taught?" for more on content standards.)

Teachers and schools that set high standards need to find some way of determining whether those standards are being met. And so too do students. Some form of **accountability** is usually required, and it most often comes in the form of standardized tests. These tests have many values, including ease of administering and scoring and the ability to compare student performance within a school, a district, a state and even a nation. Recently, educators have realized that we have overused standardized tests. On the basis of these test scores alone, the performance of school districts, teachers, and students was judged; programs were added or dropped in response; and individuals were rewarded or punished. Therefore, facing intense pressure to boost test scores, many teachers quite naturally responded by emphasizing in their instruction the knowledge and skills that were being tested. In effect, teachers began **teaching to the test**—what was tested became what was taught.

Teach to a student and not to a test.

—ERIN GRUWELL,
Teacher and Coauthor of The Freedom Writer's Diary

As instruction narrowed to concentrate more on the basics, student scores seemed to improve. State after state reported that its students were scoring above the national average on the

Assessment in the Elementary Grades: Formal and Informal Literacy Assessment

Go to the Education CourseMate website to watch the video clips, study the artifacts in the case, and reflect on the following questions:

1. What are the benefits to teachers, students, parents, and the school of each of the various types of assessment: standardized tests, informal assessments, performance assessments, and portfolio assessments?

2. Which kinds of useful information can an informal assessment, such as the running record in the bonus videos, add to that provided by standardized test scores?

3. What are the benefits and challenges for these same groups of developing a complete assessment program featuring multiple types of assessments?

> "We must put knowledge directly in the hands of teachers and seek accountability that will focus attention on "doing the right things" rather than on "doing things right."
>
> —LINDA DARLING-HAMMOND,
> Stanford University Professor of Education

standardized tests given. Overwhelmingly, communities interpreted their test results to mean that their children were above average. This phenomenon has been dubbed the "Lake Wobegon effect," so named after the mythical small town portrayed by writer and public radio humorist Garrison Keillor, where "all the women are strong, all the men are good looking, and all the children are above average."

Upon closer examination of this trend, some educators and policymakers realized that the rising scores reflected another phenomenon: children were becoming overly familiar with the test questions and were able to score well on the tests simply for that reason. Others interpreted the results to mean that the standardized tests being used were inappropriate or invalid. A common complaint was that the multiple-choice tests assessed lower-level thinking skills instead of the higher-order skills for which educators and business leaders were calling.

AUTHENTIC ASSESSMENT

Many educators and parents have expressed grave concerns about what they perceive as an overemphasis on high-stakes testing. Measuring school excellence by administering standardized tests poses a danger, which arises because of the limited and simplistic nature of the tests. Evaluation experts warn that relying on tests developed by external sources can be unduly limiting if schools organize their curricula solely to conform to the content of the tests.[33] When they adopt that perspective, schools may fail to teach what is difficult to test. In some instances, the content and actual form of a test have become the curriculum itself, with weeks of classroom drill being based on previous versions of tests. Some educators and parents see a connection between the dramatic rise in student obesity and the emphasis on high-stakes testing, because recess and physical education are often eliminated or cut back to provide more time for test drilling.

Others worry that standardized tests overemphasize technical information and underemphasize educators' professional judgments about the worthiness of a school's programs. Although there has been a national call to stress more problem-solving, critical thinking, and writing skills in the schools, most standardized tests don't measure these outcomes. As a consequence, educators are calling for more *authentic assessment,* a topic that is discussed later in this chapter. In the Video Case *Assessment in the Elementary Grades: Formal and Informal Literacy Assessment,* watch how one second-grade teacher administers several of the forms of assessment discussed in this chapter.

The pressures to "teach to the test" have increased even more in recent years, as state after state has adopted new and more rigorous academic standards.

Not long ago, educators and the business community began calling for schools to emphasize higher-order thinking skills, such as critical thinking and problem-solving abilities. These qualities are difficult to measure through multiple-choice and other objective tests, so some educators called for a different type of assessment—one that would directly measure real student performance on important tasks. For example, if we want to know how well students can write, we can examine samples of their writing. If we want to know how well students understand scientific concepts and can carry out scientific processes, we can ask them to conduct an actual experiment. In other words, the assessment would actually measure what we wanted students to be able to do rather than relying on them to choose the correct response on a multiple-choice test item. This type of assessment is known as **authentic assessment**, or **performance assessment**. Advocates claim that authentic assessment involves performance tests that get closer to how students *apply* knowledge rather than how they *store* it in their minds. The Video Case *Performance Assessment: Student Presentations in a High School English Class* shows an extended example of how one teacher goes about assessing her students' creative performance.

One method of authentic assessment involves having students collect their work over time and assemble it to create **portfolios**. See the Video Case *Portfolio Assessment: Elementary Classroom* for details on this method of assessment. These portfolios might showcase students' best work, much like an artist's portfolio. In other instances, the work in the portfolio is representative of work done throughout the semester, demonstrating students' growth over time. In either case, students and teachers can evaluate these portfolios to determine learning progress.[34] In many parts of the country, in fact, student teachers assemble portfolios of their own work to show their professional skills when they apply for employment. (See Chapter 13, "What Are Your Job Options in Education?" for more on teaching portfolios.)

Authentic assessment is not without its critics and unresolved issues. The ability of performance assessments to satisfy both the validity requirement ("Is this a true measure of what I want to assess?") and the reliability requirement ("Will this test yield a similar result when administered at different times and under different circumstances?") has yet to be determined. Cost is also a major concern. Evaluating writing samples or judging students' success in conducting a scientific experiment is much more time-consuming and therefore more costly than machine-scoring a multiple-choice exam. Standards of judgment present another difficulty. Even if testers use **rubrics** that specify criteria and standards of assessment, the subjectivity of the human evaluator is an important consideration. In addition, questions remain about how to judge excellence, originality, and creativity in art and writing, let alone math or science.

Although the quest for improved means of assessment continues, one thing is clear: any educational reform needs to include some way of knowing if students are actually meeting the standards set and becoming the well-educated individuals that society wants. Therefore, a major item on the school reform agenda is to broaden the means by which we measure student performance.

ACTIVE LEARNING: THE CONSTRUCTIVIST'S APPROACH

There is an old saying that all teachers know well: "You can lead a horse to water, but you can't make it drink." Similarly, you can have a child in a classroom, but you can't make him or her learn. Pouring information into students or forcing them to do workbooks or problem sheets won't always do it. Nor will the great majority of students learn if simply allowed to wander through a library or laboratory on their own. Something must happen *inside* learners before they learn. Curiosity? A problem

▶∎ **TeachSource VIDEO CASE**

Portfolio Assessment: Elementary Classroom

Go to the Education CourseMate website to watch the video clips, study the artifacts in the case, and reflect on the following questions:

1. In one of the bonus videos, the teacher mentions the time pressure felt by many teachers. How can teachers who are pressed for time avoid the temptation to "teach to the test"?

2. Can teachers effectively use portfolios to help them meet or cope with demands to teach students the material that will be tested on their standardized assessments? How?

3. What information would standardized test scores add—for a teacher, for parents, and for students—to the information gained from portfolio reflections?

▶∎ **TeachSource VIDEO CASE**

Elementary School Language Arts: Inquiry Learning

Go to the Education CourseMate website to watch the video clips, study the artifacts in the case, and reflect on the following questions:

1. How has this teacher prepared the lesson to allow students to take an active role in their learning, as described in this chapter? How might she have prepared differently if she did not take a constructivist view?

2. What are the benefits and the challenges for the teacher who takes a constructivist approach? What are the benefits and the challenges for students?

that they want or need to solve? And then, with the direct or indirect help of the teacher, the student "constructs" knowledge from the information available to him or her.

Constructivism is a theory of knowledge acquisition built on the idea that the learner interacts with new information to "construct" meaning from it. (See Chapters 7, "What Should Teachers Know about Technology and Its Impact on Schools?" and Chapter 9, "What Are the Philosophical Foundations of American Education?" for more on constructivism.) Constructivism provides a frame of reference for organizing classroom practices so that students learn in all content areas. Unlike educational practices in which learners passively receive information, the constructivist approach requires that learners actively interact with the information, building on their prior knowledge, attitudes, and values. The Video Case *Elementary School Language Arts: Inquiry Learning* shows a lesson that takes the constructivist's approach and, as the teacher states, "put[s] students in charge of their own learning." As learners encounter new information or experiences, they ask themselves, "What makes sense here? What happens when I do this or change that?" In this **active learning** process, learners build and add to their understanding of concepts, rules, and strategies through direct, hands-on experimentation.

Although in theory the focus is on the students, teachers play a key role in constructivist classrooms. Through a technique called scaffolding, the teacher uses clues, questions, and hints to extend students' understanding. (See Chapter 6, "What Makes a Teacher Effective?" for additional discussion of scaffolding.) In this way, the teacher helps the student construct a scaffold by linking in prior knowledge to make sense of the new information.

How does constructivism advance the goals of educational reform? First, a primary ingredient of the constructivist approach is a learner who takes responsibility for his or her own learning. The teacher and the school play important supporting roles in this effort, but the initiative of the learner is essential. In short, students can achieve excellence only if they take responsibility for their learning. Ideally, constructivist classrooms foster experiential, inquiry-based learning in an atmosphere of *intellectual play*. Constructivism incorporates many of the ideas that have been written about in this text, including inductive teaching, student–teacher interaction, cooperative learning, multidisciplinary and interdisciplinary teaching, and extensive use of new technologies.

Although constructivism has many virtues, it is merely one theory of learning, one way of thinking about how knowledge and understanding are formed. It is certainly not the only way. Indeed, critics of this approach are quick to point out that students can "construct" incorrect answers. Further, critics remind us it is a formidable task to regularly put constructivism into practice, to translate this theory of learning into a theory of teaching.[35]

Nevertheless, we believe constructivism can be a valuable corrective to much of classroom life. It can bridge the gap between teacher-centered drill or rote learning

Constructivist principles stress the importance of learners taking an active role in creating their own knowledge.

(marco mayer/Shutterstock.com)

on the one hand and excessively abstract learning on the other hand. An ancient Chinese proverb captures well the essence of constructivism: "Tell me and I forget. Show me and I will remember. Make me do it and I learn."

A SENSE OF COMMUNITY

The past few years have brought a growing realization that the largest of our schools, although more resource rich, efficient, and cost-effective, can have some destructive side effects. To some students, such large schools have an aura of impersonality that results in the disengagement of many students. It is common to hear such statements as "I'm lost here," "No one really knows me and no one cares," or "I'm just a name in someone's gradebook." Although these criticisms are directed most often at high schools, they hold for many junior high and middle schools and even some elementary schools. Clearly, the larger our schools get, and the greater the number of classmates and adults with whom students must interact, the more students disengage—and disengaged students cannot achieve excellence.

Some recent studies have found not only a decline in student engagement and therefore in academic achievement in large schools, but also a decline in faculty morale and an increase in faculty absenteeism in these facilities.[36] Large schools are often equally overwhelming for parents, who then tend to remain at a distance and uninvolved in their children's school lives.

School-as-community advocates believe that any school whose principal does not know the names of all the students is too big. Reformers such as James Comer, of New Haven's School Development Project, and Theodore Sizer, founder of the Coalition of Essential Schools, argue that a sense of community is essential to the development of an academic environment. In these reform projects, new schools are purposely kept small, and existing large schools are broken up into "houses" of 100 to 400 students. The number of teachers with whom the students interact is similarly reduced, such that these houses function as **schools-within-schools**. Because students and teachers stay in the same house for several years, they are able to establish stronger and deeper relationships. Each student is a *known* person rather than a name on a class roster.

One obvious advantage of the house plan is that it allows teachers to plan together and to bring to bear their different perceptions of a child who is having difficulties or who has special strengths. In addition, these smaller, more intimate school environments provide a more stable emotional climate for students. Faculty advisors have better knowledge of and more exposure to students and can offer them more help in dealing with students' problems or challenges. In this smaller setting, advocates argue, students are much more likely to achieve the standards of excellence set for them.

To date, the federal government has devoted close to $100 million to its Smaller Learning Communities Project. The Gates Foundation has given *$2 billion* to create small stand-alone schools and help break up large high schools into several smaller schools-within-schools. Although research suggests these changes are bringing about a better social climate, the hoped-for academic achievement results have not yet appeared. In fact, the unimpressive achievement test scores have caused the Gates Foundation to abandon its support of restructuring schools into smaller units.[37] Whether or not this was a wise move will take years of research to ferret out. The overriding idea of establishing in a school and a classroom a strong sense of community and bonds of trust and warmth among students and between teachers and students must be a priority of true educational reform.

PAUSE AND REFLECT

1. Reflecting back on your own recent schooling, did the schools you attended have this sense of community? Your elementary school? Your high school?

2. Does the college or university you are attending have this sense of community? What could be done to give it more of a sense of community?

LIFELONG LEARNING

In our global, rapidly evolving social and economic environment, people need more than a high school or college education. We must also be capable of continuous learning. Ten years from now, the jobs and tasks we perform will likely be quite different from the jobs and tasks we perform today. For this reason, schools must attend to the habits of mind and the skills that will keep people learning throughout their lives, making them **lifelong learners**. Not only must students become good learners, but they must also be enthusiastic learners. In other words, students must know *how* to learn, and they must *want* to learn.

Tools for Learning

The human brain is a glorious instrument capable of enormous feats of creativity, from writing symphonies to making scientific breakthroughs. The average brain can store and manipulate more information, by several hundred times, than the largest computers. Unfortunately, the brain has some drawbacks too. It loses or "misfiles" information. Numerous and assorted messages enter it through the eyes, ears, and other senses and somehow get lost. When we want to remember an idea, it often is simply "not there." Sometimes the information received gets modified so that when we take the exam, we are sure without a doubt that there are two quarts in a gallon and four pints in a quart. Thus, although the brain is humankind's treasure, it is hardly perfect.

In any event, to work well, the brain must be trained and well maintained. By *trained,* we mean we have to teach people how to manage and use their brains effectively. Most likely the majority of our readers have been urged a time or two by parents and teachers to "Use your brain!" Our meaning is both an extension of that request and a more specialized suggestion. We are urging that we give our brains more power through the use of new tools. In the same manner that reading extends the power of the brain by giving it access to vast amounts of important information, other tools can make the brain more efficient and better able to take in, interpret, process, store, and retrieve information. *Well maintained* means we continue to make use of these important tools long after we have left the hallowed hallways of schools.

A fresh focus on the skills of learning can and ought to be a major part of school reform. Of course, we must attend to the three R's; we are not suggesting that we give a lower priority to subject matter. Rather, to make knowledge (i.e., **intellectual capital**) more useful, students need to learn how to learn. As teachers, we must give our students the necessary **tools for learning**: advanced reading, remembering, recording, researching, test taking, analyzing, and creating. These tools can help students excel not just in school but also later in the workplace and in life in general. (See the feature A Sample of the Tools for Learning.)

a sample of the tools for learning

Here is a list of some skills, which we call *tools for learning*, that we believe ought to be taught to all students:

- *Various methods for remembering important information.* This skill largely involves teaching people how not to forget: how to move information from the fleeting short-term memory to the more enduring long-term memory.

- *Two or three methods of taking notes and saving important information.* Definite skills are associated with capturing what another person is saying, and students should systematically learn these skills.

- *Study reading.* A person practices "study reading" when the material is complex and contains information he or she wants to remember later. This technique is quite different from reading a novel or reading a telephone book. This set of skills lies at the heart of academic success, as well as success in many jobs.

- *Preparing for different kinds of tests.* Schools should teach students how to study for different types of tests, such as objective and essay tests, and how to deal with test anxiety in various situations. Because examinations and tests do not end with graduation, schools should

teach students how to cope with and master these challenges.

- *Doing research.* Students need to learn how to get answers to questions by using libraries, the Internet, expert sources, and data-gathering resources of all kinds. In essence, these skills focus on finding and accessing different data sources and using the information to solve a problem.

- *Thinking through a problem in a systematic way.* Instead of jumping to conclusions or relying on how they feel about an issue, students should learn how to think critically.

- *Generating creative ideas.* Much of life—in and out of school—requires new solutions or imaginative resolutions. Students need to learn techniques for generating novel and creative ideas individually, as well as group-oriented techniques such as brainstorming.

- *Getting the academic job done.* Students need to know how to set goals, develop a work plan, monitor their own behavior, bring a task to successful closure, and gradually become more successful at academic learning. This ability is important not simply to succeed in school but also because the modern workplace demands these same skills.

RECLAIMING CHARACTER EDUCATION

Reminding us that education is not merely about the acquisition of knowledge, Socrates (featured in Chapter 9, "What are the Philosophical Foundations of American Education?") said, "The purpose of education is to make people both smart and good." The excellence in education is not limited to just academic achievement. Many reformers have also been concerned about excellence of character. Much of the dissatisfaction with schools that has fueled recent educational reform efforts comes from parents and community leaders who believe the schools have not done enough to shape the character and ethical values of students in positive ways. Many reformers are equally convinced that a failure to address these needs of students lies at the heart of the schools' problems.

A "good student" has come to mean someone who does well on tests and achieves academically rather than someone who is a good person and who demonstrates characteristics such as responsibility, consideration for others, self-discipline, and the ability to work hard. To achieve excellence in student achievement, according to these critics, serious school reform must address the issue of **character education**, which we define as the effort to help the young acquire a *moral compass*—that is, a sense of right and wrong and also the enduring habits necessary to live a good life. Character education, then, involves helping the child *to know the good, love the good, and do the good.*[38]

Arguments Pro and Con

Some people argue that the public school has no role in character development and moral education because both are rooted in deeply held religious worldviews. As such, they are deemed "out of bounds" to public schools, which should concentrate primarily on cognitive skills such as reading, writing, and application of the scientific method.[39] According to proponents of this view, if parents want attention paid to moral values, they should put their children in private schools.

> " *Formal education is the playing field on which society vies over values.*
>
> —THEODORE SIZER (1932–2009),
> Educator and Founder of the Coalition
> of Essential Schools

Others question character education by asking, "*Whose* values should the public schools teach?" In a nation of diverse cultural backgrounds, a nation committed to freedom of thought and expression, can any one set of values be taught without infringing on someone's deeply cherished beliefs? One solution to this dilemma would have the tax-supported public schools teach the civic virtues that are necessary for life in a democratic society, such as respect for the rights of others, courage, tolerance, kindness, and concern for the underdog. Another way to seek an answer to this question is first to take a mental trip around the school described in the following paragraph and then to answer the question "Should schools stick simply to academics and skills?"

> " *Character is like a tree and reputation like its shadow. The shadow is what we think of it; the tree is the real thing.*
>
> —ABRAHAM LINCOLN (1809–1865),
> 16th President of the United States

A counselor is calling a student's home about apparently excused absences, only to find that the parent's letters have been forged. A young boy is in the principal's office for threatening his teacher with a knife. Three students are separated from their class after hurling racial epithets at a fourth. A girl is complaining that her locker has been broken into and all her belongings stolen. A small group of boys are huddling in a corner, shielding an exchange of money for drug packets. Female students complain that they are being rudely groped when their teacher leaves the room. In the playground, two girls grab a third and punch her in the stomach for flirting with the wrong boy.[40]

Schools that tolerate such behavior not only are failing to address the character education needs of their students but also have become places where the intellectual goals of schooling are impaired. In addition, such schools win little support from the general public, the people who pay for public education.

We believe that most educators know it is impossible to educate students in a moral vacuum. The process of schooling necessarily affects the way children think about issues of right and wrong and affects the ways they behave. Further, the overwhelming majority of Americans, regardless of religion, class, or racial background, support certain moral values such as respect, a thirst for justice, honesty, responsibility in our dealings with one another, consideration, compassion, persistence at hard tasks, and courage in the face of adversity.[41] For many years, we believed that teaching these moral values effectively would have the indirect and important result of helping students become more academically successful. Recent research has borne out this linkage.[42] Further, we believe that most people would wholeheartedly support schools' vigorous advocacy of these virtues. Teachers and schools can positively influence the development of desirable habits and character formation in numerous ways, but two in particular are worthy of note: using the curriculum and involving students in service activities.

Character in the Curriculum

One major approach is to use the curriculum that already exists in most schools to teach more directly and more vigorously the positive moral values that are embedded in our culture. Our history and literature are permeated with value issues and moral lessons from the past. Instead of simply having students study the facts of a historical period or read a story to build vocabulary or appreciate prose style, the teacher can confront them with ethical issues and moral lessons that are integral to the subject matter. Instead of merely teaching scientific methodologies and findings, the teacher can have students examine the real world implications of applied science, such as genetic manipulation. Through such explorations, students will see that the use of science and technologies, such as cloning, fossil fuel–based energies, and genetic manipulation, is not neutral; rather, how we use science has ethical implications. As teachers, we must see the content of our curriculum as the carrier of our moral heritage and work to engage our students in that moral heritage.

Service-Learning

Knowing about virtues, such as justice, compassion, and courage, is one thing; making them a part of one's life and practicing them diligently is another. If students are to makes these virtues part of their characters, they need real opportunities to practice them. As many reformers realize, schools can create opportunities for students, beginning in the early grades and continuing throughout the entirety of their education, to help one another and the adults in the school building. As students get older, they can be given more responsibility for working with and caring for younger students. In the later stages of high school, groups of students can take on projects in the larger community, such as helping a parent whose child has a disability or assisting with an exercise class at a senior citizens' center. Likewise, individual students can provide companionship to elderly shut-ins or peer counseling to troubled youngsters. The emphasis in such programs is not merely on the study of virtues but also on virtues in action.

Service-learning programs are growing rapidly in U.S. schools. According to a 2004 study, an estimated 4.7 million K–12 students in the US are engaged in service-learning.[43]

> *Character cannot be developed in ease and quiet. Only through experience of trial and suffering can the soul be strengthened, ambition inspired, and success achieved.*
>
> —HELEN KELLER (1880–1968), Author

A recent telephone survey of high school students showed that:

- Over 80 percent of students who participated in service-learning said they had more positive feeling about attending high school.
- Over 75 percent of students who were currently or had in the past participated in service-learning programs agreed that service-learning classes were more interesting than other classes.
- Over 75 percent of service-learning students said that service-learning had motivated them to work hard.[44]

For example, middle school students in New York City's Bronx borough chose bullying as the issue they wanted to tackle as a service-learning project. Believing that "the pen is mightier than the sword," they decided to organize a poetry slam where their peers could raise a united voice against physical and emotional bullying. Some 150 students, parents, and community members attended the slam, which featured poetry and skits exposing the fears and insecurities that motivate most bullies.[45]

Several states are considering making a certain number of hours of community service a requisite for high school graduation. In 1993, Maryland became the first state to make service an actual requirement. Currently, Maryland high school students are required to perform 75 hours of service before they can graduate.[46] We believe schools must succeed in this mission for students' sake and also because a strong program of character education makes teaching a much more satisfying profession.

T (F)

Although service-learning activities are popular with students, most believe it keeps them from working hard on academic chores.

Over 75 percent of service-learning students said that service-learning had motivated them to work hard.

PAUSE AND REFLECT

Which of the elements of school reform described to this point do you most favor? About which do you have doubts? If we made you Czar of American Education, are there any mentioned reforms you would make, and why?

VOICES from the classroom

Building Character Education into the P.E. Curriculum

Eric Gelfand has taught gymnastics and physical education to preschool through grade 12 students in Washington and Massachusetts for the past 16 years.

I can remember one of the members of my gymnastics team getting very upset about not winning. Tyler was 11 years old, and anything less than first place resulted in distress, inability to concentrate, and a feeling of failure. His reaction was stronger than others, but many on our team shared the sentiment: self-esteem and success depended on winning. I decided to initiate a discussion of our definitions of winning with the entire team.

In this discussion, we discovered that our definition of winning was based on beating others and factors over which we had no control, like the score that the judge would give us. The new definition of winning that we developed focused on giving our best effort in each moment. We also decided to concentrate only on factors that we could control, such as improving our focus and technique, supporting each other, learning from our competitors, and regulating our thoughts and

(continued)

emotions. We decided if we did these things, then we had each won.

Tyler's feelings of self-esteem and success slowly began to change, but not the first time we talked about it, or the 10th time I reminded him to refocus on our new goals, or even on the 50th time that he made himself feel good by remembering that he had done his best. Through the efforts of the entire team over a period of three to four years, Tyler arrived at a place where winning meant something very personal and attainable at all times. This evolution meant valuing respect, persistence, temperance, and compassion for ourselves and others above all else. These virtues slowly became habits, which slowly became a part of our character and who we are today. It was incredibly hard to keep ourselves focused on this goal when our society values a very different definition of winning.

In reading this chapter, you will learn that school reform depends on the efforts of individual teachers to help our children become good workers and citizens. What do you think the definition of "winning" is in academics? If the current definition is not attainable by all of your students, how can you change the system or work within it to make every child successful? I believe that the key is to value the building of character as much as achievement within a discipline. It's simple; it just takes a few years of relentless hard work and compassion.

the current state of school reform

Although the United States clearly has a new set of educational reform priorities, goals, and expectations, relatively few schools have experienced sweeping changes as a result of educational reform. Some have made fundamental changes in the way they engage children and in what they teach. Most have adopted pieces of reform, such as a new districtwide mathematics curriculum, a service program, or a career ladder for teachers. Some states have pushed through serious changes that affect the great majority of their schools, but they are the exceptions to the rule. The school experience of the first-grader or the high school senior is in many ways pretty much the same today as it was in 1983, when the current reform era began.

American education is not like an individual who, after a few life failures, looks in the mirror and says, "That's it! I'm going to get my act together starting today," and from that moment on is a "new" person. Public education in the United States is a giant institution, involving almost 15,000 centers of decision making (school boards), more than 55 million people (students, teachers, and administrators), and influences from many quarters of society. And, most importantly, like any institution it has a standard operating procedure. Everyone starting a school year in August or September (except for the newcomers, the kindergartners) has a clear set of expectations about what school ought to be like. Although chaos would result without them, these expectations make altering the course of schooling quite a demanding task.

Perhaps a better parallel than an individual trying to change the course of his or her life in short order would be that of a large luxury liner plowing through the ocean. Someone convinces the captain that dangerous icebergs lie ahead. The captain first has to be assured that the reports are reasonable, next decide where the safe water is, and then turn the wheel. Of course, because of its size and momentum, the ship may need miles to actually change course. This is where we believe American schools are today. They have heard the message; they have committed to change course and avoid the hazards; they have begun to turn the wheel. Whether the ship actually turns and misses the dangers, we must wait to see.

OUR FINAL WORD

Teachers must be at the center of educational change. Behind the somewhat head-spinning array of school reform ideas and programs, one fact is clearly discernible: the quality of our schools ultimately depends on our teachers. Educational reform is meaningless if it keeps teachers from inspiring the minds, imaginations, and characters of students on a one-on-one basis. Given the de facto connection between students and teacher, the final decisions about educational reform are, by necessity, made by teachers. Although it is discouraging (and even threatening) to know that we have not yet achieved our goal of reforming our schools, Americans are often at our best when challenged. Clearly, school reform is part of the unfinished business of America and the American teacher. A job of critical importance to all of us awaits you.

WHY TEACH? YOUR FINAL WORD

In your journal or online at this textbook's website, respond to the following questions:

1. Which three of the various reform efforts described in this chapter do you believe are most important for the improvement of American education? Why?

2. What do you believe are the most serious barriers or hindrances to the reform of U.S. schools?

3. Were any of the reform efforts described in this chapter evident in your schooling?

KEY TERMS

21st century interdisciplinary themes (382)
accountability (398)
active learning (401)
authentic (performance) assessment (400)
call for excellence (384)
career ladders (386)
character education (405)
charter schools (390)
for-profit schools (395)
intellectual capital (404)
lifelong learners (403)
magnet school (390)
national curricular standards (380)

National Education Goals for the Year 2000 (377)
performance pay (pay-for-performance) (387)
portfolios (400)
rubrics (400)
school choice (387)
schools-within-schools (402)
site-based decision making (390)
teacher competency testing (386)
teaching to the test (398)
tools for learning (404)
voucher plans (392)
within-district choice (389)
year-round education (384)

FOR FURTHER INFORMATION

TEACHSOURCE VIDEO

Ed Reform: Teachers Talk About No Child Left Behind.
This video portrays teachers and administrators discussing the issues and problems surrounding the implementation of the NCLB legislation.

WEB RESOURCES

American Diploma Project. Available at **www.achieve. org/node/337**.

Sponsored by Achieve, Inc., this nonprofit organization, created by the nation's governors and business leaders, is "working to help states raise academic standards, improve assessments, and strengthen accountability in our high schools."

ASCD SmartBriefs. Available at **www.ASCD.org**.

SmartBriefs is a free educational news service that can be received through e-mail. It contains news, commentary, and educational resources.

Center for Educational Reform. Available at **www. edreform.com/index.cfm?fuseAction=section& pSectionID=5&CFID=8224310&CFTOKEN=44734851**.

This think tank is a pro–school choice center and clearinghouse for research and information on various efforts to offer parents and educators more educational choices.

The Educational Gadfly. Available at **www. edexcellence.net**.

For a conservative slant on educational news and policy developments, you can sign up for *The Gadfly*, a weekly bulletin of policy news, book reviews, and lively commentary by Chester E. Finn.

The National Education Association's Issues and Action. Available at **http://www.nea.org/home/ IssuesAndAction.html**.

For a liberal slant on an educational reform agenda, see the website of NEA, the nation's largest teacher's union. The NEA has definite positions on many of the issues discussed in this chapter, from school choice to performance pay.

PRINT RESOURCES

John Merrow, *Below C Level: How American Education Encourages Mediocrity and What We Can do About It* (John Merrow, 2010).

This wide-ranging collection of essays covers many of the reform topics discussed above. Merrow is a former teacher and currently is the senior educational reporter for the PBS *News Hour*.

Frederick M. Hess, *Common Sense School Reform* (New York: Palgrave Macmillan, 2004).

Written by a market-oriented educator, this book offers a radically different set of reform suggestions. In the process, Hess engages in a no-holds-barred attack on most of the currently held views on education and on school reform.

Diane Ravitch, *Death and Life of the Great American School System* (New York: Basic Books, 2010).

Written by an historian and one of the leading advocates for educational reform by testing and school choice, this book is both a history of recent educational reform efforts and the author's change of heart and mind regarding school reform.

The Education CourseMate website for this text offers many helpful resources. Go to **www.cengagebrain.com** to access the TeachSource Video Cases and other TeachSource videos, flashcards, interactive quizzes, the eBook, reflection and enrichment activities, a state standards resource center, and other study aids.

13 what are your job options in education?

FOCUS POINTS

- Many factors influence the availability of teaching jobs, such as the 2007–2009 economic recession.

- Some teaching fields have a surplus of teachers, while others have shortages or are balanced in terms of supply and demand.

- Teacher salaries vary tremendously from state to state and from school district to school district.

- Certain job-hunting strategies will increase your chances of finding the right job for you.

- Licensure requirements differ from state to state.

- Being prepared as a teacher can also prepare you for jobs in other fields.

- Better prepared teachers will find it easier to gain employment, and will improve the teaching profession and its public image.

This chapter provides you with information about the availability of teaching positions in elementary, middle, and secondary schools. It also explores other career opportunities, both within and outside the educational field. Study the information carefully and discuss it with your instructors and your career planning and placement office. Your program of study may offer more job options than you have realized.

Truth OR Fiction?

T	F	Thirty to 40 percent of new teachers leave the classroom within five years.
T	F	Less than 20 percent of American teachers are from minority groups.
T	F	Salaries for private school teachers are only slightly less than those of public school teachers.

wanted

Men and women with the wisdom of Solomon, the patience of Job, and the nerves of David before Goliath. Needed to prepare the next generation for productive citizenship in the twenty-first century, often under adverse conditions. Applicants must be willing to fill in gaps left by unfit, absent, or working parents; satisfy demands of local bureaucrats and state politicians; impart healthy self-esteem; and, oh, by the way, teach content!

Hours: 50 to 60 hours per week
Pay: Growing respectable
Reward: The luxury of always knowing that you are doing something significant with your life

This fictitious ad contains many messages about the roles that teachers play. It also highlights the fact that there is a serious need for skilled new teachers in U.S. schools. As you have thought about teaching as a career, you have probably wondered whether you will be able to obtain a teaching position when you graduate. Although we would like to answer this question for you personally, we obviously cannot. We can, however, provide you with information that may help you increase your chances of obtaining the kind of teaching position you are seeking.

will there be job openings in education?

Teaching is a large occupation, with almost 3.8 million elementary and secondary teachers, representing 4 percent of the entire civilian workforce in the United States. There are more K–12 teachers than registered nurses, three times as many teachers as lawyers, and twice as many teachers as engineers in this country.[1] Given the vast size of the teaching workforce, many jobs exist. Figure 13.1 shows past, current, and projected numbers of classroom teachers in the United States.

FACTORS INFLUENCING TEACHER SUPPLY AND DEMAND

Many variables influence the supply and demand for teachers in the United States. The following sections discuss a number of these factors.

Student Enrollment in Schools

Obviously, when more students are enrolled in schools, more teachers are needed. The good news is that enrollment in public and private schools reached 55.6 million students in 2011 and is projected to increase to 58.6 million in 2019. In the United States, enrollments in secondary schools will increase by about 3.5 percent through 2019, while enrollments in elementary schools will increase by over 6 percent. The

FIGURE 13.1

K–12 Classroom Teachers in Public and Private Schools (in thousands)

Source: William J. Hussar and Tabitha M. Bailey, *Projections of Education Statistics to 2019* (Washington, DC: National Center for Education Statistics, 2011), Table 16. Available at http://nces.ed.gov/programs/projections/projections2019.

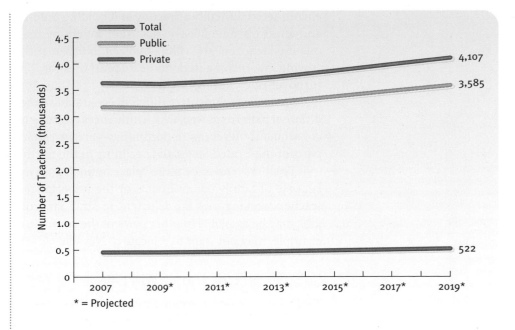

number of classroom teachers is expected to increase by almost half a million over the next eight years, increasing from 3.7 million in 2011 to 4.1 million by 2019.[2]

Class Sizes

During the 1980s and 1990s, the demand for new teachers was boosted by declining class sizes, especially in California, where the legislature tried to reduce class sizes in K–3 classrooms to around 20 students.

Nationally, current class sizes now hover around 20 students in public elementary schools and have reached over 23 students per teacher in public secondary schools. Class sizes in private schools are slightly smaller than those in public schools, averaging a bit more than 20 students per class for both elementary and secondary schools.[3] However, the changes in class sizes during the next few years are expected to be small, and they are not likely to affect the demand for new teachers in any significant fashion.

Enrollment in Teacher Education Programs

Across the United States, approximately 160,000 teachers are prepared each year; however, only 60 percent of those prepared to teach actually enter the classroom. And of these individuals, 30 to 40 percent leave teaching within the first five years.[4] Thus an adequate number of teachers are prepared to meet the demand, but because so many choose not to teach or stop teaching after a few years, the supply doesn't match the demand for new teachers.

Geographical Location

Location significantly influences the teaching job market. Some communities have far more applicants than available teaching positions. University towns, for example, usually have a great surplus of teachers. Although large urban areas historically have had more teachers available than they needed, before the economic recession of 2007–2009 they experienced a significant shortage. Rural America traditionally has encountered difficulty attracting and holding onto teachers because of lower salaries and a more sedate lifestyle than that sought by many young teachers. Not enough qualified teachers are willing to teach in urban and rural schools, particularly those serving low-income students or students of color. These schools also experience high turnover rates among teachers.

Student enrollments in different geographical regions of the country are following different patterns as well, which influences teaching opportunities. Enrollments—and consequently teaching opportunities—are increasing in the western and southern parts of the United States and declining in the northeastern states.

Teachers tend to be more "place bound" than many other professionals. That is, because of family commitments or the importance of geographical location, many teachers seeking jobs are reluctant to stray far from home. Even though teaching jobs may be available in other parts of the country, teachers from the Northeast, for example, may not want to relocate to Nevada.

Subject Matter and Grade Levels Taught

Teachers are not interchangeable units. They are prepared for different specialties (e.g., special education, elementary education, art, or secondary social studies), and the job market in each of these subfields is different. Moreover, the job market for specific subfields may change often. It is unwise, therefore, to decide whether to become an English teacher because you have heard that today there is generally either a surplus or a shortage of such teachers. There have been and continue to be chronic national teacher shortages in certain subjects, including speech pathology, hearing and visually impaired, physics and chemistry, and mathematics. There is some surplus of teachers in pre-K and elementary education, health and physical education, and social studies.[5]

In addition to looking for teachers in the subjects just listed, schools are seeking greater numbers of minorities and males. Because 76 percent of all teachers are female, schools want to increase the number of males in the teaching force, especially at the elementary school level, where only 15 percent of the nation's 1.7 million elementary public school teachers are men.[6]

Retiring Teachers, Teacher Turnover, and Returning Teachers

The United States is experiencing record teacher retirements as the teaching force continues to age. Between 2004 and 2008, more than 300,000 veteran teachers retired, and a recent report estimated that from 2010 to 2018, 1.5 million more teachers will retire.[7] One factor that bodes well for the long-term job outlook is that teachers, like much of the rest of the American workforce, are getting older. More than one-quarter of teachers are at least 53 years old.[8]

Another factor influencing job availability relates to the percentage of eligible teachers who elect not to teach or those who leave teaching after a few years. As mentioned earlier, 40 percent of those prepared to teach elect not to enter teaching, and of the 60 percent who do teach, 30 to 40 percent leave teaching within the first five years. Sadly, the brightest novice teachers, as measured by their college-entrance exams, are the most likely to leave. Factors influencing the high turnover include student discipline problems, poor working conditions, lack of support

(T) F

Thirty to 40 percent of new teachers leave the classroom within five years.

Reasons why new teachers leave the profession include student discipline problems, poor working conditions, lack of support from the school administration, poor student motivation, and lack of teacher influence over schoolwide and classroom decision making.

There is a demand for male teachers at the elementary school level, where they account for less than 15 percent of the teaching force.

(Copyright © Michael Newman/Photo Edit)

> "Teaching was the hardest work I had ever done, and it remains the hardest work I have done to date.
>
> —ANN RICHARDS,
> Former Governor of Texas

from the school administration, poor student motivation, and lack of teacher influence over schoolwide and classroom decision making.[9]

What is difficult to estimate is the number of licensed teachers, currently not teaching, who might reenter the teaching force if jobs are readily available. When teacher shortages have been predicted in the past, these returning teachers have filled the anticipated shortages. Whether this pattern will continue remains to be seen. Teachers licensed through alternative routes (like those discussed later in this chapter) are estimated to account for approximately one-third of the new teachers hired in this country.[10]

Economic Conditions

In spite of the positive long-term outlook for the teaching job market, in times of economic hardship school districts may find it necessary to reduce the size of their teaching forces to balance budgets. During the severe 2007–2009 recession, many school districts in most states found it necessary to reduce their teaching forces for lack of money. As state and local government revenues dropped dramatically, school districts' budgets were also reduced. Many school districts were forced to issue reduction-in-force (RIF) notices to teachers, informing them that they were in danger of not being rehired for the following fall. The American Investment and Recovery Act, passed by Congress in 2009, provided $785 billion dollars, much of which went to the states, to try to offset the effects of the recession. As a result of this Act, and the Job Creation Act of 2010, which provided $10 billion more, many teachers' jobs were preserved. These measures, however, were stopgap, with no guarantee of continuation in the future. What we have learned from this painful recession is that the demand for teachers is greatly influenced by school district budgets, which in turn are affected by the health of the state and local economies.

Summing Up the Job Outlook

What, then, are the job prospects for future teachers? In the long run, the situation is promising because the number of classroom teachers in elementary and secondary schools is projected to increase at least until 2019, primarily because of teacher retirements, teachers leaving the field, and increases in student enrollments. In the short run, the speed with which the U.S. economy recovers from the severe 2007–2009 recession will greatly affect the hiring picture.

In the past, if the supply of qualified teachers did not keep up with the demand, states and local school districts resorted to such practices as increasing class sizes, hiring less-than-qualified personnel, and assigning teachers trained in one field to teach in an understaffed field. These options may be less readily available now because the federal No Child Left Behind law requires all states to ensure that every public school teacher is "highly qualified," which means that the teacher has been licensed by the state and has demonstrated a high level of competence in the subjects that he or she teaches. (See Chapter 12, "How Should Education Be Reformed?" for more on this legislation.) The requirements of the No Child Left Behind law for highly qualified teachers suggest that once the country has recovered economically, the demand for teachers will remain high in years to come.

Keep in mind too that demographic projections and supply-and-demand forecasts are not just hard to apply but also very inexact and short-lived. Although their task is difficult, forecasters try to take into account the various factors we have discussed, such as retirement rates, number of former teachers reentering the field, and programs that may attract individuals from nonteaching fields into the profession. Given the fluctuating effects of these forces, what seems to be true now for a particular geographic area, a particular teaching field, or a particular year may soon be "out of date."

For all these reasons, you should make every effort to get the most up-to-the-minute information possible about teacher supply and demand. Consider such information carefully before you make a choice about pursuing a career in education and, in particular, about entering a specific subfield within education. This is especially true for people who are unable to wait for openings in their areas of teaching interest or who are unable to relocate. Sources of data with which to begin your search include your school's career counseling office, the department chairperson's or dean's office, and your state department of education. Also see the listing of useful references at the end of this chapter.

The bottom line is that demand for teachers will increase in the coming years. Remember too that there has never been a surplus of good teachers in any field.

THE SEVERE SHORTAGE OF MINORITY TEACHERS

One of the greatest teacher supply-and-demand problems concerns minority teachers. At a time when the minority school-age population is increasing rapidly, the number of minority teachers is decreasing. This shortage is severe now and appears likely to become worse in the future.

As discussed in Chapter 3, "Who Are Today's Students in a Diverse Society?" enrollments of students from minority groups are increasing; these children are currently estimated to account for about 44 percent of all students in public schools. Teaching staffs, by contrast, are becoming more and more white. Eighty-three percent of public school teachers are white, 7 percent are African American, 7 percent are Hispanic, and only 3 percent come from other minority groups, including Asian American or Pacific Islander, and Native American or Native Alaskan.[11] Most minority teachers are located in central cities rather than in suburban or rural areas.

(T) F
Less than 20 percent of American teachers are from minority groups.
Eighty-three percent of American teachers are white.

The shortage of minority teachers deprives both white and minority students of positive role models.

(© Chip Henderson)

> [Emma Belle Sweet] taught me many things. . . . But nothing could be so important to me and of such enduring quality as her simple, human act of figuratively leading me gently by the hand to a sense of self-respect, dignity, and worth.
>
> —RALPH BUNCHE,
> First African American Nobel Peace Prize Winner (1950)

During most of the 1990s, the graduation rates for minority students from teacher education programs were lower than their percentage distribution in the teaching force. Although minority enrollment in teacher education has been increasing in recent years, the need for such teachers is still acute.

This shortage of minority teachers is problematic for several reasons. First, minority children deserve to have positive minority role models who can help guide them in a world still plagued by racism. Second, white children need to have minority teachers as positive role models to help them overcome the effects of stereotyping and racism. Third, it is important for the United States' well-being to have a teaching staff that reflects the diversity of racial and ethnic backgrounds in its population. Fourth, minority teachers are needed to serve as "cultural brokers" who can help all students navigate their school environment and culture.

A number of reasons explain the shortage of minority teachers. Before desegregation efforts, nearly one-half of African American professional workers were teachers. When schools desegregated in the 1960s and 1970s, resulting in the consolidation of formerly all-black and all-white schools, thousands of African American teachers were dismissed. Today, other professions that pay more and have higher status are actively recruiting minority college students. Another causal factor has been the increasing use of competency tests at either the beginning or the end of teacher education programs.

LEADERS in education

Jaime Escalante (1930–2010)

(© Shelley Gazin/CORBIS)

It is early in the fall term at Garfield High School in East Los Angeles, once a crime-ridden school filled with low-achieving Mexican American students. It is the morning after the second game of the World Series, and as he enters the class, the teacher, known as *el professor*, shouts out his first question: "Who won the game?" After a pause, the students begin to chant enthusiastically, "Dodgers! Dodgers!" Having captured their attention, Jaime Escalante moves to the math lesson. Slapping a baseball into his mitt, he says, "As x approaches a, f of x [$f(x)$] is the trajectory. Could be a curve ball." And they are off—teacher and 59 students—on a journey into the mysteries of calculus.

Jaime Escalante, the son of an elementary school teacher, was born in La Paz, Bolivia, and began his own teaching career before age 20. While he was a high school math and physics teacher, his students began to accumulate prizes, and he soon gained national recognition. Still in his 20s, he organized the first Bolivian national symposium of physics and math teachers. In 1963, amid growing social strife in Bolivia, Escalante, now married with two sons, decided to take his wife and young family to the United States.

The next 10 years were years of adjustment and struggle, during which Escalante learned English, went back to college, and worked as a busboy and a cook. When he finally graduated, he took a job in the fast-growing computer industry and studied for the California Teaching Certificate in his free time. Soon the news came that he had passed the test and would be assigned to a rundown, troubled high school in the *barrio*—and Escalante turned his back on his substantially larger paycheck from the high-tech world and headed for Garfield High School.

When the school's accreditation was threatened because of its students' low academic performance and high dropout rate, Escalante made his move.

Supported by reform-minded administrators, he began setting high standards and making serious demands on students. They were not allowed into his class unless they proved that they had done their homework. He skillfully used the time-honored carrot-and-stick approach to cajole his pupils into reaching greater heights. In this case, the "carrot" was college and the world of opportunities higher education opened up for his students. The "stick" was his constant challenging of them: "You *burros* have math in your blood! Our Mayan ancestors were the first to develop the concept of zero!"

In 1982, his largest class of students took and passed an advanced placement test in calculus. Some of the students' test scores were invalidated by the testing company because it believed that the students had cheated since no one expected Hispanic students from an economically disadvantaged school to do so well. Despite Escalante's protests, the students had to retake the exam several months later. Once again, they did well, exceeding expectations and proving that they knew the material and that the company was wrong.

Jaime Escalante, the subject of the Academy Award–nominated film *Stand and Deliver*, later taught at Hiram Johnson High School is Sacramento, California. He hosted the PBS series, *FUTURES with Jaime Escalante*, produced by the Foundation for Advancements in Science and Education. In addition, he received numerous awards, including the prestigious U.S. Presidential Medal of Honor and the National Teachers Hall of Fame. Escalante was more than the man who has helped hundreds of Mexican American children discover self-discipline and learning and the enormous self-pride that comes with those accomplishments—he was a tide turner. He set an idea in motion, the idea that the poor and immigrant children are capable of great intellectual feats. He showed how remedial,

(continued)

slowed-down education can be replaced by demanding, accelerated education. "My skills are really to motivate these kids, to make them learn, to give them *ganas*—the desire to do something—to make them believe they can learn." Escalante was always been clear about why he taught: his love of young people and his love of his subject.

Until his death in March 2010, Escalante remained a clear and forceful spokesman for quality education, especially for minority children. He took a strong position against extensive bilingual education, believing it handicaps rather than helps Latino students. Instead, he urged a demanding education that will give minority students the knowledge and skills they need to compete in a demanding world. His educational views are captured in his famous motto: "Determination + Discipline + Hard Work = Way to Success."

Many minority teaching candidates are either having difficulties with these tests or are being discouraged from even considering teaching as a career.

What can be done to address this problem? Teaching salaries must continue to improve if teaching is to compete with other professions for well-qualified candidates. Assistance programs to help minority candidates perform well on competency tests have been effective in a number of universities and should be expanded to more colleges. Active recruitment programs for minority candidates must be developed and implemented, and they must reach down into the middle and high schools to encourage minority students to consider teaching as a career long before they enter college. As will be described later in the chapter, alternative licensure programs have been successful in recruiting minority teachers and should be continued. Scholarship and loan-forgiveness programs are needed for students who want to teach but cannot afford to pay for college. Finally, the American public must communicate in a variety of ways that it values teachers and the work they do. See the Leaders in Education box for a biographical sketch of one of America's most outstanding minority teachers, Jaime Escalante.

EMPLOYERS BESIDES THE PUBLIC SCHOOLS

Although much of the data presented in this chapter refer to public elementary and secondary schools, teachers can work in a variety of other school settings. Federal government schools and private schools are two major alternatives to teaching in a local public school.

U.S. Government

A large employer of teachers is the U.S. government. The Department of Defense operates 194 elementary and secondary schools in seven states, Puerto Rico, Guam, and 12 countries around the world. These schools enroll approximately 86,000 students and employ about 8,700 teachers. Salaries are comparable to those in the United States, but preference is given to applicants who have at least one year of successful full-time employment as a professional educator.[12]

Private Schools

Private education is a highly significant part of the American educational system. The more than 33,700 private schools in the United States have an enrollment of more than 5 million elementary and secondary school students and employ approximately 456,000 teachers. About 10 percent of all U.S. children in elementary or secondary schools attend a private school, with the overwhelming majority attending religion-affiliated schools.[13] (See Figure 13.2 for the percentage of students attending private schools affiliated with various religious denominations.)

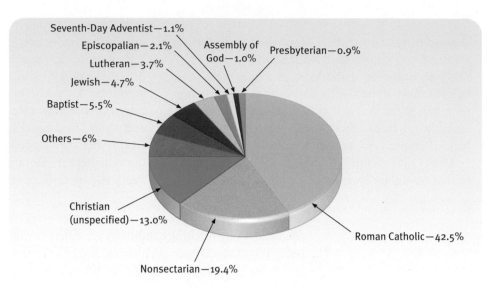

FIGURE 13.2

Percentage of Students Attending Various Kinds of Private Schools

Source: Stephen P. Broughman, Nancy L. Swaim, Patrick W. Keaton, *Characteristics of Private Schools in the United States: Results From the 2007–08 Private School Universe Survey* (Washington, DC: National Center for Education Statistics, 2009), Table 2.

Private schools employ approximately 12 percent of all elementary and secondary teachers in the United States, and more than 400,000 new teachers are expected to be needed in private schools from 2010 to 2019.[14] Thus private schools offer a growing employment opportunity for new teachers. Helpful references for finding teaching jobs in nonpublic schools are provided at the end of this chapter.

If you are considering a position at a private school, you should reflect on the relative importance of the various rewards of the job from your personal perspective. Many teachers who work in religion-affiliated schools do so because of religious motives. These teachers are often willing to work for less money than their public school counterparts; as a result, the average teacher salary in private schools is about 25 percent lower than that in public schools. In many cases, lower salaries tend to be offset by favorable working conditions. Compared with public schools, private schools have fewer classroom control problems, stricter discipline, smaller classes, fewer students using drugs, students who are absent less often, parents who are more supportive, a higher percentage of colleagues who share the school's mission, and a more supportive administration. Although private school teachers tend to work about two more hours per week than their public school counterparts, they believe they have greater influence over important school policies.[15] Thus, for many individuals, teaching in a private school represents an attractive alternative to teaching in the public schools. The Voices from the Classroom feature presents one teacher's comparison of the experience of working in public and private schools.

T (F)

Salaries for private school teachers are only slightly less than those of public school.

Most private school teachers work at religious schools, which pay teachers about 25 percent less than public schools.

PAUSE AND REFLECT

1. What are the present and projected teacher supplies in the field that currently interests you? In the geographic area you desire?

2. Are you willing to leave your current location to find a teaching position? Are you willing to teach in an urban school? A rural school? A private school?

WHAT ARE TEACHERS PAID?

We might answer this question by saying, "Not nearly enough." No one ever went into teaching because of the lure of big money. As we note in Chapter 1, "Why Teach?" the major rewards for teaching are personal rather than monetary. Most of teachers' satisfactions come from being of service to others and helping students learn. That does not mean, however, that you have to be a pauper to enjoy the satisfactions that come from teaching. Salaries are a legitimate concern for a prospective teacher—after all, everyone must have sufficient income to meet the costs of living. You will have to decide whether the salary you are likely to make as a classroom teacher will allow you to establish the lifestyle you want. This section presents some objective facts to help you make your decision.

The 2010–2011 average salary of classroom teachers in the United States was estimated to be about $56,069.[16] Figure 13.3 shows the rise in average salaries since 2001, and Table 13.1 shows how salaries vary by state and region. The Average Salary column in the table represents the average for *all* public elementary and secondary

VOICES from the classroom

Teaching in Public versus Private Schools

Karen Irving has taught chemistry and other science disciplines at the secondary and college levels, including six years of public high school teaching and six years of private high school teaching.

I loved the pulse of my urban high school, with its creative and energetic faculty. With three other chemistry teachers in our school of just under 2,000 students, we never lacked ideas or opinions about how to best help our students succeed. Sometimes we struggled to match our equipment availability to our classroom plans, but we always benefited from the sharing of experiences and expertise.

In addition to a large and diverse faculty, my urban high school boasted a large and diverse student population. However, with just three to four hours of planning time per week and 130 to 150 students in five sections, as well as science fair projects, science teams, and other extracurricular responsibilities, little time remained in my schedule to offer extra help to my students.

After six years of public high school teaching, I accepted a science teaching position at an independent, college preparatory girls' school. Because my teaching assignment at the private school included 60 to 65 students in four sections, the amount of time during the school day to plan lessons and work with students (eight hours per week) doubled from what I was used to in the public setting. In addition, because the weekly school schedule included time for faculty meetings and student clubs during the school day, teachers and students shared free time before and after school for help sessions, make-up work, and additional student enrichment. Other conditions were different too. More parents returned teacher telephone calls, provided necessary home support for learning, made arrangements for students to attend help sessions, attended school functions, and generally worked together with school personnel to ensure that their children received a quality education.

If I had the chance to create an ideal high school environment, I would blend elements of both public and private schools. Ideal High would boast a diverse, creative, and energetic faculty and student population with small classes and sufficient time for teachers to plan and deliver quality lessons. Each student would have the opportunity to reach his or her full potential. Parents, administrators, teachers, and students at Ideal High would share a common vision of an educational community of disciplined effort and academic achievement.

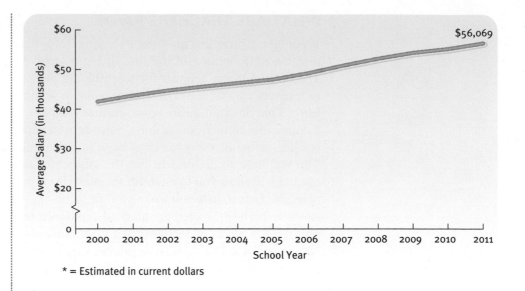

FIGURE 13.3

Average Public School Teacher Salaries

Source: Rankings and Estimates 2010 and 2011 (Washington, DC: National Education Association, 2010), Table 3.5. Available at www. nea.org/assets/docs/HE/NEA_ Rankings_and_Estimates010711. pdf.

school teachers, and the Beginning Salary column indicates the average for *first-year* teachers. For teachers in their first year, the average pay across the United States as a whole was $38,900 in 2008–2009, ranging from a low of $29, 416 (North Dakota) to a high of $48,791 (Massachusetts).[17]

Most public school salary schedules are usually determined by two factors: years of teaching experience and amount of education, usually expressed in terms of college credit-hours or advanced degrees. Thus, the longer you teach and the more college education you receive, the more money you will make. In addition, some states and school districts have used various forms of merit or performance pay (pay-for-performance) plans to reward teachers for exceptional teaching, acquiring new skills needed by the school, achieving national board certification, raising student test scores, or assuming more professional responsibilities. (See Chapter 15, "What Does It Mean to Be a Professional?" for more on national board certification.) Many politicians support performance pay plans as a way to reward those teachers who are deemed most effective. Such plans, they say, ensure that effective teachers' efforts are recognized, and should lead to fewer good teachers leaving the profession. Most teachers unions have opposed performance pay plans, maintaining that fair and equitable means for determining the salary increases under these schemes are elusive. (See Chapter 12, "How Should Education Be Reformed?" for more on performance pay plans.)

As Table 13.1 shows, salaries vary considerably from state to state. Each school district determines what it will pay its teachers, with many states setting a minimum base salary below which the school district cannot go. Generally, the large and middle-size school districts pay better than the small ones, and urban and suburban school districts pay better than rural ones. Many school districts offer extra pay for special duties such as directing the band or coaching athletic teams. Some offer summer teaching or curriculum development jobs. Most states and school districts provide public school teachers with a number of fringe benefits, including sick leave, health and life insurance programs, and retirement benefits. When applying for a teaching position, be sure to ask about these benefits; they are a major advantage for public school teachers over employees in the private sector, especially as many private employers are cutting back on such benefits.

TABLE 13.1 Estimated Average and Beginning Teacher Salaries, by State and Region

State	Average Salary ($) (2010–2011)	Beginning Salary ($) (2008–2009)	State	Average Salary ($) (2010–2011)	Beginning Salary ($) (2008–2009)
New England			**South**		
Massachusetts	71,017	48,791	Georgia	53,906	33,607
Connecticut	65,571	43,105	Virginia	51,559	41,156
Rhode Island	60,923	40,764	Kentucky	50,038	30,815
New Hampshire	52,792	32,301	Louisiana	49,634	38,580
Vermont	50,141	35,693	South Carolina	49,434	37,764
Maine	47,182	31,200	Alabama	48,282	35,246
Mideast			West Virginia	47,253	39,273
New York	72,708	46,191	Tennessee	47,043	38,517
New Jersey	66,985	48,175	North Carolina	46,850	33,743
Washington, D.C.	66,601	(NA)	Florida	46,702	41,200
Pennsylvania	60,536	38,158	Arkansas	47,700	33,112
Maryland	65,113	45,376	Mississippi	46,818	30,900
Delaware	57,934	38,439	**Rocky Mountains**		
Great Lakes			Wyoming	56,978	37,829
Illinois	63,005	39,544	Colorado	49,938	42,865
Michigan	58,595	38,647	Idaho	47,416	33,091
Wisconsin	52,031	33,210	Montana	47,132	32,657
Ohio	57,291	35,267	Utah	46,571	29,616
Indiana	50,407	33,916	**Far West**		
Great Plains			California	69,434	40,421
Minnesota	53,215	34,306	Alaska	61,093	43,423
Iowa	50,634	35,476	Oregon	56,387	34,512
Nebraska	47,521	31,223	Hawaii	55,063	38,447
Kansas	47,080	32,434	Washington	53,796	41,961
Missouri	46,411	33,806	Nevada	53,023	34,646
North Dakota	44,266	29,416	**U.S. Average**	**56,069**	**31,627**
South Dakota	35,201	29,528			
Southwest					
Oklahoma	49,039	38,579			
Texas	48,261	40,790			
Arizona	47,553	37,632			
New Mexico	46,950	33,669			

Sources: Average salaries from *Rankings and Estimates: Rankings of the States 2010 and Estimates of School Statistics 2011* (Washington, DC: National Education Association, 2010),) available at www.nea.org/assets/docs/HE/NEA_Rankings_and_Estimates010711.pdf. Beginning salaries are from the Job Search Handbook for Educators (Columbus, OH: American Association for Employment in Education, Inc., 2010), p. 64.

> ## PAUSE AND REFLECT
>
> 1. Are the average teacher salaries reported in this chapter about what you expected? How do the salaries in your geographic area compare with the national average? What might account for any differences that you note?
>
> 2. Judging from the salary information here, what do you estimate your salary as a teacher would be? Are you confident that this salary would meet your expenses?

how do you obtain a teaching position?

The job market may be encouraging for beginning teachers, but regardless of how great the demand for teachers is or how effective you may be as a teacher, school district personnel are not likely to walk up to you and offer you a job unless you have taken the steps outlined in this section. Here we suggest several courses of action that will greatly increase your chances of finding the best teaching job for you.

CAMPAIGN ACTIVELY

First, you must be determined to campaign actively for a teaching position. Draw up a plan, in writing, stating how you will proceed. Don't wait for happenstance. You might get lucky and land a job on your first try, but why take a passive attitude when you can do much more to increase your chances of obtaining satisfying employment? For example, try attending job fairs sponsored by various colleges, universities, and school districts.

Job seekers often make two common mistakes.[18] First, they try one strategy, wait for results (positive or negative), and then try something else. What you should do instead is to pursue many avenues or strategies simultaneously. Second, job seekers block themselves out at the wrong stage in the process. Some teachers halfheartedly write for information or never complete the application form; others withdraw their applications prematurely. Remember, you can always say "no" to a job offered to you, but you can never say "yes" to one that has not been offered. Keep your options open.

> " *I'm a great believer in luck, and I find the harder I work, the more I have of it.*
>
> —THOMAS JEFFERSON (1743–1826), Third President of the United States

PREPARE MATERIALS

Next, you need to get certain materials ready—namely, your résumé, cover letter, credentials, and transcripts. Your résumé allows you to present yourself the way you want to be presented to prospective employers. Its purpose is to help you get an interview with school district officials. You should make several copies of your résumé and bring extras with you to any interview.

Many sources are available to help you write your résumé. The office of career planning and placement at your college or university is a good place to start. These offices often run workshops on résumé and cover letter writing and frequently have samples of well-written résumés and cover letters available for you to examine. The American Association for Employment in Education (AAEE)'s annual *Job Search Handbook for Educators,* which is listed in the For Further Information section at the end of the chapter, is also an excellent source on how to write résumés and on other job search strategies.

Another set of materials that an increasing number of teachers are using to help them obtain jobs is called a **teaching portfolio**. Just as artists, actors, architects, and journalists use portfolios to display the products of their work, so can teachers. A teaching portfolio can include an organized collection of such items as research papers, letters of commendation or recommendation, pupil evaluations, teaching units, and digital recordings of lessons you have taught. There is no set format; you are limited only by your common sense and your own imagination. Remember, the purpose of the portfolio is to market yourself effectively, so don't be modest. A properly constructed portfolio will say much more about you than your résumé ever can.

Many beginning teachers are constructing electronic portfolios and making them available to potential employers either as websites or on DVDs. The advantage of an electronic portfolio is that it is easily accessible by potential employers and can be changed or enhanced as needed. Electronic teaching portfolios are also being used to demonstrate that prospective teachers have achieved standards—such as the InTASC (Interstate Teacher Assessment and Support Consortium) standards—required for licensure in some states. The National Board for Professional Teaching Standards (discussed in Chapter 15, "What Does It Mean to Be a Professional?") has advocated teaching portfolios as a means of assessing a teacher's work for national certification.

Almost all school districts require credentials, or the whole package from your college, recommending you for licensure. Check with the career planning and placement office about how to establish your **credential file** and what should go into it. Typically this file includes letters of recommendation, a copy of your transcript, and a résumé. Career planning and placement office personnel will help you assemble this file, and they will send copies of your file to school districts on your request. You should start working on this file early in your program so that you will have plenty of time to accumulate the required materials. Letters of recommendation should be recent, and they should come from those who are familiar with your teaching, academic knowledge, and character. Be certain to include letters from your university supervisor and your cooperating teacher in whose classroom you did your student or internship teaching. Be familiar with the Family Educational Rights and Privacy Act, also known as the Buckley amendment (discussed more fully in Chapter 8, "What Are the Ethical and Legal Issues Facing Teachers?"), which affords you certain kinds of legal protection regarding what goes into your file.*

Many applications require that job seekers submit transcripts as well. Because colleges charge several dollars per transcript, you can save money by reproducing the transcript yourself. Most school districts will accept such unofficial transcripts (i.e., transcripts sent from you rather than directly from the college) for the initial screening process. If you receive a job offer, you will then have to provide the school district with an official copy.

When you send your résumé, transcripts, and other materials to prospective school districts, the package should include a cover letter. The cover letters you write should be addressed individually. The letters may all have the same or similar content, but the recipients should not feel they are receiving a standard letter. And be sure to ask for an interview at the end of the letter—that's why you are writing it!

---

*A copy of this law appears in *Federal Register* 53, no. 69 (April 11, 1998), pp. 11942–11949. It can also be obtained by writing the U.S. Government Printing Office, Washington, DC 20402.

typical questions asked during job interviews

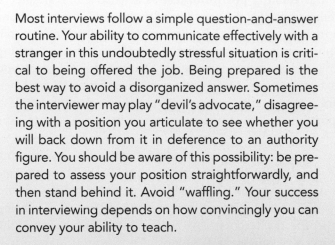

Most interviews follow a simple question-and-answer routine. Your ability to communicate effectively with a stranger in this undoubtedly stressful situation is critical to being offered the job. Being prepared is the best way to avoid a disorganized answer. Sometimes the interviewer may play "devil's advocate," disagreeing with a position you articulate to see whether you will back down from it in deference to an authority figure. You should be aware of this possibility: be prepared to assess your position straightforwardly, and then stand behind it. Avoid "waffling." Your success in interviewing depends on how convincingly you can convey your ability to teach.

interviewer a thank-you note—courtesy can make a difference.

Questions you may be asked include the following:

Motivation/Experience/Education

- Tell us about yourself.
- Why do you want to teach?
- Why do you want to work in our school district?
- Which grade levels or subjects are you most interested in teaching?
- What do you consider to be your strongest attributes as a teacher? Weaknesses?

(Brand X Pictures/Jupiterimages)

Interviews are often subjective, so your enthusiasm, self-confidence, eagerness, and believability will affect the outcome of your interview. Be sincere and mean what you say. Look the interviewer in the eye. First impressions are important, so dress conservatively. Remove visible body piercings and cover up tattoos!

At the conclusion of the interview, restate any important points you want to emphasize. Ask the interviewer for a business card and ask when the selection decision will be made. Send the

- What was your biggest problem in student teaching? How did you resolve it?
- How would you work with students who perform below grade level, especially those from poverty backgrounds?

Teaching Skills

- What is your philosophy of education?
- What are the most important learning outcomes you want your students to achieve?

(continued)

- What skills and experience do you have in employing cooperative learning strategies or computers for instructional purposes?
- How can you motivate unmotivated learners?
- How would you involve parents to help students learn?
- Describe how you have differentiated a lesson to accommodate specific students' needs.
- What is your grading philosophy?
- How have you incorporated curriculum standards into your lesson plans and units?

Classroom Management

- What ideas do you have about maintaining classroom control?
- Which rules for students would you establish in your classroom?
- How would you enforce these rules?
- Describe the most difficult student discipline situation you have faced and explain how you handled it.

Professional Responsibilities

- How do you plan to keep growing as a professional?
- Which professional journals do you read?
- Which added school responsibilities are you willing to accept?

Hypothetical Questions

- What would you do if you caught a student cheating?

- If money were unlimited, how would you improve education?
- How would you handle a student who refused to do the work you assigned?

During a job interview, you will answer many questions. But to gain the information that will help you choose among the jobs offered to you, you will also need to *ask* questions. Remember, you are interviewing the prospective employer too. Before you accept a position, you will need to know about the following:

Instructional Assignment

- Characteristics of the school district and student population
- Curriculum and resources available
- Typical class size
- Salary and benefits (medical and dental coverage and retirement)
- District's expectations and reimbursement policies for professional development
- Orientation or support services available for beginning teachers

These are just a few suggestions. For additional information on interview questions, see "Interview Questions to Answer and Ask," in *2011 Job Search Handbook for Educators* (Columbus, OH: American Association for Employment in Education, 2010), pp. 18–23.

DEVELOP INTERVIEW SKILLS

The success of your personal interview with the school district representative is one of the most important determinants of whether you get hired, so be prepared. Try to anticipate the kinds of questions that might be asked (see the accompanying box for some sample questions). Try role-playing with a friend who assumes the role of the interviewer while you play the candidate. Audiotape your "interview" so the two of you can criticize it.

One survey indicated that the major factor school officials consider as part of the decision-making process is whether the candidate has empathy for children. Be prepared to show your empathy, not by saying you have it, but rather through the examples you give from your own experience. You should also ask those who write letters of recommendation for you to emphasize this aspect of your character.

Remember, *you* are also interviewing the school district or specific school. You should look for a good fit between you and your style of teaching and what the school or district expects from you. Don't be so eager to get any position that you ignore the issue of fit. As charter schools continue to emerge (see Chapter 12, "How Should Education Be Reformed?"), new teachers will have more options to choose from in terms of work climate, educational philosophy, and learning goals. In addition, consider whether you will have access to an induction program and a mentor teacher. Research shows that having a good mentor teacher increases the likelihood of your success as a teacher. Secondary school teachers should also ask whether the number of class preparations is reduced for beginning teachers. Having only one or two types of classes to prepare for makes the first year of teaching much easier than having to complete three or four preparations for different courses.

DETERMINE JOB AVAILABILITY

Your next major task is to find out which jobs are available and where. You can use many different strategies to obtain this information. Your college's career planning and placement office receives hundreds of notifications of position vacancies, so contact that office often to see whether there are any vacancies that might interest you. Be on the lookout for job fairs, where school districts and potential teachers come together at one site to explore job opportunities. Your college or university may also sponsor such a job fair. Another source of information may be the teacher employment office operated by the state department of education. Approximately one-third of the states run such offices, and you can register with them for free or for a small charge. These offices send registered candidates a listing of openings in their specialty area for both state and out-of-state vacancies.

In addition, some private and professional organizations keep current nationwide teacher vacancy lists and will try to match your qualifications with those vacancies either for little or no cost. ASCD (formerly the Association of Supervision and Curriculum Development) has created a website called Job Ramp (**www.ascd. org/ascdjobramp.aspx**), which allows teachers to post resumes, scan job openings, and receive help in locating a teaching position free of charge. Another such organization is Teachers-Teachers.com (available at **www.teachers-teachers.com**). This service, which is offered for free to prospective teachers, allows job seekers to post their résumés online; these documents can then be accessed by thousands of schools seeking teachers. (See the For Further Information section at the end of the chapter for more information on this website.)

Personal contacts are often very effective in securing a position as well. Don't hesitate to call friends and acquaintances who might be able to help you obtain interviews. They probably can't get you a job, but they may be aware of vacancies and know whom you should contact.

Contacting specific school districts directly is another way to determine which positions are available. Call, write, or visit the personnel offices of the school districts in which you are interested to obtain current information directly from the school district. Alternatively, you can use the Internet to check the home pages of the school districts that interest you to see which job openings are listed.

GAIN EXPERIENCE THROUGH SUBSTITUTE TEACHING

Many education students develop valuable experience, earn some money, and "get a foot in the door" at a school district by serving as substitute teachers. Some universities even offer coursework in becoming an effective substitute. Besides

The First Year of Teaching: One Colleague's Story

Go to the Education CourseMate website to watch the video clips, study the artifacts in the case, and reflect on the following questions:

1. View the bonus video, where Mr. Starner reflects on his first year of teaching. Do his observations surprise you in any way? If so, how?

2. Does this teacher offer any new information about the first year of teaching?

3. What is the most important advice or information you think this teacher conveyed to you?

giving you the opportunity to refine your teaching skills, substitute teaching can provide a competitive advantage in the job market. Some school districts are apt to hire full-time teachers from their substitute ranks if the substitutes have done a good job. After all, school officials would rather hire a known teacher in whom they have confidence than take a chance on a new teacher whom they don't know. If you're interested in being a substitute teacher, visit the district personnel office to find out the requirements and attend substitute-teacher training sessions if they are offered. The Video Case *The First Year of Teaching: One Colleague's Story* depicts a fourth-grade teacher who speaks candidly about his first year of teaching.

PAUSE AND REFLECT

1. Which strategies might you use to increase your chances of being hired when you are ready to teach?

2. Which of the interview questions in the Typical Questions Asked during Job Interviews feature do you believe you would find most difficult to answer? Which would you find easiest?

how do you become licensed?

All 50 states and the District of Columbia require public elementary and secondary school teachers to be licensed to teach by the department of education in the state in which they work. The terms *licensure* and *certification* are often confused or misused. **Licensure** is the official recognition by a state governmental agency that an individual meets state requirements, whereas **certification** is the process by which the profession grants special recognition to an individual who has met certain qualifications specified by the profession. Often, the term *certification*—as in, "I'm going to get my certification to teach"—is used when *licensure* is meant. This usage is a carryover from earlier times. Today some states continue to use *certification* as a synonym for *licensure,* but in this book we have tried to distinguish between the two terms.

TRADITIONAL LICENSURE PROGRAMS

Traditionally, to qualify for licensure, a teacher has had to complete an approved teacher education program. Besides conferring a bachelor's or master's degree, which provides the necessary liberal arts background, teacher education programs fulfill the state requirement that prospective teachers take certain education courses or demonstrate certain competencies. (Links to state licensure offices appear in this book's appendix.)

Since the mid-1980s, the overwhelming majority of states have increased the requirements for licensure, adding test requirements such as the PRAXIS examinations (teacher competency exams developed by the Educational Testing Service) or, in some cases, state-developed competency tests of basic skills.

Because the No Child Left Behind law requires that "highly qualified" teachers meet standards in the content areas they teach, prospective teachers are examined on their content-area knowledge as well as pedagogical knowledge. The difficulty levels and the required scores to pass these tests vary from state to state, however. In some states, further requirements for licensure include U.S. citizenship, criminal background checks, an oath of allegiance, and in several states a health certificate.

Because the requirements for licensure differ from state to state, you should become aware of the requirements for the state in which you will seek employment. Someone in your placement office or your school of education most likely will be able to acquaint you with licensure requirements. Your education library probably contains books that list the licensure requirements for all the states. Alternatively, you can call or write directly to the teacher licensure office in the states in which you are interested. A directory of state teacher licensure offices in the United States, along with their website addresses, appears as an appendix at the end of this book. A number of states have reciprocal agreements to accept one another's licenses as valid. If you move from one state to another, you may want to check whether your teaching license is accepted by the state to which you are moving.

Besides the basic licenses for teaching at the elementary and secondary levels, many states require different licenses, or *endorsements,* for such specialization areas as special education, bilingual education, and kindergarten. If, as you gain experience, you want to move out of teaching into a supervisory, administrative, or counseling position, you will need a special license to make that transition as well.

You would be wise to become licensed or endorsed in more than one teaching area, if possible. Adding a second field of licensure will make you more attractive to prospective employers, particularly in smaller school districts, which have less flexibility to hire specialists who teach in only one area. If you plan to become an elementary school teacher, having an additional license or endorsement in reading, special education, early childhood education, or bilingual education would be very worthwhile. Another way to increase your appeal to prospective employers is to major or minor in mathematics, one of the sciences, or instructional technology. Elementary school teachers with expertise in these areas are in short supply. If you plan to teach at the secondary level, you can broaden your appeal by becoming licensed to teach in two or more subject fields. For example, if you are a Spanish major, minor in French; if you are a chemistry major, minor in physics or mathematics. Any doubling up of teaching fields will work to your advantage.

In summary, individual states use licensure requirements to assure the public that the teachers who are educating the youth of our society have been adequately prepared. Licensure requirements should present you with little difficulty as long as the teacher education institution you attend meets the general regulations of the state department of education and as long as you maintain contact with the college official responsible for coordinating the education program with the state licensure requirements.

> *Keeping young teachers in our schools is of immense importance, but keeping them there with spirits strong and souls intact is more important still. If we lose this, we lose everything.*
>
> —JONATHAN KOZOL,
> American Educational Author

ALTERNATIVE LICENSURE

In many states, the traditional route to licensure—graduation from an approved teacher education program—is no longer the sole route to gaining a teaching license. **Alternative licensure** programs have been developed as a response to (1) teacher shortages and (2) the perception on the part of some lawmakers that courses in education contribute little to a teacher's effectiveness. Generally, those licensed through alternative means hold a bachelor's degree in the subject area they will teach but have taken fewer credit hours in professional education courses than are normally required for teaching licensure. Often these candidates are required to have at least a B college grade average and to have passed a basic skills test and a test in a subject or specialty area.

One alternative program that has attracted considerable attention is *Teach for America*. This program recruits motivated undergraduate students with arts and science majors from selected colleges and universities to teach for two years in rural or urban areas that have had difficulty recruiting teachers. Although the program has been successful in attracting significant numbers of minority teachers, its dropout rate is high. Also, the number of teachers produced through the *Teach for America* program is very small compared with the number graduated through approved teacher education programs.

How successful are these alternative licensure programs? All 50 states have some form of alternative licensure option, and approximately 59,000 individuals were issued teaching licenses through an alternative route in the 2008–2009 school year. Approximately one-third of all new teacher hires in the United States now follow alternative routes to teacher licensure.[19] Few formal evaluation studies of alternative licensure programs have been carried out, however, and those that have taken place have sometimes been conducted by persons with vested interests in the outcomes. To date, a synthesis of what research has been done concludes, "Teachers who are certified through alternative routes lack adequate pedagogical skills, which are typically taught and acquired in formal teacher education programs."[20] One analysis of a national sample of teachers who entered teaching through alternative licensure routes concluded that they tended to have lower academic qualifications than those who entered through other routes, were less likely to stay in teaching, and were more likely to be teaching in inner-city schools that serve more economically disadvantaged students.[21] On the positive side, compared with graduates of traditional teacher education programs, those entering teaching through alternative licensure programs tend to be older, have more work experience in occupations other than education, are more likely to be males, and are more likely to be people of color.[22]

Supporters of alternative licensure programs argue that the ability to attract men and minorities into teaching speaks to the need for these types of programs. The federal government provides millions of dollars to help mid-career professionals and retiring military personnel become licensed as teachers.

Nevertheless, tensions exist between those who want to break college-based teacher education's monopoly and professional educators who believe that completion of an approved teacher education program is the public's best guarantee that a teacher is "safe to practice." The variety of alternative licensure programs operating across the various states is testimony to the differing views on how teachers should be prepared. The real issue is not whether traditional programs are better than alternative licensure programs, but rather what the most important elements constituting effective teacher preparation are and whether that preparation occurs through a traditional or alternative program. One thing seems certain: alternative licensure programs will continue to expand to meet the projected need for teachers.

PAUSE AND REFLECT

1. Do you have any opinions about the alternative licensure programs currently offered in most states? What do you see as their strengths? Their drawbacks?

2. Are you clear about the difference between "certification" and "licensure"?

if you don't teach, what then?

For many different reasons, a substantial number of teachers each year find themselves looking for jobs outside education. Has your preparation equipped you with skills that are in demand in fields outside education?

TRANSFERABLE SKILLS

Many noneducational employers are eager to employ teachers and people who have gone through teacher preparation programs, because they have skills that many college graduates lack. Which generic or transferable skills—that is, skills that are needed in most businesses and professions—are you likely to have developed in your preparation as a teacher? Among the skills and abilities that teachers acquire are the following:

- Planning and decision making
- Working under pressure
- Conducting performance evaluations
- Keeping records and organizing materials
- Using technology
- Establishing and maintaining good interpersonal relations
- Communicating effectively in oral and written form
- Managing groups of people

In short, many of the skills required of teachers are required for other types of work as well. Naturally, additional training may be necessary, depending on the exact type of work. Now let's examine some alternative careers.

OTHER JOBS

In addition to teaching, schools and school districts offer a number of other educational occupations, including librarian, counselor, supervisor, administrator, and school psychologist. Although these roles don't involve full-time teaching of children, they may require some minimum teaching experience and additional licensure. All these roles are important in the educational enterprise. If you decide that you are interested in education but not necessarily in long-term elementary or secondary school teaching, one of these other occupations may be right for you.

You might also investigate employment in early childhood education and day care centers. Because early childhood education is a growing field, numerous new occupations are developing within it, such as reading specialists to help diagnose learning abilities and curriculum specialists to help plan the studies. State, local, and federal government agencies need researchers, planners, evaluators, and others to administer the growing number of early childhood projects they fund.

Another area that requires teaching skills is in the field of adult education, which attempts to provide basic education and literacy skills for the many adults who lack such competencies and therefore have difficulty finding work in a technologically oriented society. Adult education occurs in many venues, including public schools, community colleges, and public service organizations.

There are many alternative careers for people who are trained as teachers but who elect not to teach in schools.

(© Elizabeth Crews)

Large businesses also conduct extensive training programs for their employees, and they require the services of people who can design and implement such programs. Many people who have been trained as teachers find their way into such jobs. Several hundreds of thousands of people are employed (full- and part-time) in training and development in the United States.*

The field of recreation and leisure activities attracts many people trained as teachers. Workers in this field plan, organize, and direct individual and group activities that help people enjoy their leisure hours. They work with people of various ages and socioeconomic groups, the sick and the well, and those with emotional and physical disabilities. Employment settings range from wilderness to rural, to suburban and urban. Examples of recreation program jobs include playground leaders; program specialists in dance, drama, karate, tennis, the arts, and other physical activities; recreation center directors; therapeutic recreation specialists; camp counselors and wilderness leaders; senior citizen program leaders; civilian special services directors in the armed forces; and industrial recreation directors. Recreation workers held about 327,500 jobs in 2008, and that figure is expected to climb to 375,500 by 2018.[23] The majority worked in local, public, tax-supported agencies, such as municipal and county park and recreation departments.

The publishing industry affords numerous job opportunities for education-oriented writers, technology experts, editors, and salespeople. If you have good writing and analytic skills, you might be interested in helping develop or edit textbooks for use in elementary and secondary schools and in colleges. If you enjoy meeting people and traveling, being a textbook sales representative might appeal to you. Another growing area is the development of computer software related to education. Individuals who combine computer skills, including web design, with an understanding of classroom instruction will have a distinct advantage in this job market.

Preparation as a teacher is also important for work related to professional organizations such as the National Education Association (NEA), American

*The American Society of Training and Development, 1640 King Street, Box 1443, Alexandria, VA 22313, can provide more information about corporate career opportunities for teachers. Available at **www.astd.org.**

Federation of Teachers (AFT), Phi Delta Kappa, Kappa Delta Pi, National Council of Teachers of Mathematics, and National Council for the Social Studies. These organizations and others like them hire people for fieldwork, writing, research, and other staff positions.

OUR FINAL WORD

Many indicators point to a strong demand for teachers in the coming years, once the country emerges from recession hangover. Impending retirements in the current teaching force and increased school enrollments are encouraging signs for prospective teachers, though some former teachers might reenter the job market to compete with recently graduated teachers for these job openings. Successful job searches may require special steps such as relocating to another area or state to secure a teaching position in your field.

There has never been a surplus of good teachers. If you and your credentials are good and you are willing to go where the jobs are, you can find a teaching job. Preparing yourself well for school districts' needs, especially by gaining expertise in more than one teaching field, can expand your job options and make you more attractive to prospective employers.

The United States has become an education-oriented society. As a nation, we now realize that reaching our individual and national goals depends on achieving high levels of education. Doing so requires being committed to more and better education, and to lifelong learning in and out of schools. Over 80 years ago, President Calvin Coolidge said, "The business of America is business." Today and into the future, the business of America is education. Teaching is where the action is and will continue to be!

WHY TEACH? YOUR FINAL WORD

In your journal or online at this textbook's website, respond to the following questions:

1. Describe your "ideal" teaching job. Which elements of that job are most important to you?

2. Now that you have surveyed the educational job market, what do you see as the pluses and minuses of preparing yourself to teach?

3. Which grade level and/or subject matter do you want to teach? How will you go about determining whether your current choice is right for you?

KEY TERMS

alternative licensure (430)
certification (429)
credential file (425)

licensure (429)
teaching portfolio (425)

FOR FURTHER INFORMATION

WEB RESOURCES

Council of Chief State School Officers. Available at **www.ccsso.org.**

This organization of the chief state school officers has a useful and informative home page, including links to each state education agency. Click on the map of State Education Agencies, and choose the state in which you are interested. Some states list telephone numbers and websites of different school districts in the state.

Preparing a Teaching Portfolio: A Guidebook. Produced by the Center for Teaching Effectiveness at the University of Texas–Austin. Available at **http:// ctl.utexas.edu/teaching-resources/advance-your-career/assemble-your-teaching-portfolio/.**

This online resource provides detailed instructions on how to prepare a teaching portfolio.

Teachers-Teachers.com. Available at **www.teachers-teachers.com.**

Sponsored by several educational organizations, this website allows schools to contact prospective teachers who have posted their résumés on the site. There is no fee for teachers.

PRINT RESOURCES

American Association for Employment in Education, *Job Search Handbook for Educators* (Columbus, OH: Author).

This annual publication is designed to assist both new and experienced educators in their job searches and is the single most important reference on this topic. The *Handbook* is usually distributed through career planning and placement offices in colleges and universities, but it may also be obtained from the AAEE office at 3040 Riverside Drive, Suite 117, Columbus, OH 43221–2550 or by calling (614) 485-1111. AAEE's website also provides links to public school systems and educational organizations and is available at **www.aaee.org.**

Richard Nelson Bolles, *What Color Is Your Parachute? 2011:A Practical Manual for Job-Hunters and Career Changers* (Berkeley, CA: Ten Speed Press, 2011).

This best-selling practical manual for job hunters and career changers is updated yearly.

Jay Mathews, *Escalante: The Best Teacher in America* (New York: Holt, 1990).

This is the biography of Jaime Escalante, who is profiled in this chapter and is the subject of the film *Stand and Deliver.* Escalante wins over his students, largely urban Hispanics, with a combination of challenges to pride, demands of dedicated hard work, and demonstrated love.

REFERENCES FOR LOCATING JOB OPPORTUNITIES

GENERAL INFORMATION

Directory of Public School Systems in the U.S. Published annually. American Association for Employment in Education, 3040 Riverside Drive, Suite 125, Columbus, OH 43221-2550, (614) 485-1111. Orders may be placed online at **www.aaee.org.**

This directory lists contact information for all public school systems in the United States.

Education Week. Available at **www.edweek.org.**

Education Week is an independent newspaper published 40 times a year. For a subscription, write to Education Week, 4301 Connecticut Avenue, NW, Suite 250, Washington, DC 20008.

Education America Network. Available at **www. educationamerica.net.**

A career site for education professionals to assist them in finding jobs.

PRIVATE SCHOOLS

National Association of Independent Schools (NAIS). Available at **http://nais.org/.**

This organization represents more than 1,200 independent schools nationwide and abroad. Contact the Associate Director of Academic Services, National Association of Independent Schools, 1620 L Street, Suite 1100, NW, Washington, DC 20036-5695, (202) 973-9700. Also visit the website for information on how to secure a teaching job at one of its schools.

TEACHING OPPORTUNITIES ABROAD

U.S. Department of Defense Dependents Schools. Available at **www.dodea.edu/home/index.cfm.**

Teachers in these American schools are U.S. government employees. Contact Department of Defense Education Activity from its website.

European Council of International Schools (ECIS). Available at **www.ecis.org.**

This organization can provide information about schools in Europe. Contact ECIS, 21B Lavant Street, Petersfield, Hampshire GU32 3EL, UK. Call (44) 1730-268244.

International Schools Services (ISS). Available at **www.iss.edu.**

This resource contains names, addresses, and other information on nearly 500 international elementary and secondary schools. Ask for the *ISS Directory of Overseas Schools.* Contact ISS, 15 Roszel Road, P.O. Box 5910, Princeton, NJ 08543, (609) 452-0990.

The Education CourseMate website for this text offers many helpful resources. Go to www.cengagebrain.com to access the TeachSource Video Cases and other TeachSource videos, flashcards, interactive quizzes, the eBook, reflection and enrichment activities, a state standards resource center, and other study aids.

14 what can the new teacher expect?

FOCUS POINTS

- Although prospective teachers may think that schools will hold few surprises, being on the other side of the desk is a very different experience and can produce a sense of culture shock.

- Administrators play an important but often confusing role in the life of the beginning teacher.

- Although fellow teachers are an enormous source of learning and support, they can sometimes be a source of difficulty.

- New teachers learn much about the job in which they are supposed to be experts: instruction.

- Some of the most intense satisfactions and disappointments experienced by new teachers come from those they came to help: students.

- Working with parents can be surprisingly complex and is rarely what the new teacher has anticipated.

- Beginning teachers can follow specific strategies to mitigate problems and heighten their chances for a successful career start.

- Teaching invariably has hidden sweetness and secret joys.

(© Bill Aron/PhotoEdit)

Starting their career is for most people one of the most exciting and energizing periods of their lives. For most young people it represents their unofficial entrance into the adult world. They are often in a new environment with new people and challenges, and they have real responsibilities. This is especially true for new teachers.

For many, the transition into full-time teaching is relatively easy and satisfying. For others, however, the first year is a struggle. Some new teachers are shocked and disappointed by their initial experience of being a teacher. For most, however, the first year of teaching is a mixed bag of highs and lows. In this chapter, we try to help prospective teachers anticipate some of the problems that lie ahead. All of the material comes directly from the experiences of beginning teachers.

Truth or Fiction?

T F One of the benefits of so many years in the classroom as students is that the first year of teaching holds few surprises for new teachers.

T F It is important for new teachers to work to eliminate the traditional social distance between themselves and students.

T F In general, it is good advice to establish good communication with your students' parents.

We have good news and bad news for you. First, the good news: forecasters predict that as a result of teacher retirement and student enrollment growth, U.S. schools will need about 2 million new teachers between 2010 and 2018.[1] Not since World War II has there been such a promising job market for teachers. As we describe in Chapter 13, "What Are Your Job Options in Education?" people entering the teaching profession in the second decade of the twenty-first century typically will have a rich variety of options and opportunities from which to choose. So much for the good news.

Now the bad news: the first year of teaching can be a rough one—too rough for many beginners. Each year, many new teachers walk into their classrooms with energy, high hopes, and rose-colored glasses, only to face unexpected problems that cause them to give up on teaching or radically lower their perceptions of their capabilities as teachers. The tips in the Voices from the Classroom feature give you an idea of what you might expect the first year.

Rather than ignoring or—even worse—sugarcoating these problems, we focus on them, even at the risk of frightening some readers. We do so because we believe "forewarned is forearmed," and many of the problems discussed in this chapter can be either prevented or radically reduced in intensity. Further, new teachers can actually find satisfaction in solving their problems and in succeeding as professionals.

Surprise is a big part of the first year too. New teachers often report their astonishment at this or that experience or event. The first year is intense because of the unexpected demands and the startling events that lurk in what was thought to be a familiar world: the classroom. These surprises often come wrapped in everyday boxes; some contain sweet treasures, and others hold booby traps. We have categorized these surprises and organized them in the following way:

- The school milieu: the shock of the familiar
- Administrators: mixed bag, as well as many hats and pressures
- Peers: a mixed blessing
- Instruction: so much to learn
- Students: friends or fiends?
- Parents: natural allies with different agendas

In this chapter, we look at each of these categories and try to take some of the surprises out of the first year of teaching. Our larger intention, however, is to help you mobilize yourself by preparing for the problems, developing your strengths, and shoring up your weaknesses.

VOICES from the classroom

Tips for Your First Year

Lauren Manganiello is currently teaching 10th-grade English at Boston Collegiate Charter School in Dorchester, Massachusetts.

The most valuable tip I can give to a prospective first-year teacher is that you should expect to work *very hard*, and sometimes *very late*, every night. The summer before I started teaching, I worked diligently at preparing units and lessons; still, I had no idea how much work I had coming to me. Granted, the amount of work you'll need to do will depend on your school and your curriculum; I have total control over what I teach, which translates to a lot of work for me. I spend between one and two hours correcting on weeknights and even more on weekends; I spend most afternoons securing the next day's lessons.

Next, expect to do a lot of learning in your first year. Most new teachers are fresh out of college or graduate school and know their specific subject matter very well; however, knowing material and knowing how to teach material are two completely different concepts! Making the switch from higher education back to high school or even elementary school education is a challenge.

Finally, expect to:

- Struggle—practice makes perfect, and if you push yourself too hard at the beginning of your career, you might burn out before your time (think of teaching as a marathon).

- Be overwhelmed with paperwork—there's a letter or form for *everything*.

- Meet amazing students who will keep you coming back to your job.

- Have responsibilities outside of your classroom, such as corridor duty; study halls; or, my favorite, bathroom duty.

- Be shocked by the sometimes cynical conversation in the lunchroom.

- Find some amazing teachers in your department and school who can be your best resources and best allies.

- Be surprised—what you worry about now will seem ridiculous once you're finally in the classroom, and what you've never even given a thought to will suddenly become your everyday amusement, pleasure, or headache!

Parents are not *always* the teacher's allies.

the school milieu: the shock of the familiar

One of the oddest occurrences related to becoming a teacher is the new teacher's sense of strangeness in what is, after all, a very familiar setting. People who become securities analysts, astronauts, or psychiatric social workers know they are moving into a strange environment, and they expect these new work worlds to present them with very different experiences from those they had as students. New teachers, however, are reentering a familiar setting, even if their schools are not the same ones in which they were taught. Nevertheless, beginning teachers are often overwhelmed by their initial exposure to school.

The new teacher's very familiarity with life in schools is a problem in that it lulls many into a false sense of understanding what is happening around them—and thus a false sense of security. "School" is a very complicated network of people, structures, and interactions.

However, having "studied" school from the perspective of a student is hardly the same as understanding it from the perspective of a teacher. Being one of 25 students sitting and listening to a teacher is quite different from being in front of 25 young people and having responsibility for their learning. Also, new teachers not only have to learn a new set of school routines for their particular school but also must understand how to administer those routines. They have to learn their way around a new building and find out how to requisition the supplies they need. They have to get acquainted with their administrators' policies, their fellow teachers, and especially their students. On top of everything else, first-year teachers often have to develop lesson plans from scratch. They must build complete units, design bulletin boards, devise an evaluation system, and make up and grade short- and long-term tests of students' understanding. The sheer volume of all this "newness" puts enormous pressure and strain on the beginners.

T (F)

One of the benefits of so many years in the classroom as students is that the first year of teaching holds few surprises for new teachers.

The new teacher's very familiarity with life in schools is a problem in that it lulls many into a false sense of understanding what is happening around them—and thus a false sense of security.

> *A teacher's day is half bureaucracy, half crisis, half monotony, and one-eightieth epiphany. Never mind the arithmetic.*
>
> —SUSAN OHANIAN,
> Writer and Educational Commentator

CULTURE SHOCK

Beginning teachers' disorientation with what they thought would be the familiar turf of school often shows up in visible signs of mental and physical stress. In the early months of the school year, many new teachers experience depression and self-doubt, outbursts of crying, physical exhaustion, insomnia, crankiness, inability to control temper, and even fits of vomiting before going to school in the morning.

One anthropologist claims that the stresses and strains many new teachers experience are similar to the phenomenon known as culture shock.[2] **Culture shock** is the feeling of dislocation that people experience when they initially live in a foreign country. Peace Corps volunteers, aid workers, exchange students, tourists, and newly arrived immigrants often report that when they are first thrust into the strange life patterns of a foreign culture, they feel numbingly disoriented, forced to assimilate too much too soon, and afraid they have made a drastic mistake by going to this strange country. It is easy to explain the

> *Rather than saying, "I have a job," I say with delight, "I am a teacher!" It's so much more than a job. It's an awakening.*
>
> —STUART D. CHANDLER,
> Fifth-Grade Teacher, Aurora, Colorado

culture shock experienced by Peace Corps volunteers and immigrants, but why teachers? Haven't we just said that teachers, as ex-students, are accustomed to the culture of school?

PAUSE AND REFLECT

1. Think of a time when you may have experienced culture shock, and try to remember, in as much detail as possible, how it made you feel.

2. Did you experience any sense of disorientation or depression during your initial months at college? Which strategies did you find helpful in getting oriented?

3. Have you ever been in a class with a teacher you thought might be experiencing culture shock?

The following account by a new second-grade teacher speaks to the kinds of culture shock problems related to the large amounts of "newness" experienced by many first-year teachers.*

from PRESERVICE to PRACTICE

Charlotte Tucker/Second Grade

The next time I hear someone say, "Teaching is an easy job," I think I'm going to slap his or her face . . . or cry! I can't believe how tired I am. I've been teaching for five weeks, and it seems as if it has been five months. I never realized that life on the teacher's side of the desk could be so different, so tiring. I remember seeing the movies set in high schools and thinking they were exaggerated. My kids are younger and don't have the kinds of problems those high school kids in the movie had, but they still have problems, and they are so demanding! They all want my attention, and they all seem to want it at the same time. "Miss Tucker, someone took my pencil! Did you do it?" "Miss Tucker, Ralph and Maxine put gum in my hair." "Miss Tucker, my father doesn't think we're doing enough arithmetic in this class and says I can tell the kids to shut up if you won't." "Miss Tucker, I need to see the nurse. I have a terrible nosebleed coming on!" And on and on.

And the forms! They never end. Forms for shots. For lockers. For parent volunteers. For books. And

we have an attendance procedure here that must have been designed by a sadist! It consumes hours of time. The principal's office continually wants information. I keep filling out forms and sending them in, only to be greeted with more forms. I can't imagine what they do with all the information.

On top of all this, I'm supposed to teach! I leave school in the afternoon—always the last one out of the building—and I'm numb from the hairline down. On some nights, I can hardly unwrap a microwavable dinner. And I spend what little free time I do have staring at my TV set and having imaginary arguments with Sandra's know-it-all father (whom I have yet to meet) about why we actually are, in fact, doing just the right amount of arithmetic. What is most discouraging is that Sandra's father wins the arguments.

Clearly, this has been the most frustrating five weeks of my life. I feel as if I've been swimming in molasses. Student teaching was a breeze compared with this!

---

*All cases in this chapter that are not accompanied by specific citations are slightly altered or fictionalized accounts of situations and problems experienced by the authors or by beginning teachers with whom the authors have worked. The names have been changed to save us all from embarrassment.

But many of the surprises of school life are very pleasant ones. There is much love and human warmth in the classroom. Some of the aspects of school life that you may have dreaded never materialize. The content about which you feel uncertain could turn out to be your strength. Also, within the four walls of the classroom, some people find a new self they didn't know existed.

administrators: mixed bag and many hats

As elementary and secondary school students, most of us had pretty simplistic notions of administrators. The superintendent, if we ever saw one at all, was a vague presence we occasionally glimpsed in the hall talking to one of the staff or in front of a microphone on ceremonial occasions. The principal was much more a part of our school lives, existing as someone beloved or feared, and occasionally both. Even though the principal was near at hand, our student's-eye view was rather one-dimensional: the principal represented AUTHORITY. In all but the rarest instances, the principal stood metaphorically directly behind the teacher, supporting the teacher and the system. [Or so we thought!] When, as students, we went to the principal's office, it almost always meant we were in trouble. Now it could mean so many things!

THE MULTIPLE ROLES OF THE PRINCIPAL

New teachers' relationships with their principals are far less one-dimensional. School principals loom quite large in the lives of beginning teachers, and the teacher–principal relationship (as well as relationships with vice principals, department heads, and master teachers) is many-faceted. Most importantly, the principal is now a *colleague,* a fellow educator joined with you in the common task of bringing civilization to the young. You are both professionals. You are both part of a common tradition. You probably share common goals (such as improving the educational opportunities of children) and attitudes (e.g., that people engaged in the important work of educating the young need more support from the public than they receive). But there is more to this relationship.

Principals are the *official leaders* in the school. They make decisions or act as the funnel for the decisions of higher authorities. Decisions made by teachers or students are normally checked with principals. Principals speak for the school community to the superintendent, the press, and the local citizens. Nothing is ever quite "official" unless the principal has been involved.

Principals are *helpers.* They can dispense information and materials, and, as experienced teachers, they are sources of tips, shortcuts, and helpful suggestions. Principals also visit classrooms and hold conferences with teachers, especially new teachers. They stand ready to aid beginning teachers who are encountering difficulties and confusion.

Principals are *policymakers.* A school system is a bureaucracy whose long arm extends from the state commissioner of education to the local district superintendent of schools to the individual school principal. That "long arm" is, in fact, educational policy—the ideas that are supposed to direct what happens in a school and, more specifically, in your classroom. Principals act on behalf of the school district's bureaucracy by introducing teachers to the policies and monitoring the policies' implementation. In addition, they often set their own policies unique to their school

from PRESERVICE to PRACTICE

Bernice Lerner: High School Mathematics

All through elementary and high school, I was bashful. In my high school graduating class, I won the "Most Shy" award. I dreaded being called on, even when I knew I had the right answer! Part of it is that I blush so easily, so my approach was to be like the furniture or the wallpaper and hope that the teacher wouldn't see me. Still, I liked school and always liked my teachers, even the ones that had fun with my blushing. When I decided to become a math teacher, I knew my shyness was going to be a problem, but I figured that I could pass my blushing off as a permanent sunburn.

Something happened, though, when I became a teacher. I began to notice a change when I was student teaching, and once I had my own class, it was quite clear: I'm a different person in my class. I feel very outgoing, almost to the point of being aggressive. Also, I've discovered that I'm a ham actor. And what a stage my classroom is! I love it. My students seem to love it, too. It seems so odd that after all these years of trying to be invisible, now I'm discovering a whole new side of myself.

CASE QUESTIONS

1. Can you think of a time when you discovered a whole new side of your personality?

2. Which personal quality of yours do you feel might be a drawback or a problem as a teacher?

---

building, such as discipline and dress codes, assembly activities, and a character education program.

Principals are *crisis managers*. When something happens that a teacher cannot handle, the principal's office is where he or she naturally turns for help. A principal needs to be fully briefed about crises, real or potential, to deal with them effectively.

Principals are *facilitators*. Schools run on things: pencils, books, paper, heat, hot lunches, sanitary toilets, lights, construction paper, petty cash, computers, and keys. It is the principal's job to keep teachers supplied so that they, in turn, can carry out the aims of the school.

Principals are *reward dispensers*. They assign classes to teachers, deciding which kind of children they will teach and whether those children will be at the level or in the subject for which particular teachers are prepared. Principals also assign teachers to extracurricular duties and activities. In addition, they can give or withhold compliments on teacher performance.

Principals are *judges*. A principal makes the decision about a new teacher's qualifications to teach in the school and later decides whether the teacher's performance merits rehiring him or her. After all, first-year teachers are neither permanent members of the faculty nor permanently licensed members of the teaching profession. Principals can write recommendations for or against teachers, thereby enhancing or destroying individuals' reputations as teachers. This role of judge is one that new teachers often don't appreciate until it is too late.

Principals act as *buffers* between teachers and angry parents (or, occasionally, angry students). Teachers can be quite vulnerable to public attack. Parents hear tales from their children or from other parents and, if they have a question or a complaint to make against a teacher, often go directly to the principal, bypassing the teacher. The principal is the official "complaint department." This delicate position requires the principal to be open and responsive to complaints and, at the same time, to support the position of the teacher involved. Such situations call for the skills of high diplomacy.

Finally, principals are *sacrificial lambs.* If the community, the teachers, or the school board become dissatisfied with what is happening in a particular school, the school's principal is vulnerable. If a school fails to make adequate yearly progress on the No Child Left Behind criteria, for example, the principal may be replaced. No one suggests replacing the students or the parents! Tenured staff cannot be dismissed (except under very special circumstances), so the principal, who may or may not be responsible for the reported problem, is likely to pay the penalty. The ease with which a principal can be dismissed is, incidentally, a characteristic shared with beginning teachers because principals typically don't have tenure as principals.

The need to wear all these hats makes for a complicated existence. Today's school principal has a most difficult job, and doing the job well requires the strengths of a field general, a philosopher, a psychiatrist, and a saint. Given that these strengths are in short supply, it is not surprising that new teachers sometimes find themselves in conflict with their principals. Principals have to make many quick and difficult decisions, often with insufficient information or time, and they are sometimes wrong.

When principals observe in teachers' classrooms, they may appear to be there as *helpers,* but they cannot put aside their role as *judges.* At some point, they must make recommendations about "their" teachers to their superiors, and they obviously are influenced by what they have seen during their "helping" observations. For this reason, confusion and potential conflict between the administrator and the new teacher may be expected. In addition, beginning teachers often do not know how to work in a bureaucracy (i.e., how to make the organization work for their ends), and they sometimes are antibureaucratic, or overly critical and complaining. This behavior can put them into direct conflict with their administrators, whose job it is to train beginners in bureaucratic procedures and whose *primary responsibility*

you know you're in trouble when . . .

- You have threatened that if there is one more sound in the classroom, you will personally call every parent to complain—and you hear a sound.
- The principal asks you what you plan to be doing next year.
- You have your students correct their own tests and the lowest mark in the class is 96 percent. And they are smirking.
- It is 10:15 A.M., and the class has ripped through three-quarters of the work you have prepared for the day.
- You return after being sick for three days, and the students chant, "We want the substitute!"
- It feels like February, and it's only late September.

- The teacher across the hall comes in and offers to show your kids how to behave.
- The parents of eleven of your students ask to see the principal, and you are not invited.
- Unsolicited, your principal offers to write a recommendation for your placement file.
- You are convinced you have finally come up with challenging and interesting work for your class, and when you present it, they chorus, "We did that last year."
- After sitting in your class for five minutes, your supervisor starts to look at the clock.
- You walk into your usually noisy classroom, and immediately all the students get in their seats and smile at you.

from PRESERVICE to PRACTICE

Steve Mellonwood: Junior High Science

During the special orientation meeting for new teachers, the principal told us all that whenever we have a problem we should come and see him. He didn't expect us to be perfect, and he told us that he felt his major job was to help new teachers. Later that week, he stopped me in the hall and warmly repeated his offer of help. I really took him at his word. So in early October, when I started having trouble planning and finding materials, I just went to see the principal. He was very cordial and, although he talked a lot about himself, he did give me some fairly helpful advice. I went to see him for three short visits. Just talking the problems out seemed to help. I started finding good materials, and my classes really improved. I felt I was really doing well, and I couldn't wait to get to school in the morning.

Then, in early December, I started getting treated in an odd way by some of the senior teachers. They were always asking me whether they could help, and could they get me a glass of water (sort of like I had some incurable disease). It was weird. Finally, I asked two of them in the lunchroom, "Why all the concern?" Well, it came out that the principal had told them that I was having "big trouble," and he had told a number of the senior teachers to do what they could for me. He had not been in to observe me once.

Later in the year the principal came in for two brief observations (to conform to minimum standards in our district), and he never had time for a conference. He did, however, write up supervisor conference reports. They were lukewarm and had no specifics. He did mention in both reports that I was improving and overcoming early problems. What improvement? What problems? All he had to go by was what I told him. I got so mad that I wrote him a note to the effect that my self-reported problems had cleared up some time ago and that I felt my teaching was better than his report had indicated. I could see the writing on the wall, though. I started looking for another position and got one without too much trouble. I liked the kids in my first school and many of the teachers. Somehow, though, early on, I had put myself in a box for the principal, and he wasn't going to let me out.

CASE QUESTIONS

1. What mistakes in judgment were made in this case?

2. Asking for help is often a two-edged sword. How would you have handled this situation?

is to ensure that the school, as a totality, runs smoothly and that students learn what is expected of them. Perhaps not surprisingly, given the many roles the administrator plays, slippage and breakdown can occur. The following account on page 446 illustrates such a case.

An error of first impressions can also work the other way: the administrator who seems severe and distant can turn out to be warm and supportive, as described in the case about Catherine Foley. As this indicates, principals (and others who have supervisory responsibility over the beginning teachers, such as lead teachers and department- and grade-level chairpersons) can be a crucial source of professional expertise and moral support. In addition, research shows that supportive administrators actually help teachers to become reflective and solve their own problems.[3] Nevertheless, new teachers need to be proactive and not wait for the help to come to them. Administrators or supervisors may potentially be able to provide the following kinds of assistance:

- They may have valuable advice on dealing with specialized problems, such as an extremely reticent student.

from PRESERVICE to PRACTICE

Catherine Foley: Fourth Grade

Quite honestly, I was afraid of Mrs. Kelly when I first went for interviews. She seemed so businesslike and talked so much about high standards that I was sure that even if I got the job, I'd end up disappointing her. And after a few weeks with my fourth-grade wigglers, I was afraid I'd never get them to settle down and work on tasks. I was wrong on both counts. The kids settled down—some too much—so that now my biggest problem is getting them excited and alive. And, boy, was I really way off on Mrs. Kelly! She is a jewel! She has so many ideas and gives them to me in the nicest way. I never feel I have to use her suggestions, but, in fact, I think I've used every one.

But what has meant the most is that she has treated me like an adult, a professional. Here I am, right out of college, and she is asking my advice about assembly programs and what to do about the cliques in our school. She has also made sure that the other teachers don't leave me out of things. I'm the only new teacher in the building this year, and they sometimes forget me.

Mrs. Kelly has a great way of weaving me into things.

I got very overtired and generally strung out after the Christmas vacation. I was depressed about my teaching and how little time or energy I had for any kind of social life. One day Mrs. Kelly intercepted me on my way to the lunchroom and took me around the corner to a sandwich shop. She knew exactly what was wrong with me and got right to the point, giving me super tips on how to organize my time and plan more efficiently. She even started me on a vitamin program that seems to give me much more energy. She has been terrific to me. She's made the year for me.

CASE QUESTIONS

1. Has your past experiences with administrators left you with particular attitudes or perceptions? What are they?

2. As a new teacher, what do you hope most to receive from an administrator?

- They can put you in contact with specialists in your building or elsewhere in the school district to help you on a range of issues, from curricular matters to dealing with disruptive students.

- They may be able to do demonstration lessons or special presentations in your class.

- They may be able to come to your classroom, observe you in action, and provide focused feedback on your early efforts to carry out a strategy such as cooperative learning.

While we suggest you seek help from administrators and supervisors, we also urge prudence. Consult them honestly, directly, and somewhat sparingly.

peers: a mixed blessing

New teachers are vulnerable to many outside forces as well as to their own insecurities. If a supportive administrator can turn a potentially disastrous year into a year of growth, a beginning teacher's professional peers can be even more influential in the process of learning how to teach and how to survive in the classroom. The following example is a case in point.

from PRESERVICE to PRACTICE

Mary Veronica: Sixth Grade

I had a hard time finding a teaching job. I had hoped to teach in my hometown, but there were just no jobs at the level I wanted to teach. The best job was on the other side of the state, and when it became clear that there were no jobs on the local horizon, I took it. I was very excited about teaching; I really felt that I was starting out on an adventure. I was, however, also moving away from my parents. Being so far away from home meant that there were lots of things that were going to be new to me. I had to get a car, find an apartment, establish a bank account, and take care of lots of other things—all at once. It was literally like a crash course in being an adult. And that's what I felt like right from the beginning: an adult. It was so different from college and even student teaching. At my school, people treated me like an adult, and they expected me to act like one. For the first months I felt as if I was play-acting at being a grown-up. Well, now I guess the role is comfortable, or maybe I just have my act down pat.

Although I made friends with a few people in my apartment building, I was really very lonely at first. I don't think I would have made it without Joan Silver. Joan teaches in the classroom next to mine. She's been, as she says, "in the trenches" for eighteen years, but she's got more ideas and energy and dedication than any of us fresh troops. Joan was a lifesaver for me. She took me under her wing even before school started. She has been a source of ideas, great materials, and inspiration, and she has never made me feel like a taker or a leech. *I* actually taught *her* some things! That's one of the reasons I admired her so much. She really wanted to

know about the new ideas I had learned in my education courses, and she put a lot of them to work in her class.

I guess we talked every day after school. A lot of the time, we just spent the hour after school laughing. A couple of times the janitor came in thinking there was something wrong, but what he found was the two of us broken up with laughter. And about once a month she would drag me home for dinner. Joan always seemed to know when I was a little low, and that's when she'd insist that I come home with her and have dinner with her family.

There's so much to learn in the first year, and not just about subject matter. Some important things—like how to get information from the school secretary and how to stay on the right side of the janitor—you never learn in education courses. Joan was my guide on everything from how to fill out my planbook to which memos from the front office I had to pay attention to and which I could put in what she called the "circular file."

It seems funny to say this, given the fact that Joan is twenty years older than I am, but I really think she's my best friend. She certainly has made this year a terrific one for me. I hope that during my career, I can mentor other new teachers in the same way.

CASE QUESTIONS

1. Do you anticipate that you will search actively for a mentor-teacher? Why or why not?

2. How might your new teaching peers be "mixed blessings"?

Although there is increasing cooperation among teachers and greater access to specialists, mentors, and aides, for the most part teachers work independently in their own classrooms and with their own students. When they are engaged in their professional work, they typically are isolated from one another. Although administrators are the official source of support and help for beginners, fellow teachers serve as a much more accessible and less threatening source of assistance. As the preceding case illustrates, a teacher's colleagues can be a powerful influence, especially in the beginning. They can be an ever-ready source of ideas and teaching tips and can initiate the newcomer into the customs of the school and lead to their desire to stay in teaching.[4] Like Joan Silver, a peer can be an inspiration and show by example what the phrase "teacher as professional" means.

Sometimes, however, teachers can have a negative influence, undermining a beginning teacher's idealism, lowering his or her standards, and offering no help at all. The teachers' lounge may be the venue for serious disillusionment. Many teachers use the lounge to "unwind" by delivering harsh criticism of students, mocking administrators, and offering negative pronouncements about the teaching profession. Although not especially different from similar "off-camera" remarks in hospitals and businesses, such comments in the teachers' lounge can blunt the new teacher's idealism and enthusiasm. The lounge is a source of much learning for beginners, but in some cases the private side of colleagues can be a rude awakening for them.

Although we strongly believe that the teaching profession has a larger percentage of dedicated, selfless people than any other profession (except, perhaps, the ministry), it also has its share of rogues and fools. Beginners should pick their way carefully among this field of new colleagues.

instruction: so much to learn

Ultimately, a teacher's only real problem is his or her students' failure to learn and to develop. All other conflicts, triumphs, and defeats pale in significance if the children are learning and developing their human potential. The degree of the children's success as learners is the best measure of a teacher's success or failure. Many pay-for-performance plans give bonuses to teachers whose students exceed expectations on the state-mandated examinations. Although the link between a teacher's instruction and a student's learning is often overstated, this relationship is crucial. Teacher effectiveness is an area in which there are few naturals, and first-year teachers generally have much to learn in this area of instruction.

> *But how do I feel at the end of each day? I feel proud of my students. I feel more knowledgeable about living, teaching, and learning. I feel lucky to be a teacher. I feel . . . full of sparks.*
>
> —IRASEMA ORTEGA-CRAWFORD,
> Biology Teacher

One major difficulty is the sheer newness of the role of teacher. After a little student teaching, you suddenly find yourself totally immersed in all the responsibilities that go with managing a classroom. You are in charge of your own class and responsible for taking it from the first day of school to the last. One particularly vexing problem for the beginning teacher is the search for effective curricular materials, as the following example illustrates.

from PRESERVICE to PRACTICE

Grace Joyce: Third Grade

The overriding question of this year has been "What works?" I'm in a constant search for materials. It is never-ending. My kids aren't especially brilliant, but they devour material and look at me as if to say, "Well, what's next?" Our school's curriculum guide is only five years old, but it is terribly dated. The students know a lot of the stuff already. They learned it in lower grades or just picked it up. They are bored by a good bit of the rest, too. I'm constantly squeezing ideas and tips from the other third-grade teachers. They are helpful, but they are in the same boat I am. Sometimes I get a big build-up on a particular workbook or special unit by a teacher who had fabulous success with it. I try it, and I fall on my face with it.

(continued)

Then there are the kids. They are so fickle! A couple of times, I took their suggestions on things they wanted to study and work on. After much work and many late hours, I'd get these classes prepared and the very same kids who were so anxious to make the suggestions couldn't have cared less.

My school district has curriculum specialists. Some of them are very good, too—particularly the math specialist. He would give me *too* much material. I'd spend hours deciding which approach to use to teach 10 minutes' worth of material. The language arts specialist was a sweet lady but very rarely available, and most of her ideas were really

out to lunch; I was on my own there. When you get right down to it, you have to make the curriculum and the materials *yours* before they are any good to you. Someone else's great materials are nothing until you have made them your own. This is hard to do the first year.

CASE QUESTIONS

1. What are the major insights about teaching that Grace recounts here?

2. How comfortable are you asking for help and advice? What are the "upsides and downsides?"

Although the curricular and instructional aspect of teaching can be a thicket of difficulty for many beginners, for others it is very exciting and inspiring.

from PRESERVICE to PRACTICE

Nicholas Briggs: Middle School Social Studies

School has always been hard for me. But then again, if the truth be known, I've always worked hard. In high school, I really got turned on to history, and I think it was then that I decided to become a teacher. In college, I took every history course I could. I was way over the required number of history courses for certification. And I was lucky to teach at a very academic high school as a student teacher. I think I did well, too. At least that's what everyone said.

I was really disappointed when I couldn't find any openings as a history teacher. I was getting very discouraged until I was finally offered a middle school job in the same school district where I had done my student teaching. My first thought was to let it go and wait for a "real" history job. What they wanted me to teach was social studies. There was some history involved, but there was also a lot of other social science material to teach. What I really wanted to teach were modern European history and the rise and fall of totalitarianism, and what they wanted was what seemed to me pretty low-level stuff. I was ready to hang it up. I could possibly work for the company my dad works for, or I could go back to school. Well, anyway, I decided I'd give middle school teaching a chance.

The great surprise of teaching for me was not the kids or anything like that. It was, on the one hand, how little I knew about my strength—history—and, on the other hand, how intellectually exciting teaching in general can be. I had taken tons of history courses and considered myself a super buff, but I had missed the essential meaning of history. That's what I have been learning these first two years, and it has been as stimulating as anything in my life. Now I feel I'm just beginning to understand the purpose of history and what should be taught. I came to teach and probably ended up learning more than my students.

Incidentally, I was offered the position I thought I really wanted, a position on the high school history faculty. I turned it down. I couldn't be happier than I am here.

CASE QUESTIONS

1. Which aspect of teaching or the instruction process do you believe will be most challenging? How sure are you?

2. Which part of teaching are you most confident about?

kevin and jim's seven additional rules for surviving the first year of teaching (or seven compelling reasons why future teachers should not try to resell this book)*

1. *When in doubt, think.* Instead of simply fretting about problems or panicking, use your best tool—your mind. Reflect. Problem solve. Try to identify the problem and possible solutions; think about the resources that are available to you; and then act and judge whether that option helped the situation.

2. *Don't look for love in the classroom.* You should definitely demand respect, but not necessarily love. Even expecting appreciation may lead to disappointment. Among many members of the "Entitled Generation," appreciation is an elusive trait. If you need love, buy a puppy.

3. *Deal with your authority problems before you enter the classroom.* Come to terms with the fact that you will be responsible for maintaining an orderly, civil, and safe environment, and think hard about how you will accomplish this feat.

4. *If you are not organized, get organized.* Coping with the planbooks, student papers, office memos, attendance records, grades, report cards, and so on requires much more organization than many beginning teachers have practiced to this point. You *must stay on top of the paperwork!*

5. *Love thy school secretaries and custodians.* Many beginners fail to realize how important the school secretaries and custodians are in enabling teachers to do an effective job and in the school's "informal communication network."

6. *Focus on learning.* Many beginners fail to concentrate on making sure their students really learn something and therefore have feelings of accomplishment. Students will put up with a great deal of "beginning teacheritis" if they sense they are learning. Remember too that they usually need to be reminded that they have learned something!

7. *Don't—we repeat, don't—get married two weeks before the start of your first teaching job.* For reasons unknown to the authors, each year thousands of new college graduates decide to simultaneously jump into two of life's most difficult undertakings: beginning a career and starting what they hope will be a lifelong relationship.

*The authors promise that if you follow these seven rules faithfully, you will survive the first year of teaching. You may even like it! If you do not survive the year, return the unused portion of this book to your instructor for a refund.

students: friends or fiends?

And now we come to the main event: students. Becoming comfortable and sensing that he or she is effective with children is a major concern for a new teacher, as it well should be—students are the main event! They make the good days good and the bad days bad. The relationship between teacher and students is multifaceted. An important aspect of the relationship is based on how well the students are achieving the goal of learning.

Although students are the primary source of a teacher's success, they can also be a source of failure. Three areas in particular cause problems: discipline, social distance, and sex. Behind each of these areas of difficulty is an inaccurate set of expectations the teacher holds about students.

In this class, a new teacher's creative lesson on DNA is paying off in student interest.

(© Bob Daemmrich)

One indication of these out-of-line expectations is the sharp change in attitudes people experience as they go through teacher education and then begin their first years of classroom teaching. Studies have shown that the longer college students stay in teacher education programs, the more positive and warm their attitudes toward students become.[5] Conversely, among beginning teachers, positive attitudes

from PRESERVICE to PRACTICE

Eileen Black: Fifth Grade

I have enjoyed my students this year, probably more than I should have. The only real down moment I had came right toward the end of the year, when something one of the sixth-grade teachers said really shook my confidence. She made some comment at lunch about how much fun-and-games was going on in my class. All of a sudden I began thinking that although I was having a great time, maybe the kids were having a great time and not really learning anything. I tried to think of what I had taught them that was really important, and my mind was blank. I tried to think of particular students who I thought had really shown a lot of progress, and I couldn't think of anyone specific. I went around that way for a couple of days, and I got sort of panicky.

Finally, almost by accident, I came across one of the student's notebooks, which had all of his work from September, even his diagnostic tests. It was really enlightening. I could almost see the change from week to week in what he knew. The problems became more difficult, but he could master them. His compositions became more interesting, and the mechanics became sounder. His handwriting looked so much more mature. I figured, though, that maybe that was just one student. I asked to look at a few other students' notebooks, and there it was. They had changed. They were different. Not just different but *better*. And I was an important part of that change.

CASE QUESTIONS

1. What are some of your hypotheses about why beginning teachers' attitudes change in this way?

2. Can you recall experiencing a new teacher's swing in attitude toward your class? What accounted for it?

toward students drop sharply. In fact, beginning teachers score significantly lower on attitude inventories than students just entering teacher education. Before going on, take a moment to consider these results.

SOURCES OF A DISTORTED VIEW

> *It's not what the teacher does that's important. It's what the teacher gets the children to do.*
>
> —PHIL SCHECHTY,
> Educational Reformer

Our experience in working with college students (for more years than we care to report) has convinced us that most students who are preparing to become teachers have high ideals in general and become particularly idealistic about children and education during their preparation. They believe that as teachers they should have warm relations with students, and they want to make the classroom more relaxed and more responsive to the needs of students than the traditional classroom in which they were educated. As college students take more education courses and observe in classrooms, their views of children become even more idealistic and, as a result, more positive. By graduation, the rose-colored glasses are firmly affixed.

Also, college students have managed to shut out many less positive memories of their own childhood and adolescence. They forget things like the time they joined with the other seventh-graders to put four tacks on Miss Derriere's chair. They blot out all the juicy stories other students have told about the young physical education teacher, even though they knew most were untrue. They forget about how they enjoyed reading (or writing) obscenities about their math teacher on the lavatory wall. They forget how cruel kids can be to kids. Somehow the dark side of human nature recedes from view during teacher education. But fear not—it reappears in the beginning teacher's classroom. New teachers rediscover human fallibility, in their students and in themselves, and all too often the sad result is that their positive attitudes toward children plummet. (The Video Case *Elementary Classroom Management: Basic Strategies* shows how two teachers at different levels keep things flowing smoothly in their classes.)

Normally, teachers' positive attitudes make a comeback, although they rarely regain the heights they reached during the latter stages of teacher preparation.

The class clowns who were so amusing to you in high school are often a very different story when they reappear in your classroom.

(Brad Wilson/Getty Images)

Nevertheless, the beginner's unrealistic expectations are a great source of his or her problems in the classroom. Although problems of this kind abound, here we look at just the three areas mentioned earlier: discipline, social distance, and sex.

" Teaching is leaving a vestige of yourself in the development of another. And surely the student is a bank where you can deposit your most precious treasures.

—EUGENE P. BERTIN (1922–2008),
Humanitarian

CLASSROOM MANAGEMENT

Classroom management, classroom control, or discipline (pick your euphemism) is one of those problems that shouldn't exist. After all, school is an opportunity for children. The teacher works hard to help them. It's simple: the teacher is there to teach, and the students are there to learn. Unfortunately, things do not always work out that way.

The great majority of schools, whether kindergartens or high schools, are organized with the expectation that the teacher will be "in charge" of the class. You may not like this structure, but there are things you can do about it. (For example, zero-tolerance policies in many schools regarding weapons or illegal substances take some of the burden of enforcement off teachers.) But being in charge is still what is generally expected of a teacher by the children, your teacher-peers, and the administration. (We return to this matter of expectations in the section on social distance later in this chapter.) Few (and lucky) are the teachers who do not have to come to grips with their role as disciplinarian.

Unaccustomed to Being in Charge

A discipline problem occurs when someone violates the expected orderly pattern of classroom behavior. In most cases, the breach of discipline is an overt act by one or more students that distracts attention from or interrupts the performance of the task at hand. Few teacher education students of traditional college age have had much opportunity to be "in charge," give orders, coordinate the activities of a group of people, or say such things as "Quiet down!" or "Stay in your seat!" Students, by contrast, are accustomed to being taught by experienced teachers who know how to manage and control them, usually rather effortlessly.

Students can sense uncertainty and hesitancy in a new teacher. Moreover, school is not fun-and-games for children, who can get restless and bored in the classroom. (Remember how long the school day was when you were in elementary and secondary school, how long you had to sit still at a stretch, and how much you had to do that didn't interest you?) These conditions, plus the potential for friction that always exists in any group containing so many people, make it almost inevitable that first-year teachers will have some trouble establishing the kind of productive relationship with students that they seek. (In the Video Case *Secondary Classroom Management: Basic Strategies*, a teacher discusses maintaining a consistent social distance, as well as other aspects of classroom management.)

As we have implied, many new teachers start out with a rather idealized picture of children as victims. They assume that misbehavior is a result of some condition external to the child, such as a disruptive home life or poverty. Often the suggestion is made that something in the teacher's class provokes or brings forth the problem.

▶❚❚ TeachSource VIDEO CASE

Secondary Classroom Management: Basic Strategies

Go to the Education CourseMate website to watch the video clips, study the artifacts in the case, and reflect on the following questions:

1. This teacher echoes the point made in this chapter that teachers should maintain a consistent social distance, either relaxed or strict. How does his teaching demonstrate this point?

2. How does this teacher demonstrate that he is "in charge," as described in this chapter?

3. What is the most important piece of advice this case offered for you, as a preservice teacher?

If only the teacher would "establish the right environment" or "reach out to the child in just the right way," the problem would be solved. This idea is a subset of the larger view that people are not capable of evil, only social arrangements are capable of evil—an idea that had many adherents in education at one time and still has some advocates today. This idea that all children are innately good, combined with the first-year teacher's insecurities and search for approval, makes it difficult for many new teachers to deal confidently with their role as disciplinarian. (See Kevin and Jim's Suggestions for Classroom Management Problems and Table 6.1, Different Approaches to Classroom Management, both in Chapter 6, "What Makes a Teacher Effective?")

SOCIAL DISTANCE

Establishing an appropriate **social distance** from students occupies a good deal of a beginning teacher's attention and energy. Like disciplinary techniques, the ability to establish the correct social distance does not come with a teaching license or one's first job. The accompanying feature provides some advice on how beginning teachers can begin developing the appropriate distance on the very first day of school.

from PRESERVICE to PRACTICE

Carole Foster: Fourth Grade

I was convinced that a good class was a happy class and that I wasn't going to be like those grouchy teachers I remember from my own elementary school. So in the first part of the year, I let a lot of small infractions go unnoticed: talking during silent reading period, lateness on assignments, yelling out the window to students on the playground, and the like. It was a little hard on my nerves, but I thought I was establishing an open and creative environment. It soon became clear that it was open, but not particularly creative. In fact, I first discovered reality when a friendly parent suggested that the room was too noisy and disorderly for the children to get their work done. I tried to "tighten up," but the students were already used to my "open and creative" environment. I just couldn't get them to settle down.

Finally, the straw that broke the camel's back—and almost broke mine—was when the principal came in to observe. The kids behaved horribly. I

felt as if they were trying to make me look bad. Whatever their intentions, the situation was not lost on the principal. During the follow-up conference, he was very frank with me, telling me that if I couldn't maintain better discipline, he might have to "relieve" me. One thing I particularly remember him saying was, "Carole, if you can't *keep* school, you can't *teach* school." Then he gave me some specific suggestions. Even with those good suggestions, I had a very difficult time working my way back in charge and establishing a more civil and orderly classroom. Next year things will be different!

CASE QUESTIONS

1. Do you remember having an inexperienced teacher like Carole who was always "running hot and cold"?

2. What problems, if any, do you anticipate with relating to students?

"HECKUVA DAY, WASN'T IT, MS. CARPENTER? NO HARD FEELIN'S?"

(© James Estes)

Beginning teachers often take refuge in one of the two extremes of behavior. Many hide their insecurities by acting harshly and maintaining a strict and extremely businesslike manner, sometimes bordering on hostility. Others attempt to be completely "natural," rejecting the stiff "teacher" image and seeking to break down all barriers between themselves and their students. The first extreme, the overly strict teacher, can give rise to long-term difficulties, whereas the "natural" teacher usually has short-term but rather severe problems.

Kevin and Jim's guide to the first day of school

In many areas of life, from job interviews to dating, first impressions are powerful. The same is true at the beginning of the school year—students' first impressions set the tone for how the rest of the school year will proceed. With that in mind, we offer a few tips we have picked up along the way.

1. *Teach your very best lesson.* Often teachers use the first day for filling out forms, assigning lockers, and handling essential but boring "administrivia." Such a day can set a tone for students that this year will be just like all the other years, like all the other classes. Students, by contrast, will be fresh from the summer at this point, carrying renewed expectations that this year may be different. Capitalizing on this attitude with a really interesting lesson will create important momentum for your class. You can catch up on the forms and other items later in the week.

2. *Establish class rules and procedures.* Although a good lesson is most important on the first day, setting the stage for good classroom management cannot be stressed too much. Let your students know you plan to maintain an orderly classroom with rules that foster respect and a healthy work environment. You need not take a "lay-down-the-law" stance,

but you should let your students know that your classroom will have clear rules to enhance the chances of everyone succeeding.

3. *Start learning and using students' names.* As soon as you receive your class lists or rosters, start familiarizing yourself with the students' names. Once you meet your students, start matching names with faces and, whenever possible, use their names. Nothing signals your interest in them and your capacity for being on top of the situation like using their names on Day One.

4. *Be friendly but businesslike.* Often the insecurities of new teachers get the best of them. They vacillate between being Mr. or Ms. Nice Guy and Attila the Disciplinarian. The beginning teacher's early commitment to a friendly but task-oriented atmosphere is the key to its realization.

5. *Share with students your vision for the year ahead.* Students want to succeed. Even the ones with a history of difficulty with other teachers want the new school year to be better. Don't tell students how hard they are going to work; tell them how much they are going to know at the end of the year and what they can do with this new knowledge.

6. *Establish procedures for communicating with parents.* You need parental support, and students want to know whether you'll contact parents about both good and bad events. Let them know that you plan to establish communication with their parents and that you see parents as your partners, as your co-teachers.

from PRESERVICE to PRACTICE

Jane Candis: Middle School Math

Most of my year was spent alternating between being Wanda the Witch and sweet little Miss Muffet. I started out determined to be different from all those cold teachers I had growing up. I was going to be everyone's sweet Big Sister. I really was surprised when this plan didn't work. The children didn't respond; if anything, they seemed to be confused. Some of them actually started treating me like their big sister, and I found myself getting annoyed. They became very familiar and started asking me both in and out of class all sorts of embarrassing questions such as "Are you going on a date this weekend?" or "Did you ever do drugs in college?" The final straw came when one of my boys—one of my favorites too—came up to me in the hall while I was talking to a senior teacher. Smiling, he patted me on the back and said, "How's it going, Miss Candis?" I was mortified.

After that little incident, I became tough. I was all business. If anyone got close to being familiar, I cut him or her off at the knees. I really said some nasty things. I was just so uptight that I overreacted. I guess I was hurt that my Big Sister routine didn't work. Later, I realized that one reason behind my wanting to be Big Sister was simply that I wanted to be liked, at any cost. I guess my insecurities led me to seek approval from my students. Anyway, I spent most of the year going back and forth on this issue—one week being Wanda and the next being Miss Muffet. It was really a strain for both the kids and me. Finally, toward the end of the year, I got my sea legs and I stopped playing a role. The class settled into a serious work routine. It was much more fun that way. I think everyone was relieved.

CASE QUESTIONS

1. Have you considered the issue of social distance between teacher and students? How much social distance do you believe is appropriate for you?

2. What are your ideas about how to establish effective discipline in a classroom?

3. Do you anticipate that classroom control will be a strength or weakness for you?

T (F)

It is important for new teachers to work to eliminate the traditional social distance between themselves and students. Students expect the teacher to interact with them in certain recognizable ways; that is, they expect a certain degree of social distance. They are confused or put off when the teacher acts like "one of the gang."

The problem with playing the role of the overly strict, aloof teacher is that it may become a permanent habit. Acting like a Prussian officer may appeal to a hidden need to make others submissive. Also, one may begin to believe that "a quiet class is a good class."

The problem confronting overly "natural" teachers is that their view of natural behavior often clashes with students' expectations. Students expect the teacher to interact with them in certain recognizable ways; that is, they expect a certain degree of social distance. They are confused or put off when the teacher acts like "one of the gang." The crux of the problem, then, is that the beginning teacher often wants to be a friend or a pal, whereas students expect and want the teacher to be an adult. Because they are uncertain and striving to be adults themselves, students seek strength and maturity in their teachers. Often they interpret the beginning teacher's efforts at naturalness and informality as weakness.

SEX

Sexual attraction and romance between students, and even between teachers, is alive and well in the American school—and most people recognize this fact. Nevertheless, the idea of sexual attraction or romance between students and teachers generally remains a taboo subject (except, of course, on TV and in the movies!). In fact, there is no surer way to end your career quickly and unhappily than to become, or even appear to become, romantically involved with a student.

Beginning teachers are more likely than experienced ones to confront this problem. For one thing, many of them are nearer in age to their students than they are to the majority of teachers in their building. For another, they are often single, new to the community, and lonely. The strain of the new job may increase their need for affection, and this need may find expression in their relationships with students.

from PRESERVICE to PRACTICE

Gary Cornog: High School English

In one class, there dwelt a fair young creature who found me to be an easily flustered appreciator of her many charms. She was a coquette and, to my way of thinking, a dangerous one. She had me at a great disadvantage. Although she could liltingly ask special favors of me (such as my continued toleration of her misbehavior in class), I could not cope with her in anything like a spontaneous way. Unless I was in a phenomenally commanding mood, I could expect to hear such daily entreaties as "Oh, Mr. Cornog! Mr. Cornog! Could you come here and help me?" or "Mr. Cornog, I just don't understand!" (All this spoken in a voice of tender urgency.) She would have her left arm raised, her right arm aiding

it, and would be leaning forward and upward from her desk so that (I thought) I would not fail to notice her finer endowments (I didn't).

"What is it, Julie?" I would reply, hoping the fear in my heart would not be evident in my voice. It nearly always was.

"Mr. Cornog, there's something here I don't understand. Could you come here and look at it?"

"*Don't,*" I tell myself. "*Don't.*"

"Read it to me and I'll explain it." (*From here,* I almost added, but that would be too obvious.) No. She's getting up.

"I'll bring it up there."

(continued)

She approaches. She arrives at my left side. I note a scent of lemony perfume, an attempt at makeup about the eyes. She leans over to place the book in front of me, and some of her long dark hair grazes my shoulder. By this time, I feel thoroughly unwilling to answer any question regarding syntax. *What about private tutoring?* I hear my lecherous innards suggesting. Heaven forbid! My frustration causes me to blurt a response to her query, hoping that she'll return to her seat. The class, by this time, has observed me melting into a limpid pool behind the desk. She must be smiling triumphantly above me, her glory reflected in my devastation.

If only she had been as innocent of malice in her manipulations as I had been tender in my innocence, then all would have been well. Alas, she was not. She thought it great sport to exercise her arts for the benefit of her friends, and I could think of no way to break the spell. I could not ignore her, because then the class would notice my attempt and think that she had really gotten to me. I could not allow her to continue to dominate me, for then the respect I sought would never appear. Who could respect a hen-pecked English teacher? The befuddled teacher doing battle with the temptress every day—what a tableau! What a cliché. It pained me to see myself in such a humiliating posture. It was so absurd.[6]

CASE QUESTIONS

1. What are your thoughts about keeping proper social distance between yourself and students?
2. How should Gary have handled this situation?

protecting against accusations of sexual misconduct

In recent years, heightened sensitivity toward sexual behavior in our schools has emerged. Because of their age, new teachers are particularly vulnerable to accusations of sexual misconduct. Being new to a particular school environment and lacking a reputation, a first-year teacher can be a victim of damaging rumors or even false charges. Here are five practical steps you can take to limit false accusations of sexual misconduct:

1. Avoid being in a private space alone with a student. If a student wants to have a private conversation with you, take him or her to a public space, such as a hallway, and speak in a low voice.

2. Do not give students your home phone number. If you have to call a student at home, be sure that a parent is on the phone during the conversation.

3. Avoid being in a car alone with a student. If it is necessary to transport a student, have another adult in the car. Also, notify your administrator and the student's parents before doing so.

4. If anything of a sexual nature occurs in your classroom (such as suggestive remarks, leering, sexual drawings or notes), take careful notes or keep a computer log of the event. If the number of such events increases, share the issue with your administrator. Don't try to resolve the situation on your own.

5. Be exceedingly careful about speaking about sexual topics or using language that might have sexual connotations in front of students. If this happens inadvertently and an "innocent" comment is left open to misinterpretation, document the situation.

Even though these rules may appear excessively fussy, we urge you to follow them. A little caution may save you a messy "he said/she said" confrontation—or worse.

Source: Adapted from "Protect Yourself," written by LaRae G. Munk, director of legal services for the Association of American Educators. Reprinted by permission of the Association of American Educators and the author.

In much the same way, students often become attracted to their teachers. They sometimes get what is best described as a "crush" on their teachers, becoming emotionally attached to them, greeting them eagerly in the morning, sending them personal e-mails, and walking them to their cars after school. This can be a very awkward situation in that the student wants to be treated as special and to feel that the affection is reciprocated. If the teacher rejects or embarrasses the student, the student can be hurt deeply.

Besides the platonic attachments teachers can form to young children, a 22-year-old teacher quite conceivably can find a 16-year-old student sexually attractive. Thus, as the following account indicates, high school teachers are particularly vulnerable to sexual attraction or manipulation. Our only advice in this area is an emphatic *don't*.

A final comment on your relations with students: some first-year teachers become terribly discouraged by their relationships with students. Most of us teach because we like young people and want to work with them. When we are rejected or fail in some aspect of teaching, it is painful. Developing satisfying relationships with students usually involves some initial uncertainty. Most problems with students are a result of inexperience, and the majority of second-year teachers find that most of their first-year problems disappear and they feel very much at ease with their students. Experience with young people before beginning teaching—as a parent, camp counselor, or tutor—can also help you learn about how you relate best to them and ease the transition.

parents: natural allies with different agendas

The parent and the teacher are natural partners. Both are working to help the child become a more fully developed person, and both want the child to be happy, sensitive, intelligent, and well balanced. Therefore, it is crucial for teachers to establish and maintain effective channels of communication with parents. Sometimes, though, the relationship between teacher and parent runs amok and the natural allies become antagonists. Instead of devoting their energies toward understanding and aiding the child, they waste them on conflict with each other.

The great majority of parent–teacher conferences are cordial, constructive, and characterized by mutual respect. Although problems of perception or communication may arise initially, the parents' and teacher's shared interest in the child is typically enough to overcome these minor blocks. At other times, more persistent problems develop—and they are not always the fault of the parents.

The sources of teacher–parent problems are the same as those involved in any human relationship, but these encounters are more highly charged than in most relationships. This intensity is natural, because a child and his or her future are at issue. The account on pages 460–461 of Brenda's mother and a new teacher, Ruth Billsbury, illustrates some of the dynamics that are usually hidden from view.

(T) F

In general, it is good advice to establish good communication with your students' parents.

Therefore, it is crucial for teachers to establish and maintain effective channels of communication with parents.

"As teachers we should be able to identify strengths in every child. It might not be an academic strength. It could be your kid gets along well with others.

—LAURIE CURTIS,
Assistant Professor, Kansas State University

from PRESERVICE to PRACTICE

Walter Connor: High School History

In the late winter, we had our annual parents' night. All the teachers were to work with students on displays and projects. And, of course, we had to get lots of students' work up on the board. The drab old school building looked like the Rose Bowl Parade by the big night.

We met the parents in our rooms and gave them an overview of what we were doing for the year. I thought I would be nervous, but somehow I wasn't. I was so distracted and fascinated by their faces. I never suspected that they would look so much like their kids! Or rather, vice versa.

When I finished my talk, I handed out folders of the children's work and told the parents I would be happy to talk with them individually. Most of my students had been doing fairly well, so most of the evening went well. The parents of my two prize ding-a-lings didn't show, an event I greeted with mixed emotions.

One set of parents hung back. I hadn't met them yet, but I knew immediately who they were. They were Bill Russell's parents. Bill is a great big happy kid. He is not bright, and he struck me as being quite lazy. All he likes to do is play his guitar, which he is pretty good with. The only time I have gotten any work from him was during a unit on the Civil War. I persuaded him to look up the folk songs and marching chants of the Civil War. He gave a "singing and strumming" report to the class. But after that—nothing! (Bill was carrying something between a D and an F at that time.) Well, the Russells asked a lot of questions, and I stayed with the straight-facts-no-sugar-coating approach, which I was convinced was

the right approach. Then Mr. Russell glanced anxiously at his wife, looked over his shoulder to see that none of the other parents was within earshot, and said, "Tell me, Mr. Connor. We're both college men. My son, Bill . . . is he, you know, college material?"

I didn't know what to say, so I said, "What do you mean?"

"We just want to know if we should be saving to send him to college. Is he, you know, college material?"

All I thought of was that here was a guy who really wanted a straight answer, so I said, "Well, no. I don't think so." Then I looked at Mrs. Russell. I should have looked at her before answering because I saw tears beginning to run down her cheeks. But after the tears came the hostility. "How dare you prejudge my boy! Bill was right! Admit it, you don't like Bill. You are trying to ruin his chances. We work hard to raise our only son, and then some young know-it-all teacher ruins everything!"

Underneath the hysteria, which subsided in about five long minutes, she was right. I was way off base. I had no right to make that judgment. I had known their son for a half year in one course that clearly didn't interest him much. I didn't have enough data. Well, I made another appointment with them. During that meeting, I saw the frightening intensity of their desire to get my class's number-one guitar player into college. Some good things came out of this conference. Bill's work picked up. He actually ended the year with a C. I was the one who learned a good lesson, though. Wanting to be honest doesn't mean arrogantly abandoning good judgment.

from PRESERVICE to PRACTICE

Ruth Billsbury: Sixth Grade

It happened in late March. Ten days earlier, Brenda Carson's mother had called me. She said she wanted to talk to me and asked whether there was any day that I stayed late at school. She didn't get off work until 4:30 P.M. and couldn't make it to school until

5:15. I often worked late at school, so I made an appointment for two days later.

I was curious about why she wanted to see me, and I began to worry. Brenda had something of a reputation in the school. In September, during the

(continued)

teachers' workshop before the opening day, two teachers "sympathized" with me when they heard I had Brenda as one of my students. They didn't go into great detail why, and I didn't want to ask. I was watching Brenda out of the corner of my eye during those first months, and I guess I paid particular attention to her. In recent months, there had been no problems, and I hadn't thought much about her—that is, until her mother called.

Brenda's mother showed up right on time, and after a few pleasantries she said, "Well, I know you're busy, so I'll come right to the point. Three weeks after Brenda started kindergarten, Brenda's father and I separated. After a terrible on-again, off-again year, we decided to get a divorce. It was hard on both of us, but it was crushing for Brenda. She's an only child. Maybe she blamed herself for the breakup. I don't know. In any event, she went into a kind of tailspin. She was trouble at home, and she's been in trouble in school almost from the moment of the breakup. She's no genius, but she's bright enough to do better than she's done. She just dug in her little heels and wouldn't try. She wouldn't bring books home. She wouldn't do assignments. Every time I asked her about school, her standard answer was, 'I hate school.'

"Once I got working and my life started to settle down, we were able to make a life together. But the school situation was still rotten. None of the other girls played with Brenda. She was never invited to any parties. I even suggested that she invite one of her classmates to stay overnight one Friday night, and the kid refused. We were both heartbroken.

"Then you came along. I don't know what you did to her, but you certainly have turned her around.

I sensed it the first day of school. She came home with a funny look in her eye and said, 'This year is going to be different. I can just tell.' She wouldn't say why, but after a few days I guessed. She was continually talking about you—from what you said to her to what kind of car you drive. Honestly, one weekend when we were out grocery shopping, she made me drive by your apartment, she was so curious to find out what it looked like.

"And I guess you know how she's doing in school. I don't think she's missed her homework once. I'm sure she's not your best student, but I know she's doing pretty well, particularly considering the hole she was digging for herself.

"You look surprised at all this. I figured you might be. Brenda can really keep her feelings to herself when she wants to. But honestly, you have touched that girl in a special place. The difference in her is like night and day. You can't imagine what all this has meant to me. Her pain was my pain, and now it's gone away. Brenda even has friends now.

"Anyway, I just wanted you to know. I just wanted to see you and to thank you personally."

Brenda's mother was out the door before I could respond. It was so unexpected; I don't know what I could have said anyway. That one event has given me a great, great deal to think about.

CASE QUESTIONS

1. What sorts of complexities do you see in teacher–parent relationships?

2. What direct steps can teachers take to establish good relationships with parents?

REASONS FOR PARENT–TEACHER PROBLEMS

The two case studies you have just read illustrate a number of reasons that parents and teachers may have a difficult relationship with each other or even fall into direct conflict.

1. *Varied perceptions.* Teachers and parents are quite likely to perceive the same phenomenon in very different ways. The hassled teacher may perceive a particular child as a wild, undisciplined, troublemaker, whereas the parents may see their child as energetic, spontaneous, and sociable. An apparently quiet, shy child may turn out to be a chatterbox in the security of home.

2. *Judgments on students.* Evaluation is another area of difficulty. It is part of the teacher's job to make judgments about a child's performance, a process that can touch on some deep insecurities. It can dash the parents' hopes and put

brakes on their aspirations, particularly in this age of anxiety when parents see education as their children's royal road to success. In our competitive society, being average is taken by some as failure. For these reasons, the teacher needs to be especially sensitive when dealing with issues of evaluation and would do well to stay away from judgments such as students being "above average" or "below average" or comparing certain children with other students. (Remember what happened to Walter Connor.)

3. *Differences of social class and experiences.* Issues of social distance have been at the hub of much parent–teacher antagonism in recent years. Because most teachers are middle class or aspiring to the middle class, they normally have relatively few problems communicating with middle-class people. By contrast, when they deal with parents from a lower or higher socioeconomic class or a different ethnic group, or both, the potential for communication difficulties heightens. Upper-class parents may look down on public schools and treat teachers condescendingly. Poor parents may have had unfortunate and unpleasant experiences with schools and, as a result, regard them with fear or suspicion. Often, these parents speak a different language or dialect than the teacher. What the teacher sees as a humble classroom is to some parents a strange, uncomfortable part of a huge, impersonal bureaucracy. In many urban areas, this impression of the school as a cold, unfriendly, and impersonal institution is supported by the evidence: the school doors are locked, and parents have to pass by police officers and assorted hall guards before receiving a pass to see the head secretary and obtain permission to see the teacher. The fact that many lower-class parents, as children, encountered prejudice in schools and found going to school more discouraging than helpful makes communication even more difficult.

4. *Overburdened parents.* Another factor, as noted in Chapter 4, "What Social Problems Affect Today's Students?" is the changes that are occurring in the American family. Increasingly, mothers—who, in an earlier era, stayed home, kept house, and guided their children through school—have full-time jobs. Usually, it is very difficult for working parents to leave work so as to meet with their children's teachers or attend parent–teacher organization (PTO) meetings and after-school functions that would put them in closer contact with teachers. Often these events are unwelcome chores in an already stressful life.

5. *The pain of change.* Going to school changes children. School, in fact, exists to help children change in specified ways: to read, to solve problems, to speak a foreign language, and to discover new worlds. And students do change. They master things. They acquire confidence—or they lose confidence. They become increasingly independent of their parents. Some parents rejoice at their child's growing freedom from them. For others, the process in which their child's independence grows is painful. Hearing her little girl talk about how much she loves her teacher may arouse jealousy in a mother and cause her to act in a hostile manner when the mother meets the teacher. When a high school student comes home from school with political, social, or religious views that conflict with those of his parents, resentment, and confusion can result. When faced with these sometimes unsettling changes, parents often approach a conference with the teacher with a sincere mixture of appreciation and hostility.

6. *Special problems.* Not all homes are traditional and peaceful. Many children come from chaotic households filled with anger and frustrations, which can spill over

from PRESERVICE to PRACTICE

Scott D. Niemann: Third and Fourth Grades

When the bell rang at 8:15 A.M. on August 28, a new reality entered my mind. Parents stopped by the classroom to familiarize themselves with the new third- and fourth-grade teacher in the village. Some of the concerned looks I spied on the parents' faces as they left their children were heartfelt. Breaking out in a cold sweat, I realized the amount of trust the parents were handing over to me. There was one term that entered my mind: *in loco parentis*, a legal term meaning "in place of the parents." I was taking on the responsibility of a parent!

Following the first day, I expressed my concern to a fellow teacher and he replied, *"Encargada!"* He explained how parents in Mexico often use this Spanish term when they are putting their child's

life in a teacher's hands. It means, "We are handing our child over to you and now you are in charge." Wow! What a responsibility.

CASE QUESTIONS

1. How did your own parents feel about your schools and your teachers? Were their attitudes different when you were in the earlier grades than when you were in later grades? If so, why did their attitudes change?

2. Which of these six potential problem areas do you believe represents the greatest threat to you? What are you going to do about it . . . now?

into a parent–teacher conference. Conferences with divorced parents can be particularly tricky and quickly lead to "the blame game" ("I thought you promised to monitor his TV watching!"). If anger flares up in a conference, gently, but firmly end it. In military parlance, "Terminate engagement and withdraw!"

7. *Privilege and responsibility.* It is often the parents who give new teachers the sense of what a privilege *and* a responsibility it is to be a teacher, as reported by a new teacher in Alaska.

surviving the first year of teaching

When one of the authors was about to begin his first year of teaching, his battle-scarred department chairman cryptically commented to him, "Promise yourself today that you will teach a second year." At the time, the meaning behind the remark was unclear. However, after the emotional yo-yo ride of that initial year had taken a few swoops and plunges, the chairman's message came into sharp focus. A person's first year of teaching is too unusual, too filled with extremes and emotional highs and lows to provide a sound basis for deciding whether teaching is the work on which one wants to spend one's life. Nevertheless, fully one-third of all new teachers leave the profession by the end of their third year.[7]

But these kinds of statistics need not determine your personal fate. Many of the problems and issues that cause teachers to leave the field are preventable through planning and a few resolutions. Most importantly, be aware that a single—and nontypical—year is rarely the basis for a sound career decision.

Being happy in your work will make you a more effective teacher.

(© Will Hart / Photo Edit)

BEGIN NOW

Start now to prepare for the predictable events and problems of the initial year. Make a systematic study of your strengths and weaknesses, with an eye toward using your strengths in the classroom and gradually eliminating your trouble areas. With both problematic areas and your strengths, seek the advice and help of trusted friends, family, and teachers.

For instance, if you have an especially good reading voice, plan to capitalize on it as a teacher. Students from preschool through college love to be read to.

If you are painfully self-conscious and shy, develop a plan to overcome this shortcoming. Don't try to defeat your shyness with big, dramatic gestures, such as trying out for the lead in the college play. Take an incremental approach, using small steps. Plan to speak to someone standing in line next to you whom you don't know; volunteer answers in class. Realize that your shyness may never completely go away, but you will gradually feel more and more comfortable speaking and working with people if you push yourself to make small advances regularly. You may surprise yourself. (Remember Joan Kinney.)

KEEP A TEACHING JOURNAL

A **teaching journal** can be any notebook that is large enough to hold your teaching thoughts and suggestions. If you prefer working at a keyboard, a computer file can serve the same purpose. Although some teachers started such books in grade school when they first decided to teach, the beginning of one's formal preparation as a teacher is a very good time to begin a journal.

You can use your teaching journal to record all the useful ideas and helpful strategies you discover, saving them for the time when you are actually teaching. This material can include teaching skills learned in lectures or observed in the field, such as how to grade papers effectively or how to give students evaluative feedback on in-class presentations. In addition, it could include methods of disciplining in different situations, easy and efficient ways to take attendance, ways to present particularly difficult concepts, things to do when students get restless or overexcited, and sources of good curricular materials.

Having such a journal serves two functions. First, the teaching journal serves as a constant reminder that you are preparing to actually be in charge of your own classroom (a fact that often is not in sharp focus for preservice teachers). Second, the journal can be a lifesaver when you are struggling during the first year. A typical journal entry might look like this:

Tuesday, October 7
Ninth-grade English

Began the introductory lesson on Shakespeare and the Globe Theater today. The biographical info went over only minimally well. Brian and Mark loudly wanted to know why they needed to know when he was born and died and what difference it made. Some of the other kids looked bored as I went into my spiel, and I realized I was probably lecturing too much.

Next time, I should review the information that I present and figure out what's important for them to know and what's extraneous. Just because I'm fascinated with it doesn't mean that it's all appropriate or necessary for a ninth-grader's introduction to Shakespeare. Also, maybe some sort of question–answer sheet about Shakespeare would work better and get more involvement from the kids.

On the bright side, they all seemed to love the Globe Theater model. They really liked the way it opened, showing the cross-section with all the various stage areas. Brian and Mark were among the most interested in the model. The kids also seemed to be able to follow along on their photocopied drawing of the Globe. Jon and Elizabeth (who usually aren't impressed with anything) told me that it was "pretty cool." The next time, maybe I'll start with the theater and allow more time for them to explore it.

Besides offering professional advantages, the teaching journal can serve as a valuable personal record. One 20-year teaching veteran in Massachusetts has kept a journal about his teaching experiences throughout his career. He finds that it has "captured the moment," recording what he was thinking and experiencing as he taught throughout the years.

An alternative form of this idea is a card file of "teaching tips," utilizing either with index cards or in a similar computerized format. This file of tips can provide quick, easy reference for planning or problem solving.

Keeping a journal is one of the chief characteristics of the *reflective practitioner,* a goal and ideal we have stressed throughout this book.

MAINTAIN THE PROPER FRAME OF MIND

It is important to maintain the right frame of mind during your first year of teaching—that is, to realize that you are someone who is untested and who has a great deal to learn. Humility is a virtue that has been all but drowned out in our modern, "We're Number One" culture. Zen masters and teachers of the spiritual life urge the beginner to assume an attitude of submissiveness before what is to be learned—showing not weakness, but humility. Many new teachers strive hard to *avoid* humiliation, not realizing that a humble person cannot be humiliated. Instead of assuming a false confidence, acknowledge that you have much to learn and open yourself up to that learning.

Making use of this suggestion is somewhat tricky. The humble frame of mind we urge you to adopt is one of alertness and quiet observation of your new context,

> *The love of nurturing and observing growth in others is essential to sustaining a life of teaching. This implies that no matter what you teach or how you present yourself to your students, you have to be on the learners' side and to believe that they can and will grow during the time that you are together.*
>
> —HERBERT KOHL,
> Teacher and Educational Writer

expecting difficulties of some sort but being quietly confident that solutions will come. By all means, it does *not* mean becoming a *doormat*. In a way, the new teacher should be like a good apprentice: working hard, keeping eyes open, asking questions, and being eager to learn everything possible about the craft.

One key aspect of having a proper frame of mind is understanding the social and economic context within which your new school exists. Schools vary immensely, depending on their social, ethical, religious, and economic make-up. (You will find background information in Chapter 2, "What Is a School and What Is It For?" and Chapter 11, "How Are Schools Governed, Influenced, and Financed?") Study your new community and ask questions, so you are not blindsided by attitudes and behaviors that you may be encountering for the first time.

FIND A MENTOR

A first-year teacher can have no greater gift than a good **mentor,** an experienced teacher who is willing to act as a guide and confidant through the first year. Besides all of the information and tips that a mentor can give you, a good mentor is an interpreter-guide on what is essentially foreign turf. A mentor can tell you which pieces of paper from the principal's office must be responded to immediately, who has the formal power and who has the real power, what administrators emphasize most in teacher evaluations, and which teachers are most willing to share ideas and which ones are not. Perhaps even more important, a mentor is a friend. (Remember Mary Veronica and Joan Silver.)

> *In a completely rational society, the best of us would be teachers and the rest of us would have to settle for something less, because passing civilization along from one generation to the next ought to be the highest honor and the highest responsibility anyone could have.*
>
> —LEE IACOCCA,
> Automotive Innovator and Executive

A growing body of research provides solid support for the benefits of mentoring programs. In one study, beginning teachers who had no mentor were three times more likely to leave the profession than those who had mentors.[8] Sixty-seven percent of teachers who have been mentored claim that the experience significantly improved their teaching. Unfortunately, only 47 percent of public school teachers report having received such guidance.[9]

In recent years, many school districts have developed special arrangements to help beginning teachers. Some offer special induction programs, some support mentor programs, and some have both. In situations where there is no induction program or a mentor is not assigned, we nevertheless urge you to make finding a mentor a high priority.

MAKE YOUR STUDENTS' PARENTS YOUR ALLIES

We suggest that all teachers—but particularly new teachers—take a very proactive, positive approach toward parents. Instead of having parents get to know you indirectly through the often-distorting eyes and mouths of their children ("My new teacher, Miss Sniddly, hates me. And besides, she can't teach. How come I got stuck with a new teacher?"), help them get to know you and engage them with what you will be doing with their children this school year. Here are some practical suggestions for how to do so.

First, prepare a short statement to be carried home, signed, and returned, introducing yourself to parents and outlining your major goals for the year. Stress that you and they are in a partnership to help their child have a productive year. Let them know how to get in touch with you. Tell them the date for Back-to-School Night and that you are looking forward to meeting them. One new first-grade teacher we know sent a letter with an insert photo of herself to her first-graders and their parents once she received her class list in the summer. She wrote a little about herself, told them some of the things they would do during the coming school year, and (for the parents) explained her approach to teaching. Besides being exciting for the students, this technique helped the new teacher start the year (and, more importantly, finish the year) with her students' parents as strong allies.

Second, once you have established disciplinary and homework policies, send a copy of those policies home for parental sign-off and return.

Third, on the first day, get the home, work, and cell telephone numbers of each student's parents or guardians. The fact that you possess these valuable bits of information will not go unnoticed by your students, particularly those who might be inclined to push the disciplinary envelope.

Fourth, it is a good idea to call all parents early in the fall. In particular, call the parent(s) as soon as a student appears to be falling behind, tuning out, or misbehaving: "Mrs. Tate, this is Philip's teacher. Philip's performance has begun to slip. What can we do to get him back on track?" "Mr. Dee, this is Joan's teacher. Joan just won't stop talking in class. It is interfering with other students and keeping her from doing the work she is capable of. What can we do to make this the good year we all want for Joan?" The key word in dealing with parents is *we*, as in "What can *we* do?" Phone calls should be made and brief notes sent home for positive reasons as well. Such a "good news" call can make a parent's month!

Finally, if problems persist, insist on a parent visit. (Conversations that include messages such as "We need to work together to get little Adolph involved in his schoolwork" are helpful for everyone involved.) There is no surer way to get children's attention than to have them realize they are the reason their parents had to leave work early to come to school. Although this is an upsetting bother for many parents, the extra effort is usually worth it because of the positive effect it can have on their child's school experience.

TAKE EVALUATION SERIOUSLY

The news that they are to be evaluated by their principal or some other administrator often comes as a surprise to novice teachers. Even more shocking is the revelation that the related evaluation reports are sometimes the cause of not being rehired.

Typically, it is a major job responsibility of principals and other district administrative personnel to visit systematically and evaluate the performance of new teachers. Depending on the district and the conscientiousness of the administrator, this type of observation and evaluation can take place anywhere from once to a dozen times during the first year. Usually, the administrator makes three or four evaluative visits, which are followed up closely by feedback conferences during which the administrator goes over his or her observations of the individual's teaching. Together these evaluative visits play an important part in the school district's decision to rehire the teacher or terminate his or her employment.

It is important, then, for new teachers to understand thoroughly how their work will be evaluated. Before you accept a teaching position, be clear about how and when your work will be evaluated. Most school districts have an official evaluation and feedback form, and you should know this form well. Check out the department of education's website in your state to see how new teachers are evaluated. If the school or district's evaluator gives you advance notification of a visit, prepare for the occasion. Find out from your mentor teacher what the administrator really stresses in teaching. And do your best. If the evaluator raises issues or makes suggestions for improvement, take them very seriously. You do not necessarily have to agree, but you should not casually ignore the issues. In most cases, the comments are legitimate, and the new teacher should strive to repair or strengthen the area that was criticized.

TAKE CARE OF YOURSELF

One of the greatest surprises of full-time, fully responsible teaching (as opposed to student teaching) is how tiring it is. Teaching is physically, mentally, and emotionally draining, particularly until one gets conditioned to it—that is, until one gets into "teaching shape." This is true for many jobs. The stress and strain of new employment wear newcomers down and set them up for colds, flu, and other mild ailments. This problem is compounded in teaching because it is such an "in your face" occupation (referring to all those coughing, sniffling, and wheezing faces

Regular large muscle exercise can relieve much of the stress of teaching.

(Pete Saloutos/Shutterstock.com)

you encounter every day). A classroom is a magnificent germ factory, with viruses claiming new victims daily. The teacher who is exhausted, run down, and regularly staying up late reworking lesson plans and correcting papers is a prime target for whatever is circulating in the environment.

The stress and strain of a new teaching position also can cause mild depression. In their first year, few teachers live up to their own expectations. Often, new teachers are separated from their regular support system of family and friends. Having not yet established realistic standards, they really don't know whether they are succeeding or failing. A bad class or even a single resistant or disrespectful student can emotionally unseat them. To counter this vulnerability to sickness of body and spirit, new teachers need to give special attention to their health. When you feel yourself becoming overstressed or burned out, take deliberate steps to rectify the situation. Reduce stress directly by trying to solve key problems that are bothering you, and look for ways to relieve stress indirectly as well. Plan a weekend away, take vitamins, or join an aerobics class. Instead of getting overtired and run down, beginners need to take special pains to get enough rest, eat well, and get adequate exercise.

OUR FINAL WORD

Much of this chapter has dealt with the trials and tribulations of being a new teacher. Nevertheless, most new teachers have a great sense of accomplishment and are proud of themselves at the end of their first year. They have learned an enormous amount in 9 or 10 months. Along with the undoubtedly difficult challenges, teaching has its pleasures and bright moments, making it a rewarding and fulfilling occupation for most. English novelist Joyce Cary has written that human joy comes not from the great events but from the little, everyday things, like a good cup of tea.* The joys and satisfactions of teaching can lie in mundane happenings and small surprises. As a teacher, you may find joy in the following:

- Experiencing those electric moments when you can *feel* the students thinking and *see* those new connections being made

- Watching two lonely kids whom you brought together walk down the hall side by side, now friends

- Getting your planbook back from your supervisor with the comment, "These are *excellent* lessons"

- Finding in your box, on a rainy Friday afternoon, a note written in a childish scrawl: "You are my most favorite teacher. Guess who?"

- Shopping at the mall and meeting one of your students, who proudly introduces you to her mother as "my teacher," and being able to tell by the mother's response that you are respected in their household

- Having a former student call to tell you that he has a problem and needs your advice

- Chaperoning a dance and having what you thought was your most hostile student happily introduce his girlfriend to you

- Hearing in the teachers' lunchroom that your supervisor called you "a real professional"

- Being observed by the principal and having your students make you look terrific

- Surviving until June, being bone-tired but proud of what you and your kids have been able to do

- Cleaning out your desk on the last day of school after the kids have been dismissed and finding a box of candy with a card signed by the whole class

- Realizing—be it daily, weekly, or monthly—that what you are doing with your life *really does make a difference*

*Translated into "U.S. speak," that means joy comes from a good cuppa coffee.

WHY TEACH? YOUR FINAL WORD

In your journal or online at this textbook's website, respond to the following questions:

1. Can you remember any new teachers you have had who fit the scenarios described in this chapter? Did they encounter any situations similar to those described in this chapter?

2. What do you expect to be your major problems as a beginning teacher? What steps can you take now to prevent those problems?

3. Make a list of your potential teaching strengths. How can you sharpen them and use them effectively in your teaching?

KEY TERMS

culture shock (440)
mentor (466)

social distance (454)
teaching journal (464)

FOR FURTHER INFORMATION

TEACHSOURCE VIDEO

Mentoring First-Year Teachers: Keys to Professional Success

This video shows how mentoring works and the benefits of having this professional assistance from an experienced colleague.

WEB RESOURCES

About Teaching and the First Year. Available at **www2. ed.gov/teachers/become/about/edpicks.jhtml**

The U.S. Department of Education has a special website to support first-year teachers. Comprehensive and current, it can provide you with many answers to everyday questions.

Beginning Teacher's Tool Box. Available at **www. inspiringteachers.com.**

Manned by veteran teachers, this site offers everything from an "Ask Our Mentor a Question" section, where you can e-mail questions to a veteran teacher, to "Tips for New Teachers" (click "archives") that include inspiration, humor, and the top 10 things to do before school starts.

EZ School. Available at **www.ezschool.com.**

This website, associated with Amazon.com, is a treasure of resources for the new teacher. It is filled with good ideas, teaching plans for a range of subject matter, and worksheets.

Teachers First. Available at **www.teachersfirst.com.**

This website is a treasure trove of information, good ideas, lesson plans, and even humor. It is well organized and easy to search for the topic or need of choice.

PRINT RESOURCES

Esme Raji Codell, *Educating Esme: Diary of a Teacher's First Year* (Chapel Hill, NC: Algonquin Books, 1999).

This book is the account of a new fifth-grade teacher in a Chicago inner-city school. Hip, imaginative, and irreverent, the book takes the reader through the teacher's triumphs and travails with students and a particularly dense administrator.

Jonathan Kozol, *Letters to a Young Teacher* (New York: Crown, 2007).

A compilation of sage advice to "Francesca," a beginning first-grade teacher in an urban elementary school.

Harry K. Wong and Rosemary T. Wong, *The First Days of School: How to Be an Effective Teacher* (Sunview, CA: Harry Wong, Paperback, 2009).

This highly acclaimed handbook abounds with tips and strategies to help the new teacher get a strong start through motivation and minimizing discipline and the other problems that plague new teachers.

 The Education CourseMate website for this text offers many helpful resources. Go to www.cengagebrain.com to access the TeachSource Video Cases and other TeachSource videos, flashcards, interactive quizzes, the eBook, reflection and enrichment activities, a state standards resource center, and other study aids.

15 what does it mean to be a professional?

(© Radius Images/Alamy)

I n this chapter, we focus on the teacher as a professional—that is, as a member of an occupational group. We will see how this rather abstract concept of *professionalism* affects the daily life of the classroom teacher. In effect, we examine the role of the individual teacher within the larger context of being a member of a profession.

FOCUS POINTS

- Teachers can become involved in different types of situations and conflicts in which they will need counsel or support.

- Teachers have become more powerful in recent years, but they don't have the same kinds of power that members of some other professions have.

- The question of whether teaching is a profession can be judged by reference to specific criteria. Although cases can be made both for and against teaching being a profession, there is a third option for you to consider.

- The teaching profession is still evolving, and much depends on its capacity to maintain the public's trust.

- Various levels of professionalism exist, and the National Board for Professional Teaching Standards and its standards for certification are having a substantial effect on teachers.

- The National Education Association and the American Federation of Teachers—the two most influential teacher organizations—have quite different origins and are competing for the support of classroom teachers.

Truth or Fiction?

T F   It is a clear-cut matter that teaching is and always has been not just a career, but a profession.

T F   The National Education Association and the American Federation of Teachers, professional organizations that represent the majority of the nation's teachers, neither take positions on political issues nor endorse individuals running for office.

T F   The term *professional development* refers to moving through and up the ranks in the educational hierarchy.

The essence of a career in teaching is close, hands-on work with the young. When people think about becoming teachers, their thoughts and musings usually revolve around working with students. Rarely do they bother with hypothetical issues beyond the scope of the classroom. This narrow focus is both natural and appropriate because the teacher's success or failure depends on his or her effectiveness with students. Nevertheless, there is much more to being a teacher. Teachers work within a system that exposes them to pressures from many quarters. Prospective teachers are often somewhat naive about these pressures and forces, and that naiveté can be dangerous, both in making a career decision and in making a successful career.

To help you see this point, we would like you to indulge in a set of thought experiments for a few moments. We will offer you a few brief scenarios, and after reading each one, you should reflect on how you might react. As you read each scenario, imagine yourself as a first-year teacher in that ideal classroom you carry around in your head. Assume that you appear to be doing a fine job. You are really enjoying your teaching experience. Your students are making nice progress, and they seem to be interested in their work. A few "helicopter" parents have indicated that although they were initially worried that their precious children were to have a new (in other words, *untested*) teacher, they are pleased with their children's progress in your class. So, things are going very well, until . . .

Scenario One

You get a special-delivery letter from a group called Patriotic American Parents (PAP). You have heard they are very active in your area and are especially interested in schools. Their letter informs you that their lawyer is preparing a case against you for using books on their disapproved list. (You didn't know there was such a list, but sure enough, there is, and you have been using books from it!) They claim they have evidence that you are "waging a subtle but nevertheless vicious war against the cause of justice and liberty and have succeeded in temporarily deflecting the minds of some of your students from the truth." Furthermore, they want to know why you display the United Nations flag and why there are no pictures of past presidents on your classroom walls. Finally, you are said to recite the Pledge of Allegiance in a much too hasty fashion, which is clearly a sign of your disrespect for your country. This is the first you have heard of these charges or even of the Patriots' interest in you. You think of yourself as patriotic and are shocked by the letter. They have requested that you respond in writing by next week or they will begin legal proceedings.

> *The only way to keep our kids foolproof is to keep them away from fools.*
>
> ——WILL ROGERS (1879–1935),
> Cowboy Humorist

Scenario Two

In late January, the principal, who holds a conference with each new teacher, told you she thought you were doing a fine job and that she wanted you to return next year. In passing, she remarked that she would be getting a contract to you in the spring. Toward the end of April, you got a little nervous and called her office. You spoke to her executive secretary, who said not to worry, that you were on the list and that a contract would be coming before long. You stopped worrying. Today is the last day of school, and you find a very nice personal note from the principal in your school mailbox. She thanks you for your fine work during the year and says she is sorry you will not be back next year. You call the principal's office. She is "in conference," and her executive secretary says they are not renewing your contract. She cannot remember speaking to you in April. She knows nothing about the case. She does know, however, that the Board of Education has put on a lot of pressure for cuts in next year's personnel budget. She ends by telling you, "You must be very disappointed, dear. I know how you must feel." No, she doesn't!

Scenario Three

One lunch hour, you noticed something peculiar when you sat down at the faculty dining table. Conversations stopped, and you had the distinct impression your colleagues had been talking about you. A few days later, an older teacher stopped you in the hall after school and said, "I don't want to butt in, but you really are upsetting Mrs. Hilary and Mr. Alexander." Mrs. H. and Mr. A. have the classrooms on either side of yours. Apparently, they claim your class makes so much noise that they can't get anything done. Both are very traditional in their approach to education, whereas you believe in a more activity-oriented approach. Although your class is rather noisy occasionally, it is never chaotic, and its noise is usually a byproduct of students' involvement in a task. Twice Mr. Alexander has sent messengers with notes asking that your class be quieter. You have always complied. You hardly know either teacher. You have never really talked to Mr. Alexander except to say hello. Mrs. Hilary, with whom you've chatted, prides herself on being a strict disciplinarian. What she means, you have inferred, is that she is able to keep the children quiet. You know Mr. Alexander is chummy with Mrs. Hilary. You go to the vice-principal, who seems to know all about the case, but only from the Hilary–Alexander angle. Inexplicably, the vice-principal gets quite angry and claims that until you came along, the faculty got along beautifully. Furthermore, you are being very unprofessional in making complaints against experienced teachers. You feel as if you are trapped in a bad dream.

These horror stories, of course, are not everyday occurrences. Also, keep in mind that entrance into any profession has its trials and booby traps. These accounts are intended to help you realize that you can be an effective teacher and still have

Part of being a professional is being ready to stand up and be heard.

trouble keeping your job. What is the common theme running through each of these anecdotes? You, the teacher, were succeeding in your work with children, but forces outside your classroom began to impinge on you. PAP wanted to make a target case of you. The school system bureaucracy was ready to put you on the unemployed rolls. Two of your colleagues damaged your reputation with the faculty and administration. Other than that, it's been a super year.

Although you may feel confident that you could handle some of these situations, it is doubtful that you could cope with all such cases that might arise. In some instances, you would be powerless to respond effectively to your adversaries, and you might end up a helpless victim of circumstance. Fortunately, a teacher is not alone. Like people in many other occupational groups, teachers have organizations whose job it is to protect them from such indignities and injustices. These organizations function on several levels, from the local to the national, and usually their very existence keeps situations like those described from occurring. When they do occur, these organizations are there to support the teacher. At least, that is the way they should work.

In becoming a teacher, you are not just committing yourself to work with children. You are joining an occupational group composed of other individuals with similar responsibilities, concerns, and pressures whose help you may need and who, in turn, will need your help.

the status of teaching: a profession or not?

The question "Is teaching a profession?" probably arouses deep yawns in many of our readers. Most people thinking about a career in teaching are more interested in whether it will be a personally rewarding way to spend their time than in whether it is a "true profession." Will teaching bring me personal satisfactions? Will it provide an outlet for my talents and energies? Will I be effective with kids? These questions are, we suspect, closer to your skin. Nevertheless, the question of professionalism and the related issues are important to teachers and influence the quality of education teachers provide for children. They will also affect the quality of your life as a teacher.

So what is a profession? A **profession** is more than a group of individuals all engaged in the same line of work. Professions have a more or less recognizable set of characteristics that distinguish them from nonprofessions.[1] As you read the following list of characteristics, check whether you think teaching qualifies on each premise:

1. A profession renders a unique, definite, and essential service to society. Only the people in the particular profession render the service; for instance, only lawyers practice law. The service rendered must be considered so important that it is available to all the people in a society.

   ❏ yes   ❏ no

2. A profession relies on intellectual skills in the performance of its service. This does not mean that physical actions and skills are not needed; rather, the emphasis in carrying on the work is on intellectual skills and techniques.

   ❏ yes   ❏ no

3. A profession entails a long period of specialized training. Because professional work requires special intellectual skills, it requires specialized intellectual training. General education such as that represented by a bachelor's degree is valued but is not considered adequate. The specialized training must cover a substantial period and not be obtained in cram courses or correspondence schools.

❑ yes ❑ no

4. Both individual members of the profession and the professional group enjoy a considerable degree of autonomy and decision-making authority. Professional groups regulate their own activities rather than having outsiders set policies and enforce adherence to standards. Whereas factory workers have very limited decision-making power and are closely supervised in the performance of their work, professionals are expected to make most of their own decisions and be free of close supervision by supervisors.

❑ yes ❑ no

5. A profession requires its members to accept personal responsibility for their actions and decisions and, in general, for their performance. Because the professional's service is usually related to the client's human welfare, this responsibility is an especially serious one.

❑ yes ❑ no

6. A profession emphasizes the services rendered by its practitioners more than their financial rewards. Although the personal motives of any individual professional are not necessarily any higher than any other worker's, the professional group's public emphasis is on service. The "Leaders in Education" feature provides one example of the teaching field's emphasis on service.

❑ yes ❑ no

7. A profession is self-governing and responsible for policing its own ranks. As a consequence, professional groups perform a number of activities aimed at keeping the quality of their services high and looking out for the social and economic well-being of the professional members. Also, these self-governing organizations set standards of admission and exclusion for the profession.

❑ yes ❑ no

8. A profession has a code of ethics that sets out the acceptable standards of conduct for its members.

❑ yes ❑ no

These characteristics, then, are the major requirements of a profession. Although few professions satisfy all of them fully, this list does serve as a benchmark against which occupational groups can measure themselves and direct their development if they wish to enjoy professional status. With these criteria in mind, let's look at some of the arguments that people have made for and against teaching as a profession.

THE CASE *AGAINST* TEACHING AS A PROFESSION

The roots of teaching as an occupation go back to ancient Greece, where slaves called *paidagogos*, or pedagogues, taught children to read and write and helped them memorize passages of poetic history. Despite this long history, a careful look at current practices reveals that teaching does not qualify as a profession.

A Child's Many Teachers

If education is a teacher's unique function, the teacher certainly has a great deal of competition. Children today learn a tremendous amount from media offerings, including *Sesame Street,* the History Channel, YouTube.com, and *Sports Illustrated.* The *non*-teacher-educators include parents, ministers, older friends, neighbors, employers, best friends, coaches, scout leaders, camp counselors, and grandparents. The world is bursting with teachers, and those who hold forth in school buildings have only a small piece of the action.

LEADERS in education

Kay Toliver

(Courtesy of Kay Toliver, Teacher)

Kay Toliver has been instilling a love of knowledge in middle school students in Spanish Harlem for more than 30 years. Toliver teaches on the cutting edge of mathematics, stressing thinking and application over computation, and weaving history and art through class discussions into the study of mathematics. Because many of her students come from poor, unstable backgrounds and have poor language skills, she emphasizes writing, reading, and research. Toliver's students must always be prepared to explain their solutions orally, in complete and clear sentences. They are required to keep daily journals, in which they write about what they have learned in class, ideas about how to apply the concepts they study, or simply observations about the class or the teacher. "We don't need different methods to teach so-called disadvantaged children," says Toliver. She believes that students' ability to express themselves in well-written English must be acquired hand in hand with mathematical discovery. In addition to enhancing writing skills, the journals allow the teacher to gain a glimpse of her students' confusions in mathematics. "A teacher can stand in front of the class and think she's giving a great lesson. But that's not always the truth," she explains.

Kay Toliver's influence is spreading beyond her classroom to videos. In 1995, she was featured in a Peabody Award–winning public television special, *Good Morning Miss Toliver.* Also, with Jaime Escalante, Toliver contributed to "Interactions: Real Math—Real Careers," a multimedia tool that connects pre-algebra math principles to real life in scenarios featuring career professionals. Along with Escalante, Toliver sees the way to future jobs through mathematics, especially for students from the inner city. In addition to the mathematical tools, P.S. 72 children use computers. Toliver feels her students must be technologically competitive. With money she received from one of her many awards, the Presidential Award for Excellence in Science and Mathematics Teaching, she purchased software and computers for her school's computer lab.

Recently Toliver retired from full-time teaching. She is still involved in education, however, and is in demand as a keynote speaker and teacher trainer. She is the host of a Peabody Award–winning classroom series for elementary math students, *The Eddie Files,* and has passed along her classroom strategies in two staff development series, *The Kay Toliver Files* and *Teacher Talk.* These materials are influencing a new generation of teachers through their use in professional development workshops and teacher training programs at universities. Most recently, she has worked with The Futures Channel to present staff development institutes and parent engagement events at schools and districts throughout the country.

Toliver has seen many students who have been exposed to drugs or crime, or both. Frequently, one parent is gone, or a child may be in foster care. Too often a sibling is in jail, and the students' peers are dealing with everyday street life in East Harlem. But having grown up in the South Bronx and East Harlem, Toliver is well acquainted with the world of her students. As a result, discipline is not a problem in Toliver's class. Students understand she is serious and works hard to make math interesting.

"Becoming a teacher was the fulfillment of a childhood dream," says Toliver. "My parents always stressed that education was the key to a better life. By becoming a teacher, I hoped to inspire African American and Hispanic youths to realize their own dreams. I wanted to give something back to the communities I grew up in."

Learn more about Kay Toliver's approach at www.nationalmathtrail.org/ktmathtrail.html.

Limited Training

Although teaching has intellectual and theoretical foundations, it requires a rather short period of specialized training (considerably less than some of the skilled trades), and entrance into the occupation is not especially competitive, particularly on intellectual grounds. If teaching is a profession, it is one composed of college graduates with a sweeping span of academic abilities, varying levels of commitment, and a wide range of motivations for becoming teachers.

Constraints on Autonomy

Although a good deal of talk touts teachers' autonomy and decision-making power (and teachers have come a long way since the early days of the United States, as described in the feature on rules and duties for nineteenth-century teachers), in today's classrooms teachers still have a very low level of autonomy and decision-making power. Teachers are at the second rung from the bottom (superior only to students) of the "school hierarchy," which is ultimately commanded by the local board of education. Unlike lawyers and doctors, who can reject clients, teachers have students assigned to them. They also have supervisors: their principal, lead teacher, department head, and others farther up the chain of command. They teach a curriculum and are responsible for their students' meeting content standards that have been chosen or developed by others.

Unlike other professions, teachers do not formally evaluate other teachers; instead, administrators do so. Moreover, most of the important decisions that affect teachers' daily lives—even those that bear directly on the standards of their own profession—are made by non-teachers (administrators and citizen school board members). Although teachers are beginning to get more involved in teacher preparation programs and are acquiring some influence in the licensing and certification of teachers, laypeople and bureaucrats still wield a great deal of the decision-making power. Some teachers, like factory workers, even have to punch a time clock (or, put more genteelly, they "sign in" and "sign out"). In sum, they have very little to say about what goes on in their "shop."

Responsibility for Their Profession

Although things are beginning to change, it is a rare event, indeed, when a teacher loses his or her job because Johnnie can't read or Samantha failed calculus. After a teacher achieves tenure, it takes some form of gross negligence, clear incompetence, or serious sexual offense for him or her to be fired. As professionals, teachers do very little policing of their own ranks. Their professional organizations are just like other

It is important to remember that parents are your students' first teachers.

(© Ephraim Ben-Shimon/Corbis)

self-serving organizations, whether composed of teamsters or autoworkers—that is, the primary energies of teacher associations and unions and professional associations are devoted to their own survival and growth. Secondarily, they attempt to protect their members, increase their salaries, and expand their benefits.

Most teachers, however, are only minimally involved in the major professional associations and their activities. Except when the organization calls a strike—a rare but still somewhat contradictory activity for a "profession" supposedly dedicated to serving children—teachers generally just pay their dues. Most teachers claim they are too busy to take an active role in professional affairs. This lack of fully engaged

rules and duties for teachers in the nineteenth century

- Teachers will fill the lamps and clean the chimney each day.
- Each teacher will bring a bucket of water and a scuttle of coal for the day's session.
- Make your pens carefully. You may whittle nibs to the individual tastes of the pupils.
- Men teachers may take one evening each week for courting purposes, or two evenings a week if they go to church regularly.
- Women teachers who marry or engage in improper conduct will be dismissed.
- Every teacher should lay aside from each day's pay a goodly sum of his earnings. He should

use his savings during his retirement years so that he will not be a burden to society.
- Any teacher who smokes, uses liquor in any form, visits pool halls or public halls, or gets shaved at a barber shop will give good reasons for people to suspect his worth, intentions, and honesty.
- The teacher who performs his labor faithfully and without fault for five years will be given an increase of twenty-five cents per week in his pay.

Source: From the rules and duties for teachers teaching in an 1872 Missouri school district.

involvement in professional activities may stem from the fact that so many teachers have second jobs, either as homemakers or in the after-school labor market.

Job Security and Salary

Teachers work in circumstances very different from those encountered by other professionals. Like other public servants, they are hired, rather than operating as independent agents. They are on a fixed salary schedule and are protected by tenure laws rather than independently having to find a market for their services. In effect, teaching is a low-paying, relatively high-security job rather than a high-paying, low-security profession. Seniority as a teacher appears to be more important than competence. Talk about professionalism may be personally satisfying to teachers, but it does not conform to the reality of the teacher's occupational life.

THE CASE *FOR* TEACHING AS A PROFESSION

The evidence for the status of teaching as a profession is witnessed and attested to by the very nature and nobility of the teacher's work. Society has entrusted teachers with its most important responsibility: the education of its young. Throughout history, many great thinkers have acknowledged how crucial the work of the teacher is to the fulfillment of personal and national goals. As this realization has spread in recent decades, opportunities and rewards for the teacher have continued to improve.

Teachers' Commitment to Service

Service to others lies at the very heart of what it means to be a professional. Teachers make large material sacrifices to serve children. The overwhelming percentages of people who teach could find work that, at least in material terms, is much more rewarding. Many could command large salaries in business or more lucrative professions. A 2010 study found that teachers surveyed said they spent that school year an average of $398 of their own money on school supplies and an additional $538 on instructional materials—a total of $936—for their classrooms.[2] This is truly service above and beyond the call of duty!

The Teacher's Unique Skills

> *What office is there which involves more responsibility, which requires more qualifications, and which ought, therefore, to be more honorable than that of teaching?*
>
> —HARRIET MARTINEAU (1802–1876),
> Nineteenth-Century Feminist and Abolitionist

Although children learn from many people—from parents to television personalities—teachers are the specialists who pass on to the young the key skills they need to participate effectively in the culture. They aid the young in acquiring the most difficult, if not the most important, skills—those that involve thinking and manipulating ideas. Neither reading nor geometry is often learned on the street. Teachers are the indispensable midwives of the "knowledge society." Although teachers do not undergo a particularly lengthy period of specialized training, they are in a sense continually educating themselves. Further, teachers are expected (and, in most states, required by law) to upgrade their teaching skills and content knowledge periodically.

The Teacher's Autonomy

Teachers have an immense span of personal control. They normally determine the method of instruction. They decide which aspects of the curriculum they will highlight and which they will cover quickly. The limits on their creativity in the classroom are few, if any. After the initial few years of teaching, they are seldom observed and evaluated. Teachers' classrooms are their castles. If teachers believe they do not have enough autonomy or do not agree with their administrators, they are free to move to another school.

A teacher's autonomy is accompanied by a responsibility to teach effectively. Like other professionals, teachers must be able to justify the manner in which they render their social services, whether it is grading or disciplinary actions. Teachers take responsibility for their actions and, like other professionals, are open to criticisms of their performance.

PAUSE AND REFLECT

1. Where do you stand on the question, "Is teaching a profession?" Is the designation "a profession" important to you?

2. To you, what are the best arguments for and against the professional status of teaching?

A THIRD POSSIBILITY: AN EVOLVING PROFESSION

Like most other complex questions, our query about whether teaching is a profession cannot be answered satisfactorily with simple pro-and-con arguments such as those just offered. Also, the conditions under which teachers work differ so dramatically, and teachers possess such varying degrees of knowledge, commitment, and expertise, that it is difficult to come up with a definitive, one-size-fits-all answer. In most schools, teachers fulfill many of the criteria of professionals. In other schools, they seem to function somewhat as clerks and technicians.

In certain ways, teaching clearly is eligible for professional status; in other ways, it deviates sharply from accepted canons of professionalism. On the one hand, teachers provide an intellectual service to the community. They undergo specialized training to master the theoretical basis of their work. Ethical standards guide their work with students. On the other hand, they too often function like many other lower-level white-collar workers and civil servants. Too often seniority and job security are the rules that guide their path rather than excellence and independence. Like many other occupational groups that are considered professional, at this moment in history, teachers only partially qualify for this sobriquet. For these reasons, some educators call teaching a "semiprofession," a label we reject as pejorative and demeaning.

Another way to look at the issue (and one we favor) is to think of teaching as an *evolving profession*—that is, it is in the process of becoming a full profession. Today, great efforts are being made to increase the professionalism of teaching. What will determine whether teaching becomes a full-fledged profession during your lifetime? Among the key factors are the trends toward greater self-determination, better preparation, and recognizing excellence in teaching.

T (F)

It is a clear-cut matter that teaching is and always has been not just a career, but a profession.

Like most other complex questions, our query about whether teaching is a profession cannot be answered satisfactorily with simple pro-and-con arguments such as those just offered. Also, the conditions under which teachers work differ so dramatically, and teachers possess such varying degrees of knowledge, commitment, and expertise, that it is difficult to come up with a definitive, one-size-fits-all answer.

"

A professional is someone who can do his best when he doesn't feel like it.

—ALISTAIR COOKE (1908–2004),
British Commentator on American Culture

Greater Self-Determination

Perhaps the teacher does lack the autonomy of, say, a small-town lawyer. Yet every profession has limits on its autonomy. For example, an increasing number of doctors and dentists are now employed by health maintenance organizations (HMOs) and are forming unions to protect their rights against their HMO managers. The crucial point for teachers, though, is the direction in which teaching is moving.

In the same way that the United States is committed to civilian control of the military, Americans are committed to civilian (i.e., parents, community leaders, and school boards) control of their schools. Control over the teaching profession is a different matter, however, and should be largely in the hands of teachers. In particular, to make teaching a full profession, teachers must assume a larger role in the governing of their career affairs. Up to now, the great majority of teachers have taken the attitude "Let George do it," allowing others to make the major decisions about who should teach, how teachers should be trained, and under what conditions they should render their services. This situation will not substantially change until teachers take the lead in making it change.

Better Preparation

To make teaching a full profession, teachers must also demand better preparation requirements. As long as the public believes that any college graduate with a smattering of education courses can walk in off the street and do a teacher's job, people will tend not to treat teachers as professionals. As described in Chapter 13, "What Are Your Job Options in Education?" this dangerous perception may even worsen if, owing to teacher shortages, states issue alternative licenses to individuals without any professional training at all! We are definitely not suggesting that teachers should adopt artificial trappings, like a doctor's smock or a general's braided uniform, so that they will appear more distinctive and impressive. Rather, teachers must appear better because they *are* better. Like architects and surgeons, teachers must know their work, and their vocation must be imbued with a sense of high purpose. When that happens, the public will decide affirmatively that teachers should be treated as full professionals.

> *To erect fine buildings and to seek to meet the needs and abilities of all individuals who desire to avail themselves of the opportunities so generously offered without providing teachers with qualifications commensurate with the ideal is a sham.*
>
> —I. L. KANDELL,
> Educational Philosopher and Teacher

Recognizing Excellence in Teaching

Not all of the nearly 4 million people working in U.S. schools are interested in and, in some cases, capable of measuring up to the standards of professionalism discussed earlier. At present, what we are calling (and will continue to call) the *teaching profession* is a mixed bag, with a great many transients "just passing through," a great many rather uncommitted teachers, and a great many truly excellent, dedicated career teachers.

Almost 50 years ago, an educator captured what we believe to be the essence of the professional teacher in the following statement:

> Let us define a career teacher as one who plans to, and actually does, make a life occupation of teaching; one who is philosophically, emotionally, and spiritually committed, who is never satisfied with what he does and how well he's doing it, and who fully intends to keep on growing for the rest of his life.[3]

This educator estimated that only one out of four practicing teachers fit his definition. Herein lays the difficulty: until the great majority of teachers satisfy this educator's definition or until there is a qualitative regrouping of those presently identified as "teachers," the designation of teaching as a full-fledged profession will be in doubt.

LEVELS OF PROFESSIONALISM

What people (yourself included) think of the professional status of teaching is clearly important. Even so, this issue is dwarfed in importance by how you will live out your professional life and how you *will be* as a teacher. One way to think about this point is to conceive of teaching as having three levels, or three ways that teachers go about their work.[4] Level One is the *imitative-maintenance* teacher, Level Two is the *meditative* teacher, and Level Three is the *generative-creative* teacher.

The Level One Teacher

Individuals functioning at Level One are essentially going through the motions prescribed by someone else in a rather mechanical fashion. They tend to be preoccupied with classroom discipline and keeping students busy. Such teachers may be successful at getting students *through* their lessons and examinations, but they are somewhat robotic in narrowly following preset patterns—namely, patterns set out in curriculum guides or textbooks. Level One teachers find security in *teaching to the test* and in what are pejoratively called *teacher-proof materials*, rigid instructional materials that offer step-by-step guidance for teachers' actions. Many new teachers, before they get their "sea legs," operate for a time at this level.

Although not in itself a problem, the imitative-maintenance approach doesn't allow the teacher to respond to the unique needs of students or to the special circumstances that continually arise in a classroom. Level One teachers don't know how to respond to the interesting, off-the-wall question or what to do when something unexpected happens. Instead, they let the "teachable moment" float by. This kind of unimaginative teaching makes teaching more of a technical occupation than a profession.

The Level Two Teacher

As the label "meditative" implies, teachers at Level Two mentally reflect on what they are doing in a classroom, but their reflection lies within a narrow range. They have an awareness of the uniqueness of their classroom and their students, and they go beyond their curricular guides and materials, but their adaptations are few and seem more like tinkering around the instructional edge. They may, for example, deviate from the prescribed teaching guide, but not very far. Level Two teachers may vary their instructional patterns to fit certain classroom events—that is, the obvious boredom of students—or they may bring in supplemental materials. However, they are hardly innovative.

The Level-Three Teacher

There is a large jump to the generative-creative level. These teachers focus on their individual students, and they take a wide view of knowledge. They attend to their curricular guides and the prescribed materials, but those materials serve as launching pads rather than being the sole targets of their instruction. These teachers' classrooms are characterized by a wide variety of instructional approaches and problem-centered materials. Level Three teachers play off the interests and talents of

Who says learning can't be fun?

(© Susie Fitzhugh)

their students, but not in a casual or pandering way. Their expectations for students are high and transcend required tests and examinations. They approach instruction as diagnosticians, seeking the best ways to engage students in their own mental growth. They do not simply transmit knowledge, but rather create: they create in students a desire to learn and they create classroom environments where individual students become self-directed learners.

Few new teachers burst on the educational scene as Level Three generative-creative teachers. Many start at Level Two or attain this status quickly. As a beginning teacher, it is important to have an understanding of your current behavior and to work toward this highest level. The very embracing of the goal will put you on the road to full professionalism. This concept of levels of teaching, besides offering a path to excellence, points to a challenging professional opportunity, an opportunity to which we now turn.

NATIONAL BOARD FOR PROFESSIONAL TEACHING STANDARDS

Since it began in 1987, the **National Board for Professional Teaching Standards (NBPTS)** has been working to recognize and provide greater support to superior (or Level Three) teachers. In the process, this organization attempts to strengthen the claim of professionalism for the career of teaching and to play a leading role in this effort.

Over the years, the lack of recognizable high standards has discouraged some potentially outstanding people from entering teaching and has lowered the level of aspiration of others. High standards tend to focus people's attention and harness their energies. For example, in long-distance running, the four-minute mile was long considered an unbreakable barrier. For many years, sports commentators pontificated that it was beyond the capacities of humans to run a mile in four minutes or less. Then, in 1957, Roger Bannister, a relatively obscure British medical student, broke the magic barrier. A new standard was set, and runners reset their sights. The following year, *37* runners broke that "unbreakable barrier." Today, breaking the four-minute barrier is commonplace, simply because a new standard has been set and people have risen to it in great numbers. The NBPTS is trying to perform a similar function for the teaching profession.

The NBPTS has established standards for teaching practice and has developed a series of board certification assessments based on these standards. As of 2010, slightly more than 82,000 teachers, from all 50 states and the District of Columbia, had achieved board certification.[5] Board advocates believe that these standards allow teachers to gain a highly regarded, professional credential like that available to physicians, accountants, architects, and other professionals. So far, however, while 90 percent of all U.S. physicians and 30 percent of U.S. architects are board certified, only 3 percent of U.S. teachers have achieved that feat.[6]

Core Propositions and Characteristics

The NBPTS is dedicated to and directed by five core propositions:

1. Teachers know the subjects they teach and how to teach these subjects to students.
2. Teachers are committed to their students and their learning.
3. Teachers are responsible for managing and monitoring student learning.
4. Teachers think systematically about their practice and learn from experience.
5. Teachers are members of a learning community.[7]

In addition, the organization has five distinguishing characteristics:

1. The NBPTS supports experienced teachers—that is, teachers with a baccalaureate or an advanced degree who have graduated from an accredited college or university and have at least three years of teaching experience.
2. "Taking the boards" is completely voluntary. It is not intended to be a condition of work, like state licensure, but rather an achievement testifying to an individual teacher's attainment of a high level of professionalism.
3. "Taking the boards" involves submitting oneself to a set of examinations and assessments in particular areas or subject matters such as early childhood, English language arts, and physical education and health. Currently, board certification is offered in 27 different teaching fields, and there are plans for adding more.
4. These assessments are not typical paper-and-pencil tests. Teaching, by its very nature, is a mixture of thought and action and is not measured well by traditional "sit-down" testing. Among the means of assessment are videotapes of the individual's teaching and an evaluation of his or her professional portfolio. Such a portfolio might include examples of students' work, sample lesson plans, and other items that the teacher believes will support his or her candidacy. Candidates do, however, take examinations to assure depth of knowledge in their field. They are also asked to respond to and justify their responses to classroom circumstances that are presented to them on CDs.
5. The primary control of the NBPTS is in the hands of a 63-person board of directors. Although administrators, teacher-educators, and the general public are represented on the NBPTS, two-thirds of the board members are teachers—a further step toward achieving professionalism in teaching.

Advantages of Board Certification

In recent years, NBPTS certification has meant a salary bonus for those teachers so designated. However, in 2009 and 2010, the amounts of these awards, which recently reached $20,000 as a one-time bonus,[8] have been reduced, victims of recession-driven budget cuts. The states remain committed to NBPTS certification, as is the federal Department of Education. Eight of the 10 recipients of Race to the Top federal education funding grants announced by the U.S. Department of Education referenced programs administered by the National Board for Professional Teaching Standards (NBPTS) in their proposals.[9]

Board certification also means that school boards have a recognizable basis on which to award merit pay or pay for performance other than arbitrary and impressionistic criteria, such as "Her children do well on tests" or "He seems to work long hours and is popular with the brightest students."

Besides raising salaries, board certification offers a number of other advantages for teachers. Teachers who have achieved NBPTS certification are professionally more portable, meaning that they can move more freely across state lines. Also, this effort should stimulate research on what constitutes superior teaching. Likewise, it should trigger more attention to this research-based knowledge within teacher education and throughout the teaching force. Most of all, it should contribute to the essential but difficult mission of creating a system of recognition for highly skilled and dedicated professionals.

Criticisms of the NBPTS

The NBPTS is not without critics. Some educators claim that there is no solid knowledge base in teaching (as opposed to medicine or architecture) on which to ground the board's assessments. Others see the NBPTS as a public relations move to enhance the status and salaries of teachers with artificial trappings ("Yep, Eloise got herself board certified, but we all know she couldn't teach a stone to drop!"). Still others, suspicious that the NBPTS is controlled by its majority of teacher members, see it becoming a vehicle by which to serve the economic interests of teachers and to insulate them further from their "clients" (the students and their parents). Finally, some critics dismiss the NBPTS as just another organization promoting a failed "progressive ideology" (i.e., self-esteem, multiculturalism, and cultural relativity) rather than focusing on content knowledge and whether students are *actually* learning.[10]

For two decades critics of board certification for teachers were uncertain that the process was sound and that it really made a difference, particularly in the classroom where the educational rubber meets the road. Finally, in 2008, the National Research Council completed a congressionally mandated study and confirmed that National Board Certification has a positive impact on student achievement, teacher retention, and professional development. In particular, the research showed that board-certified teachers brought about more higher-level thinking, or more of the "deep thinking" needed by a competitive twenty-first-century workforce.[11]

WHAT EVERY NEW AND OLD TEACHER SHOULD POSSESS: THE INTERSTATE TEACHER ASSESSMENT AND SUPPORT CONSORTIUM STANDARDS

In the same year that the NBPTS began its work, the Council of Chief State School Officers (CCSSO) began parallel work that focuses on what prospective teachers ought to know and be able to do to attain initial teaching licenses in their states. Called the Interstate New Teacher Assessment and Support Consortium, the effort sought to lay out standards for a common core of teaching skills and knowledge for all beginning teachers at all grade levels and subject areas. Recently, the CCSSO has shifted its focus from standards for beginning teachers to all teachers, new and old. In the process, the name was changed, dropping the "new," now to be called the Interstate Teacher Assessment and Support Consortium (InTASC). Together with the NBPTS, it is working to create model standards for "board-compatible" teacher licensing. Although their focuses are different, they are, however, complementary. The InTASC standards are seen as core standards that apply across grade levels and subject matter for all teachers, whereas the NBPTS has developed standards that apply across a grade-level range and are subject specific.

Although all this talk of NBPTS, CCSSO, and InTASC may seem like so much alphabet soup, the educators behind these letters are working hard to develop clear and practical standards. The purpose behind these standards is not only to have teachers across the country possess a common core of professional abilities, but also to lay the foundation for a seamless transition to acquiring the board certification later on. The INTASC standards are, in effect, the "first tier" of skills and knowledge that all new teachers should possess.

Currently, 34 states have developed and implemented teacher-licensing standards that are based on 10 core principles developed by INTASC.[12] These 10 INTASC standards for all beginning teachers are listed on the inside covers of your book. Find more information on INTASC and the standards at the website that accompanies this book.

> ### PAUSE AND REFLECT
>
> 1. What are you doing now to ensure that you meet the INTASC standards as a beginning teacher?
>
> 2. Does the idea of working toward board certification appeal to you? Why or why not?

professional associations

Like other occupational groups such as doctors and teamsters, teachers have associations whose function is to protect their interests and attempt to improve their lot in life. For example, teacher salaries (which are the major cost of schooling) and other educational expenses come out of taxpayers' pockets. Tax revenues are used for many purposes, and intense competition occurs among groups that rely on tax money to support their efforts to fight crime and delinquency, increase aid to the elderly and to the poor, and so on. In the rough-and-tumble world of a democracy, teachers need someone or something to look out for their interests and the interests of the recipients of their services: children. This is the avowed function of many teachers associations. Protection of teachers' rights and improvement in their rewards and working conditions will not just happen. There is an old saying: "Nobody gives you nothin' for nothin'." The advances teachers make will occur largely as a result of their hard work and their willingness to stand up for what they believe.

Our primary focus in this section is on the large "umbrella organizations" of teachers, the **National Education Association (NEA)** and the **American Federation of Teachers (AFT)**. These two groups have the most immediate and sustaining effects on the lives of teachers. Although private-sector unionism fervor has waned in recent decades, the NEA and AFT have emerged as major forces in U.S. education and in the labor movement itself. In 2010, NEA membership numbered 3.2 million; in the same year, the AFT reported a membership of 1.5 million.[13,14] Both associations claim to represent teachers to the federal, state, and local governments; to educational authorities at the state and local levels; and, finally, to the general public. Both organizations also come to the aid of teachers, like those in the vignettes on pages 473 and 474, whose legal rights are being violated or who are being treated shoddily or unethically. It is important to know something about the NEA and the AFT because if you become a teacher, they will claim to be speaking for *you*. In fact, many new teachers report being asked to join a professional association their first day on the job.

As you read the following pages, be aware that the NEA and the AFT are and have been engaged in a struggle for the hearts, minds, and membership dues of teachers for decades. Further, each is concerned with advancing its cause and gaining the support of future teachers. In addition, there is a short feature about one of the newer, smaller professional associations, the Association of American Educators (AAE), which is taking a very different approach than the major professional organizations of teachers.

THE NATIONAL EDUCATION ASSOCIATION

Founded in 1857, the NEA today is a complex institution that operates on the national, state, and local school district levels and serves a diverse clientele of rural, suburban, and urban teachers. The bulk of its 3.2 million or more members are classroom teachers, but also included are teacher aides, administrators, professors, retired educators, and college students preparing to become teachers. The NEA has some 14,000 local affiliate chapters in approximately 80 percent of the nation's school districts.[15]

Services to Members

The NEA offers its members a wide range of services, from an extensive array of publications, to research on issues such as comparative salary scales and the attitudes of teachers on various topics. In addition, its UniServ program has some 1,800 professionals in the field working with teachers, ready to give local teachers help in such specialized areas as collective bargaining.[16] A number of special services are available to members as well, such as travel programs, insurance policies, mutual fund programs, and book club programs.

The NEA and Political Issues

Since the NEA's inception, its goal has been "to elevate the character and advance the interests of the profession of teaching and to promote the cause of education in the United States." In advancing this goal, it regularly comes out against issues such as competency testing of teachers. Despite this stance, since 1987 the NEA has supported the NBPTS, and it has long been a champion of small class sizes and special programs for linguistic and ethnic groups within schools.[17] Further, it has taken forceful positions on other issues. It has, for example, been a vigorous opponent of various voucher plans that call for using public tax monies for religious and other private schools. In addition, the organization has given only lukewarm and qualified support for charter schools.[18]

When it was started a century and a half ago, the NEA tried to speak for all public educators, including both teachers and

> *If one is going to change things, one has to make a fuss and catch the eye of the world.*
>
> —ELIZABETH JANEWAY (1913–2005),
> Novelist and Feminist

"

I ask for philosophy from my union and it gives me politics, partisanship, and public relations. Teachers learn to be pragmatists or they don't survive. Underneath their veneer of practicality, they are dreamers. Truck drivers and longshoremen might not need a philosophical guiding light from their union leaders, but teachers do. Teachers yearn for commitment, for caring, and for conscience.

—SUSAN OHANIAN,
Author and Educational Commentator

administrators alike. That all changed about 40 years ago, when two things happened: first, the work of the organization became more concentrated on improving the lot of public school teachers; and, second, it started to flex its muscles in the political arena. In 1976, the NEA for the first time formally backed a presidential candidate (Jimmy Carter). Since then, it has consistently backed Democratic candidates for national and most state offices.

The NEA has become a strong political player for various reasons. At the time, one political commentator referred to teachers as "bright, articulate, and reasonably well informed, making them naturals for political activism."[19] What was true then is even truer now. Further, the NEA is big and rich. NEA gets its money from mandatory dues. In the 2009–2010 school year, it received $162 from each member teacher and $93.50 from each full-time education support staff member. The NEA's total budget for 2010 is $356 million.[20] That same year, the organization donated $40 million to the Democratic Party for its election races.[21]

Its sheer size, money, and presence in many congressional districts are huge assets to any candidate or party it would care to support. However, the Democratic Party has been the recipient of the great majority of the NEA's political help. In the 2007–2008 election cycle, NEA donated more than $56 million almost exclusively to Democratic races and by a wide margin was the nation's leading political contributor. On the other hand, NEA teachers lean no further to the left than any other large group of Americans. In fact, consistent with previous results, the NEA's own 2005 survey found that members "are slightly more conservative (50%) than liberal (43%) in political philosophy."[22] Many, however, question the wisdom of putting all these human and financial "eggs" into one political basket.

THE AMERICAN FEDERATION OF TEACHERS

The AFT's membership is approximately one-third the size of the NEA's, but this organization represents teachers in key urban areas across the country. Currently, it bargains for teachers in New York City, Chicago, Philadelphia, Cleveland, Pittsburgh, Kansas City, St. Louis, Detroit, Boston, Houston, Dallas, Atlanta, and Washington, D.C.[23]

The AFT's leadership is very clear about placing the organization squarely within the American labor movement. The organization itself is affiliated with the American Federation of Labor and Congress of Industrial Organizations (AFL-CIO), which has a membership of more than 14 million. The AFT alone has more than 1.5 million members, with 43 state affiliates and 3,000 local affiliates nationwide.[24] Much of the AFT's growth in the past five decades has resulted from its success in introducing the collective bargaining process into the annual salary negotiations of teachers. Its aggressive techniques, which include strikes and the threat of strikes, are credited with achieving substantial salary increases for teachers and with forcing the NEA to adopt more militant tactics. On the downside, the shrinking student enrollments in some major cities, which are the AFT's real power base, have preoccupied the organization and sapped its energies.

The AFT's Stance on Issues

Although the AFT is noted for its hard bargaining on bread-and-butter issues such as salaries and benefits, it has also been a defender of academic freedom and greater

reformers in the ranks: the association of american educators

Established in 1994, the **Association of American Educators (AAE)** represents a fresh approach for teachers who are dissatisfied with the two major professional groups. Since its inception, AAE has become the largest nonunion teacher association in the United States. As such, it offers educators an alternative to the nation's teacher unions. Currently, AAE helps to lead a coalition of over 300,000 teachers in all 50 states, teachers whom it claims are focused on professionalism and putting the needs of our children first. Although not necessarily strictly anti-union, AAE is opposed to many of the stands taken by the NEA and the AFT, such as teacher strikes, forced unionism, and opposition to performance pay. AAE has the following key goals:

1. To encourage and support teachers who embrace certain views on education in the United States, such as the view that schools should aim to improve a young person's character as well as his or her intellect.

2. To keep the governance of the organization in the hands of practicing teachers. Currently, more than half the AAE's board of directors comprises classroom teachers who have won national teacher-of-the-year awards.

3. To keep the focus on educational issues and to stay out of politics. In contrast to the $500 to $700 combined annual local, state, and national dues charged by the major organizations, AAE dues are a mere $180, and much of that goes for liability insurance.

This lean organization does not try to offer its members all of the supportive services of its larger rivals. It is, however, turning out to be an alternative for those who are tired of paying hefty dues and who disagree particularly with the political stands and social views of the larger organizations.

---

participation in decision making by teachers. In spite of the fact that the AFT opposes many of the same issues as the NEA, such as vouchers, and shares with it only qualified support for charter schools, the AFT has a more progressive reputation, owing largely to the efforts of its long-time leader Albert Shanker, who died in 1997. Once seen by many as the champion of raw "teacher power" and as concerned only with the good of teachers, Shanker became a strong advocate of educational reform in his later years. He lobbied both his own organization and the public in support of many reform efforts such as the NBPTS, certain kinds of merit pay, higher minimum standards for teachers, and longer and more intense teacher education. In contrast, the NEA has only recently come to support many of these reform efforts.

A Possible Merger?

For more than thirty years, the leaders of both the NEA and the AFT (along with many members of the press) have been discussing the possibility of merging the two groups into one organization that would represent the entire teaching force. The advantages of one giant organization are attractive to many people. It has been suggested that a merged organization's vast political strength in national elections and ability to call for a nationwide school shutdown would give teachers enormous power. Also, the NEA and the AFT historically have spent much of their energy competing with each other to represent teachers in contract talks with local school systems, wasting resources that could otherwise be used to improve education and the professionalism of teachers.

Although a merger would do much to solidify the power of teachers to effect change, internal organizational issues and jealousies have kept the NEA and AFT apart. In 2001, the two organizations stopped fighting and signed the "NEAFT Partnership" agreement, launching "an ongoing effort by the two groups to collaborate in projects ranging from education conferences to political and legal campaigns." A decade later, it would appear that this on-again, off-again romance has fizzled, at least temporarily.[25] In effect, they remain separate and independent, but come together to lobby for common causes.

PAUSE AND REFLECT

1. Once you are established as a teacher, does the idea of becoming active in one of these two professional organizations or unions appeal to you personally? If so, what is the attraction?

2. What questions or concerns, if any, do you have about joining one of the two major teacher organizations?

OTHER PROFESSIONAL ASSOCIATIONS

In addition to the NEA and AFT, many other educational organizations exist. Each supports certain constituents and serves their special interests. Table 15.1 offers a sample of these groups. The ones listed under the heading "Specialized Associations

TABLE 15.1 Nationwide Organizations of Interest to Teachers

Specialized Associations of Teachers

Council for Exceptional Children (www.cec.sped.org)
National Science Teachers Association (www.nsta.org)
National Council of Teachers of English (www.ncte.org)
National Council for the Social Studies (www.ncss.org)
National Association for Music Education (www.menc.org)
National Association for the Education of Young Children (www.naeyc.org)
Association of Career and Technical Education (www.acteonline.org)
International Reading Association (www.reading.org)
National Council of Teachers of Mathematics (www.nctm.org)
American Council on the Teaching of Foreign Language (www.actfl.org)
National Art Education Association (www.naea-reston.org)
American Alliance for Health, Physical Education, Recreation and Dance (www.aahperd.org)
Association for Education Communications and Technology (www.aect.org)
National Association for Gifted Children (www.nagc.org)

Nationwide Special-Interest Groups in Education
National School Boards Association (www.nsba.org)
American Association of School Administrators (www.aasa.org)
Association for Supervision and Curriculum Development (www.ascd.org)
American Educational Research Association (www.aera.net)
Council of Chief State School Officers (www.ccsso.org)

Nationwide Groups Supporting Teacher Education
Association of Teacher Educators (www.ate1.org)

of Teachers" are primarily for teachers of a particular subject matter or area within the life of the school. Under the second heading, "Nationwide Special-Interest Groups in Education," are more broad-based organizations that typically include members of the public, administrators, people from higher education, and teachers. The third heading, "Nationwide Groups Supporting Teacher Education," identifies an organization involved in teacher education. Through journals, in-service training, or professional development institutes, as well as conferences and conventions, such organizations play a vital role in keeping teachers informed about research and developments in their fields. It is here where much of the teacher's professional activity goes on. We urge you to consider joining those associations closest to your interests.

There are also professional associations dedicated specifically to future teachers. The largest of these is the NEA's *Student* Program, which consists of over 60,000 members across more than 1,000 college/university campus chapters and 50 state programs.[26] As a branch of the NEA, the SNEA offers many of the benefits of NEA membership, such as liability insurance when members student teach, access to the NEA's research files, and subscriptions to its regular publications, *The NEA Handbook* and *Today's Education*.

Three other professional groups that are open to prospective teachers include the honor societies of Pi Lambda Theta, Phi Delta Kappa, and Kappa Delta Pi. These associations are international in scope but typically organize around chapters on university or college campuses. They hold regular meetings to discuss recent developments in the field, such as constructivist approaches to learning, brain research, and character education. These organizations provide an excellent opportunity for students to meet other education students in a nonclassroom setting and particularly to meet practicing teachers and administrators in a professional yet informal setting. If membership in such honorary associations interests you, we suggest that you check out their websites; speak to one of your education professors about which, if any, of the organizations are on your campus and how you can learn about them; and call, write, or e-mail the headquarters of these organizations to obtain general information and to learn whether there are chapters on your campus. It is not unheard of for beginning education students to initiate new chapters on their campuses.

WANTED: A NEW PROFESSIONALISM

The era of aggressive trade unionism in the U.S. private sector of the economy has receded in recent years. In its place, a new cooperative spirit has brought about a revival of many of our industries. By putting slogans such as "excellence" and "reengineering" into practice, workers and management have altered the economic landscape. Many see a similar pattern being followed by members of public school teachers' public sector unions. Serious, prolonged teacher strikes are becoming a rarity. Also, we are witnessing the beginnings of a revival similar to that seen in U.S. industry in the guise of the "educational excellence" movement and the "restructuring" efforts currently sweeping through our schools. In our view, the issue of teacher professionalism is very much wrapped up in these broader school renewal efforts. Whether teachers are treated as professionals will depend on the bottom line: the performance of our schools. To promote that performance, teachers must begin, both individually and collectively, with a personal commitment to excellence.

The term *professionalism* in education, however, has begun to acquire some negative connotations. Although professional organizations for teachers have existed for more than a century, only in the last 50 years have they employed aggressive trade union tactics. However, the fear of teachers' unions potential to strike and thus radically disrupt the work world of parents with school-age children has been replaced. Currently, films like *Waiting for "Superman"* and others are portraying teachers' unions as more interested in protecting its members rather than the good of children. Specifically, critics point to their protecting clearly incompetent teachers and resisting educational choices of minority children trapped in failing public schools. If *professionalism* is to mean anything, first and foremost it means looking out for the concerns of one's clients, who in this case are our children.

> *So to all of you who teach, hats off. Yours is an invaluable profession, a calling sure and high and noble, a model we cannot live without if we expect to remain strong and free. Don't quit. Don't even slack off. If ever we needed you, we need you today.*
>
> —CHARLES SWINDOLL,
> Pastor and Radio Broadcaster

your own professional development

Think back over your education and the teachers you have had. Were any of them sincere souls but deadly dull? People of good will, whose classes were unfortunately morgue-like? Teachers who seemed to have a magic touch enabling them to stretch an hour into a week? If you haven't had one of these mind-numbing teachers, think of the social studies teacher in the movie *Ferris Bueller's Day Off* ("Anyone? Anyone?").

> *Education must not any longer be confined to the young. The young must not look forward to its completion; the old must not look back on it as an accompaniment of immaturity. For all people, education must be made to seem a requirement of human life as long as that endures.*
>
> —ISAAC ASIMOV (1920–1992),
> Author of Science Fiction

Once upon a time, these teachers most likely were filled with energy, ideas, and idealism, but something happened—or something didn't happen. They probably survived their first years of teaching and then quietly settled into routines. Then with the passage of time, those routines became mindless. Now, when they enter the classroom, these teachers unknowingly switch over to autopilot. These autopilot teachers undoubtedly went to all of the in-service days, did graduate work after school or during the summers, and probably hold advanced degrees. But something *didn't* happen, because they failed to take personal control of their **professional development**.

WHAT *IS* PROFESSIONAL DEVELOPMENT, ANYWAY?

Professional development is a large term encompassing the efforts both by a school (or school district) and by individual teachers to improve their skills and competencies. In this final chapter, we focus on the professional development efforts of new teachers. Teaching, and particularly "sage-on-the-stage" teaching (where the teacher is the center of attention and information), can be draining, both intellectually and emotionally. Without recharging one's batteries through professional development and learning new theories, methods, and skills, many of the embedded joys and satisfactions of teaching go flat over time. In the 1990s, the U.S. Army had a motto: "Be all you can be! Join the Army." The essence of the professional development activities described here is that they offer ways and means for you as a teacher to "be all you can be."

T (F)

The term *professional development* refers to moving through and up the ranks in the educational hierarchy.

Professional development is a large term encompassing the efforts both by a school (or school district) and by individual teachers to improve their skills and competencies.

THE NEW IMPERATIVE: YOUR OWN PROFESSIONAL DEVELOPMENT

As we have stressed throughout this text, schooling in the United States is changing. Where once schools could be satisfied with teaching basic skills and conveying preset bodies of information, today the shifting societal and economic landscapes are demanding change. We are becoming a "knowledge society" in which the demands on our students, who face the challenge of surviving and thriving in a global economy, increase yearly. A dramatic example can be seen in the rising interest in technological literacy: as American society has become increasingly dependent on electronic information services, the needs and advantages of being comfortable and competent with computers, the Internet, CDs, videodiscs, and networking have become more evident. Of course, the demands on today's students go much further than that.

The field of education has a great deal to learn in this regard from U.S. industry. For two decades, successful businesses and corporations have made a major commitment to "reengineering" or "reinventing" themselves. A good example of this continual growth and development is Apple, the organization led by Steve Jobs, which has introduced a stream of novel electronic products, from the Mac to the iPod, and the iPhone to the iPad. Creatively oriented firms such as Apple make a major investment in their employees; those individuals, in turn, know they must grow as employees.

Similarly, our schools must become **learning organizations**, where the goals and priorities are driven by questions such as "What does this student need to get past his or her individual learning barrier?" and "How can I find the right material or right question to ignite this student's mind?" At the same time, classical educational questions such as "What is most worth knowing?" and "Are students *really* understanding this material?" must be continually revisited and augmented by a new priority for student learning.

This shift in the ground beneath the feet has profound implications for teachers. Rather than a skills trainer or an information dispenser, the new teacher must be a "learning professional." In today's world, that means becoming a continuous learner, committed to one's growth both as a person and as a professional. It means knowing the most current information in one's field and knowing how to share it with students. It means being part of a community of learning with other teachers, both giving and taking knowledge.

Not many decades ago, it was considered adequate for a teacher to obtain an undergraduate education and a teaching license and then have no further training. Today, most states have legislated continuing education for teachers. In fact, in more than half of the states, it is no longer possible to gain permanent licensure. An increasing number of states are requiring teachers to keep up with developments in their fields or specific areas of education.

> *The improvement of understanding is for two ends: first, our own increase of knowledge; second, to enable us to deliver that knowledge to others.*
>
> —JOHN LOCKE (1632–1704),
> English Philosopher

Although we have known a few of what might be called "born teachers" or "naturals," the overwhelming majority of teachers have to learn our craft. In addition, because this "craft" is continually evolving, we need to be continuous learners. The broad, operational vehicle for becoming a continuous learner is professional development. This term refers to a whole range of activities available to help a teacher "stay alive" professionally.

One of the great stumbling blocks to professional development is time. When does a teacher have the time? A recent study

Some of the most productive staff development is done working on projects with close colleagues.

(Thomas Barwick/Jupiterimages.)

by the National Staff Development Council found that teachers in the United States are given significantly less time and support for high-quality professional learning than their counterparts in other developed nations. The study compared U.S. teachers' average of 1,080 hours per year in classroom teaching time with that of teachers from European and Asian counties, where primary school teachers teach 803 hours per year and secondary teachers only 664 hours per year.[27] The report states, "A significant number of schools in high-achieving countries build time into teachers' work day or week for professional development, prominently including forms of collaborative work on instructional issues."[28] As this report strongly suggests, more time for professional development should become a major educational priority.

PROFESSIONAL DEVELOPMENT OPPORTUNITIES

Teachers have two broad categories of professional development available to them: programs offered by institutions and self-initiated activities.

Most schools and their districts sponsor professional development in the form of **in-service programs** such as courses, workshops, or short retreats. These professional development programs often focus on some particular problem or issue such as communication with parents, or target some new area such as environmental education. (The Video Case *Parent–Teacher Conference* shows two teachers role-playing how the conversation between parent and teacher might go at conference time.) Or, for instance, if students in a particular school are getting unsatisfactory grades on standardized mathematics achievement tests, the district may choose to provide special training for the faculty, or the district may decide to switch to a new, supposedly better mathematics program, a change that will also require special training for the faculty.

A recent study found that two out of three teachers reported that they had structured opportunities for collaboration with fellow teachers. However, this collaboration time amounted to only 2.7 hours each week. Teachers named four areas they believe are most essential for their continuing professional development: content or subject matter, classroom management, students with special needs, and technology. On the other hand, fewer than half reported their professional development focused on teaching students with disabilities (42%) and on English language learners (27%).[29]

Supervision

Another form of professional development comes through supervision. During a teacher's early years in the profession, school districts provide professional advice that amounts to one-on-one help. For instance, if you are a new high school teacher, your department head may observe your classes regularly and discuss the observations with you; if you are an elementary school teacher, your building principal or lead teacher may make regular visits and follow them up with feedback sessions. Although supervision can sometimes be quite threatening, particularly to nontenured teachers, it offers an opportunity to obtain valuable insight and information about your teaching techniques and skills.

Mentoring

In recent years, many school districts have instituted mentoring programs whereby more experienced teachers are assigned to assist beginners. The same study cited above found that three out of four new teachers were participating in special induction programs, and four out of five had been assigned mentors. Regrettably, these supports were available for a significantly lower percentage of teachers in high-poverty, high-minority schools.[30] (Mentoring is discussed in more detail in Chapter 14, "What Can the New Teacher Expect?") Along with special training, these mentors may receive a reduction in teaching responsibilities, a salary increase, or both. Mentoring programs formalize and make more systematic the time-honored process in which an experienced teacher takes a rookie under his or her wing, helping the beginner make the theory-into-practice transition and serving as a nonjudgmental colleague.

TeachSource VIDEO CASE

Parent-Teacher Conference

Go to the Education CourseMate website to watch the clips, study the artifacts in the case, and reflect on the following questions:

1. Several types of continuous learning opportunities are described in this chapter. Which are depicted in this case?

2. Earlier in the chapter, the authors described several aspects of teaching that either contributed to the case *for* teaching as a profession or contributed to the case *against* teaching as a profession. Do you believe that conducting parent–teacher conferences is a responsibility that can be used as evidence either for or against teaching as a profession? Explain your opinion.

Group Study

Group study is yet another common form of continuous learning for the teacher. It often takes the form of committee work. When a problem arises in the school, for which there is no apparent solution, a group of people takes upon itself the task of exploring the problem, with a view toward recommending an enlightened course of action. In recent years, to obtain opinions from outside the school, teachers and administrators have begun inviting community residents to these study groups. Typical issues these groups might address include curricular alternatives, dealing with bullying on the playground, an analysis of the unused education resources in the community, a writing-across-the-curriculum program, and the potential benefits and costs of using support professionals in a high school.

Graduate Study

A popular form of self-initiated professional development, and a way for you to continue to learn, is to take courses or to work toward an advanced degree. Most colleges and universities offer courses suitable for and interesting to teachers. Special and regular courses are offered in the evening, on weekends, and during the summer vacation. Many universities are now offering computer-based distance-learning courses, which enable teachers (and others) to do advanced study without leaving their homes. These courses and degree programs not only allow teachers to gain a deeper understanding of their work but also make it possible for some teachers to train for other jobs in education, such as guidance counseling, administration, or college teaching.

Independent Study

One aim of education is to develop the ability to engage in independent study. Independent study is jargon for being able to "go it alone." Although this approach is much discussed among educators, students seem to get little actual practice in choosing and systematically investigating their own areas of interest. Nevertheless, self-initiated independent study is one of the most important means for continual self-renewal available to you as a teacher. Teachers are confronted daily with things they do not understand about children and knowledge and about human learning:

- Is there anything in this discussion about learning styles, and how I can apply it in my classroom?
- What does the new brain research suggest about teaching topic A and subject B?
- What are the fundamental skills of composition that children should know?
- How can I help my students use history for their own benefit?

Such questions are daily grist for the teacher's independent study mill. Answering them—that is, engaging in this kind of independent study—used to mean traipsing off to a library and haunting the stacks for information. Today, online search engines, such as Google, bring with a few keyboard clicks a flood of information, theory, and advice. Even if you cannot find teachers in your own building who are interested in a particular question or issue, you don't have to go on this quest alone. The Internet has come to the rescue! Google, for example, has established the Google Teachers Center, a portal to all sorts of useful resources and materials. One of these resources is Google for Educators Discussion Groups, where you can join a "virtual group" centered on a particular topic or start your own group.

Of course, your study should not be confined to professional problems. Your own personal interests may lead you into such areas as organic gardening, physical fitness, classic movies, the politics of colonial America, the humanizing of the corporate state, or harnessing the media. Not by professional problems of teaching and learning alone doth the teacher live!

Systematic Reflection on Practice

As we said at the beginning of this book, of all the approaches to professional development mentioned here, *the most important* is developing the habit of reflecting on one's practice. If teachers, whether new or old, are to improve, they need to make systematic reflection on what is happening in their classrooms a regular part of their professional lives. In the "spaces" in their lives—the time between classes, driving home, working out at the gym, or cooking dinner—they need to ask themselves questions like these:

- What went right in class today?
- What didn't work?

- Which students am I not reaching, and what should I do about it?
- What can I do to get my uninvolved students more engaged?
- Are there other ways of presenting this material that will connect with students who have different learning styles?

Becoming a reflective practitioner—that is, developing the habit of systematic reflection on your work—is *the royal road* to excellence in teaching!

CHARACTERISTICS OF EFFECTIVE PROFESSIONAL DEVELOPMENT

For many practicing teachers, the notion of professional development often conjures up memories of trudging off to after-school gatherings where they were lectured to by strangers on topics that held little interest or relevance to their teaching. Or maybe it meant spending the summer taking state-mandated courses or workshops required to renew their licenses. Such activities are, at best, minimal means to keep up to date with the teaching field, and, at worst, major stumbling blocks to true educational reform. Although a school district that hires a teacher and a state that licenses a teacher have the right to require a teacher's continuing education, such a top-down approach is not likely to serve the needs of children in this new century.

Effective professional development, then, does the following for teachers:

- Enables teachers to develop further expertise in subject content, teaching strategies, uses of technologies, and other essential elements of teaching to high standards
- Focuses on teachers as central to student learning, yet includes all members of the school community
- Focuses on individual, collegial, and organizational improvement
- Respects and nurtures the intellectual and leadership capacity of teachers, principals, and others in the school community
- Reflects the best available research and practice in teaching, learning, and leadership
- Promotes continuous inquiry and improvement of schools
- Is planned collaboratively by those who will participate in and facilitate that development
- Requires substantial time and resources
- Is driven by a coherent long-term plan
- Is evaluated ultimately on the basis of its effects on teacher instruction and student learning, and uses this assessment to guide subsequent professional development efforts

> *The teacher who has stopped learning is a deadening influence rather than a help to students being initiated into the ways of learning.*
>
> —MORTIMER ADLER (1902–2001),
> American Educator and Philosopher

Educational reform expert Michael Fullan suggests that teachers seeking to improve themselves are characterized by four attitudes: (1) They accept that it is possible to improve; (2) they are ready to be self-critical; (3) they recognize better practice than their own; and, (4) most importantly, they are willing to learn what they have to learn to do what needs to be done.[31] In our view, a teacher who is not engaged in learning activities because of lack of opportunity or lack of personal incentive is stunting his or her own career and is a barrier to the educational reform we need. In the Voices from the Classroom feature, one teacher describes the moment she first realized how deeply the commitment to lifelong learning can run among teachers.

QUESTIONS YOU SHOULD ASK ABOUT PROFESSIONAL DEVELOPMENT OPPORTUNITIES

The qualities of the professional development opportunities should be a key factor when you are considering taking a teaching position. In particular, you should find answers to the following questions:

1. Are the schools conceived of as **learning communities**, in which everyone—adults and children alike—are always learning?

2. Do teachers, specialists, and administrators see their continuing educational growth as an integral part of their workday?

3. Does the district's definition of "professional development" take into account whatever contributes to making an educator more effective?

4. What professional development costs are to be borne by you or by the school district or the state?

> " *A child, unlike any other, yet identical to all who have preceded and all who will follow, sits in a classroom today—hopeful, enthusiastic, curious. In that child sleeps the vision and the wisdom of the ages. The touch of a teacher will make the difference.*
>
> —SHARON M. DRAPER,
> Teacher of the Year 1997, Board-Certified Teacher

VOICES from the classroom

Professionalism

Theresa Madison teaches 10th-grade language arts at Brighton High School in Brighton, Massachusetts.

Before I began teaching, I had a certain vision of what the world of teachers would be like. I prepared myself for hearing a lot of "when you've been around as long as I have" and "when you get to be my age, you'll understand." I felt a sort of pre-embarrassment for all the mistakes I would probably make before I "got it." To me, the profession presented itself as a kind of hierarchy where the big cheese of the school would offer condescending advice and rolled eyes at my rookie mishaps.

Now, only six months into the experience, I am happy to say that my fears were quite wrong. Not too long ago, I went to visit a colleague of mine, Jane, in her classroom during one of her planning periods. She's been a teacher for about six or seven years and at our school for only three. About a minute or two into our conversation, I noticed that the door that adjoined her room with Mrs. Conner's room was open and students were moving between the two. Soon Mrs. Conner herself came bustling in and out of Jane's room, looking for glue sticks and getting a clarification about some graphic organizer.

After asking what was going on, I made a concerted effort to hide my surprise. Jane was asked to take on a smaller class load this year and to spend the remaining time as a literacy coach. She told me that the job included sitting in on classes for a week or so and then working one-on-one with that particular teacher to experiment with different instructional practices and techniques. But Mrs. Conner? She had been teaching for 30 years. This was a woman who had a way with students, parents, and other teachers that I wished I could bottle and sell. It was one thing to smile and nod at staff meetings when younger teachers spoke, but to invite a teacher with far fewer years on the job into your classroom was quite a different scenario.

I could only describe the feeling as humbling. Nobody, it seemed, was out to get me or laugh at my naiveté. The more I began to look around, the more I noticed that many of my colleagues were "age blind." The task at hand was to educate students, and if someone had a better way of doing things or if some workshop came along that could benefit a teacher's practice, then many of these educators were up for another learning experience. I had always heard that teachers were learners for life, but I wasn't sure how many of them bought that old cliché. As it turns out, seeking more for our students and our own practice is not considered a sign of weakness or a stigma by all of those scary veterans; it's simply part of being a professional.

OUR FINAL WORD

Becoming a teacher may be compared with sculpting a work of art from a piece of stone. The difference is that the teacher is both the sculptor and the stone. The teacher begins with a vision of what he or she wants to be and then sets to work transforming the vision into a reality. The process requires an understanding of the material with which one is working—the self—and of the tools one can use. It also requires a vision of the teacher one desires to become. Finally, it takes long hours of chipping away and then polishing the surfaces. To be a teacher, particularly a teacher who is continuously moving forward, is a lifelong commitment to be an artist.

WHY TEACH? YOUR FINAL WORD

In your journal or online at this textbook's website, respond to the following questions.

1. Do you aspire to become board certified? Why or why not? Explain your answer.

2. Which of the ideas for lifelong professional development described in this chapter appeal to you most? Why?

3. Do teachers need a professional organization? Ideally, which essential functions would such a group perform?

KEY TERMS

American Federation of Teachers (AFT) (487)
Association of American Educators (AEE) (490)
in-service programs (495)
learning communities (499)
learning organizations (494)

National Board for Professional Teaching Standards (NBPTS) (484)
National Education Association (NEA) (487)
profession (475)
professional development (493)

FOR FURTHER INFORMATION

WEB RESOURCES

American Federation of Teachers. Available at **www.aft.org.**

The AFT's website provides information on the organization and its programs, commentary on current issues, and links to other interesting web pages. Contact the American Federation of Teachers, 555 New Jersey Avenue, NW, Washington, DC 20001.

National Board for Professional Teacher Standards. Available at **www.nbpts.org.**

This website has extensive information on the organization and the standards as well as extensive resources of interest to teachers.

National Education Association. Available at **www.nea.org.**

This website offers a great deal of information about the NEA and its programs. Contact the National Education Association, 1201 16th Street, NW, Washington, DC 20036, (202) 833-4000, fax: (202) 822-7974.

PRINT RESOURCES

Dan C. Lortie, *Schoolteacher: A Sociological Study* (Chicago: University of Chicago Press, 1975).

This classic book presents a sociological view of the ethos of the teaching profession, that pattern of orientations and sentiments that are peculiar to teachers. Although somewhat dated, the book nevertheless provides striking insights into the work of the teacher.

National Commission on Teaching and America's Future, *No Dream Denied: A Pledge to America's Children* (Washington, DC: Author, 2003). Available at **www.nctaf.org.**

This report is a follow-up to the bipartisan commission's initial report, *What Matters Most: Teaching for America's Future.* It examines issues related to teacher retention; strengthening teacher preparation, accreditation, and licensure; and ways to build a professionally rewarding career in teaching.

Rod Paige, *The War Against Hope: How the Teachers' Unions Hurt Children, Hinder Teachers, and Endanger Public Education* (Nashville, TN: Thomas Nelson, 2007).

This strongly opinionated book by former U.S. Secretary of Education Rod Paige lays out a case against the major teachers unions, explains how Paige thinks they are hurting teachers and children, and suggests how the profession ought to be reformed.

The Education CourseMate website for this text offers many helpful resources. Go to www.cengagebrain.com to access the TeachSource Video Cases and other TeachSource videos, flashcards, interactive quizzes, the eBook, reflection and enrichment activities, a state standards resource center, and other study aids.

Before You Close the Book ...

... Let's return to our first question, "Why teach?" Why should you select a career in

the teaching profession from the myriad of occupational choices open to you? While only you can answer these questions, we would like to offer a few final thoughts to help you grapple with them. First, however, we need to acknowledge up-front that we are biased. We both have loved being teachers, as have our wives. Also, the people we like and admire most in the world are teachers. And the individuals whose lives have inspired us most throughout our lives have been our teachers.

But we have worked hard in *Those Who Can, Teach* to present an honest, warts-and-all picture of the teaching profession. Like every occupation, it has its pluses and minuses. Teaching is special, however; it affects people in a deeply personal way. Think again about some of the details we reported in the first chapter, "Why Teach?"

- An incredible 96 percent of new teachers said they teach because it "is the work they *love* to do"! Surely there isn't another occupation that generates such enthusiasm.
- In a survey of school administrators, these school leaders are enormously enthusiastic about the new generation of teachers entering their schools. *Ninety-eight percent* described their new teachers as "motivated" and "energetic."
- In another study, high school graduates were asked about who they believe has most influenced them, and *three out of five* said that person was a teacher.
- The general public, too, holds teachers in extremely high regard. When asked to rate which of eight professions (including physician, lawyer, nurse, and journalist) provided the greatest benefit to society, 62 percent selected teachers. Teachers were cited *four times more* than the second choice, physicians.

This is compelling evidence that teaching is a deeply satisfying and much appreciated occupation. But here are some other points we think you should consider:

- Unless you are the next Bill Gates or Paris Hilton, you will have to work. Whether you are a worker in a Dilbert-like office cubicle or a forest ranger in a national park, some questions will regularly occur to you, such as, "Is what I'm doing, what I'm spending my life on, *really* significant? Is what I'm doing with my life making a difference or simply putting bread on my table and clothes on my back?" One of the greatest benefits of being a teacher is that you never have to worry about these kinds of questions. You will always be aware that you are doing profoundly important work. As a teacher, you will be changing people. You will always know that you are making *marks* on students' minds and characters. After a few years of teaching, it will be a regular occurrence to get calls and letters from former students thanking you for what you have done for them.
- You will be working with high-minded, dedicated individuals. Of course, there will be the occasional person who rushes into school in the morning unprepared and almost runs over students in her race to get out of the building at three o'clock. But they are rare. Individuals who select careers in education represent a subgroup of people who are deeply concerned about the next

generation. They want children to get a good start in life, to gain the knowledge that will give them real access to a good life. They are concerned that young people forge the habits that constitute good character. In surveys stretching over thirty years and more, *seven out of ten* practicing teachers report that their primary reason for originally selecting teaching is their "*desire to work with young people.*" Their second reason is their conviction about the importance of education to society. These are the kinds of people you will be working with and be surrounded by as a teacher. Not a bad team to be on!

- It is a truism that no one goes into teaching for the big money. On the other hand, there are important quality-of-life issues to consider. We quipped earlier in the book about the three best reasons to be a teacher: June, July and August. But summer vacations, along with winter and spring breaks, are not to be dismissed. Only having to show up for work about half the days in the year gives teachers a great deal of control over their own lives. While much of this so-called free time is spent in study and professional development, much of it is at your own disposal.

- All work, whether as a plumber or a lawyer, falls after a while into a pattern. You have done it before . . . and before that. The work becomes routine. And, yes, teaching has its patterns and its routines. Still we know of no other career where there are more elements that fight against the work become routine or boring. Each student is different, with different talents and learning styles and different learning barriers or problems. Each class has its own personality. The content you teach, whether as a second-grade teacher or a high school social studies teacher, has built-in mysteries and challenges. You will never know all there is to know about your content or about the various ways to teach it. The work of teachings is endlessly fascinating.

the habit of reflection

The "Why teach?" question is one theme of this book. The other is reflection, the practice of getting the full richness of the meaning out of your experiences. The teacher without this habit is like the golfer who plays regularly but never really thinks about what he is doing. In essence, he is *practicing his mistakes*. The unreflective teacher, too, makes the same mistakes over and over. Before you lay aside this book, we urge you—one last time—to stop and reflect on some important issues. You can respond on the blank lines that follow, on a separate sheet of paper, or online at the Education CourseMate website, where an interactive version of this exercise is available. In the exercise, we ask you to think about three main questions: things you have learned about yourself; things you have learned about teaching and education, and aspects of teaching and education you still want to know more about.

    Visit the Education CourseMate website and answer these questions online.

1) What are the three most important things you have learned about yourself during this course?

1. _____

2. _____

3. _____

2) List at least five qualities you have that will make you a successful teacher.

1. _____

2. _____

3. _____

4. _____

5. _____

3) What are the three most important things you have learned about teaching and education, things that you did not know before the course began?

1. _____

_____

2. _____

_____

3. _____

_____

4) What aspects of teaching and education do you want to know more about? Questions you still want to have answered? Concerns you still have? List at least three questions or concerns.

1. _____

_____

2. _____

_____

3. _____

_____

The habits of continually probing and examining your reasons for teaching and of routinely reflecting on what you have done in the classroom will make you a true professional, one like the teacher in the poem below.

ONE TEACHER'S ANSWER

This story-poem, "What Teachers Make," by poet Taylor Mali provides us with a stirring answer to the question, "Why teach?"

What Teachers Make

by Taylor Mali (www.taylormali.com)

He says the problem with teachers is
What's a kid going to learn
from someone who decided his best option in life
was to become a teacher?
He reminds the other dinner guests that it's true
what they say about teachers:
Those who can, do; those who can't, teach.

I decide to bite my tongue instead of his
and resist the temptation to remind the dinner guests
that it's also true what they say about lawyers.

Because we're eating, after all, and this is polite company.
I mean, you're a teacher, Taylor.
Be honest. What do you make?

And I wish he hadn't done that—
asked me to be honest—
because, you see, I have this policy:
if you ask for it, then I have to let you have it.

You want to know what I make?

I make kids work harder than they ever thought they could.
I can make a C+ feel like a Congressional Medal of Honor
and an A— feel like a slap in the face.
Don't waste my time with anything less
than your very best.

I make kids sit through 40 minutes of study hall
in absolute silence.

I make parents tremble in fear when I call home.
I make parents see their children for who they are
and what they can be.

You want to know what I make?

I make kids wonder,
I make them question.
I make them criticize.
I make them apologize and mean it.
I make them write, write, write.
I make them read.
I make them spell *definitely beautiful, definitely beautiful, definitely beautiful*
over and over and over again until they will never misspell either
one of those words again.
I make them show all their work in math
and hide it on their final drafts in English.
I make them understand that if you've got *this,*
then you follow *this,*
and if someone ever tries to judge you
by what you make, you give them *this.*

Here, let me say it simply, so you know what I say is true:
Teachers make a difference! Now what about you?

and one final, final word

When we were racking our brains for a title for this book, someone reminded us of the nasty comment George Bernard Shaw, the late-nineteenth-century Irish playwright, made about teachers: "Those who can, do. Those who can't, teach." While possibly true then (which we doubt), it certainly is false now. In recent decades, the importance of education for the well-being of individuals *and* society has become more and more clear. Much of America's power and prosperity has resulted from our deep commitment to education. And teachers have been the keys to our educational achievements. One thing is crystal clear to thoughtful observers: we need even better schools and better teachers, and people are answering the call. Shaw was dead wrong. **Those who can, teach.**

websites of U.S. state teacher licensure offices

A teaching license is valid only in the state for which it is issued, and licensure and testing requirements are never static. If you are planning to move to another state, you should contact that state's licensure office, as listed below. Because the websites for these offices often change, if you experience difficulty reaching anyone of them, you can link to any state agency by going to www.ccsso.org and clicking on the state education agencies bar. When you contact the state licensure office, indicate the type of license you are receiving from your current state and which national tests you have taken, and ask for application materials and procedures for obtaining licensure in the new state. Another source of information about licensure requirements will be the actual districts to which you apply.

On the Education CourseMate website, you will be able to find information about your state's certification and licensure requirements, the Council for Exceptional Children, and even state standards for specific teaching areas like literacy, science and social studies. Check it out!

Alabama	www.alsde.edu/html/home.asp
Alaska	www.educ.state.ak.us/teachercertification
Arizona	www.ade.state.az.gov/certification
Arkansas	www.arkansased.org/educators/licensure.html
California	www.ctc.ca.gov
Colorado	www.cde.state.co.us/index_license.htm
Connecticut	www.sde.ct.gov/sde/site/
Delaware	www.doe.state.de.us
District of Columbia	http://dcps.dc.gov/portal/site/DCPS/
Florida	www.fldoe.org/edcert
Georgia	www.gapsc.com/Certification/index.asp
Hawaii	http://doe.k12.hi.us/teacher/index.htm
Idaho	www.sde.idaho.gov/site/teacher_certification/
Illinois	www.isbe.net/certification/
Indiana	www.doe.in.gov/educatorlicensing/
Iowa	www.state.ia.us/boee/
Kansas	www.ksde.org/
Kentucky	www.kyepsb.net/certification/index.asp
Louisiana	www.doe.state.la.us/lde/tsac/home.html
Maine	www.maine.gov/education/cert/index.html
Maryland	www.marylandpublicschools.org/MSDE/divisions/certification/certification_branch/
Massachusetts	www.doe.mass.edu/educators/e_license.html
Michigan	www.michigan.gov/mde
Minnesota	http://education.state.mn.us/MDE/Teacher_Support/Educator_Licensing/index.html
Mississippi	www.mde.k12.ms.us/ed_licensure/index.html
Missouri	http://dese.mo.gov/divteachqual/teachcert/
Montana	http://opi.mt.gov/Cert/index.html
Nebraska	www.education.ne.gov/tcert/
Nevada	http://nvteachers.doe.nv.gov/
New Hampshire	www.education.nh.gov/certification/index.htm
New Jersey	www.nj.gov/education/educators/license/
New Mexico	www.ped.state.nm.us/licensure/
New York	http://ohe33.nysed.gov/tcert/
North Carolina	www.dpi.state.nc.us/work4ncschools/employment/
North Dakota	www.nd.gov/espb/licensure/
Ohio	www.ode.state.oh.us/
Oklahoma	http://sde.state.ok.us/
Oregon	www.tspc.state.or.us/
Pennsylvania	https://www.tcs.ed.state.pa.us/
Puerto Rico	http://de.gobierno.pr/tags/certificacion-de-maestros
Rhode Island	www.ride.ri.gov/educatorquality/certification/
South Carolina	www.scteachers.org/Cert/index.cfm
South Dakota	http://doe.sd.gov/oatq/teachercert.asp

Tennessee	www.tn.gov/education/lic/
Texas	www.sbec.state.tx.us
Utah	www.schools.utah.gov/cert/
Vermont	http://education.vermont.gov/new/html/maincert.html
Virginia	www.doe.virginia.gov/teaching/licensure/index.shtml
Washington	www.k12.wa.us/certification/
West Virginia	http://wvde.state.wv.us/certification/
Wisconsin	http://dpi.wi.gov/tepdl/

Wyoming	http://ptsb.state.wy.us/
U.S. Virgin Islands	www.doe.vi/
United States Department of Defense Dependent Schools	www.dodea.edu/home/

Chapter 1

1. The Apple Monster: Where Teachers Meet and Learn has an additional list of positive reasons: Fifty Reasons to Love Teaching, available at **http://theapple.monster.com/benefits/articles/9628-50-reasons-to-love-teaching.**

2. Sharon Feiman-Nemser and Robert E. Floden, "The Culture of Teaching," in Merlin C. Witrock, ed., *The Handbook of Research on Teaching* (New York: Macmillan, 1986), pp. 510–511.

3. David Haselkorn and Louis Harris, The Essential Profession: A National Survey of Public Attitudes Toward Teaching, Educational Opportunity and School Reform (Belmont, MA: Recruiting New Teachers, Inc., 1998), p. 2.

4. Dan Lortie, *Schoolteacher* (Chicago: University of Chicago Press, 1975), p. 102.

5. David Haselkorn and Louis Harris, The Essential Profession: A National Survey of Public Attitudes Toward Teaching, Educational Opportunity and School Reform (Belmont, MA: Recruiting New Teachers, Inc., 1998), p. 2.

6. Mihaly Csikszentmihalyi and Jane McCormack, "The Influence of Teachers," *Phi Delta Kappan* 67, no. 6 (February 1986), pp. 415–419.

7. *A Man for All Seasons*, DVD, directed by Fred Zinneman, 1966, Highland Films Company.

8. John Goodlad, *A Place Called School* (New York: McGraw-Hill, 1984); Judith W. Little, "The Persistence of Privacy," *Teachers College Record* (Summer 1990), pp. 509–536.

9. Leslie A. Swetnam, "Media Distortion of the Teacher Image," *The Clearing House* (September/October 1992), p. 30.

10. Ibid., pp. 30–32.

11. The Public Agenda, *A Sense of Calling: Who Teaches and Why* (New York: Public Agenda, 2000), p. 13.

12. Ibid.

13. Ibid., p. 36.

14. Ibid., p. 10.

15. Ibid.

16. Ibid., p. 12.

17. Ibid.

18. The MetLife Survey of the American Teacher: Collaborating for Student Success, April, 2010, p. 45. Available at **http://www.metlife.com/assets/cao/contributions/foundation/american-teacher/MetLife_Teacher_Survey_2009.pdf.**

19. Ibid.

20. Ibid., p. 12.

21. The Public Agenda, *Attitudes About Teaching* (New York: Public Agenda, 2003), p. 14.

Chapter 2

1. Elliot Eisner, *The Educational Imagination: On the Design and Evaluation of School Programs*, 3d ed. (Belmont, CA: Wadsworth, 1976).

2. Mike Rose, *Possible Lives* (New York: Penguin, 1995).

3. James Shaver and William Strong, *Facing Value Decisions: Rationale Building for Teachers* (Belmont, CA: Wadsworth, 1976).

4. Among the leading spokesmen for this position are Michael Apple and Henry Giroux. See Michael Apple, *Education and Power*, 2nd ed. (New York: Routledge, 1995); Henry Giroux, "Critical Pedagogy: Cultural Politics and the Discourse of Experience," *Journal of Education* 67, no. 2 (1987), pp. 23–41.

5. Paulo Freire, *The Pedagogy of the Oppressed* (New York: Herder and Herder, 1970).

6. Jacques Barzun, *Begin Here: The Forgotten Conditions of Teaching and Learning* (Chicago: University of Chicago Press, 1991), pp. 4, 14.

7. International Baccalaureate: Country Information for the United States. Available at **http://www.ibo.org/country/US/index.cfm.**

8. Thomas Jefferson, "A Bill for the More General Diffusion of Knowledge," in *Public and Private Papers*, ed. Tom Wicker (New York: Vintage Books/Library of America, 1990), p. 39.

9. Jean Anyon, "Ghetto Schooling: A Political Economy of Urban Reform," in *Exploring Education: An Introduction to the Foundations of Education*, 2nd ed., ed. A. Sadovnik, P. Cookson, and S. Semel (Boston: Allyn & Bacon, 2001), p. 53.

10. Emile Durkheim, "Education; Its Nature and Role," in *Exploring Sociocultural Themes in Education*, 2nd ed., ed. J. Strouse (Columbus, OH: Merrill Prentice Hall, 2001), p. 57.

11. Philip W. Jackson, *Life in Classrooms* (New York: Teachers College Press, 1990).

12. Ibid., p. 16.

13. Benjamin S. Bloom, *Taxonomy of Educational Objectives* (Boston, MA: Allyn and Bacon, 1956). Copyright (c) 1984 by Pearson Education.

14. C. Yecke, *The War on Excellence: The Rising Tide of Mediocrity in America's Middle Schools* (Westport, CT: Praeger, 2003).

15. Ibid.,

16. Hayes Mizell, Keynote speech, 2004 Conference of the National School Board Association's Council of Urban Boards of Education.

17. Elissa Gootman, "Trying to Find Solutions in Chaotic Middle Schools," *The New York Times*, January 3, 2007. Available at **http://www.nytimes.com/2007/01/03/education/03middle.html?ex=1325480400&en=a632ad2a32cd6973&ei=5090&partner=rssuserland& emc=rss.**

18. Jaana Juvonen, Vi-Nhuan Le, Tessa Kaganoff, Catherine Augustine, and Louay Constant, *Focus on the Wonder Years: Challenges Facing the American Middle School* (Santa Monica, CA: RAND, 2004). Available at **http://www.rand.org/publications/MG/MG139/.**

19. Mizell, op. cit.

20. Grace Chen, "Should Sixth Grade Be in Elementary School or Middle School?" *Public School Review*, March 30, 2008. Available at **http://www.publicschoolreview.com/articles/13.**

21. Bob Herbert, "Putting Our Brains on Hold," *The New York Times*, August 6, 2010. Available at **www.nytimes.com/2010/08/07/opinion/07herbert.html?_r=1.**

22. Peter D. Hart Research Associates/Public Opinion Strategies, Rising to the Challenge: Are High School Graduates Prepared for College and Work? A Study of Recent High School Graduates, College Instructors, and Employers (Washington, DC: Achieve Inc., February 2005).

23. Janet Quint, Saskia Levy Thompson, and Margaret Bald, with Julia Bernstein and Laura Sztejnberg, *Preface of Relationships, Rigor, and Readiness: Strategies for Improving High Schools*, MDRC Publication, October 2008. Available at **http://www.mdrc.org/publications/498/preface.html.**

24. High School Dropout Crisis Threatens U.S. Economic Growth and Competitiveness, Witnesses Tell House Panel, May 12, 2009 6:15 PM. Available at **http://edlabor.house.gov/newsroom/2009/05/high-school-dropout-crisis-thr.shtml.**

25. Bill Gates, Untitled Speech, Governors' National Education Summit on High Schools, February 26, 2005. Available at **http://www.admin.mtu.edu/ctlfd/EdPsychReadings/BillGate.pdf.**

26. Arthur G. Powell, Eleanor Farrar, and David K. Cohen, The Shopping Mall High School: Winners and Losers in the Educational Marketplace (Boston: Houghton Mifflin, 1985).

27. Theodore Sizer, Horace's Compromise: The Dilemma of the American High School (Boston: Houghton Mifflin, 1984).

28. About the International Baccalaureate. Available at http://www.ibo.org/general/who.cfm.

29. "Find an IB World School." Available at http://www.ibo.org/school/search/index.cfm?programmes=&country=US&region=&find_schools=Find.

30. In preparing this section, we have drawn on the following studies: W. B. Brookover, Effective Secondary Schools (Philadelphia: Research for Better Schools, 1981); R. Edmonds, "Effective Schools for the Urban Poor," Educational Leadership 32 (1979), pp. 15–17; M. Rutter et al., Fifteen Thousand Hours (Cambridge, MA: Harvard University Press, 1979); J. Stallings and G. Mohlman, School Policy, Leadership Style, Teacher Change and Student Behavior in Eight Secondary Schools (Mountain View, CA: Stalling Teaching and Learning Institute for the National Institute of Education, 1981); R. Blum, Effective Schooling Practices: A Research Synthesis (Portland, OR: Northwest Regional Education Laboratory, April 1984); H. J. Walberg, "Productive Teaching and Instruction: Assessing the Knowledge Base," Phi Delta Kappan 71 (February 1990), pp. 470–478; T. Toch, In the Name of Excellence (New York: Oxford University Press, 1991); Richard J. Murname and Frank Levy, "What General Motors Can Teach U.S. Schools About the Proper Role of Markets in Education Reform," Phi Delta Kappan 78 (October 1996), pp. 113–116; P. J. Kannapel and S. K. Clements with D. Taylor and T. Hibpshman, Inside the Black Box of High-Performing High-Poverty Schools (Lexington, KY: Prichard Committee for Academic Excellence, 2005), retrieved February 17, 2005, from http://www.prichardcommittee.org/FordStudy/FordReportJE.pdf.

31. David C. Berliner, "Effective Classroom Teaching: The Necessary but Not Sufficient Condition for Developing Exemplary Schools." In Research on Exemplary Schools, ed. Gilbert R. Austin and Herbert Garber (Orlando, FL: Academic Press, 1985), pp. 127–154.

32. Peabody-Vanderbilt University website. Accessed August 18, 2010, from http://peabody.vanderbilt.edu/x12192.xml.

Chapter 3

1. Susan Aud, Mary Ann Fox, and Angelina Kewal Ramani, Status and Trends in the Education of Racial and Ethnic Groups (Washington, DC: U.S. Department of Education, National Center for Education Statistics, 2010), p. iii. Available at http://nces.ed.gov/pubsearch/pubsinfo.asp?pubid=2010015.

2. Ibid., pp. 8–9.

3. James A. Banks and Cherry A. McGee Banks, Multicultural Education: Issues and Perspectives, 6th ed. (Somerset, NJ: John Wiley & Sons, 2007), p. 1.

4. Carl A. Grant and Christine E. Sleeter, "Race, Class, Gender, and Disability in the Classroom," in James A. Banks and Cherry A. McGee Banks, eds., Multicultural Education: Issues and Perspectives, 6th ed. (Somerset, NJ: John Wiley & Sons, 2007), pp. 66–73.

5. Leonard Davidman and Patricia T. Davidman, Teaching with a Multicultural Perspective: A Practical Guide (New York: Addison-Wesley, 2001), pp. 76–80.

6. Geneva Gay, Culturally Responsive Teaching: Theory, Research, and Practice (New York: Teachers College Press, 2000); and Gloria Ladson-Billings, Crossing Over to Canaan: The Journey of New Teachers in Diverse Classrooms (San Francisco: Jossey-Bass, 2001).

7. National Clearinghouse for English Language Acquisition, "The Growing Number of Limited English Proficient Students, 1997/98–2007/08." Available at www.ncela.gwu.edu/publications.

8. Office of English Language Acquisition, Language Enhancement, and Academic Achievement for Limited English Proficient Students, Biennial Report to Congress on the Implementation of the Title III State Formula Grant Program, School Years 2004–06 (Washington, DC: 2008), p. 12.

9. Urban Institute, Children of Immigrants: Facts and Figures (Washington, DC: 2006). Available at www.urban.org/publications/900955.html; and Jeanne Batalova, Spotlight on Limited English Proficient Students in the United States (Washington, DC: Migration Policy Institute, 2006).

10. The Condition of Education, 2010 (Washington, DC: National Center for Education Statistics, 2010). Available at http://nces.ed.gov/programs/coe/2010/section1/indicator05.asp.

11. [414 U.S. 56]. Available at www.nabe.org/files/LauvNichols.pdf.

12. Russell Gersten and John Woodward, "A Case for Structured Immersion," Educational Leadership 43 (September 1985), p. 75.

13. Raul Yzaguirre, "What's Wrong with Bilingual Education?" Education Week (August 5, 1998), pp. 46, 72.

14. Mary Ann Zehr, "Bilingual Ed., Immersion Found to Work Equally Well," Education Week (April 9, 2010). Available at www.edweek.org/ew/articles/2010/04/09/29bilingual_ep.h29.html?qs=bilingual+education+effectiveness.

15. U.S. Department o.f Education, "Fiscal Year 2011 Budget Summary." Available at www2.ed.gov/about/overview/budget/budget11/summary/edlite-section3a.html#ela.

16. Howard Gardner, Frames of Mind (New York: Basic Books, 1985); and Howard Gardner, Multiple Intelligences: The Theory in Practice (New York: Basic Books, 1993).

17. Seana Moran, Mindy Kornhaber, and Howard Gardner, "Orchestrating Multiple Intelligences," Educational Leadership 64 (September 2006), pp. 22–27.

18. Howard Gardner, Five Minds for the Future: Cultivating Thinking Skills, (Boston, MA: Harvard Business School Press, 2006).

19. Jay Mathews, "21 Years Later, 'Multiple Intelligences' Still Debated," The Washington Post (September 7, 2004), p. A9.

20. 29th Annual Report to Congress on the Implementation of the Individuals with Disabilities Education Act, 2007, vol. 2 (Washington, DC: U.S. Department of Education, 2010), Table 1-3. Available at www2.ed.gov/about/reports/annual/osep/2007/parts-b-c/index.html#download.

21. U.S. Department of Education, "Fiscal Year 2011 Budget Summary." Available at www2.ed.gov/about/overview/budget/budget11/summary/edlite-section3b.html#spedstate.

22. "Special Education and the Individuals with Disabilities Education Act," National Education Association. Available at www.nea.org/specialed/index.html.

23. Ronald M. Hager and Diane Smith, The Public School's Special Education System as an Assistive Technology Funding Source: The Cutting Edge (Buffalo, NY: National Assistive Technology Advocacy Project, Neighborhood Legal Services, Inc., 2003). Available at www.nls.org/specedat.htm.

24. The Appalachia Educational Laboratory, The Link 14, no. 1 (Spring/Summer 1995), p. 21.

25. Sarah Wernick, "Hard Times for Educating the Highly Gifted Child," The New York Times (May 30, 1990), p. B8.

26. Digest of Education Statistics, 2009 (Washington, DC: National Center for Education Statistics, 2010), Tables 53 and 54. Available at http://nces.ed.gov/pubsearch/pubsinfo.asp?pubid=2010013.

27. John Cloud, "Failing Our Geniuses," Time (August 27, 2007), p. 42.

28. William Glasser, Choice Theory in the Classroom (New York: Harper Perennial, 1998).

29. David Sadker and Karen Zittleman, "Gender Bias: From Colonial America to Today's Classrooms," in James A. Banks and Cherry A. McGee Banks, eds., Multicultural Education: Issues and Perspectives, 6th ed. (Somerset, NJ: John Wiley & Sons, 2007), p. 149.

30. Rae Lesser Blumberg, "Gender Bias in Textbooks: A Hidden Obstacle on the Road to Gender Equality in Education," paper commissioned for the EFA Global Monitoring Report 2008, Education for All by

2015: Will We Make It? (UNESCO, 2007). Available at **http://unesdoc. unesco.org/images/0015/001555/155509e.pdf.**

31. Debra Viadero, "Researchers Mull STEM Gender Gap," *Education Week* (June 17, 2009), pp. 1, 15.

32. Ibid.

33. Michelle Galley, "Boys to Men," *Education Week* (January 23, 2002), pp. 26–29.

34. Jay P. Greene and Marcus A. Winters, "Leaving Boys Behind: Public High School Graduation Rates," Civic Report, no. 48, April 2006 (New York, NY: Manhattan Institute for Policy Research). Available at **www. manhattan-institute.org/html/cr_48.htm.**

35. "Annual Earnings of Young Adults," findings from *The Condition of Education, 2006* (Washington, DC: U.S. Department of Education, National Center for Education Statistics, 2006), Table 22-14, p. 156; and Deb Perelman, "In Big Cities, Young Women Outearn Men." Available at **http://blogs.eweek.com/careers/content001/wages/young_ women_earn_more_than_men_in_big_cities.html.**

36. "The 2009 National School Climate Survey: Executive Summary," (New York, NY: Gay, Le.sbian, and Straight Education Network, 2010). Available at **www.glsen.org/cgi-bin/iowa/all/research/index.html.**

37. Rex Wockner, "N.Y. Governor Signs Law Protecting LGBT Students," *Pride Source* (November 6, 2010). Available at **www.pridesource.com/ article.html?article=43255**; and Revised Sexual Harassment Guidance (Washington, DC: Office of Civil Rights, U.S. Department of Education, 2001). Available at **www2.ed.gov/about/offices/list/ocr/docs/ shguide.html.**

38. C. Emily Feistritzer, *The Context of Teaching in the U.S.*, Table 13. Available at **www.teach-now.org.**

Chapter 4

1. Lisbeth Bamberger Schorr, "Effective Programs for Children Growing Up in Concentrated Poverty." In A. C. Huston, ed., *Children in Poverty* (Cambridge, UK: University of Cambridge Press, 1991), pp. 261–262.

2. Federal Interagency Forum on Child and Family Statistics, "America's Children: Key National Indicators of Well-Being, 2010," Table FAM1.A. Available at **www.childstats.gov/americaschildren.**

3. Ibid.

4. Ibid, Table ECON1.A.

5. Ibid, Table. ECON2.

6. Ibid.

7. *Health in Schools* (Washington, DC: Center for Health and Health Care in Schools, 2010). Available at **www.healthinschools.org/en/Health-in-Schools.aspx.**

8. Carmen DeNavas-Walt, Bernadette D. Proctor, and Jessica Smith, U.S. Bureau of the Census, *Income, Poverty, and Health Insurance Coverage in the United States: 2009.* Current Population Reports P60-238 (Washington, DC: U.S. Government Printing Office, 2010), p. 9. Available at **www.census.gov/prod/2010pubs/p60-238.pdf.**

9. Ibid., p. 14.

10. Ibid., pp. 14, 55.

11. Ibid, Table 4, p. 15.

12. *2010 Kids Count Data Book,* (Baltimore, MD: Annie E. Casey Foundation, 2010), p. 32.

13. Federal Interagency Forum on Child and Family Statistics, "America's Children: Key National Indicators of Well-Being, 2007," p. 16. Available at **www.childstats.gov/pdf/ac2007/ac_07.pdf.**

14. National Center on Family Homelessness. Available at **www.family-homelessness.org/facts.php?p=sm.**

15. Education for Homeless Children and Youth Program, Title VII-B of the McKinney–Vento Homeless Assistance Act (As Amended by the No Child Left Behind Act of 2001), Non-Regulatory Guidance (Washington, DC: U.S. Department of Education, 2004). Available at **www.ed.gov/programs/homeless/guidance.pdf.**

16. Ruby Payne, "Understanding and Working with Students and Adults from Poverty," *Instructional Leader* 9 (March 1996). Available at **www.enc.org/features/focus/archive/urban/document. shtm? input=FOC- 002943-index.**

17. *U.S. Teenage Pregnancies, Births, and Abortions: National and State Trends by Race and Ethnicity* (New York, NY: Guttmacher Institute, 2010), Table 2.1. Available at **www.guttmacher.org/pubs/USTPtrends.pdf.**

18. The National Campaign to Prevent Teen and Unplanned Pregnancy, "By the Numbers." Available at **www.teenpregnancy.org/costs/.**

19. National Campaign to Prevent Teen and Unplanned Pregnancy, "Teen Pregnancy, Out-of-Wedlock Births, Healthy Relationships, and Marriage." Available at **www.thenationalcampaign.org/why-it-matters/wim_teens.aspx.**

20. *Kids Count Data Book 2004*, p. 38.

21. Centers for Disease Control and Prevention, "Sexually Transmitted Diseases in the United States, 2008." Available at **www.cdc.gov/std/ stats08/trends.htm.**

22. Centers for Disease Control and Prevention, "Questions and Answers: HIV Prevalence Estimates—United States, 2006." Available at **www. cdc.gov/hiv/topics/surveillance/resources/qa/prevalence.htm.**

23. Kaiser Family Foundation, "Sexual Health of Adolescents and Young Adults in the United States" (September 2008). Available at **www.kff. org/womenshealth/3040.cfm.**

24. Rob Stein, "Obama Administration Launches a Sex-Ed Program," *The Washington Post* (October 28, 2010), p. A3.

25. *Child Maltreatment 2008* (Washington, DC: U.S. Department of Health and Human Services, Administration for Children and Families). Available at **www.acf.hhs.gov/programs/cb/pubs/cm08/index.htm.**

26. Cynthia Crosson Tower, *The Role of Educators in Preventing and Responding to Child Abuse and Neglect* (Washington, DC: U.S. Department of Health and Human Services, Child Welfare Information Gateway, 2003). Available at **www.childwelfare.gov/ pubs/usermanuals/educator/.**

27. University of Michigan, Institute for Social Research, *Monitoring the Future: National Results on Adolescent Drug Use: Overview of Key Findings, 2010*, Table 7. Available at **www.monitoringthefuture.org/.**

28. Ibid., Table 7.

29. *Youth Suicide Fact Sheet* (Washington, DC: American Association of Suicidology, 2007). Available at **www.suicidology.org/web/guest/ stats-and-tools/fact-shccts.**

30. Ibid.

31. *Indicators of School Crime and Safety: 2010* (Washington, DC: National Center for Education Statistics, 2010, Figure 1.1, p. 7. Available at **http://nces.ed.gov/pubsearch/pubsinfo.asp?pubid=2011002.**

32. Ibid., Indicators 4 and 5, pp. 16, 20.

33. Ibid., Indicator 8, p. 34.

34. National Gang Center. Available at :**www.nationalgangcenter.gov.**

35. *Indicators of School Crime and Safety: 2010,* Indicator 11, p. 42.

36. Sameer Hinduja and Justin W. Patchin, "Cyberbullying: Identification, Prevention, and Response," Cyberbullying Research Center, 2010. Available at **www.cyberbullying.us.**

37. Susan M. Swearer, Dorothy L. Espclage, Tracy Vaillancourt, and Shelley Hymel, "What Can Be Done about School Bullying? Linking Research to Educational Practice," *Educational Researcher* 39 (January/ February 2010), p. 42.

38. Regan McMahon, "Everybody Does It," *The San Francisco Chronicle* (September 7, 2007), p. 18.

39. Ibid.

40. Ibid.

41. "High School Dropouts in America," (Washington, DC: Alliance for Excellent Education (September 2010). Available at www.all4ed.org/files/HighSchoolDropouts.pdf.

42. Ibid.

43. J. Laird, M. DeBell, G. Kienzl, and C. Chapman, *Dropout Rates in the United States: 2005* (Washington, DC: National Center for Education Statistics, 2007), Table 1. Available at http://nces.ed.gov/pubs2007/dropout05/tables/table_01.asp.

Chapter 5

1. Catherine Cornbleth, "Hidden Curriculum," in James W. Guthrie, ed., *Encyclopedia of Education,* 2nd ed. (New York: Macmillan Reference USA, 2003), pp. 537–539.

2. Elliot W. Eisner, *The Educational Imagination,* 3rd ed. (Upper Saddle River, NJ: Prentice Hall, 2001), pp. 87–97.

3. Karin Chenoweth, "Reading Wars, Take 2," *The Washington Post Magazine* (May 16, 1999), p. 17.

4. Steve Leinwand and Steve Fleischman, "Teaching Mathematics Right the First Time," *Educational Leadership* 62 (September 2004), p. 86.

5. *Science for All Americans* (Washington, DC: American Association for the Advancement of Science, 1989).

6. Arthur W. Foshay, "Knowledge and the Structure of the Disciplines," in William A. Jenkins, ed., *The Nature of Knowledge: Implications for the Education of Teachers* (Milwaukee: University of Wisconsin Press, 1961).

7. National Council for the Social Studies, *Expectations of Excellence: Curriculum Standards for Social Studies* (Washington, DC: Author, 1994).

8. *Digest of Education Statistics, 2009* (Washington, DC: National Center for Education Statistics, 2010), Table 56. Available at http://nces.ed.gov/pubsearch/pubsinfo.asp?pubid=2010013.

9. U.S. Department of Education, Office of Vocational and Adult Education, *Carl D. Perkins Career and Technical Education Act of 2006, Report to Congress on State Performance, Program Year 2007–08,* Washington, DC, 2010, p. 2.

10. Ibid., p. 15

11. NAEP 2009 Reading Assessment, *The Nation's Report Card.* Available at http://nces.ed.gov/nationsreportcard.

12. NAEP, U.S. History 2006, *The Nation's Report Card.* Available at http://nces.ed.gov/nationsreportcard/pdf/main2006/2007474_1.pdf.

13. *The Nation's Report Card.* Available at http://nces.ed.gov/nationsreportcard.

14. Trends in International Mathematics and Science Study, 2007. Available at http://nces.ed.gov/timss/results07.asp.

15. Highlights from PISA 2009: Performance of U.S. 15-Year-Old Students in Reading, Mathematics, and Science Literacy in an International Context (Washington, DC: National Center for Education Statistics, 2010).) Available at http://nces.ed.gov/pubsearch/pubsinfo.asp?pubid=2011004.

16. *Digest of Education Statistics, 2009,* Table 151.

17. William Schmidt, "Are There Surprises in the TIMSS Twelfth Grade Results?" in *TIMSS United States, Report No. 8* (East Lansing, MI: United States National Research Center [TIMSS], April 1998), p. 4.

18. National Education Commission, *Prisoners of Time: A Report of the National Education Commission on Time and Learning* (Washington, DC: U.S. Government Printing Office, 1994), p. 23.

19. Larry Cuban, How Teachers Taught: Constancy and Change in American Classrooms, 1890–1980 (New York: Longman, 1984).

20. Robert E. Slavin, *Cooperative Learning,* 2nd ed. (Boston: Allyn and Bacon, 1995), pp. 3–4.

21. Ibid., pp. 14–70.

22. Scott Willis and Larry Mann, "Differentiating Instruction," *Curriculum Update,* Association for Supervision and Curriculum Development (Winter 2000), p. 2.

23. *Prisoners of Time,* pp. 10, 31, 34.

24. Mortimer Adler, *The Paideia Proposal* (New York: Macmillan, 1982).

25. E. D. Hirsch, Jr., *Cultural Literacy* (Boston: Houghton Mifflin, 1987). Also see the Core Knowledge Foundation's website at www.coreknowledge.org.

26. Debra Viadero, "On the Wrong Track," *Teacher Magazine* (January 1999), pp. 22–23.

27. Dominic Brewer, Daniel Rees, and Laura Argys, "Detracking America's Schools: The Reform without Cost?" *Phi Delta Kappan* 77 (November 1995), pp. 210–212+.

28. Ian Quillen, "More Top Scores Found in Tracked Schools," *Education Week* (December 16, 2009), p. 4.

Chapter 6

1. J. W. Getzels and P. W. Jackson, "The Teacher's Personality and Characteristics," in N. L. Gage, ed., *Handbook of Research on Teaching* (Chicago: Rand McNally, 1963), p. 574.

2. Thomas L. Good and Jere E. Brophy, *Looking in Classrooms,* 10th ed. (Boston: Allyn and Bacon, 2008), pp. 49–51.

3. Lee S. Shulman, "Knowledge and Teaching: Foundations of the New Reform," *Harvard Educational Review* 57 (February 1987), p. 8.

4. Chris Argyris and Donald A. Schon, *Theory in Practice: Increasing Professional Effectiveness* (San Francisco: Jossey-Bass, 1974), pp. 3–19.

5. B. O. Smith et al., *Teachers for the Real World* (Washington, DC: American Association of Colleges for Teacher Education, 1969), p. 44.

6. Richard Kindsvatter, William Wilen, and Margaret Ishler, *Dynamics of Effective Teaching* (White Plains, NY: Longman, 1996), pp. 2–3.

7. Carol Weinstein and Wilford A. Weber, "Classroom Management," in James M. Cooper, ed., *Classroom Teaching* Skills (Belmont, CA: Wadsworth, Cengage Learning, 2011), p. 217.

8. David C. Berliner, "Effective Classroom Teaching: The Necessary but Not Sufficient Condition for Developing Exemplary Schools," in Gilbert R. Austin and Herbert Garber, eds., *Research on Exemplary Schools* (Orlando, FL: Academic Press, 1985), pp. 136–138; Gary D. Borich, *Effective Teaching Methods,* 6th ed. (Upper Saddle River, NJ: Pearson Education, 2007), pp. 14–15.

9. Jacob S. Kounin, Discipline and Group Management in Classrooms (New York: Holt, 1970).

10. Good and Brophy, *Looking in Classrooms,* p. 94.

11. Alfie Kohn, "Beyond Discipline," *Education Week* (November 20, 1996), pp. 37, 48.

12. Good and Brophy, *Looking in Classrooms,* pp. 55–56, 320–322.

13. Ibid., pp. 320–322.

14. Ibid., pp. 317–320; William W. Wilen and Ambrose A. Clegg, Jr., "Effective Questions and Questioning: A Research Review," *Theory and Research in Social Education* (Spring 1986), pp. 153–161.

15. Greta Morine-Dershimer, "Instructional Planning," in J. M. Cooper, ed., *Classroom Teaching Skills,* 9th ed. (Belmont, CA: Wadsworth, Cengage Learning, 2011), p. 51.

16. Ibid.

17. Mardell Raney, "*Technos* Interview with Jonathan Kozol," *Technos* 7, no. 3 (Fall 1998), p. 10.

Chapter 7

1. This example is loosely based on a class at Ligon Middle School in Raleigh, North Carolina. Available at www.ncsu.edu/midlink/gis/hazardous_waste.htm.

2. David A. Dockterman, "A Teacher's Tools," *Instructor* 100 (January 1991), pp. 58–61.

3. Gene White, "From Magic Lanterns to Microcomputers: The Evolution of the Visual Aid in the English Classroom," *English Journal*, 73 (March 1984), p. 59.

4. Paul Saettler, *The Evolution of American* Educational *Technology* (Englewood, CO: Libraries Unlimited, 1990), p. 98.

5. Mark Hofer, Robb Ponton, and Kathleen Swan, "Reinventing PowerPoint: A New Look at an Old Tool," *Social Studies Research and Practice* 1 (Winter 2006), pp. 457–464.

6. Douglas Levin and Sousan Arafeh, *The Digital Disconnect: The Widening Gap Between Internet-Savvy Students and Their Schools* (2002). Available at **www.pewinternet.org/Reports/2002/The_ Digital_Disconnect_The_widening_gap_between_Internetsavvy_ students_and_their_schools.aspx.**

7. North Central Regional Educational Laboratory and the Metiri Group, *enGauge 21st Century Skills: Literacy in the Digital Age* (Naperville, IA/ Los Angeles, 2003). Available at **Document2 http://pict.sdsu.edu/engauge21st.pdf.**

8. Ray Kurzweil, *The Age of Spiritual Machines: When Computers Exceed Human Intelligence* (New York: Viking, 1999).

9. David H. Jonassen, *Modeling with Technology: Mindtools for Contemporary Change*, 3rd ed. (Englewood Cliffs, NJ: Prentice Hall, 2005), p. 3. The concept of a computer application as a cognitive tool follows from the idea that "learning is a consequence of thinking"; see David Perkins, *Smart Schools: Better Thinking and Learning for Every Child* (New York: Free Press, 1992), p. 8.

10. Beaumie Kim and Thomas C. Reeves, "Reframing Research on Learning with Technology: In Search of the Meaning of Cognitive Tools," *Instructional Science* 35 (January 2007), pp. 207–256.

11. Cleborne D. Maddux, D. LaMont Johnson, and Jerry W. Willis, *Educational Computing: Learning with Tomorrow's Technologies*, 3rd ed. (Boston: Allyn and Bacon, 2001), pp. 204–205.

12. Matthew Maurer, "Supporting Language and Literacy Development with Technology." In Matthew Maurer and George Steven Davidson, eds., *Leadership in Instructional Technology* (Upper Saddle River, NJ: Merrill, 1998), p. 79.

13. Andrew Trotter, "Teaching the Basics: Beyond Drill and Practice," *Technology Counts '98, in Education Week* (October 1, 1998), pp. 25–27.

14. Diann Boehm, "I Lost My Tooth!" *Learning and Leading with Technology* 24 (April 1997), pp. 17–19.

15. Randy L. Bell, John C. Park, and Doug Toti, "Digital Images in the Science Classroom," *Learning and Leading with Technology* 31 (May 2004), pp. 26–28.

16. Jennifer Underdah, Joycelyn Palacio-Cayetano, and Ron Stevens, "Practice Makes Perfect: Assessing and Enhancing Knowledge and Problem-Solving Skills with IMMEX Software," *Learning and Leading with Technology* 28 (April 2001), pp. 26–31.

17. Candy Beal and Cheryl Mason, "Virtual Fieldtripping: No Permission Notes Needed. Creating a Middle School Classroom Without Walls," *Meridian* 2 (January 1999). Available at **www.ncsu.edu/meridian/ jan99/vfieldtrip/index.html.**

18. Hollylynne Stohl Drier, Kara M. Dawson, and Joe Garafalo, "Not Your Typical Math Class," *Educational Leadership* 56 (February 1999), p. 21.

19. Jeffrey Hovermill Shamatha, Dominic Peressini, and Kirsten Meymaris, "Technology-Supported Mathematics Activities Situated Within an Effective Learning Environment Theoretical Framework," *Contemporary Issues in Technology and Teacher Education* 3, (2004), pp. 362–381.

20. National Council of Teachers of Mathematics, *Principles and Standards for School Mathematics* (Reston, VA: The National Council of Teachers of Mathematics, 2000), p. 24. Available at **www.nctm.org/standards.**

21. Kelsey J. Sinclair, Carl. E. Renshawa, and Holly A. Taylor, "Improving computer-assisted instruction in teaching," *Computers & Education* 42 (2004), pp.169–180.

22. Robyn Pierce, and Kaye Stacey, "Monitoring Progress in Algebra in a CAS Active Context: Symbol Sense, Algebraic Insight and Algebraic Expectation," *The International Journal of Computer Algebra in Mathematics Education* 11 (2004), pp. 3–11.

23. Ann M. Farrell, "Teaching and Learning Behaviors in Technology-Oriented Precalculus Classrooms," Ph.D. dissertation, Ohio State University, *Dissertation Abstracts International* 51 (1990), p. 100A.

24. Lori Langer de Ramirez, *Empower English Language Learners with Tools from the Web.* (Thousand Oaks, CA. Corwin, 2010).

25. Peter West, "Support Pilot Distance-Learning Projects, Congress Urged," *Education Week* (March 17, 1993), p. 16.

26. Carole Vinograd Bausell and Elizabeth Klemick, "Tracking U.S. Trends," *Education Week* (March 29, 2007), pp. 42–44.

27. Sam Dillon, "Online Schooling Grows, Setting off a Debate," *New York Times* (February 1, 2007). Available at **www.nytimes.com/2008/02/01/ education/01virtual.html.**

28. Patricia Hutinger, Carol Bell, Gary Daytner, and Joyce Johanson, *Disseminating and Replicating an Effective Emerging Literacy Technology Curriculum: A Final Report* (Washington, DC: U.S. Office of Special Education Programs, July 2005), pp. 6–7.

29. Mary Seegers, "Special Technological Possibilities for Students with Special Needs," *Learning and Leading with Technology* 29 (November 2001), pp. 32–39.

30. National Educational Technology Standards for Students (**http://cnets. iste.org/**).

31. Sara Dexter, Aaron Doering, and Eric S. Riedel, "Content Area Specific Technology Integration: A Model for Educating Teachers," *Journal of Technology and Teacher Education* 14 (April 2006), pp. 325–345.

32. Thomas C. Reeves, "Technology in Teacher Education: From Electronic Tutor to Cognitive Tool," *Action in Teacher Education* 17 (1996), p. 74.

33. David Jonassen, Jane Howland, Rose M. Marra, and David Crismond, *Meaningful Learning with Technology*, 3rd ed. (Upper Saddle River, NJ: Pearson, 2008).

34. Henry Jay Becker and Jason Ravitz, "The Influence of Computer and Internet Use on Teachers' Pedagogical Practices and Perceptions," *Journal of Research on Computing in Education* 31 (Summer 1999), pp. 356–384. See also Laura M. O'Dwyer, Michael Russell, and Damian J. Bebell, "Identifying Teacher, School and District Characteristics Associated with Elementary Teachers' Use of Technology: A Multilevel Perspective," *Education Policy Analysis Archives* 12 (September 2004), pp. 1–31; and Peter E. Doolittle and David Hicks, "Constructivism as a Theoretical Foundation for the Use of Technology in Social Studies," *Theory and Research in Social Education* 31 (2003), pp. 72–104.

35. Sarah M. Butzin, "Using Instructional Technology in Transformed Learning Environments: An Evaluation of Project CHILD (Computers Helping Instruction and Learning Development)," *Journal of Research on Technology in Education* 33 (Summer 2001), pp. 367–373.

36. Glen Bull, Gina Bull, and Sara Kajder, "Mining the Internet: Tapped In," *Learning and Leading with Technology* 31 (February 2004), pp. 34–37.

37. Cheryl Mason Bolick and James M. Cooper, "Classroom Management and Technology." In Carolyn M. Evertson and Carol S. Weinstein, eds., Handbook *of Classroom Management: Research, Practice, and Contemporary Issues* (Mahwah, NJ: Lawrence Erlbaum, 2006), pp. 541–558.

38. Ronald E. Anderson and Amy Ronnkvist, "The Presence of Computers in American Schools," *Teaching, Learning and Computing: A National Survey* (1998). Available at **www.crito.uci.edu/tlc/findings/computers_in_american_schools/**.

39. Joe Garafolo, Glen Bull, Randy Bell, and Stephanie van Hover, "Interactive Whole-Class Display Systems," *Learning and Leading with Technology* 32 (October, 2004), pp. 28–31.

40. Sunya Collier, Molly H. Weinburgh, and Mark Rivera, "Infusing Technology Skills into a Teacher Education Program: Change in Students' Knowledge about and Use of Technology," *Journal of Technology and Teacher Education* 12 (2004), pp. 447–468.

41. Reenay R. H. Rodgers and Vivian H. Wright, *You've Got Mail: Using Technology to Communicate with Parents.* Paper presented June 25, 2007, at the National Educational Computing Conference, Atlanta, GA.

42. Peter Steinberg, Mitch Morehart, Stephen Vogel, John Cromartie, Vince Breneman, and Dennis Brown, USDA: Economic Research Service, *Broadband Internet's Value for Rural America Economic Research Report No. (ERR-78)* 70 pp. (August 2009). Available at **www.ers.usda.gov/publications/err78/**.

43. *A Nation Online: Entering the Broadband Age* (Washington, DC: U.S. Department of Commerce, 2006). Available at **www.ntia.doc.gov/reports/anol/NationOnlineBroadband04.pdf**.

44. Robert C. Johnston, "Money Matters," *Education Week* (May 10, 2001).

45. Alec MacGillis, "Law, Software Fuel New 'Digital Divide,'" *The Baltimore Sun* (September 21, 2004). Available at **www.baltimoresun.com/news/bal-te.software21sep21,1,6949097.story**.

46. Victoria, J. Rideout, Ulla G. Foehr, and Donald F. Roberts, *Generation M² Media in the Lives of 8- to 18-Year-Olds*, A Kaiser Family Foundation Study (2010). Accessed at **http://kff.org/entmedia/upload/8010.pdf**.

47. Cornelia Brunner, Dorothy Bennett, and Margaret Honey, "Technology, Gender, and Education: Defining the Problem," paper prepared for the AAUW Commission on Gender, Technology, and Teacher Education, October 1998.

48. Cornelia Brunner, "Opening Technology to Girls," *Electronic Learning* 16 (February 1997), p. 55.

49. Amanda Lenhart and Mary Madden, "Teen Content Creators and Consumers" (2005). Available at **www.pewinternet.org/Reports/2005/Teen_Content_Creators_and_Consumers.aspx**.

50. International Society for Technology in Education, "National Educational Technology Standards: Connecting Curriculum and Technology" (2000). Available at **www.iste.org**. Reprinted with permission.

51. Jill Casner-Lotto and Linda Barrington, Are They Really Ready to Work? Employers' Perspectives on the Basic Knowledge and Applied Skills of New Entrants to the 21st Century U.S. Workforce (New York, 2006). Available at **www.21stcenturyskills.org/documents/FINAL_REPORT_PDF9-29-06.pdf**.

52. Larry Cuban, "Techno-Reformers and Classroom Teachers," *Education Week* 16 (October 9, 1996).

53. Judi Harris, *Virtual Architecture: Designing and Directing Curriculum-Based Telecomputing* (Eugene, OR: International Society for Technology in Education, 1998).

Chapter 8

1. From Kenneth R. Howe, "A Conceptual Basis for Ethics in Teacher Education," *Journal of Teacher Education* 37 (May/June 1996), p. 6. Reprinted with permission.

2. Ibid, p. 6.

3. Steven Tigner, *Educator's Affirmation* (Boston and Toledo, OH: Boston University and University of Toledo, 1989). Reprinted by permission of Steven Tigner.

4. Kern Alexander and M. David Alexander, "Due Process Rights of Teachers," in *American Public School Law*, 7th ed. (Belmont, CA: Thomson West, 2009), pp. 887–919.

5. *U.S.L. Week 4223,* March 24, 1970, quoted in Louis Fischer and David Schimmel, *The Rights of Students and Teachers* (New York: Harper and Row, 1982), p. 323. Much of this chapter is drawn from the material presented in this excellent and highly readable book and also from Louis Fischer, David Schimmel, and Cynthia Kelly, *Teachers and the Law,* 4th ed. (1995), 5th ed. (1998), and 6th ed. (2002) (New York: Addison-Wesley Longman).

6. Fischer, Schimmel, and Kelly, *Teachers and the Law,* 5th ed., p. 20.

7. *Smith v. School District of the Township of Darby,* quoted in Fischer, Schimmel, and Kelly, *Teachers and the Law,* 5th ed., p. 31.

8. Davis Guggenheim, *Waiting for "Superman,"* 2010.

9. *Smith v. School District of the Township of Darby,* p. 38.

10. Ibid., p. 47.

11. Ibid., pp. 76–77.

12. Ibid., p. 101.

13. *Pickering v. Board of Education,* 225 N.E. 2d 1 (1967); 391 U.S. 563 (1968).

14. Alexander and Alexander, "Due Process Rights of Teachers," pp. 555–556.

15. Ibid., 640–641.

16. *Scoville v. Board of Education,* 425 F. 2d 10 (7th Cir. 1970).

17. *Anderson v. Evans,* 660 F. 2d 153 (6th Cir. 1981).

18. *Stroman v. Colleton County School District,* 981 F. 2d 152 (4th Cir. 1992).

19. Fischer, Schimmel, and Kelly, *Teachers and the Law,* 5th ed., p. 166.

20. Perry A. Zirkel, "MySpace?" *Phi Delta Kappan* 90 (January 2009), pp. 388–389

21. Mark G. Yudof, David L. Kirp, Betsy Levin, and Rachel F. Moran, *Educational Policy and the Law,* 4th ed. (Belmont, CA: West/Thomson Learning), pp. 255–256.

22. Ibid., p. 256.

23. Ibid., p. 257.

24. Fischer, Schimmel, and Kelly, *Teachers and the Law,* 5th ed., p. 169.

25. Ibid., p. 169.

26. Thomas R. McDaniel, "The Teacher's Ten Commandments: School Law in the Classroom," *Phi Delta Kappan*, 60, no. 10 (June 1979), p. 707.

27. Fischer, Schimmel, and Kelly, *Teachers and the Law,* 5th ed., p. 451.

28. Ibid., p. 324.

29. Ibid., pp. 297–298.

30. Ibid., p. 307.

31. Ibid., p. 306.

32. Bill Mears, "Court Dismisses Pledge Case," CNN.com. Available at **www.cnn.com/2004/LAW/06/14/scotus.pledge/**.

33. *Lee v. Weisman* (90-104) 505 U.S. 557 (1992).

34. *Santa Fe Independent School District* v. *Department of Education* (99-62) 168 F. 3d 806.

35. Benjamin Senor, "Even After the Supreme Court Ruling, We're Still in the Dark about Religion Clubs at School," *American School Board Journal* 173 (August 1986), p. 17.

36. Cheryl D. Mills, "Important Education-Related U.S. Supreme Court Decisions," in Cordon Cawalti, ed., *Challenges and Achievements of American Education* (Alexandria, VA: Association for Supervision and Curriculum Development, 1993), p. 192.

37. Caroline Hendrie, "Teacher May Lead Bible Lessons at Her Own School, Court Rules," *Education Week* (September 9, 2002).

38. Stephen Arons, "Separation of School and State," *Education Week* (November 17, 1984), p. 24.

39. Thomas J. Flygare, "Supreme Court Strikes Down Louisiana Creationism Act," *Phi Delta Kappan* 69 (September 1987), pp. 77–79.

40. Associated Press, "Science Standard Debates in Kansas," August 11, 1999.

41. *Mozert* v. *Hawkins County Board of Education,* U.S. Dist. Ct. (E.D. Tenn.) 647 F Supp. 1194 (1987).

42. *Smith* v. *Board of School Commissioners of Mobile County* no. 87-7216 (11th Cir., 26 September 1987).

43. Thomas R. McDaniel, "The Teacher's Ten Commandments: School Law in the Classroom," *Phi Delta Kappan* 60 (June 1979), p. 703. Reprinted with permission of the author.

44. Richard Riley, Secretary of Education, and Walter Dellinger, Assistant Attorney General, White House press release, July 12, 1995, pp. 2–4.

45. *Tinker* v. *Des Moines Independent Community School District,* 393 U.S. 503 (1969).

46. Fischer, Schimmel, and Kelly, *Teachers and the Law,* 5th ed., p. 271.

47. Nelda Cambron-McCabe, Martha McCarthy, and Stephen Thomas, *Public School Law: Teacher's and Student's Right,* 5th ed. (Boston: Allyn & Bacon, 2004).

48. Early Warning, Timely Response: A Guide to Safe Schools. Available at **www.athealth.com/Consumer/issues/EW_Section1.html.**

49. *Goss* v. *Lopez,* 95 S.Ct. 729 (1975).

50. *Honig* v. *Doe,* 108 S.Ct. 592, 605 (1988).

51. *Fuller* v. *Decatur Public School Board of Education School District 61, 78* F. Supp. 2d 812 (C.D. Ill. 2000).

52. Yudof, Kirp, Levin and Moran, *Educational Policy and the Law,* p. 525.

53. Darcia Harris Bowman, "District Dress Code Attracts Nationwide Attention," *Education Week* (October 15, 2003), p. 10.

54. "Fashion Dictates," *Education Week*'s Wednesday Blog. Available at **http://blogs.edweek.org/teachers/webwatch/2006/09/fashion_dicates.html?qs=dress +codes.**

55. Discipline at School, Center for Effective Discipline. Available at **www.stophitting.com/index.php?page=statesbanning.**

56. Ibid. Also U.S. Department of Education, Office for Civil Rights: Available at **http://ocrdata.ed.gov/.**

57. Fischer, Schimmel, and Kelly, *Teachers and the Law,* 5th ed., p. 268.

58. Ibid., p. 279.

59. *New Jersey* v. *T.L.O.,* 105 S. Ct. 733 (1985).

60. Perry A Zirkel, "Turning the Tide," *Phi Delta Kappan* (September 2009), p. 76–77

61. *Vernonia School District 47J* v. *Acton,* 115 S.Ct. 2386 (1995) as reported in Yudof, Kirp, Levin, and Moran, *Educational Policy and the Law,* pp. 317–320.

62. Censorship and Challenges, American Library Association. Available at **www.ala.org/ala/aboutala/offices/oif/ifissues/censorshipchallenges.cfm.**

63. *Tinker* v. *Des Moines Independent Community School District.*

64. *Bethel School District no. 403* v. *Fraser,* 106 S. Ct. 3159 (1986).

65. Linda Greenhouse, "Vote Against Banner Shows Divide on Speech in Schools," *New York Times Online* (June 26, 2007). Available at **www.nytimes.com/2007/06/26/washington/26speech.html?_r=1&adxnnl=1&oref=slogin&adxnnlx=1182860348-+JKe2p4I+8N5fnutayh8Lw.**

66. *Hazelwood School District* v. *Kuhlmeier,* 56 U.S.L.W. 4079, 4082 (January 12, 1988).

67. Ibid.

68. American Association of University Women, *Hostile Hallways: The AAUW Survey on Sexual Harassment in America's Schools* (New York: Louis Harris Associations, 1993), p. 6.

69. *Davis* v. *Monroe County Board of Education,* 119 S. Ct. 1661 (1999).

70. Ibid.

71. *Owasso Independent School District* v. *Falvo,* 534 S. Ct. 00–1073.

Chapter 9

1. Aristotle, *Politics.* Translated by T. A. Sinclair. (Middlesex, England: Penguin, 1978).

2. Richard M. Felder and Barbara A. Soloman, *Learning Styles and Strategies.* Available at **www4.ncsu.edu/unity/lockers/users/f/felder/public/ILSdir/styles.htm.**

3. In a national survey of deans and department chairpersons of education schools and departments, 91.4 percent "agreed" or "strongly agreed" with the following statement: "There exists a set of core values/virtues upon which most Americans agree, regardless of race, creed, class or culture, which can and should be taught in schools." See Emily Nelsen Jones, Kevin Ryan, and Karen E. Bohlin, *Teachers as Educators of Character: Are the Nation's Schools of Education Coming Up Short?* (Washington, DC: Character Education Partnership, 1999), p. 7; Association of Supervision and Curriculum Development, *Moral Education in the Life of the School* (Alexandria, VA: ASCD, 1989). Both former Presidents Bill Clinton and George W. Bush have called for greater emphasis on character education in U.S. schools.

4. Personal communication from Katie Birkhead, Director Professional Development, K–8 Program, Core Knowledge Foundation, Charlottesville, VA.

5. Bob Kizlik, "Assertive Discipline Information" (June 28, 2007). Available at **www.adprima.com/assertive.htm.**

6. Website of the North Central Regional Educational Laboratory. Available at **www.ncrel.org/sdrs/areas/issues/students/learning/lr1scaf.htm.**

7. Charlotte, Allen, "Read It and Weep: Why Does Congress Hate the One Part of No Child Left Behind That Works?" *The Weekly Standard,* 012, no. 41, (2007). Available at **www.weeklystandard.com/Content/Public/Articles/000/000/013/850gvneh.asp.**

8. Cited by David T. Hansen in a speech at Teachers College, Columbia University, Winter 2007. Available at **http://quicktime.tc.columbia.edu/users/dls2141/hansenOrig-0001.mp3**

9. David T. Hansen. *Ethical Visions of Education* (New York: Teachers College Press, 2007), preface.

Chapter 10

1. Marvin Lazerson, "Access, Outcomes, and Educational Opportunity," *Education Week* (January 27, 1999), p. 46.

2. Willystine Goodsell, *Pioneers of Women's Education in the United States* (New York: AMS Press, 1970/1931), p. 5.

3. R. Freeman Butts and Lawrence A. Cremin, *A History of Education in American Culture* (New York: Holt, 1953), p. 245.

4. Butts and Cremin, *A History of Education in American Culture,* p. 408.

5. John D. Pulliam, *History of Education in America,* 3rd ed. (Columbus, OH: Merrill, 1982), pp. 157–159.

6. Butts and Cremin, *A History of Education in American Culture*, p. 260.

7. Merle Curti, *The Social Ideas of American Educators*, 2nd ed. (Totowa, NJ: Littlefield, Adams, 1959), p. 183.

8. Butts and Cremin, *A History of Education in American Culture*, p. 443.

9. Thomas D. Snyder, *120 Years of American Education: A Statistical Portrait* (Washington, DC: U.S. Department of Education, National Center for Education Statistics, 1993), pp. 36–37; *Projections of Education Statistics to 2018* (Washington, DC: National Center for Education Statistics, 2010), Table 1. Available at **http://nces.ed.gov/programs/ projections/projections2018/tables/table_01.asp?referrer=list**.

10. William T. Gruhn and Harl R. Douglass, *The Modern Junior High School*, 3rd ed. (New York: Ronald Press, 1971), pp. 46–53.

11. Jaana Juvonen, Vi-Nhuan Le, Tessa Kaganoff, Catherine Augustine, and Louay Constant, *Focus on the Wonder Years: Challenges Facing the American Middle School* (Santa Monica, CA: RAND Corporation, 2004). Available at **www.rand.org/pubs/monographs/2004/RAND_ MG139.pdf**.

12. Ibid.

13 .National Catholic Educational Association, *United States Catholic Elementary and Secondary Schools 2009–2010*: The Annual Statistical Report on Schools, Enrollment and Staffing. Available at **www.ncea. org/news/AnnualDataReport.asp#schools**.

14. Stephen P. Broughman, Nancy L. Swain, and Patrick W. Keaton, *Characteristics of Private Schools in the United States: Results From the 2007–2008 Private School Universe Survey, First Look.* (Washington, DC: National Center for Education Statistics, March 2009.) Available at **http://nces.ed.gov/pubsearch/pubsinfo.asp?pubid=2009313**.

15. Ibid.

16. Herbert M. Kliebard, *Religion and Education in America: A Documentary History* (Scranton, PA: International Textbook, 1969), p. 119.

17. The Religious Freedom Page. Available at **http://religiousfreedom.lib. virginia.edu**.

18. Earle H. West, *The Black American and Education* (Columbus, OH: Merrill, 1972), pp. 7–8.

19. Eric Lincoln and Milton Meltzer, *A Pictorial History of the Negro in America*, 3rd ed. (New York: Crown, 1968), pp. 108–109.

20. *Historical Statistics of the United States, Colonial Times to 1970*, vol. I, Table Series H 433–441 (Washington, DC: U.S. Government Printing Office, 1975), p. 370.

21. Franklin Frazier, *The Negro in the United States*, rev. ed. (New York: Macmillan, 1957), pp. 427, 432–436, 438.

22. Gary Orfield, Susan E. Eaton, and the Harvard Project on School Desegregation, *Dismantling Desegregation* (New York: New Press, 1996), pp. 105–106; Jomills Henry Braddock II, Robert L. Crain, and James M. McPartland, "A Long-Term View of School Desegregation: Some Recent Studies of Graduates as Adults," *Phi Delta Kappan* 66 (December 1984), pp. 259–264.

23. Anthony Lukas, *Common Ground* (New York: Knopf, 1985).

24. Howard Ozmon and Sam Craver, *Busing: A Moral Issue* (Bloomington, IN: Phi Delta Kappa Educational Foundation, 1972), pp. 33–34.

25. Thomas D. Snyder and Sally A. Dillow, *Digest of Education Statistics 2009*, Table 90. (Washington, DC: National Center for Education Statistics, 2010. Available at **http://nces.ed.gov/programs/digest/d09/**.

26. Gary Orfield, *Reviving the Goal of an Integrated Society: A 21st Century Challenge*, a report of the Civil Rights Project, January 2009, p.13. Available at **http://civilrightsproject.ucla.edu/research/k-12-education/ integration-and-diversity/reviving-the-goal-of-an-integrated-society- a-21st-century-challenge**.

27. Richard M. Merelman, "Dis-integrating American Public Schools," *Education Week* (February 6, 2002), p. 37.

28. R. Freeman Butts, *The Education of the West: A Formative Chapter in the History of Civilization* (New York: McGraw-Hill, 1973), p. 279.

29. Bureau of Indian Education website: **www.bie.edu/Schools/index.htm**.

30. *Status and Trends in the Education of American Indians and Alaskan Natives: 2008* (Washington, DC: NCES, 2008. Available at **http://nces. ed.gov/pubs2008/nativetrends/index.asp**.

31. Susan Aud, Mary Ann Fox, and Angelina KewalRamani, *Status and Trends in the Education of Racial and Ethnic* Groups (Washington, DC: NCES, 2010, p. 46.) Available at **http://nces.ed.gov/pubsearch/ pubsinfo.asp?pubid=2010015**.

32. Ibid., p. 140.

33. Ibid.

34. Ibid., p. 7.

35. Ibid., p. 46.

Chapter 11

1. Frederick M. Hess and Olivia Meeks, *School Boards Circa 2010: Governance in the Accountability Era* (Washington, DC: National School Boards Association, The Thomas B. Fordham Institute, and The Iowa School Boards Foundation, 2011), pp. 20–21.

2. Larry Cuban, "Conflict and Leadership in the Superintendency," *Phi Delta Kappan* 67 (September 1985), p. 8. See also Arthur Blumberg with Phyllis Blumberg, *The School Superintendent: Living with Conflict* (New York: Teachers College Press, 1985), p. 32; and Susan Moore Johnson, *Leading to Change: The Challenge of the New Superintendency* (San Francisco: Jossey-Bass, 1996), pp. 77–78.

3. *The State of the American School Superintendency: A Mid-Decade Study* (Alexandria, VA: American Association of School Administrators, 2007).

4. Thomas D. Snyder, Sally A. Dillow, and Charlene M. Hoffman, *Digest of Education Statistics 2006* (Washington, DC: National Center for Education Statistics, 2007), p. 16.

5. Alex Molnar, *School Commercialism* (New York: Routledge, 2005), p. 6.

6. Partnership for 21st Century Skills. Available at **www.p21.org**.

7. U.S. Department of Education, Fiscal Year 2012 Budget Summary. Available at **http://www2.ed.gov/about/overview/budget/budget12/ summary/edlite-section1.html**.

8. *Rankings and Estimates: Estimates of School Statistics 2010* (Washington, DC: National Education Association, 2010), p. 81.

9. Ibid., p. 94.

10. Ibid., p. 96.

11. Rob Greenwald, Larry V. Hedges, and Richard D. Laine, "The Effect of School Resources on Student Achievement," *Review of Educational Research* (Fall 1996), pp. 361–396; Eric A. Hanushek, "Spending on Schools," in Terry Moe, ed., *A Primer on American Education* (Palo Alto, CA: Hoover Press, 2001), pp. 69–88.

12. Deborah A. Verstegen, "Financing the New Adequacy: Towards New Models of State Education Finance Systems That Support Standards Based Reform," *Journal of Education Finance* 27 (Winter 2002), pp. 749–782.

13. Improving Basic Programs Operated by Local Educational Agencies (Title I, Part A) (Washington, DC: U.S. Department of Education). Available at **www2.ed.gov/programs/titleiparta/index.html**.

14. U.S. Department of Health and Human Services, Administration for Children and Families, Early Childhood Learning and Knowledge

Center, Head Start Program Fact Sheet Fiscal Year 2010.. Available at **http://eclkc.ohs.acf.hhs.gov/hslc/HeadStartProgram/HeadStartProgramFactsheets/fHeadStartProgr.htm**.

15. Linda Jacobson, "Research Offers Competing Data on Effectiveness," *Education Week* (April 25, 2007), p. 30.

16. Michael Holzman, "Preschool's Effects at 40," *Education Week* (January 19, 2005), p. 33.

17. *National Assessment of Title I, Final Report, Executive Summary* (Washington, DC: National Center for Education Evaluation and Regional Assistance, 2007).

Chapter 12

1. Conway Dorsett, "Multicultural Education: Why We Need It and Why We Worry About It," *Network News and Views* 121, no. 3 (March 1993), p. 31.

2. Marc Tucker, "Making Tough Choices," *The Kappan* 88, no. 10 (June 2007), pp. 728–732. Available at **www.pdkmembers.org/members_online/publications/Archive/pdf/k0706tuc.pdf**.

3. Education Commission of the States, "Exit Exams: State Requires Passage of Exit Exam for High School Graduation," June 25, 2007. Available at **http://mb2.ecs.org/reports/Report.aspx?id=1359**.

4. Eric Hirsch, Julia E. Koppich, and Michael S. Knapp, *Revisiting What States Are Doing to Improve the Quality of Teaching: An Update on Patterns and Trends* (Seattle: Center for the Study of Teaching and Policy, University of Washington, February 2001), p. 16.

5. For further information on portfolios and authentic assessment see Susan Black, "Portfolio Assessment," *The Executive Educator* (February 1993), pp. 28–31.

6. There are several good websites dealing with constructivism in education. Among them are Funderstanding (available at **www.funderstanding.com/constructivism.cfm**) and Concept to Classroom (available at **www.thirteen.org/edonline/concept2class/constructivism/index.html**). For a critical perspective, see A. MacKinnon and C. Scarff-Seatter, "Constructivism: Contradictions and Confusion in Teacher Education," in V. Richardson, ed., *Constructivist Teacher Education: Building New Understandings* (Washington, DC: Falmer Press, 1997).

7. Anthony Bryk and Yeow Meng Thum, "The Effects of High School Organization on Dropping Out," unpublished paper, University of Chicago, 1988, pp. 54–68. See also Anthony Bryk and Mary Erina Driscoll, "An Empirical Investigation of the School as a Community," unpublished paper, University of Chicago, 1988, pp. 54–63.

8. Kevin Ryan and Thomas Lickona, eds., *Character Development in Schools and Beyond* (Washington, DC: Council for Research on Values and Philosophy, 1987), pp. 21–26.

9. Barry Chazan, "Against Moral Education." In *Contemporary Approaches to Moral Education* (New York: Teacher College Press, 1985).

10. William Damon, quoted by Amitai Etzioni, *The Spirit of Community* (New York: Crown, 1993), pp. 100–101.

11. "Values Education: Time for Greater Emphasis!" *Phi Delta Kappan* 75, no. 2 (October 1993), p. 145.

12. J. S. Benninga, M. W. Berkowitz, P. Kuehn, and K. Smith, "The Relationships of Character Education and Academic Achievement in Elementary Schools," *Journal of Research in Character Education* 1, no. 1 (2003), pp. 17–30.

13. *Service Learning Is …* (Scotts Valley, CA: National Service Learning Clearinghouse). Available at **www.servicelearning.org/article/archive/35/**.

14. Daniel Hart, Thomas M. Donnelly, James Youniss, and Robert Atkins, "High School Community Service as a Predictor of Adult Voting and Volunteering," *American Educational Research Journal* 44, no. 1 (March 2007), pp. 197–219.

15. National Service-Learning Clearinghouse, June 2009. Available at **www.servicelearning.org/instant_info/fact_sheets/tribal_facts/americorps_and_service-learning_101**

16. History of Service Learning. Maryland State Board of Education. Available at **http://www.marylandpublicschools.org/MSDE/programs/servicelearning**.

17. Thomas Toch, *In the Name of Excellence* (New York: Oxford University Press, 1991), p. 9.

18. Goals 2000: Educate America Act (March 31, 1994); *The National Education Goals* (Washington, DC: U.S. Department of Education, 1994).

19. The No Child Left Behind Act of 2001 Reauthorization of the Elementary and Secondary Education Act Policies and Legislation. Available at **www.whitehouse.gov/news/reports/no-child-left-behind.html**.

20. E. D. Hirsch, as quoted by Sara Mosle, *The New York Times Book Review*, September 29, 1996, p. 15.

21. Northwest Regional Educational Laboratory, *Catalog of School Reform Models*. Available at **www.nwrel.org/scpd/catalog/modellist.asp**.

22. Theodore Sizer, *Horace School: Redesigning the American High School* (Boston: Houghton Mifflin, 1992), pp. 207–208.

23. American Diploma Project. Available at **www.achieve.org/node/604**.

24. Lynn Olson, "State Leaders Pledge to Reform Nations High Schools," *Education Week* (February 28, 2005), Web version.

25. Quoted by the editors of *Education Week*, "From Risk to Renewal" (February 10, 1993), p. 187.

26. IES Educational Statistics, "Special Analysis 2007: High School Course Taking." Available at **http://nces.ed.gov/programs/coe/2007/analysis/sa01a.asp**.

27. The NAEP High School Transcript Study: Trends in Course Taking: Major Findings. Available at **www.nces.ed.gov/nationsreportcard/hsts/results/trends/findings.asp**.

28. Ibid.

29. Table 167. Minimum amount of instructional time per year and policy on textbook selection, by state: 2000, 2006, and 2008 , *Digest of Educational Statistics*, 2009, National Center for Educational Statistics. Available at **http://nces.ed.gov/programs/digest/d09/tables/dt09_167.asp?referrer=list**.

30. Statistical Summaries of Year-Round Educational Programs: 2006-2007, National Association for Year-Round Education. Available at **www.nayre.org**.

31. Robert Marzano and John Kendall, "The Fall and Rise of Standards-Based Education," *National Association of State Boards of Education Issues in Brief* (1998).

32. Toch, In the Name of Excellence, p. 158.

33. Bess Keller, "'Qualified' Teachers: A Victory on Paper?" *Education Week* (December 8, 2004).

34. Vaishali Honawar, California Approves Teacher Test, in Teacher Magazine, October 15, 2007.

35. Marc Tucker, "Making Tough Choices," p. 732.

36. Education World. Available at **www.education-world.com/a_issues/issues374a.shtml**.

37. Center for Teaching Quality, 2007. Available at **www.teacherleaders.org/teachersolutions/index_ctq.php**.

38. U.S. Charter Schools. Available at **www.uscharterschools.org/cs/dia/view/dai/95**.

39. Center for Education Reform. Available at **www.edreform.com/_upload/ncsw-numbers.pdf**.

40. Magnet Schools of America. Available at **www.magnet.edu/modules/news/**.

41. Jeanne Allen and Anna Varghese Marcucio, *Charter School Laws Across the States* (Washington, DC: Center for Education Reform, 2004). Available at **www.edreform. com/index.cfm?fuseAction=section&pSectionID= 14&cSectionID=122**.

42. Center for Educational Reform, *Charter Schools*. Available at **www.edreform.com/index.cfm?fuseAction=document&documentID=1964**.

43. Vouchers and Charter Schools: The Latest Evidence, The Brookings Institute, Oct. 19, 2010. Available at **www.brookings.edu/events/2000/0224education.aspx**.

44. Center for Educational Reform, "Education Programs Constitutional; Growth Steady," July 26, 2007 Available at **www.edreform.com/index.cfm?fuseAction=section&pSectionID=14&cSectionID=122**.

45. National school voucher plan deepens debate, *Religion Newswriters*. July 31, 2006. Available at **www.religionlink.org/tip_060731.php**.

46. Amy Goldstein, "Bush Proposes, Vouchers for All Displaced Students," *Washington Post,* September 20, 2005; p. A08. Available at **www.washingtonpost.com/wp-dyn/content/article/2005/09/19/AR2005091901428.html** .

Chapter 13

1. *Occupational Outlook Handbook, 2010–2011 Edition* (Washington, DC: Department of Labor, 2010. Available at **www.bls.gov/oco/**.

2. William J. Hussar and Tabitha M. Bailey, *Projections of Education Statistics to 2019* (Washington, DC: National Center for Education Statistics, 2010), Tables 2 and 32. Available at **http://nces.ed.gov/programs/projections/projections2019.8**

3. Thomas D. Snyder and Sally A. Dillow, *Digest of Education Statistics, 2009* (Washington, DC: National Center for Education Statistics, 2010), Table 67. Available at **http://nces.ed.gov/programs/digest/d09/tables/dt09_067.asp**.

4. Erling E. Boe, Lynne H. Cook, and Robert J. Sunderland, "Teacher Turnover: Examining Exit Attrition, Teaching Area Transfer, and School Migration," *Exceptional Children*, 75, no. 1, September 2008, pp. 7–31; and C. Emily Feistritzer, *The Context of Teaching in the U.S.* Available at **www.teach-now.org**.

5. *The 2011 Job Search Handbook for Educators* (Columbus, OH: American Association for Employment in Education, 2010), p. 59.

6. C. Emily Feistritzer, *The Context of Teaching in the U.S.* Available at **www.teach-now.org**.

7. Thomas G. Carroll and Elizabeth Foster, *Who Will Teach? Experience Matters,* (Washington, DC: National Commission on Teaching and America's Future, 2010), pp. 3–4.

8. Ibid., p. 8.

9. Richard M. Ingersol and Thomas M. Smith, "The Wrong Solution to the Teacher Shortage," *Educational* Leadership, May 2003, pp. 30–33.

10. C. Emily Feistritzer, "The Impact of Alternative Routes," *Education Week*, November 19, 2009, pp. 26, 32.

11. *An Emerging Picture of the Teacher Preparation Pipeline* (Washington, DC; American Association of Colleges for Teacher Education, 2010), p. 7.

12. *Department of Defense Education Activity*. Available at **www.dodea.edu/home/facts.cfm**.

13. Stephen P. Broughman, Nancy L. Swaim, and Patrick W. Keaton, *Characteristics of Private Schools in the United States: Results from the 2007–08 Private School Universe Survey* (Washington, DC: National Center for Education Statistics, 2009). Available at **http://nces.ed.gov/pubsearch/pubsinfo.asp?pubid=2009313**.

14. *Projections of Education Statistics to 2019* (Washington, DC: National Center for Education Statistics, 2011),) Table 32. Available at **http://nces.ed.gov/programs/projections/projections2019**.

15. Council for American Private Education, "Why Teach in a Private School?" Available at **www.capenet.org/teach.html**.

16. *Rankings and Estimates* (Washington, DC: National Education Association, 2010),) p. 92.

17. *Job Search Handbook for Educators* (Columbus, OH: American Association for Employment in Education, Inc., 2010), p. 64.

18. Most of the ideas in this section are taken from John William Zehring, "How to Get Another Teaching Job and What to Do If You Can't," *Learning*, 6 (February 1978), pp. 44, 46–51.

19. C. Emily Feistritzer, *The Context of Teaching in the U.S.* Available at **www.teach-now.org**.

20. Julie Ranier Dangel and Edith M. Guyton, *Research on Alternative and Non-traditional Education: Teacher Education Yearbook XIII* (Lanham, MD: Rowman and Littlefield, 2005), p. 77.

21. J. Shen, "Has the Alternative Certification Policy Materialized Its Promise? A Comparison of Traditionally and Alternatively Certified Teachers in Public Schools," *Educational Evaluation and Policy Analyses*, 19 (1997), pp. 276–283.

22. C. Emily Feistritzer, *The Context of Teaching in the U.S.* Available at **www.teach-now.org**.

23. *Occupational Outlook Handbook,2010-11 Edition, Recreation Workers* (Washington, DC: U.S. Department of Labor, 2010). Available at **www.bls.gov/oco/ocos058.htm#projections_data**.

Chapter 14

1. William J. Hussar and Tabitha M. Bailey, *Projections of Education Statistics to 2018* (Washington, DC: National Center for Education Statistics, 2009), Tables 2 and 32. Available at **http://nces.ed.gov/programs/projections/projections2018**.

2. The Peace Corps, "Adjusting to a New Culture," in The Peace Corps Cross-Cultural Workbook, Peace Corp Information Collection and Exchange, Washington, D.C. [no date], pp. 183–194. Available at **www.peacecorps.gov/wws/publications/culture/pdf/chapter6.pdf**.

3. S. M. Kardos, S. M. Johnson, H. G. Peske, D. Kauffman, and E. Liu, E, "Counting on Colleagues: New Teachers Encounter the Professional Cultures of Their Schools," *Educational Administration Quarterly* 37, no. 2 (2001), 250–290.

4. T. M. Smith and R. M. Inglesoll, "What Are the Effects of Induction and Mentoring Programs on Beginning Teacher Turnover?" *American Educational Research Journal* 41, no. 3 (2004), p. 682.

5. R. Fessler, "Dynamics of Teacher Career Stages," in T. Guskey and M. Huberman, eds., *Professional Development in Education: New Paradigms and Practices* (New York: Teachers College Press, 1995).

6. Gary Cornog, "To Care or Not to Care," in Kevin Ryan, ed., *Don't Smile until Christmas: Accounts of the First Year of Teaching* (Chicago: University of Chicago Press, 1970), pp. 18–19. Copyright © 1970. Reprinted by permission of Kevin Ryan.

7. National Commission on Teaching and America's Future, "No Dream Denied: A Pledge to the American Children." Available at **www.NCTAF.org**.

8. Y. Gold, "Beginning Teacher Support," in J. Sikula, T. Buttery, and E. Guyton, eds., *Handbook of Research in Teacher Education,* 2nd ed. (New York: MacMillan, 1999), pp. 458–594.

9. Alliance for Excellent Education, *Issue Brief* (August 2005), p. 2. Available at **www.all4ed.org/publications/TeacherAttrition.pdf**.

Chapter 15

1. Myron Lieberman, Education as a Profession (Englewood Cliffs, NJ: Prentice Hall, 1956.)

2. Canan Tasci, "Teachers Still Spending Their Own Money on Classroom Supplies," *Redlands Daily Facts*, September 20, 2010. Available at **www.redlandsdailyfacts.com/news/ci_16120598**.

3. Walter Boggs, quoted at 1963–1964 Convention of the National Commission on Teacher Education and Professional Standards; Myron Brenton, *What's Happened to Teachers?* (New York: Coward-McCann, 1970), p. 242.

4. D. Tanner and L. N. Tanner, *Curriculum Development: Theory into Practice*, 3rd ed. (New York: Macmillan, 1995).

5. The website of the National Board for Professional Teaching Standards (NBPTS). Available at **www.nbpts.org/about_us/2009_national_board_cert/national_board_certifica**.

6. Based on recent figures extrapolated from data reported by National Board for Professional Teaching Standards (NBPTS), *55,000 Reasons to Believe* (Arlington, VA: Author, 2007), p. 4.

7. Ibid., p. 3.

8. Ibid., p. 4.

9. "80% of Race to the Top Winners Name National Board Programs," National Board for Professional Teaching Standards, August 26, 2010. Available at **www.nbpts.org/about_us/news_media/press_releases?ID=672**.

10. Chester Finn and Danielle Wilcox, "Board Games: Failure of the National Board for Professional Teaching Standards to Accomplish Objective of Improving Quality of Teaching in the US; Business Backs a Losing Educational Strategy," *National Review* (August 9, 1999); and Frederick M. Hess, *Common Sense School Reform* (New York: Palgrave Macmillan, 2004).

11. "New Report Affirms National Board Certification's Positive Impact on Student Achievement and Learning," National Board for Professional Teaching Standards, June 11, 2008. Available at **www.nbpts.org/about_us/news_media/press_releases?ID=422**.

12. Telephone conversation with staff of The Council of Chief State School Officers.

13. National Education Association website. Available at **www.nea.org**.

14. About AFT. American Federation of Teachers, AFL-CIO. Available at **www.aft.org/about/**.

15. Available at **www.nea.org/home/2580.htm**.

16. NEA Handbook: Program and Administration. Available at **www.nea.org/assets/docs/2011_NEA_Handbook_Program_and_Administration_redacted.pdf**.

17. Available at **www.nea.org/home/12584.htm**.

18. "Charter Schools," National Education Association website. Available at **www.nea.org/home/16332.htm**.

19. Steven Chaufmann, "The NEA Seizes Power: The Teachers' Coup," *The New Republic*, October 11, 1980, pp. 9–11.

20. Mike Antonucci, "The Long Reach of Teachers Unions: Using money to win friends and influence policy," *Education Next*, vol. 10, no. 4 (Fall 2010). Available at **http://educationnext.org/the-long-reach-of-teachers-unions/**.

21. Ibid.

22. *Wall Street Journal*, October 20, 2010, p. 1.

23. American Federation of Teachers. Available at **www. aft.org**.

24. Ibid.

25. Intercepts, *NEA Convention 2010: NEA-AFT Relations*. Available at **www.eiaonline.com/intercepts/2010/07/04/nea-convention-2010-nea-aft-relations/**.

26. National Education Association. Available at **www.nea.org/student-program www.nea.org/aboutnea/NEAFTPartnership.html**.

27. Anthony Rebora, "Report: U.S. Lagging in Teacher Learning," *Education Week*, March 16, 2009. Available at **www.edweek.org/tsb/articles/2009/03/16/02nsdc.h02.html**.

28. Ibid.

29. "Double Take: Research Alert," *Educational Leadership*, vol. 68, no. 4 (December 2010), p. 8.

30. Ibid.

31. Quoted by Mark Edwards in "Turbo-Charging Professional Development," *The School Administrator*, December 9, 1998, p. 36.

1890 institutions Colleges and universities created for African Americans as a result of the second Morrill Act passed by Congress in 1890.

academic engaged time The time a student spends on academically relevant activities or materials while experiencing a high rate of success.

academic freedom The freedom of teachers to teach about an issue or to use a source in teaching without fear of penalty, reprisal, or harassment.

academy A type of secondary school during the early national period that tried to combine the best of the Latin and English grammar schools. During the nineteenth century, it took on a college preparation orientation.

acceleration A method of teaching gifted and talented students in which they do the same work as other students but at a faster pace.

acceptable use policy A statement of rules governing student use of school computers, especially regarding access to the Internet.

accountability The reform movement that embraces the idea that schools and educators should be required to demonstrate what they are accomplishing and should be held responsible for student achievement and learning.

active learning Learning in which the student takes control of or is positively involved in the process of his or her education; strongly associated with constructivism.

adequate yearly progress (AYP) Students must show demonstrable improvement toward meeting state standards. Under NCLB, schools with students who do not make adequate yearly progress are subject to a variety of corrective measures.

aesthetics A branch of philosophy that examines the perception of beauty and distinguishes beauty from that which is moral or useful.

alternative licensure A procedure offered by many states to license teachers who have not graduated from a state-approved teacher education program.

American Federation of Teachers (AFT) The nation's second largest teachers' association or union. Founded in 1916, it is affiliated with the AFL-CIO, the nation's largest union.

American Recovery and Reinvestment Act A 2009 act of Congress designed to create jobs, spur economic activity, and foster accountability and transparency in government spending.

app An abbreviation for an application that runs on a mobile device such as a iPod Touch or an iPhone or android phone.

assimilation The absorption of an individual or a group into the cultural tradition of a population or another group.

assistive technology The array of devices and services that help people with disabilities to perform better in their daily lives. Such devices include motorized chairs, remote control units that turn appliances on and off, computers, and speech synthesizers.

Association of American Educators (AEE) Established in 1994, the Association of American Educators is the nation's largest nonunion professional organization of teachers.

at-risk students *See* students at risk.

authentic (performance) assessment A recent trend in student evaluation that attempts to measure real student performance on significant tasks; the focus is on what we want the student to be able to do. Also called *performance assessment.*

axiology The philosophical study of values, especially how they are formed ethically, aesthetically, and religiously.

behaviorism A psychological theory asserting that all behavior is shaped by environmental events or conditions.

bilingual education A variety of approaches to educating students who speak a primary language other than English.

block scheduling An approach to class scheduling in which students take fewer classes each school day but spend more time in each class.

blog (Web log) A personal website that the user updates frequently. Most are used like a journal or as a place to share personal opinions and information.

breach of contract A failure to fulfill the requirements of a legal agreement.

Brown v. Board of Education of Topeka U.S. Supreme Court ruling in 1954 holding that segregated schools are inherently unequal.

Buckley Amendment Shorthand name for the Family Educational Rights and Privacy Act, which outlines who may and may not have access to a student's records.

call to excellence An educational slogan pointing students to high standards.

career ladder A series of steps in an occupation. Usually the higher steps ("rungs" on the ladder) bring new tasks, more responsibility, increased status, and enhanced rewards.

categorical grants Federal aid to education that must be spent for purposes that are specified in the legislation and by the federal agency administering the funds. Compare *block grants.*

certification Recognition by a profession that one of its practitioners has met certain standards. Often used as a synonym for *licensure,* which is governmental approval to perform certain work, such as teaching.

character education Efforts by the home, the school, the religious community, and the individual student to help the student know the good, love the good, and do the good and, in the process, to forge good qualities such as courage, respect, and responsibility.

charter schools Public schools in which the educators, often joined by members of the local community, have made a special contract, or charter, with the chartering agency. Usually the charter allows the school a great deal of independence in its operation.

chief state school officer The executive officer of a state's board of education who is usually responsible for the administration of that state's public education. This person is also the head of that state's department of education. Also called *superintendent of education, commissioner of education,* and *superintendent of public instruction.*

choice theory A theory articulated by psychiatrist William Glasser, holding that humans have fundamental needs such as survival, love, power, freedom, and fun, and that throughout our lives, our actions are attempts to satisfy these needs.

civic learning (civic education) A part of social studies that emphasizes preparing students to be good citizens by becoming aware of our common heritage and engaging issues related to character and values. Students learn to apply principles of democracy to everyday concerns they will face and/or already face as citizens.

classroom management The set of teacher behaviors that create and maintain conditions in the classroom, thus permitting instruction to take place efficiently and effectively.

cognitive tools Computer applications that are used to engage and enhance thinking.

Common Core State Standards An initiative that lays out learning standards in mathematics and English language arts, and which will develop assessments to measure student achievement of the standards. Over 40 states have adopted the standards as of 2011.

common schools Public elementary schools that are open to children of all classes. During the nineteenth century, the common school became the embodiment of universal education.

common school A nineteenth-century school in the United States that was designed to serve students of all classes and religions.

compensatory education Educational support to provide a more equal opportunity for disadvantaged students through activities such as remedial instruction and early learning.

comprehensive high school The most common form of high school in the United States, designed to offer a range of preparation programs, including college preparation and vocational education.

constructivism A theory, based on research for cognitive psychology, that people learn by constructing their own knowledge through an active learning process rather than by simply absorbing knowledge directly from some other source.

content standards Statements of the subject-specific knowledge and skills that schools are expected to teach and students are expected to learn.

continuing contract An agreement between a school district and a teacher outlining the conditions and terms of work.

contract A binding agreement between two or more parties.

cooperative learning An instructional approach in which students work together in groups to achieve learning goals. A variety of cooperative learning strategies exist.

core curriculum A common course of study for all students, often called for by essentialist reforms in the 1980s.

core knowledge See *cultural literacy.*

credential file A file established by college students—typically with the school's career planning and placement office—that contains materials important for securing a teaching job, for example, letters of recommendation, a transcript, and a résumé.

critical thinking The intent to help students evaluate the worth of ideas, opinions, or evidence before making a decision or judgment.

cultural literacy Being aware of the central ideas, stories, scientific knowledge, events, and personalities of a culture; also known as *core knowledge.*

cultural pluralism An approach to diversity of individuals that calls for understanding and appreciating cultural differences.

culturally responsive teaching A method of embracing students' cultural backgrounds by modifying classroom conditions or activities to include elements that relate to the students' culture.

culture A group that shares beliefs about what is right and wrong, and what is good and bad; it also includes the dominant ideas, stories and myths, artistic works, social habits, organizations, and language of the group.

culture shock The feeling of disorientation experienced by individuals when initially immersed in a society with different values, customs, and mores.

curriculum All the organized and intended experiences of the student for which the school accepts responsibility.

cyberbullying Bullying through information and communication technologies, such as mobile phone text messages, e-mail messages, Internet chat rooms, and social networking websites such as MySpace, Facebook, and Bebo.

dame school A school run by a housewife during early colonial days.

deductive reasoning A type of reasoning from the general to the particular; reasoning in which the conclusion follows from the premise stated.

***de facto* school segregation** Segregation in the schools resulting primarily from residential patterns.

***de jure* school segregation** Segregation in the schools that occurs by law.

democratic reconstructionists Subscribers to an educational perspective that focuses on developing students who are prepared to make positive changes in a democracy.

differentiated instruction A variety of techniques used to adapt instruction to the individual ability levels and learning styles of each student in the classroom.

digital storytelling An instructional approach in which students use images, often digital photos, accompanied by their own written and recorded narrative to create a story that is stored digitally.

distance education The use of technology to link students and instructors who are separated in terms of location.

district school The type of school that succeeded the town school and moving school in New England. A township was divided into districts, each with its own school, its own schoolmaster, and funding from the town treasury.

drill-and-practice In educational technology, software programs that give students a series of tasks to reinforce a concept or to initially diagnose a student's level. These programs monitor progress, provide feedback, and present tasks accordingly.

due process The deliberative process that protects a person's constitutional right to receive fair and equal protection under the law.

economic reconstructionists Subscribers to an educational perspective or motivation that focuses on developing students who take a critical stance toward the dominant social and economic status quo.

education The process by which humans develop their minds, their skills, and their character. It is a lifelong process marked by continual development and change.

effective schools Schools that provide a significantly better education (usually measured by student test scores) for a much larger percentage of their students than do other schools serving similar student populations.

Elementary and Secondary Education Act (ESEA) The federal government's single largest investment in elementary and secondary education, including Title I. Originally passed in 1965 and periodically reauthorized by Congress, most recently in 2001 as the No Child Left Behind Act.

English grammar school A form of secondary education in the latter half of the colonial period that provided a practical alternative education for students who were not interested in college.

English language learners (ELLs) Students whose native language is not English and who have difficulty understanding and using English.

enrichment A method of teaching gifted and talented students in which they are allowed or assigned to do additional work to make regular class assignments more challenging or meaningful to them.

epistemology A branch of philosophy that examines the nature of knowledge, its origins, its foundations, its limits, and its validity.

equality of educational opportunity A concept that students from less advantageous backgrounds should have equal opportunities to experience success in school. Disagreement exists on whether this implies simply providing equal resources or ensuring equal success compared to more privileged students.

essentialism An educational philosophy that emphasizes a core body of knowledge and skills necessary for effective participation in society. Proponents believe that an educated person must have this core of knowledge and skills and that all children should be taught it.

ethics A branch of philosophy that examines the right and wrong of human conduct. The term can also refer to a particular moral code or system.

extrinsic rewards Rewards to an individual that are external to the activity itself, such as grades, gold stars, and prizes.

fair use A legal principle defining specific, limited ways in which copyrighted material can be used without permission from the author.

for-profit schools Financially driven businesses that typically contract with a community or school district to provide educational services.

generational poverty Families living in poverty for two generations or longer.

grievance A formal complaint about working conditions. Procedures for filing grievances are often part of teachers' employment contracts.

Head Start A federally funded compensatory education program, in existence since the mid-1960s, that provides additional educational services to young children suffering the effects of poverty.

inclusion The commitment to educate each child, to the maximum extent appropriate, in the regular school and classroom rather than moving children with disabilities to separate classes or institutions.

individualized education program (IEP) A management tool required for every student covered by the provisions of the Individuals with Disabilities Education Act. It must indicate a student's current level of performance, short- and long-term instructional objectives, services to be provided, and criteria and schedules for evaluation of progress.

individualized family services plan (IFSP) Similar to an individualized education program for school-age children, the IFSP specifies the services to be provided to developmentally delayed children from birth through age two. The IFSP is authorized by PL 99–457, the Education of the Handicapped Act Amendments.

inductive reasoning A type of reasoning, from the particular to the general, in which one can make a general conclusion based on a number of facts.

in loco parentis The responsibility of the teacher to function "in the place of the parent" when a student is in school.

in-service training The efforts by a school or school district to improve the professional skills and competencies of its professional staff. Also called *professional development* or *staff development.*

integrated curriculum See *interdisciplinary curriculum.*

intellectual capital Another term for knowledge.

intellectual property A product of the intellect that has commercial value, including copyrighted property such as literary or artistic works, and ideational property, such as patents, appellations of origin, business methods, and industrial processes.

intelligent design theory A theory about the origins of life that suggests that the complexity of life is too great to be accounted for by standard evolutionary theories and that "an intelligence" either created or somehow guided its development.

interdisciplinary curriculum Also known as integrated curriculum. A curriculum that integrates the subject matter from two or more disciplines, such as English and history, often using themes such as inventions, discoveries, or health as overlays to the study of the different subjects. Also known as *integrated curriculum.*

intrinsic rewards Rewards to an individual that come from within, such as personal satisfaction or happiness.

junior high school A separate kind of school created typically for grades 7, 8, and 9. The first junior highs were founded in 1909–1910. In recent years, they have been gradually replaced by middle schools.

Kalamazoo **case** The 1874 U.S. Supreme Court decision (*Stuart and Others* v. *School District No. 1 of the Village of Kalamazoo and Others*) that upheld the right of states to tax citizens to create public high schools.

kindergarten A division of school for children below the first grade, usually for children between ages 4 and 6; the concept, which means "garden of children" was imported into the United States from Germany during the nineteenth century.

Latin grammar school First type of secondary school in the American colonies. Its main purpose was to prepare students for college.

law The system of rules that governs the general conduct of a particular community's citizens.

LCD projector A projector that allows projection of the material seen on a computer screen to a larger screen for the whole class to see.

learning communities Organizations in which all members are engaged in continuous learning and improvement efforts.

learning organization An organization that systematically learns from its experience what works and what does not work, with the goal to increase innovation, effectiveness, and performance.

learning style Characteristic way a student learns; includes factors such as the way an individual processes information, preference for competition or cooperation, and preferred environmental conditions such as lighting or noise level.

least restrictive environment (LRE) A requirement of the Education for All Handicapped Children Act that students with disabilities should participate in regular education programs to the greatest extent appropriate.

lesbian, gay, bisexual, and transgendered (LGBT) An initialism used since the 1990s to describe what was formerly called the "gay community." The term is intended to emphasize a diversity of sexuality- and gender identity–based cultures.

liability A legal obligation.

licensure The approval given to an individual by a governmental agency, usually the state, to perform a particular work, such as teaching.

lifelong learners People who continue throughout their lives to learn new things after they leave school.

limited English proficient (LEP) Term for students whose native language is not English and who have difficulty understanding and using English.

local school board The policymaking body of a school district; it represents the citizens of the district in setting up a school program, hiring school personnel, and generally determining local policy related to public education.

logic A branch of philosophy that involves the study of reasoning or of sound argument. In a more specific sense, logic is the study of deductive inference.

looping An educational practice of multiyear teaching in which the teacher follows students to the next grade level and stays with the group for several years.

magnet school An alternative school that provides instruction in specified areas such as the fine arts, for specific groups such as the gifted and talented, or for using specific teaching styles such as open classrooms. In many cases, magnet schools are established as a method of promoting voluntary desegregation in schools.

mainstreaming The practice of placing special education students in general education classes for at least part of the school day while also providing additional services, programs, or classes as needed.

McGuffey Readers A six-volume series of readers developed by William Holmes McGuffey that sold more than 100 million copies between 1836 and 1906. The readers served to create a common curriculum for many students.

mentor A person who gives both personal and professional guidance to a novice.

metaphysics A branch of philosophy devoted to exploring the nature of the existence of reality as a whole rather than to studying particular parts of reality as the natural sciences do. Metaphysicians try to answer questions about reality without referring to religion or revelation.

middle school A school that bridges the grades between elementary school and high school, usually grades 6–8. It differs from a junior high school because it is specifically designed for young adolescents, with a strong emphasis on personal growth and development, rather than mimicking the high school's emphasis on academics and sports, as junior high schools often did.

mind maps Graphical representations of a story or concept. See also *webs*.

Morrill Act Federal legislation passed in 1862 that granted each state federal land to establish colleges for the study of agriculture and mechanical arts. A second Morrill Act, passed in 1890, provided similar federal support to create "separate but equal" colleges for African Americans.

multicultural curriculum Several approaches to multicultural curriculum exist, but in essence, it promotes an understanding of and appreciation for cultural pluralism. It attempts to address issues of social injustice related to racism, sexism, and economic inequality by reducing prejudice and fostering tolerance through the formal curriculum.

multicultural education An approach to education that recognizes cultural diversity and fosters cultural enrichment of all children and youth.

multiple intelligences A theory of intelligence put forth by Howard Gardner that identifies at least eight dimensions of intellectual capacities that people use to approach problems and create products.

National Board for Professional Teaching Standards (NBPTS) The professional agency that sets voluntary standards for what experienced teachers should know and be able to do in more than 30 different teaching areas.

national curricular standards Nationally dictated or recommended curriculum and levels of educational achievement.

National Education Association (NEA) The nation's largest teachers' association, founded in 1857 and having a membership of over 3.2 million educators.

National Education Goals (Goals 2000) Goals for U.S. education, established by the president and the 50 state governors and legislated by Congress, that were intended to be reached by the year 2000.

New England Primer The basic text used in schools during the eighteenth century. It was an illustrated book composed of religious texts and other readings.

news group A worldwide electronic network of users who share a common interest and post messages to one another.

No Child Left Behind Act (NCLB) The name of the 2001 reauthorization of the Elementary and Secondary Education Act. NCLB adds many new requirements for states and school districts.

Northwest Ordinances Passed by Congress in 1785 and 1787, these ordinances were concerned with the sale of public lands in the Northwest Territory (from present-day Ohio to Minnesota). Every township was divided into 36 sections, one of which was set aside for the maintenance of public schools. The 1787 ordinance reaffirmed that religion, morality, and knowledge were necessary to good government.

Old Deluder Satan Act A Massachusetts law passed in 1647 that strengthened an earlier law requiring parents to educate their children. It required every town of 50 or more families to pay a teacher to teach the children reading and writing so they could read the Bible and thwart Satan, who would assuredly try to keep people from understanding the scriptures.

parent-teacher organization (PTO) A local organization, usually centered around each school, that consists of both parents and teachers at that school. Its purpose is to serve as a communication mechanism between the school and the parents of the school's students.

pedagogical content knowledge Teachers' knowledge that bridges content knowledge and pedagogy with an understanding of how particular topics can best be presented for instruction, given the diverse interests and abilities of learners.

perennialism A particular view of philosophy that sees human nature as constant, with few changes over time. Perennialism in education promotes the advancement of the intellect as the central purpose of schools. The educational process stresses academic rigor and discipline.

performance pay (pay for performance) A financial reward given to teachers, based on the special quality of their work.

personal practical knowledge The set of understandings teachers have of the practical circumstances in which they work.

philosophy The love or search for wisdom; the quest for basic principles to understand the meaning of life. Western philosophy traditionally contains five branches of philosophy: metaphysics, ethics, aesthetics, epistemology, and logic.

phonics An approach to reading that teaches the reader to decode words by sounding out letters and combinations of letters.

Plessy v. Ferguson A Supreme Court decision in 1896 that upheld the constitutionality of separate but equal accommodations for African Americans. The ruling was quickly applied to schools.

portfolio A collection of a person's work. For students, portfolios are used as a relatively new form of authentic assessment. They can contain a great range of work, from pencil-and-paper drawings to sculpture.

private venture school A type of school in the middle states during colonial times, licensed by the civil government but not protected or financed by it.

privatization A movement to contract with private organizations, often for profit, to operate particular public schools whose students have been performing poorly on academic tests, or to provide specific educational services to public schools. The Edison Schools and Sylvan Learning Centers are examples of such providers.

problem solving The process of either presenting students with a problem or helping them to identify a problem and then observing and helping them become aware of the conditions, procedures, or steps needed to solve the problem.

productivity tools Applications, such as word processors, e-mail programs, and spreadsheets, that let a person accomplish tasks more efficiently than if he or she had to use a typewriter, a calculator, or postal mail.

profession An occupation or occupational group that fulfills certain criteria. Among other things, it must require training and knowledge, perform a social service, have a code of ethics, and have a sense of autonomy and personal responsibility.

professional development The efforts by a school or school district to improve the professional skills and competencies of its professional staff. Also called *in-service training* in education. Also called *staff development*.

Program for International Student Assessment (PISA) An international assessment of 15-year-old students in mathematics, science, and reading, administered every three years.

progressivism A form of educational philosophy that sees nature as ever-changing. Because the world is always changing and new situations require new solutions to problems, learners must develop as problem solvers.

project approach An instructional method through which students engage in an in-depth investigation of a real-world topic worthy of their attention and effort. The process often includes fieldtrips or expert guests and a culminating event through which children present the results of their research.

project method A method of education in which students work in groups on a topic of interest to them. Developed by William Heard Kilpatrick, who believed that because students learn only what is of interest to them, they should be the ones to determine topics of study.

psychic reward Mental and spiritual benefits. Teaching has many.

public comprehensive high school The predominant form of secondary education in America in the twentieth century. It provides both preparation for college and a vocational education for students not going on to college.

Race to the Top A $4 billion federal program initiated in 2011 by the Obama administration to encourage states to institute reforms regarding standards, recruitment and training of teachers, establishment of data systems to track student growth, and programs to reform failing schools.

real encounters Face-to-face experiences that are powerful sources of learning.

reduction in force (RIF) The elimination of teaching positions in a school system because of declining student population or funding.

reflection Conscious and analytical thought by an individual about what he or she is doing and how the action affects others.

reflective practitioner A individual who has established the habit of reviewing his or her performance to continually improve practice.

reflective teaching A teacher's habit of examining and evaluating his or her teaching on a regular basis.

resegregation Schools returning to a pattern of more racial segregation after a period of progress toward desegregation.

response to intervention (RTI) A method of academic intervention used in the United States which is designed to provide early, effective assistance to children who are having difficulty learning. RTI seeks to prevent academic failure through early intervention, frequent progress measurement, and increasingly intensive research-based instructional interventions for children who continue to have difficulty.

romanticism A child-centered philosophy of education that condemns the influences of society and suggests instead that a child's natural curiosity and the natural world should be used to teach.

rubric A scoring tool that lists the criteria for a piece of work or "what counts" toward a grade.

scaffolding Providing assistance—some structure, clues, help with remembering certain steps or procedures, or encouragement to try—when a learner is on the verge of solving a problem but can't complete it independently.

school choice Allowing parents to select alternative educational programs for their children, either within a given school or among different schools.

school culture The prevailing mores, values, and rituals that permeate a school.

school vouchers See *voucher plans*.

schooling Formal instruction typically conducted in an institution, adhering to standardized practices.

schools-within-schools In large schools, the establishment of "houses" of teachers and 100 to 400 students.

self-fulfilling prophecy Students' behavior that comes about as a result of teachers' expectations that the students will behave in a certain way. Teachers expect students to behave in a certain way and communicate those expectations by both overt and subtle means, and students respond by behaving in the way expected.

sexual harassment Unwanted and unwelcome sexual attention that interferes with one's life.

simulation A technique for learning or practicing skills that involves dealing with a realistic but artificial problem or situation. Typically, it provides an opportunity for safe practice with feedback on performance.

site-based decision making A school reform effort to decentralize, allowing decisions to be made and budgets to be established at the school-building level, where most of the changes need to occur. Usually teachers become involved in the decision-making process. Also known as *site-based management, school-based management,* or *school-based decision making.*

social distance The psychological relationships between individuals, ranging from the formal to the familiar.

social media Media that features content created by nonprofessionals; examples include postings by bloggers and digital photos posted at online photo-sharing sites.

social reconstructionists Proponents of the theory of education that schools and teachers need to engage in the restructuring and reforming of society to eradicate its ills and shortcomings.

socialization The general process of social learning whereby children learn the many things they must know to become acceptable members of society.

society A grouping of individuals bound together by a variety of connections, such as shared geographic space, similar racial features, or a shared culture.

socioeconomic status (SES) A system for measuring the economic conditions of people using the family's occupational status, income, and educational attainment as measures of status.

special education Educational programming provided by schools to meet the needs of students with disabilities.

spreadsheet An interactive software program allowing users to perform multiple calculations and view more than one answer at a time.

staff development The efforts by a school or school district to improve the professional skills and competencies of its professional staff. Also called "in-service" training in education.

state board of education The state's primary education policy-making body for elementary and secondary education.

state department of education The state bureaucracy, operating under the direction of the state board of education, whose responsibilities typically include administering and distributing state and federal funds, licensing teachers and other educational personnel, providing educational data and analyses, and approving college and university educational licensure programs.

STEM (science, technology, engineering, and mathematics) An acronym referring to educational programs in science, technology, engineering, and mathematics.

students at risk Students judged to be in serious jeopardy of not completing school or not succeeding in school.

subject-matter curriculum A curriculum that focuses on bodies of content or subject matter, usually the traditional subject disciplines.

superintendent of schools Typically, a professional educator selected by the local school board to act as its executive officer and as the educational leader and chief administrator of the local school district.

teacher competency testing Examinations given to teachers to assess their professional knowledge and skills.

teaching journal A professional record of reflections, instructional ideas, and observations by a teacher or future teacher.

teaching portfolio Collection of items such as research papers, pupil evaluations, teaching units, and video clips of lessons to reflect the quality of a teacher's teaching. Portfolios can be used to illustrate to employers the teacher's experience or to obtain national board certification.

teaching to the test Instruction that is driven by the requirements or characteristics of a test rather than the needs of students or the substance of a particular subject.

tenure A legal right that confers permanent employment on teachers, protecting them from dismissal without adequate cause.

Title I The section of the 1965 Elementary and Secondary Education Act that delivers federal funds to local school districts and schools for the education of students from low-income families and supplements the educational services provided to low-achieving students in those districts.

tools for learning Cognitive skills that make independent learning possible. They include advanced reading, remembering, recording, researching, test taking, analyzing, and creating.

town school A New England elementary school during the early colonial period, required in every town of 50 or more families.

tracking The homogeneous grouping of students for learning tasks on the basis of some measure(s) of their abilities.

Trends in International Mathematics and Science Study (TIMSS) An international assessment of fourth-, eighth-, and twelfth-graders in mathematics and science.

tutorials A software application designed to provide initial instruction in a given topic, check for understanding throughout the process, and evaluate the learner's grasp of the topic once the program is completed.

ubiquitous computing Situations in which each student is provided access to some type of mobile computing device to use inside the classroom, out in the field, and at home.

universal education Schooling for everyone.

vicarious experiences Learnings gained not through direct experiences, but through observations or readings.

virtual fieldtrip Computer software that simulates the experience of an actual fieldtrip with the use of digital images and multimedia tools.

vlog An abbreviation for video blogging, a type of blogging using audio and video.

vocation A spiritual calling to do certain kinds of work. For many, teaching is more than a job; it's a vocation.

voucher plans A type of educational choice plan that gives parents a receipt or written statement that they can exchange for the schooling they believe is most desirable for their child. The school, in turn, can cash in the received vouchers for the money to pay teachers and buy resources. Also called *school vouchers.*

wait-time The time a teacher spends waiting for an answer after posing a question. Research indicates that good questioning practices involve giving students sufficient time to think about and respond to each question.

WebQuest An inquiry-based learning activity that directs learners in using information from the Web.

webs Graphical representations of a story or concept. See also *mind maps*.

whole language approach A teaching approach emphasizing the integration of language arts skills and knowledge across the curriculum. It stresses the provision of a literate environment and functional uses of language.

wiki A website developed collaboratively by a community of users, allowing any user to add and edit content.

within-district choice Allows parents to choose from among the various public schools that a school district or state operates.

word processor A computer application used for the production of any sort of printable material, including composition, editing, formatting, and possibly printing.

writing across the curriculum An instructional approach using writing as a tool for learning in all subject areas.

year-round education An educational reform, adopted in some states, where students go to school the same number of days as in traditional schools, but the school days are more evenly distributed throughout the school year.

zero-tolerance policies School policies calling for automatic suspension or expulsion of students who bring forbidden items, such as drugs or weapons, to school or who engage in undesired behavior.

zone of proximal development A range of tasks that a person cannot yet do alone but can accomplish with assistance. This zone is the point at which instruction can succeed and real learning is possible.

Index

Note: Figures and tables are denoted by "f" and "t," respectively.